Insider Guide

Careers in Investment Banking

2005 Edition

Helping you make smarter career decisions.

WetFeet, Inc.

609 Mission Street
Suite 400
San Francisco, CA 94105

Phone: (415) 284-7900 or 1-800-926-4JOB
Fax: (415) 284-7910
Website: www.WetFeet.com

Careers in Investment Banking

ISBN: 1-58207-432-1

Table of Contents

Investment Banking at a Glance

Opportunity Overview

Undergrads and MBAs from top schools are recruited for a number of openings that is small even in the best of times. Competition is fierce, so if you're not from a top-tier school, you may need to be more resourceful and persistent than those who are. Doing an internship in investment banking is essential to breaking into the field in today's business environment. Networking is key; make use of your alumni network. Undergrads vie for 2-year positions as analysts. If you do well, depending on the firm, you may get to stay for a third year, perhaps even abroad. MBAs compete for fast-track associate slots, and international assignments may be available for those who want them. Midcareer people are recruited by headhunters or hired on an ad hoc basis for positions at various levels. Though relatively few people come into the industry from other fields, it can be done, especially by those who have a technical background in a specific industry and an aptitude for and interest in finance. Otherwise, expect to start at the bottom.

Major Pluses about Careers in Investment Banking

- Big bucks. Despite the fact that investment banking compensation is down in recent years from its apex during the tech and dot-com boom, this industry still pays more than just about any other you can think of.

- Excellent opportunity to learn the financial aspects of business inside out.

- Work with talented, intelligent, hardworking people.

- Build a network of networked people.

- Your life is the market—riding a bull is exciting and lucrative.

Major Minuses about Careers in Investment Banking

- How many different ways can you say, "Work your tail off?"

- No job security—only the unemployment line has more people who have been fired.

- The work can be tedious, especially at the lower levels.

- The industry has more than its share of big egos, abrasive personalities, and workaholics.

- Your life is the market—a bear could put you out of work.

Recruiting Overview

- Very formalized and extremely competitive process at the entry level; it's exceedingly difficult to get in the door these days if you haven't done an internship in the industry.

- Primary channel is on-campus recruiting, but there are opportunities for midcareer hires, non-MBA advanced-degree holders, and candidates from non-top-tier schools.

- Heavy emphasis on quantitative and analytical abilities.

- Hard work is rewarded regardless of race or gender; however, white males dominate the industry.

The Industry

- Overview

- The Bottom Line

- The Basics of Investment Banking

- From the Inside

- Emerging Industry Trends

- Industry Performance

- Industry Rankings

Overview

You've seen all the headlines, over the past few years, deriding Wall Street firms. You've seen the news photos of disgraced research analysts who recommended certain stocks to the public even while they trashed them in e-mails to colleagues; you've heard about the nine-figure fines investment banks have had to pay for transgressions like conflicts of interest. Still, there's something intriguing about the industry—the legendary long hours and mega-bonuses—and you like to imagine yourself a pinstripe-wearing, jet-setting investment banker. But suddenly it dawns on you. What the heck is investment banking? You panic. What do investment bankers do? What's the difference between sales and trading and corporate finance? More to the point, why do you want to be a banker?

The intensely competitive, action-oriented, profit-hungry world of investment banking can seem like a bigger-than-life place where deals are done and fortunes are made. In fact, it's a great place to learn the ins and outs of corporate finance and pick up analytical skills that will prove useful throughout your business career. But investment banking has a very steep learning curve, and chances are you'll start off in a job whose duties are more *Working Girl* than *Wall Street*.

Wall Street is filled with high-energy, hardworking young hotshots. Some are investment bankers who spend hours hunched behind computers, poring over financial statements and churning out spreadsheets by the pound. Others are traders who keep one eye on their Bloomberg screen, a phone over each ear, and a buyer or seller on hold every minute the market's in session. Traders work hand in hand with the institutional sales group, whose members hop from airport to airport trying to sell big institutions a piece of the new stock offering they have coming down the pipeline. Then there are the analytically minded research analysts, who read, write, live, and breathe whichever industry they follow.

So where do you begin, and how do you focus your job search? Let's begin with an important reminder: Investment banking isn't one specific service or function. It is an umbrella term for a range of activities:

- Underwriting, selling, and trading securities (stocks and bonds)
- Providing financial advisory services, such as M&A advice
- Managing assets

Investment banks offer these services to companies, governments, nonprofit institutions, and individuals.

Traditionally, commercial banks and investment banks performed completely distinct functions. When Joe on Main Street needed a loan to buy a car, he visited a commercial bank. When Sprint needed to raise cash to fund an acquisition or build its fiber-optic network, it called on its investment bank. Paychecks and lifestyles reflected this division, too, with investment bankers reveling in their large bonuses and glamorous ways while commercial bankers worked 9 to 5 and then went home to their families. Today, as the laws requiring the separation of investment and commercial banking are reformed, more and more firms are making sure they have a foot in both camps, thus blurring the lines and the cultures. The action and players are still centered in New York City and a few other money centers around the world, but the list of players is getting smaller as the industry consolidates. Today, leading banks include Merrill Lynch, Goldman Sachs, Morgan Stanley, Citigroup (whose investment banking arm was until recently known as Salomon Smith Barney), Credit Suisse First Boston, and J.P. Morgan Chase. These and other firms are regular visitors to campus career centers.

But before you get excited about the promise of riches (and bid all your on-campus interview points), you'll want to do a little research on the industry and think about whether investment banking is a good career for you. One thing is certain: You shouldn't go into investment banking just for the money—the lifestyle is too demanding. To survive in investment banking, much less to do well, you'll need to like the work itself. And, even if you love the work, an investment banking career can still be a tough road. If the market or your industry group is in a slump (or if your firm suddenly decides to get out of a certain segment of the business), there's always the chance that you may find a pink slip on your desk Monday morning.

Things were tough on Wall Street for a few years after the stock market tumble of the early 2000s. The demise of the dot coms and the drop in the stock market ended one major source of revenues for I-banks: IPOs, which became all but impossible to bring to market. In 1999, there were 480 initial public offerings, which raised a total of $91.7 billion. In contrast, the first quarter of 2003 saw only five IPOs, worth a total of $1 billion. At the same time, M&A activity all but dried up. The extended market decline hurt the profits of investment banks' brokerage operations, as investors (and the commissions they pay each time they trade) dropped out of the market. And September 11, 2001, hit the industry hard: Morgan Stanley and Merrill Lynch both had offices in the World Trade Center, and bankers throughout the Street had a frightening new understanding of how they make ideal symbolic targets for those who hate the West. One result of all this turmoil on the Street has been layoffs: By 2003, according to some, Wall Street employment levels were some 25 percent lower than they were at their peak in 2000.

But things have been looking better of late. The economy has gotten stronger, and industry is spending money again, meaning more mergers and more acquisitions. Indeed, in the first half of 2004, M&A dollar volume clocked in at $891 billion, up from $625 billion in the first half of 2003. The stock market is up, meaning more equity underwriting and rising brokerage volume. Indeed, global equity and equity-related dollar volume was $256 billion in the first half of 2004, up from $149 billion in the first half of 2003.

Still, firms are always looking for new (read: cheaper) bodies; even though they might not be hiring to the extent they did back in the late 1990s, banks are still bringing on best-and-brightest hires for analyst and associate programs.

So if you like fast-paced, deal-oriented work; are at ease with numbers and analysis; have a tolerance for risk; and don't mind putting your personal life on hold for the sake of your job, then investment banking may be a great career choice. But if this doesn't sound like you, a job in investment banking could turn out to be a bad dream come true.

The Bottom Line

Investment banking is one of the best ways a young person can learn about finance and make good money right out of school. Even if you ultimately decide to reclaim your personal life by pursuing other options, the skills you learn on Wall Street will be valuable in most business careers. But before you can cash in on those potential returns, you'll have to put up with some very substantial hardships, including high pressure, long days and nights of hard work, a few difficult personalities, and the expectation—no, the requirement— that all personal plans are subject to the demands of work.

In addition, you'll find that life on the Street is very much at the mercy of the markets. Bull markets bring more work to do than is humanly possible, but you'll be rewarded with a paycheck that can sometimes double year-to-year. Bear markets can leave you sitting at your desk with a pile of deals on hold, hoping that the rumored layoffs and smaller-than-usual bonuses don't come to pass. Despite this inherent uncertainty, the field remains an extremely popular destination for undergraduates and MBAs. Indeed, Citigroup, Goldman Sachs, Bank of America, Morgan Stanley, Lehman Brothers, J.P. Morgan Chase, Merrill Lynch, UBS, and Deutsche Bank are all on *Fortune*'s 2004 list of the "50 Most Desirable MBA Employers." And, because of the current difficult economic environment and the resulting lower demand for employees among investment banks, competition for open spots is especially stiff. As a result, getting your foot in the door by doing an internship with a bank should be your top priority if you want to start a career in investment banking.

The Basics of
Investment Banking

You're beginning your job search, and from what you've heard so far, you want to give investment banking a shot. But there's one small problem: You're not exactly sure what an investment bank does, so convincing the recruiter that you're perfect for the job is going to be a challenge. We'll help solve that problem by giving you a basic introduction to investment banking and a view of its different job opportunities.

The terms *brokerage firm*, *broker-dealer*, and *investment bank* are used interchangeably in popular conversation, but they actually represent different types of companies:

- A **brokerage firm** executes trades, acting as an intermediary between investors and stock exchanges. For this, it takes a commission.

- A **broker-dealer** works similarly, except that it also trades for its own account. That means that if you purchase a stock, it may be bought through an exchange, or it may be bought from the dealer's own account. You pay the current market price, regardless of what the dealer paid for it.

- An **investment bank** is a broker-dealer that provides financing services to corporations, including stock and bond offerings, merger and acquisition advice, and some strategic planning.

These activities are supported in part by the sales, trading, and research functions of the firm.

An investment bank is an advisor to corporations. It's a middleman in the creation and issuance of financial products (stocks, bonds, etc.), it's a sales and distribution organization for those same financial products, it's a major investor and position-taker in the financial markets, and it's a research organization. All of these activities support each other, but it might be helpful to look at them individually.

Capital Raising and Underwriting Services

A primary service of an investment bank is to raise capital for corporations, governments, and other institutions by selling those clients' stock, debt, or other financial paper. The bank helps the client determine a reasonable price for the stock or bond issue and then buys the securities and resells them to investors. The investment bank makes its money on the *spread*, or the difference between the price it pays the client for the securities and the price at which it resells the securities.

Financial Advisory Services

Investment banks advise companies, government entities, and other institutions about their financial strategies and the most effective use of the financial markets. A very high-profile service is mergers and acquisitions (M&A) advice. Examples of other services include assisting companies with their option programs, providing pension-fund managers with up-to-the-minute information and advice on investment strategies, and helping international companies understand how to best minimize their exposure to foreign currency exchange risks.

Sales and Distribution

To be an effective underwriter, an investment bank must have a wide distribution network and a knowledgeable sales force that can consistently find buyers for all of the stocks, bonds, and other financial instruments that the I-bank underwrites. The bulk of the underwritten securities are sold to institutional investors such as pension funds, money management firms, mutual funds, and other large-quantity buyers. The institutional sales force advises and cultivates these important buyers (a job that requires a lot of traveling, schmoozing, and hand-holding) and executes the sales. In addition to these institutional salespeople, many banks have or are adding a retail sales force of stockbrokers plus online discount brokerage services that funnel offerings into the hands of the average investor. However, retail sales— sales to individual investors—is usually considered a completely separate business unit unrelated to investment banking.

Trading and Market-Making Services

To support the institutional and retail sales efforts, most investment banks actively trade securities in the marketplace, thereby providing liquidity (cash) and market prices for their investors. When a firm decides to make a market in a particular stock, it stands ready with its own capital to buy and sell the stock at publicly quoted prices. A firm can make a market either on the exchange floor for listed stocks or on its own trading desk for over-the-counter stocks. Traders usually focus on one group of stocks at a time, often becoming specialists in a particular industry.

Research Services

Nearly all banks have a staff of research analysts who study economic trends and news, individual company stocks, and industry developments to provide proprietary investment advice to institutional clients and in-house groups, such as the sales and trading divisions.

Until recently, the research division has also played an important role in the underwriting process, both in wooing the client with its knowledge of the client's industry and in providing a link to the institutions that own the client's stock once it's publicly traded. Indeed, in many cases, research analysts' compensation was tied to investment banking revenues. However, in recent times banks have faced public and regulatory outcries over conflicts of interest inherent in having bankers and researchers work hand in hand.

As a hypothetical example, consider Bank A, which counts Company X, which is facing financial difficulties, among its banking clients. Should Bank A's research team pan Company X's stock, which would benefit investors who subscribe to Bank A's research, but might upset Company X to the point that it drops Bank A and hires another firm to be its investment banker? Or should it recommend the purchase of Company X stock, which would help Company X financially and keep the banking revenues from Company X rolling in—and pump up research analysts' bonuses, which are based in part on the success of Bank A's banking operations?

In an effort to end the legal scrutiny of their operations, investment banks are now attempting to reinforce the separation between their banking and research arms. You can certainly count on research playing a lesser role in selling banking deals.

Also, independent research houses (e.g., Needham & Co., Sidoti & Co., and JMP Securities) are benefiting in a big way from a settlement between the investment banking industry and regulators that requires investment banks to spend a total $432.5 million over 5 years to give clients independent research. And as the full-service investment banks move to purchase independent research, as they're required to do by regulators, certain research specialists—Standard & Poor's and BNY Jayhawk (which actually aggregates research from more than 100 research organizations)—are looking like they're going to make out handsomely.

From the Inside

Everything coming into focus? Before you say yes, understand that although the services provided by investment banks are relatively standard, different firms can have significantly different market niches and client bases. It's especially easy to get confused when you start paging through the corporate brochures, since every firm has a slightly different way of organizing and marketing its activities. So as you're reading, think in terms of the basic banking functions, and suddenly "capital markets" will reveal itself to be plain old sales and trading.

Keep in mind that although most investment banking org charts look complex, there are essentially three major professional divisions to a full-service investment bank:

- Investment banking
- Sales and trading
- Research

It's important to understand which is which, because the specific tasks (as well as the skills and personalities of the people themselves) are very different. You'll be dinged if you walk into the interview cubicle without some idea of whether you want to structure deals, trade financial products, or do research—and if you pursue and end up getting a job that you're not really a good fit with, work will make you miserable. To help you avoid either fate, we will now take you on a brief tour of a few of the basic jobs within a typical investment bank.

Corporate Finance

The corporate finance group (frequently known as banking or CorpFin) serves the sellers of securities. These may be either Fortune 1000 companies that are looking to raise cash to fund growth or private companies that are looking to go public (i.e., to sell stock on the public markets for the first time). Think of investment bankers as financial consultants to corporations. This is where CEOs and CFOs turn when they're trying to figure out how to finance their operations, how to structure their balance sheets, or how best to move ahead with plans to sell or acquire a company. (M&A can fall under the CorpFin umbrella, but we've written it up separately in this guide.)

The activities of the CorpFin department can range from providing pure financial advice to leading a company through its first equity issue (or IPO). As a result, industry or product knowledge is key, and many investment banks divide their corporate finance departments into industry subgroups, such as technology, financial institutions, health care, communications, entertainment, utilities, and insurance, or into product groups like high-yield, private equity, and investment-grade debt.

As a whole, the corporate finance group will do any and all of the following:

- Underwrite equity offerings (translation: The investment bank buys all of the shares of stock for sale from the corporation or government entity and then sells them on the market to investors.)

- Underwrite fixed-income (debt/bond) offerings

- Help firms analyze their financial needs

- Help firms devise and implement financial strategies (e.g., how to structure their balance sheets, and when and how to proceed with funding initiatives)

- Determine valuations for offerings (i.e., what the opening price for the stock should be)

Who Does Well

Investment banking jobs like corporate finance require critical, detail-oriented thinking. If you have a knack for using numbers to understand patterns that influence business, you're going to be valuable to a company. If you can't crunch and analyze them, this isn't going to be the right job for you. You should also enjoy and excel at solving problems and be able to think critically about the numbers you're working with.

They also require excellent communication and people skills, both to work on banking teams and to build solid relationships with clients.

Lawyers can make as good a fit in this career as MBAs, and experienced candidates with strong experience in a given industry make good candidates for investment banking positions.

Undergrad and grad students should try to get an internship—it's the best way to secure an eventual offer.

An advanced degree (an MBA or other degree) is all but required to advance in this career, and some sales ability is necessary to sell banking business to potential clients.

Sample Project

When a private company's growth demands larger and larger amounts of cash, management will often turn to an investment bank to develop a financing strategy that's more economical than, say, the revolving stack of credit cards it's been using to meet payroll. By selling a portion of its stock to the public in an IPO, a private company can raise a significant amount of capital without increasing its debt burden. An analyst's or associate's role in the process begins once the bank has been invited to pitch for the underwriting business. First, you and the rest of the deal team (senior bankers from your group, plus the appropriate research analyst) will put together a pitch book that includes a preliminary valuation of the company and a description of how the bankers will position the company to make its stock most attractive to investors. If your firm is selected as an underwriter, you and the other analysts and associates staffed on the deal will do most of the legwork to finalize the valuation, prepare and submit the prospectus to the SEC for review, accompany management on the road show, and coordinate with the company's lawyers and other underwriters during the process. After the market has closed on the day the deal is scheduled to price, the deal team will gather for a conference call with the other underwriters and company management to decide the final price for the offering. The next morning, the stock begins trading (with any luck, up!) and you start making plans for the deal team to gather with the company at a posh restaurant for a celebratory closing dinner.

Job Tips

This department generally hires a significant number of MBAs and undergraduates to develop financial models, create the offering memorandum (an important document that can run 200 pages), and facilitate the due diligence process. If you are hired into one CorpFin industry group, think of your relationship with that group as dating rather than marriage. Don't necessarily plan to spend the rest of your 2 or 3 years or career in that group. Market trends are ever changing, and so are the compositions of specific industry groups.

Mergers and Acquisitions

The mergers and acquisitions group (known as *M&A*) provides advice to companies that are buying another company or are themselves being acquired. M&A work can seem very glamorous and high profile. At the same time, the work leading up to the headline-grabbing multibillion-dollar acquisition can involve a Herculean effort to crunch all the numbers, perform the necessary due diligence, and work out the complicated structure of the deal. As one insider puts it, "You have to really like spending time in front of your computer with Excel." Often, the M&A team will also work with a CorpFin industry group to arrange the appropriate financing for the transaction (usually a debt or equity offering). In many cases, all this may happen on a very tight timeline and under extreme secrecy. M&A is often a subgroup within corporate finance; but in some firms, it is a stand-alone department. M&A can be one of the most demanding groups to work for.

M&A groups will

- Advise firms on merger and acquisition strategies.
- Determine target company valuations.
- Help the target of a hostile acquisition arrange a defensive strategy.
- Conduct due diligence on a target or acquiring company (i.e., examine the financial results and other business factors that will affect the value of an acquisition).
- Negotiate price, terms, and conditions of an acquisition or merger.
- Work with the other company's advisory team and the lawyers to structure the deal.

Who Does Well

Like corporate finance, M&A requires detail-oriented thinking, a knack for using numbers to understand business patterns, problem-solving skills, an ability to think critically about the numbers you're working with, and excellent communication and people skills.

Also like corporate finance, lawyers, MBAs, and experience candidates with specific industry knowledge make good M&A candidates. Entry-level candidates should try to get an internship to increase their chances of eventually getting full-time offers.

Sample Project

IBM Corporation decides it has an opportunity to strengthen its hardware business by acquiring an innovative developer of communications software. It approaches an investment bank to get advice on the potential deal. The bankers help IBM secretly value the target company's assets and the potential value of its products to IBM (which may be higher than their current value because of the opportunities to link with IBM hardware and because of Big Blue's marketing muscle). The M&A group then develops IBM's acquisition strategy and makes contact with the target company. Once the offer is made, the target company will consult its own investment bankers. They help the target evaluate IBM's proposal, determine various strategies for defending against or negotiating with IBM, and work out a deal that will be in the best interest of the company's shareholders. After some back and forth, the sides agree on a price (usually a combination of stock and cash), sign the documents, and become one. (Meanwhile, the advisors take their own hefty fees to the bank.)

Job Tips

The M&A department usually recruits under the CorpFin or investment banking umbrella, although within the group you may find further specialization along industry lines. The work here tends to be intense and very deal-focused, and the hours are unpredictable. "You might be staffed on five transactions and not much is happening. Then one turns live, and you have to cancel your weekend plans," says an insider. "Or you could be very busy, and the next day something happens and work gets pushed back a week and suddenly your weekend is free." The job provides an excellent introduction to the high-stakes, high-power push and pull of the corporate world. Insiders tell us that personal ambition is a big success factor in M&A. "You can learn the technical skills like accounting and modeling," says one first-year associate. "It's not so easy to learn how to be driven and to take responsibility, to own the deal." If you're depressed by the thought of spending 3 or more weeks of your life crunching numbers for a deal that never happens, there may be better alternatives in CorpFin.

Public Finance

Public finance is similar to corporate finance except that instead of dealing with corporations, it works with public entities such as city and state governments and agencies, bridge and airport authorities, housing authorities, hospitals, and the like. Although the basic services (financial advisory and underwriting) and the financial tools (bonds and swaps, but no equity) are similar to those used for private-sector clients, numerous political and regulatory considerations must be assessed in the structuring of each deal. A particular key issue involves how to get and maintain tax-exempt status for the financial instruments the client will use.

The public finance group will

- Advise public entities on capital-raising strategies.
- Advise public entities on portfolio management.
- Arrange project finance.
- Help municipal entities restructure their debt.
- Determine a valuation for a debt/bond offering.
- Underwrite tax-exempt notes, bonds, derivatives, and other municipal securities.

Who Does Well

These jobs require strong numbers skills and excellent analytical ability. They also require strong communication skills, since people in this area spend a lot of time dealing with clients. People with experience working in or with government are especially attractive when it comes to landing jobs in public finance, as are lawyers.

An internship is the best point of entry for inexperienced candidates.

Sample Project

Let's say the city of San Francisco wants to give the 49ers a new stadium. The city invites a number of I-banking firms to help it determine the lowest-cost financial structure to pay for the new stadium. The firms research the financial, political, and regulatory issues involved in raising the necessary cash, develop a strategy for raising the funds through tax-exempt instruments, price the deal, and prepare a proposal. The proposal will include a profile of the strategy and its cost, as well as reasons for choosing the presenting firm for the deal. Once a bank is chosen to execute the financing, it will prepare all the necessary financial and regulatory documentation and work with other departments in the bank to shop the offering.

Job Tips

Public finance specialists tend to spend more time with each other than with the rest of the people in the bank. Because it helps to have an understanding of government, many people in public finance come from government backgrounds. Municipal positions were hot in the '70s and '80s, when firms could earn fat underwriting fees for their work. However, as competition has heated up and clients have become more sophisticated, bank fees have fallen, causing the public finance business to become more of a marginal activity for many banks on the Street.

Sales and Trading

Job opportunities in sales and trading—an investment bank's distribution arm—differ from those in the investment banking divisions. Remember, I-banking is more than just corporate finance. You can think of sales and trading as being similar to the sales force for any corporation. This group is responsible for selling all of the financial products (stocks, bonds, and their derivatives) sponsored by the investment banking department. As such, it serves as the vital link between the sellers (corporations and government entities) and the buyers (investors). Depending on the firm, the buyers may be institutions (pension funds, mutual funds, insurance companies, hedge funds, and other asset managers), high-net-worth individuals, or private investors. Although frequently lumped together, salespeople and traders actually perform different functions.

Who Does Well

Sales jobs and trading jobs have many overlapping skill requirements, such as verbal communication skills, sales skills, and a facility for numbers. But the people who do well in each area are not identical. For example, salespeople have to be good at building relationships with a variety of personality types, whereas traders only have to be good at building relationships with other traders. Salespeople have to be good at giving presentations, whereas traders have to be good at making snap decisions based on constantly changing information. Sales jobs typically require a lot more travel than do trading jobs. People in both careers have to be aggressive self-starters.

People in both of these careers will have to take exams to become licensed in their area of specialty. For example, most salespeople have to pass the Series 7 exam.

Unlike investment banking careers, it's not always necessary to get a graduate degree to advance up the ladder in sales or trading.

Sales

Sales professionals typically have a list of institutional clients to whom they pitch new offerings, offer portfolio management advice, and sell securities. The sales department may be divided by account size, security type (debt or equity), geography, or product line. The department is typically divided into large institutional, middle market, and retail (or private-client services) sections.

In other words, a salesperson who manages a high-volume institutional account would not likely handle a smaller, low-volume buyer as well. Groups may be further divided based on the complexity of a bank's financial products, such as government securities, corporate securities, asset-backed securities, futures, options, foreign exchange, derivatives, and others. Because a salesperson works largely on commission, there are major bucks to be made, especially with some of the high-volume accounts.

Sales will typically perform the following:

- Develop strong relationships with institutional investors
- Meet with economic and equity research departments to discuss economic and industry trends and their impact on the markets
- Work with the investment banking department to market new debt and equity issues
- Assist and advise clients in developing and executing investment strategies
- Watch company/industry/economic/political news and market activity, and advise clients about the likely impact on their portfolios
- Attend company presentations and research conferences, typically with clients
- Arrange meetings between clients, research analysts, and company management

Sample project. You're sitting at your desk when suddenly the live news feed on your computer flashes an article about a Fortune 100 company that is firing its CEO and replacing him with a highly respected industry veteran and current board member. You immediately get on the phone to four of your major institutional clients who own big chunks of the company's stock and tell them that this seems to indicate that potential merger talks between the company and its rival have been called off. Two of the clients had been expecting a buy-out and decide to sell a portion of their shares. The third client wants more information about the new CEO's likely plans, so you bring in your head research analyst who covers the company, for a conference call with the client. The fourth client wants to maintain its position unless there's a further drop in the stock price.

Job tips. Along with corporate finance, the sales and trading area typically hires the largest number of MBAs and undergraduates. This is a particularly desirable job for people who love to sell and make money. Along with the big bucks, however, comes a great deal of stress. Because salespeople are essentially account managers, they're the ones who have to take the heat from a client who is irate that a particular stock in his portfolio is falling. It's not easy keeping all of the people happy all of the time, especially in a down market. As you progress up the ranks, you'll typically get more (and more important) clients to manage.

Trading

Traders are responsible for taking positions in the market through purchases and sales of equities (stocks), debt (bonds), and other securities. Trading functions are typically divided by the product lines offered by the investment bank. It's not a job for the meek, timid, or easily offended. During market hours, all trading floors are loud, high-energy environments. Traders must juggle several phone lines, scan computer screens flashing headlines and quotes, and respond to orders from salespeople—all while executing trades with precision timing. The firm's capital is on the line, and every second can be worth millions.

Traders typically

- Develop a solid knowledge of market, company, and industry information. (An insider says, "A good trader is constantly on top of what's going on.")

- Evaluate market activity and supply/demand indications from salespeople and clients.

- "Make markets"—maintain a position in a stock the firm has underwritten, quote bid and ask prices, and buy and sell at those prices.

- Advise salespeople, clients, and research analysts on market activity and pricing for different stock and equity issues.
- Put major trades together by negotiating with salespeople/clients and other dealers.
- Perform valuation analysis of derivatives, convertibles, or baskets of stocks.
- Manage the firm's investment risk.

Sample project. The life of a trader is less project-driven and more market-driven. For instance, let's assume you're at an equity trading desk responsible for trading stocks in timber companies. If you're good at your job, you're constantly reading the news about the economy and the real estate and stock markets. You're also good at picking up the phone and chatting with others in the business about what's going on behind the scenes in government and industry.

Over time, in your reading, you've seen a few articles about some big homebuilding companies, which included anecdotal evidence that demand for their services in some regions may be slackening. Then, one morning, during your daily morning phone call with the research associate covering the same companies you trade for your bank, you learn that he's learned from his homebuilding-industry contacts that a couple of the major players in the sector have definitely experienced lower demand in the past month or so. You also know that this afternoon, new-housing starts will be announced; this is a closely watched number, and the current consensus on the Street is that today's is going to be a high number.

You know that a lower-than-expected number will send the timber sector tumbling. You think the problem through, doing some risk analysis, and decide that odds are very good that the housing-starts number will not come in as high as expected. So you take medium-sized short positions for your bank in the couple of companies in the industry with the worst fundamentals.

Late in the day, during a trading lull, you're talking on the phone with a buddy at another desk about how great the Pistons looked against the Lakers in the first game of the NBA Finals, when the new housing-starts figure flickers across the computer screen in front of you. The number's lower than expected!

Immediately, most of the phones in front of you are ringing, with (you know) sell orders for the companies you trade. You say good-bye to your buddy, smile to yourself, and pick up a phone, knowing that as the market for timber stocks tumbles you'll be able to close out your short position at a sizeable profit for the firm—and a sizeable positive impact on your bonus.

Job tips. On the trading floor of an exchange, the action never stops while the market is in session. (In case you haven't seen a trading floor, it looks something like NASA's Mission Control, only instead of dozens of sleepy-looking engineers, the room is dominated by clean-cut twenty-somethings, most of whom have their sleeves rolled up and are often talking on several phones at once.) Most exchanges have different departments or "desks" focusing on different types of securities. While the market is open, traders are pretty much tied to their spot on the desk, which is an inch away from the next guy's and jam-packed with multiple computer screens. But don't worry: Not every day is a hectic nightmare. Fridays in August will find the floor more concerned with Nerf balls and sports scores than frantic trades. Better yet, the job is essentially done after the market closes and all orders have been reconciled. Unlike your colleagues in most other areas of the bank, you're almost guaranteed your personal time. A special note to University of Chicago MBAs: No one on a trading desk believes that markets are efficient.

Research

Every full-service investment bank has a research department that provides analytical support for investment banking, sales, and trading activities. Research may seem a lot less glamorous than some of the other departments, but these analysts' industry knowledge can often be the most important factor in winning a new CorpFin client or convincing Fidelity to buy shares in an unknown company's IPO. Investment banks regularly lose and gain business as a result of the annual rankings of research analysts that come out in *Institutional Investor* magazine.

Research departments are generally divided into two main groups: fixed-income research and equity research. Both types of research can incorporate several different efforts, including quantitative research (corporate financing strategies, specific product development, and pricing models), economic research (economic analysis and forecasts of U.S. and international economic trends, interest rates, and currency movement), and individual company research. It's important to understand that these are "sell-side" analysts (because they in effect "sell" or market stocks to investors), rather than the "buy-side" analysts who work for the institutional investors themselves.

An equity research analyst will become an expert on a particular group of companies in software, semiconductors, health care, oil and gas, or some other industry group. Unlike the deal-oriented work in investment banking, research is responsible for maintaining a long-term relationship with corporate clients, long after the deal is done. Researchers meet regularly with company management, analyze the company's position relative to its competitors, and provide investors and the sales and trading departments with recommendations about the company's stock (usually rating the stock according to some system, e.g., "strong buy," "buy," or "hold"). Depending on the number of companies in his or her universe, the analyst is responsible for writing one or two reports every quarter on each company, updating interested clients on the company itself, and following market trends that may affect the company's performance. Insiders tell us that though there are different models for the way researchers cover their industries or sectors, those who hope to rank well in the *Institutional Investor* research team ratings tend to cover a small number of companies in great depth. One insider who covers the biotech sector regularly follows the eight companies with the largest market caps.

When you hear on the news that "Microsoft exceeded Wall Street's expectations," newscasters are referring to the average of the earnings estimates published by all research analysts who follow Microsoft. Research analysts listen to presentations from the management of companies they follow, run the new information through their financial models, and relay the information and their predictions about the companies' future performance to investors and the sales force. Their predictions are tested four times a year, when companies release quarterly results, prior to which the company's research department works long days for several weeks (insiders refer to these periods as "reporting seasons" or "earnings"). Companies usually report earnings after the market closes for the day, so analysts must rush to prepare investment recommendations based on the earnings reports, in order to provide them to clients before the market opens the next morning.

Research insiders have long told us that one of the trickiest aspects of the job is to mediate the competing needs of CorpFin, traders, and the companies the analyst covers. "Investment banks are paid for doing deals," says one insider. "On the other hand, I have an obligation to my buy-side clients, who trade stocks on my recommendation. . . . If I sell people deals that don't perform well, they won't listen to me and I won't have a career anymore. I also have a relationship with the companies I cover and [which my bank] might want to take public. They don't take kindly to negative recommendations about them. You put a sell recommendation on somebody's stock, and management might not return your call."

Indeed, with the decline in the markets hurting investors' portfolios, analysts are facing tremendous criticism for helping create the market bubble by recommending stocks of companies that turned out to be dogs—and sometimes even recommending stocks publicly while deriding them internally. And banks are facing criticism for the way they have tied research analysts' compensation to the performance of their banking operations, which can cause conflicts of interest.

The research analyst position involves

- Meeting with company management and analyzing (modeling) the company's financial statements and operations.
- Providing written and oral updates on market trends and company performance to sales and trading as speedily as possible.
- Attending or organizing industry conferences.
- Speaking with the sales force, traders, and investment bankers about company or industry trends, and recommending positions on stocks.
- Developing proprietary pricing models for financial products.
- Making presentations to clients on relevant market trends and economic data, and offering investment recommendations and forecasts.
- Staying on top of emerging new companies in the industry.

Sample Project

Merck & Co. announces that it has requested FDA permission to begin clinical testing of several antistroke medications. The research analyst who covers the pharmaceutical industry calls up contacts at Merck and the FDA and makes a preliminary assessment of Merck's likelihood to receive final approval for the drug. Based on this analysis, and the prospect that this could blossom into a

$300-million-a-year business within 5 years, the analyst issues a "buy" recommendation on the stock. The analyst writes a report, including information about the drug and the impact an FDA green light will have on Merck's business. Before the market opens the following day, the report will be distributed to institutional clients and the sales force. Also, during the daily morning conference call, the analyst will share his or her findings and predictions with all of the traders and salespeople and recommend that they contact their clients and encourage them to purchase the stock.

Who Does Well

This is a detail-oriented career and a very analytical career. If you can't bear studying something (in this case, a company, industry, or financial instrument) from all possible angles, research probably isn't for you. Also, if you require a lot of external stimulus to get you through the workday, you're better off looking into other career tracks in investment banking.

Research could be right up your alley if you have the skills to interact with clients, bankers, and traders (people skills); if you enjoy and are good at analyzing data and figuring out puzzles; and if you can make persuasive arguments verbally and in writing (communication skills).

Research may be especially right for you if you have all of the above skills plus deep knowledge about a particular industry. For example, if you're a biochemist and can show you have the other skills necessary for this career, and you're interviewing for a position analyzing companies in the biotechnology and pharmaceutical industries, your resume will go straight to the top of the pile. As with a number of other careers in investment banking, many lawyers fit well into this career.

Job Tips

The research field tends to be a relatively specialized group within an investment bank. Because the department usually hires for the long term rather than for positions that turn over every 2 or 3 years, there are not as many openings for MBAs and undergrads as there are in banking. Those who are hired generally start as associates and move up to become senior analysts after a couple of years.

Associates generally work long hours, conducting research and working on financial models for the analyst, who may be on the road, meeting with company management or making marketing presentations to institutional clients. One insider tells us that the associates at his firm pull all-nighters on a weekly basis: "You have to be a senior vice president before you start going home at a reasonable hour."

Although research departments take people from a wide variety of backgrounds, they especially appreciate people with financial analysis skills or experience in a particular industry. (PhDs take note: The research department may be your best bet for breaking into banking.) "There's an extreme requirement for trust and discretion," says an insider. "I'm frequently privy to knowledge of upcoming events that will have a dramatic effect on stock prices. There's a huge temptation to tell your cousin, and, of course, you can't do that."

In research, there's less movement between groups than in investment banking, and a research associate must live and breathe the industry he or she covers. A lucky analyst will get a good industry right off the bat. A mediocre analyst with a good industry will have an easier time collecting a nice bonus than will a good analyst covering a dog of an industry.

If you take a job in research, you may find your job description altered somewhat as your bank takes steps to reinforce the separation of its research and banking functions. At the very least, you can count on having less of a role in selling banking business than your more senior colleagues have had in the past.

Controlling

The controlling function oversees the financial details of an investment bank, from the micro level (e.g., making sure trades are booked accurately) to the macro level (e.g., setting budgets for all the departments of the bank). It keeps track of the bank's finances, overseeing the P&L and balance sheet for everything from individual departments and trading desks to the bank as a whole. It advises senior management on the financial state and performance of all the areas of the bank, as well as on ways to lower costs, manage risk, and increase financial performance, and forecasts financial performance and budgetary needs. It also delivers information to external entities such as shareholders, creditors, tax authorities, regulatory authorities, and the bank's auditors.

At the lower levels, people in the controlling function are generally assigned to a specific department or sales or trading desk. They conduct activities such as producing daily P&L reports, checking the accuracy of bookings, creating reports assessing risk or whether the products they are overseeing are priced properly given market conditions, updating balance sheets, and so on. At higher levels, people in the controlling function oversee more areas of the bank, develop annual business plans and budgets, and advise management on overall business strategy, risk management, and reporting processes.

A controller in an investment bank requires the following skill set:

- Often requires a bachelor's degree or better in economics, accounting, or a related field
- Strong analytical and problem-solving skills
- Strong attention to detail
- Excellent communication skills
- Facility with numbers and an understanding of accounting
- Demonstrated interest in or understanding of investment banking

Information Technology

Investment banks have a growing need for IT experts—people to develop, install, manage, and troubleshoot the various technologies banks use as part of conducting business. These technologies vary from internal sales and trading and accounting systems to corporate intranets, online trading systems, and big enterprise systems, like those offered by SAP or Oracle, that manage everything from customer relationships to human resources. Investment banks employ software engineers, system administrators, Web developers, database administrators, and those in similar careers to fill these and related IT roles. Often the IT specialist in an investment bank will work closely with the specific department or departments that use or are developing the technology that the IT person specializes in—for example, techies focused on HR systems will work closely with the human resources department, making sure that a bank's HR system meets the needs of that bank's HR department. Many banks now offer internships to IT types; this is the best way to get a foot in the door in the field.

The specific skills required for investment banking IT positions vary according to the specific role. Most, however, will require the following skill set:

- A bachelor's degree or better in a technology field
- Strong analytical and problem-solving skills
- Certification in or experience with the specific technology on which the job is focused
- Attention to detail
- Solid communication skills
- The desire and ability to continuously update one's tech skills
- Demonstrated interest in or understanding of investment banking

Operations

At the highest levels, people in operations help decide how to structure the bank so that it can perform at the highest possible level, advising management on things such as where the bank should be based, who its vendors should be, what technology systems can optimize the bank's various businesses, and what its employment policies, business processes, and accounting practices should be.

At the lower levels, people in operations are responsible for activities such as transaction processing, handling account transfers, balancing daily entries, and other administrative functions. Lower-level operations professionals are generally assigned to a specific product, department, or sales or trading desk, for which they handle the clearing and settlement of trades and funds transfers, accurately record security positions, make sure regulatory requirements are met, and so on. Lower-level operations professionals may also play a role in improving systems and processes for their department, product, or desk.

Required skills include the following:

- Bachelor's degree or better
- Strong analytical and problem-solving skills
- Attention to detail
- Excellent communication skills
- Facility with numbers and an understanding of accounting
- Demonstrated interest in or understanding of investment banking

Emerging Industry Trends

Warming Trend?

As the global economic climate cooled down following the economic and financial swoon of the early 2000s, so did investment banking performance. IPO and M&A activity all but dried up; the only bright spots on the Street were areas in which lower interest rates drive business, such as mortgage-backed and municipal securities. At the same time, the big banks found themselves tremendously overstaffed, having hired new employees like gangbusters in the boom years of the 1990s. As a result, investment banks laid off tens of thousands of employees. Reports vary, but some say employment levels were 25 percent lower in 2003 than they were at their peak. At the same time, I-banking bonuses, which can account for half or more of some employees' total annual compensation, fell by 50 percent and then some.

But things are looking up today, in mid-2004. The economy is adding jobs. The stock market is up. Businesses are spending money again. More companies are going public. More companies are spending money to acquire other companies. Emerging markets like China promise vast new banking opportunities. And investment banks are enjoying stronger revenues than they've had in years.

One result is that all those banks that laid off employees when the markets tumbled are now hiring. And because it's cheaper to employ a recent grad than someone with more experience, there are a growing number jobs to be had for the cream of the crop from the best schools. Remember: Those who do I-banking internships will have the best shot at full-time openings.

Or Stormy Weather Ahead?

Although many believe the industry is moving into a growth period, confidence in the financial markets today is still not what it was 5 years ago. A number of things are making investors nervous. One is the threat of terrorism. Another is uncertainty about the 2004 presidential elections. And then there's the fact that interest rates look to be on the rise. Some wonder whether the inflation threat can be avoided. Others wonder whether the rise in rates will pull the chair out from under the housing boom or will cause money to flee the equity markets.

Industry Consolidation

Investment banking has witnessed a rash of cross-industry mergers and acquisitions in recent times, largely due to the late-1999 repeal of the Depression-era Glass-Steagall Act. The repeal, which marked the deregulation of the financial services industry, now allows commercial banks, investment banks, insurers, and securities brokerages to offer one another's services. As I-banks add retail brokerage and lending to their offerings and commercial banks try to build up their investment banking services, the industry is undergoing some serious global consolidation, allowing clients to invest, save, and protect their money all under one roof. These mergers have added a downward pressure on employment in the industry, as merged institutions make an effort to reduce redundancy.

Among the M&A activity in recent years: First Boston and Donaldson, Lufkin & Jenrette were both acquired by Credit Suisse; J.P. Morgan and Hambrecht & Quist were swallowed by Chase; Robertson Stephens was acquired by FleetBoston; and Alex. Brown was acquired by Deutsche Bank.

Meanwhile, foreign firms like Deutsche Bank and UBS are moving aggressively into U.S. markets. The result: Firms in the United States and abroad are looking for partners or acquisitions to beef up their global presence. "Almost everything we do now has some cross-border component. More than 50 percent of my work is in foreign investments," says one insider. "Every day I see a wire come across about something going on somewhere like Kenya or India."

Scandals on the Street

The swing in the markets from up, up, up to down, down, down focused a lot of scrutiny on firms on the Street. One of the biggest issues was the fact that banks overrated the investment potential of client companies' stocks intentionally, deceiving investors in the pursuit of favorable relationships—and ongoing banking revenue opportunities—with those companies. Firms also came under fire for the methods by which they allocated stock offerings (specifically, for whether they charged excessive commissions to clients who wanted to purchase hot offerings), as well as for possible manipulation of accounting rules in the course of presenting clients' financial info to potential investors.

By now, almost all of the important investment banks have paid fines totaling in the billions of dollars to settle allegations against them, and the scrutiny of regulators remains sharp. And banks are paying millions to purchase independent research to provide to their customers. In addition, big-time players on the Street, including research analysts like Henry Blodget (Merrill Lynch) and Jack Grubman (Citigroup) and bankers like Frank Quattrone (CSFB) have been accused or convicted of misdeeds and/or fined and fired.

Will the effects of changes coming out of the banking scandals be lasting? Probably not; as the markets improve, and everyone involved starts doing better

> **"**
> **Almost everything we do now has some cross-border component. More than 50 percent of my work is in foreign investments. Every day I see a wire come across about something going on somewhere like Kenya or India.**

off than they were in bad times, regulators ease up on doing their jobs, and companies and their employees become more greedy and prone to breaking the rules to make more money.

New Relationships between Research and Banking

All that said, several changes in the way banks do business seem sure, all of them relating to research: less of a link between research analysts' compensation and firms' banking revenues, less of a role for research analysts in seeking banking business, and more objectivity in research reports. Already, banks are enforcing new degrees of separation between bankers and research analysts: Some banks have even thought about spinning off their research arms into separate entities. The SEC is now requiring research analysts to affirm in writing that the recommendations in their reports are truly what they believe, and that they have received no payment for specific research opinions (a requirement designed to de-link research analysts' compensation from their firms' banking efforts). It's also requiring firms to provide investors with independent research.

The tricky thing about all this is that separating research from banking makes it harder for banks to justify the costs of conducting research. Without revenues that are directly or indirectly the result of their research departments, research becomes purely a cost center. As a result, banks are more likely to look to cut costs in research. That means some investment banks' research departments will either have to cover fewer companies or cover a greater number of companies per analyst—or both.

Industry Performance

Just 5 or 6 years ago, it was much easier to put together a list of the most important investment banking concerns for job seekers to be aware of. But since then, industry consolidation and deregulation breaking down the walls between investment banking and other types of financial services operations in the United States have resulted in fewer pure investment banking and securities companies, and many more diversified financial services companies that include investment banking and securities services among their operations. The list on the following page will give you an idea of some of the major companies engaged in investment banking around the world; for a more accurate idea of the top companies focused primarily on investment banking and securities, check out the league tables. In general, these days, the bulge bracket is thought to include Citigroup Global Markets, Credit Suisse First Boston, Goldman Sachs, Lehman Brothers, Merrill Lynch, and Morgan Stanley.

Key Investment Banks by 2003 Revenue

Company	Revenue ($M)	1-Yr. Change (%)	Employees
HSBC Holdings	56,077	38.9	232,000
Deutsche Bank AG	54,064	−6.6	67,682
BNP Paribas	52,096	8.3	89,100
UBS AG	49,961	8.2	69,061*
Bank of America Corp.	49,006	5.7	133,549
J.P. Morgan Chase & Co.	44,363	2.3	110,453
Morgan Stanley	34,933	7.8	51,196
Barclays PLC	32,577	17.8	74,420
Merrill Lynch & Co.	27,745	−1.8	48,100
Goldman Sachs Group	23,623	34.0	19,476
Societe Generale*	22,939	−14.4	88,278
Citigroup Global Markets Holdings	20,722	−2.5	39,000
Royal Bank of Canada	18,828	26.2	59,549
Lehman Brothers	17,287	3.0	16,200
The Bank of Nova Scotia	13,089	11.3	43,986
Credit Suisse First Boston LLC	11,718	−9.8	18,341
Nomura Holdings**	10,554	48.2	14,385
The Bear Stearns Companies	7,395	7.3	10,532
Daiwa Securities Group	3,235	−12.1	11,559

*2002 figures. **2004 figures.
Sources: Hoover's; WetFeet analysis.

Global Debt (Including ABS, MBS, and Taxable Munis)

During the first half of 2004, debt issuance rose to $2.73 trillion, from $2.69 trillion in the first half of 2003. Citigroup, Merrill Lynch, and J.P. Morgan came in first, second, and third in global debt issuance in the first half of 2004, but Credit Suisse First Boston slipped into the top three, in place of Merrill Lynch, in the rankings for the second quarter of 2004.

Sources: Thomson Financial; WetFeet analysis.

Global High Yield

High-yield issuance came in at $86 billion during the first half of 2004, compared to $70.5 billion in the same period of 2003. Junk debt issuance heated up in the telecom sector, rising to $9.3 billion in the first half of 2004, compared to $2.4 billion in the same year-earlier period.

Sources: Thomson Financial; WetFeet analysis.

Global Equity and Equity-Related

Proceeds from global equity and equity-related new issues rose to $256 million in the first half of 2004, up from $149 million in the first half of 2003. Morgan Stanley was the number-one bookrunner during the first half of 2004, with transactions including Belgacom SA's $4.4 billion IPO and a $3.8 billion secondary equity offering for General Electric. Goldman Sachs came in second, with transactions including Royal Bank of Scotland's $4.79 billion equity offering and Belgacom's IPO. Citigroup ranked third.

Sources: Thomson Financial; WetFeet analysis.

Global IPOs—U.S. Issuers

IPO activity picked up in the first half of 2004, with issues totaling some $17 billion, more than in the whole of 2003. After some bone-dry years, strength in the IPO market looks to continue in coming months, as there are more than 180 companies that have filed to go public.

Sources: Thomson Financial; WetFeet analysis.

Municipal Securities

Excluding short-term notes and private placement issues, volume decreased in the first half of 2004 to $187.0 billion from $204.3 billion in the year-ago period. However, second quarter volume increased to $101.9 billion, from $85.1 billion in the first quarter of 2004. California's $15.2 billion debt issuance was the biggest issuance in the first half of the year.

Sources: Thomson Financial; WetFeet analysis.

Mergers & Acquisitions Advisory

The M&A market, like other areas of Wall Street, looks like it's undergoing a revitalization in 2004, after a long dry spell. Announced worldwide dollar volume came in at $891 billion in the first half of 2004, up 42 percent from $625 billion in the same period in 2003. But observers fear that rising interest rates may end up hurting M&A activity, due to higher financing costs.

Sources: Thomson Financial; WetFeet analysis.

Industry Rankings

To see who's number one in securities underwriting, investment banking insiders look to the quarterly league tables. The league tables show overall industry underwriting activity by security type and the ranking/market share of the individual firms as measured by underwriting volume. You can find the league tables in *Investment Dealers' Digest*, which publishes and reports on the underwriting volumes and industry rankings each quarter. The league tables are produced by Thomson Financial.

To see who's number one in investment research, take a look at *Institutional Investor*'s All-America Research Team (published each fall) and Global Research Team. More subjective than the league tables, these are the result of *I.I.* polls of buy-side analysts and portfolio managers. *I.I.*'s annual rankings are closely watched and often have a direct impact on an analyst's compensation and job security. (Along with All-America and Global Research Teams, *I.I.* puts out rankings for All-Europe, All-Asia, All-Japan, Emerging Markets, and Latin American Research Teams.)

The *Wall Street Journal* also ranks analysts each year. These rankings don't have quite as much clout as *I.I.*'s, but they're still considered important.

Here's a taste of how the firms stacked up in the league table results for the first half of 2004, along with the most recent research rankings when we went to press. For more details on each firm, check out individual WetFeet Company Insider Guides (see the last two pages of this book for a complete list of available WetFeet Insider Guides).

Global Debt, Equity and Equity-Related, First-Half 2004

Rank	Bookrunners	Proceeds ($M)	Market Share (%)	Issues (#)	First-Half 2003 Rank
1	Citigroup	284,874.1	9.5	1,019	1
2	Morgan Stanley	225,969.7	7.6	770	3
3	Merrill Lynch	216,496.9	7.2	920	4
4	J.P. Morgan	209,593.7	7.0	845	2
5	Credit Suisse First Boston	198,490.9	6.6	804	6
6	Lehman Brothers	195,943.3	6.6	682	5
7	Deutsche Bank	187,581.3	6.3	749	8
8	UBS	163,840.1	5.5	655	9
9	Goldman Sachs	150,570.2	5.0	454	7
10	Banc of America Securities	101,506.8	3.4	429	10

Source: Thomson Financial, www.thomson.com/league.

Global Equity and Equity-Related, First-Half 2004

Rank	Bookrunners	Proceeds ($M)	Market Share (%)	Issues (#)	First-Half 2003 Rank
1	Morgan Stanley	33,622.5	13.1	116	2
2	Goldman Sachs	29,657.0	11.6	106	1
3	Citigroup	22,608.6	8.8	127	3
4	UBS	19,879.2	7.8	110	6
5	Merrill Lynch	19,644.7	7.7	88	5
6	Deutsche Bank	15,396.1	6.0	77	10
7	J.P. Morgan	14,302.2	5.6	92	4
8	Credit Suisse First Boston	11,832.6	4.6	77	7
9	Lehman Brothers	10,606.4	4.1	63	9
10	Nomura	7,318.2	2.9	76	11

Source: Thomson Financial, www.thomson.com/league.

Global Common Stock—U.S. Issuers, First-Half 2004

Rank	Bookrunners	Proceeds ($M)	Market Share (%)	Issues (#)	First-Half 2003 Rank
1	Morgan Stanley	12,671.5	18.6	47	5
2	Goldman Sachs	10,903.9	16.0	44	1
3	J.P. Morgan	6,318.6	9.3	39	7
4	Citigroup	6,104.1	9.0	36	2
5	Merrill Lynch	4,961.6	7.3	36	4
6	Credit Suisse First Boston	4,739.1	7.0	33	6
7	Lehman Brothers	4,484.7	6.6	40	3
8	UBS	3,541.5	5.2	33	9
9	Banc of America Securities	2,469.1	3.6	21	8
10	Bear Stearns	2,182.7	3.2	17	10

Source: Thomson Financial, www.thomson.com/league.

Global Initial Public Offerings—U.S. Issuers, First-Half 2004

Rank	Bookrunners	Market Proceeds ($M)	Share (%)	Issues (#)
1	Morgan Stanley	4,412.0	26.2	10
2	Goldman Sachs	3,299.1	19.6	12
3	J.P. Morgan	1,597.0	9.5	11
4	Credit Suisse First Boston	1,232.3	7.3	10
5	Merrill Lynch	1,003.5	6.0	8
6	Friedman Billings Ramsey	980.4	5.8	8
7	Citigroup	826.1	4.9	4
8	Banc of America Securities	723.2	4.3	8
9	UBS	629.7	3.7	6
10	Lehman Brothers	468.5	2.8	7

Source: Thomson Financial, www.thomson.com/league.

Global Debt, First-Half 2004

Rank	Bookrunners	Proceeds ($M)	Market Share (%)	Issues (#)	First-Half 2003 Rank
1	Citigroup	262,265.5	9.6	892	1
2	Merrill Lynch	196,864.6	7.2	833	4
3	J.P. Morgan	195,291.6	7.2	753	2
4	Morgan Stanley	192,347.3	7.0	654	3
5	Credit Suisse First Boston	185,692.4	6.8	726	6
6	Lehman Brothers	185,336.9	6.8	619	5
7	Deutsche Bank	172,185.2	6.3	672	7
8	UBS	143,960.9	5.3	545	8
9	Goldman Sachs	120,913.1	4.4	348	9
10	Barclays Capital	97,550.1	3.6	340	12

Source: Thomson Financial, www.thomson.com/league.

Global High-Yield Corporate Debt, First-Half 2004

Rank	Bookrunners	Proceeds ($M)	Market Share (%)	Issues (#)	First-Half 2003 Rank
1	Credit Suisse First Boston	12,432.1	14.4	73	2
2	Citigroup	11,011.5	12.8	64	1
3	Deutsche Bank	10,290.2	11.9	58	4
4	Banc of America Securities	9,118.6	10.6	58	5
5	J.P. Morgan	8,998.9	10.4	54	3
6	Morgan Stanley	7,721.7	9.0	32	9
7	Lehman Brothers	5,025.3	5.8	38	6
8	UBS	4,503.0	5.2	34	8
9	Goldman Sachs	4,336.9	5.0	29	7
10	Bear Stearns	3,019.7	3.5	26	10

Source: Thomson Financial, www.thomson.com/league.

U.S. Investment-Grade Corporate Debt, First-Half 2004

Rank	Bookrunners	Proceeds ($M)	Market Share (%)	Issues (#)	First-Half 2003 Rank
1	Citigroup	66,832.4	20.5	278	1
2	J.P. Morgan	46,911.4	14.4	249	2
3	Lehman Brothers	29,339.5	9.0	98	4
4	Goldman Sachs	29,219.1	9.0	100	7
5	Credit Suisse First Boston	28,898.4	8.9	161	9
6	Morgan Stanley	28,627.7	8.8	80	3
7	Merrill Lynch	20,676.9	6.3	97	5
8	Banc of America Securities	16,988.2	5.2	82	6
9	UBS	12,233.2	3.8	43	11
10	Deutsche Bank	10,699.6	3.3	55	8

Source: Thomson Financial, www.thomson.com/league.

U.S. Mortgage-Backed Securities, First-Half 2004

Rank	Bookrunners	Proceeds ($M)	Market Share (%)	Issues (#)	First-Half 2003 Rank
1	UBS	45,001.3	12.5	55	2
2	Bear Stearns	42,612.6	11.9	64	3
3	Lehman Brothers	34,883.8	9.7	42	4
4	Banc of America Securities	32,977.3	9.2	42	6
5	Citigroup	27,763.6	7.7	36	7
6	Morgan Stanley	26,899.5	7.5	40	8
7	Royal Bank of Scotland	23,799.6	6.6	42	9
8	Credit Suisse First Boston	22,017.1	6.1	39	5
9	Goldman Sachs	20,391.9	5.7	39	1
10	Deutsche Bank	18,238.7	5.1	29	13

Source: Thomson Financial, www.thomson.com/league.

The Industry

U.S. Long-Term Municipal New Offerings, First-Half 2004*

Rank	Managing Underwriter	Proceeds ($M)	Market Share (%)	Issues (#)	First-Half 2003 Rank
1	UBS Financial Services	25,721.2	13.8	420	2
2	Citigroup	20,721.2	11.1	324	1
3	Lehman Brothers	17,628.1	9.4	114	6
4	Goldman Sachs	14,832.7	7.9	104	7
5	Merrill Lynch	12,640.5	6.8	137	3
6	Bear Stearns	11,423.2	6.1	92	5
7	J.P. Morgan Securities	9,908.1	5.3	95	8
8	Morgan Stanley	9,706.0	5.2	116	4
9	RBC Dain Rauscher	7,456.3	4.0	346	9
10	Banc of America Securities	6,830.5	3.7	153	10

*Full credit to bookrunner.

Source: Thomson Financial, www.thomson.com/league.

Worldwide Announced Mergers & Acquisitions, First-Half 2004

Rank	Firm	Value ($M)	Deals (#)	First-Half 2003 Rank
1	Goldman Sachs	252,266.2	172	1
2	Merrill Lynch	237,206.4	96	4
3	Morgan Stanley	218,632.1	154	9
4	Citigroup	206,773.6	175	2
5	J.P. Morgan	201,071.5	178	3
6	Lehman Brothers	140,871.9	86	10
7	UBS	120,198.5	111	7
8	Lazard	103,084.8	87	6
9	Rothschild	91,512.0	105	11
10	Credit Suisse First Boston	82,076.5	141	5

Source: Thomson Financial, www.thomson.com/league.

U.S. Completed Mergers & Acquisitions, First-Half 2004

Rank	Firm	Value ($M)	Deals (#)	First-Half 2003 Rank
1	Goldman Sachs	134,552.5	55	1
2	Morgan Stanley	92,119.2	56	4
3	Banc of America Securities	70,798.1	28	13
4	Merrill Lynch	50,235.9	39	5
5	Citigroup	48,173.4	61	9
6	Lehman Brothers	45,217.3	46	7
7	J.P. Morgan	37,558.1	48	8
8	Credit Suisse First Boston	33,661.7	56	6
9	Lazard	27,962.2	20	2
10	Houlihan Lokey Howard & Zukin	20,521.3	39	16

Source: Thomson Financial, www.thomson.com/league.

Overall Research Strength

See the following tables for the number of analysts from each investment bank on *Institutional Investor*'s research teams.

Rank 2002	Rank 2003	Firm	Total Positions 2003	Total Positions 2002	1st Team 2003	1st Team 2002
		***Institutional Investor* 2003 All-America Research Team**				
2	1	Lehman Brothers	50	52	7	9
5	2	Morgan Stanley	36	42	8	9
2	3	Merrill Lynch	35	52	9	11
1	4	Smith Barney Citigroup	34	53	8	14
-	5	UBS	32	0	8	0
4	6	Credit Suisse First Boston	27	44	5	8
6	6	Goldman Sachs	27	36	5	5
7	8	Bear, Stearns & Co.	23	29	6	6
11	8	J.P. Morgan Securities	23	16	4	3
-	10	Deutsche Bank Securities	18	0	1	0

Sources: *Institutional Investor*; WetFeet analysis.

Institutional Investor 2003 All-America Fixed-Income Research Team

Rank 2002	Rank 2003	Firm	Total Positions 2003	Total Positions 2002	1st Team 2003	1st Team 2002
1	1	Lehman Brothers	35	35	15	12
2	2	Credit Suisse First Boston	33	31	9	7
2	3	J.P. Morgan	30	31	6	12
4	4	Citigroup	19	25	3	2
-	5	UBS	17	0	7	0
7	6	Morgan Stanley	16	17	4	8
9	7	Bear, Stearns & Co.	15	10	4	2
9	7	Deutsche Bank	15	10	4	2
8	9	Goldman Sachs	14	13	1	2
5	10	Merrill Lynch	13	22	3	6

Sources: *Institutional Investor*; WetFeet analysis.

Institutional Investor 2003 Global Research Team

Rank 2002	Rank 2003	Firm	Total Positions 2003	Total Positions 2002	1st Team 2003	1st Team 2002
4	1	UBS	23	18	9	5
3	2	Merrill Lynch	22	19	4	4
1	3	Morgan Stanley	20	21	5	6
5	4	Deutsche Bank Securities	19	13	5	5
5	5	Smith Barney Citigroup	18	13	1	1
1	6	Credit Suisse First Boston	15	21	2	6
8	7	J.P. Morgan	9	6	1	0
7	8	Goldman Sachs	8	7	2	1
9	9	Lehman Brothers	6	4	0	0
10	10	Dresdner Kleinwort Wasserstein	2	2	0	0

Sources: *Institutional Investor*; WetFeet analysis.

The Industry

Wall Street Journal's 2004 "Best on the Street" Survey

Rank	Firm	Total Awards	Qualifying Analysts (#)	"Batting Average"*
1	Merrill Lynch & Co.	13	59	.220
2	UBS	12	48	.250
3	Raymond James	11	32	.344
4	Legg Mason	8	25	.320
5	A.G. Edwards	8	37	.216
6	Bear Stearns	8	42	.190
7	Needham & Co.	7	15	.467
8	Sidoti & Co.	7	16	.438
9	Wachovia Securities	7	28	.250
10	Piper Jaffray	6	20	.300
11	SG Cowen	6	23	.261
12	JMP Securities	5	8	.625
13	Morgan Keegan	5	14	.357
14	Robert W. Baird	5	17	.294
15	Prudential Equity Group	5	33	.152

*Firms are ranked by total awards; "batting averages" (ratio of a firm's total awards to its total number of research analysts who qualified for the survey) were used to break ties.
Source: Thomson First Call.

The Firms

- The Big Picture

- Major Players

- Other Firms

The Big Picture

Until the wave of consolidation and convergence that started in the 1990s in the financial services industry, the playing field had changed very little and was easy to understand. Commercial banks and investment banks each had their roles, as defined by federal regulations, and seldom did the two meet. And within investment banking, firms could be neatly categorized by their size, market focus, or both. At the top was the bulge bracket, which consisted of the six largest firms: Merrill Lynch, Goldman Sachs, Morgan Stanley, Salomon Smith Barney, First Boston, and Lehman Brothers. These firms still dominate the securities underwriting and M&A markets, though you'll notice a few name changes in the past few years. All firms beyond the bulge bracket were labeled *boutiques* or *regionals*. Boutiques are niche firms that focus on a particular industry, such as technology, or financing vehicle, such as munis. Regionals, as the name implies, focus on financing and investment services in a particular geographic region.

These labels are still used (although the smaller firms scorn the boutique image), but as the rapid pace of mergers and acquisitions continues to alter the landscape, the traditional categories are becoming less and less meaningful. Large commercial banks that have acquired investment banks are bringing large amounts of capital to the playing field, along with a mix of financial services more varied than ever before.

To help you understand who the major players are today, we've profiled a number of the largest investment banks, plus a number of second-tier banks. To give you an idea of the broader range of options available in investment banking, we've also listed a number of other firms that you can research on your own.

Major Players

Banc of America Securities LLC

9 West 57th Street
New York, NY 10019
Phone: 212-583-8000
www.bofasecurities.com

Overview

Banc of America Securities is the U.S. investment banking arm of Bank of America, one of the biggest commercial banks around. Together with Bank of America's U.K. investment banking subsidiary, Banc of America Securities Ltd., it offers a full range of investment banking and brokerage services.

The company was created in 1998, when its parent bank acquired Montgomery Securities. Later, Bank of America was acquired by NationsBank, and the combined entity took on the Bank of America name.

Banc of America Securities' main offices are in San Francisco, New York, and Charlotte. It employs people in areas including corporate and investment banking, the global markets group (debt capital raising, sales, trading, and research), portfolio management, e-commerce, global treasury services, and asset management.

Banc of America Securities offers full-time and summer associate and analyst programs in the United States and in Europe. In the United States, it recruits at a long list of schools across the country, everywhere from Amherst, Dartmouth, and Yale, to Indiana and Illinois, to Stanford and University of California—

Berkeley, to Texas A&M and University of Texas, to Wake Forest, Vanderbilt, and Duke. It also recruits at top schools in Europe. For a complete list of schools where Banc of America Securities recruits, visit its career website (www.bofasecurities.com/corporate/content/oncampus.asp).

Key Facts

- A senior foreign-exchange officer in the New York office sued Bank of America for gender discrimination in April 2004.

- Has been poaching bankers of late. Hired a top telecom banker away from CSFB in April 2004 to run its media and telecom mergers group, and hired a team of bank analysts from UBS AG in March 2004. Also hired three new European M&A bankers in March.

- In March 2004 agreed to a censure and a fine of $10 million to settle SEC charges of improper record-keeping and failure to produce requested documents in a timely manner.

- Recently settled a class action suit brought by investors in Enron for $69 million and may have to pay $250 million or more to settle SEC charges that it allowed a client to trade mutual fund shares illegally.

Key Financial Stats

2003 revenue: $8,933

1-year growth rate: 3 percent

Personnel Highlights

Not available.

The Bear Stearns Companies Inc.

383 Madison Avenue
New York, NY 10179
Phone: 212-272-2000
www.bearstearns.com

Overview

It was the end of an era in 2001, when longtime Bear Stearns CEO Ace Greenberg stepped down from his leadership post. Greenberg had instilled the firm with an aggressive, no-frills, no-bull corporate culture that is Bear Stearns's calling card to this day. Founded in 1923 by Joseph Ainslee Bear, Robert B. Stearns, and Harold C. Mayer, Bear Stearns built its business reputation around strong trading and clearinghouse operations. In the 1990s, the firm began an effort to build its banking and advisory operations, as well as its asset management business. Still, it has one of the largest clearing operations in the country.

The firm has a big presence in Latin America and has long done a lot of business in Europe. Anticipating bigger and bigger business in Asia, along with the other big banks on Wall Street, Bear is currently building its presence in that region.

Bear Stearns is on the lookout for experienced candidates in asset management, controlling, IT, operations, and private client services. It hires MBAs and other advanced-degree holders for positions in asset management, commercial mortgages, financial management, investment banking, research, and sales and trading. Undergrads can find jobs here in asset-backed securities, asset management, capital markets, collateralized debt obligations, controlling, fixed income and equity, global credit, investment banking, mortgages, operations, and private client services. All candidates should apply online. If you're a student, you should also attend Bear Stearns's campus events and sign up for an on-campus interview.

Key Facts

- Sued in March 2004 by insurance commissioners alleging that the firm helped financier Martin Frankel steal $200 million.

- Bear's mortgage-backed business has been very strong during the active housing market, but rising rates in 2004 are a threat to this business.

- Considered a prime candidate for a merger or acquisition as banks consolidate to enhance their market power.

- Was one of a number of major banks paying between $80 million and $125 million as part of a $1.335 billion settlement with regulators for research misdeeds, in 2002.

Key Financial Stats

2003 revenue: $7,395 million

1-year growth rate: 7 percent

Personnel Highlights

Number of employees: 10,532

1-year growth rate: 0 percent

Citigroup Global Markets Holdings Inc.

388 Greenwich Street, 38th Floor
New York, NY 10013
Phone: 212-816-6000
www.citigroupcib.com

Overview

In 1997, the insurance conglomerate Travelers Group, owner of Smith Barney, acquired the investment bank Salomon Inc., creating Salomon Smith Barney. In 1998, Travelers acquired Citicorp, creating the financial services giant Citigroup. Until recently, the investment banking arm of Citigroup went by the name Salomon Smith Barney, but in the spring of 2003, it dropped the SSB name and replaced it with Citigroup's Corporate & Investment Bank.

The bank operates in areas including capital raising, advisory, lending, risk management, trading, cash management, trade finance, and custody. It operates in more than 100 countries. A major player on the street, in the first half of 2004 it finished at or near the top of the league tables in junk debt, investment-grade corporate debt, municipal debt, mortgage-backed debt, global equity and equity-related business, and M&A advisory. You can learn in great detail about the bank's operations and strategy by downloading the Citigroup Global Corporate & Investment Banking Day Presentation, available at www.citigroup.com/citigroup/fin/gcib.htm.

Citigroup's Corporate & Investment Bank recruits at top schools across the United States and Europe. It recruits undergrads, MBAs, and other advanced-degree candidates for positions in capital markets, equities, fixed income, research, corporate finance, investment banking, transaction services, operations, and technology. Check www.citigroup.com/citigroup/oncampus/homepage/calendar.htm to learn whether the bank recruits at your school. The career section also has information for experienced candidates.

Key Facts

- Federal and state investigations into research misdeeds at the firm resulted in Citigroup paying a $400 million fine in 2002, and onetime star telecom research analyst Jack Grubman resigned, was barred from the securities industry, and agreed to pay a $15 million fine.

- On to-do list: Continue to grow coverage in Europe; continue to grow M&A/advisory business; focus on restructuring opportunities around the world.

- Announced in February 2004 that it is restructuring its global corporate and investment banking business segment into two main groups, the capital markets group and the banking group.

- Beefed up its trade execution capabilities by acquiring Lava Trading in July 2004.

Key Financial Stats

2003 revenue: $20,722 million

1-year growth rate: −3 percent

Personnel Highlights

Number of employees: 39,000

1-year growth rate: −3 percent

Credit Suisse First Boston LLC

11 Madison Avenue
New York, NY 10010
Phone: 212-325-2000
www.csfb.com

Overview

Credit Suisse First Boston is the result of the 1988 merger of the investment bank First Boston and Credit Suisse, a European commercial bank. In 2000, the firm acquired Donaldson, Lufkin & Jenrette, a leading underwriter of high-yield bonds with a golden reputation in research. A bulge-bracket bank, CSFB ranked fifth among all banks in 2003 in terms of global debt, equity, and equity-related issuance.

CSFB has experienced trouble in recent years, with business slackening in key areas (e.g., IPO underwriting) and regulatory trouble (the firm paid a $200 million fine in 2002 for research improprieties and another $100 million in 2002 to settle charges that it received kickbacks in the form of higher commissions from clients to whom it allocated hot IPO shares—and in the process rock-star tech banker Frank Quattrone resigned and eventually was convicted of criminal charges). The firm has also been losing key bankers in recent times; epitomizing this trend, the CEO of the investment bank, John Mack, announced plans to leave the firm in the summer of 2004, reportedly due to the fact that his desire to merge Credit Suisse with another firm was not in line with the desires of the majority of the directors of Credit Suisse. After that announcement, the firm's head in China announced plans to leave the firm, and as this guide goes to press the firm must surely be worried that an exodus of the firm's talent in Asia will ensue.

The bank recruits undergrads and MBA and other grad students for positions in IT, asset management, private client services, sales and trading, research, private equity, and investment banking. CSFB has a presence at top schools across the country. Experienced job candidates and students at schools where CSFB does not recruit can apply through the company's website.

Key Facts

- Known for excellence in high-yield debt; ranked first among all banks in junk debt underwriting in the first half of 2004.

- 69 locations in some 34 countries.

- For minority students, offers all-expenses-paid trip to New York in June to learn more about investment banking and CSFB (application deadline: March 15).

- Considering responding to demands for stronger separation of banking and research by creating an independent research business bearing the DLJ name.

- Named co-lead underwriter for 2004's Google IPO, along with Morgan Stanley.

- Sold its Pershing clearinghouse to Bank of New York in 2003.

Key Financial Stats

2003 revenue: $11,718 million

1-year growth rate: –10 percent

Personnel Highlights

Number of employees: 18,341

1-year growth rate: –20 percent

Deutsche Banc Securities Inc.

60 Wall Street
New York, NY 10019
Phone: 212-469-4000
www.db.com

Overview

Deutsche Banc Securities is the full-service North American investment banking arm of German financial services giant Deutsche Bank AG. It includes Deutsche Bank Alex. Brown, which provides M&A, acquisition finance, and project finance advisory to clients in the health-care, media, real estate, technology, and telecom sectors.

The bank has been undergoing some changes, with some key employees leaving the firm and the addition of a number of senior-level hires. In March 2004, Deutsche announced it was laying off 50 employees in the equity group, including nine senior research analysts, dropping coverage of 100 of the 731 companies it used to cover in the process. Observers report that layoffs could continue as the bank cuts back on research coverage, a common trend on the Street.

Overall, though, Deutsche Bank has been focused on building its presence in North America. The bank's investment banking arm hires undergrads and MBA and other grad students for entry-level positions in global corporate finance, global capital markets, global equities, technology, operations, controlling and finance, risk management, HR, and private wealth management.

DB recruits for region-specific positions on campuses around the world, but all job applicants, even those on campuses where the bank has a presence, must start the application process by completing an online application form. The bank then screens candidates and sets up interviews with those it wants to learn more about. The bank interviews MBA, undergrad, and other entry-level candidates on campus or, if the bank isn't recruiting on a given campus, in an arranged location (e.g., a hotel) or in a Deutsche Bank office. Check the DB website to learn whether the bank comes to your campus or to learn more about the careers available at the bank or the application and interview process, including deadlines in various regions and for various positions.

Key Facts

- As of July 2004, Deutsche Bank is reportedly planning on settling charges brought by the SEC and the New York DA over alleged conflicts of interest between research and investment banking.

- Launched a correspondent mortgage lending group in June 2004 and is looking to staff up the group in following months.

- Is geared up for an increase in investment banking activity, having hired 12 new senior bankers in late 2003.

Key Financial Stats and Personnel Highlights

Not available.

Friedman, Billings, Ramsey Group, Inc.

1001 19th Street North
Arlington, VA 22209
Phone: 703-312-9500
www.fbr.com

Overview

Friedman, Billings, Ramsey has made a big splash on the Street in recent times. In 2003, the bank ranked third in U.S. initial public offering underwriting, behind only Goldman Sachs and Credit Suisse First Boston. And it continues to do well: In the first quarter of 2004, FBR's underwriting revenues increased to $62.8 million from $8.8 million in the year-earlier period, its corporate finance revenue grew to $28.3 million from $5.7 million in the year-earlier period, and its institutional brokerage revenues came in at $35.2 million, up 211 percent from the year-earlier period. And the bank's investment banking deal pipeline included $5 billion in potential deals at the start of 2004.

All this growth means more jobs at Friedman, Billings, Ramsey; indeed, the bank is in the process of staffing up in a number of areas. FBR offers top students internships in areas such as asset management, equity research, investment banking, institutional sales, accounting/finance, corporate communications, human resources, information technology, and legal/compliance. Students should check the firm's website to learn more, as should those interested in full-time jobs.

Friedman Billings Ramsey has offices in Arlington, Atlanta, Bethesda, Chicago, Cleveland, Dallas, Denver, Houston, Irvine, New York, Portland, San Francisco, Seattle, London, and Vienna.

Key Facts

• Hired six new research analysts in April 2004, increasing the number of industries it covers from six to eight: consumer, diversified industrials, energy, financial services, health care, insurance, real estate, and technology, media, and telecommunications.

• In February 2004 announced plans to hire 60 new bankers during the year.

• Said in February 2004 that it plans to grow its capital markets business, with an emphasis on the technology, health-care, and consumer sectors.

• Sponsors the FBR Open, formerly the Phoenix Open, a stop on golf's PGA Tour.

Key Financial Stats

2003 revenue: $629 million

1-year growth rate: 134 percent

Personnel Highlights

Number of employees: 496

1-year growth rate: 3 percent

The Goldman Sachs Group, Inc.

85 Broad Street
New York, NY 10004
Phone: 212-902-1000
www.gs.com

Overview

Goldman Sachs was founded in 1869 when Marcus Goldman, an immigrant from Europe, began a small enterprise to provide an alternative to expensive bank credit. In the 1950s, Goldman played a lead role in establishing the municipal bond market, and in the 1970s the firm formed the first official M&A and real estate departments on Wall Street. Today it continues to sit at or near the top in most areas of investment banking advisory, sales, and trading. In the first 6 months of 2004, Goldman ranked second in global equity and equity-related business, second in global IPO underwriting, fourth in global investment-grade corporate debt, fourth in muni underwriting, and first in M&A advisory. Perhaps even more significant, it is probably considered by the majority of people in the industry as the gold standard in terms of the quality of its employees (a belief that's especially true among Goldman employees, naturally), what an investment bank should be, and how a bank should do business. (A fact that's a bit ironic given that Goldman has faced as much scrutiny as any other bank as the SEC and other regulators try to clean up Wall Street in the wake of the early-2000s banking scandals—and has had to pay a pretty penny to settle charges of misdeeds brought against it.)

The bank is very sophisticated—and successful—in its recruiting practices. Its website includes a "Where Do I Fit?" quiz to help visitors understand where it might make sense for them to work within Goldman Sachs. The bank recruits on campuses around the globe. Students should check the site to learn more about whether Goldman recruits on their campus, what they should do if it doesn't, and how the Goldman interview process works. Students and experienced candidates can also apply for jobs online.

Key Facts

- In 2002, the firm was one of a number of major banks paying between $80 million and $125 million as part of a $1.335 billion settlement with regulators for research misdeeds.

- Agreed to pay $2 million in 2004 to settle SEC charges that it improperly marketed IPOs in 1999 and 2000. Also in 2004, agreed to pay $40 million to settle SEC charges that it received higher commissions from investors who were offered in-demand IPO shares and that it gave client executives IPO shares for agreeing to give Goldman more banking business.

- In 2004, is the target of an SEC investigation into improper handling of Dutch auctions in the bond market.

- In 2004, Spear, Leeds & Kellogg, the clearinghouse unit of Goldman Sachs, agreed to pay a total of $45.5 million to settle charges that it violated New York Stock Exchange rules.

- Former President and COO John Thain left the firm to head the NYSE in 2004.

- Has hired S&P to provide independent research to Goldman clients, per new industry regulations.

- Hasn't had an M&A department since disbanding its M&A group after the 2000 market tumble, but is considering reviving the group in 2004.

- In February 2004 laid off several dozen traders and salespeople, with those in the cash equities group the primary victims of the ax, as the bank focuses more on selling and trading more complex financial instruments.

Key Financial Stats

2003 revenue: $23,623 million

1-year growth rate: 3 percent

Personnel Highlights

Number of employees: 19,476

1-year growth rate: –1 percent

Jefferies Group, Inc.

520 Madison Avenue, 12th Floor
New York, NY 10022
Phone: 212-284-2300
www.jefco.com

Jefferies, which was founded in 1962, serves small- and middle-market corporate clients, offering investment banking, including M&A, research, off-exchange institutional brokerage, research, asset management, and equity and debt underwriting, sales, and trading, with an emphasis on high-yield debt.

It is in the process of expanding both organically and via acquisition. In December 2003, for example, it acquired Broadview International, a global M&A advisor focused on the technology sector, and the fixed-income desk of Mellon Securities. It acquired Quarterdeck Investment Partners, a boutique bank specializing in M&A for the aerospace and defense and federal IT industries, in 2002.

Meanwhile, it has expanded existing business groups including the general industrial group in investment banking, the private placement group in the fixed income department, the equity research department, private client services, and health care investment banking in recent months—largely by picking up talent laid off by the bulge bracket banks. Indeed, Jefferies has grown from 77 bankers in 1999 to more than 165 in 2004. It also has some 80 research professionals covering some 500 companies.

Visit the Jefferies website to learn more about job opportunities with the firm.

Key Facts

- Had major business difficulties way back in 1987, when it was revealed that Jefferies had illegally "parked" stock for Ivan Boesky for his corporate takeover attempts.

- Looking to expand in Asia and Europe.

- Has offices in London, Paris, Zurich, and Tokyo.

Key Financial Stats

2003 revenue: $927 million

1-year growth rate: 23 percent

Personnel Highlights

Number of employees: 1,626

1-year growth rate: 20 percent

J.P. Morgan Chase & Co.

270 Park Avenue
New York, NY 10017
Phone: 212-270-6000
www.jpmorganchase.com

Overview

This firm was formed by a mega-merger when Chase Manhattan, one of the largest commercial banks around, paid $33 billion to join with J.P. Morgan, one of the oldest and most prestigious commercial and investment banks in the world. Subsidiaries include J.P. Morgan Fleming Asset Management, which serves institutional investors; J.P. Morgan Partners, a private-equity house; J.P. Morgan H&Q, an investment banking arm focused on areas like tech and health care; and J.P. Morgan Private Bank, which serves wealthy private clients. And now, with the 2004 acquisition of Bank One, it's getting even bigger. (However, the acquisition probably won't have a major effect on the way things are done in the investment bank, J.P. Morgan.)

J.P. Morgan is a major player in terms of debt and equity issuance worldwide; in the first half of 2004, it was third in the league tables in global equity underwriting, in U.S. IPO underwriting, and in overall debt underwriting. It is also a player in M&A—fifth best in the business, in terms of worldwide announced deals in the first half of 2004.

The bank hires undergrads and MBAs and other grad-degree holders in areas including corporate finance, fixed-income sales and trading, equity research, fixed-income research, derivatives research, investment management, and private banking. It recruits at schools across the United States. Check the bank's website and with your career services center to learn more about how you can apply for positions at J.P. Morgan. Both experienced candidates and students can apply for jobs online.

Key Facts

- In 2002, the firm was one of a number of major banks paying between $80 million and $125 million as part of a $1.335 billion settlement with regulators for research misdeeds.

- In 2003, paid $25 million to settle charges of illegal IPO allocation and $135 million to settle Enron-related charges.

- $58.7 billion acquisition of Bank One completed in July 2004.

- Reported by Reuters in May 2004 to be looking to add 50 to 100 people in operational roles in its equities and fixed-income groups in Europe.

- J.P. Morgan's investment banking business posted earnings of $1.11 billion in the first quarter of 2004, a big jump from $897 million in the same year-earlier period. The bank's investment management and private client arm earned $115 million in the first quarter, up from $27 million in the first quarter of 2003.

Key Financial Stats

2003 revenue: $44,363 million

1-year growth rate: 2 percent

Personnel Highlights

Number of employees: 110,453

1-year growth rate: 17 percent

The Firms

Lazard LLC

121 Boulevard Haussmann	**U.S. Headquarters:**
75382 Paris Cedex 08, France	30 Rockefeller Plaza
Phone: 33-1-4413-01-11	New York, NY 10020
	Phone: 212-632-6000

www.lazard.com

Lazard, the biggest remaining private investment bank on the Street, is a full-service investment bank, operating in areas including securities origination, sales and trading, research, asset management, and investment banking. Its reputation in M&A and corporate restructuring advisory is the bank's biggest strength. Bruce Wasserstein, a legend on Wall Street, has been CEO since 2002.

Currently the firm is considering going public, at Wasserstein's urging; analysts have given the bank a valuation of between $3.5 billion and $4.1 billion.

Lazard is known for having an entrepreneurial, nonhierarchical culture. In other words, if you need to be managed to be at your best, or you want a clear career path, there are other places that might be a better fit for you.

In North America, Lazard recruits MBAs for associate programs on-campus at Haas, Columbia, Harvard, Stanford, University of Chicago, and Wharton. It also recruits undergrads for analyst programs at University of California—Berkeley, Claremont McKenna College, Columbia, Florida A&M, Georgetown, Harvard, Northwestern, Howard, McGill, Princeton, Queens College, Stanford, University of Chicago, University of Illinois, University of Michigan, Notre Dame, University of Virginia, Wellesley, Penn, and Yale. If you're an experienced candidate, check Lazard's website for information on opportunities and how to apply for them.

Key Facts

- Has about 550 banking professionals and about 2,500 employees overall.

- Various arms of Lazard merged into a single organization in 2000. Its resulting one-firm structure allows for greater cross-border collaboration than was possible before the merger.

- In the United States, has offices in New York, Chicago, San Francisco, Los Angeles, Houston, and Atlanta.

Key Financial Stats and Personnel Highlights

Not available.

Lehman Brothers Holdings Inc.

745 Seventh Avenue
New York, NY 10019
Phone: 212-526-7000
www.lehman.com

Overview

Traditionally one of the bulge-bracket firms, Lehman Brothers went through a troubled marriage to American Express in 1989; it was spun off from Amex in 1994. Curiously, the firm started out in 1850 as a dry goods store in Alabama and quickly became a force in the cotton industry. The firm is known for its excellence in fixed-income underwriting and research but is also strong in other areas. Lehman has put in strong performances in some recent years, but it doesn't have the size or clout of some of its rivals. In the first half of 2004, Lehman ranked sixth in M&A, sixth in debt underwriting, and sixth in global debt, equity, and equity-related proceeds.

The firm is currently beefing up its Hong Kong operations, in anticipation of ample financing and equity origination opportunities in the region, and expanding its European derivatives capabilities. In April 2004 it announced that it is looking to acquire overseas banks and investment companies, and that it plans to expand its European operations.

While other banks have been making heavy cuts in their research departments during the business and market slowdown of the past few years—as well as company and industry coverage—Lehman has been less aggressive in trimming research positions. As a result, while other banks are responding to the pick-up in the economy by making lots of research hires, landing a research position at Lehman is going to remain extremely difficult.

Lehman has associate and analyst summer and full-time programs for MBA and other grad degree candidates and undergrads. Check its website for recruiting contacts, information on how to apply, and whether Lehman recruits on your campus, as well as information for experienced candidates.

Key Facts

- In 2002, the firm was one of a number of major banks paying between $80 million and $125 million as part of a $1.335 billion settlement with regulators for research misdeeds.

- Chosen by California to lead management of its $15 billion bond offering, which will be the largest Lehman has ever handled, worth double the amount of the previous largest bond offering lead managed by the firm.

- Lehman has a reputation of being a bit less white-shoe (i.e., less formal) than most other banks and a bit more street-wise than those banks.

Key Financial Stats

2003 revenue: $17,287 million

1-year growth rate: 3 percent

Personnel Highlights

Number of employees: 16,200

1-year growth rate: 31 percent

Merrill Lynch & Co., Inc.

4 World Financial Center
250 Vesey Street
New York, NY 10080
Phone: 212-449-1000
www.ml.com

Overview

Merrill was founded in 1914, when Charles Merrill opened the first U.S. retail brokerage firm, winning his company the nickname "the firm that brought Wall Street to Main Street." He was joined a year later by his friend Edmund Lynch.

In recent years, the company has worked to increase its presence in the global marketplace. The firm's strength lies in its vast retail brokerage network and large asset management business, as well as its position near the top of the global underwriting and advisory league tables.

All has not been rosy for Merrill of late. Poor performance has forced the firm to drop thousands of employees over the past several years. In 2002, the firm was forced to pay $100 million to New York State after evidence supporting allegations of fraudulent stock recommendations by Merrill research analysts came to light. Also in 2002, the firm was one of a number of major banks paying between $80 million and $125 million as part of a $1.335 billion settlement with regulators for research misdeeds. In 2003, the firm was charged by the SEC with helping Enron fraudulently pump up its profits in 1999, and Merrill agreed to pay $80 million to settle.

Merrill recruits undergrads for positions in debt, equity, and relationship management; investment banking; private client; credit; investment management; services and operations; technology; and accounting and finance. It hires MBAs into debt, equity, investment banking, private client, private wealth, research, and business development. If you're a student, check with your career center to see whether Merrill Lynch holds on-campus interviews or resume drops at your school and whether the center has an application procedure that you must follow in addition to completing the firm's online application. Experienced candidates can apply for jobs at the Merrill website.

Key Facts

- Rumor has it that Merrill may sell some or all of its $513 billion investment management business. Companies that moved into investment management, looking at the business as a way to add a predictable revenue stream, are now looking at getting out of the business, citing increased regulatory scrutiny.

- Reportedly considering making a $2 billion acquisition of energy trader Entergy Koch LLP.

- Ordered to pay $2.2 million after an arbitration panel found the firm guilty of discriminating against female stockbrokers in April 2004.

Key Financial Stats

2003 revenue: $27,745 million

1-year growth rate: −2 percent

Personnel Highlights

Number of employees: 48,100

1-year growth rate: −6 percent

Morgan Stanley

1585 Broadway
New York, NY 10036
Phone: 212-761-4000
www.morganstanley.com

Overview

Morgan Stanley is one of the leading firms in underwriting, retail distribution, and asset management. Indeed, in the first half of 2004, the bank was ranked first in global equity and equity-related proceeds, global IPO underwriting, and global debt underwriting and second in U.S. completed M&A business.

Morgan Stanley was formed in 1935 after the Glass-Steagall Act forced banks to cease underwriting and other investment banking activities, when Henry Morgan and Harold Stanley left J.P. Morgan and established a separate I-banking firm. A 1997 merger with Dean Witter gave Morgan Stanley access to that company's extensive retail brokerage business. In 2002, the firm was one of a number of major banks paying between $80 million and $125 million as part of a $1.335 billion settlement with regulators for research misdeeds.

Morgan Stanley hires undergrads and MBAs around the globe for programs including equity research, fixed income, IT, investment banking, investment management, public finance, and strategic planning. For more information, check www.morganstanley.com/careers/recruiting/programs/index.html. While there, you can check whether Morgan Stanley recruits at your campus and apply for programs online if it doesn't.

Key Facts

- More than 600 offices in 27 countries.

- Settled for $54 million in July 2004 over charges by the Equal Employment Opportunity Commission that it engaged in gender discrimination; specifically, that it denied women promotions and raises and subjected them to groping, crude sexual comments, and the likes. The *Wall Street Journal* reported on June 2, 2004, that the firm tried to silence witnesses in the case via cash settlements.

- In 2004 tentatively agreed to pay $40 million to settle SEC charges over improper IPO allocation practices.

- In 2003, reached $50 million settlement with SEC over charges that it offered sales incentives to staff to sell Morgan Stanley funds and variable annuities; in 2004, the firm faces a civil suit over the same charges.

- Expanding operations in Russia in 2004, despite the shaky economic climate in that country, and plans to make 40 hires as part of the effort.

- Purchased portfolio risk management firm Barra Inc. and U.K. property firm Canary Wharf in 2004. Hopes that Barra's products will differentiate Morgan Stanley from competitors and boost its institutional equities and prime brokerage businesses.

- Announced plans in March 2004 to physically separate research staff from fixed-income sales and trading staff in order to avoid conflicts of interest.

- Expanded foreign exchange business in 2004.

Key Financial Stats

2003 revenue: $34,933 million

1-year growth rate: 8 percent

Personnel Highlights

Number of employees: 51,196

1-year growth rate: −8 percent

Piper Jaffray Companies

800 Nicollet Mall, Suite 800
Minneapolis, MN 55402
Phone: 612-303-6000
www.piperjaffray.com

Overview

Piper Jaffray is a full-service investment bank serving the middle market. It offers investment banking, securities underwriting, mergers and acquisitions, institutional equity sales and trading, and equity research services. Piper Jaffray's two main lines of business are private client services and capital markets; its investment research group supports both. Piper Jaffray also has a private capital group, which offers investment funds to institutions and high-net-worth individuals, and a venture arm that focuses on health-care investments.

In 1913, H. C. Piper Sr. (the grandfather of the firm's current vice chairman) and C. P. Jaffray formed a commercial paper company called Piper, Jaffray & Co. In 1917, Piper, Jaffray merged with George B. Lane & Co., another commercial paper business, started in 1895, to become Lane, Piper & Jaffray. Over the years the firm branched into a variety of other business areas, until it became a full-service investment bank. In 1997, the firm was acquired by U.S. Bancorp; at the end of 2003, it once again became an independent entity, when it was spun off by U.S. Bancorp.

Piper Jaffray believes the middle market is attractive due to the fact that investment banking industry consolidation has resulted in fewer smaller banks focused on middle-market corporate clients.

With the funds raised by the public offering of Piper Jaffray shares, the firm is engaged in a major expansion effort. In the first half of 2004, the firm made steps to build its research capabilities by adding analysts in the health-care, specialty finance and insurance, credit card, commercial and consumer finance, and mortgage REIT sectors. (Look for Piper Jaffray to try to chase new banking business in these areas.) In addition, the firm has hired new technology bankers and new fixed-income sales and trading professionals.

The bank recruits for investment banking and research positions. It offers summer investment banking internships to undergrads and MBA candidates. It recruits undergrads and MBAs at University of California—Berkeley, UCLA, University of Michigan, University of Minnesota, and Stanford; MBAs at University of Chicago, Kellogg, and Wharton; and undergrads at University of Colorado, Duke, University of Illinois, University of Iowa, University of Kansas, Macalaster College, Notre Dame, University of St. Thomas, University of Texas, and University of Wisconsin—Madison. If Piper Jaffray does not come to your school, or if you're an experienced job candidate, contact the firm directly.

Key Facts

- In the first quarter of 2004, Piper Jaffray revenue clocked in at $209 million, up from $162 million in the first quarter of 2003.

- Spun off as a newly traded public company by U.S. Bancorp on December 31, 2003.

- Equity research covers some 400 companies; fixed-income research covers some 100 companies.

- Has locations in London, New York, Chicago, San Francisco, and Menlo Park in addition to Minneapolis.

Key Financial Stats

2003 revenue: $702 million

1-year growth rate: 6 percent

Personnel Highlights

Number of employees: 2,992

1-year growth rate: 3 percent

UBS Investment Bank

1/2 Finsbury Avenue
London EC2 M2PP, United Kingdom
Phone: 44-20-7567-8000

U.S. Headquarters:

677 Washington Boulevard
Stamford, CT 06901
Phone: 203-719-3000

www.ibb.ubs.com

Overview

UBS Investment Bank is part of UBS AG, which is the world's largest private bank. UBS AG is based in Switzerland, so UBS Investment Bank has a wealth of valuable European and other international connections. The current incarnation of the firm was created through a series of acquisitions, starting with Swiss Bank Corp.'s purchase in the 1990s of O'Connor & Associates, an equity-derivatives trading firm in Chicago. SBC next bought SG Warburg, a London- and New York–based investment bank. Next, SBC acquired Dillon Read, a small, distinguished U.S. investment banking firm, to increase its presence in the United States. In 1998, SBC merged with the Union Bank of Switzerland. And finally, in 2000, Paine Webber was added to the fold, enhancing UBS Warburg's distribution capability as well as its business with high-net-income individuals.

The investment bank operates in three main areas: equities, investment banking, and fixed income, rates, and currencies. Its equities business has membership on 82 stock exchanges in 31 countries, and has a physical presence in 40 cities around the world.

The equity research group's 700 analysts around the world follow some 2,900 companies, as well as producing economic, strategy, and derivative research. The investment banking group advises clients on mergers and acquisitions, strategy reviews, and restructuring. It's known for expertise in cross-border mergers and acquisitions and capital raising strategies. The fixed income, rates, and currencies group employs some 2,200 professionals and operates in major markets around the world. UBS is especially strong in foreign exchange.

The bank is a major player in Europe. Indeed, a 2004 poll of European companies by the Institutional Investor Research Group named UBS the best investment bank for equity transactions. And in recent years, it's been growing its U.S. business. It was recently crowned the number-one U.S. equity bookrunner for 2003 as part of The EuroWeek Awards.

Key Facts

- Expecting big results from the Asian markets in coming years and allocating resources accordingly.

- During the first half of 2004, the research group was named by *Institutional Investor* as the number-one research firm in Emerging Markets in Europe, the Middle East, and Africa; number one in the All-Asia research survey; and number one in *I.I.*'s All-Europe research survey. It also came in second on the *Wall Street Journal*'s Best on the Street research survey and in *Institutional Investor*'s All-Japan research survey. And it came in first in the 2004 *Institutional Investor* All-Europe poll in sales, trading, and execution.

- Number one among investment banks outside the United States in terms of its share of the investment banking fee pool, and the fastest growing in the United States.

- Has the largest FX business in the world, by market share, and finished number one in the 2003 Euromoney FX poll for the second year in a row. It also ranked third in the United States in the 2003 *Institutional Investor* fixed-income sales and trading rankings.

Key Financial Stats

2003 revenue: $10,430 million
1-year growth rate: 30 percent

Personnel Highlights

Number of employees: 15,500
1-year growth rate: −3 percent

Other Firms

Firm	Headquarters	Website
Adams Harkness	Boston	www.adamsharkness.com
Allen & Company	New York	n/a
Brown Brothers Harriman & Co.	New York	www.bbh.com
C.E. Unterberg, Towbin	New York	www.unterberg.com
CIBC World Markets Holdings	Toronto	www.cibcwm.com
Daiwa Securities Group	Tokyo	www.daiwausa.com
Dresdner Kleinwort Wasserstein	London	www.drkw.com
Fox-Pitt, Kelton	New York	www.foxpitt.com
FTN Midwest Research	Cleveland	www.midwestresearch.com
Greenhill & Co.	New York	www.greenhill-co.com
Hoenig	Rye Brook, NY	www.hoenig.com
JMP Securities	San Francisco	www.jmpsecurities.com
Keefe, Bruyette & Woods	New York	www.kbw.com
Legg Mason	Baltimore	www.leggmason.com
McDonald Investments (KeyBanc Capital Markets)	Columbus, OH	www.mcdinvest.com
Merriman Curhan Ford & Co.	San Francisco	www.merrimanco.com
Morgan Keegan & Co.	Memphis	www.morgankeegan.com
Needham & Co.	New York	www.needhamco.com
Nomura Holdings	Tokyo	www.nomura.com
Oppenheimer Holdings	Toronto	www.opco.com
Prudential Equity Group	New York	www.cm1.prusec.com
Ragen MacKenzie Group	Seattle	www.ragen-mackenzie.com

The Firms

Firm	Headquarters	Website
Raymond James Financial	St. Petersburg, FL	www.rjf.com
RBC Dain Rauscher Corp.	Minneapolis	www.rbcdain.com
Robert W. Baird & Co.	Milwaukee	www.rwbaird.com
Roth Capital Partners	Newport Beach, CA	www.rothcp.com
Ryan Beck & Co.	Livingston, NJ	www.ryanbeck.com
Sanders Morris Harris Group	Houston	www.smhgroup.com
Sandler O'Neill & Partners	New York	www.sandleroneill.com
Sanford C. Bernstein & Co.	New York	www.bernstein.com
Schwab Soundview Capital Markets	Jersey City	www.schwabsoundview.com
SG Cowen & Co.	New York	www.sgcowen.com
Sidoti & Co.	New York	www.sidoti.com
Stephens Inc.	Little Rock	www.stephens.com
Stifel Financial Corp.	St. Louis	www.stifel.com
Sun Hung Kai & Co.	Hong Kong	www.shkco.com
SunTrust Robinson Humphrey	Atlanta	www.suntrustrh.com
SWS Group	Dallas	www.swsgroupinc.com
TD Securities	Toronto	www.tdsecurities.com
The Advest Group	Hartford	www.advest.com
Thomas Weisel Partners	San Francisco	www.tweisel.com
Wachovia Securities	Richmond, VA	www.wachoviasec.com
Wedbush Morgan Securities	Los Angeles	www.wedbush.com
William Blair & Co.	Chicago	www.williamblair.com
WR Hambrecht + Co.	San Francisco	www.wrhambrecht.com

The Workplace

- Lifestyle
- Culture
- Hours
- Workplace Diversity
- Travel
- Compensation
- Vacation and Perks
- Training
- Career Path
- Insider Scoop

Lifestyle

If you talk to people in the industry about what they really do, you'll find that the life of an investment banker is both more mundane and more demanding than Hollywood filmmakers would have us believe. No matter what area of an investment bank you join, you'll need to make a substantial commitment to your work. But the particular nature of that commitment will vary according to the department you join.

Work in trading generally revolves around the daily cycle of the market and is relatively predictable. The days start early and the work can be intense while the market is in session. The trading day, however, usually finishes shortly after the markets close. As a result, it actually is possible for people in this area to make plans to get together with friends in the evening.

By contrast, investment banking (CorpFin, M&A) revolves around the deal of the moment and can be completely unpredictable. When a deal is hot, everybody on the team will be expected to put all plans on hold and grind away until the work is done. Before the champagne corks start popping, there's a lot of heavy-duty quantitative analysis and extensive back and forth with the attorneys.

There is one tenet you'll need to accept right off the bat: In the minds of most investment bankers, there is no such thing as a personal life. "You have to be willing to make this your top priority," says an insider. "I'm single, and it's tough to start dating when you're working these hours and traveling to Jakarta. It's not like I'm working 100 hours every week, but at a moment's notice, I could fly to Albuquerque for 3 days. I was seeing someone last fall and had to cancel a number of dates, and she must have thought, 'This guy is bailing on me. He can't be gone at 2:00 a.m. that many times in a row.'"

By choosing one of the best-paying careers right out of school, you are also opting to forgo most social activities your friends will be enjoying (though likely with smaller paychecks). Everyone you work for will expect you to be available almost 24 hours a day, 365 days a year. Don't even try to weasel out of an emergency call back to the office with some lame excuse like, "Gee boss, it's my anniversary, and I have these tickets for a Broadway show. . . ." If that's a problem—and many decide that it is, either before they start or after a year or two—there are plenty of other jobs WetFeet can help you research and plan for.

Culture

Investment banks are filled with young, hardworking, intelligent people. Some find that they're also filled with arrogant, master-of-the-universe know-it-alls. So be prepared for the possibility of a few nightmare colleagues who may try your patience. And prepare to be surrounded by people whose primary motivation in choosing their career was money. Indeed, a recent study by management professor Peter Cappelli and executive search firm Spencer Stuart found that 73 percent of investment banking professionals surveyed said getting rich was their primary career objective, and just 14 percent said they'd stay in the industry if they couldn't. These are people who believe that a quality life necessitates getting the best that money can buy—whether it's your car, your kitchen appliances, or your vacations.

Beyond that, culture depends on the firm and your particular group. Your managing director (MD) sets the tone. Some firms, such as Goldman and Merrill, are renowned for their team ethic. (They are also sticklers for fairly conformist behavior.) Others have more of a "star system" that encourages individuals to shine on their own—or be cut from the team. Such an environment is often labeled "entrepreneurial," but the word has a very different meaning within a huge corporate structure than it does at a hungry start-up.

A number of the big players, including Goldman and Morgan Stanley, have long been known as "white-shoe" firms, while Merrill Lynch is known as the firm that "brought Wall Street to Main Street," and it tries hard not to be as elitist.

Your ability to adapt to the culture of a firm may determine whether you sink or swim. Therefore, in gauging your interest in a firm, a particular function, or a group, it's important to think carefully about what aspects of a job matter most to you.

Hours

People who work on the Street tend to work a lot and also tend to exaggerate how much time they actually spend working. For example, one insider claimed to work 110-hour weeks "regularly"—which works out to 15-hour days, 7 days a week. But even taking some exaggeration into account, the young minions of investment banking work an enormous number of hours, especially compared to just about anybody else right out of school. "My attitude going in for the first 3 years is that I want to be working long hours and learning as much as I can," says an insider. "I don't consider [90 hours per week] to be bad at all."

Within a bank, the hours do vary from department to department. They also vary depending on the time of year, the amount of new business a firm is generating, and the bull/bear market cycle. Employees in investment banking/ corporate finance work the longest hours. According to insiders, 80-plus hour weeks are the rule rather than the exception, and most people spend at least 1 weekend day at the office. Nearly all employees can tell war stories about periods when they virtually lived out of a briefcase and didn't see the insides of their own apartments for days on end. "Equity research is more civilized than banking, but it's still a lot of hours," says a research analyst, who told us that the associates at his bank work all night on a weekly basis. "I pull very few all-nighters. But you have to be a senior vice president before you start going home at a reasonable hour."

On the sales and trading side, the market drives the hours. When the market's in session, you're on. That means that sales and trading staff arrive at the office early enough to review all the news and overnight developments before the opening bell and then work intensely until the closing bell. According to our insiders, this makes for about a 60-hour week. One special note for those interested in doing their sales and trading out of a West Coast office: You'll need to be up and running full steam by 5:00 a.m. at the latest, but then you'll usually be out the door by 2:00 or 3:00 p.m. Your afternoons will be free, but no one will be around to play with you.

Workplace Diversity

The investment banking stereotype is the WASP male who attended a prep school and an Ivy League college and who knows of no other stores but Brooks Brothers and L.L. Bean. The stereotype is and isn't true. Says an insider, "You don't see a lot of black people and you don't see a lot of Latinos, but there are a lot of Asians. All of the top people are white men." On the other hand, firms have an interest in changing, although most firms are highly evasive when discussing specifics. Two factors are leading the change: The first is that firms have realized they can be more effective if they look more like their clients, and more and more Fortune 500 companies have diverse management teams. Second, many departments at investment banks are meritocracies, particularly at lower levels and on trading desks. There is a glass ceiling, but it is getting thinner. Still, this remains an issue for the industry: Merrill Lynch, Morgan Stanley, and Salomon Smith Barney (now Citigroup's Corporate & Investment Bank) have all faced sex-discrimination charges in recent years—and in 2004 Morgan Stanley paid $54 million to settle a gender discrimination suit. But if you bring in the clients, make winning stock picks, generate commissions, and get deals done, your gender or skin color shouldn't hold you back too much. After all, two of the most prominent people on Wall Street are women: Abby Joseph Cohen of Goldman Sachs and Mary Meeker of Morgan Stanley.

As for family-friendly practices, well . . . anyone in or considering a two-career family should keep in mind that the long hours and high travel demands of most investment banking jobs can make a tough balancing act even tougher. As a result, the higher ranks seem to be populated mostly by men with stay-at-home wives raising children. Your boss might not understand that you need to be at your daughter's school because your wife is out of town on a business trip. Generally speaking, corporate finance has the most demanding hours and travel requirements, while trading has the least (in terms of the investment banking industry).

The bottom line on gender and other diversity issues is that Wall Street is more open now than at any time in its history, but it still has a ways to go.

Travel

Travel requirements in investment banking can be significant, especially on the banking side of the business. Unlike management consulting, however, where a consultant may take the same flight to Kansas City every Monday morning for 6 months and the same flight back home every Thursday evening, in investment banking most people tend to make shorter, less predictable trips. People in corporate finance, for example, may travel to visit prospective client offices or facilities. Or they might go on road shows, during which a team of bankers and client executives hit as many as 20 cities in a period of 8 to 10 days to "shop" an upcoming issue. Salespeople and traders visit clients, and research analysts visit companies and institutions around the globe. Get yourself a passport if you don't already have one, because more than one investment bank employee has been ordered to be on the next flight to London (including one trading assistant we know who had to courier IPO papers).

The good news? You'll get to stay in nice hotels, your firm may pay for business class, and you will collect so many frequent-flyer miles that you may never pay for a plane ticket again. One research analyst told us that 1 year he put 100,000 miles on his frequent-flyer account for one airline and 50,000 on another. "And that was with no travel to Asia and almost none to Europe." Insider tip for the mileage-rich who can't bear to get near an airport on that rare day off: Plane tickets make great wedding and graduation presents.

Compensation

All right, like any good banker you want the bottom line. Exactly how much are these guys going to pay you to sign your life away? We'll get to the numbers in a minute. But before we do, there are several things to keep in mind. First, salaries at investment banks, even for nonprofessional staff, almost always consist of a base salary plus a fiscal year-end bonus. Second, bonuses are determined at the end of each year and are based on the performance of Wall Street, as well as the performance of your firm and department and your contribution to them. Third, base salaries tend to be relatively low at the entry level (well, let's say moderate), and bonuses are discretionary. As a result, your take-home pay from year to year can go through swings of more than 100 percent, especially when you move up in seniority.

One other useful point: Firms often have different methods of calculating employee bonuses. Some allocate a portion of profits to a particular department while others may divvy up the proceeds among the departments according to performance. Others may use a commission structure based on revenue instead of profits. Some firms are more generous than others with regard to bonuses, and policy can change, too.

Because of the tremendous decline in investment banking revenues over the past few years, bonuses have plummeted. Indeed, investment banks have cut bonuses by as much as 60 percent over the last several years.

Due to scrutiny of research-analyst compensation, research analysts are almost certain to see their total compensation level off or fall in coming years. During the boom years, many research analysts received bonuses based on the amount of banking business they attracted to their firms. Due to concerns about conflicts of interest in research, banks are separating research bonuses from underwriting and other banking business results.

A final note: Investment banking opportunities, of course, exist outside the bulge bracket and outside New York. If you go to work for a boutique or regional bank, don't be surprised if your compensation is not as hefty as that of your bulge-bracket peers.

Undergraduates

In the bulge bracket, starting salaries for undergrads average $45,000 to $55,000. In the boom times of the late 1990s, year-end bonuses for analysts usually fell within a range of $10,000 to $20,000; that ended as soon as the bottom dropped out of the markets. Now, as the United States moves out of recession, bonuses are on the rise, but you probably wouldn't notice much of a difference. We know this isn't what you want to hear, but it's better to know up front what can happen when the market loses steam.

MBAs

Pay increases of 30 percent were reported for 1999 and 2000, but those days are over. Recruiting competition from dot coms is practically nonexistent today, and consulting firms' recruiting efforts have been in a nosedive, while at the same time investment banks are hiring fewer MBAs. As a result, salaries have flatlined. Still, at bulge-bracket banks, MBAs from top-tier B-schools should start at around $85,000 in base salary, plus a signing bonus in the low $20,000s. Any year-end bonus will be contingent on what the market does in the second half of the year.

Summer Hires

Dreading another summer of being the office flunky—fetching coffee and smiling and filing, all for a measly wage? Well, have no fear. It isn't like that for summer interns at investment banks. Many firms use intern programs to attract future analysts and associates, offering challenging work and substantial pay to college sophomores and juniors in hopes of being at the top of their lists come recruiting time. Successful interns at some firms reportedly earn up to $1,200 a week. The price tag for this juicy summer salary is often your social life; some interns report working 70 to 80 hours a week.

On the other hand, successful interns have a better shot at landing a full-time spot after graduation.

The Workplace

Vacation and Perks

What vacation? Are you kidding? Actually, it's rumored that most investment banks offer employees at least 2 or 3 weeks of vacation a year. However, you'll have a hard time taking it all. Moreover, no matter where in the world you go, you can expect to have to check your voice mail multiple times a day and be ready to drop all plans and take the first flight back to New York at a moment's notice. (You might start preparing your potential vacation partners for this as you get ready to interview.)

Do you relish the thought of unlimited long-distance calls, free take-out dinners at the office, and a prepaid limo back to your apartment at 3:00 a.m.? These are regular perks in the world of investment banking. But don't expect a luxurious office. "It's amazing to me that you can go into the office of someone you know is making more than a million a year and it's no bigger than that of an insurance agent," says an insider who made the switch from another industry. Employees may usually set up any investment or other type of financial account with the firm without the usual fees—in fact, you are usually required to do so.

Training

Given the highly technical, jargon-laden nature of jobs in an investment bank, the training program is critical for most people. The specifics of training programs vary from department to department and firm to firm. Many resemble a mini B-school experience, with case studies, work projects, lessons, and post-case discussions, all designed to help new employees better understand how the bank functions. Some banks conduct their programs, which may last anywhere from a few weeks to several months, in a highly structured classroom setting. Others start people off with a few classes and then let them do a lot of on-the-job learning. Another difference between firms: Some training programs take a generalist approach; others a specialist approach. That is, some firms use the training period to give you experience on as many desks in as many divisions as possible, so that you (and the bank) can determine where you fit best when it comes time to commit to a group. Other firms start you off in one group (with any luck, one of your top choices) and focus most of your training in that area; then, if you're not happy in a few months, you can ask to try something else.

Your training will almost surely include help in preparing for the NASD's licensing exams. The basic Series 7 General Securities license is required for most people who will be involved in selling securities, including corporate finance and research professionals as well as salespeople and traders. Take these seriously; you may be given a limited number of chances to pass (and you will probably have to do most of the studying on your own time). A caution against lying: Your fingerprints will be taken and will be checked by the NASD as part of the registration process. We know of a mutual fund employee who lost her job when her prints were run and it turned out that she had been convicted of felony shoplifting—on her job application, she said she'd never been convicted of a crime.

Career Path

Opportunities for Undergraduates

All investment banks are looking to hire the best, the brightest, and the most motivated undergraduates they can find, because the work is very, very demanding. Undergraduates are usually hired as analysts. Note the derivations of that word: anal + yst. Anal is important because you have to cross all of your *T*s and dot all of your *I*s carefully and twice. Banks typically hire undergraduates with some background in accounting, finance, or economics, because those majors teach you many of the basics you'll need and demonstrate your interest in the industry. However, if you're an engineer or a liberal arts major from a top school, you'll find yourself in good company on Wall Street, too. Just be sure you can present a strong case for what you have to offer and why you are interested in the bank you are courting.

Opportunities for MBAs and Other Advanced-Degree Holders

Each year investment banks hire significant numbers of MBAs from programs across the country. Although the banks also take people with advanced degrees in economics, law, math, computers, and other less obviously related fields, it is less common for people to enter investment banking midcareer. If, after a few years elsewhere, you suddenly realize that investment banking is your true calling, chances are you'll have to start on the ground floor with all of the newly graduated MBA recruits. One possible exception: People with wide industry experience or specific skills (or a Rolodex full of rich and powerful connections in government or industry) may be able to fill a specialized function, such as research analyst or product specialist, higher up within a firm. Although a pedigree from a top university may help you get a foot in the door, becoming a partner or managing director depends much more on your performance and endurance. In fact, insiders tell us that people from lesser-known institutions often outperform people from brand-name schools. As one ex-banker says, "You gotta really want it to give up your life the way they want you to. The people who came out of second-tier schools and worked hard enough to get a spot with a firm are often the hungriest."

> " "
>
> **You gotta really want it to give up your life the way they want you to. The people who came out of second-tier schools and worked hard enough to get a spot with a firm are often the hungriest.**

The career trajectory of an investment banker usually follows one of two paths. Those who grind away on the career track move from associate to VP to managing director over the course of 4 to 8 years. Others will tire of the work, put in enough time to collect a bonus or two, and then leave the industry (or be fired). Investment banking experience can open many doors to future opportunity. "You certainly have a great Rolodex when you're done," says one insider. "You can go work with a company, with venture capital, with funds on the buy side, or you can go off and write a novel."

Although it is very common for people to move around the industry, insiders recommend that new MBAs spend several years with their first firm, to establish a track record.

Insider Scoop

What Employees Really Like

Experience

The world of high finance is, like New York City itself, fast-paced, high-energy, and go, go, go. This is no place for loafers. It's also no place for the sensitive, hesitant, or meek. Insiders tell us that the experience you gain in investment banking comes at twice the speed of that acquired in many other professions. This may be due in part to the fact that investment bankers put in twice as many hours as those in other professions, but other factors are involved as well. There may be times in your first year when you are juggling four projects, for four different people, at once. "You work with lots of different personalities, fight a lot of fires, and get a crash course in time management," one insider says. Furthermore, you may have the opportunity to meet and interact with the CEOs and CFOs of major public corporations. Be on your best behavior. It's not uncommon for an impressive young investment banker to be recruited into a client's finance or business development department.

Education

Many insiders tell us that the education and skills you gain in investment banking are invaluable. There is no better way to learn about finance, the inner workings of Wall Street, and how the business world generally works. When you read a headline stating that IBM is acquiring a hot new software developer, you can be sure a team of investment banking analysts is grinding out spreadsheet model after spreadsheet model to tell IBM how much it should pay and what return it will get on the investment. Those analytical skills, in conjunction with the introduction investment banking gives you to the world of finance, provide a great launching pad for almost any career path you may ultimately choose. Just don't get used to the big paycheck.

Money

Okay, let's face it. You're not considering a career in investment banking because you want to save the world. You have the rest of your life for that, and you probably won't be spending the rest of your life on Wall Street. If you're an undergraduate or MBA steeped in debt, or you want to be at the top of your peer group in terms of salary, investment banking is a good choice. Even with big-city rents and restaurant prices, you'll almost certainly build up a hefty savings account. While starting salaries and bonus packages are similar in the first 2 years for both consultants and bankers, when business is good investment bankers usually continue up a steep salary curve while consultants do not.

Watch Out!

Hours

Has anyone seen my social life? Being an analyst or associate at an investment bank is like being a doctor on call. This doesn't just mean that you'll regularly be working 60 to 80 hours a week. It means canceling vacations, receiving phone calls between 4:00 and 6:00 a.m., and, probably worst of all, just when you're wrapping up your mellow day around 6:00 or 7:00 in the evening, having the new hotshot banker come over and add an urgent item to your to-do list. And hotshot needs it before tomorrow's 8:00 a.m. flight to Chicago. You go back to your desk, order dinner, and settle in for the night. In the banking business, your life comes second to your job. Though this varies both by firm and by department, insiders tell us that you can generally plan on working at least 12-hour days—and count yourself very lucky if that's all you do.

" "

The politics and personalities in investment banking are not the easiest to deal with, particularly as an analyst. First-year analysts often deal with hazing, practical jokes, and the worst assignments.

Three Ps

Investment banking revolves around the three Ps—power, politics, and personalities. Most of the investment bankers you'll work with will be hardworking, goal-oriented young people like you, but when you have a lot of motivated, competitive Type As jockeying for their shares of the year-end bonus pot, political skirmishes are bound to erupt. Here's what one of our undergraduate insiders says: "The politics and personalities in investment banking are not the easiest to deal with, particularly as an analyst. This is ultimately why I left investment banking. First-year analysts often deal with hazing, practical jokes, and the worst assignments. (MBA-laden associates are generally excluded.) Second-year analysts often delegate their own grunt work to the first-years and horde the more interesting and challenging work. And management often doesn't manage; life is the deal, and everything else is secondary. You don't move up the ranks of an investment bank because you are a good manager, but rather because you work hard, understand finance, and bring in deals."

One insider from a non-top-tier business school tells us that some firms can get arrogant about whom they interview. If you run into a firm that interviews candidates only from top-tier schools and you're not, consider it a reason to think twice about working there. "If management is a bunch of Harvard guys, you have to wonder how many jokes you'd have to take about not attending Harvard. And what are the odds the choice assignments would go to a Harvard guy?" Others, however, tell us firms are easing up on this a bit.

The Work

It might be sacrilegious to say this in the company of corporate recruiters, but insiders tell us that the work you do as an investment banker is not always interesting. Don't be blinded by dreams of a Wall Street job filled by constant excitement, glamour, and wheeling and dealing. All insiders tell tales of coma-inducing spreadsheet work that would threaten analysts' lives if they weren't jolted back to reality by the endless blinking of their voice-mail lights. In most offices, the assistants go home at 5:00 p.m. or so, and who do you think handles copying and faxing after that hour? Not the senior managing directors, that's for sure. The adrenaline junkie in you ought to be pleased.

Getting Hired

- Recruiting Overview

- The Recruiting Process

- Interviewing Tips

- Getting Grilled

- Grilling Your Interviewer

Recruiting Overview

Being hungry for an investment banking job is at least as important as having a top-tier school on your resume. Wall Street firms see a lot of flashy pedigrees, but what really makes a candidate stand out is enthusiasm and commitment to work.

With fewer job offers available from banks, and increased demand for those offers due to cutbacks in recruiting by consulting firms and most other types of companies, today it's more important than ever to do an internship in the field if you want to break into investment banking. Banks take this as proof that you are dedicated to working in investment banking and as an opportunity to see whether you have what it takes to make it in the business. So make landing an internship a top priority.

In addition, be sure to research the banks you end up interviewing with. With the increased competition for each open position, these days you won't stand a chance of receiving a job offer if you don't know how each bank works and has been performing, or if you haven't networked your way into talking to some of the professionals at the banks you're interested in.

The Recruiting Process

The investment banking recruiting process begins with the scheduling of a first-round interview. While it's true that banks are looking to fill fewer openings in the current difficult economic environment, all of the bulge-bracket investment banks recruit analysts and associates from top colleges and universities across the country, typically in the fall for MBAs and in the winter for undergrads. (Typically, banks make most of their campus hires into their investment banking departments, such as corporate finance or mergers and acquisitions; fewer hires into sales and trading; and fewer hires still into research, though MBAs stand a chance of landing a research job if they have the right skills and demonstrated interest in the field.) If you attend a school at which the big firms recruit, sign up for an on-campus interview. Firms typically fill their schedules through a combination of closed- and open-schedule interviews; if you're signing up under an open schedule, bid a lot of points. Increasingly, investment banks post their schedules and a lot of other very useful information on their websites. Make those websites the first stop in your research. WetFeet also has a rich array of information on investment banking firms and recruiting online at www.WetFeet.com.

The Interview Cycle

Regardless of where your interests lie (sales and trading, research, corporate finance), your first-round investment banking interview will typically be a traditional 30-minute resume review and informal get-to-know-you session. Many of the firms send alumni of schools they recruit at to conduct first-round campus interviews, so interviewers will often be familiar with your classes and school activities. Insiders tell us that your interviewer will be looking for you to communicate two points very clearly:

1. Why you want to go into the investment banking business

2. Why you want a job with this firm in particular

If you make it through the initial round, you'll be invited to second-round interviews in New York (or in a regional office, if that's where you're applying). Second rounds are half- to full-day affairs (often held on a Saturday and called "Super Saturday"), during which you'll be grilled by at least a half-dozen people with varying degrees of seniority. Sometimes you'll be interviewed one-on-one, other times two-on-one. Some firms sit you in a conference room while the recruiters cycle through; others will send you out to meet your interviewers on their turf, whether that's the trading floor or the analyst pit. Don't bother packing a sandwich; you'll probably be taken to lunch by an analyst or associate. Some firms also conduct third-round interviews, which are similar to second rounds, before extending their offers.

Beyond the Ivies

What if you're not currently a student or the big-name firms don't recruit at your school? Well, your job seeking is going to be a little tougher, but you have several options. One is to use your alumni network to identify a colleague within the firm who can serve as your advocate. First, ask lots of thoughtful, informed questions about the firm and demonstrate your commitment to an investment banking career, and then ask for the colleague's advice in pursuing your job search. Perhaps he or she can persuade the appropriate recruiting manager to watch for your resume and find you a spot in the interview cycle. Basically, the name of the game when you're not recruited is to find any way to make your resume stand out from the thousands of others that investment banks receive every week. It's important to be in sync with the firm's recruiting schedule, so be sure to start contacting alumni early in the fall. Most firms fill their new hire rosters by early spring.

The Aggressive Option

Some investment banking insiders have told us that if you're serious about getting a job on Wall Street and the big firms don't recruit at your school, your best bet is to go to them. "You can drop your resume and play, or you can take fate into your own hands and go to Wall Street and kind of load the deck," says an insider who used this strategy to garner seven Wall Street offers. It may cost you a few bucks, but if you land a job on Wall Street, your salary will more than pay back the investment. Schedule a job-hunting trip to New York and set up as many appointments as you can with the firms you're most interested in. Making the effort to arrange interviews and visit the firms on your own demonstrates your commitment to landing a job on Wall Street; anyone can send in a cover letter and resume, but relatively few go the extra mile.

One insider tells us he made regular trips to New York (it helped that he went to school not far from there) for informational interviews. He said people rarely turned down his requests. "The same five people get calls every week. Instead, try for that senior person that most people don't know about. You want that person to write 'good guy' on your resume and forward it on to HR." He says the informational format helped prepare him for his actual job-hunting trip. "By the time you have your first real interview with Merrill Lynch," he says, "you're much more polished. You've been asked those questions ten different times. You have a battle-tested response."

Extra initiative will also be required of all candidates wishing to work with one of the smaller boutique banks. For the most part, smaller firms don't have the recruiting budgets to support an extensive on-campus recruiting program, so you'll have to contact them on your own.

Also, since investment banking is a meritocracy, you may well be able to start in a clerical position and move up. This possibility is most likely in trading and least likely in corporate finance. Be nice to everyone you meet, do a knockout job, and make it clear that you don't want to be the receptionist or mailroom clerk forever. A lot of firms encourage ascent from below, in part because they like the idea of well-scrubbed, nicely dressed college graduates answering the phones. Ace Greenberg, until recently the longtime chairman of Bear Stearns, started in the mailroom. The whitest of the white-shoe firms are probably least open to such back-door entry, whereas smaller and regional firms (and Bear Stearns) are more open.

Honesty Is the Best Policy

Whatever you do, don't lie on your typo-free resume. You may well get caught (finance is a small world), which will pretty much ruin your career on Wall Street forever. Do people do it? One recruiter says, "We once had a guy who claimed he was a Navy SEAL. We checked it out because it seemed so interesting. It turned out he had never even been in the military. Needless to say, we didn't hire him, and we made some calls, and I don't think anyone else did either. You expect a 15 percent exaggeration factor on resumes, but some people just go crazy."

Interviewing Tips

Experienced Wall Street insiders tell us that the recruiting process should begin before your first-round interview. The first step, before you sign up for that interview, is to determine whether you're applying for a corporate finance, sales and trading, or research position. It's true that the content of first-round interviews will be similar in any case. However, insiders tell us that focus on a goal is important, and a lack of focus will earn you a ding. If you're an undergrad, are you interested in being a sales and trading analyst or a corporate finance analyst? MBAs, are you gunning for a research associate position, or is public finance your top choice? Pick one as early as possible, and be sure to clearly communicate your choice to your interviewer.

A great way to learn which area of investment banking turns you on most is to participate in a "Day on the Job" program. When the banks visit your school, ask them about it. Or approach alums from your school or friends already in the business and ask if you can shadow them for a day. (This is a great way to get your foot in the door if you want to work at a firm that doesn't recruit at your school.) Most of the major Wall Street firms have regional offices in which you can spend a day observing traders, bankers, or researchers at work. Even if you don't live near a city in which one of the major banks is represented, visit a smaller bank. If you choose correctly, the work and the atmosphere will be similar. Taking the time to do a "Day on the Job" will not only be highly informative for you, it will demonstrate to your recruiter that you're serious about your job search.

If your recruiter casually asks you, "So, what other firms are you interviewing with?" it isn't a trick question. However, here's a bad answer to this question: "Well, of course an M&A job with your firm is my first choice, but I'm also talking to Lehman Brothers about a trading job and Credit Suisse First Boston about a job in their research group." Remember, focus is important. Pick one area of concentration and stick with it.

An insider tells us not to underestimate the power of this question. "You've got to build momentum for yourself. If you answer with names they've never heard of, they wonder if you're just grabbing at whatever's out there. You need to know the hierarchy of the firms and what it means when you answer that question." If you're serious about a career on Wall Street, you'll be talking to a lot of firms, and your recruiter wants to hear that. The fact that you're talking to other firms is fine. But don't drop names unless you're really interviewing there. "When someone tells me they're talking to Merrill, Goldman, and Lehman, I call my buddies at Merrill, Goldman, and Lehman and ask if they've heard of the guy. We all went to school together and keep in touch," says an insider. "Once you get the really competitive candidate, you stop talking to your buddies, but in the informational phase, we talk across firms a lot."

Your recruiters will be looking for different skill sets depending on the type of investment banking job you're pursuing. One insider who worked in corporate finance after college and pursued a sales position after business school observes that in her corporate finance interviews, the recruiters focused on her analytical skills and experiences, while her sales interviews were more weighted toward evaluating her people skills, particularly those related to negotiation, relationship building, and persuasion.

In a corporate finance interview, the recruiter will be evaluating your analytical prowess. Expect to be asked about relevant coursework (economics, finance, accounting) and professional experiences. Before your interview, walk through your resume and identify an experience or two that required your supreme powers of analysis (even if it was just writing an investment plan for your summer job earnings). One insider says, "Even if you're an undergrad without previous experience in the financial industry, emphasize the analytical aspects of those things you have done."

In a sales and trading interview, demonstrate your ability to persuade. Expect to be asked questions like:

- What kind of sales experience do you have?
- Tell me about a negotiation you've been involved in.
- Convince me to hire you.

All candidates should be prepared to discuss how to value a company. Know which numbers to look for. If you're an MBA, elementary concepts such as discounted cash flow and the weighted average cost of capital should be as familiar as the back of your hand. You should also be prepared to work with a few numbers without breaking into a cold sweat. Undergrads won't be expected to perform quantitative Olympics at an MBA level, but they should be familiar with the basic concepts of valuation. Have a look at WetFeet's *Beat the Street* Insider Guide series for a succinct how-to overview of these and other interview questions as well as a first-person perspective by a student who snagged several job offers.

As stated above, there are two questions you'll certainly be asked in your first-round interviews, and you'll hear them again as you proceed through further rounds:

1. Why do you want to go into the investment banking business?

2. Why do you want a job with this firm in particular?

Our insiders tell us that it's very obvious when a candidate has prepared an answer to these questions before the interview; they typically come off as well-polished and committed. Those who aren't prepared come across as wishy-washy. We're not going to tell you how to answer the first question—you've got to figure that out for yourself (though several tools in this guide can help).

As for the second, know what distinguishes one firm from another. If you're interested in M&A, which firm is on top? A good answer might be, "I want to work for you because you're the best in this category, have been for the last 5 years, and offer the most extensive training program on the Street." Obviously, it's important that this all be true; toward that end, be sure to spend some quality time with the company profiles in this book and with the league tables. For substantive detail, you should also read WetFeet's Company Insider Guides and online company interviews and profiles, and articles on the firms with which you're interviewing.

Wall Street insiders tell us that liberal arts majors have a bit more selling to do to land a finance job. It's not that the banks don't hire English majors, but they hire a lot more economics and finance majors. So if you followed your bliss in college and are now deciding to explore career opportunities on Wall Street, be prepared to demonstrate your analytical skills up front. Play offense, not defense. Tell your interviewer that although you have a liberal arts background, your analytical skills are sharp as a tack because of X, Y, and Z experiences.

Don't forget, all the investment banks are aggressively building their foreign operations, so speak up about any overseas work experience or foreign language skills. Just don't exaggerate. If you claim to speak Japanese, for example, don't be surprised if a native speaker conducts your interview in that language.

Getting Grilled

WetFeet interviewed industry insiders and asked them what questions an investment banking job candidate can expect—and prepare for—before an interview. Here are several representative questions. Be prepared for these, and you'll probably have an easier time with the unexpected material.

- What most excites you about a (corporate finance, research, sales, trading) job?
- What can you tell me about a couple of stocks that you follow?
- Why do you want to work for this bank versus our competitors?
- Who is our competition (in the major categories)?
- Sales/trading: Pretend that I'm a portfolio manager for Fidelity. Explain to me why I should buy the latest IPO the firm has underwritten.
- Research: You've just been hired as our firm's new XYZ industry analyst. In 2 weeks, you're scheduled to address a growth-stock conference on industry trends. How would you prepare?
- Corporate finance: In a merger discussion, Moon Microsystems says Plum Computing is worth $23 per share; Plum says $34 is more in the ballpark. Who's right, and how would you arrive at a valuation?
- Tell me about your leadership experience.
- Tell me about a high-stress situation you've been in. How did you handle it? What could you do better the next time?
- What did the stock market do last week?
- The Fed recently lowered interest rates. Do you think the move will be sufficient to stimulate the stock market? Why, or why not?
- In which areas is our firm the strongest? The weakest?
- What other banks are you interviewing with?
- What career opportunities are you exploring other than investment banking?

Grilling Your Interviewer

You know it's coming: that moment when the interviewer turns to you and says, "Okay, do you have any questions for me?" Ostensibly an opportunity for you to learn about the company and the recruiting process, it's also an opportunity for the interviewer to learn how much you know about the firm, how well you've prepared for the interview, and whether you're really interested in working for the firm. The following are good generic questions that will fit most investment banking interviews. However, you'll want to think of additional ones that apply specifically to the company with which you're interviewing. One important reminder: If you've already covered any of this material in your interview, don't revisit it. You'll appear inattentive and unfocused.

A word to the wise: We've grouped our questions according to our sense of relative risk. Those in the "Rare" section are meant to be boring and innocuous, while those in the "Well Done" section will help you put the fire to your interviewer's feet. But beware: They may also turn you to toast!

Rare

- What kind of person are you looking for? (This question will provide useful information on personal characteristics you should emphasize.)

- What makes a person successful in this business?

- What made you choose this firm over other firms?

- What is a typical career path in the (corporate finance, sales, trading, research) department?

- How much of an analyst/associate's time is spent pitching new business?

- Is there a formal mentoring program for new analysts/associates?

- If I'm a CEO, why would I choose your firm to take my company public?

Medium

- Beyond the league tables, what differentiates your firm from other firms?

- How is an analyst/associate assigned from the generalist pool to a project?

- Can one request specific teams, industries, or product groups?

- How well do the firm's different divisions work together?

- How long does it take most people here to become managing directors? What's the path? Are there specific benchmarks you have to hit?

- What are the firm's biggest challenges and opportunities in the next 2 years?

- What aspect of your job do you find most frustrating?

Well Done

- How has increased consolidation in the industry affected your firm, both positively and negatively?

- If the company has merged: What new business has resulted from the merger? How well have the two cultures mixed?

- If the company has not merged: Do you think the company needs to acquire or merge with a competitor in the near future?

- What percentage of the managing directors are female or minority?

- How would your firm fare relative to the competition if interest rates suddenly skyrocketed? If oil prices plummeted? (Or whatever else you can think of along these lines, to help you gauge how prepared the firm is for future possibilities.)

- How committed is the firm to building its XYZ business? (Investment banks are known to eliminate entire departments when they underperform against expectations, and if you happen to work for one of those departments, that means bye-bye.)

For Your Reference

- Investment Banking Lingo

- Recommended Reading

- Online Resources

Investment Banking Lingo

To become an investment banker, you'll need to talk the talk. While what follows is by no means a complete list of the terms you'll encounter on Wall Street, it's a good start. Some of these might help you in an interview; others won't. Know them anyway.

Bake-off. The meeting where groups of Hermès-tied and -scarved bankers (analyst minions trailing behind, furiously scribbling into Palm Pilots) parade into a company's boardroom one after another to pitch their underwriting or advisory services as the only choice for the company's upcoming deal. Also known as a "beauty contest."

Bulge bracket. Generally defined as the top five to ten full-service investment banks on Wall Street. It is not a fixed set, as firms move into and out of the bulge bracket over time. The name derives from the top bracket on a tombstone ad (see also: Tombstone) in the *Wall Street Journal.*

Bloomberg. Also known as *Pandora's Box* or the *black box.* This funky little computer, used daily by almost every investment banker, is a one-stop shop for a very wide range of company, economic, and market news, provided you can learn its idiosyncratic navigational commands. Bloomberg (the name of the company that sells the service) was one of the first providers of real-time stock quotes, news feeds, and economic reports. Increasingly, other online services are encroaching on its turf, but some banks still prefer Bloomberg's "closed" system and encourage using it in conjunction with other Internet resources. Bloomberg gives you published estimated future earnings for specific companies and can graph performance. It tells you how many shares of the company the president owns as well as the president's salary. It even gives current sports scores, Vegas odds, cartoons, and philosophical quotes about the market.

Buy side and sell side. *Buy side* refers to institutional buyers of securities, specifically asset management firms, mutual funds, and pensions. At an investment bank, you're working on the sell side, providing research and selling securities to investors. Your clients, the investors, are on the buy side.

Chinese wall. The boundaries that separate research, corporate finance, and sales and trading, with the aim of preventing transmission of inside information. The wall may be physical (different departments on different floors of the same building, or trading on Wall Street and corporate finance in Midtown), or it may be an intangible series of procedures to control documents. When a research analyst is finally told of a deal, usually right before it's announced to the public, he or she is "brought over the wall" and becomes restricted from commenting on the stock. See also: Insider Trading.

Comps. Also known as *comparable company analysis* and *competitive pricing analysis*, comps are an endless part of an analyst's work. Comps are spreadsheet models (generally done in Microsoft Excel) that compare the vital financial statistics of companies in the same industry, such as Nike, Reebok, and Converse. Comps help bankers value a company's financial position relative to others in the same industry by comparing data such as current stock prices, earnings, and financial ratios. An analyst can expect to run comps for just about every deal.

CYA. Roughly, "cover your posterior region."

Deals. Deals are deals, but investment bankers are ultimately neither buyer nor seller. For them, a deal is the process and completion of a security issuance or acquisition/merger of a company. The number of deals completed in a year is one of the most important measures of success of both the bank and the individual banker.

Derivatives. The only thing you remember from calculus. A derivative is also a financial instrument with no inherent value other than what it derives from some other underlying asset. For example, one type of derivative is an interest rate cap. Let's say a company has a floating rate loan. In order to manage its interest rate risk, the company might purchase a 7 percent interest rate cap from the issuer for $200,000. The issuer of the cap assumes the risk of an increase in interest rates above 7 percent. If rates exceed 7 percent, the issuer pays for the excess cost owed by the company. If rates stay below 7 percent, the issuer pockets the whole $200 grand. Other types of derivatives include swaps (referring to the swapping of variable- for fixed-rate cash flows) and reinvestment products.

Due diligence. When a bank decides to do a deal for a client, it goes through a process of due diligence, in which the bankers and their lawyers sit down with management and their accountants and ask them every question they can think of that may uncover possible risks. The bank must do this because if it issues a security for a company with undisclosed risks and then the business falters, causing the security to tank, investors could lose a lot of money and the bank could be sued. See also: CYA.

Dutch auction. One of several processes for selling an offering, this one is designed to be highly objective. Interested investors place bids indicating the number of shares they want and the price they will pay. The deal closes at the lowest price at which all the shares would be sold. Bid too low and you don't get any shares (even if you're a Fidelity fund manager); bid too high and you risk driving up the price more than necessary. So far, they haven't caught on.

Face time. This is the time after 8:00 p.m. when you choose to stay at work just because others, particularly senior others, are there, even though you don't have anything to do. The significance of this around bonus time each year is unclear. (Do not ask during your interview how much face time is required.)

Hedge fund. Don't take the name literally. Hedge fund is the term used to describe a private investment partnership. Since they are private, hedge funds (unlike mutual funds that are sold to the public) are not regulated by the SEC and cannot advertise. There are consultants who specialize in reviewing hedge funds and disseminating the information to potential investors. A share of profits/losses is allocated to all partners based on their percentage ownership; the general partner is paid an additional incentive fee.

High yield. High-yield bonds, also called *junk bonds* or *junk*, are bonds to which Moody's or Standard & Poor's gives low ratings. They produce high yields, unless they go into default. See also: Investment grade.

Insider trading. Crack a joke about insider trading around bankers, and you'll certainly be warned that it's not to be taken lightly. As an investment banker, one is privy to a huge amount of information that cannot be acted on. Imagine, for example, that you were part of the team advising IBM in its acquisition of a publicly traded software developer. Knowing that IBM would be offering a 30 to 50 percent premium over the going market price for the company's stock, you could buy a couple of hundred (or thousand) shares of the company and sell them a month later after the deal goes through, making a tidy profit. Unfortunately, this is illegal, and if you're caught, you may be banned from the securities industry for life, fined, and/or thrown in jail. (See the movie *Wall Street* for a Hollywood portrayal of such an event.) See also: Chinese wall.

Investment banker. A term used by outsiders only. If you are in the business, you are a banker. The opposite is commercial banker.

Investment grade. Low-risk bonds, as determined by Standard & Poor's (AAA to BBB) or Moody's (AAA to Baa). Both Standard & Poor's and Moody's provide independent credit ratings, research, and financial information to the capital markets. See also: High yield.

IPO. An initial public offering (IPO) occurs when a privately owned company sells shares of stock to the public for the first time and the shares are then publicly traded through a stock exchange. In 1999 and 2000, being "pre-IPO" was a bigger draw than "dental plan" in *San Jose Mercury News* want ads. In 2003, "dental plan" is more than holding its own.

LBO. Leveraged buyout. This term was more widely used in the '80s, but the activity is still alive and kicking. An LBO happens when a company is purchased using very little equity and a lot of debt. Let's say you buy an ailing automobile for $100, using $10 of your own cash and a $90 loan from your parents. You agree to pay your parents back the full $90, plus 1 percent interest per month until the loan is paid off. You then proceed to sell the wheels for $10 each, the muffler for $8, the stereo and speakers for $25, the engine for $50, the axle and drive train for $17, and the body to the junkyard for $5. You give your parents back their $90 plus 2 months' interest ($1.80), and you still have $53.20 left over, which is a 532 percent return on your initial $10 investment. An LBO is significantly more complicated, but, in general, a corporation is purchased at a low price, its assets are sold off at a much greater value, and the bank in charge makes a handsome profit.

LTM. Last 12 months. For example, a senior banker may say to you, "Get me the company's LTM revenue and earnings numbers."

Lucite. Brand name for a durable clear plastic material, as well as versions of tombstones (see: Tombstone) encased in Lucite that are distributed to members of the deal team. Lucites are highly coveted tchotchkes among bankers, and different firms compete to see which can create the cleverest designs. You may need to keep your pill-shaped, jewel-cut, and working-slot-machine Lucites at home to protect them from covetous coworkers.

M&A. Get used to this shorthand, as virtually no insiders bother saying "mergers and acquisitions."

Make the quarter. When a publicly held company meets or beats an analyst's quarterly or annual earnings estimates.

Municipal bond. Debt issued by local or state government body. Usually the interest is exempt from federal (and sometimes local and state) taxes.

NASD. The National Association of Securities Dealers, the parent company of the Nasdaq Stock Market, is responsible for operating and regulating Nasdaq and other over-the-counter (OTC) securities markets.

Nasdaq. The Nasdaq Stock Market is a decentralized network of competitive market makers, or firms that stand ready to buy or sell securities at publicly quoted prices.

OTC. Over-the-counter securities are those that aren't traded on an organized exchange like the New York Stock Exchange. A broker-dealer will "make a market" for OTC securities.

PE multiple. The price-to-earnings multiple is a very important ratio on Wall Street. It can tell you if a stock is over- or under-valued relative to its historical performance and relative to other firms. To get it, divide the market price of a share of common stock by the earnings per share of common stock for the last 12 months. A forward PE uses estimated earnings in the denominator.

Printer. A company that prints financial documents for a deal. Young bankers and lawyers spend a lot of time here before a deal, checking and rechecking the progress of a prospectus or proxy statement.

Pitch book. Investment bankers spend as much time pitching deals as they do actually working on deals. Every time one of the calling officers (top two or three levels of bankers) goes to a meeting with the management of a potential client, he or she takes along a slide presentation or bound stack (or "deck") of bullet-point pages and charts, which is called a pitch book. It discusses the client's industry and why your bank is the best one for the client to use in any deal it contemplates. The upside of putting together a pitch book? It's one of your initiation rites as an investment banker. Moreover, you'll learn a lot about a company and an industry, and maybe you'll even meet someone cute in the copy center (where you'll be for long, long hours). The downside? Insiders tell us that putting together pitch books can be pretty dull and repetitive, especially for low-on-the-totem-pole analysts. If you're an associate, you'll generally be writing and designing a pitch book, while the undergrad analysts put together the charts and graphs, compile the statistics, and make all of the edits.

Red herring. The preliminary prospectus on a deal. Printed along the side of the front cover, in red ink, is a notice indicating that it is preliminary. A road show (see below) starts once a firm is cleared by the SEC to "print the reds."

Road show. A sales trip around the country (and sometimes other countries) with the upper management of a company during the month or so before the company's securities issue. During the road show, the company management, investment bankers, and research analysts on the deal team will visit institutional investors to tell the story behind the company and convince them to buy into the offering. At times, this means breakfast in San Francisco, lunch in L.A., an evening flight to Denver for meetings the next morning (spending the night at a posh hotel), then on to Chicago, and so on. Exhausting, but a lot of good meals and a chance to see some interesting new faces.

Secondary offering. When a publicly traded company offers more stock on the market. Any offering after the company's IPO is a secondary offering. Also known as a "follow-on."

Share of voice. The amount of credibility a securities analyst has with respect to a particular stock. Usually earned by making accurate calls on the stock's price movement. The analyst with the most share of voice is often called the "ax" on a stock.

Synergy. Often an attempt to explain CEO hubris. In doing an analysis of one company acquiring another, a banker may say that a company makes $50 million per year, and that a company it hopes to acquire makes $20 million per year, but together they'll make $100 million. Nobody taught you this in college math, did they? The basic idea is that neither company can reach its full potential on its own, but by linking with a well-positioned strategic partner, both parties achieve the stuff that dreams are made of.

Tombstone. If you read the *Wall Street Journal* (which you should be doing regularly if you're interested in investment banking), keep an eye out for the big box advertisements in Section C declaring, "Company X completed the issuance of X hundreds of millions of shares (or dollars of debt)" and then listing all of the investment banks involved in the deal. The size and grouping of the bank names show the level of involvement each had on a particular deal. The largest name on the left side of the tombstone is the one to pay attention to, as it is the lead manager—the bank that did most of the work and received the lion's share of fees. See also: Lucite.

Wallpaper. Worthless securities. The issuing company has gone bankrupt or defaulted.

White shoe. Anachronistic (but still often used) characterization of firms that see themselves—or would like others to see them—as upper-crust and above activities as distasteful as hostile takeovers. The term comes from an old Ivy League tradition of wearing white buck shoes in elite fraternities and clubs.

Recommended Reading

Against the Gods: The Remarkable Story of Risk

Peter L. Bernstein (Wiley, 1998)

A cool study of the history of man's understanding of risk and probability, starting with early gamblers in Greece, going through 17th century probability theory, and ending up with chaos theory. Fun reading for those interested in markets and investing.

Barbarians at the Gate: The Fall of RJR Nabisco

Bryan Burrough and John Helyar (HarperCollins, 1991)

The ultimate inside story of the largest takeover in history, this book also provides an insightful look at the culture and personalities of Wall Street. Ross Johnson, CEO of RJR Nabisco at that time, needed a new PR agent after this book came out.

Bombardiers

Po Bronson (Penguin, 1996)

A black comedy about life on a trading desk, this story cuts mighty close to the bone. Bronson worked as a fixed-income sales analyst at Credit Suisse First Boston's San Francisco office.

Den of Thieves

James B. Stewart (Simon & Schuster, 1992)

This is a classic about the 1980s insider trading scandals, which featured names like Michael Milken, Ivan Boesky, and Dennis Levine, changed the world of M&A, and brought down the bank Drexel Burnham Lambert.

Goldman Sachs: The Culture of Success

Lisa Endlich (Knopf, 1999)

Hagiography, but still interesting. If you're interviewing at Goldman, you should definitely read this. Even if you are interviewing with one of Goldman's competitors, you might want to read this for more information about one of the Street's biggest names.

Heard on the Street: Quantitative Questions from Wall Street Job Interviews

Timothy Falcon Crack (Timothy Crack, 2000)

This book is indispensable if you're a PhD or other job candidate vying for a quantitative position (for example, derivatives analysis) on Wall Street.

The House of Morgan:
An American Banking Dynasty and the Rise of Modern Finance

Ron Chernow (Atlantic Monthly Press, 1990)

At 720 pages, this isn't exactly beach reading, unless you need something to keep your towel from blowing away. Nevertheless, this is a surprisingly readable history of J. Pierpont Morgan and his empire, which still operates as the modern firms Morgan Stanley and J.P. Morgan Chase. Founded in England in 1838, the firm financed American wars, both foreign and civil; ruled over many of the turn-of-the-century trusts such as U.S. Steel, General Electric, and Standard Oil; survived disasters including the sinking of the Morgan-owned Titanic, the 1929 stock market crash, and tight regulation of banking and underwriting practices; and continues to thrive today. Because of the Morgans' power, this book is also a history of investment banking in Europe and the United States. Highly recommended for anyone interviewing with one of the Houses of Morgan as well as anyone interested in financial history.

Liar's Poker: Rising Through the Wreckage on Wall Street

Michael Lewis (W.W. Norton & Company, 1989)

This fun, easy read provides tremendous insight into the culture of Salomon Brothers, sales and trading, and Wall Street in general during the boom of the '80s. You'll also learn a fair amount about how investment banking works. Though much has changed since this era, the personality types remain exactly the same.

Monkey Business: Swinging Through the Wall Street Jungle

John Rolfe and Peter Troob (Warner Books, 2000)

This book takes readers behind the scenes at Donaldson, Lufkin & Jenrette (absorbed in 2000 by Credit Suisse First Boston), depicting the ridiculous lengths that entry-level grunts on Wall Street can go to cope with long hours, stress, and despotic managers; fit in with their peers; and stand out in the eyes of those who can advance their careers.

The Predators' Ball:
The Inside Story of Drexel Burnham and the Rise of the Junk Bond Raiders

Connie Bruck (Penguin, 1989)

Today, Michael Milken is a philanthropist, raising money to fight prostate cancer. This is the story of Milken before he was enjoined from working in investment banking—when he was hot and investment banking was about junk bonds and raids. A nice slice of the '80s.

Online Resources

The Web is loaded with information on investment banking and the securities industry, but most of it exists to attract the interest of individual investors. Trying to find information relevant to your investment banking job search can be a frustrating experience—plugging the term "investment bank" into a typical search engine produces over 500,000 hits. So we did some legwork, surfed for hours, and found the finance sites that are worth a job seeker's look. If you've got the time and want to do some exploring on your own, these are some great places to start.

Finance Site List

www.cob.ohio-state.edu/fin/journal/jofsites.htm

It's hard to imagine that there could be a more comprehensive list of finance links than this one, maintained by the *Journal of Finance*. It's neatly categorized, too, which makes it manageable.

Careers in Business

www.careers-in-business.com

This site provides descriptions of job opportunities in investment banks, some salary information, and industry trends. Careful with the data, though—it's a bit outdated. The site includes a career reference section, which directs you towards help with cover letters, resumes, interviewing, and so on.

Securities Industry Association

www.sia.com

The SIA is the industry trade group. Download the Securities Industry Briefing Book. The briefing book offers a nice history of the capital markets and a summary of the markets' performance last year.

Thomson Financial

www.tfibcm.com

This is the firm that compiles all the data for the underwriting league tables. You can find the latest month's tables here along with some interesting commentary.

Investor Words

www.investorwords.com

Some of that industry jargon still have you confused? Try looking it up on this online encyclopedia of finance. (It's actually more like a dictionary.)

Knowledge @ Wharton: Finance and Investment

knowledge.wharton.upenn.edu

This publication, put out by the Wharton School of Business, offers a lot of timely content regarding news and issues of interest to people on the Street.

Investopedia.com

www.investopedia.com/dictionary

This site provides an extensive dictionary of terms used by the investment community. So if you want to sound like an insider, and use terms like "Guns and Butter Curve," "Big Uglies," and "Bo Derek" like you know what you're talking about, this is a good site to check out.

McKinsey Quarterly: Financial Services and Corporate Finance

www.mckinseyquarterly.com

The *McKinsey Quarterly*, a product of one of the preeminent strategy consulting firms in the world, offers in-depth analysis of news and issues of interest to bankers and potential bankers.

Finance and Business Publications

Most major business publications can be found on the Web. Some are completely free—try Euromoney magazine for a great source of free content—some offer current issues free and then charge for archive searches, and others require paid membership to access any part of their sites. The *Wall Street Journal* Interactive Edition is one that requires a membership, but it's definitely worth paying for. You get a personalized version of the *Journal*, plus access to *Barron's* Online, *SmartMoney* Interactive, the *WSJ* career site, the Dow Jones Publications Library, and the *WSJ* online business glossary.

- *Wall Street Journal Interactive Edition*: www.wsj.com
- *Business Week*: www.businessweek.com
- *The Economist*: www.economist.com
- *Euromoney*: www.euromoney.com
- *The Financial Times*: www.ft.com
- *Forbes*: www.forbes.com
- *Fortune*: www.fortune.com
- *Institutional Investor*: www.institutionalinvestor.com
- *Investors Business Daily*: www.investors.com

WetFeet.com has a number of current articles on the state of investment banking and other financial services careers. Last, but far from least, check out WetFeet's online company mini-sites, where leading financial service firms discuss jobs, recruiting, and themselves in their own words.

WETFEET'S INSIDER GUIDE SERIES

JOB SEARCH GUIDES

Getting Your Ideal Internship

Job Hunting A to Z: Landing the Job You Want

Killer Consulting Resumes

Killer Investment Banking Resumes

Killer Resumes & Cover Letters

Negotiating Your Salary & Perks

Networking Works!

INTERVIEW GUIDES

Ace Your Case: Consulting Interviews

Ace Your Case II: 15 More Consulting Cases

Ace Your Case III: Practice Makes Perfect

Ace Your Case IV: The Latest & Greatest

Ace Your Case V: Return to the Case Interview

Ace Your Interview!

Beat the Street: Investment Banking Interviews

Beat the Street II: I-Banking Interview Practice Guide

CAREER & INDUSTRY GUIDES

Careers in Accounting

Careers in Advertising & Public Relations

Careers in Asset Management & Retail Brokerage

Careers in Biotech & Pharmaceuticals

Careers in Brand Management

Careers in Consumer Products

Careers in Entertainment & Sports

Careers in Human Resources

Careers in Information Technology

Careers in Investment Banking

Careers in Management Consulting

Careers in Manufacturing

Careers in Marketing & Market Research

Careers in Nonprofits & Government

Careers in Real Estate

Careers in Supply Chain Management

Careers in Venture Capital

Consulting for PhDs, Doctors & Lawyers

Industries & Careers for MBAs

Industries & Careers for Undergraduates

COMPANY GUIDES

Accenture

Bain & Company

Boston Consulting Group

Booz Allen Hamilton

Citigroup's Corporate & Investment Bank

Credit Suisse First Boston

Deloitte Consulting

Goldman Sachs Group

J.P. Morgan Chase & Company

Lehman Brothers

McKinsey & Company

Merrill Lynch & Co.

Morgan Stanley

25 Top Consulting Firms

Top 20 Biotechnology & Pharmaceuticals Firms

Top 25 Financial Services Firm

Praise for previous editions of Childhood Cancer

"This practical guide will empower parents to understand the disease better and participate more actively in the treatment process. Recommended for all consumer health collections."

— *Library Journal*

. . . . .

"There's only one word to describe this book—terrific! It is definitive, comprehensive, and easy to read...I recommend this guide to health professionals in pediatric oncology and all parents coping with a child with a solid tumor."

— Denise Cain-Jones, MSW, ACSW
Update Newsletter, Association of Pediatric Oncology Social Workers

. . . . .

"In my 15 years of experience as a pediatric oncology nurse, I have never come across a book as informative, easy-to-read, honest, and encouraging as Childhood Cancer... [It] will truly empower those who read it to be better advocates for their children. I am recommending this book to all the pediatric oncology nurses, social workers, and family support personnel I know."

— Kari Yarwood, ND, RN, CPON
Pediatrics Special Interest Group Newsletter, Oncology Nursing Society

. . . . .

"Having a child diagnosed with cancer is an emotional time that often leaves a family feeling helpless and without control. Written by parents who have walked in the shadow of childhood cancer, this book provides detailed information, open-armed support, and the arsenal of tools needed to fight the battle that lies ahead."

— Clarke Anderson, MD
Children's Center for Cancer and Blood Diseases,
Children's Hospital Los Angeles

. . . . .

"Childhood Cancer is an exceptional resource for parents who are forced to navigate the complex world of childhood cancer. It is invaluable for all family members."

— Eleanor Pask, RN, MScN, EdD, Executive Director
Candlelighters Childhood Cancer Foundation ~ Canada

. . . . .

"This guide is written specifically for the families and caregivers of newly diagnosed children...The authors blend technical information in easy-to-understand language with advice from scores of parents and survivors...The book is sensitively and thoughtfully rendered."

— *Today's Librarian*

"An excellent, supportive, and well-needed book."

— Alan Rees
Consumer Health, A Majors Report

• • • • •

"This book uniquely succeeds in meshing clinical knowledge of impeccable scientific quality with a pragmatic, 'been there done that' sensibility of what is important to parents and caregivers. I recommend it most highly for those in need of helpful knowledge that will empower and help parents and caregivers to cope."

— Mark Greenberg, MD
Professor of Paediatrics & Surgery, University of Toronto
Chair, Paediatric Oncology Group of Ontario

• • • • •

"We are eternally grateful for the invaluable information and advice found in this book! As parents, a patient, and participants in this project, it is truly a gift of guidance, hope, and comfort. Not only would I recommend it for anyone in need, but it definitely should hold a proud place on the book shelf of every pediatric facility."

— Cheryl, Michael, and Shoshana Tobias
Childhood cancer survivor and her parents

• • • • •

"Patient empowerment is the theme, and this new book gives parents and caregivers the knowledge and skills to partner for the best medical care possible."

— *School Nurse News*

• • • • •

"I am a physician and the parent of a child with cancer. The toll that pediatric cancer takes on families is unquantified, but it includes physical and psychiatric illness in the child and in family members, divorce, and tremendous financial stress. Having a resource for coping with all the hardships is the first step toward putting the world back together, and Nancy Keene's books are the best solution I have found."

— Catherine L. Woodman, MD, parent of a childhood cancer survivor
Departments of Psychiatry and Family Medicine, University of Iowa

Childhood
Cancer

A Parent's Guide to Solid Tumor Cancers

Third Edition

Anne Spurgeon and Nancy Keene

Childhood
Cancer Guides

Childhood
Cancer Guides

Childhood Cancer: A Parent's Guide to Solid Tumor Cancers, Third Edition

by Anne Spurgeon and Nancy Keene

Published by Childhood Cancer Guides, P.O. Box 31937, Bellingham, WA 98228. Printed in the United States of America.

Printing History:
1997: First Edition
2002: Second Edition
2016: Third Edition

ISBN 978-1-9410-8990-3

Library of Congress Cataloging-in-Publication Data

Names: Spurgeon, Anne, author. | Keene, Nancy, author.
Title: Childhood cancer : a parent's guide to solid tumor cancers / Anne
   Spurgeon, Nancy Keene.
Description: Third edition. | Bellingham, WA : Childhood Cancer Guides, 2016.
   | Series: Childhood cancer guides | Revision of: Childhood cancer / Honna
   Janes-Hodder & Nancy Keene. 2002. 2nd ed. | Includes bibliographical
   references and index. | Description based on print version record and CIP
   data provided by publisher; resource not viewed.
Identifiers: LCCN 2015045112 (print) | LCCN 2015044034 (ebook) | ISBN
   9781941089910 (pdf) | ISBN 9781941089927 (mobi) | ISBN 9781941089934 (eBook) | ISBN
   9781941089903 (pbk. : alk. paper)
Subjects: LCSH: Cancer in children--Popular works.
Classification: LCC RC281.C4 (print) | LCC RC281.C4 J36 2016 (ebook) | DDC
   362.19892/994--dc23
LC record available at http://lccn.loc.gov/2015045112

To our children—Alison, Julia, Kathryn, Nate, Peter

and

To all children with cancer—past, present, and future—and those who love them

Table of Contents

Foreword

Considerable progress has been made in the last 20 to 30 years in treating children with cancer. Currently, about 80 percent of all children diagnosed with cancer can be cured, including those diagnosed with solid tumors. Nevertheless, having a child with cancer must be one of the most traumatic experiences one can imagine. This book was developed to help educate parents and caregivers of children with solid tumors to make the experience easier to endure.

For most people, it is easier to cope with a difficult situation if they understand what is happening and why. This book will help parents gain a much better understanding of childhood cancer, its treatments, and their consequences. It also provides suggestions and guidelines for dealing with the practical, as well as the emotional, aspects of this experience. The more parents understand about their child's disease, the more effectively they can participate in their child's care and the decisions about treatment.

This book presents a comprehensive view addressing many of the common experiences of having a child with cancer: understanding clinical trials; general principles of surgery, radiation therapy, chemotherapy, and their side effects; stem cell transplantation; novel approaches to therapy; choosing a central venous catheter; coping with procedures; and dealing with hospitalizations. These chapters can be extremely helpful in preparing for therapy. Nutrition can be a very important component in tolerating chemotherapy, and this is also addressed in considerable detail. There are also practical tips about record keeping and finances, as well as dealing with schools and addressing your child's educational needs.

Six chapters are devoted to the major solid tumors of childhood (excluding brain tumors): neuroblastoma, kidney tumors, retinoblastoma, liver tumors, soft tissue sarcomas, and bone sarcomas. These chapters provide information about the origin and spread of these tumors; the signs and symptoms of disease; diagnosis and staging; prognostic indicators; treatment (surgery, chemotherapy, radiation, stem cell transplants); and future directions. The chapters are organized in a very consistent manner, so information is easy to find. Furthermore, many points are illustrated with stories from the experiences of individual patients to make some of the information more accessible.

Finally, there are chapters dealing with more emotional and psychological components of the experience: the importance of siblings, family, and friends; other sources

of support; dealing with feelings, behavior, and communication; anticipating the end of treatment and beyond; and even preparing for the possibility of relapse or death. Again, these sections are generously illustrated with stories that provide examples from real-life situations.

There are general themes that pervade this book that make it particularly valuable. For example, there is considerable empowerment in having a better knowledge base and understanding about the disease and its treatment. It is important for parents to participate in an active way in their child's care, and in the decision-making process. Also, it is important to be realistic but optimistic. Cancer is a serious and life-threatening illness, even in the best of circumstances. There are some cancers that can be cured reliably in the majority of cases, and others in which only a minority survive. Nevertheless, it is difficult to say with certainty at diagnosis whether any individual patient will survive or not, so there is always reason for optimism. Indeed, the majority of children with solid tumors can be cured, but the chances of cure depend on the diagnosis, extent of disease, and certain other biological or genetic features that influence response to therapy and prognosis.

The rate of improvement in cure rates has reached a plateau, and we are encountering long-term effects of cancer and its treatment in the survivors. Nevertheless, this is also a time of great optimism. Laboratory studies of cancer cells have revealed a number of clues about what genetic changes are responsible for cells becoming malignant. These genes, proteins, and pathways represent unique features of cancer cells that should allow us to develop more targeted approaches to therapy. These novel approaches should substantially improve the cure rates and have much less toxicity than current approaches.

— Garrett M. Brodeur, MD
Audrey E. Evans Endowed Chair, Professor of Pediatrics
Chief, Division of Oncology
Children's Hospital of Philadelphia

Introduction

*We are all in the same boat, in a stormy sea,
and we owe each other a terrible loyalty.*

— G. K Chesterton

Anne and Nancy each have children who survived cancer—Anne's son had rhabdomyo-sarcoma and Nancy's daughter had high-risk leukemia. Both children were diagnosed as preschoolers and each had surgery, radiation, and chemotherapy. We understand that nothing prepares a parent for the utter devastation of having a child diagnosed with cancer. We have walked the path from that life-changing moment through information gathering, treatment, and rehabilitation. We know that fear and worry are lessened by having accurate information and through hearing the stories of other children and families who have walked the path before us. We are honored to share with you what we and many other parents and healthcare providers have learned.

What this book offers

This book is not autobiographical. Instead, we wanted to blend basic technical information in easy-to-understand language with stories and advice from many parents and children. We wanted to provide the insights and experiences of parents who have all felt the hope, helplessness, anger, humor, longing, panic, ignorance, warmth, and anguish of their children's cancer treatment. We wanted parents to know how other children react to treatment, and we wanted to offer tips to make the experience easier.

Obtaining a basic understanding of topics such as medical terminology, common side effects of treatment, and how to interpret laboratory results can help improve quality of life for the whole family. Learning how to develop a partnership with your child's doctor can vastly increase your family's peace of mind. Hearing parents describe their own emotional ups and downs, how they coped, and how they molded their family life around hospitalizations is a tremendous comfort. And knowing there are other parents out there who hold their breath with each scan hoping for good news can help you feel less alone. Our hope is that parents who read this book will find understandable medical infomation, obtain advice that eases their daily life, and feel empowered to be strong advocates for their children.

The parent stories and suggestions in this book are absolutely true, although some names have been changed to protect children's privacy. Every word has been spoken by the parent of a child with cancer, a sibling of a child with cancer, or a childhood cancer survivor. There are no composites—just the actual words of people who wanted to share what they learned with families of children newly diagnosed with a solid tumor.

How this book is organized

We have organized the book sequentially in an attempt to parallel most families' journeys through treatment. We all start with diagnosis, then learn about the tumor and its treatment, try to cope with procedures, adjust to medical personnel, and deal with family and friends. We all seek out various methods of support and struggle with the strong feelings felt by our child with cancer, our other children, and ourselves. We also try to work with our child's school to provide the richest and most appropriate education for our ill child.

Because it is tremendously hard to focus on learning new things when you are emotionally battered and extremely tired, we tried to keep each chapter short. The first time we introduce a medical term, we define it in the text. Because both boys and girls get cancer, we did not adopt the common convention of using only masculine personal pronouns (e.g., he, him). We do not like using he/she, so we alternated personal pronouns (e.g., she, he) within chapters. This may seem awkward as you read, but it prevents half of the parents from feeling that the text does not apply to their child.

All the medical information contained in this third edition of *Childhood Cancer* is current as of 2015. As treatment is constantly evolving and improving, there will inevitably be changes. For example, the technology that supports surgery and radiation treatments continues to improve. Scientists are currently studying some new medications and genetically determined responses to specific drugs that may dramatically improve treatments. You will learn in this book how to discover the newest and most appropriate treatments for your child. However, this book should not be used as a substitute for professional medical care.

We have included three appendices for reference: blood tests and what they mean; resource organizations; and books, websites, and support groups.

How to use this book

While conducting research for this book, we were repeatedly told by parents to "write the truth." Because the "truth" varies for each person, more than 140 parents, children with solid tumors, and their siblings share portions of their experiences. This book is full of these snapshots in time, some of which may be hard to read, especially by

families of newly diagnosed children. Here are our suggestions for a positive way to use the information contained in this book:

- Consider reading only the sections that apply to the present or the immediate future.
- Realize that only a fraction of the problems that parents describe will affect your child. Every child is different; every child sails smoothly through some portions of treatment but encounters difficulties during others.
- Take any concerns or questions that arise to your child's oncologist and/or nurse practitioner for answers. The more you learn, the better you can advocate for your child.
- Share this book with family and friends. Usually they desperately want to help and just don't know how. This book not only explains the disease and treatments but also offers dozens of concrete suggestions for helpful things family and friends can do.

Best wishes for a smooth journey through treatment and a bright future for your entire family.

Acknowledgments

This book is truly a collaborative effort—without the help of many, it would simply not exist. We give heartfelt thanks to our families and friends who supported us along the way. Special thanks to our editor, Sarah Farmer, for her excellent editorial skills, as well as humor, patience, tact, and honesty when needed. Thanks to Alison Leake, who used her eagle eye to copyedit the book, despite her busy work schedule. She did a great job! Special thanks to Susan Jarmolowki for making the interior design and layout look great. Michele Keen of Creative Freedom designed a gorgeous cover. Garrett Brodeur, MD, graciously took time from his busy schedule to update his Foreword from the second edition. Thank you! We deeply appreciate all of you for helping make this a comprehensive, up-to-date resource for families of children with solid tumors and those who love them.

We send many thanks and much appreciation to the co-author of the first two editions of this book—Honna Janes-Hodder. Honna gathered stories from her friends in the childhood cancer community that captured so many of the experiences and emotions of each member of their family.

We also are grateful for generous support from the O'Reilly Foundation, Genentech, and other donors who wish to remain anonymous for providing funding to support publication of this book.

All three editions of this book are true collaborations between families of children with solid tumors and medical professionals. Many well-known and respected members of the pediatric oncology community, members of national organizations, and parents

carved time out of their busy schedules to review chapters, make invaluable suggestions, and catch errors. We especially appreciate the patient and thoughtful responses to our many emails and phone calls. Thank you: Clarke P. Anderson, MD; Peter C. Adamson, MD; D. M. Bass, MD; David Beele, LSW; Jean B. Belasco, MD; Kristin Bradley, MD; Garrett Brodeur, MD; Nancy J. Bunin, MD; Stan Calderwood, MD; William Carroll, MD; D. R. Chaulk, MD; Susan Cohn, MD; Lynne Conlon, PhD; Max Coppes, MD, PhD; Ruth Daller, CRNP; Kenneth DeSantes, MD; Connie DiDomenico, CRNP; Jeffrey S. Dome, MD, PhD; Debra Ethier, RTT; Christina Falcone, Financial Counselor; Daniel Fiduccia; Debra L. Friedman, MD; Joel W. Goldwein, MD; Richard G. Gorlick, MD; Mark Greenberg, MD; Stephan Grupp, MD, PhD; Jack Hand, MD; Bruce Himelstein, MD; Wendy Hobbie, RN, MSN, PNT; JoAnne Holdt, MA; Lawrence F. Jardine, MD; F. Leonard Johnson, MD; Anne E. Kazak, PhD; Beverly J. Lange, MD; Ann-Marie Leahey, MD; Laurie D. Leigh, MA; Susan J. Leclair, MS, CLS (NCA); John M. Maris, MD; Anna T. Meadows, MD; Grace Monaco, JD; Linn Murphree, MD; Ann Newman, RN; Mark Newman, MD; Cal Peddle, BSc, PhD; Greg Peddle, PhD; C. Patrick Reynolds, MD, PhD; Robert C. Seeger, MD; Hiro Shimada, MD; Susan Shurin, MD; Steven Simms, PhD; Douglas Strother, MD; Heidi Suni, MSW; Susan DiTaranto, RN, BSN; Ellen Tracy, RN; David R. Ungar, MD; Judith G. Villablanca, MD; Daniel von Allmen, MD; Leonard H. Wexler, MD; and Richard B. Womer, MD.

More than words can express, we are deeply grateful to the parents, children with cancer, and their siblings, who generously opened their hearts while sharing their experiences with us. To all of you whose words form the heart and soul of this book, thank you: Brenda Andrews; Robin B.; LeeAnn Barnard; Sheila Batten; Terry Beck; Theresa Beech; Anne Beecher, mom to Charlie and Max; Mike and Kathy Blaker, parents of Adam; Patrice Boyle and Sean Boyle; Ted and Michele Bozarth; Jocelyne Brent; Sue Brooks; Nancy and Ernie Bullard; the Burge family; Noreen Burgess, Coley's mom; Dottie Bradford Buttafogo; Ricky C. (Garrett's dad); Nicole Canfield, Wyatt's mommy; Christopher and Angela Carson; Nicole Carter, mother of the brave Mary Tipton Carter; Jennifer Cartwright, mom to Aaron and Zach; Alicia Cauley; Naomi Chesler; Jennifer Click; Cathy and Tim Cooley; Cynthia Diaz; Corinne Eiriksson, Jamshid's mum; Allison E. Ellis; E. Engelmann; Dana Erickson; Mel Erickson; Kellie Espinoza; Donna Evans, Cienna's mommy; Sarah Farmer; Art Farro; Rene Fernandez; Kate Foley, mom to Cameron, 4/25/94 to 5/31/98; Tamra Lynn Sparling Fountaine; Alana Freedman; Jenny Gardner; Sandra Gaynor; Judy Gelber; Shirley Enebrad Geller; Roxie Glaze; Lynn Goering; Sharon Gould, Leah Wicklund, and her awesome big brother Jacob Wicklund; Jamie Griffith, mom to Ellie; Kris H.; Lisa Hall; Erin Hall; Daphne Hardcastle; Jessica Hargin; Jodi and Cameron (Super Cam) Harris; Linda Harrison; Susan Harvey; Kathryn G. Havemann; Kristen Hebberth, proud mama to Super Jayden; Nikki Henning, proud mommy of sweet Tala; Douglas L. Herstrom; Heidi Hicks, proud mommy of our brave brown-eyed beauty, Brinley Hicks; Connie Higbee-Jones; David Hodder; Ruth Hoffman;

Chris Hurley; David and Esther Hurst; Lorie Jager; the Jordan family; Erin A. Jordan; Fr. Joseph; Peggy Kaiser; Susan Kalika; Joyce Kammerman; Beth Karanicola; Winnie Kittiko; Terri Kluey; Lisa Korenko; Karen L. Krajewski; Kori Lamb, Tanner's mom; Missy Layfield; Bob Ledner; Susanne Lehrman; Elinor Lemky; the Peter G. Lewis Family; Pam Lim; Gail and John Lindekugel, parents of Levi; Maryanne Macaluso; Julie Macedo; Cyndi and Andrew MacKinlay; Alice Mauck, mom to TJ; Dierdre McCarthy-King; Sara McDonnall; Gigi McMillan; Keeley Mendez; Lori Michelle Miller; Marilyn Brodeur Morin; Wendy Mitchell; Holly Moisa; Amanda Moodie; Jean Morris; Leslee Morris; Laura Myer; Carolyn Nordberg; M. Clare Paris; Jeff Pasowicz; Jennifer Peterson; Donna Phelps; Laura Randall, RN, mother of Matthew; Jim and Vickie Reilly; Mary Riecke; Lynne A. Rief; Amanda Riel; Wendy Rigden McCurley; Jennifer E. Rohloff; Kevin Rufener, Charlotte's father; Steve and Shirlene S.; Maria Sansalone; Heidi Schoenecker; Carole Schuette; Angela Schuldies; Mark W. Schumann; Sharon Schuster; Janice Scott; Susan Sennett; Erin Shanahan; Lynnette Shanahan; Lori Shipman; Lorrie Simonetti; Cathi Smith; Carl and Diane Snedeker; Anne Spurgeon; Michaela Stokes-Noonan; Jenni Swink; Leeann T.; Iris Taylor; T. Terwilliger; Megan Thomas; Wendy Thompson; Marie Thomsen; Gigi N. Thorsen; Robyn Thurber; Lisa Tignor; Sarah, Tim, and John Allen Tinkel; Michael and Cheryl Tobias; Shoshana Tobias; Laura Todd-Pierce; Michele Trieb; Cathy Tschumy; Susan E. Tuccio; Kathleen Tucker; Bridget Tuxen; Dina Van Yperen; Dawn Veltri; Melissa L. Walhovd; Annie Walls; Ralene Walls; Kim Warren; Sheri White; Kimbra Suzanne Wilder; Jean Wilkerson; Catherine Woodman, the Yantis Family; Lise Yasui; Cheryl Zeichner; Ellen Zimmerman; Carla, mom of Nelson; and those who wish to remain anonymous.

Despite the inspiration and contributions of so many, any errors, omissions, misstatements, or flaws in the book are entirely our own.

Chapter 1

Diagnosis

"WE HAVE THE RESULTS OF THE SCAN BACK; I'm afraid it's bad news. Your child has a tumor." For every parent who has heard those words, it is a moment frozen in time. In one shattering instant, life forever changes. Families are forced into a strange new world that feels like an emotional roller coaster ride in the dark. Every member of the family will feel strong emotions. However, with time and the knowledge that many children survive cancer, hope will grow.

Signs and symptoms

Cancer begins with the transformation of a single cell. The malignant changes that occur in these renegade cells can cause several signs and symptoms, many of which mimic common childhood illnesses.

Parents are usually the first to notice that something is wrong with their child, and they seek medical attention. Occasionally, a diagnosis of cancer is based on chance findings during a routine examination by a pediatrician, eye doctor, or dentist. Rarely, it is discovered on an x-ray done for other reasons.

Following are some of the signs and symptoms that may indicate the presence of a solid tumor:

- Swelling or persistent pain in bones, joints, the back, or legs
- A lump, especially in the abdomen, neck, chest, pelvis, armpits, or legs
- A whitish color behind the pupil
- Continued, unexplained weight loss
- Frequent infections
- Nausea that persists
- Fatigue
- Paleness
- Eye or vision changes that occur suddenly and persist
- Recurrent or persistent fevers

Most parents react to their concerns by taking their child to a doctor. Usually, the doctor performs a physical exam and may order blood work or x-rays.

> *Ten days after a well-baby check, I was changing 3-month-old Estele's diaper and noticed that the right side of her belly felt hard. I felt around and found a lump. It was a Sunday, so I called the nurse line at the pediatrician's office and was told it was probably constipation. Estele had gone several times that day, and I just knew it wasn't that. My husband and I took her to the emergency room where an ultrasound was done. They didn't tell us what was wrong but said we had to go to the children's hospital right away and not to stop anywhere.*

Sometimes the diagnosis is not as easy and fast as Estele's:

> *When Hailee was a baby, we noticed that sometimes her eye appeared white and sometimes it looked reddish. We were worried, but the pediatrician said that she was healthy. He eventually gave us a referral to see an ophthalmologist when we insisted. Since he didn't feel it was an emergency, we had to wait 3 months to see the eye specialist, who diagnosed her unilateral retinoblastoma. By that time, Hailee's retina was detached, and her eye had to be enucleated. I remember feeling completely shocked when the specialist said that she had a disease that would kill her if left untreated.*

Where should your child receive treatment?

After a tentative diagnosis of cancer, most physicians refer the family to the closest major children's hospital for further tests and treatment. It is very important that the child with cancer be treated at a facility that uses a team approach, including pediatric oncologists, oncology nurses, specialized surgeons and pathologists, pediatric nurse practitioners, pediatric radiologists, psychologists, child life specialists, rehabilitation specialists, education specialists, and social workers. State-of-the-art treatment is provided at these institutions, offering your child the best chance for remission (disappearance of the disease in response to treatment) and ultimately, cure.

> *The day that I took Cassandra (age 5) to the pediatrician, I had assumed she would be sent home on antibiotics for some type of infection. She had been complaining of pain in her left knee and had developed a large lump on her left buttock. Instead, we left with instructions for her to eat nothing, since she was going to be sedated the following morning for some scans at the children's hospital. From that point on, things happened very fast. I remember only bits and pieces of those first few days at the hospital. I was told that Cassandra had rhabdomyosarcoma, that the following day they would do a biopsy and implant a central catheter, and that chemotherapy would be started as soon as possible.*

Physical responses

Many parents become physically ill in the weeks following their child's diagnosis. This is not surprising, given that most parents stop eating or grab only fast food, have trouble sleeping, and are exposed to all sorts of illnesses while staying in the hospital. Every waking moment is filled with excruciating emotional stress, which makes the physical stress much more potent and weakens the body's immune response.

> The second week in the hospital I developed a ferocious sore throat, runny nose, and bad cough. Her counts were on the way down, and they ordered me out of the hospital until I was well. It was agony.

• • • • •

> That first week, every time my son threw up, so did I. I also had almost uncontrollable diarrhea. Every new stressful event in the hospital just dissolved my gut; I could feel it happening. Thank God this faded away after a few weeks.

To help prevent illness, try to eat nutritious meals, get a break from your child's bedside to take a walk outdoors, and find time to sleep. Care needs to be taken not to overuse drugs or alcohol in an attempt to control anxiety or cope with grief. Although physical illnesses usually end or improve after a period of adjustment, emotional stress often continues throughout treatment.

Emotional responses

The shock of diagnosis results in an overwhelming number of intense emotions. Cultural background, individual coping styles, basic temperament, and family dynamics all affect an individual's emotional response to stress. There are no set stages of response, and parents frequently find themselves vacillating from one emotional extreme to another. Many of these emotions reappear at different times during the child's treatment. All of the emotions described below are normal responses to a diagnosis of cancer in a child.

The emotional responses of children and teens are discussed in Chapter 21, *Communication and Behavior*.

Confusion and numbness

In their anguish, most parents remember only bits and pieces of the doctor's early explanations of their child's disease. This dreamlike state is an almost universal response to shock. The brain provides protective layers of numbness and confusion to prevent emotional overload. Pediatric oncologists understand this phenomenon and are usually quite willing to repeat information as often as necessary. Children's hospitals have nurse

practitioners, physician assistants, nurses, and child life specialists who translate medical information into understandable language and answer questions for both parents and children. Do not be embarrassed to say you do not understand or that you forgot something you were told. It is sometimes helpful to write down instructions and explanations, record them on a small audio recorder or smartphone, or ask a friend or family member to help keep track of all the new and complex information. These notes can be transcribed and kept with the written materials you receive from the medical providers so you can refer to them later.

> When I left the doctor's office, I was a mass of hysteria. I couldn't breathe and felt as if I was suffocating. Tears were flowing nonstop. I had lost total control of myself and had no idea of how to stop my world from turning upside down.

· · · · ·

> For a brief moment I stared at the doctor's face and felt totally confused by what he was explaining to me. In an instant that internal chaos was joined with a scream of terror that came from some place inside me that, up until that point, I never knew existed.

Denial

Denial is when parents simply cannot believe that their child has a life-threatening illness. Denial helps parents survive the first few days after diagnosis, but gradual acceptance must occur so the family can make the necessary adjustments to accommodate cancer treatment. Life has dramatically changed. When parents accept what has happened, understand their fears, and begin to hope, they are better able to advocate for their child and their family. This process takes time.

> I walked into the empty hospital playroom and saw my wife clutching Matthew's teddy bear. Her eyes were red and swollen from crying. I had no idea what had happened. A minute later the doctor came into the room with several residents [doctors who are receiving specialized training]. He told me that Matthew had cancer and that he was very sick. I remember thinking that there had to have been a mistake. Maybe he was reading the wrong chart? My initial reaction was that it was physically impossible for one of my children to have cancer. Cancer is a disease of the elderly. Kids don't get cancer!

Guilt

Guilt is a common and normal reaction to a diagnosis of childhood cancer. Parents sometimes feel they have failed to protect their child, and they blame themselves. It is especially difficult because the cause of their child's tumor, in most instances, cannot be explained. There are questions: How could we have prevented this? What did we do wrong? How did we miss the signs? Why didn't we bring her to the doctor sooner?

Why didn't we insist that the doctor do a scan? Did he inherit this from me? Why didn't we live in a safer place? Was it because of the fumes from painting the house? Why? Why? Why? Nancy Roach describes some of these feelings in her booklet *The Last Day of April*:

> Almost as soon as Erin's illness was diagnosed, our self-recrimination began. What had we done to cause this illness? Was I careful enough during pregnancy? … I wondered about the toxic glue used in my advertising work or the silk screen ink used in my artwork. Bob questioned the fumes from some wood preservatives used in a project. We analyzed everything—food, fumes, and TV. Fortunately, most of the guilt feelings were relieved by knowledge and by meeting other parents whose children had been exposed to an entirely different environment.

It may be difficult to accept, but parents need to understand that they did nothing to cause their child's illness. Years of research have revealed little about what causes childhood solid tumors or what can be done to prevent them.

Fear and helplessness

Fear and helplessness are two faces of the same coin. Nearly everything about this new situation is unknown, and what parents do know—that their child has a life-threatening illness—is too terrifying to contemplate. Each new revelation about the situation raises new questions and fears: Can I really flush a catheter or administer all these drugs? What if I mess something up? Will I be fired if I miss too much work? Who will take care of my other children? How do I tell my child not to be afraid when he can see I am scared to death? How will we pay for this? The demands on parents' time, talents, energy, courage, and strength are daunting.

> Sometimes I would feel incredible waves of absolute terror wash over me. The kind of fear that causes your breathing to become difficult and your heart to beat faster. While I would be consciously aware of what was happening, there was nothing I could do to stop it. It's happened sometimes very late at night, when I'm lying in bed, staring off into the darkness. It's so intense that for a brief moment, I try to comfort myself by thinking that it can't be real, because it's just too horrible. During those moments, these thoughts only offer a second or two of comfort. Then I become aware of just how wide my eyes are opened in the darkness.

A child's diagnosis strips parents of control over many aspects of their lives and can change their entire world view. All the predictable and comforting routines are gone, and the family is thrust into a new world that is populated by an ever-changing cast of characters (interns, residents, fellows, pediatric oncologists, surgeons, nurses, social workers, and technicians); a new language (medical terminology); and seemingly endless hospitalizations, procedures, and drugs. This transition can be hard on all parents,

particularly those who are intimidated by doctors and medical environments, and those who are used to a measure of power and authority in their home or workplace.

> *My husband had a difficult time after our son was diagnosed. We have a traditional marriage, and he was used to his role as provider and protector for the family. It was hard for him to deal with the fact that he couldn't fix everything.*

Parents often feel utterly helpless. For example, physicians they have never met are presenting treatment options for their child. Parents are also faced with the fact that they cannot do anything that will take away their child's illness or make everything better, and parents' inability to relieve their child's suffering can lead to feelings of great helplessness. Even if parents are comfortable in a hospital environment, they may feel helpless because there is simply not enough time in the day to care for a very sick child, deal with their own changing emotions, educate themselves about the disease, notify friends and family, make job decisions, and restructure the family schedule to deal with the crisis.

> *It's not a nice way to have to live. What's waiting around the next corner? That's a scary question. One of my biggest fears is the uncertainty of the future. All that we can do is the best we can and hope that it's enough.*

Many parents explain that helplessness begins to disappear when a sense of reality returns. They begin to make decisions, study their options, learn about the disease, and become comfortable with the hospital and staff. As their knowledge grows, so does their ability to participate constructively as members of the treatment team (for more information, see Chapter 11, *Forming a Partnership with the Treatment Team*). However, do not be surprised if feelings of fear, panic, and anxiety erupt unexpectedly throughout your child's treatment.

Anger

Anger is a common response to the diagnosis of a life-threatening illness. It is nobody's fault that children are stricken with solid tumors. Because parents cannot direct their anger at the cancer, they may target doctors, nurses, spouses, siblings, or even their ill child. Because anger directed at other people can be very destructive, it is necessary to find ways to express and manage the anger.

> *Life isn't fair, yet the sun still comes up each morning. To be angry because your child has a cancer is normal. The question is where to direct that anger. Sometimes I feel as if I'm angry at the entire world. In my heart, though, my outrage is directed solely at each and every tumor cell feeding on my child.*

Expressing anger is normal and can be cathartic. Trying to suppress this powerful emotion is usually not helpful. Some suggestions from parents for managing anger follow.

Anger at the healthcare team:

- Try to improve communication with the doctors. Scheduling time to talk away from your child's bedside may make it easier to have a more in-depth discussion.

- Discuss your feelings with one of the nurses or nurse practitioners.

- Ask the hospital social workers for advice on how to productively address your concerns if you become angry or frustrated with members of the medical staff, your insurance company, or others involved in your child's care.

- Talk with parents of other ill children, either locally or by joining an online support group.

Anger at family:

- Exercise a little every day

- Do yoga or relaxation exercises

- Keep a journal or make an audio recording your feelings

- Cry in the shower or pound a pillow

- Listen to music

- Read other people's stories about childhood cancer

- Talk with friends

- Talk with parents of other ill children in person or online

- Try individual or family counseling

- Live one moment at a time

Anger at God:

- Share your feelings with your spouse, partner, or close friends

- Discuss your feelings with clergy or church, synagogue, or mosque members

- Know that anger at God is normal

- Pray or meditate

- Give yourself time to heal

It is important to remember that angry feelings are normal and expected. Discovering healthy ways to cope with anger is vital for all parents.

> My husband went to the gym and lifted weights during and after treatment to get his anger and worry out. I saw a therapist for a period of time, and I got on medications. I didn't want to go on meds, I didn't want to need that, but it leveled me out.

Sadness and grief

No one is prepared to cope with the news that their child has cancer. Intense feelings of sorrow, loss, and grief are common, even when the prognosis is good. Parents often describe feeling engulfed by sadness. They fear they may simply not be able to deal with the enormity of the problems facing their family. Parents grieve the loss of normalcy and realize life will never be the same. They grieve the loss of their dreams and aspirations for their child. They may feel sorry for themselves and may feel ashamed and embarrassed by these feelings.

> *I have an overwhelming sadness and, unfortunately for me, that means feelings of helplessness. I wish I could muster up a fighting spirit, but I just can't right now.*

> • • • • •

> *While I have moments of deep sadness and despair, I try not to let them turn into hours and certainly not days. I am too aware of the fact that I may have the rest of my life to grieve.*

Parents travel a tumultuous emotional path where overwhelming emotions subside, only to resurface later. All of these are normal, common responses to a catastrophic event. For many parents, these strong emotions become more managable as hope grows.

Hope

After being buffeted by illness, anger, fear, sadness, grief, and guilt, most parents welcome the growth of hope. Hope is the belief in a better tomorrow. Hope sustains the will to live and gives us the strength to endure difficult times. Hope is not a way around; it is a way through. Many children survive childhood cancer and live long and happy lives. There is reason for hope.

Many families discover a renewed sense of both the fragility and beauty of life after the diagnosis. Outpourings of love and support from family and friends provide comfort and sustenance. Many parents speak of a renewed appreciation for life and feel like each day with their child is a precious gift.

> *When we were given the diagnosis, it took time and layers of understanding before we could come to grips with everything. We realized that the adjustment wouldn't be made in a single step, but that we'd reach plateaus of "new normal" along the way. In other words, don't be surprised if you feel like you have a pretty good grip on things and then suddenly lose it one day. As with life as usual, some days will be better than others. If you feel deeply sad or completely overwhelmed one day, remind yourself that it's a mood like all the others in your repertoire, and there is an excellent reason for it, but in time you will feel better able to cope.*

A Japanese proverb says: "Daylight will peep through a very small hole."

The immediate future

You are not alone. The rest of this book contains stories from parents of children with childhood cancer, as well as practical information about the disease and its treatment. You'll learn about the choices other parents made and how they adjusted, learned, and became active participants in their child's treatment. Many have traveled this path before you, and reading about their experiences may help your family develop its own unique strategy for coping with the challenges ahead.

A Mother's View

Memory is a funny thing. I'd be hard pressed to remember what I had for dinner last night, but like many people, the day of the Challenger explosion and, even further back, the day of John Kennedy's death, are etched in my mind to the smallest detail.

And like a smaller group of people, the day of my child's cancer diagnosis is a strong and vivid memory, even seven years later. Most of the time, I don't dwell on that series of images. It was, after all, a chapter in our lives, and one that is now blessedly behind us. But early each autumn, when I get a whiff of the crisp smell of leaves in the air, it brings back that dark day when our lives changed forever.

Many of the memories are painful and, like my daughter's scars, they fade a little more each year but will never completely disappear. While dealing with the medical and physical aspects of the disease, my husband and I also made many emotional discoveries. We sometimes encountered ignorance and narrow-mindedness, which made me more sad than angry. Mistakes were made, tempers were short, and family relations were strained. But we saw the other side, too. Somehow, our sense of humor held on throughout the ordeal, and when that kicked in, we had some of the best laughs of our lives. There was compassion and understanding when we needed it most. And people were there for us like never before.

I remember two young fathers on our street, torn by the news, who wanted to help but felt helpless. My husband came home from the hospital late one night to find that our lawn had been mowed and our leaves had been raked by them. They had found a way to make a small difference that day.

Another time, a neighbor came to our house bearing a bakery box full of pastries and the message that his family was praying for our daughter nightly around their supper table. The image of this man, his wife, and his eight children joining in prayer for us will never leave me.

A close friend entered the hospital during that first terrible week we were there to give birth to her son. I held her baby, she held me, and we laughed and cried together.

Sometimes, when I look back at that time, I feel as though everything that is wrong with the world and everything that is right is somehow distilled in one small child's battle to live. We learned so very much about people and about life.

Surely people who haven't experienced a crisis of this magnitude would believe that we would want to put that time behind us and forget as much of it as possible. But the fact is, we grew a little through our pain, like it or not. We see through new eyes. Not all of it is good or happy, but it is profound.

I treasure good friends like never before. I view life as much more fragile and precious than I used to. I think of myself as a tougher person than I was, but I cry more easily now. And sure, I still yell at my kids and eagerly await each September when they will be out of my hair for a few hours each day. But I hold them with more tenderness when they hop off the school bus into my arms. And I like to think that some of the people around us, who saw how suddenly and drastically a family's life can change, hold their children a little dearer as well.

Do I want to forget those terrible days and nights seven years ago? Not on your life. And I hope the smell of autumn leaves will still bring the memories back when I'm a grandmother, even if I can't remember what I had for dinner last night.

— Kathy Tucker
CURE Childhood Cancer Newsletter
Rochester, NY

Chapter 2

Bone Sarcomas

BONE SARCOMAS ARE a group of several different cancerous tumors of the bone. The most common bone sarcomas diagnosed in children and adolescents are osteosarcoma and Ewing sarcoma.

This chapter first explains the structure and function of the skeletal system. It then describes osteosarcoma and the four diagnoses known as the Ewing sarcoma family of tumors (ESFT)—Ewing sarcoma of the bone, extraosseous Ewing sarcoma, Askin's tumor, and peripheral primitive neuroectodermal tumor (PPNET). The sections on each type of bone sarcoma include information about signs and symptoms, how it is diagnosed, and how it is treated.

The skeletal system

The human skeleton contains 206 bones, all held in place by connective tissues such as ligaments and tendons. Several types of bone make up the skeletal system, each classified according to its shape: long, short, irregular, and flat. Together, they perform several different functions.

The skeleton is a mechanical framework that muscles pull on to create movement. It gives structure to the body, protects the internal organs, and determines body size and shape. The skeleton also works as a factory, because various blood cells are manufactured in the marrow of the bones. Bones also act as storage depots, holding minerals such as calcium and phosphorus for the body to use later.

Bone is a living tissue and its structure is continuously changing. For example, the skeleton of the fetus in the womb is mostly cartilage. As pregnancy continues, bone develops. After the child is born, certain areas are still a combination of bone and cartilage. These areas are called growth plates. In the long bones, such as the arms and legs, there are growth plates at each end. Growth plates are what allow bones to lengthen as a child ages. By the time a child reaches age 20, the 270 softer bones she was born with have fused to form the 206-bone structure of the skeleton.

Osteosarcoma

Osteosarcoma is a malignant tumor of the bone and the most common bone sarcoma. Scientific advances over the past 50 years have dramatically improved the outcome for children and adolescents diagnosed with osteosarcoma. Advances in surgical techniques have also improved their quality of life.

Who gets osteosarcoma?

In the United States, osteosarcoma is diagnosed each year in approximately 450 children, teens, and young adults. The peak incidence occurs between the ages of 10 and 24. Researchers believe there is an association between the disease and the rapid period of bone growth during adolescence.

In adolescents, osteosarcoma is the third most common cancer, following leukemia and lymphoma. The disease is slightly more common in males than in females and is slightly more common in Black and Hispanic children than in White children. Osteosarcoma is believed to be more common in individuals who will grow to be taller than average.

In children and adolescents, about half of these tumors arise in the end of the thigh bone (femur) closest to the knee or in the end of the shin bone (tibia) closest to the knee. About 10 percent of the time it appears in the end of the upper arm bone (humerus) nearest the shoulder. Less common sites are the pelvis, jaw, spine, and ribs. Twenty percent of children diagnosed with osteosarcoma have metastases (cancer that has spread to other places in the body) at the time their cancer is found. Of this group, approximately 85 percent have tumors in their lungs.

> The day our daughter was diagnosed with osteosarcoma, I was sick with a fever of 103° and had to stay home while her dad took her to the appointment. My husband told me it was the worst day of his life when she looked up at him and asked him if she was going to die. Both he and the doctor immediately responded that we were all going to do everything to keep that from happening. She trusted that we would take care of the cancer and she would recover.

Genetic factors

The cause of osteosarcoma is not known, but some associations with other conditions have been identified. For example, retinoblastoma, a rare eye cancer of childhood, is associated with osteosarcoma. Children who have the inherited form of retinoblastoma have a substantial risk of developing osteosarcoma. The risk appears to be increased by treatment with radiation to the bones of the eye socket. But the increased frequency of osteosarcoma in non-irradiated sites (e.g., arms and legs) indicates a genetic

abnormality predisposing the child to these two cancers. For more information, see Chapter 5, *Retinoblastoma*.

Other genetic syndromes that may predispose young people to developing osteosarcoma include Bloom syndrome, Werner syndrome, Li-Fraumeni syndrome, and Rothmund-Thomson syndrome.

Environmental factors

Exposure to radiation increases the risk of developing osteosarcoma—about 3 percent of children diagnosed with the disease had previous irradiation of the site. Studies have found that osteosarcoma occurs 4 to 40 years after irradiation. Children and adolescents with osteosarcoma in a former radiation field have the same cure rate as any other person with the disease, as long as they are treated with standard surgery and chemotherapy. Osteosarcoma has also been associated with bone-seeking radioisotopes, such as radium 224, which is used to treat tuberculosis.

Osteosarcoma signs and symptoms

Osteosarcoma occurs most frequently in the long bones such as the femur and humerus. Symptoms usually include pain, with or without associated swelling. The affected area also may have an increased temperature. Often, the child will limp, as about 80 percent of these tumors are located near the knee, and the joint's range of motion may be decreased.

Some people attribute the beginning of this cancer to an injury, but trauma to the bone does not cause cancer. Sometimes the child or teen may be diagnosed with a broken bone—even when there has been no injury to the area—and that is how the cancer is discovered.

Because symptoms can come and go, and often involve pain in the legs of active young people, signs of osteosarcoma can be present for weeks or months before a diagnosis is reached.

> When Leeann was diagnosed with osteosarcoma in the left femur, I remember feeling total and utter shock. She had been complaining of pain in her knee for months, but since she was physically active playing basketball, baseball, and gymnastics, I assumed it was something minor like a pulled ligament. I also told her more than once that it was just "growing pains." Fortunately, she persisted and we took her to a local orthopedist. The orthopedist asked us to make an appointment with a pediatric orthopedist two and a half hours from home. I knew at this point it was something much more serious than a pulled muscle. Once the initial diagnosis was made, we went into a fog.

At diagnosis, about 20 percent of young people with osteosarcoma have x-ray evidence of disease that has spread to other parts of the body (called metastatic disease). When metastatic disease is in the lungs, there are usually no symptoms, although it occasionally causes shortness of breath, chest pain, and coughing. Children with advanced metastatic disease may have fever and weight loss.

Diagnosis of osteosarcoma

Specific tests and procedures are performed before a diagnosis of osteosarcoma can be reached. Any child or teen with suspected osteosarcoma should be seen by a pediatric oncologist and an orthopedic oncologist (a surgeon) who have experience treating this disease. The oncologist obtains the child or teen's medical history and performs a complete physical examination. A complete blood count (CBC) and differential are ordered (see Appendix A, *Blood Tests and What They Mean*), along with other bloodwork and a urinalysis.

The first imaging studies done are often x-rays of the area suspected of having a malignancy. Because these tumors have a distinct appearance when viewed on plain x-ray films, a radiologist may suspect osteosarcoma is present based on the x-ray alone. A magnetic resonance imaging test (MRI) of the affected region is usually done, and a computerized tomography (CT) scan and a bone scan may also be performed. To read about these imaging tests, see Chapter 10, *Coping with Procedures*.

A definitive diagnosis of osteosarcoma can only be made by examining part of the tumor under a microscope. A complete evaluation by the orthopedic or pediatric oncologist, including imaging studies, should be done before the initial biopsy, because a poorly performed biopsy may jeopardize the option of future limb-sparing surgery. An experienced surgeon or an interventional radiologist (a doctor who specializes in diagnosing and treating diseases using medical imaging and minimally invasive treatments) who has extensive experience with the treatment of pediatric sarcomas should perform an open biopsy (when a surgical incision is made through the skin to expose and remove tissues) or a needle biopsy (a thin needle is used to take tissue or fluid samples from muscles, bones, or organs). The samples of the mass that are removed will be examined by a pathologist.

> *I was a 16-year-old cheerleader preparing for a national competition when my knee started to hurt. I thought it was just a sports injury, and I put ice on it. When it didn't improve, I went to physical therapy and then to a specialist in sports medicine. He took an x-ray and then sent me for an MRI. That night he called to say, "I'm so sorry, but you have a tumor." I had a biopsy the next day. It was osteosarcoma.*

Staging

Once osteosarcoma has been diagnosed, the pediatric oncologist will perform more tests to determine whether the cancer has spread to other parts of the body.

> *My daughter Shoshana is now 19. She was diagnosed with osteosarcoma just before her sixteenth birthday. The tumor was located in her right fibula. She also had lung metastases. Pain was her basic symptom, especially at night. We started out at the pediatrician, then an orthopedic doctor, and finally an orthopedic oncologist who did a biopsy. We were then passed on to a pediatric oncologist, who is our primary doctor. The latter two are a great team!*

A CT scan or MRI of the bones, a CT scan of the chest, and a nuclear bone scan can be performed to check for metastases at sites distant from the main tumor. A bone scan that uses a radiopharmaceutical, called technetium-99m, is frequently ordered to provide the physician with clear images of the entire skeleton. These bone scans are helpful in detecting the presence of metastatic disease and "skip lesions." Skip lesions are areas of disease occurring at different sites, but within the same bone as the primary tumor. Bone scans are sensitive to many other normal events, such as minor strains and injuries to the bone, so an abnormality on the bone scan does not always mean the tumor has spread.

There are two stages of osteosarcoma:

- **Localized.** A localized tumor is limited to the bone of origin.
- **Metastatic.** Tumors are found in other parts of the body, particularly the lungs or other bones. Other sites of metastatic disease are rare but can occur.

Prognosis

Since the 1970s, the treatment of osteosarcoma has dramatically improved. The majority of children and adolescents now survive the disease, most (90–95%) with limbs still intact. The prognosis and best treatment for each child with osteosarcoma are determined by analysis of several clinical and biological features.

The most significant factors used to determine prognosis for the child with osteosarcoma are the extent of the disease at diagnosis and whether or not it has metastasized.

For children or adolescents with localized disease, important factors are the tumor's resectability (ability of the surgeon to remove the tumor, which is determined by its size and location) and how it responds to chemotherapy.

For children or adolescents with metastatic disease at diagnosis, prognosis depends on the site of the metastases and the resectability of the metastatic tumors (either at diagnosis or after chemotherapy).

Treatment of osteosarcoma

At diagnosis, many parents do not know how to find experienced doctors and the best treatments for their child. State-of-the-art care is available from physicians who participate in the Children's Oncology Group (COG). This study group includes pediatric surgeons and oncologists, neurologists, radiation oncologists, researchers, and nurses. COG conducts studies to discover better therapies and supportive care for children with cancer. You can learn more about COG and find a list of its member treatment centers at *www.childrensoncologygroup.org*.

The orthopedic and pediatric oncologists will explain to the family the best options for treatment (standard treatment or a clinical trial, if open). For more information, see Chapter 9, *Choosing a Treatment*. For children and teens with osteosarcoma, treatment typically consists of chemotherapy, followed by surgery, and then more chemotherapy. Osteosarcoma is not very responsive to radiation, so it is rarely used.

Surgery

Improvements in the surgical management of osteosarcoma over the past few decades have significantly improved long-term survival rates and the quality of life for children diagnosed with this disease.

Surgery usually occurs after a period of preoperative chemotherapy, although some treatment plans require surgery before chemotherapy. Successful surgical removal of the primary tumor most often consists of limb-salvage surgery or, in less than 10 percent of cases, amputation. A surgical procedure called a thoracotomy (opening the chest cavity) is used to biopsy or remove tumors in the lungs.

> *Eric was diagnosed at age 15 with osteosarcoma in his left femur. He had chemotherapy and successful limb salvage surgery. Before cancer he was a baseball player, aggressive in-line skater, and a real on-the-go kid. I'm proud to say, he took his new limitations very well. He was able to remain very active despite his reconstructed leg. Although high-impact activities were discouraged, he continued to ride his bicycle and go canoeing, hiking, and camping in the mountains. He played softball with his friends, but preferred to let someone else do his base running.*

The doctors, the young person with osteosarcoma, and the parents need to have thorough and honest discussions about surgical options. There are pros and cons to both amputation and limb salvage procedures. For instance, lower leg amputations allow survivors to continue playing sports, whereas limb salvage procedures generally do not. Youngsters who are still growing when limb salvage surgery is done will have marked leg length discrepancies as they age, sometimes requiring multiple surgeries, although this has improved with the development of expandable prostheses. Limb salvage, however,

can sometimes provide a good cosmetic result. There are many, many factors to consider. Given the same information, different families may make different decisions.

The treatment team will discuss several factors that affect treatment options, including the size, location, and extent of the primary tumor; the presence or absence of distant metastases; the age of the child; skeletal development; presence of fractures in the bone; and patient and family preferences. Remember, only surgeons who have a great deal of experience treating osteosarcoma should operate on your child. If you do not feel your child's surgeon has enough experience, it is your right to request another surgeon or to find another treatment center that has a surgeon who has considerable experience with osteosarcoma.

> Shoshana had limb-sparing surgery after weeks of chemotherapy (all high-dose through her central line). The surgery took 9 hours. She got back onto her chemo-therapy protocol a few weeks later. We did the wheelchair, then crutches (for a long time), then a cane, then walking, dancing, running! She had surgery to remove the lung tumors later that same year.

Amputation

Amputation involves removal of all or a portion of an arm or a leg. Two forms of surgery have been developed in recent decades to improve the mobility of children who require an amputation of a portion of the leg. Both methods still require the use of a prosthetic device, but they better preserve the leg's functionality. One form of this is a tibia turn-up, where the leg is amputated above the knee and the tibia bone from the lower leg is turned upside down; this makes it possible for the lower end of the tibia to be fused to the bottom of the femur.

The other surgery used to improve function in children who require a leg amputation above the knee is called rotationplasty. The length of the lower portion of the leg is adjusted, then rotated 180 degrees, and attached to the femur. The ankle joint serves as a replacement for the surgically removed knee joint. An artificial limb is then designed to fit over the ankle. Rotationplasty surgery can cause cosmetic and psychosocial difficulties because of the appearance of the reconstructed limb, but it can be a good choice to help promote maximum function for an active young person.

Children or teens who have a limb amputated need a great deal of rehabilitation and psychological support. Although amputation is traumatic at any age, osteosarcoma typically occurs during the teenage years, when appearance is especially important to an adolescent's emotional well-being. State-of-the-art prosthetic limbs allow great mobility, as well as cosmetic appeal. Studies have demonstrated similar quality of life between osteosarcoma survivors who had amputation and those who had limb-salvage surgery.

Limb-salvage surgery

Advances made in limb-salvage procedures have enabled this technique to be used with an increasing number of children and teens. The challenge for the surgeon is to remove all evidence of disease while maintaining surrounding nerves and blood vessels. The structural integrity of the bone is then restored through the use of bone grafts or metallic devices. The survival rate for children or teens who have limb salvage surgery is equivalent to that of amputation.

The potential benefits of limb-salvage procedures are both functional and psychological, although this has been difficult to prove. However, limb-sparing surgery is not used if there is any doubt about whether the surgeon will be able to completely remove the tumor. The first priority is to remove the entire tumor.

> Vince has played baseball since he was 18 months old and his great grandmother would patiently spend hours pitching a foam ball to him. By age 8, he was on a travel baseball team that was amazing. He was diagnosed with osteosarcoma in his left distal femur at age 11. He had limb salvage surgery and his orthopedic surgeon told him no running, no jumping, no contact sports, certainly no baseball. He suggested he switch to swimming or golf. We as parents knew baseball had to remain a factor for his own mental health. So we fought against the surgeon and said just tell us what the limitations of his parts are, and what are the consequences of broken pieces. From that, we as a family came up with what could and could not be done on the baseball field (and what we did was against the doctor's advice).
>
> As parents, we tried to protect our son, so when he went back on the field (even during treatment) we made him wear extra padding to protect his port, and we all knew he was more of an inspirational player than a force to be reckoned with. But every milestone he made encouraged him to set the next one. First, he wanted to get back in uniform and sit on the bench. Then, he wanted to play toss before the game. Then he wanted an at bat. Then he wanted to play in the field. The bottom line is cancer does indeed take things away: it steals your ability to run fast enough, it costs you time that should have been spent improving skills, it might affect self-esteem when you aren't as good as you "might have been."
>
> But Vince is now almost 18, and has worked himself into playing at a high school level. He played 2 years of JV and now this will be his second year on varsity. I find that I still have those bitter thoughts, why didn't he get the chance to reach his full potential. When some of his friends have been having their official signing days with colleges (and baseball scholarships) I had my weepy times. But I also think this is more of a problem for us parents than for the kids. The thing right now is that while he is considering which college to attend, he has several other options that do not include baseball. At some point, he may walk away from baseball teams to be at a bigger school or a different location or in a program that he likes. We will always think we made the right choice to allow Vince to go as far as he could.

Children or teens who have a broken bone at the time of diagnosis may not be good candidates for limb-salvage surgery. Chemotherapy before surgery may cause poor healing of the fracture, which creates added obstacles when attempting limb-sparing techniques. The fracture also creates the risk that the tumor will spread locally. Tumor location, as well as the age of the child, also affect the likely success of limb-salvage surgery, and in some cases amputation may be a more suitable approach.

> Leeann's limb-salvage surgery kept her leg in an immobilizer for 6 weeks, day and night. There was a big problem getting her flexibility back, even with a year of painful physical therapy. The pain was manageable with the help of morphine, but getting her around was very difficult. Even the 3-hour car ride home was a trial. Once at home, we rented a wheelchair for the first month until she felt comfortable on crutches. I spent many hours on the floor of the bathroom, holding her leg up while she used the toilet. She became a real pro on those crutches!

Several different bone replacements are available for use in limb-salvage surgery:

- Autologous grafts involve removing a healthy bone from another area of the child's body to replace the diseased bone. Sometimes the blood vessels that feed the bone can be moved along with it to keep the bone alive in its new location. Allografts use bone from cadaver donors and are preferred when more bone is needed than can be removed from another part of the child's body.

- An endoprosthesis, usually made of steel or titanium, is a manufactured replacement for the diseased bone.

> My daughter was 16 when she was diagnosed with osteosarcoma. During her surgery, they wrapped a muscle from the back of her calf around to the front to hold the bone graft in place. It left a large open area that was covered by a skin graft from her thigh. It certainly worked in holding her graft in place, but left her leg looking pretty awful (even though we had a plastic surgeon assist with that part of the surgery), and I haven't seen a scar like it on anyone else. They also put small bone slivers from other bones around the graft sites in hopes of faster grafting, and that apparently worked as well. She walks much better than they expected—a slight limp but no braces necessary. She never did regain feeling in the bottom of her right foot. Sometimes she thinks amputation would have been better, because with a prosthesis she'd be able to run and jump and roller blade and participate in sports, things she can't do now with the bone graft and complete knee replacement.

Possible problems with limb replacement are infection, graft failure, and longevity of the manufactured bone replacement.

> Tyler was diagnosed with osteosarcoma of his left femur when he was 7. Half of his femur had to be removed. When Tyler was 8 years old, we approached a surgery

decision. We had three options: One option was a rod in place of half his femur and knee, which really wasn't an option

because the rod couldn't be lengthened to meet the needs of a growing child. The other two options were rotationplasty and amputation. Tyler had one last MRI of his leg to see how the tumor had responded to chemotherapy. Imagine our surprise when the surgeon said to us, "I'm going to make your decision a little harder." The tumor had shrunk enough so his growth plate could be saved. With this good news came another surgery option, a donor bone. We left feeling good and had some research to do. We talked with several osteosarcoma patients who had gone through all the options we were faced with, and we also spoke with other surgeons. After long consideration and praying about our new option, we decided the best surgery for Tyler would be a vascularized fibular allograft. Tyler's fibula was inserted down the center of the cadaver bone to give him blood flow and added strength. The surgery took about 16 hours because attaching all the blood vessels was a long process. He stayed in the ICU for 3 days with a fever and low oxygen levels. Once everything was under control, they moved him to the orthopedics floor for a week.

Lung surgery

Tumors located in the lungs can often be removed during a procedure called thoracotomy (surgery in which an incision is made to open the chest cavity). Disease located within the ribs sometimes requires the removal of affected bones and replacement with a synthetic material to reconstruct the chest wall.

Chemotherapy

Chemotherapy has greatly improved the long-term survival of children with osteosarcoma. Before the use of chemotherapy, the prognosis was very poor for a young person diagnosed with osteosarcoma, despite amputation. This is because almost all children, including those with no obvious signs of metastatic disease, have microscopic disease in the lungs at the time of diagnosis.

Current protocols for osteosarcoma usually use doxorubicin and two or three other chemotherapy drugs from this list: high-dose methotrexate, cisplatin, ifosfamide, or etoposide (also called VP-16).

After chemo, Tyler was feeling sick but ice cream really seemed to help. For a while he was getting so sick and losing weight because he couldn't keep any food down, so they put him on medicine that encouraged him to eat and then he ate like crazy. When Tyler started getting mouth sores from chemo, we reached out to our support group to see if anyone had some suggestions. One of the moms suggested that we use aloe vera juice. When her son was going through treatment, a nurse recommended it. Tyler would swish it around and swallow it three times a day. It helped relieve a

lot of pain with existing mouth sores and prevented them from appearing. As long as we started him on aloe before treatment and continued it throughout, he wouldn't get mouth sores.

Chemotherapy is generally given before and after surgery. Giving chemotherapy before surgery may facilitate limb-salvage procedures by shrinking tumors before they are removed. Children who respond well to pre-surgical chemotherapy (more than 90 percent tumor death) have a better prognosis than those who do not respond as well to initial chemotherapy.

Overall, Leeann survived chemotherapy without too many side effects. The usual nausea was controlled with Zofran® and Benadryl®. The hardest part was losing her hair. She was at such a critical time in her growing up that showing up at a new school wearing a wig caused a lot of anxiety.

For information about current clinical trials and the newest treatments, see the section at the end of this chapter called "Information on standard treatments."

Ewing sarcoma family of tumors

Ewing sarcoma gets its name from the physician who first described it in 1921, Dr. James Ewing. He noted that this bone cancer was different from osteosarcoma, because it was particularly sensitive to radiation. For several years it was felt that Ewing's sarcoma occurred only within the bone; however, other similar tumors were found within soft tissues. These tumors include extraosseous Ewing sarcoma (EES), Askin's tumor, and peripheral primitive neuroectodermal tumor (PPNET). Together, these four malignancies are called the Ewing sarcoma family of tumors (ESFT).

Who gets ESFT?

Each year, about 250 children and adolescents in the United States are diagnosed with an ESFT malignancy. Ewing sarcoma of the bone accounts for 87 percent of these diagnoses.

Most ESFT occur in young people between the ages of 10 and 20, and the median age of children diagnosed with Ewing sarcoma is 15. Only 27 percent of ESFT cases are diagnosed in children younger than age 10, but Ewing sarcoma has been diagnosed in infants and small children. Boys are diagnosed with this disease more often than girls, and there is a much higher incidence in White children compared with those of other ethnic groups (93% of all Ewing sarcoma of the bone and 85% of EES are diagnosed in White children).

surgeons and oncologists, radiation oncologists, researchers, and nurses. COG conducts studies to discover better therapies and supportive care for children with cancer. You can learn more about COG and find a list of its member treatment centers at *www. childrensoncologygroup.org*.

The goals of ESFT treatment are to cure the child, maintain as much function of the affected area as possible, and minimize the possible long-term effects of treatment. Treatment for an ESFT tumor includes chemotherapy plus surgery and/or radiation. If the tumor is completely removed with good margins of normal tissue, radiation is generally not given.

> *When Cameron (age 10) was diagnosed with localized Ewing sarcoma, the oncologist, a nurse, and the resident sat us down and presented us with the standard protocol and a clinical trial. They explained that if we chose to put him on the clinical trial we could pull out at any time throughout treatment. They told us he would have 11 total cycles of inpatient chemotherapy and 6 weeks of radiation over 9 months, but we know now it will be longer than that. It is hard to accept the delays but the chemo is hard on his body and it takes him a while to recover and get ready for his next treatment.*

Surgery

It is essential that the surgeon who will remove the tumor has experience with ESFT. The type of surgery depends on the location of the mass and the impact surgery will have on the function of the affected part of the body (see Chapter 14, *Surgery*).

During the operation, the surgeon removes all or some of the tumor and then takes samples from surrounding tissues. The pathologist determines whether the entire tumor has been removed, or whether some cells remained behind. If the surgeon is able to remove the entire tumor, it is referred to as a total gross resection. If there is evidence of remaining disease, it is referred to as residual disease. If the residual disease is visible to the naked eye or can be felt by the surgeon's hand, it is called gross residual disease. If it is only visible under the microscope, it is called microscopic residual disease.

> *My son Jeremy had Ewing's in his left distal femur. He was diagnosed at age 11. He had chemo from February to April of that year and then limb-salvage surgery in May. He was on crutches for a very long time. They were able to spare his distal growth plate in the initial surgery. However, three surgeries later (problems with the "hardware"), they finally screwed bolts into his growth plate. Since then, he has had to have surgery once to shorten his "unaffected" leg.*

Before the development of limb-salvage surgery, most children with extremity tumors had the affected limb amputated and received high-dose radiation therapy. Many children now have limb-salvage procedures using autologous grafts, allografts, an

endoprosthesis, or rotationplasty (see pages 17 to 20 for descriptions of these surgeries) or targeted radiation therapy to treat their tumor.

> When we decided that amputation was the best treatment, we spent the next few weeks talking about it. It was almost as if we were mourning the loss of his leg and foot—saying goodbye to his toes. The surgery to remove his leg just below the hip took 14 hours. Troy's femur was removed, and the tibia was moved up and flipped to act as the upper leg bone. The foot was amputated. His prosthesis was attached at the knee.
>
> I have never regarded my son as handicapped. Troy is able to do almost all things other kids his age enjoy doing. He climbs, rides a bike, skateboards, and even spends time on his boogie board. Today he is a healthy, happy 13 year old. I have no anger about what has happened. In fact, I feel very fortunate. My son has adjusted very well, physically and emotionally, to losing his leg. He doesn't let it slow him down.

Radiation

Radiation is often needed to treat children diagnosed with ESFT. Radiation is used for tumors that cannot be completely removed with clear margins. The entire pre-chemotherapy tumor area, with 2 centimeter margins, is usually included in the radiation field. Children or teens with gross residual disease are usually given a total dose of 5,580 cGy. For those with microscopic residual disease, the standard dose is 5,040 cGy. Radiation is given over a period of 4 to 6 weeks. No radiation therapy is recommended for children who have no evidence of microscopic residual disease following surgery. For more information, see Chapter 17, *Radiation Therapy*.

Research to evaluate the potential benefits of proton beam radiation and intensity modulated radiation therapy is ongoing. These types of more focused radiation therapy decrease the dose of radiation to healthy tissue around the tumor. However, it will be a number of years before enough information is available to determine whether either proton radiation or intensity modulated radiation therapy might allow for greater function and reduce the risk of secondary cancers.

Chemotherapy

Before chemotherapy became a standard way to treat ESFT in the 1960s, very few children survived. Chemotherapy reduces the size of the tumor before surgery, kills microscopic cancer cells, and improves the long-term survival rate. All children or teens with Ewing sarcoma receive chemotherapy as part of treatment.

> Troy (age 5) was diagnosed with Ewing's sarcoma. The disease was in his right femur. He had a total of 18 courses of chemotherapy consisting of ifosfamide, VP-16, vincristine, and doxorubicin. Less than halfway through the protocol, the doctors

decided that it was time to operate to remove the tumor. He had surgery to remove the femur and the knee. He then continued on with several more months of chemotherapy. Treatment was hard on Troy, and he struggled with nausea and vomiting, along with loss of appetite.

Current standard chemotherapy includes vincristine, doxorubicin, and cyclophosphamide, alternating with ifosfamide and etoposide (also called VP-16). For more information about these medications, see Chapter 15, *Chemotherapy*.

Information on standard treatments

Treatments for various types of childhood cancers evolve and improve over time. The treatments described in this chapter were the ones most commonly used (called standard treatments) when this book was written. You can learn about the newest treatments available by calling (800) 422-6237 and asking for the PDQ (physician data query) for childhood bone cancers. This free information, also available online at *www.cancer.gov/cancertopics/pdq/pediatrictreatment* (scroll down to "Osteosarcoma" or "Ewing sarcoma.") explains the disease, state-of-the-art treatments, and ongoing clinical trials. Two versions are available:

• One for families—uses simple language and contains no statistics; and

• One for professionals—is technical, thorough, and includes citations to scientific literature.

To learn about current Phase III clinical trials for bone sarcomas in children or teens, you can visit the National Cancer Institute's website *www.cancer.gov/clinicaltrials/search* and type "Osteosarcoma" or "Ewing sarcoma/PNET" in the "Cancer type/condition" box, and then choose Phase III in the "Trial status/phase" box. Then click the red "Search" button at the bottom of the page.

My daughter Casey was treated for osteosarcoma by an orthopedic oncologist. As soon as she stopped vomiting from chemotherapy, she returned to her beloved cheerleading, took up jazz dancing (she claims it was the best physical therapy), and is now on the varsity springboard diving team at her high school. She sends her orthopedic oncologist photos and videotapes of her doing these things that he claims give him heart pains. But, one day, when he observed her sitting cross-legged in his examining room, he finally admitted that she has had the best physical response of any of his patients and he took a picture of her sitting that way for a brochure. I can't explain to you how wonderful it makes me feel to see this doctor actually glow when he sees Casey (now only once a year). He calls the whole office together to behold her!

Chapter 3
Liver Cancers

CHILDHOOD LIVER CANCERS ARE RARE, as less than 2 percent of all childhood cancers grow in the liver. The most common form of liver cancer in children is hepatoblastoma. Hepatocellular carcinoma is the second most common, but it occurs infrequently. Although extremely rare, two other types of tumors—undifferentiated embryonal sarcoma and infantile choriocarcinoma—sometimes develop in children's livers.

This chapter first explains the structure and function of the liver. Then it describes the signs and symptoms of cancer in the liver and how a diagnosis is made. The chapter then delves into the four types of liver cancers, explains how doctors determine the best treatment, and describes the current standard treatment for each of the cancers.

The liver

The liver is the body's largest internal organ and one of its most complex. Located beneath the rib cage in the upper right part of the abdomen, this wedge-shaped organ is divided into two main lobes—right and left—and two smaller lobes (see Figure 3-1).

The liver is like a chemical refinery that operates 24 hours a day. It receives blood from both the hepatic artery and the portal vein, and it modifies substances contained in the blood that pass through it. For example, after food is digested and absorbed into the bloodstream, the liver metabolizes, or chemically changes, the food into forms that are easier for the rest of the body to use.

Another major function of the liver is to filter blood to remove harmful materials. The liver changes toxic substances, including some drugs, into material that can be easily eliminated from the body in urine and feces. The liver also produces bile, a greenish-brown fluid that is needed for proper digestion. Bile is stored in the gallbladder.

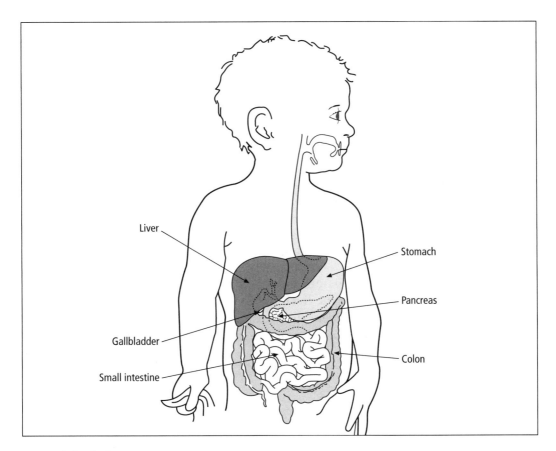

Figure 3-1: The liver

The liver performs hundreds of complex and necessary bodily functions, such as:

- Producing, storing, and releasing glucose (blood sugar), which is a form of energy that keeps the body active.

- Producing, storing, and releasing fat to help regulate the supply of fuel for the body.

- Regulating the balance of many important hormones including adrenal, thyroid, and sex hormones.

- Regulating the supply of essential minerals and vitamins, such as copper and iron.

- Producing, excreting, and converting cholesterol into other important substances that the body needs.

- Manufacturing key proteins, such as those used to transport other substances in the blood and those providing resistance to infection.

- Making proteins that aid in the clotting of blood.

The liver has an amazing ability to regenerate, which allows large amounts of liver tissue to be removed without any major risk to the well-being of the child.

Signs and symptoms

Liver cancer is often found when parents notice a mass in their child's abdomen (usually in the upper right or middle part). The abdomen may be swollen, and some children have abdominal pain. A child with liver cancer may have a poor appetite and recent weight loss. Nausea and vomiting, in addition to weakness, may also be present. All of these symptoms can mimic other illnesses, and sometimes it takes several trips to the doctor to get a diagnosis.

> Logan had been sick for 3 months prior to the diagnosis with severe vomiting, weight loss, a hard abdomen, and irritability. He cried day and night and was very clingy. He had a lot of trouble sleeping. Four different doctors saw Logan and said it was just a stomach bug. He continued to have all the same symptoms, but only worse. I took Logan to the emergency room because I had had enough. Scans were performed and we were told that Logan had a mass in his liver and they were 99.9% sure it was cancer.

Diagnosis

Several tests and procedures are necessary to diagnose liver cancer and determine its type. In addition to completing a medical history and thorough physical examination of the child, the doctor will order several blood tests, including:

- **Complete blood count (CBC).** A sample of blood is checked for the number of red blood cells, white blood cells, and platelets; the amount of hemoglobin in the red blood cells; and how much of the blood is made up of red blood cells.

- **Serum tumor marker tests.** Certain types of cancer cause the body to release substances into the blood called tumor markers. Depending on the type of liver cancer, the blood may have increased amounts of a protein called alpha-fetoprotein (AFP) or a hormone called beta-human chorionic gonadotropin (β-hCG). The AFP levels of children with liver cancer are followed throughout treatment to evaluate the effectiveness of therapy and later to screen for recurrence.

- **Liver function tests.** The liver sometimes releases substances into the bloodstream that signal the presence of cancer in the liver or liver damage from treatment.

- **Lactate dehydrogenase levels.** Measurements of this substance are used to help diagnose liver cancer.

- **Hepatitis B and C.** In some circumstances, blood tests are used to check for the hepatitis virus, which is related to hepatocellular carcinoma, but not hepatoblastoma.

For more information on these blood tests, see Appendix A, *Blood Tests and What They Mean*.

When liver cancer is suspected, imaging studies such as ultrasonography (US) and computerized tomography (CT) of the liver and abdomen are performed. The doctor may also order a magnetic resonance imaging (MRI) of the liver. For more information about these tests, see Chapter 10, *Coping with Procedures*. The definitive test for liver cancer is a liver biopsy, which is a diagnostic procedure used to obtain a small piece of the mass in the liver. This may be done during an open surgical biopsy or by a fine needle biopsy guided by CT or US. The sample of tissue is viewed under a microscope and tested for certain antibodies and gene mutations. For information about biopsies, see Chapter 14, *Surgery*.

At diagnosis, many parents do not know how to find experienced doctors and the best treatments for their child. State-of-the-art care is available from physicians who participate in the Children's Oncology Group (COG). This study group includes pediatric surgeons and oncologists, radiation oncologists, researchers, and nurses. COG conducts studies to discover better therapies and supportive care for children with cancer. You can learn more about COG and find a list of its member treatment centers at *www. childrensoncologygroup.org*.

Hepatoblastoma

Hepatoblastoma is the type of liver cancer most often diagnosed in young children. Almost all (95%) children with hepatoblastoma are diagnosed before they are 3 years old. The incidence of hepatoblastoma has doubled in the last 20 years. It is thought that this rise in incidence may be related to the increase in rates of survival of very low birth weight, premature infants who are known to have a higher risk of developing hepatoblastoma than children who were not born prematurely.

Children with certain syndromes (e.g., Beckwith-Wiedemann syndrome, familial adenomatous polyposis, and Aicardi syndrome) are at higher risk of developing this cancer. Children with a condition called hemihypertrophy (when one side of the body grows more quickly than the other side) are also at increased risk of developing hepatoblastoma. However, most children with these conditions do not develop hepatoblastoma.

Wyatt was diagnosed when he was 9 months old. He wasn't sitting up very well, so I asked the pediatrician about it and he said Wyatt had hypotonia (low muscle tone) and referred us to a physical therapist. She was checking the muscles in Wyatt's abdomen and she felt a lump. I took him to the pediatrician that afternoon, and he thought it might be an enlarged liver. He sent us to the closest children's hospital, and they found a huge tumor—6 x 7 cm. He had imaging, was admitted, then the next

day they did a biopsy and placed a central line. His tumor was Stage III because it was in three lobes. He gets 5-FU, vincristine, and cisplatin and it's shrunk by 50%, but he's on the transplant list because it's only 2 mm away from a major blood vessel. So, they can't resect it and leave clean margins.

Staging

Once hepatoblastoma has been diagnosed, the pediatric oncologist will order more tests and scans to determine the extent of the disease. Imaging studies, such as a CT, MRI, or bone scan, should be performed to check for metastases (spread of the cancer to other parts of the body).

Staging is needed to choose the best treatment. In the United States, staging is based on whether the tumor can be completely removed surgically and whether it has metastasized.

- **Stage I.** The tumor was completely removed.
- **Stage II.** The tumor was removed surgically, but microscopic traces of disease were still present. Children with tumors that rupture during surgery are classified as having stage II disease.
- **Stage III.** The tumor cannot be removed surgically or is partially removed, and disease was found in the lymph nodes.
- **Stage IV.** The disease has spread to distant areas in the body. Ten percent of children with hepatoblastoma have metastatic disease in the lungs at diagnosis. Rare areas of spread can include the central nervous system (brain and spinal cord) and the abdomen.

   Logan was 19 months old when he was diagnosed with hepatoblastoma. At diagnosis, the tumor was the size of a grapefruit and had spread to his lymph nodes and also to the right atrium of his heart.

After surgery, approximately 20 to 30 percent of children are found to have stage I or II hepatoblastoma, 50 to 70 percent have stage III disease, and 10 to 20 percent have stage IV disease.

An alternative staging system (called PRETEXT), widely used in Europe, is based on the number of liver lobes that contain cancer. The amount of tumor in each lobe is determined by MRI, and sometimes through CT or ultrasound. This staging system is used before surgery.

- **PRETEXT stage 1**: Tumor is in only one lobe.
- **PRETEXT stage 2**: Tumor is in two adjoining lobes.

- **PRETEXT stage 3**: Tumor is in three adjoining lobes or two non-adjoining lobes.

- **PRETEXT stage 4**: Tumor is in all four lobes. Tests are conducted to determine whether cancer has spread outside of the liver.

In international treatment protocols, all children with hepatoblastoma are treated with chemotherapy prior to surgery.

Treatment

To choose the best treatment for children with hepatoblastoma, pediatric oncologists consider the child's stage of disease, characteristics of cancer cells (called histology), and the level of AFP in the blood. An initial AFP level of less than 100 ng/ml, regardless of stage, puts children in a higher risk category.

> My infant daughter was diagnosed with stage III hepatoblastoma. It was in two lobes but couldn't be removed because it was so close to the blood vessels in the liver. There is another spot on her liver, not near the tumor, that they don't know if it's more tumor or a bile duct. So, we don't know if the surgeon is going to take the spot and the tumor, or just the tumor. I hope they can take it all so we'll never have to worry about the mystery spot. Her AFP has gone way down, and they said that the scans show that the tumor might be dead and won't shrink any more. They are going to do the surgery next week, then two more rounds of chemo after that. We know the surgeon—he did her biopsy, both Hickmans (had to have the first one removed due to a blood infection), and also put in her G-tube.

All children with hepatoblastoma need surgery. Because of the relationship between the quality of the surgery and children's outcomes, surgery should be done by pediatric surgeons who have experience removing tumors in the liver and who have access to liver transplant programs (see section later in this chapter called "Liver transplantation").

> Logan's chemotherapy was hung and dripping within 2 hours of the pathology report. Logan received cisplatin, vincristine, and 5-FU [fluorouracil]. He had chemotherapy every 3 weeks that usually took an average of 2 days. After Logan received the first round, there was a small decrease in size of the tumor. After the second, there was a little more. Since his tumor was responding, we decided to stay on the protocol.

> Just 10 days after his second birthday, Logan had a 5-hour operation to remove the entire right lobe of his liver and his gallbladder. During surgery he lost quite a lot of blood and was given five units while in the operating room. He was transferred to ICU [intensive care unit] and was given another unit of blood and one of platelets. He remained there for only 36 hours and was transferred to the pediatric oncology floor.

By the third day, he was walking around. He had very little pain and he never complained. By the fourth day, he was running up and down the hall feeling wonderful. You would never guess that he had just had a major operation. On the fifth day, we were able to take him home. Two weeks after the operation, he went back to have one more round of chemotherapy and then we were done.

The most common treatment plans, based on stage of disease and the kind of cancer cells, are described below.

Stages I and II: Treatment of stages I and II hepatoblastoma of pure fetal histology (when the cancer cells look exactly like fetal liver cells under a microscope) usually involves surgery to completely remove the tumor. This is followed by regular monitoring of AFP levels and periodic imaging studies to see whether the cancer returns (called watchful waiting). Chemotherapy is generally not given. However, care must be taken to ensure that the histology diagnosis was accurate, because sometimes pockets of other types of hepatoblastoma cells are found in the tumor (called non-pure fetal histology). Children with these mixed types of cancer cells need more aggressive treatment, usually involving four courses of three chemotherapy drugs (cisplatin, vincristine, and fluorouracil) after surgical removal of the tumor. The chemotherapy is given to ensure any tumor cells that may have spread outside the liver are killed.

Stage III: Children with stage III disease are first treated with chemotherapy to try to shrink the tumor so it can be completely removed. The most commonly used combination of chemotherapy drugs includes cisplatin, vincristine, and fluorouracil. If the tumor shrinks enough, it is removed surgically. If the tumor cannot be completely removed, liver transplantation is sometimes recommended. Occasionally, a two-step treatment called transarterial chemoembolization is used. This involves giving chemotherapy directly to the tumor via a catheter and then cutting off the blood supply to the tumor by plugging the artery with material (e.g., metal coils or gelatin sponges).

A clinical trial ended right before Wyatt was diagnosed, so he is on standard treatment for his stage III tumor. He takes 5-FU, cisplatin, vincristine, doxorubicin, and also Zinecard® to protect his heart from the doxorubicin. Our go-to drugs are Zofran® and Benadryl® for the nausea and vomiting. After the fifth cycle, he vomited for 5 days despite the antinausea drugs, and he got really dehydrated and was hospitalized. They added Ativan® and Reglan® for the 2 weeks he was in. We just had a 3-week break and he gained a pound a week. I'm grateful that he seems to be luckier than some of the other kids we've met—he just hasn't been as sick.

Stage IV: The standard treatment for stage IV hepatoblastoma is four courses of cisplatin, vincristine, and fluorouracil, followed by surgery to remove the primary tumor and any tumors in the lungs. If the primary tumor is completely removed, the tumors in other parts of the body can no longer be seen on scans, and the AFP returns to normal,

then two more courses of the same three chemotherapy drugs are given. If the cancer in the liver cannot be removed through surgery and there are no signs of cancer in other parts of the body, the treatment is generally a liver transplant. If a liver transplant is not possible, treatment may include additional chemotherapy (e.g., ifosfamide, cisplatin, and doxorubicin), radiation therapy, or transarterial chemoembolization—giving chemotherapy directly to the tumor via a catheter and then cutting off the blood supply to the tumor by plugging the artery with material (e.g., metal coils or gelatin sponges).

To find out how to learn about the most current treatments available, see the section at the end of this chapter called "Information on standard treatments."

Hepatocellular carcinoma

Hepatocellular carcinoma is a rare cancer that is more common in boys than in girls and that is diagnosed most often in children who are older than 10. Risk factors for this form of liver cancer are:

- The hepatitis B virus (if passed from mother to child at birth).

- Certain inherited metabolic conditions, including glycogen storage disease and tyrosinemia.

- Biliary cirrhosis, Alagille syndrome, or progressive familial intrahepatic cholestasis.

One particular form of hepatocellular carcinoma, fibrolamellar carcinoma, occurs most often in adolescents.

> Kennedy had just turned 12 at the time of her diagnosis. She had been struggling with intermittent vomiting. I noticed that she had lost some weight but attributed it to her very busy and active basketball season. I took her to the doctor for an exam on a Friday. She didn't comment on anything regarding her physical exam but ordered a few blood tests, just to check out organ function. On the following Monday, the clinic called and said Kennedy had increased liver enzymes and wanted her to have an ultrasound, which was scheduled for the following day. I knew right then that something was horribly wrong. We barely made it home from the ultrasound appointment and the clinic was calling telling us to come back in. When we got there, they told us that there was a large tumor on her liver and they had already set us up for an appointment at the closest children's hospital the following morning.

> Her morning consisted of an MRI, CT scan, and lots of blood work. A few hours later, the oncologist took us in a room and told us they were pretty sure Kennedy had hepatocellular carcinoma, a liver cancer that is extremely rare in kids in the United States. She actually had three areas of cancer on her liver—a very large tumor hanging off the left lobe and two large, ill-defined areas of cancer in her right lobe.

The only good news was that there were no signs of cancer anywhere else; it was all contained to her liver.

In addition to the signs and symptoms listed earlier in the chapter for all liver tumors, 15 to 20 percent of children with hepatocellular carcinoma have jaundice (yellowing of the skin and whites of the eyes caused by excess bilirubin in the blood) or fever. Poor appetite and weight loss are common. If the tumor ruptures, bleeding into the abdominal cavity may occur.

Staging

After hepatocellular carcinoma is diagnosed, the staging process is identical to the process used to stage hepatoblastoma (see pages 31–32).

Treatment

Hepatocellular carcinoma cancer cells are very aggressive. These tumors often involve all lobes of the liver, making surgery difficult. This is why pediatric oncologists carefully consider the child's age, stage of disease, and type of cancer cells to choose the treatment with the best chance for cure. All surgeries for children with hepatocellular carcinoma should be done by pediatric surgeons with experience removing liver tumors and who have access to liver transplant programs. The most commonly use treatment plans, based on stage of disease, are described below.

Stages I and II: Treatment of stages I and II hepatocellular carcinoma usually consists of surgery to completely remove the tumor, followed by chemotherapy (using cisplatin and doxorubicin). If tumor tissue is in more than one lobe of the liver, it is not always possible to remove the tumor completely at diagnosis. In these instances, preoperative chemotherapy may shrink the tumor to a size that makes removal possible.

Stages III and IV: Children with stage III or IV disease are treated with chemotherapy to try to shrink the tumor so it can be completely removed. The most commonly used combination of chemotherapy drugs includes cisplatin and doxorubicin. If the tumor shrinks enough, it is removed surgically. If it cannot be completely removed, liver transplantation is sometimes recommended. Occasionally, a two-step treatment called transarterial chemoembolization is used. This involves giving chemotherapy directly to the tumor via a catheter and then cutting off the blood supply to the tumor by plugging the artery with material (e.g., metal coils or gelatin sponge). Other treatment options include cryosurgery (freezing all or part of the tumor), injecting the tumor with alcohol, or radiation therapy.

We took Kennedy to a different and well-known hospital for a second opinion. The pediatric oncologist there was honest in telling us that there wasn't a protocol for

this type of cancer in kids. We also met with a surgeon who worked exclusively with livers. He informed us that attempting resection at this time would be a huge mistake. Treatment was to consist of cisplatin and doxorubicin infusions done inpatient at the hospital. Then, she would start the newer oral chemo medication called sorafenib and take it twice daily until her next IV chemo. The entire cycle was 21 days in length. Honestly, I questioned whether or not we should even do chemo. The prognosis was grave and I didn't want the last days of her life to be full of the type of suffering she was about to go through. I talked to her oncologist about my feelings and she assured me that we would know early on if this was working or not. We would do two cycles and then repeat scans. They also followed a tumor specific protein called AFP to give us an indication of tumor response.

After two rounds of chemo, she had repeat scans. We were all shocked to hear that her tumors had shrunk 50%! Each round continued to bring a drop in her AFP and shrinkage of her tumors. After five rounds of chemo and one round of chemoembolization, she was listed for transplant with a Status 1B, which is a rare listing type reserved for kids. Within 5 days of her Status 1B listing, we received a call that 5 months prior wasn't even a possibility. On May 27, 2012, Kennedy received a lifesaving liver transplant.

A child with a previously damaged liver who is diagnosed with hepatocellular carcinoma may not be eligible for surgery. For example, a child with liver damage from hepatitis B or C could not survive if large portions of the liver were surgically removed. In such cases, only small tumors are removed.

Coley's surgery was very scary, I think more for us than for her. She has been my role model for bravery throughout the entire process. The surgery took a few hours and has left her with a large scar that goes from one side of her stomach to the other in an upside down U. I was very scared to see her in intensive care, because I was afraid that I would break down when I saw her with all those tubes. But after waiting all those hours, when we were finally able to see her, she looked so beautiful. She had made it!

Undifferentiated embryonal sarcoma

Undifferentiated embryonal sarcoma of the liver is a rare liver cancer in children and is most commonly diagnosed in those who are 5 to 10 years old. At diagnosis, the cancer has often spread throughout the liver and to the lungs. It's very important to differentiate between embryonal sarcoma of the liver and biliary tract rhabdomyosarcoma, which are very similar clinically, but which require very different treatments.

Treatment of undifferentiated embryonal sarcoma of the liver involves complete surgical removal of the tumor, followed by chemotherapy (some combination of vincristine,

cyclophosphamide, dactinomycin, doxorubicin, or ifosfamide is usually used). Tumors that cannot be completely removed after diagnosis are first shrunk with four cycles of chemotherapy and then reevaluated. Liver transplantation is sometimes necessary when tumors cannot be surgically removed.

Choriocarcinoma of the liver

Choriocarcinoma of the liver is a very rare tumor that is usually found in the first few months of an infant's life. The baby might be anemic if the tumor has hemorrhaged. Clinical diagnosis can be made without biopsy based on MRI of the liver, extremely high serum β-hCG levels, and normal AFP levels for age.

Surgery usually follows chemotherapy because the tumors often hemorrhage. The combination of cisplatin, etoposide, and bleomycin has been effective in some children. After chemotherapy, the remaining tumor is surgically removed.

Liver transplantation

A small number of children with liver tumors need a liver transplant. Before selecting a transplant center, research your options. Institutions may just be starting a transplant program, or they may have lots of experience. Some may be excellent for adults, but have limited pediatric experience. Some may use a team approach (including hepatologists, pediatric surgeons, pediatric social workers, nutritionists) and others may not. Additionally, your insurance plan may require that your child go to a specific transplant center.

Choosing a transplant center

To help you learn about the policies of different transplant centers, here are some questions you can ask:

- How many pediatric transplants did your institution do last year?

- How successful is your program? What are the 1-year, 2-year, and 5-year survival rates for children with the same type and severity of disease my child has? (Some institutions accept very high-risk patients, and these statistics would not compare to those of a place that only performs less risky transplants.)

- What is the nurse-to-patient ratio? Do all the staff members have pediatric training and experience?

- What support staff is available (educator, social worker, child life therapist, chaplain, etc.)?

- Will my child be in a pediatric or combined adult–pediatric unit?

- What are the institution's rules about parents staying in the child's hospital room?

- What on-site or nearby housing is available for families of children undergoing transplantation? What are the costs for this housing?

- Describe the transplant surgery in detail, including anticipated complications.

- Explain the risks and benefits of this procedure.

- What is the average length of time before a child leaves the hospital? For a child who has been discharged from the hospital but whose home is far away, how long before he can leave the area to go home?

- What will my child's life be like, assuming all goes perfectly? What will it be like if there are problems?

- What are the long-term side effects of this type of transplant? What long-term follow-up is available?

- How will we be notified when a donor liver is available?

- How much will this procedure cost? How much will my insurance cover? (This is not applicable in Canada, where provincial health programs cover the cost of the procedure.)

Many transplant centers have videos and booklets for patients and their families that explain services and describe what to expect before, during, and after the transplant. You can call any transplant center that you are considering and ask staff to send you all available materials.

> We talked with several parents about the two transplant programs that are closest to our home. We visited both programs and picked the one a little farther away just because the services for the kids and the quality of life for the family sounds much better. If all goes well, we will be there less than 3 months. If problems develop, it could be much longer.

Paying for the transplant

Liver transplants are expensive. Insurers might cover the cost of the procedure without question if the transplant is considered the standard of care. However, if your insurance company considers the type of transplant proposed for your child to be experimental, it might not be covered. Most insurance plans have a lifetime cap, and many only pay 80 percent of the costs of the transplant up to the cap. The Children's Organ Transplant Association (*http://cota.org/learn-more*) can help with fundraising efforts.

Most transplant centers employ financial counselors who will work with your family to sort through insurance issues. In addition, most insurance companies will assign your child's care to a transplant coordinator or case manager, who is responsible for making

arrangements with the transplant center and handling financial issues. Getting to know your hospital financial counselor and your insurance coordinator and voicing your needs and concerns may help during this stressful time.

Finding a liver

Children who need a liver transplant may need an entire liver (from a deceased donor) or a portion of a liver from a living donor. If your child needs an entire liver, he or she will be put on a transplant list. Your family will be given a device to notify you the moment a liver is available. If only a portion of a liver is needed, it can come from a parent, family member, or family friend, as long as the donor meets age, size, blood type, and health requirements. If a relative donates part of a liver, it is called a "living-related donor transplant." Within a few weeks, the donor's liver will regrow to a normal size (called regeneration).

> We are doing two things. Wyatt is on transplant list for a whole liver, but two of my relatives have the right blood type to donate a portion of their livers. But, they need to lose weight to be in the right BMI [body mass index] to be a donor for the surgery. We are working with Angel Flight Northeast, and they sent me a list of pilots who would fly us to the hospital if a liver becomes available. So, I basically go to bed with anxiety and wake up with anxiety.

The transplant and beyond

Before the surgery, you child will have many tests, including blood and urine tests, echocardiogram, electrocardiogram, and a chest x-ray (these procedures are described in Chapter 10, *Coping with Procedures*). During surgery, the surgeon will remove the diseased liver and will connect the new liver (whole or part) to your child's hepatic artery, hepatic vein, portal vein, and bile duct. The surgery usually lasts 5 to 10 hours. Your child may spend 2 or 3 days in the intensive care unit and then a week or so in the hospital. After discharge, you'll need to stay in the area so the transplant team can monitor your child's health and manage the medications needed after the transplant.

One possible problem after a liver transplant is rejection of the organ by the body's immune system. Medications (called immunosuppressants) are given to help minimize the risk of rejection. Although the risk of rejection is greatest in the first few weeks after the transplant, your child will have to take anti-rejection medications for the rest of his or her life. These medications also leave children vulnerable to certain infections, so care must be taken to avoid people who are sick.

In some rare cases, the body rejects the new organ and another liver transplant is necessary. However, most children do very well after this life-saving procedure.

Information on standard treatments

Treatments for various types of childhood cancers evolve and improve over time. The treatments described in this chapter were the ones most commonly used (called standard treatments) when this book was written. You can learn about the newest treatments available by calling (800) 422-6237 and asking for the PDQ (physician data query) for childhood liver cancer. This free information, also available online at *www.cancer.gov/cancertopics/pdq/pediatrictreatment* (scroll down to "Liver cancer, childhood") explains the disease, state-of-the-art treatments, and ongoing clinical trials. Two versions are available:

- One for families—uses simple language and contains no statistics; and

- One for professionals—is technical, thorough, and includes citations to scientific literature.

To learn about current Phase III clinical trials for liver cancers in children, visit the National Cancer Institute's website *www.cancer.gov/clinicaltrials/search* and type "liver cancer, child" in the "Cancer type/condition" box and then choose Phase III in the "Trial status/phase" box. Then click the red "Search" button at the bottom of the page.

Matthew's only symptom was an enlarged belly. He seemed to be a normal, active 18-month-old. His medical team estimated that his tumor was initially the size of a grapefruit. Four months of chemotherapy shrank the tumor to about the size of an egg, making surgery safer and more likely to be successful. Two additional months of chemotherapy were used as follow-up after his surgery. His alfa fetoprotein level returned to normal following the surgery and remained normal for 3 years, when it started to slowly climb. After ruling out all other possible causes, we knew it would only be a matter of time before our fears were confirmed. A CT scan found the liver mass.

Surgery was scheduled right away to attempt to resect the tumor. We tried several different chemotherapy protocols in the next five months, but Matthew was not improving. We met with the liver transplant team and Matthew was placed on the list. As the clock continued to tick and his AFP continued to climb, he continued on chemotherapy.

Matthew had his liver transplant. It was thrilling for us to see him recover from major surgery so quickly! At almost 2 years following his transplant, his AFP has remained normal and our hospital visits are not so frequent. Matthew played ball this past summer, completed his kindergarten year with very few absences, and is now a first grader learning to read!

Chapter 4

Neuroblastoma

NEUROBLASTOMA IS A CANCER of newly developing cells in the sympathetic nervous system (described below). The average age at diagnosis is around 2 years old. Most children are diagnosed before the age of 5, and diagnosis is rare after age 10. Although neuroblastomas can develop anywhere in the sympathetic nervous system, from the neck to the pelvis, more than half of these cancers originate in an adrenal gland in the abdomen. Symptoms of this disease vary depending on the location of the primary tumor.

First, this chapter looks at the structure and function of the sympathetic nervous system. Then it describes who gets neuroblastoma, what the signs and symptoms are, how it is diagnosed, and how doctors determine the prognosis. The chapter ends with a discussion about the newest treatment options.

The sympathetic nervous system

The human body is equipped with an impressive information system made up of the central nervous system (CNS) and peripheral nervous system (PNS). The CNS includes the brain and spinal cord, and the PNS connects the CNS to limbs and organs. The network of nerves that make up the PNS include the sympathetic nervous system and the parasympathetic nervous system, but neuroblastomas only arise in the sympathetic system. The sympathetic nervous system responds to a person's environment and emotions. For example, if a child is surprised or frightened, the sympathetic nervous system leaps into action by accelerating the heartbeat, increasing blood sugar, and cooling the body through perspiration.

The adrenal glands

The adrenal glands are small glands that sit on top of each kidney and are responsible for producing many different hormones. Each adrenal gland has two parts (see Figure 4-1). The outer portion, called the cortex, secretes hormones such as cortisone and aldosterone that the body uses to balance fluids and electrolytes. The central portion, called the medulla, produces hormones that help the body respond to stress.

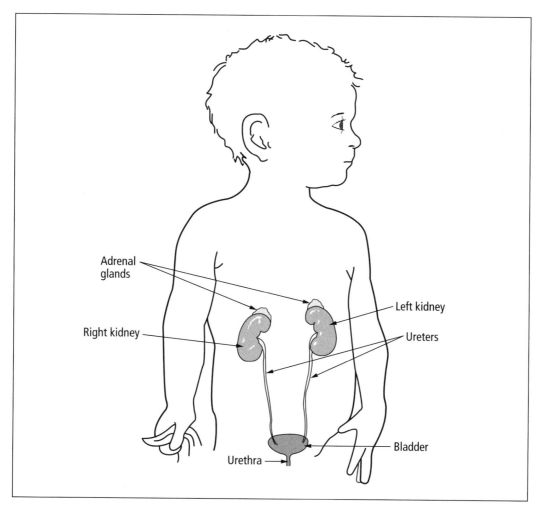

Figure 4-1: The adrenal glands

Who gets neuroblastoma?

Neuroblastoma is the second most common solid tumor in children (brain tumors are the most common). Each year more than 800 children are diagnosed with neuro-blastoma in North America. Boys are diagnosed more often than girls, and there is a slightly higher incidence among White children than among Black children, although Black children are more likely to be diagnosed with high-risk disease. More than half of all neuroblastomas are diagnosed in children ages 2 years or younger, 89 percent are

diagnosed before age 5, and 98 percent are diagnosed by age 10. Neuroblastoma is the most common cancer diagnosed in the first year of life.

> My son was only 2 years old when his first symptoms began. It was on the day of his third birthday that we received the diagnosis of neuroblastoma. A tumor was attached to his left adrenal gland, and cancer cells were also discovered in his bones and bone marrow. I remember thinking that I had never heard such a strange and ugly sounding word as neuroblastoma before in my life.

For reasons that are not understood, sympathetic nerve cells that are at the very beginning of their growth cycle sometimes begin to divide rapidly and form tumors, instead of maturing normally. To stop this process, the cancer cells must be killed with chemotherapy drugs and radiation, removed with surgery, or encouraged to mature into normal nerve cells with help from drugs called retinoids. Another way to stop this disease is to stimulate the immune system to attack and kill the tumor cells.

Genetic factors

Most neuroblastoma tumors arise spontaneously, and there is no known environmental cause. Approximately 1 to 2 percent of diagnosed children have a family history of neuroblastoma. Affected children from these families are usually diagnosed as infants, and they may have multiple primary tumors. Children with familial neuroblastoma have tumors that develop in various ways. In some cases, they spontaneously disappear; in others, they rapidly grow and spread.

The major neuroblastoma predisposition gene is called *ALK*, and this gene maps to the short arm of chromosome 2. Mutations in this gene account for 75 percent of hereditary cases. Another gene called *PHOX2B* predisposes to neuroblastoma in 5 percent of hereditary cases. However, most of these children also have a disorder called central hypoventilation syndrome, or "Ondine's curse." The gene responsible for the remaining hereditary cases is not currently known, although there may be a slight increased probability in children with Hirschsprung disease of Neurofibromatosis type 1.

Environmental factors

Although certain types of cancer have been linked to environmental factors, this is not true for neuroblastoma. Many research studies have been conducted to evaluate possible environmental causes, but no prenatal or environmental exposures have consistently or conclusively been associated with an increased risk of developing neuroblastoma. There is nothing parents could have done to prevent their child from developing this disease.

Signs and symptoms

Children with neuroblastoma often experience a number of different signs and symptoms, depending largely on the location of the primary tumor and whether the disease has spread (metastasized) to other locations in the body.

> Mikey (4 years old) was always a sickly child and he was constantly on antibiotics for one ailment or another. The night before we took him to the emergency room, he had fallen into his toy box and hurt his abdomen. He wasn't in any pain, but overnight a huge mass began to appear. He was asleep on my bed lying on his side and we could see a mass protruding from his upper left abdomen area. We never imagined it could be a tumor.

· · · · ·

> Nelson (age 6) was having a lot of trouble with constipation. The pediatrician did a lot of x-rays to see where he was blocked. On the last x-ray, they caught the bottom of his lung field and saw that one lung was full of fluid. The pediatrician sent us to the local hospital to tap the fluid and then they found a huge mass. It was pushing his kidney into his intestines and blocking them. It came up behind his liver and lungs.

In many cases, parents find a lump or mass in the abdomen while dressing or bathing their young child. The abdomen may appear enlarged, or the child may experience intermittent abdominal pain. The child may stop eating, lose weight, or experience diarrhea and vomiting. Children with neuroblastoma may have fever and they may be unusually tired and irritable. If disease has spread to the bones, the child may begin to limp, refuse to stand, or describe pain in the bones. Neuroblastoma sometimes spreads to the bones of the skull and orbits (bones around the eyes). This may make one or both of the eyes protrude, or the child may develop dark circles around the eyes due to bleeding into the tumor. This is often referred to as "raccoon eyes."

> Initially, when our son began limping, we attributed it to normal growing pains. There were no other signs that it could be a more serious situation. We took him to a doctor a few days after the limping started, and he didn't seem to feel it was a cause for great concern, either. Shortly after that, our son began to complain of leg pains and soon he was unable to walk at all.

If the tumor involves the spinal cord, the child may have back pain and difficulty passing urine or stool. Tumors located in this area sometimes cause spinal cord compression that can result in stumbling, weakness, or paralysis. Children whose disease has spread to the bone marrow may have pale skin from low numbers of red blood cells, and/or tiny red dots under the skin (petechiae) due to low numbers of platelets. Tumors growing in the chest may cause a chronic cough or difficulty breathing.

Charlotte was ahead on every single milestone by 4 months old. She was very active and could sit alone. It was very noticeable when, on Father's Day, her legs stopped moving. Her legs were spread out in "frog pose" and she looked uncomfortable when we sat her up. We went to see her pediatrician the next day, and he said there was something wrong but he didn't know what it was.

Horner syndrome is a rare disorder that is sometimes associated with a mediastinal (in the chest) or cervical (in the neck) neuroblastoma. It occurs when the nerve to the eye is damaged or disrupted by a tumor high in the chest. It may also occur after surgery to remove a tumor in the neck or chest. With this syndrome, the eyelid droops, the pupil looks small, and the child may not sweat on the side of the face with the affected eye.

My son had a strange reaction after his surgery in which he developed a red flush on exactly one side of his face and neck. The anesthesiologist called it Horner syndrome, and was interested in it enough to take a photograph of it for research purposes.

Opsoclonus-myoclonus syndrome (OMS) is another rare manifestation that can accompany neuroblastoma. It is sometimes referred to as "dancing eyes–dancing feet syndrome" because of rapid, uncontrollable movement of the eyes, and sudden, jerky movements of the feet and legs. OMS is usually associated with a localized, mature tumor that has a good prognosis. However, OMS may be associated with developmental delay, and these symptoms may persist or recur. Only about half of OMS cases are associated with neuroblastoma.

Rachel was 3 years old when she first developed symptoms. One of her eyes started turning in and she lost most of her vision in that eye (she regained it after treatment). The doctor did some scans and a biopsy, and diagnosed her neuroblastoma. She had a primary tumor on her right adrenal gland, but there was a much larger tumor in her sinus cavity, behind her right eye. Her urine catecholamine levels were never elevated.

Another unusual syndrome associated with favorable, mature neuroblastomas is vasoactive intestinal peptide (VIP) syndrome. Children with this syndrome have abdominal distension and watery diarrhea, but because it is caused by a protein made by the tumor, VIP syndrome goes away once the tumor is removed.

Diagnosis

Many tests are necessary to confirm a diagnosis of neuroblastoma because symptoms of this disease can mimic other illnesses, including other cancers. A pediatric oncologist

will perform a thorough physical examination and order a complete blood count (CBC). The following tests should also be done:

- Bone is assessed by a meta-iodobenzylguanidine (mIBG) scan (performed in the nuclear medicine department) and, if the results of the mIBG scan are negative, by a technetium 99 scan.

- Enlarged lymph nodes are examined and biopsied. Lymph nodes that cannot be felt on exam should be assessed by a magnetic resonance imaging (MRI) scan with three-dimensional (3D) measurements.

- The abdomen (including liver) and pelvis are best evaluated with an MRI, but a computerized tomography (CT) scan with oral contrast can be used to distinguish tumor from loops of intestines.

- Chest x-rays are done from the front and side. CT scans and/or MRI scans are necessary if the chest x-ray shows a tumor or if an abdominal tumor extends into the chest.

To minimize unnecessary radiation, MRI scans are often done instead of CT scans. For more information on these procedures, see Chapter 10, *Coping with Procedures*.

> *Little alarm bells started going off when the radiologist had the technician scan Cam's abdomen twice. She wanted to get a good look at his liver and all the way to the bottom of his kidneys. A few hours later, the oncologist, psychologist, and nurse clinician all showed up and my stomach sank.*

Blood and urine tests, biopsies, and evaluation of many tumor cell characteristics also help a pediatric oncologist make or confirm a neuroblastoma diagnosis. Over 90 percent of neuroblastomas secrete hormones called catecholamines. When catecholamines break down, they produce VMA and HVA, which are found in the urine. A 24-hour urine collection or a single urine sample will be tested for VMA and HVA levels. This test is valuable for making the initial diagnosis and for following the child's response to treatment.

> *At the age of 19 months, Justina lost all her motor skills. At first she was clumsy and staggering, but it progressed very rapidly (over a period of 4 days) to a point where she was not able to pull herself up or even sit. Her eyes would bounce, roll back, and circle. She was scared, since she had no concept of where her body was in space. She always felt as if she was falling. Justina was misdiagnosed for 4 months until we finally learned she had neuroblastoma.*

To make a diagnosis, the pediatric oncologist needs tumor tissue obtained from a biopsy or surgical removal of tumor (see Chapter 14, *Surgery*). Every child with suspected neuroblastoma will also have a bone marrow aspiration and bone biopsy done on each hip. These procedures are described in Chapter 10, *Coping with Procedures*. A pathologist

will study the tumor sample, the bone marrow biopsy, and the bone marrow aspirate (liquid part of the bone marrow), and these materials will then be tested for a variety of biologic and genetic factors.

> *The local hospital did a chest and abdominal CT before they sent him to the children's hospital. The pediatrician said it was cancer. He said, "We think it's neuroblastoma but you need a biopsy." We got a definite diagnosis at the children's hospital—solid mass 20 centimeters high! It didn't cross the midline. They speculated he'd had it since he was born.*

Staging

Once a diagnosis of neuroblastoma has been made, the pediatric oncologist will order additional tests and scans to determine the stage (extent of the disease). Using the International Neuroblastoma Staging System (INSS), neuroblastoma is categorized into one of the following stages:

- **Stage 1.** The tumor is limited to the site of origin and can be completely removed (resected), with or without microscopic residual disease (extremely small amounts that are visible only with the aid of a microscope). Lymph nodes on both sides of the abdomen or chest are negative, which means that no cancer is found when the lymph node tissue is examined under a microscope.

- **Stage 2A.** The tumor affects only one side of the body and is limited to the site of origin; the cancer cannot be completely removed (visible amounts of disease remains); and lymph nodes on both sides of the body are negative microscopically.

- **Stage 2B.** The tumor affects only one side of the body and is limited to the site of origin; complete removal may or may not be possible; lymph nodes on the same side of the body near the tumor are positive (contain neuroblastoma cells); and lymph nodes on the opposite side of the body are negative microscopically.

- **Stage 3.** The tumor has grown across the midline and cannot be easily removed; regional lymph nodes may or may not be positive; the tumor affects only one side of the body with lymph node involvement on the opposite side of the body; or the tumor begins in the midline with lymph node or tumor involvement on both sides of the body.

- **Stage 4.** The tumor has spread to distant lymph nodes, bone, bone marrow, liver, and/ or other organs (except as defined for stage 4S).

- **Stage 4S.** This stage includes only infants younger than 1 year of age. The tumor is confined to the site of origin described in stages 1 or 2, with spread limited to the liver, skin, and/or bone marrow.

When Adam was 3 weeks old, we took him to the pediatrician because his abdomen was swollen. We were shocked to learn that it was cancer—stage 4S neuroblastoma. He didn't receive any treatment for his disease at that time, because his doctor felt he didn't need it. Instead, we just watched him very closely. His tumors eventually calcified, and he was fine until 5 years later when he suffered a relapse and required chemotherapy. He has done very well, and recently we celebrated his twelfth birthday.

The INSS system has been used for the past 25 years, but staging can vary depending on how skilled or aggressive the surgeon is. The medical community is now evaluating a new staging system (called the INRG staging system) that is based on image-defined risk factors, rather than the extent of surgical removal.

Prognosis

Treatment for childhood neuroblastoma has steadily improved in the last 2 decades. In the 1960s, over 75 percent of all children with neuroblastoma died. Now, the success rate of treatment varies with the stage at diagnosis.

To determine the best possible treatment for each child, doctors consider the stage of disease as well as the factors below to decide whether the child is in a low-, intermediate-, or high-risk category:

- **MYCN amplification.** *MYCN* is a normal gene that contributes to some neuroblastomas developing or becoming very aggressive. Amplification means that instead of two copies of *MYCN* in every cell, the neuroblastoma cells have 100 to 200 copies of the gene. This occurs in 20 to 25 percent of tumors.

- **Tumor pathology.** Using the International Neuroblastoma Pathology Classification method, the tumor is graded as favorable or unfavorable, based mainly on how it looks under a microscope (called histopathologic classification).

- **DNA index.** This is a measurement of the amount of DNA material in neuroblastoma cells. Diploidy (also known as a DNA index of 1, corresponding to 46 chromosomes) is the normal amount of DNA in a human cell. Children with diploid or near-diploid tumors tend to have a worse outcome. Having more than the diploid amount of DNA (or chromosomes) is called hyperdiploidy (also known as DNA index >1). Most cells in hyperdiploid tumors have 60 to 70 chromosomes, which is associated with a favorable outcome.

- **Child's age.** Previously, oncologists thought that an age of 12 months or younger was associated with favorable outcomes. However, several recent studies suggest that 18 months is a better age cut-off to distinguish likely outcomes.

June 24 was a big, big day. We met the pediatric neurologist at 10 a.m., and he used a lot of scary words. He had a list of five or six dangerous diseases it might be, and

he had her in an MRI at 1 p.m. At 3:30 p.m., a team of 20 doctors and nurses walked in—oncologists, neurologists, nurses—and Charlotte wasn't even back from the MRI yet. They told us they found a mass; they thought it was cancer and wanted to do a biopsy. They called in a special surgeon who did the biopsy around 7 p.m. A couple of hours later, they had confirmed it was cancer, and by 11 p.m. they knew it was Stage 4 intermediate-risk neuroblastoma. By 1 or 2 a.m. on June 25, they started her on chemo.

Treatment

At diagnosis, many parents don't know how to find experienced doctors and the best treatment for their child. State-of-the-art care is available from physicians who participate in the Children's Oncology Group (COG). This study group, composed of pediatric surgeons and oncologists, neurologists, radiation oncologists, researchers, and nurses, provides the best current treatments for childhood cancers and conducts studies to discover better therapies and supportive care for children with cancer. You can learn more about COG and find a list of its member treatment centers at *www. childrensoncologygroup.org*.

After diagnosis and staging, the pediatric oncologist will discuss with you the best-known treatment or a clinical trial (see Chapter 9, *Choosing a Treatment*) based on the following risk categories:

- **Low risk.** Children with low-risk disease do not require aggressive treatment. They usually have surgery or biopsy, followed by observation. The following are included in the low-risk category:

  – All children with INSS stage 1 disease

  – Children with INSS stage 2 disease, except those older than age 1 at diagnosis with *MYCN* amplification and unfavorable pathology

  – Infants with 4S disease with hyperdiploidy, favorable pathology, and non-amplified *MYCN*

- **Intermediate risk.** Children with intermediate-risk disease generally require surgery and 12 to 24 weeks of chemotherapy. Radiation therapy is occasionally necessary. The following are included in the intermediate-risk category:

  – Children younger than age 1 with INSS stage 3 disease with non- amplified *MYCN*

  – Children older than age 1 with INSS stage 3 disease with non-amplified *MYCN* and favorable pathology

  – Children younger than age 1 with INSS stage 4 disease with non-amplified *MYCN*

  – Children younger than age 1 with stage 4S disease, non-amplified *MYCN*, diploidy, or unfavorable pathology

- **High risk.** Children with high-risk neuroblastoma need aggressive treatment, which usually lasts 10 to 12 months and is divided into three phases: 1) an induction phase of chemotherapy and surgery; 2) a consolidation phase with peripheral stem cell transplantation and radiation and; 3) a maintenance phase that includes 6 months of isotretinoin and immunotherapy. The following are included in the high-risk category:
  - Children older than 1 year with INSS stage 2 disease with amplified *MYCN* and unfavorable pathology
  - Children younger than age 1 with INSS stage 3 disease with amplified *MYCN*
  - Children older than 1 year with INSS stage 3 disease with non-amplified *MYCN* and unfavorable pathology or with amplified *MYCN*
  - Children older than 1 year with INSS stage 4 disease
  - Infants with stage 4 or 4S disease with amplified *MYCN*

The goal of treatment is to achieve a complete remission by killing all cancer cells as quickly as possible. Complete remission occurs when all signs and symptoms of neuroblastoma disappear and abnormal cells are no longer found by any standard evaluation (MRI/CT scan, bone scan, bone marrow aspiration, or biopsy). Newer methods are being evaluated that can detect a much smaller amount of tumor in the blood or marrow. This is called the detection of minimal residual disease (MRD).

> *They did a biopsy of the tumor, a bone marrow biopsy, mIBG scan, bone scan, a full staging. Once we had a diagnosis, they sat us down and said, "This is what's going to happen," and presented the stages of treatment. They added, "We'll tell you what you can expect at each stage when we reach it." I made the nurse practitioner sit down and explain everything to me, and told her, "I need you to tell me what is coming down the line." I saw kids up there whose parents were really detached. They didn't understand, and they didn't want to understand. They didn't need to know like I needed to know.*

Chemotherapy

Chemotherapy is used to treat almost all children with intermediate- and high-risk neuroblastoma, and some children with low-risk disease. Response rates have improved considerably through the use of multi-drug regimens (treatments using more than one chemotherapy drug). The most commonly used chemotherapy drugs include carboplatin, cyclophosphamide, doxorubicin, and etoposide. Cisplatin, vincristine, and topotecan are also used for children with high-risk disease. For more information, see Chapter 15, *Chemotherapy*.

Tanner (13 months) went immediately into the pediatric intensive care unit [PICU] because the tumor was pushing on his lungs. His belly was huge and he was having trouble breathing. He was intubated, but he was awake and on a lot of pain meds. It took several days after the biopsy to get the results, then we got a treatment plan and he started chemotherapy in the PICU. We stayed in the PICU through the first two chemo treatments, and then he stayed on the regular oncology unit for the third one.

• • • • •

Luke (2 years old) had side effects from his chemo protocol that were relatively minor compared to what other children experience. He did have nausea, but it usually consisted of one to three vomiting episodes over 1 or 2 days and was over quickly. Over the entire 8-course cycle, he did have numerous neutropenic bouts, with several visits to the emergency room for night-onset fevers resulting in short-term hospitalizations to get IV antibiotics. He did get two or three infections in his Broviac® that also required hospitalizations for antibiotics. However, he only needed one blood and one platelet transfusion during the entire protocol.

Generally, parents receive an outline of the chemotherapy treatment plan (called a protocol) that includes the drugs that will be used, the doses, and a treatment schedule.

Surgery

Almost all children with neuroblastoma need to have surgery. It is used to obtain tumor tissue for diagnosis, to stage the disease, to remove the tumor, and for second-look surgeries. If the tumor hasn't spread and appears resectable, surgery is performed soon after diagnosis. However, this usually is not possible, and chemotherapy is used to shrink the tumor before surgery. Even after chemotherapy, surgical removal is often incomplete in children with stage 3 and 4 disease, and radiation is required to destroy remaining tumor cells.

Tanner's tumor shrank quite a bit before the surgery. The surgery took 6 to 7 hours, and the surgeon who saw him in the beginning told me, "I will get this tumor out." He had a great attitude. An MRI showed some tumor or necrotic [dead] tissue afterwards, so the second surgeon went in a couple of weeks after the first surgery to make sure no live tumor was left in. Tanner did fine. They bounce back really quickly when they're little.

The goals of the initial surgery will depend on a variety of factors, including tumor location, resectability, proximity to major blood vessels and nerves, and your child's prognosis. Lymph nodes near the tumor are usually sampled to determine whether the disease has spread. Sometimes a liver biopsy is done to determine whether an infant has stage 4S disease. However, in older children, the value of this practice is unclear if the liver appears normal on the scans and during surgery.

The surgery to remove the tumor took about 4 hours, and there were no major complications. Scott spent 3 hours in the recovery room before being ready to go to the ward. His first words after waking were, "I love you, Mom." While in the recovery room, we realized that Scott's stuffed Yoshi® toy, which also went to the operating room, returned with a neck bandage identical to Scott's. Someone had a sense of humor!

Complications can occur during or after aggressive surgeries. Common complications are bleeding, adhesions after surgery (internal scars that make tissues or organs stick together), injuries to vessels leading to the kidneys, and neurological problems such as Horner's syndrome. When surgery is done after chemotherapy has been given to shrink the tumors, fewer complications occur.

Scott has a minor complication from surgery called Horner syndrome. His left eyelid droops, and the pupil is smaller than that of the right eye. It doesn't impact his vision, but it is clearly noticeable when you look at him.

Spinal cord compression, often called "dumbbell" extension, occurs when a tumor invades the spinal canal. Chemotherapy is often used to treat this condition, but in some cases, a surgical procedure called laminectomy is done instead. A laminectomy removes part of the bone covering the spinal canal, relieving symptoms caused by compression of the cord and nerve roots.

Radiation therapy

Neuroblastoma is very sensitive to radiation. Radiation therapy is used for some children with intermediate-risk disease when their tumors do not respond well to chemotherapy. It also is a standard part of the treatment protocol for children with high-risk disease, and is sometimes used to relieve pain. For more information, see Chapter 17, *Radiation Therapy*.

My son experienced very few side effects from the local radiation he received to his abdomen and chest. He was premedicated each time with Zofran® and only had a few bouts of vomiting over a 2-week course. Other than diarrhea, he tolerated it great and wasn't even very fatigued.

Stem cell transplantation

Peripheral blood stem cell transplant (also referred to as hematopoietic stem cell transplant or HSCT) is often part of the protocols used to treat children with high-risk or relapsed neuroblastoma. The child's own blood stem cells are removed and frozen early in treatment, then transplanted back during the consolidation phase of treatment. Some treatment centers are experimenting with doing tandem transplants (two transplants in a row) in an attempt to increase the likelihood of destroying all the neuroblastoma cells.

Chemotherapy drugs such as melphalan, cisplatin, teniposide, and doxorubicin are used to prepare children for transplant. For more information, see Chapter 18, *Stem Cell Transplantation*.

> *Preparation for the transplant was harder on me than it was on 7-year-old Nelson. They had given him a month off from chemo so he was feeling really good, and they explained to him that he was going to get a whopping big dose of chemotherapy and he wasn't going to feel too well. And he didn't. We had some issues of him not want-ing to eat since he completely lost his appetite. He was like a limp rag and felt really, really lousy. His counts bounced back really fast after the transplant, and he was only in the hospital 4.5 weeks before we got out of there. He's a major fighter.*

Differentiation therapy and immunotherapy

13-cis-retinoic acid (isotretinoin) is in a category of drugs called retinoids (relatives of Vitamin A), which are thought to cause normal cells to differentiate, or mature, into normal cells more rapidly. Thus, treatment with isotretinoin is sometimes called dif-ferentiation therapy. Isotretinoin is taken by mouth daily for 2 weeks (followed by a 2-week rest) for 6 months after a stem cell transplant to stop the growth and spread of neuroblastoma. This treatment only works when there is minimal residual disease (MRD), not when there's a substantial amount of tumor left.

The monoclonal antibody ch14.18 is an important immunotherapy treatment used to treat children with high-risk neuroblastoma. It is given in five cycles along with two substances (GM-CSF and interleukin-2) that help the white blood cells use the anti-body to more effectively destroy the neuroblastoma.

Information on standard treatments

Treatments for various types of childhood cancers evolve and improve over time. The treatments described in this chapter were the ones most commonly used for newly diagnosed children (called standard treatments) when this book was written. You can learn about standard treatments by calling (800) 422-6237 and asking for the PDQ (physician data query) for neuroblastoma. This free information, also available online at *www.cancer.gov/cancertopics/pdq/pediatrictreatment* (scroll down to "Neuroblastoma, childhood") explains the disease, state-of-the-art treatments, and ongoing clinical tri-als. Two versions are available:

- One for families—uses simple language and contains no statistics; and

- One for professionals—is technical, thorough, and includes citations to scientific literature.

To learn about current Phase III clinical trials for neuroblastoma, you can visit the National Cancer Institute's website *www.cancer.gov/clinicaltrials/search.* Type "neuroblastoma" in the "Cancer type/condition" box and then choose Phase III in the "Trial status/phase" box. Then click the red "Search" button at the bottom of the page.

Newer treatment approaches

For children with neuroblastoma that does not go away after standard treatment, or that recurs, newer, targeted therapies are used. Newer drugs target specific genes, proteins, and pathways (such as ALK or TRK) that are critical to neuroblastoma cell survival.

Cellular immunotherapy (treating disease by stimulating the body's natural immune response) has proven very effective against acute lymphoblastic leukemia and may be modified to target neuroblastoma. Another new treatment is the targeted delivery of conventional drugs to the tumor using nanoparticles (microscopic particles of matter engineered to do specific tasks). Some of these approaches have been used successfully in recurrent disease and are now being tested in newly diagnosed children. However, others are still being developed or are being tested in children for the first time. There is great promise for more effective, less toxic therapy for neuroblastoma in the near future.

Charlotte was 4 months old at diagnosis with stage 4, intermediate risk neuroblastoma. The tumor had crossed the midline, was pressing on her lungs and liver, and was wrapped around her spine. It was the size of a man's fist in a 16-pound baby. In the MRI pictures, it looked like the tumor was literally grasping her spine. At diagnosis, she could not move her legs at all. She had a few rounds of chemotherapy starting in June but no other treatments. All of a sudden one day in September she grabbed her leg. She was sitting on the changing table and reached down and held her leg. Then we saw her move the leg a little. The doctor warned us that it might not be deliberate movement, but soon we could see that she was really moving it. After that she started rolling over and sitting up. She was declared in remission in March at 13 months old, and she is now a healthy 5 year old.

Chapter 5

Retinoblastoma

RETINOBLASTOMA IS A CANCEROUS tumor of the eye that primarily affects young children. It is the most common eye cancer of childhood and occurs in both hereditary and non-hereditary forms. At diagnosis, there may be one or more tumors present in one or both eyes.

This chapter first describes the structure and function of the eye. Then it explains who gets retinoblastoma, what the signs and symptoms are, how it is diagnosed, and how the prognosis is determined. The chapter ends with a discussion of current treatments and how to find out about the newest standard treatments.

The eye

Each structure within the eye has a specific task to help transmit information from the outside world through the optic nerve to the brain (see Figure 5-1).

The cornea is the curved outer portion of the eyeball that transmits light to the retina. Behind the cornea is the iris, which is the colored portion of the eye. The iris controls the amount of light entering the eye by making the opening at the center, called the pupil, either larger or smaller.

As light rays pass through the curved surface of the cornea, they are bent and then passed through the pupil. Inside the eye, sitting behind the pupil, is a disc-shaped structure called the lens. The lens is clear in a healthy eye, and it has two curved surfaces that refract light two more times on its journey to the back of the eye. As light rays travel from the front to the back of the eye, they pass through a colorless, jelly-like material, called the vitreous, which fills the eyeball behind the lens.

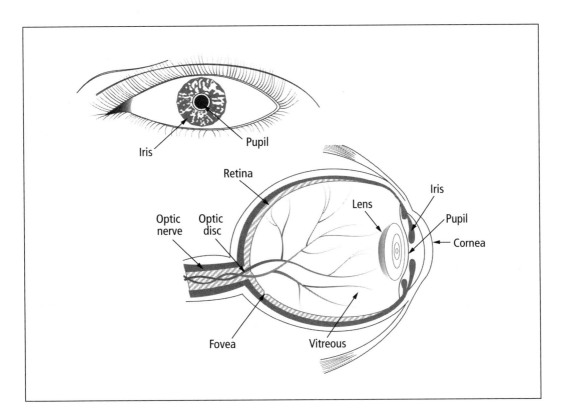

Figure 5-1: The anatomy of the eye

The inside lining of the eyeball consists of a structure called the retina. The retina converts light energy into electrical impulses that are transmitted to the brain. The fovea is the area of the retina that is the center of vision, and the optic disc is the area of the retina where the optic nerve enters the eye. Retinoblastoma tumors develop in the retina of the eye because of a genetic mutation, either inherited or acquired. This mutation causes abnormal growth of immature retinal cells called retinoblasts.

> *Thirty years ago, when I was 18 months old, I was diagnosed with retinoblastoma. I had one tumor in just one eye. The eye was surgically removed, and I had no chemotherapy or radiation. I have no late effects other than wearing a prosthesis and having vision in only one eye.*

Who gets retinoblastoma?

Retinoblastoma is usually diagnosed in very young children, and may be present at birth. In fact, over 95 percent of children are diagnosed before they are 5 years old. Approximately 350 children are diagnosed with retinoblastoma every year in the United States. There is no higher incidence in any particular race, and boys are affected as often as girls.

There are hereditary and non-hereditary forms of this disease. At diagnosis, 60 percent of children have a single tumor in one eye (unilateral retinoblastoma) and 40 percent have multiple tumors in one or both eyes (bilateral retinoblastoma). Unilateral retinoblastoma tends to be non-hereditary, whereas bilateral retinoblastoma is usually hereditary. Children with bilateral retinoblastoma are typically diagnosed at a younger age than those with only one tumor and one eye involved.

> *John Allen was 15 months old when he was diagnosed with unilateral retinoblastoma. The doctor didn't give us any information other than it was a fast-growing cancer and that it needed to be taken care of right away. We couldn't see the specialist for another 5 days, so we cried and prayed. We didn't know whether we were going to lose our baby or not. When we saw the specialist, she answered all of our questions in detail. We were then referred to a pediatric oncologist and pediatric ophthalmologist surgeon. They, too, were fantastic. We were relieved when they explained the enucleation [removal of the eye] to us. What mattered most was that our little boy had an excellent chance of beating his disease.*

Children who have the hereditary form of retinoblastoma and have disease in both eyes have a very small risk of also developing a tumor in the pineal gland of the brain, called pineoblastoma. Sometimes this is referred to as trilateral retinoblastoma.

Genetic factors

The exact cause of retinoblastoma is unknown. However, much is known about the genetics and inheritance of this tumor.

A change, called a mutation, in a gene called *RB1* is involved in the development of retinoblastoma. Genes are located and organized on chromosomes inside the body's cells. They are passed from parent to child through the egg and the sperm. The nuclei of human cells contain 22 chromosomes plus the sex chromosomes X and Y. There are two copies of each of these chromosomes, except for the sex chromosomes. Children get one copy of each of the 22 chromosomes from their biological mother and the other copy from their biological father.

The genes on these chromosomes contain material called DNA. The DNA instructs the cells to make proteins that determine such things as eye color, skin color, and blood type.

The *RB1* gene is located on chromosome 13. In roughly 60 percent of children with retinoblastoma, there is a change in both copies of the *RB1* gene, but only in the cells of the tumor in the eye. If you look at cells from any other area in the body, chromosome 13 is completely unchanged with no mutation in the *RB1* gene. Scientists don't know what causes the mutation in this gene. Most of the time, these children develop one tumor only in one eye. This is called the non-hereditary form of the disease (see table below on inheritance of retinoblastoma).

The hereditary form of retinoblastoma occurs in around 40 percent of children with the disease. In these cases, the mutated *RB1* gene is found in all the cells of the body. In 85 percent of children with the hereditary form of retinoblastoma, no one else in the family has retinoblastoma (called the non-familial or sporadic form). In these cases, a spontaneous mutation occurs in the copy of the *RB1* gene when the child is conceived. The parents do not carry a mutation of the *RB1* gene in every cell of their bodies.

The remaining 15 percent of children with the hereditary form of retinoblastoma have a family member with the disease (usually a parent). This is called the familial form. In these cases, a parent had an abnormal copy of the *RB1* gene in every cell in his or her body and passed it on to the child through the sperm or egg. All of these children started their lives with one mutated copy of the *RB1* gene in every cell in their bodies, including all the retinoblasts in the eye. After conception, if a mutation occurs in the other copy of the *RB1* gene in one or more retinoblasts in the eye, retinoblastoma develops. In these children, the disease can occur in one or both eyes and more than one tumor may be present at diagnosis. New tumors may form during the first 5 years of life.

Non-hereditary form Approximately 60% of all children diagnosed	Hereditary form Approximately 40% of all children diagnosed	
	Non-familial form (85%)	Familial form (15%)
Child usually has one tumor in one eye	No family history of retinoblastoma	Family history of retinoblastoma
Mutation is found only in tumor cells	Spontaneous mutation is found in all cells of body	Inherited mutation is found in all cells of body
Survivors cannot pass mutation on to offspring	Survivors can pass mutation on to offspring (50% risk for each child)	Survivors can pass mutation on to offspring (50% risk for each child)

It is not known what causes the changes in the *RB1* gene in either of these forms of retinoblastoma. It is known that there is nothing parents can do to prevent retinoblastoma.

> *I am a long-term survivor of bilateral retinoblastoma, diagnosed when I was 10 months old. My first enucleation [surgical removal of the eye] was the left eye in May 1971, with radiation to the right eye. The enucleation of the right eye was in March 1972. I have had no subsequent treatment since then. Due to my loss of sight at such an early age, I had no traumatic adjustment period that losing sight later in life might have caused. I really can think of no significant effects that my retinoblastoma has had on my adult life other than the usual adaptations required for dealing with blindness.*

Pediatric oncologists help determine whether the disease is hereditary or non-hereditary based on a number of factors, including family history, age at diagnosis, number of tumors, and whether one or both eyes are involved. They will then discuss the benefits of genetic testing to verify whether your child has the hereditary or non-hereditary form of the disease. Genetic testing and counseling should be offered to all families of children with retinoblastoma.

If the pediatric oncologist has not told you which type of retinoblastoma your child has, you should ask. The oncologist can then explain whether other family members need to be checked for retinoblastoma and how often.

The type of retinoblastoma your child has affects:

- Treatment options
- Risk for having another child with retinoblastoma
- Risk of your child having a child with retinoblastoma
- Risk of your child getting other cancers later in life

Children with the hereditary form of retinoblastoma are at a higher risk of getting another cancer later in life than children with the non-hereditary form of the disease are.

> *When Westley was diagnosed with retinoblastoma at 7 months old, our ophthalmologist immediately ordered genetic testing to determine if he had the hereditary form of the disease and if he had inherited a mutation from my husband, who was diagnosed with unilateral retinoblastoma 35 years ago when he was 18 months old. Westley was found to have bilateral, hereditary retinoblastoma, with multiple tumors in both eyes.*
>
> *When my husband was diagnosed with retinoblastoma, they removed his eye and he was examined every 6 months until he was 5 years old. He didn't have chemotherapy*

or radiation, and he never had any more tumors. He had multiple prosthetics because he would hide or flush his eye down the toilet sometimes when he was a grumpy toddler. Now he gets a new one every 10 years.

I am bothered by the fact that even though we had amniocentesis and genetic testing when I was pregnant with Westley because I was 35, and they knew my husband was a retinoblastoma survivor, no one warned us of the genetic risk to our child and that we should have him examined carefully by his pediatrician to watch for signs of tumors in his eyes. Since he was diagnosed, we have had good genetic counseling. Sometimes my husband feels guilty that he passed this on to our son, but we know that no one is to blame. Because of the high risk of having another child with retinoblastoma, we have decided not to have any more biological children.

Environmental factors

No environmental factors have been linked to increased risk of retinoblastoma.

Signs and symptoms

The most common symptom of retinoblastoma is when a child's pupil appears white when a light is shined in the eye. This is called leukocoria (Greek for "white pupil") and is sometimes referred to as "the cat's eye reflex." This is often first noticed when parents look at photographs of their child and see that one pupil appears white instead of black or red.

Another symptom of retinoblastoma is strabismus—when the affected eye drifts inward (esotropia) or outward (exotropia). However, most children who have strabismus do not have retinoblastoma. Occasionally, children with retinoblastoma have irises of different colors. Very large tumors can cause pain or swelling, but this is not common. Vision loss is another symptom of retinoblastoma, but parents rarely know about it because young children generally do not talk about vision problems. Apart from the symptoms above, a child with retinoblastoma will likely seem healthy.

It took a few days to get a diagnosis. On a Friday morning, at Noah's 2-month checkup, the pediatrician noticed a white reflex in one of his pupils and showed me the difference between the eyes. When I asked what would cause it, he was vague and said he would call an ophthalmologist for an appointment for us. When the ophthalmologist's office called asking us to come in that same day, we began to realize that something quite serious must be going on.

The ophthalmologist said Noah either had cancer or another progressive condition and he would need to be seen by a retina specialist in Seattle (a 1 hour and 45 minute drive away). When we asked if he would be able to see out of the eye, he very

matter-of-factly informed us that there was no question that he could not see and would not see again from that eye.

On Monday morning, we were told that Noah had retinoblastoma, the tumor was very large, and the eye would need to be removed. We were in shock and scared of the tests and surgery he would need. It was hard to imagine what it would be like for him to lose his eye, and we were worried about the possibility of metastases [spread of the tumor]. Everything seemed very unreal, but we just did what had to be done.

Diagnosis and staging

After a parent or doctor notices the abnormality in a child's eye(s), an ophthalmologist should examine the child. If retinoblastoma is suspected, the child should be referred to a major medical center with expertise in treating children with cancer. There, a pediatric oncologist and an ophthalmologist with expertise in retinoblastoma will obtain a full medical history, perform a thorough physical examination, and examine the child's eyes under anesthesia. An ophthalmic ultrasound, a magnetic resonance imaging (MRI) scan, and/or a computerized tomography (CT) scan may be done at this time. The ophthalmologist will often use a microscope with a camera attached (called wide-field fundus photography) and an imaging technique that uses light rather than sound waves or radiation (called spectral domain optical coherence tomography) to carefully examine all areas of the retina. Once these tests are completed and retinoblastoma is diagnosed, the pediatric oncologist will work with the ophthalmologist and other specialists to formulate the best treatment plan.

I first noticed the weird reflection in Jayden's right eye in photos when he was 9 months old. I asked the pediatrician three times about it, but he said it was nothing. Jayden was rubbing his eye a lot, and now I know he must have had a lot of pressure and it hurt. We were at his 15-month visit when the doctor said it was fine for the third time. He didn't dilate his eye or do a close examination, or he would have seen the tumor and noticed that Jayden's eye didn't respond to light at all since he was already blind. One week later the swelling was so bad I took him to the urgent care, and when it was even worse the next day I drove him to the emergency room where he was finally diagnosed. The ophthalmologist told us later that given the size of the tumor, he had probably been blind since he was 7 months old. He hit all his development milestones early, and I really didn't suspect anything was wrong. I'm in early childhood education so I know what to expect. I felt bad that I didn't catch the fact that he couldn't see.

A process called staging is done to find out the extent of the disease. Results from the CT or MRI are used to establish the extent of disease in both eyes, orbits (bones around the eyes), optic nerves, and the brain. If the CT or MRI shows that the disease has

spread outside the eye, the pediatric oncologist may perform a lumbar puncture (spinal tap), nuclear bone scan, bone marrow biopsy, and/or bone marrow aspiration. These procedures are described in Chapter 10, *Coping with Procedures*.

> *From the beginning, we always talked to our son about what was happening, about what he might be feeling, about how sorry we were that we couldn't avoid having him go through a specific procedure. He understood our love and concern. We always felt it was important to be honest with him about what was happening because he had a right to know. We bought him a doctor kit, a Playmobil® operating room, and kept one of his anesthesia masks for him to play with. We gave him empty dilating drop bottles so he could be the one to put the eye drops in a willing patient (stuffed animal).*

Treatment options for retinoblastoma depend on the location and size of the tumor and the extent of tumor cell growth near the original tumor (called tumor seeding). Tumors may be intraocular (within the eye) or extraocular (spread beyond the eye). In North America, the International Classification for Intraocular Retinoblastoma is the most widely used method for staging retinoblastoma in children.

International Classification for Intraocular Retinoblastoma

- **Group A.** Tumors with a width of 3 mm or less that are in the retina and not near the foveola (center of vision) or the optic disc

- **Group B.** All tumors in the retina that don't fit the Group A criteria.

- **Group C.** Distinct local tumor(s) with minimal seeding under the retina or minimal seeding in the vitreous (the gel portion of the eye)

- **Group D.** Large tumors, tumors with indefinite edges, or tumors with diffuse seeding under the retina or vitreous

- **Group E.** A very large tumor that may reach to the front of the eye and cause high eye pressure (glaucoma), bleeding, or other extreme damage

Children with retinoblastoma should be followed closely by their medical team from diagnosis to age 5 to monitor for recurrence or spread of the cancer outside the eye. The frequency of these exams depends on many factors, including:

- Whether the disease is in one or both eyes

- The number, size, and location of tumors

- Family history

- The type of treatment.

After age 5, the chance of recurrence or spread is very low, but children should still be seen at least once a year by an ophthalmologist and a pediatric oncologist to monitor for late effects resulting from treatment.

Prognosis

The prognosis for cure from retinoblastoma that is confined to the retina (Groups A and B) is excellent (more than 95%). In less developed countries where diagnosis and treatment of retinoblastoma are often delayed, metastatic disease is common and survival rates are lower. Vision in the affected eye may be saved depending on the extent of the disease at the time of diagnosis.

Treatment

At diagnosis, many parents do not know how to find experienced doctors and the best treatments for their child. State-of-the-art care is available from physicians who participate in the Children's Oncology Group (COG). This study group includes pediatric surgeons and oncologists, radiation oncologists, researchers, and nurses. COG conducts studies to discover better therapies and supportive care for children with cancer. You can learn more about COG and find a list of its member treatment centers at *www. childrensoncologygroup.org.*

It is also important that your child be seen by a pediatric ophthalmologist who has experience treating retinoblastoma. The pediatric ophthalmologist should work closely with your child's pediatric oncologist throughout treatment. Together, they will identify the treatment options (e.g., the current standard of care or a clinical trial) based on the stage and classification of the disease within the eye and whether it has spread outside the eye (see Chapter 9, *Choosing a Treatment*). Depending on the situation, treatment may include surgery, radiation, chemotherapy, and/or local eye treatments, including cryotherapy and laser therapy. The goals of therapy are to cure the disease and to preserve as much vision as possible.

> *We relied on the opinions of the surgeon, retina specialist, two pathologists, a retinoblastoma specialist from Canada, parents of children with retinoblastoma, and material from medical journals when deciding on treatment for Hailee (14 months old). They all offered pieces of the puzzle, which allowed us to make an informed decision. Hailee had her eye enucleated, and since all the cancer was removed, further treatment wasn't necessary. She is followed every 6 months with EUA [exam under anesthesia] and MRI, and has done very well. She has coped well with the enucleation, and she looks beautiful.*

Surgery and local eye treatments

Several types of procedures are used to treat retinoblastoma: enucleation, cryotherapy, laser thermotherapy, and laser photocoagulation. The ophthalmologist may also deliver chemotherapy locally to the tumor (see section about chemotherapy later in this chapter). The most appropriate treatment is chosen on an individual basis. An important component of treatment is support from psychologists, social workers, and genetic counselors to help families deal with the cancer, its treatment, the possible loss of an eye and vision, and the potential risk of other family members developing retinoblastoma.

Enucleation

Enucleation is the surgical removal of an eye. It may be necessary if:

- The tumor is very large and there is no hope that the eye will have useful vision.
- The eye has glaucoma.
- The tumor has spread extensively within the eye, to the optic nerve or orbit.
- Other treatment methods have failed to destroy the disease.
- The retina cannot be examined because of vitreous hemorrhage or cataract.

Enucleation is a relatively simple operation that is done under general anesthesia. In addition to gently removing the eye, the surgeon will also remove a section of the optic nerve. An implant is placed into the socket immediately after the eyeball is removed. The child will be fitted for an artificial eye several weeks after the procedure.

> Jayden was 17 months old when his right eye was enucleated. He had a clear conformer [plastic device] placed in the socket so the tissues wouldn't grow and his prosthetic would fit. I kept him patched so people wouldn't stare, but they stared anyway. Jayden got his first prosthetic 3 months later, and he looked amazing. The surgeon carefully kept a lot of his nerves so he has great movement and no one can tell his eye isn't real.
>
> Jayden has allergies, so there's a lot of buildup on his prosthesis and we have to take it out and clean it every couple of weeks. He has Elli the Elephant from the German Children's Eye Cancer Foundation. She has a fake eye that pops out. Jayden will talk to her and say, "OK, Elli, we have to wash your special eye." He sometimes pops his eye in her eye socket, just to be silly. He likes reading a coloring book with me called Joey's Special Eye about a boy with retinoblastoma who has a prosthetic eye and wears glasses [see Appendix C, Books, Websites, and Support Groups].

$$\bullet \quad \bullet \quad \bullet \quad \bullet \quad \bullet$$

Hailee (14 months) never experienced any difficulties with her prosthetic eye. We spent a great deal of time preparing Hailee when the eye was about to be enucleated. We read her My Fake Eye [see Appendix C, Books, Websites, and Support Groups], which helped a great deal with the prosthesis. She took the book to daycare and the caregiver read it to the other children. It has never been a big deal for her. She is now 4 years old and continues to do well.

After the enucleation, a pressure patch is placed over the eyelid. When the patch is removed, antibiotic drops are put in the socket for about a week. The eyelid is usually swollen and bruised for the next few days.

Noah had his left eye enucleated at age 2 months. We were able to take him home a couple of hours later. The most difficult part for me was handing him over to the nurse who took him into the operating room, and not getting to see him until he had awakened. We were impressed that he recovered quickly from anesthesia, and, when the bandages were removed 3 days later, that there was virtually no bruising.

After enucleation, the prosthesis needs to be replaced periodically to foster orbital growth. Children who have one or both eyes removed before age 3 may have an altered facial appearance when they mature.

Cryotherapy

Cryotherapy, a freezing treatment, is used to treat small primary tumors or new tumors that develop on the anterior (front part) of the retina. It is most successful if used to treat tumors up to 5 mm in diameter and 3 mm in thickness, and it may have to be repeated numerous times to eliminate all the tumor cells. It is often used in combination with chemotherapy and can also be used after radiation therapy.

During cryotherapy, extreme cold is applied by a small probe placed directly on the part of the eyeball closest to the tumor. The surgeon uses ultrasound to guide the probe to ensure that healthy tissue around the tumor remains unharmed. The procedure is done under local or general anesthesia. The eye and eyelid will swell for one or more days, and an ointment or drops can be used to help decrease the swelling.

One advantage of cryotherapy is that it may help prevent the need for enucleation or radiation therapy. However, it cannot successfully treat larger tumors, and it may cause retinal scars, tears, or detachments that damage vision.

Zachary was 10 months old when he was diagnosed with unilateral retinoblastoma in the left eye. He had several eye exams since birth because I had retinoblastoma when I was a child. He was treated with cryotherapy and radioactive plaques.

Zachary did well, so our experience with cryotherapy was pretty positive. Of course, being so young, he didn't really know what was going on.

Laser thermotherapy

Laser thermotherapy (also known as transpupillary thermal therapy or TTT) is a method of delivering heat directly to the surface of the tumor using infrared radiation and a diode laser. It is used to treat tumors smaller than 3 mm in size. Like cryotherapy, it can be combined with chemotherapy or radiation therapy to treat larger tumors. Children are sedated during this procedure. It leaves a relatively small scar, preserving more vision.

> *Westley was 7 months old when he was diagnosed with bilateral retinoblastoma. He had 6 months of chemotherapy (etoposide, carboplatin, and vincristine) one time per month, with monthly eye exams done under anesthesia [EUA] to track his progress. We started cryotherapy and laser treatments on individual tumors after 4 months of initial chemotherapy, to shrink the tumors as much as possible with chemotherapy first. For the first 18 months, he had EUAs once a month, then we moved to EUAs every 6 weeks.*

> *He is almost 3, and he has had 29 EUAs. All but two times so far the regular EUA has shown new tumor growth that has been immediately treated with cryotherapy or laser therapy. We learned quickly that this is the norm; it's what happens with bilateral retinoblastoma. We find the tumors and get rid of them when they're little so we can save as much vision as possible. We assume he will continue to have sedated exams every 6 weeks until his sixth birthday. If his tumors become stable, it could stretch out.*

Laser photocoagulation

Laser photocoagulation is another method for treating small tumors. It is used to treat small tumors located at the back of the retina that are not close to the optic nerve or blood vessels.

This technique cauterizes (burns) tissues around the tumor with focused light from an argon laser, delivered while the child is anesthetized. The light is delivered through the pupil and kills the tumor by destroying its blood supply. Laser photocoagulation is often used in combination with radiation, sometimes used in combination with chemotherapy, and occasionally used alone. Many treatment/cancer centers have replaced this procedure with laser thermotherapy.

Radiation therapy

Retinoblastoma is very sensitive to radiation, which is sometimes used to destroy local disease while attempting to maintain vision. The use of radiation has decreased in recent decades because of the risk of damage caused by high doses of radiation to growing tissues in small children. Two methods of radiotherapy are used to treat retinoblastoma: external beam radiotherapy and plaque radiotherapy.

External beam radiotherapy

External beam radiation therapy (also called EBRT) is generally required if the tumor has extended outside of the orbit, but it is sometimes used for retinoblastoma that is still contained within the eye. Due to advances in other therapies and the potential for adverse long-term effects, radiotherapy isn't generally used to treat retinoblastoma that's outside the eye. Because young children must be sedated for external beam radiotherapy, and the delivery of the radiation doses must be very precise to minimize damage to other tissues, only professionals who specialize in pediatric radiation therapy should treat your child.

External beam radiotherapy has traditionally been delivered by a linear accelerator targeted at the tumor. The current standard protocol is a total dose of 3,500 to 4,000 centigrays (cGy), given in daily doses over a 4- to 5-week period. Some centers give a lower total dose of external beam radiation to children who have already had their tumors treated with local therapies. The actual radiotherapy treatment takes approximately 2 or 3 minutes, but the preparation takes significantly longer. A number of centers now offer a newer type of radiotherapy (called proton beam), which is associated with fewer long-term side effects and is becoming a more common treatment for retinoblastoma. For more information, see Chapter 17, *Radiation Therapy*.

> The doctor had been optimistic that Noah would have unilateral disease, so we were all quite devastated to learn 5 months later that he had new tumors in his remaining eye. Both were small enough to treat with laser, but unfortunately one was adjacent to the optic nerve so Noah had to have radiotherapy. The treatment was very localized. His white blood cell count dropped some, but not seriously. He experienced a mild radiation burn on the opposite side of the treated eye and some eyebrow hair loss.

Late effects may develop in the months or years after external beam radiation. They may include cataracts, slowed growth of the bones in the orbit, vision loss, reduced tear production, chronic conjunctivitis, damage to retina and optic nerve, and an increased risk of second cancers in the radiation field. Children with the hereditary form of the disease are more likely to develop subsequent cancers outside the radiation field, and

the use of radiotherapy increases this risk. Children who have had radiation to the eye need expert follow-up evaluations on a routine basis.

Plaque radiotherapy

Plaque radiotherapy, also called brachytherapy, is a type of radiation therapy that places small pellets (sometimes called seeds) of radioactive material (iodine, cobalt, or ruthenium) near the tumor. The seeds are contained in a carrier that shields healthy tissue from the radiation. The radioactive material and the carrier together are called a plaque.

This type of radiotherapy is used primarily to treat small, single tumors in children with unilateral, early-stage disease that cannot be treated successfully with other local therapies. It is very effective and can be used in combination with chemotherapy. The pediatric oncologist, ophthalmologist, and a medical physicist will work closely together to plan the appropriate radioactive materials to use, their placement, and the dosage. The placement is done under general anesthesia, and the child stays in the hospital for the amount of time needed to deliver the correct dose of radiation (often 2 to 4 days). The child and the hospital room are monitored for radiation, and a parent staying with the child usually wears a radiation badge or other device for monitoring, as well. Surgery to remove the plaque usually takes less than an hour, and your child may be able to go home the same day. The full effect of the radiation on the tumor is not seen for several months.

Chemotherapy

Until the 1990s, systemic (intravenous) chemotherapy was primarily used to treat retinoblastoma that had spread outside the eye. To prevent the long-term problems that can occur after enucleation or radiation, more doctors are now using chemotherapy to treat intraocular (within the eye) retinoblastoma. The decision to use chemotherapy is complex and depends on a number of factors, including your child's age; family history; the number, size, and location of tumors; and the ability of the ophthalmologist to use local treatments. Chemotherapy works better for smaller tumors and for tumors that have not spread.

For intraocular retinoblastoma, intravenous chemotherapy is generally used in conjunction with local therapies (e.g., cryotherapy, thermotherapy, laser photocoagulation, plaque radiation therapy) to shrink the tumor and help prevent new ones from growing. This is called chemoreduction therapy. This technique can help avoid the use of enucleation or external beam radiation.

Chemotherapy is also sometimes delivered directly to the eye. The ophthalmologist can do this in a variety of ways. The most common method is directly injecting

chemotherapy drugs into the vitreous to try to attack small pieces of tumor; this method is called selective intra-arterial chemotherapy.

Another way to administer chemotherapy is through the arteries. In this case, an interventional neuroradiologist puts a fine catheter into the femoral artery in the groin area and, using a special type of x-ray guidance called fluoroscopy, feeds the catheter all the way into the ophthalmic artery in the eye. The ophthalmologist then injects the chemotherapy into this artery.

The chemotherapy drugs most commonly used intravenously to treat retinoblastoma are vincristine, etoposide, carboplatin, cyclophosphamide, and doxorubicin. Melphalan, topotecan, and carboplatin are delivered via intra-arterial chemotherapy. For more information about these drugs, see Chapter 15, *Chemotherapy*.

> *Jayden was diagnosed at 15 months with retinoblastoma. Because his tumor was so large and had spread to his optic nerve, he had two high-dose rounds of IV chemotherapy in July and August and then he had the enucleation of his right eye in September. The tumor caused enough pain and swelling that he stopped talking. He went back to using the sign language I taught him as a baby. To help relieve the pain and pressure, I gave him oxycodone, steroids, and dilating eye drops. The chemotherapy reduced the size of the tumor dramatically. Three days after the surgery he was talking, smiling, and playing again. Afterwards, he had 4 months of standard chemotherapy and finished in January. He just celebrated one year off treatment and he is doing very well.*

Information on standard treatments

Treatments for various types of childhood cancers evolve and improve over time. The treatments described in this chapter were the ones most commonly used (called standard treatments) when this book was written. You can learn about the newest treatments available by calling (800) 422-6237 and asking for the PDQ (physician data query) for retinoblastoma. This free information, also available online at *www.cancer.gov/cancertopics/ pdq/pediatrictreatment* (scroll down to "Retinoblastoma") explains the diseases, state-of-the-art treatments, and ongoing clinical trials. Two versions are available:

• One for families—uses simple language and contains no statistics; and

• One for professionals—is technical, thorough, and includes citations to scientific literature.

To learn about current Phase III clinical trials for retinoblastoma in children, you can visit the National Cancer Institute's website *www.cancer.gov/clinicaltrials/search*. In the "Cancer type/condition" box, choose "retinoblastoma" and choose "Phase III" in the "Trial status/phase" box. Then click the red "Search" button at the bottom of the page.

I am a long-term survivor of bilateral retinoblastoma. I think that parents can be very instrumental in their child's recovery. Even though it may not be easy, I feel that it is important to be strong and positive. Seek all of the information possible, and don't hesitate to ask questions. Times will be tough, so please find support, whether it be family counseling focusing on cancer or corresponding with other parents who have had similar experiences. Don't hold all of your feelings in. Have the same expectations for your child with retinoblastoma as you would for any other. Don't set limitations for your child; there are already plenty of those out there.

Although I am blind, when I was a child I tap danced, rode horses, and I was a competitive roller skater. I attend college full-time and have many good friends. I have matured into a woman with strong character, spirit, and motivation, and this has helped me overcome many challenges.

Chapter 6

Soft Tissue Sarcomas

SOFT TISSUE SARCOMAS ARE cancerous tumors that develop in various soft tissues of the body. Soft tissues connect, surround, and support body structures and organs. They include muscles, tendons, fat, nerves, blood vessels, connective tissues, and synovial tissues (connective tissue around joints and tendons).

Several types of soft tissue sarcomas are diagnosed in young people—the most common one is rhabdomyosarcoma. Other soft tissue sarcomas include alveolar soft part sarcoma, fibrosarcoma, hemangiopericytoma, leiomyosarcoma, liposarcoma, malignant fibrous histiocytoma, malignant peripheral nerve sheath tumor (also known as neurofibrosarcoma or malignant schwannoma), and synovial sarcoma. About 700 children and teens are diagnosed with a soft tissue sarcoma in the United States every year; almost half of those tumors are rhabdomyosarcoma.

This chapter first looks at the structure and function of muscles and connective tissues. Then it describes who gets soft tissue sarcomas, what the signs and symptoms are, how they are diagnosed, and how the prognosis is determined. Finally, the chapter discusses current treatments for rhabdomyosarcoma and other soft tissue sarcomas.

Muscles and connective tissues

The human body comes equipped with more than 650 muscles. These muscles, together with other connective tissues (joints, ligaments, and tendons), form the support system for the skeleton and allow the body to move. The three types of muscles are:

- **Skeletal muscles.** These muscles manipulate the skeleton to cause movement. Skeletal muscles are *voluntary* muscles because their actions can be controlled.

- **Smooth muscles.** These muscles are found in many places in the body, such as the bladder, arteries, veins, and the digestive tract. Smooth muscles are *involuntary* muscles because their actions occur without conscious control.

- **Cardiac muscle.** This type of involuntary muscle is found only in the heart. Several layers of cardiac muscles make up the heart wall, which contracts and relaxes to keep the heart pumping.

71

Joints, ligaments, and tendons work with the different types of muscles to keep the body moving and working. Joints and tendons are surrounded by synovial tissue—a sheath that secretes a clear, thick lubricating fluid.

- **Joints.** The main function of joints is to connect bone to other bone and to allow movement where it is needed. Some joints, such as those found in the skull, do not move at all; others, such as those found in the spine, have restricted movement. Joints in the arms, legs, and shoulders permit a great deal of movement.

- **Ligaments.** Ligaments cross over joints and help join bone to bone. The ligaments support joints and help prevent dislocation.

- **Tendons.** Tendons connect skeletal muscles to bones. These cords of tissue are flexible and very strong. They transfer force to the bones to cause movement. For example, the Achilles tendon connects the calf muscles to the bone in the heel and allows the foot to push against the ground when walking.

Signs and symptoms

The signs and symptoms of a soft tissue sarcoma largely depend on the location of the primary tumor (where the tumor first grew) and whether or not the disease has metastasized (spread) to other areas. Often, a lump or mass is one of the first signs of a soft tissue sarcoma.

> Cassandra had been complaining for a month of pain in her left knee while sleeping at night. I brought this to the attention of her pediatrician at a well-child visit. The doctor looked her over and said that it was probably growing pains, and to elevate her leg in the evening and see if that might help. Following his advice, I began to elevate her leg at night with a pillow— a practice that my mother used when I had similar pains in my legs as a child. This didn't help alleviate the pain, though, and in fact, it seemed to intensify as days went by. One week later we were at a local coffee shop and Cassandra had to go to the bathroom. I went in with her, and while I was helping her with her tights I noticed a large lump on her left buttock.

Primary tumors located in the head or neck region can cause many different signs and symptoms. Tumors in the tissues around an eye can cause the eyelid to droop. The eye may appear to protrude or bulge, and a child may also develop double vision.

> I called a dear friend who had graduated from being our babysitter during her four years of college to her current status as second-year medical student. I told her I needed to do some research, listed Joseph's symptoms, told her what the ophthalmologist said, then asked about tumors in the eye area. She opened her cancer book and under orbital tumors found a word—a cancer—I'd never heard of before. "Okay,"

she said, "this is the most common orbital tumor in children, it causes ptosis (drooping eye) and proptosis (protruding eye), hits kids most commonly between the ages of 2 and 6, is more common in boys than in girls, and is highly malignant."

As she described these symptoms, she was literally describing Joseph's face. She spelled the word out for me, and I still have the piece of paper on which I took those notes, on which I first wrote the word "rhabdomyosarcoma."

A soft tissue sarcoma in the head can paralyze cranial nerves controlling eye movement or sight, causing blurred vision, blindness in one eye, or one side of the face to droop. Tumors that arise in the sinus area or the middle ear can cause nasal obstruction, sometimes resulting in discharge and intermittent bleeding. Also, the child's voice may sound different.

Rhabdomyosarcomas are often found in the bladder and prostate. Symptoms include blood in the urine, difficulty passing urine, urinary obstruction, and pain. Prostate tumors tend to be found as a large mass, sometimes accompanied by constipation.

Boys with tumors in the paratesticular area (the area near the testicles) may have a painless enlargement of the scrotum.

Vaginal tumors (usually seen in infants) may look like a bunch of grapes at the vaginal opening, often accompanied by vaginal discharge. Tumors originating in the cervix or uterus are diagnosed more frequently in older girls, and they usually consist of a mass that can cause vaginal discharge.

Tumors that occur in the extremities and trunk press on nerves or muscles, resulting in swelling, pain, and redness in the affected area. These masses are usually hard and not tender to the touch. Invasion of the disease into peripheral nerves can cause pain or weakness in the pelvis and extremities. Tumors that develop on the chest wall can cause breathing difficulties, and an abdominal mass can block the gastrointestinal or genitourinary tract.

The pediatrician looked concerned as she examined Cassandra and told me that it was some type of "mass." I didn't think the word "cancer" at all. She made an appointment for her to see a surgeon at Children's Hospital later that afternoon. I knew that this was something serious, but had no idea just how bad until later that evening when the surgeon gave me the results of the CT scan [computerized tomography scan]: cancer in her left buttock, with metastatic lesions in her lungs. When I heard this news, I was reeling. My sister had died just 2 years before of breast cancer, and my younger brother had just finished treatment for testicular cancer. I thought, "This can't be happening again!"

Diagnosis of soft tissue sarcomas

The doctor will obtain your child's medical history, perform a physical examination, and order a battery of tests including a complete blood count (CBC), liver function tests, and other blood tests including electrolytes and kidney function levels. Ultrasounds, computerized tomography (CT) scan, and magnetic resonance imaging (MRI) are often done to evaluate the size of the mass and its relationship to surrounding structures. Once the mass has been examined through imaging, a biopsy is needed so the cells can be tested to determine whether the mass is cancer and, if so, what type. The three kinds of biopsy are:

- A needle biopsy, usually done through the skin (sometimes under the guidance of ultrasound or CT scan).

- An incisional biopsy, where the surgeon only removes a small piece of the tumor.

- An excisional biopsy, where the surgeon tries to remove most or all of the tumor.

The biopsy should be done by a surgeon who has experience with pediatric solid tumors so:

- Enough tissue is removed to allow for a definite diagnosis; but

- The procedure does not make it more difficult for the entire mass to be removed in a future surgery (if additional surgery is needed).

For further information on these procedures, see Chapter 14, *Surgery*.

Tests are necessary to establish a specific diagnosis, especially because non-rhabdomyo-sarcoma soft tissue sarcomas can appear very similar, even at the microscopic level. The different types of tumor cells have distinctive molecular and genetic characteristics that can be used to help doctors establish the exact diagnosis, determine a prognosis, and find the most appropriate treatments.

> TJ was 2¾ when he came to me to help get his pants back up after using the bathroom. I saw one testicle was twice as large as the other and a darker color, almost purplish red. He said it didn't hurt. I called the pediatrician, who did an exam and thought he had some trauma to the area. We went to the local hospital for an ultrasound, and they thought it looked like there was bleeding in his scrotum, so from there they sent us to a major research hospital to see a pediatric urologist. The urologist said TJ had a hernia and to come back for surgery, but I questioned that because it felt like a mass, like a third testicle. The pediatric urologist wanted us to wait 6 weeks for the surgery, but I knew there was something else wrong with my baby so I called the next day and I said I don't want to wait 6 weeks. We were able to schedule the surgery for 3 weeks later.

The doctor came out after 20 minutes in surgery and said that the lump was not a hernia, so he wanted to keep him under and do a biopsy, although he did not think it could be cancer. An hour after that he returned and said, "I'm really sorry, I was wrong. One of the best pathologists in the world looked at your son's tumor and it is cancer. It is rhabdomyosarcoma. We need to remove his testicle and the tumor right now."

Rhabdomyosarcoma

Childhood rhabdomyosarcoma is a soft tissue cancer that arises in the muscles. It accounts for 3 to 4 percent of all cases of childhood cancer and for nearly 50 percent of all childhood soft tissue sarcomas.

Rhabdomyosarcoma can start in any muscle in the body, and tumor origin is often associated with age. Most head and neck tumors occur in children younger than age 8, whereas tumors in the arms and legs are most commonly diagnosed in adolescents. Rhabdomyosarcoma is also found in the genitourinary tract, including the bladder, prostate, and vagina.

There are two distinct subtypes of rhabdomyosarcoma. In the past, these subtypes were defined exclusively by how the tumors looked under the microscope, but today the presence or absence of a specific genetic mutation is considered the most accurate way of identifying the two subtypes. The mutation is a *translocation*—a genetic accident that results in a piece of one gene (called *PAX*) getting stuck next to a piece of another gene (called *FOXO1*), creating a new cancer gene that is only found in the tumor cells. The subtypes are:

- **Embryonal (also called ERMS).** This type accounts for 70 to 80 percent of all childhood rhabdomyosarcomas. Tumors with this histology usually arise in the head, neck, and genitourinary areas. Botryoid and spindle cell tumors are subtypes of embryonal tumors accounting for about 10 percent of rhabdomyosarcoma diagnoses, and they are most often diagnosed in very young children. Botryoid tumors are found under the mucosa (moist tissues) of the vagina, bladder, or nasopharynx (space between the back of the nose and the top of the mouth). Spindle cell tumors most often occur in the tissues around the testes (called the paratesticular area) in boys. These tumors do not contain the *PAX-FOXO1* translocation.

- **Alveolar (also called ARMS).** Approximately 20 percent of rhabdomyosarcoma tumors have alveolar histology. These tumors are a more aggressive form of rhabdomyosarcoma. Alveolar rhabdomyosarcoma is found more frequently in adolescents and in children with tumors of the trunk, limbs, anus, scrotum (in boys), or external genital area (in girls). These tumors always contain the *PAX-FOXO1* translocation, although there are two different variants of this translocation.

Who gets rhabdomyosarcoma?

Rhabdomyosarcoma is the most common childhood soft tissue sarcoma. Approximately 400 children and adolescents are diagnosed with rhabdomyosarcoma in the United States each year, and half of them are younger than age 6. The disease has a slightly higher incidence in males than in females. The occurrence of disease found in White and Black males is very similar; however, the incidence in Black females is only half of that in White females.

> Charlie was 16 months old and had been completely healthy. One day, he dropped to his knees in pain and showed us that his belly hurt. He had gone a day without pooping and we called the pediatrician who recommended juice, and later a suppository. Over a couple of days it wasn't better and in the middle of the night I just felt like something was wrong, so I took him to the emergency room. They could tell his bladder was very full, and he was in pain. He had reached the point where he wasn't urinating any more. They did an ultrasound and an x-ray, and they saw a mass. They scheduled an appointment with a urologist for us that afternoon at the pediatric hospital 45 minutes away.
>
> The doctor did a rectal exam and said, "Folks, it's not good" after he felt the mass. We stayed at the hospital, and they did a CT scan and a biopsy. The oncologist came to the hospital room and spent hours explaining what rhabdomyosarcoma was and answering questions about what to expect.

Genetic factors

The cause of rhabdomyosarcoma is not known, but it is associated with some other conditions. For example, children with Li-Fraumeni syndrome, neurofibromatosis, or Beckwith-Wiedemann syndrome have a higher chance of developing rhabdomyosarcoma than children without them.

Staging

Once rhabdomyosarcoma has been diagnosed through surgical biopsy and microscopic analysis of the tissue, more tests are done to determine whether the cancer has spread to other parts of the body. Computerized tomography (CT), magnetic resonance imaging (MRI), and nuclear bone scans are used to evaluate the extent of the disease and to see whether the tumor has spread. Many hospitals now do positron emission tomography (PET) scans instead of bone scans.

The most common sites that rhabdomyosarcoma spreads to are the lungs, nearby lymph nodes, lymph nodes in other parts of the body, bones in other parts of the body, and bone marrow. To check to see if the disease has spread to any of these locations, doctors

do additional procedures. For example, a bone marrow aspiration and biopsy may be performed to see whether the disease has spread to the bone marrow. For tumors located in the sinuses or at the base of the skull, a spinal tap is done to see whether tumor cells have spread to the lining of the brain. If the mass is located in the pelvic area, ultrasonography may be done along with the CT scan. This process is called staging, and it helps the doctor choose the most appropriate treatment for the child.

> *Cassandra had to undergo a myriad of tests and procedures when she was initially diagnosed. The CT scans showed that the tumor in her bottom had spread to the lungs, so we knew that first night that she was fighting a malignant cancer. The second day at the hospital she had an MRI. While she was under anesthesia for that procedure, the doctors implanted a Hickman® line in her chest that would be used for administering chemo, antibiotics, fluid, food, etc. over the next 8 months. They also took samples of her bone marrow to see if the cancer had spread there—it hadn't.*

> *The next day she had a bone scan to detect any bone involvement (there was none). They also ran tests on her kidney function to use as a baseline. An ultrasound of her heart was done as well, also to use as a baseline, since one of the chemo drugs, Adriamycin®, can cause heart problems.*

The staging of rhabdomyosarcoma involves three steps.

Step 1: Assigning a stage. The stage is determined by the location of the tumor (also known as the primary site), its size, the extent of nearby lymph node involvement, and whether the tumor has metastasized (spread to distant sites in the body). Primary sites are divided into two groups—favorable and unfavorable.

- **Stage 1.** The tumor is in a favorable site: this includes the orbits, eyelids, head (excluding the parameningeal area of the middle ear, nasal cavity, and sinuses), neck, gall bladder, bile ducts, or the genitourinary region (excluding the kidney, bladder, and prostate). Tumor cells may be present in nearby lymph nodes, but have not spread to other parts of the body.

- **Stage 2.** The tumor is in an unfavorable location, such as the sinuses, nasal cavity, extremities, bladder, prostate, perineum (in boys, area between the anus and scrotum; in girls, the area between the anus and vagina), chest wall, or around the spine. Primary tumors must be less than or equal to 5 centimeters (cm) in diameter and nearby lymph nodes cannot contain tumor cells. No distant metastases are present.

- **Stage 3.** The tumor is in an unfavorable site and is either more than 5 cm, or any size with nearby lymph node involvement. No distant metastases are found.

- **Stage 4.** The tumor has spread to distant sites.

Step 2: Assigning a surgical-pathologic group.

- **Group I.** A tumor is completely removed, no disease is found in the tissue taken from around the tumor (called margins), and lymph nodes in the region do not contain any tumor cells. No distant metastases are found.

- **Group II.** A tumor is completely removed but either microscopic disease has been detected in the margins or disease is found in nearby surgically removed lymph nodes. No distant metastases are found.

- **Group III.** A tumor could not be completely removed during surgery. This is the most common tumor group. No distant metastases are found.

- **Group IV.** Distant metastases are present at diagnosis.

Step 3: Assigning a risk group.

- **Low risk.** Children are considered to have low-risk disease if their stage and group are: (1) embryonal histology Stage 1 and Group I, II, or III; or (2) embryonal histology Stage 2 or 3 and Group I or II.

- **Intermediate risk.** Children are considered to have intermediate-risk disease if their stage and group are: (1) histology Stage 2 or Stage 3 and Group III; or (2) alveolar histology Stage 1, 2, or 3 and Group I, II, or III.

- **High risk.** Children are considered to have high-risk disease if their stage and group are embryonal or alveolar Stage 4 and Group IV.

Prognosis

Since the 1970s, the treatment of rhabdomyosarcoma has dramatically improved. A child's prognosis is determined through the analysis of several clinical and biological features. For tumors that have not spread to other parts of the body (Stages 1, 2, and 3), the most important risk factor is the presence or absence of the *PAX-FOXO1* translocation. Children or teens who have tumors that are completely resected (removed) often have the best prognoses.

Treatment of rhabdomyosarcoma

At diagnosis, many parents do not know how to find experienced doctors and the best treatments for their child. State-of-the-art care is available from physicians who participate in the Children's Oncology Group (COG). This study group includes pediatric surgeons and oncologists, radiation oncologists, researchers, and nurses. COG conducts studies to discover better therapies and supportive care for children with cancer. You can learn more about COG and find a list of its member treatment centers at *www.childrensoncologygroup.org*.

A pediatric oncologist will explain the child's treatment options: a standard treatment or a clinical trial, if open (see Chapter 9, *Choosing a Treatment*). For children and teens with rhabdomyosarcoma, treatment can include surgery, chemotherapy, and radiation.

> After 16-month-old Charlie had lab work and scans and a biopsy of his tumor, the oncologist gave him a diagnosis of Stage 2, Group III embryonal rhabdomyosarcoma of the prostate. He was classified as intermediate risk. They presented treatment options and we chose to put him on a study that included 42 weeks of vincristine, actinomycin-D, and cyclophosphamide plus radiation, randomized to either add an additional drug or not.
>
> He was hospitalized for the first night of his chemotherapy each round so he could receive IV hydration and mesna to protect his bladder from the cyclophosphamide. Ondansetron worked very well to keep him from having nausea, and he walked the halls of the hospital the whole time we were there.
>
> Charlie was scheduled to begin photon radiation therapy a few weeks after he began chemotherapy, but the radiation oncologist was concerned about administering radiation to such a small child in that sensitive area, so he met with the tumor board to ask them to refer Charlie for proton radiation therapy. The closest hospital to us with proton radiotherapy was in Boston, so he and I went there for 6 weeks for his treatments.

Surgery

All children diagnosed with rhabdomyosarcoma will have some type of operation to determine the diagnosis. This may be a needle biopsy or small incisional biopsy, or it may be a larger operation that removes some or all of the primary tumor. An experienced pediatric surgeon who has extensive experience with the treatment of pediatric sarcomas should perform any biopsy or surgery.

Surgery usually happens very early in the course of treatment because it can reduce the amount of the disease. However, the tumor may not be completely removed if it is located near vital blood vessels, if it invades surrounding normal tissue, or if its removal will have a significant functional or cosmetic effect.

> The doctor showed us the MRIs, and we got to see the monster in Joseph's head. It was a creepy top-down view, and we could see a big white blob behind his right eyeball, pushing it much farther out and down than the left one. Still no one used the word cancer. He explained how he would do the biopsy, cutting across the width of the whole eyelid to retrieve a bit of the mass, leaving packing and stitches that would make the eye look puffy and scary for a few days, but which would retreat into invisibility within a few months.

During surgery, the pediatric surgeon removes some or all of the tumor and then may sample surrounding tissues that are later examined by a pathologist (doctor who examines tissues under a microscope). The pathologist looks at the margins (tissue around the tumor that is removed during surgery) and determines whether the entire tumor has been removed, or whether some cancer cells remain. If the surgeon is able to remove the entire tumor, it is referred to as a gross total resection. If there is evidence of remaining disease, it is referred to as residual disease. If the surgeon can see or feel remaining tumor, the tumor that could not be surgically removed is called gross residual disease. If tumor cells in the margins are only visible under the microscope, it is called microscopic residual disease.

Approximately 15 percent of newly diagnosed children have tumors that can be completely removed. In the other 85 percent of children, some disease remains after surgery. As a result, chemotherapy is used in all treatment protocols, and radiation is used in most. Second-look surgical procedures, done after a period of chemotherapy, are sometimes recommended to remove any remaining residual disease and to determine whether further treatment is necessary. For more information, see Chapter 14, *Surgery*.

> *Sean had a 10-hour surgery during which they removed a 3-pound tumor from his shoulder. He was cut from the top of his ear down to his mid-chest area. I believe they could not find the point of origin of the tumor and cut to the top of his ear searching for it. The MRI technicians told me that the surgeon must have been a magician to leave the area so incredibly clean. Two MRIs since surgery have shown that the site remains tumor free.*

Chemotherapy

All children diagnosed with rhabdomyosarcoma receive chemotherapy to kill tumor cells that remain after surgery. Giving several chemotherapy drugs in combination has markedly improved the survival rate for this disease. The most commonly used drugs include vincristine, dactinomycin, cyclophosphamide, ifosfamide, etoposide, doxorubicin, and irinotecan. For information on these drugs, see Chapter 15, *Chemotherapy*.

> *Sean's treatment included surgery, 14 rounds of chemotherapy, and 30 radiation treatments. He had every side effect imaginable. Aside from very low blood cell counts, he also had raised liver counts and had jaundice a few times. He has had pneumonia and klebsiella [a type of bacterial infection] when neutropenic [low numbers of a type of white blood cell that fights infections]. His eyes were blood red from capillaries breaking. Amazingly, with all of the side effects he experienced, he had very little nausea during and after chemotherapy. I have seen him sit and eat greasy fried chicken and fries during chemo.*

Holden (age 2) had 42 weeks of chemotherapy and 28 radiation treatments for Stage 3, Group III, intermediate-risk embryonal rhabdomyosarcoma of the prostate and bladder. We initially thought he would have to have surgery, but we were glad that the tumor responded to chemotherapy so he was able to avoid having his prostate removed. He had vincristine, dactinomycin, and cyclophosphamide until about 9 or 10 weeks into his treatments and then our oncologist said that they had seen research indicating that they were getting good results alternating irinotecan with dactinomycin and cyclophosphamide, so we did that for the remainder of his treatments. He had very little nausea except when he had irinotecan—that made him very sick. He had few problems with neutropenia and his treatments were only delayed once because of low blood counts.

Radiation therapy

Radiation therapy is an important tool used to treat children with rhabdomyosarcoma. Radiation is a form of energy that can be passed from a machine through the air and into a child's body. It is used to kill tumor cells that remain following surgery and chemotherapy. Radiation may also be given in the operating room during surgery (intraoperative radiation therapy) or with seed implants (brachytherapy).

Three main types of energy beams are used: electrons, photons, or protons. Electrons tend to be used for superficial tumors, and photons or protons are usually used for deep-seated tumors. Proton-beam radiation may be recommended for very young children or for tumors at the skull base or in the pelvis to try to minimize the risk of radiation damage to surrounding tissues. Recommendations for radiation therapy depend on the site of the primary tumor and on the amount of tumor left after surgery.

The 15 percent of children whose tumors are completely removed (Stage 1, Group I) do not usually receive radiation treatments. The 85 percent of children who have residual disease after surgery are usually treated with radiation to the primary tumor site. Most protocols call for radiation therapy to begin 6 to 12 weeks after the first doses of chemotherapy are given; however, children with Stage 4 rhabdomyosarcoma often have radiation delayed until 22 to 24 weeks after the start of chemotherapy.

Children with residual disease receive doses of 180 to 200 centigray (cGy) of external beam radiation a day for up to 6 weeks. The total amount of radiation given to the pre-chemotherapy tumor site may reach 3,600 to 5,040 cGy.

Joseph had 6 weeks of daily photon radiation delivered to his right orbit. His treatments began 3 weeks before his fifth birthday. The radiotherapy staff handled him with patience, affection, and respect from the first day they met him, and gave us a lot of support as a family. They invited him in for a couple of trips to their

treatment rooms to get used to the equipment and meet all the people before they did any of the preliminary measurements or scans. He got all the time he wanted to ride up and down on the tables and ask questions about the machines. Using me as a sample patient, they made a mold of the type of plastic mesh mask Joseph would need for his treatments so he could see what it would be like. Having my head screwed down to that table was NOT FUN! I'm glad I did it, though, because just as I tasted all his medicines, this gave me a chance to try a physical experience from his perspective, too.

A child or teen receiving radiation therapy must be completely still so the radiation beam is aimed at the right spot. Young children may require daily anesthesia so they can safely receive radiation therapy. For more information, see Chapter 17, *Radiation Therapy*.

We traveled to Boston so that Charlie could receive 6 weeks of proton radiotherapy for rhabdomyosarcoma of the prostate. We went to the hospital once per day so he could be sedated and treated. He had no radiation burns, and he only had one day of diarrhea. He did not have peeling or blackened skin as we have heard about with kids on traditional photon radiation. He really had no problems at all.

Non-rhabdomyosarcoma soft tissue sarcomas

Childhood soft tissue sarcomas develop in soft tissues such as muscles, tendons, fat, blood vessels, nerves, and synovial tissues (tissues around joints). Just over 50 percent of all childhood soft tissue sarcomas have a histology (how the cells look under a microscope) that is different from rhabdomyosarcoma. As a group, non-rhabdomyosarcoma soft tissue sarcomas comprise about 4 percent of all malignant tumors in children. They include:

• **Alveolar soft part sarcoma.** This rare and slow-growing sarcoma is found most often in older children. It arises in skeletal muscle of the extremities, head, and neck.

• **Extraosseous Ewing sarcoma.** Ewing sarcoma is usually a bone sarcoma, but it can also occur in soft tissues. It is most often diagnosed in older adolescents and young adults; the median age at diagnosis is 20. The most common tumor sites are the trunk, arms, legs, head, and neck. For more information on the treatment of Ewing sarcoma, see Chapter 2, Bone Sarcomas.

• **Fibrosarcoma.** This soft tissue sarcoma is the most frequently occurring non-rhabdomyosarcoma soft tissue sarcoma in children younger than age 1. These tumors occur most often in the arms and legs, and the majority of children diagnosed have tumors that have not spread to other parts of the body (metastasized). Children younger than 4 diagnosed with this disease have an excellent prognosis after treatment with only surgery.

- **Hemangiopericytoma.** This tumor of the blood and lymph vessels occurs most often in infants.

- **Leiomyosarcoma.** This sarcoma develops in smooth muscle and most often occurs in the gastrointestinal tract, especially the stomach.

- **Liposarcoma.** This sarcoma arises in fatty tissue and is found most frequently in young teenagers. The most common sites of origin are the legs or trunk.

- **Malignant fibrous histiocytoma.** This form of soft tissue sarcoma most frequently occurs in the lower extremities and the trunk area. Other sites include the arms, scalp, and kidney.

- **Malignant peripheral nerve sheath tumor (also known as neurofibrosarcoma or malignant schwannoma).** This aggressive cancer often occurs in association with neurofibromatosis. The most common site of origin is an arm, hand, foot, or leg.

- **Synovial sarcoma.** This sarcoma is diagnosed most often in children ages 10 and older. The disease occurs frequently in the legs, especially in the area of the thigh or knee. It is also found in the arms, head, neck, and trunk.

Leah was around 10 or 11 years old when she noticed a lump in the front of her armpit. She was starting to go through puberty so she thought it was part of that. She would play with it. She first made me aware of it early in 7th grade. It started to interfere with the nerves in her arm, and she connected the lump to that feeling of having a pinched nerve. We showed it to her pediatrician at her annual checkup the day after her 13th birthday. The doctor was concerned and gave us a referral to the adult breast clinic at the university hospital. Leah was examined by the breast surgeon who told us he was 99% sure after a needle biopsy and ultrasound that it was benign, but something about it concerned him, and he told us he would like to remove it. After the surgery he told us that it was obvious that the mass was cancerous, a 2 cm x 3 cm tumor in her pectoral muscle. She was in the 1% that had cancer. Lab testing showed that it was alveolar soft part sarcoma (ASPS), a rare sarcoma that makes up only 1% of all sarcomas, so the surgeon told her she was in the 1% of the 1%.

Leah had a full battery of tests after that—MRIs, CT scans, bone scans, and so on. They couldn't find any evidence that the cancer had spread. ASPS grows very slowly, but if it spreads there are limited treatments for it. She had a second surgery to make sure all the margins were clear of any cancer cells. Because chemotherapy and radiation are not effective for this type of tumor, she did not have any other treatments. Leah was transferred to pediatric oncology for all of her follow up care. We joined the childhood cancer family support group and it really helped us to talk to people who understood. I made her go to camp with the other teens, and she connected with a great group of friends and attended camps every year after that. It has been 7 years since the surgery and her scans have all been clear.

Genetic factors

Many soft tissue sarcomas are distinguished by particular chromosome abnormalities that are identified after the tumor is biopsied. These are usually not inherited chromosomal abnormalities, but are mutations in the tumor cells. Because many soft tissue sarcomas look very similar under the microscope, identification of these unique genetic changes helps the treatment team diagnose your child's particular type of tumor. This allows them to understand how aggressive the cancer is and tailor the treatment plan and follow-up care.

Staging

There is no standard staging or grading system that applies to all non-rhabdomyosarcoma soft tissue sarcomas. To determine the most promising treatment, oncologists will consider the grade of the tumor (how aggressive it looks under the microscope), the size of the tumor, the extent of tumor spread, and how much of the tumor has been surgically removed.

Treatment

At diagnosis, many parents do not know how to find experienced doctors and the best treatments for their child. State-of-the-art care is available from physicians who participate in the Children's Oncology Group (COG). This study group includes pediatric surgeons and oncologists, radiation oncologists, researchers, and nurses. COG conducts studies to discover better therapies and supportive care for children with cancer. You can learn more about COG and find a list of its member treatment centers at *www.childrensoncologygroup.org*.

Non-rhabdomyosarcoma soft tissue sarcomas are rare in children, so the treatments are based on experience with adults. Generally, the size and location of the tumor, as well as tumor histology (how the cells look under a microscope), are used to choose the best treatment. Treatments should be individually tailored to the child's tumor and designed to give the best chance of survival with the fewest long-term effects.

Surgery is the cornerstone of treatment for soft tissue sarcomas (see Chapter 14, *Surgery*). Many of the non-rhabdomyosarcoma soft tissue sarcomas can be treated successfully with just surgery, and they do not respond as well to chemotherapy or radiation therapy as rhabdomyosarcomas do. An experienced pediatric surgeon who has extensive experience with the treatment of pediatric sarcomas should perform biopsies and surgeries.

Ideally, the pediatric surgeon will attempt to remove the mass completely with wide margins (portions of the surrounding tissue) to ensure that no microscopic disease remains. The most important prognostic factor is whether the surgeon is able to completely remove the primary tumor.

Radiation is generally recommended for:

- All large (more than 5 cm), high-grade soft tissue sarcomas, even if the tumor is completely removed and no tumor cells are found in the margins.

- High-grade sarcomas of any size when tumors cells are present in the margins.

- Large tumors that cannot be completely removed surgically.

The dose and field of radiation therapy are based on the age of the child and the size and location of the tumor. Children who receive radiation therapy for non-rhabdomyosarcoma soft tissue sarcomas generally have better outcomes than those who do not. However, radiation therapy without complete surgical removal of the tumor is rarely successful at permanently controlling the tumor.

Chemotherapy is often recommended:

- After the removal of large (more than 5 cm), high-grade sarcomas, because they are associated with a greater risk of spread to other parts of the body.

- For tumors that cannot be removed surgically or have already spread to other parts of the body.

Some types of non-rhabdomyosarcoma soft tissue sarcomas do not respond to chemotherapy, so it may not be recommended even in the above situations.

Although medical science has made advances in treating non-rhabdomyosarcoma soft tissue sarcomas while reducing the side effects and long-term impact to the child, amputation is sometimes necessary. For older children and teens, limb-sparing procedures are sometimes used instead of amputation. For information about amputation and limb-sparing procedures, see Chapter 2, *Bone Sarcomas*.

Information on standard treatments

Treatments for various types of childhood cancers evolve and improve over time. The treatments described in this chapter were the ones most commonly used (called standard treatments) when this book was written. You can learn about the newest treatments available by calling (800) 422-6237 and asking for the PDQ (physician data query) for soft tissue sarcomas or rhabdomyosarcoma. This free information, also available online at *www.cancer.gov/cancertopics/pdq/pediatrictreatment* (scroll down to "Sarcoma,

Childhood Soft Tissue" or "Rhabdomyosarcoma, Childhood"), explains the diseases, state-of-the-art treatments, and ongoing clinical trials. Two versions are available:

- One for families—uses simple language and contains no statistics; and

- One for professionals—is technical, thorough, and includes citations to scientific literature.

To learn about current Phase III clinical trials for soft tissue sarcomas in children, you can visit the National Cancer Institute's website *www.cancer.gov/clinicaltrials/search*. In the "Cancer type/condition" box, choose the type of cancer ("soft tissue sarcoma, child" or "rhabdomyosarcoma, child") and choose "Phase III" in the "Trial status/phase" box. Then click the red "Search" button at the bottom of the page.

Kenny was the most beautiful baby. He laughed a great deal and very rarely cried until the age of 2 when he was diagnosed with stage IV, embryonal rhabdomyosarcoma. Kenny had tumors from his pelvis up to his aorta. Because of the extensive disease, our surgeon couldn't remove them. He began chemotherapy the day after Christmas and continued until July when he began radiation. He had 27 rounds of radiation throughout July, all under anesthesia. It was very difficult and draining, but toward the end, Kenny would set up all the equipment, hook his pulse oximeter up, turn his oxygen on, and hold his mask to be anesthetized. He was just shy of his third birthday.

In September, we began to see the light at the end of the tunnel. Kenny's tumors seemed to disappear and a biopsy of the scar tissue found no cancer, but he continued chemotherapy until January. Kenny recently celebrated his fourth birthday. He whooped with delight as he put on his new helmet, gloves, and kneepads and took off down the hill on his new bright blue skateboard.

Chapter 7

Kidney Tumors

ABOUT 600 CHILDREN AND TEENS in North America are diagnosed each year with cancer that originates in the kidney. The most common kidney cancer is Wilms tumor, which gets its name from a German doctor, Max Wilms, who wrote one of the first medical articles about it in 1899. Eighty percent of all kidney cancers in children are Wilms tumor. The remaining 20 percent includes renal cell carcinoma, clear cell sarcoma of the kidney, malignant rhabdoid tumor of the kidney, and congenital mesoblastic nephroma. Sometimes a kidney tumor is not cancerous, and its removal is curative. Examples of these tumors are cystic nephroma and nephrogenic rests.

This chapter first explains the structure and function of the kidneys and the symptoms of kidney tumors. It then covers each of the four main types of kidney tumors and describes who gets them, what the signs and symptoms are, how they are diagnosed, and how they are treated. It ends with a brief discussion about how parents can find out about the newest treatments available.

The kidneys

The kidneys are located near the middle of the back and are responsible for filtering the blood. These two bean-shaped organs are each about the size of a fist. The kidney operates as a recycling depot complete with high-tech sanitation engineers. Its main job is to filter harmful waste products from the blood and to regulate the return of reusable chemicals—sodium, phosphorus, and potassium—back into circulation.

Inside each kidney are millions of microscopic structures that filter out large particles, such as proteins and white and red blood cells, and allow them to return to the bloodstream. What remains in the kidney after this process is called urine. Urine flows from the kidney through a long tube (ureter) into the bladder, where it is stored until it leaves the body through urination (see Figure 7-1).

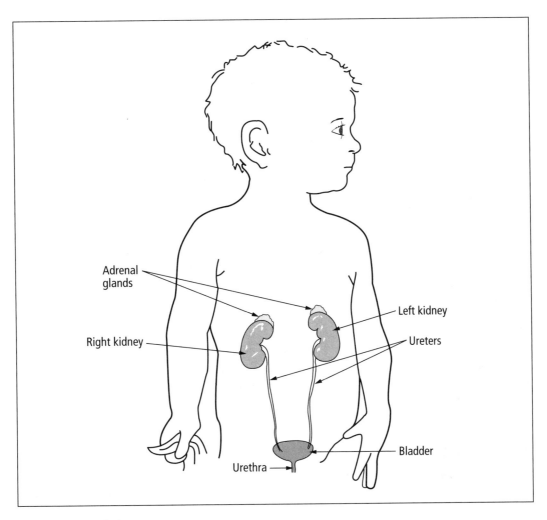

Figure 7-1: The kidneys

Signs and symptoms of kidney tumors

Kidney tumors are often difficult to diagnose. Usually, a parent notices a lump or mass in the abdominal area while dressing or bathing a child who has no other symptoms. By this time, the tumor is generally very large. Sometimes the tumor is found during routine doctor visits when the pediatrician palpates the toddler's abdomen. Kidney tumors are occasionally diagnosed when the child is evaluated for other unrelated reasons, such as accidental trauma to the abdominal area.

Some children with kidney tumors have abdominal pain, and up to 25 percent have blood in the urine. Blood may be visible to the naked eye or it may only be seen with a microscope. About 25 percent of children have high blood pressure at diagnosis.

> The vomiting and the lump were the only symptoms that Elizabeth had. I have seen the list of symptoms for Wilms tumor, and I'm always startled by them. She never had signs of any of those things. I feel very fortunate that we caught her cancer so soon and with so little indication of anything being wrong. This is especially true since I know Wilms tumor is a fast growing cancer and we were fighting against time.

Other signs and symptoms of kidney tumors include fever, diarrhea, weight loss, shortness of breath, urogenital infections, and anemia (low number of red blood cells). The child may feel tired and unwell.

Wilms tumor

Approximately 550 to 600 children are diagnosed with Wilms tumor in North America every year. It is more common in children of European and African descent than in Asian children. Girls are slightly more at risk of developing Wilms tumor than boys.

The average age at diagnosis is between 3 and 4 years when the disease is unilateral (affecting only one kidney), but it is generally diagnosed at a younger age when the disease is bilateral (affecting both kidneys). Seventy-five to 80 percent of children with Wilms tumor are diagnosed before the age of 5. Five percent of children with Wilms tumor have tumors in both kidneys at diagnosis.

> Matthew was 1 year old when he was diagnosed with Wilms tumor. Everyone used to tell me how lucky I was because he was so young and he probably wouldn't remember anything. Funny, because lucky was not a word I would use to describe the scenario.

Genetic factors associated with Wilms tumor

Wilms tumor is believed to result from mutations in certain genes. These genes are associated not only with Wilms tumor, but with several other rare conditions. Roughly 10 percent of children diagnosed with Wilms tumor also have one of the following birth defects or syndromes:

- **WAGR syndrome.** WAGR is an acronym for Wilms tumor, aniridia (incomplete formation of the iris of the eye), genitourinary tract abnormalities, and mental retardation. A child with this syndrome, caused by a deletion of the short arm of chromosome 11 (called 11p), has a greater than 30 percent chance of developing Wilms

tumor. Aniridia is caused by alterations of a gene called *PAX6,* which sits on chromosome 11p adjacent to a gene called the Wilms tumor suppressor gene *(WT1). WT1* is responsible for formation of the genitourinary system and is implicated in Wilms tumor development. If a child has a deletion of 11p that includes both *PAX6* and *WT1,* there is an increased risk of Wilms tumor. If the deletion affects only *PAX6,* the risk of Wilms tumor is much lower.

- **Denys-Drash syndrome.** This syndrome is characterized by abnormal kidney function and genital abnormalities. It is also associated with mutations of *WT1* on chromosome 11p.

- **Beckwith-Wiedemann syndrome.** This congenital disorder is characterized by larger-than-normal internal organs, a large tongue, hemihypertrophy (one side of the body grows larger than the other), and hernia of the navel at birth. Sometimes hemihypertrophy can be seen in the absence of the other features of Beckwith-Wiedemann syndrome. Approximately 5 to 10 percent of children with Beckwith-Wiedemann syndrome or hemihypertrophy develop Wilms tumor or other childhood cancers.

- **Nephroblastomatosis.** The presence of small pockets of embryonal kidney tissue called *nephrogenic rests* in the kidney is called nephroblastomatosis. This precancerous condition is usually found in both kidneys. Nephrogenic rests can shrink and disappear, or multiply and develop into Wilms tumor. The condition should be closely monitored and may be treated with chemotherapy.

- **Hereditary Wilms tumor.** Inherited Wilms tumor, characterized by tumors in both kidneys and a family history of the disease, is uncommon. Only about 2 percent of all children diagnosed have a family history of Wilms tumor.

Wilms tumor has also been reported in association with other syndromes, such as Perlman syndrome, Simpson-Golabi-Behmel syndrome, Sotos syndrome, mosaic variegated aneuploidy, Fanconi anemia, DICER1 predisposition syndrome, and Bloom syndrome.

Environmental factors

No link has been found between development of Wilms tumor and any environmental factors.

Diagnosis of Wilms tumor

Several tests and procedures are necessary to diagnose Wilms tumor. The doctor will first perform a physical examination and obtain the child's medical history. Then, the child usually has an abdominal ultrasound and/or a contrast-enhanced computerized tomography (CT) scan. Because some children have tumors in both kidneys, both kidneys need to be examined. A complete blood count (CBC) is ordered, as well as

urinalysis to check for signs of blood in the urine. The child will receive blood chemistry tests to evaluate kidney function.

> *I have to say that on diagnosis day our pediatrician was wonderful. When I called the doctor's office and told them about the lump that I had found in her abdomen and the vomiting, no one even hinted at what might be wrong. I was simply told to bring her in as soon as possible. The doctor was examining her less than 2 hours after my call to his office. He didn't tell me initially what he suspected. Later, he told me that he wanted to be sure before he even mentioned the word to me. He sent us to the local hospital where she underwent her first CT scan. The pediatrician was waiting for us with the news when we returned to his office.*

Staging Wilms tumor

Once Wilms tumor has been diagnosed, more tests are done to determine whether the cancer has spread to other parts of the body. This process is called staging and it helps the doctor choose the best treatment for the child. Computerized tomography (CT) scans of the chest should be ordered because approximately 20 percent of children with Wilms tumor have lung metastases at diagnosis.

> *Elizabeth's cancer was found by CT scan. That probably gave the doctors up front a good indication of what they were facing (how large the tumor is, how far it has spread). They said that she had a cancerous tumor called Wilms, and we were sent to the children's hospital. Surgery was immediately scheduled. I was told that what happened following the surgery would depend on what they found in surgery. I was also told at the very beginning that she would lose her kidney. If they discovered that the cancer had progressed beyond the kidney (e.g., to the lung), it was possible that further surgery would be done. Following the surgery, tissues were typed and staged. A few days after the surgery, the doctors and I sat down in the conference room. It was then that I was given the staging information and the list of all of the stages so that I could see how we fit into the big scheme of things.*

These are the stages of Wilms tumor:

- **Stage I (approximately 20%).** The tumor is limited to the kidney and can be completely removed surgically. No tumor cells are found in the lymph nodes.

- **Stage II (approximately 22%).** The tumor extends beyond the kidney, but is completely removed surgically.

- **Stage III (approximately 32%).** The tumor is not completely removed surgically or is ruptured during surgery, or disease is found in one or more abdominal lymph nodes.

- **Stage IV (approximately 20%).** The disease has spread to the lung, liver, bone, or brain, as well as distant lymph nodes.

- **Stage V (approximately 6%).** The tumor is found in both kidneys at the time of diagnosis.

> *We sat and waited for hours and then the door clicked and white coats entered the room. The doctors sat on the couch and gave us the diagnosis. They explained it was bilateral Wilms tumor, a pediatric kidney cancer that was quite common, but being on both kidneys made it unusual. I asked what stage it was and when they said "Stage V" I just lost it. Tala was 14 pounds, how could she survive this? I don't remember what they were saying after that, I just remember it was very dark in the room. They explained that they would do 6 weeks of chemotherapy to try and destroy the tumors in her chest and they said we would start chemo the next day.*

Prognosis

Treatment of Wilms tumor in children is one of medicine's success stories. Due to improvements in surgical techniques, drug therapies, and radiation therapy, 90 percent of children with Wilms tumor who receive standard treatment are cured. The best treatment for each child with Wilms is determined by analysis of several clinical and biologic features.

After a biopsy or surgery, a pathologist examines the cancer cells under a microscope. If the nuclei of some of the cells appear larger than normal or irregular in shape, it is called anaplasia. If anaplasia is scattered throughout the tumor, it is called diffuse anaplasia and that means a poorer prognosis. If anaplasia is found in only one area of the tumor (called focal anaplasia) the prognosis is intermediate—between diffuse anaplasia and no anaplasia.

Tumor cells that are not anaplastic are said to be Wilms tumor of favorable histology. The vast majority of children diagnosed with Wilms, approximately 90 percent, have tumor cells with a favorable histology.

The pediatric oncologist will determine the prognosis using many criteria, including stage of disease and presence of anaplasia in the tumor cells. These factors affect the intensity of treatment needed.

> *The initial pathology was Stage 1, favorable histology with no lymph node involvement, and we left hoping and praying we were done. We were told we'd get a call from oncology on Monday or Tuesday. A senior pathologist reviewed the slides and he felt one of the lymph nodes had involvement, which took Victoria from stage 1 to stage 3. They sent the tissue on to a third party to evaluate, so they wouldn't over treat or under treat her. We waited another week for that to come back, and they agreed that the one lymph node was likely involved. So the same day that we got that confirmation, we took her to the hospital for chemotherapy. We were on a research study that required her to start chemo within 2 weeks of surgery.*

Treatment of Wilms tumor

At diagnosis, many parents do not know how to find experienced doctors and the best treatments for their child. State-of-the-art care is available from physicians who participate in the Children's Oncology Group (COG). This study group includes pediatric surgeons and oncologists, radiation oncologists, researchers, and nurses. COG conducts studies to discover better therapies and supportive care for children with cancer. You can learn more about COG and find a list of its member treatment centers at *www. childrensoncologygroup.org*.

After diagnosis and staging, your child's pediatric oncologist will propose the standard treatment or a clinical trial (see Chapter 9, *Choosing a Treatment*) based on many factors, including your child's stage of disease and the histology of the tumor. Following is a discussion of treatment for tumors in only one kidney.

Surgery

A pediatric surgeon with experience operating on children with kidney cancer should do all biopsies and surgeries. In North America, children diagnosed with Wilms tumor usually have surgery to remove the kidney, called a nephrectomy, before any other therapy is given (see Chapter 14, *Surgery*). Occasionally, if the diagnosis is uncertain, a biopsy is performed prior to nephrectomy. Only children with Wilms tumor in both kidneys (bilateral Wilms tumor) or inoperable tumors receive chemotherapy prior to surgery.

> We walked Brinley (age 3) down to surgery at 7:45 in the morning. We loved that we were able to stay with her until the moment she closed her eyes. The next time we got to see her was 5:30 that night when she went into recovery. It was a long day. She was groggy and in some pain. My sister-in-law saw her and burst into tears, but we were happy because we had talked to the doctor and knew he thought she was doing very well. It's funny how two people can see the same thing in a completely different way.

Two types of nephrectomies are used to remove Wilms tumor:

- **Radical nephrectomy.** Removal of the tumor, as well as the entire kidney and surrounding tissues, including part of the ureter. The remaining kidney is able to compensate for the loss of the other kidney.

- **Partial nephrectomy.** Removal of the tumor and a portion of the affected kidney. This type of surgery is usually done for bilateral Wilms tumor or if the other kidney is damaged or has already been removed.

During surgery, the pediatric surgeon takes samples from lymph nodes in the area. The surgeon may also biopsy other areas in the abdomen or the liver if she suspects the cancer might have spread.

> We had an awesome surgical team. Victoria went in for surgery at 1 in the after-noon and we didn't get back to her until 7. They had told us that it would take 3 to 7 hours. They texted us status updates on a pager during the surgery and let us know where to meet her for recovery. She had an epidural when she came out of surgery, so that is how they managed her pain until the next day. They placed her port while she was in surgery. They removed and examined over 22 lymph nodes from her abdomen. We stayed at the hospital until Saturday.

Chemotherapy

The vast majority of children diagnosed with Wilms tumor receive chemotherapy (drugs that kill cancer cells) as part of the standard treatment. Several chemotherapy drugs are effective against this type of cancer. The use of dactinomycin and vincristine has dramatically increased survival rates. Children with stage I or stage II disease with favorable histology usually are treated with just these two drugs. Children who are diagnosed with Wilms tumor at a more advanced stage also receive doxorubicin. Children with diffuse anaplasia are treated with doxorubicin, etoposide, cyclophosphamide, vincristine, and sometimes other drugs such as irinotecan and carboplatin. For information about these drugs, see Chapter 15, *Chemotherapy*.

Children with stage I and stage II disease with a favorable histology are treated for 18 weeks. Children whose tumor has anaplasia and/or a higher stage are treated for 24 weeks. Infants younger than 12 months are given 50 percent of the chemotherapy given to older children to reduce possible long-term effects.

Because chemotherapy can damage healthy, normal cells, the pediatric oncologist may need to adjust the doses. The goal is to minimize potential side effects (see Chapter 16, *Common Side Effects of Treatment*), while providing adequate treatment for the disease.

> My daughter's main side effects from the dactinomycin and vincristine were constipation and nausea. She was given a standard dose of Senecot® every day for the constipation, and we were given a standing prescription for Zofran® to control the nausea. Both of these drugs worked wonders for her. She really suffered very little discomfort during chemotherapy.

Radiation therapy

The decision to use radiation therapy to treat a child with Wilms tumor is based largely on the stage and histology of the tumor. Children with stage I and stage II favorable

histology disease do not require radiation. For children with more advanced stages of disease, external beam radiation therapy is given (see Chapter 17, *Radiation Therapy*). This type of treatment uses high-energy rays, delivered from outside the body, to kill cancer cells. The amount of disease present will determine the size of the area that will be radiated. Usually, 1,050 centigrays (cGy) is the recommended dose of radiation used in children with advanced stage disease or tumors with unfavorable histology. Children with stage IV disease also receive radiation to treat metastases in the lungs and elsewhere.

> My 1-year-old son had a huge tumor that went from his diaphragm to his bladder and crossed the midline. He had a simulation that lasted one and a half hours, then radiation to the spinal cord and abdomen, once a day for 5 days. He tolerated it very well. The only side effect he had was red peeling skin. He did have doxorubicin for the following 6 months, and had radiation recall several times. His peeling skin would return for a couple of days, then disappear.

Treatment for bilateral tumors

Tumors in both kidneys are found in approximately 5 percent of children diagnosed with Wilms tumor. CT scans and ultrasound usually identify tumors in both kidneys, and at some treatment centers 18F-fluorodeoxyglucose positron emission tomography (FDG-PET) scans are used to highlight active disease in the main tumor and metastases.

The goal of treatment for stage V Wilms tumor is to try to destroy the tumors while preserving as much healthy kidney tissue as possible. Current treatments use chemotherapy (vincristine, dactinomycin, and doxorubicin) to reduce the size of the tumors before surgery. After 6 weeks of treatment, the kidneys are re-evaluated to see whether the tumors have shrunk sufficiently to allow surgery that leaves part of the kidney in place. If not, chemotherapy continues until week 12, when surgery is performed. After surgery, the chemotherapy regimen may be adjusted based on the tumor histology. Radiation therapy may be used, depending on the tumor's histology and extent of spread.

> The doctor sat us down to tell us the initial plan for my daughter's treatment: 6 weeks of chemotherapy, which they hoped would shrink the kidney tumors enough to do surgery; if not, they would add 6 more weeks of chemo and then do the surgery. The goal was to save as much of each kidney as they could. She was given vincristine, dactinomycin, and doxorubicin. We stayed in the hospital just short of 3 weeks because her counts were low and because she was on intravenous feedings. We had a lot to learn to be able to take her home. After the surgery, her last 19 weeks of chemo were done as an outpatient in the day treatment facility.

Follow up

After treatment, there is a chance that the Wilms tumor will return (called a relapse or recurrence). The likelihood of relapse depends on the initial stage and histology, but the average relapse rate is only 10 percent. Tumor relapse most commonly occurs in the lungs, the original tumor site, or the liver. In 1 to 3 percent of children, a second tumor develops later in the remaining kidney—most of these children were younger than 12 months old when they were originally diagnosed and/or their kidney tumor contained pockets of embryonal tissue called nephrogenic rests. To detect relapse or second tumors, chest x-rays and abdominal ultrasound tests are recommended on the following schedule:

- Both tests should be performed every 3 months for first 2 years after completion of therapy, followed by every 6 months for the second 2 years, followed by every 12 months for 1 additional year.

- For children with nephrogenic rests, abdominal ultrasounds should be performed every 3 months until age 7 or 8.

Other types of childhood kidney cancers

Rare childhood kidney cancers include renal cell carcinoma (RCC), clear cell sarcoma of the kidney, rhabdoid tumor of the kidney, and congenital mesoblastic nephroma. Treatment for these aggressive cancers is more intensive than treatment for Wilms tumor. A combination of surgery, radiation, and chemotherapy is used to treat these types of kidney cancers.

Renal cell carcinoma

Renal cell carcinoma (RCC) is the second most common cancer of the kidney in children. It is the most common kidney cancer in adults, but the genetics and the cell histology (the microscopic structure) of pediatric renal cell carcinoma are different than the adult version. RCC is very rare in children younger than age 15, but makes up about two-thirds of kidney cancers in young people ages 15 to 19.

RCC is associated with a variety of genetically linked conditions, including von Hippel-Lindau (VHL) disease, tuberous sclerosis, and a hereditary form of RCC. Children with hereditary leiomyomatosis, which causes benign tumors of the uterus or skin, have a 10 to 15 percent chance of developing RCC, and may need to be screened for it on a yearly basis for the rest of their lives.

The most common signs and symptoms of RCC include abdominal pain, an abdominal mass, and blood in the urine.

RCC is an aggressive cancer that spreads to other sites much more readily than does Wilms tumor. About half of children and teens with RCC are found to have stage III or stage IV cancer at diagnosis. Metastases are often found in the bone, brain, lungs, and soft tissues. Children with renal cell carcinoma that has spread to nearby lymph nodes have a significantly higher cure rate than do adults with the same cancer.

Your child or teen with renal cell carcinoma should be treated at a regional pediatric hospital that has specialists in childhood cancer who are knowledgeable about the most promising treatments. Pediatric RCC is currently treated with surgery if the tumor has not spread to distant areas of the body. There is no standard treatment for RCC that has spread, but biologically targeted therapy with tyrosine kinase inhibitors is a promising new treatment.

Clear cell sarcoma of the kidney

Clear cell sarcoma of the kidney is a very rare cancer (found in about 3 percent of the children with kidney cancer) that is usually diagnosed in the first 4 years of life. The initial symptoms are the same as other pediatric kidney tumors, and may also include fever or high blood pressure. Clear cell sarcoma of the kidney is more aggressive than Wilms tumor. It often spreads to the lungs, bones, brain, and soft tissues. Survival rates have improved markedly in the last 2 decades with the development of multi-drug chemotherapy regimens.

Clear cell sarcoma of the kidney is staged in the same way Wilms tumor is staged (see the earlier section called "Staging Wilms tumor"). Current treatments for all stages include surgery; 24 weeks of chemotherapy with doxorubicin, cyclophosphamide, etoposide, and vincristine; and radiation therapy.

> My son, Andy, was diagnosed with Stage III clear cell sarcoma of the kidney. His tumor was very close to the inferior vena cava but they were able to do surgery right away to get the tumor before it got into that major blood vessel. Andy's treatment is 24 weeks total: vincristine for 13 weeks, doxorubicin every 6th week, etoposide every 6th week, and cyclophosphamide every 3rd week. We are through week 10, and Andy is doing very well. No fevers, no nausea. They cut out one of his antinausea medications (Decadron®), because it was making him nuts. One minute he was happy; the next he was screaming and throwing things and kicking people. When they stopped the Decadron®, he returned to normal. He just had his first abdominal ultrasound and chest x-ray since diagnosis, and all was clear.

Rhabdoid tumor of the kidney

Malignant rhabdoid tumor of the kidney was first identified in 1978. It is a very rare cancer, diagnosed in about 25 children every year in the United States. It occurs most frequently in infants and toddlers, with a median age at diagnosis of 15 months. Rhabdoid tumors can also originate in other organs, soft tissues, and in the brain, where they are known as atypical teratoid/rhabdoid tumors (AT/RT). Rhabdoid tumor of the kidney can metastasize all over the body, and 10 to 15 percent of children with this tumor will also have tumors in their brain or spinal cord at diagnosis.

Indicators at diagnosis of rhabdoid tumor of the kidney include fever, blood in the urine, plus very young age and advanced disease with distant spread (stage IV). Rhabdoid tumor of the kidney is staged in the same way Wilms tumor is staged (see the earlier section called "Staging Wilms tumor"). A tumor biopsy is required to determine a diagnosis of rhabdoid tumor of the kidney.

The cell origin of rhabdoid tumors is not known, and no cause has been identified. However, research on rhabdoid tumor tissue has given scientists clues about what genetic mutations are involved in the development of these tumors. Some physicians recommend genetic testing of direct relatives of children with rhabdoid tumors to determine whether they carry a family predisposition to developing these tumors.

Rhabdoid tumors are rare and very aggressive, so it is extremely important that your child be treated at a regional pediatric hospital with specialists who are knowledgeable about the most promising treatments. All stages of rhabdoid tumor of the kidney are currently treated with surgery and chemotherapy using some combination of vincristine, cyclophosphamide, doxorubicin, etoposide, ifosfamide, and carboplatin.

Congenital mesoblastic nephroma

Congenital mesoblastic nephroma is the most common kidney cancer diagnosed in children younger than 3 months of age. Twice as many boys as girls are diagnosed with this cancer. Tumor diagnosis and staging are done in the same manner as for Wilms tumor (see "Diagnosis of Wilms tumor" and "Staging Wilms tumor" sections earlier in this chapter). The tumor can only be distinguished from Wilms tumor by looking at the tumor cells under a microscope. There are two major cell types:

- **Classic.** Classic mesoblastic nephroma is often diagnosed in a fetus during a prenatal ultrasound or in a child during the first 3 months of life.

- **Cellular.** Cellular mesoblastic nephroma has a genetic translocation (an exchange of parts) between chromosomes.

The standard treatment for mesoblastic nephroma is surgical removal of the kidney. The survival rate for patients diagnosed by the age of 7 months is nearly 95 percent. A higher stage at diagnosis, an older age, and a diagnosis of cellular mesoblastic nephroma are associated with a higher rate of relapse. Some physicians prescribe chemotherapy for children who are older than 3 months of age and have stage III cellular tumors to avoid recurrence or spread of tumor cells that might remain after surgery.

Information on standard treatments

Treatments for various types of childhood cancers evolve and improve over time. The treatments described in this chapter were the ones most commonly used (called standard treatments) when this book was being written. You can learn about the newest treatments available by calling (800) 422-6237 and asking for the PDQ (physician data query) for childhood kidney tumors. This free information, also available online at *www.cancer.gov/cancertopics/pdq/pediatrictreatment* (scroll down to "Kidney tumors of childhood, Wilms tumor and other") explains the disease, state-of-the-art treatments, and ongoing clinical trials. Two versions are available:

- One for families—uses simple language and contains no statistics; and

- One for professionals—is technical, thorough, and includes citations to scientific literature.

To learn about current Phase III clinical trials for kidney cancers in children, visit the National Cancer Institute's website *www.cancer.gov/clinicaltrials/search* and choose the type of kidney cancer in the "Cancer type/condition" box and choose Phase III in the "Trial status/phase" box. Then click the red "Search" button at the bottom of the page.

I had Wilms tumor in 1962 when I was 2 years old. I had one kidney removed, then radiation and chemotherapy. I recovered and had a perfectly normal childhood. Other than not wearing bikinis because of the big scar right around my waist, it didn't affect me much. I played hockey, basketball, and other contact sports without problems. I have no late effects from the treatment other than slight curvature of the spine and a few less pockets of fat on the side they irradiated. They told me that one of my fallopian tubes was damaged, but I have had three sons, all over seven pounds. My childhood cancer experiences created a deep fascination with medicine, and I am now a nurse.

Chapter 8
Telling Your Child and Others

YOU HAVE JUST LEARNED your child is gravely ill. There is so much to take in, so much to do, and all you really want to do is wake up and end this nightmare; but you are the only one who knows this news. What will you tell your sick child? And what can you say to your other children, or your parents? Should you tell your friends and neighbors? What can you possibly say?

Telling your child

It is important to provide age-appropriate information soon after diagnosis and to create a supportive climate so your child begins to understand what is happening and feels comfortable asking questions. In the past, shielding children from the painful reality of cancer was the norm. Most experts now agree that children feel less anxiety and cope with treatments better if they are given age-appropriate explanations. Your child needs to know what is happening now and be prepared for what is to come. Because you are coping with a bewildering array of emotions yourself, sharing information and providing reassurance and hope may be difficult. Remember that sharing strengthens the family, allowing all members to face the crisis together.

> *Our daughter was 8 at diagnosis. She had emergency surgery to fix a "twisted" ovary, which turned out to be an ovarian germ cell tumor. The surgeon removed the mass and our daughter's ovary along with it. We got the initial pathology before we left the hospital, but wanted to wait for final pathology before we told her of the cancer diagnosis. We took our daughter to her regular pediatrician the next week and gave her the news. I told her the surgeon found cancer on her ovary and took it out, but she would need special medicine called chemotherapy to get rid of any cancer that was left. Our daughter loves her pediatrician so we thought it would help to tell her with him so he could answer questions and reassure her. We were honest with her and she handled it very well.*

When to tell your child

You should tell your child as soon as possible after diagnosis. Sick children know they are sick, and all children know when their parents are upset, frightened, and withholding information. In the absence of the truth, children imagine—and believe—scenarios far more frightening than the reality. It's nearly impossible for children to make sense of their new world without an explanation: they're in a strange place, none of their normal activities continue, strangers are performing scary and painful procedures on them, their parents are upset, and they see sick children everywhere they look. They may not talk about their fears, but they know something is very wrong.

> We felt we had to tell Jessica the truth from the very beginning. She needed to know that she could trust us. Talking about it helped her understand why the treatments were necessary. We told her that her hair would fall out, but that it didn't matter. She would still be beautiful to us, with or without hair. We told her when something would hurt and when it wouldn't. We told her we were all in this together and that we would discuss everything every step of the way.

The most loving thing a parent can do is to tell the truth before the child is overwhelmed by fear of what she has imagined. Staying silent has another side effect: it undermines the credibility of the parent with the child. This will be a long and frightening journey, and your child must believe you are in this together and that she can always count on you to support her and tell her the truth.

Who should tell your child

You can decide who should first talk to your child about the cancer based on his age, level of understanding, and how comfortable he is in his current environment. If your child is very ill due to the cancer or has had to be rushed to surgery, this conversation may need to take place in the hospital at a quiet time. In most cases, however, you will be able to gather your thoughts after receiving the initial diagnosis and talking with the medical team about the best way to explain the diagnosis to your child.

Some parents tell their child in private, while others prefer to have a family physician, oncologist, social worker, member of the clergy, or other family member present. Most children's hospitals have child life specialists who can help explain the diagnosis and treatment to young children in an age-appropriate manner. Often, they have age-appropriate materials (books, pictures, dolls) to help with the conversation.

> When we first found out that the MRI showed a moderately large tumor, we didn't tell Billy, who was 2 years old, until a few days later. I think we needed to be clear for ourselves what the plan was going to be. Over the next few days, we started to tell him that the MRI pictures showed that he had a boo-boo, and soon we would take a trip to a hospital with Grammie where the boo-boo would be fixed. When the

day came for surgery, Grammie was with us when we told him again about the boo-boo, that this was the day for it to be fixed, and that he would take a nap while the doctors fixed the boo-boo. He asked if we would be with him, and we each reassured him that we all would be there when he woke up. I had decided not to mention the pain or bandages, but I think now that we know a little better, we might have said something about that, too.

Children ages 4 to 12 sometimes benefit from having the treatment team (oncologist, nurse, social worker, child life specialist, or psychologist) present when told about their diagnosis. It promotes the sense that everyone is united in their efforts to help your child get well. Staff members can answer the child's questions and provide comfort for the entire family. Children in this age group sometimes feel guilty and responsible for their illness. They may harbor fears that the cancer is a punishment for something they did wrong. Parents, social workers, psychologists, child life specialists, and nurses can help explore these concerns and provide reassurance.

My 6-year-old son Brian was sitting next to me when the doctor called to tell me that he had cancer. I whispered into the phone, "What should I tell him?" The doctor said to tell him that he was sick and needed to go to a special children's hospital for help. As we were getting ready to go to the hospital, Brian asked if he was going to die, and what were they going to do to him. We didn't know how to answer all the questions, but told him that we would find out at the hospital. My husband told him that he was a strong boy and we would all fight this thing together. I was at a loss for words.

At the hospital, they were wonderful. What impressed me the most was that they always talked to Brian first, and answered all his questions before talking to us. When Zack (Brian's 8-year-old brother) came to the hospital 2 days later, the doctors took him in the hall and talked to him for a long time, explaining and answering his questions.

I was glad that we were all so honest, because Brian later confided to me that he had first thought he got cancer because he hadn't been drinking enough milk.

Adolescents have a powerful need for control and autonomy that should be respected. At a time when most teens are becoming independent, teens with cancer are suddenly dependent on medical personnel to save their lives and on parents for emotional support. Teenagers sometimes feel more comfortable discussing the diagnosis with their physician in private. In some families, a diagnosis of cancer can force unwelcome dependence and add new stress to the already turbulent teen years. Other families report that the illness helped forge closer bonds between teenagers and their parents.

Just when I had expected her to become a rebellious teenager, Florence (15 years old) became even closer to me than before. She knew that I had believed her when she started having symptoms from the tumor and sometimes she said I'd saved her life.

It is not always possible to control how your child or teen finds out about the cancer diagnosis, especially if you find out at the same time she does. Finding out about the cancer abruptly or with little warning can be difficult, but be assured that both you and your child can recover from this upsetting experience by gathering more information and building a trusting relationship with the medical team.

> We were told that Kasey (age 13) had a massive sinus infection that was resisting treatment, and on Thursday they had taken a biopsy of the infection to determine what antibiotic to use on it. On Sunday, we were an hour from home, leaving my daughter's soccer game. The ENT [ear, nose, and throat doctor] called from the children's hospital while the girls and I were sitting in the car waiting for my husband to pack up the last of our things. She didn't ask me where I was or if I was alone, she just said "Your daughter has cancer and you need to come in tomorrow." We had never suspected cancer. I jumped out of the car and just yelled it to my husband. He got on the phone to talk to the doctor and fell to his knees on the sidewalk. Kasey came to us saying, "What is going on?" So we told her there on the sidewalk. We couldn't keep that from her when she saw we were so upset.

Children and teens react to the diagnosis of cancer with a wide range of emotions, as do their parents. They may lapse into denial, feel tremendous anger or rage, or be extremely optimistic. As treatment progresses, both children and parents often experience a variety of unexpected emotions.

> We've really marveled as we watched Joseph go through the stages of coping with all of this just as an adult might. First of all, after he was diagnosed in April, he was terrified. Then for 3 months, he was alternately angry and depressed. When we talked to him seriously during that time about the need to work with the doctors and nurses against the cancer no matter how scary the things were that they asked him to do, he looked us right in the eye and screamed, "I'm on the cancer's side!" Over the course of a few weeks, he seemed to calm down and made the decision to fight it, to cooperate with all the caregivers as well as he possibly could and to live as normal a life as he could. It's hard to believe that someone could do that at 4 years old, but he did it. By his 5th birthday in late July, he'd made the transition to where he is now: hopeful and committed to "killing the cancer."

What to tell your child

Children need to be told that they have a tumor in their body and what that means, using words and concepts that are appropriate for their age and level of emotional development. The sooner they are comfortable with the word cancer, and with the name of their disease, the less mysterious it will seem and the more powerful they will feel as they deal with it. Very young children might be satisfied to hear, "A tumor is growing in your arm and it should not be there. We are going to the hospital so the

doctors can take it out." Older children may benefit from reading books alone or with a parent, reading information on reliable internet sites, or asking members of the treatment team questions to get the information that matters most to them.

It is important to share the name of the disease and an age-appropriate description of it with your child. Here are some other key concepts to talk about:

- No one knows what causes cancer, and it is not the child's fault she got sick.
- Some things about cancer are scary—for the child and the parents—and it is okay to feel afraid, confused, angry, or sad.
- It may be necessary to spend a lot of time in the hospital.
- There might be some unpleasant side effects, such as hair loss and nausea, but most of them are temporary.
- The parents, the child, and the healthcare team all have jobs to do to help the child get well, and everyone will work together to make that happen.
- Questions or worries are normal, and your child should feel free to ask a parent or someone on the healthcare team any questions she wants to ask.
- There are many things you as parents cannot control, but you will never lie to him and will always try to make sure there are no surprises.
- School-age children might not be able to go to school for a few months, but there are ways they can keep in touch with their classmates while they are out of school.
- Cancer is not contagious; friends and family cannot catch it, and your child did not catch it from anyone.
- Cancer is caused by cells that grow the wrong way, and it is no one's fault.

> My 4-year-old daughter told me very sadly one day, "I wish that I hadn't fallen down and broken inside. That's how the cancer started." We had explained many times that nothing she did, or we did, caused the tumor, but she persisted in thinking that falling down did it. She also worried that if she went to her friend Krista's house to play that Krista would catch cancer.

Older children and teens may have some knowledge of cancer, which might mean they will need a more detailed explanation of their cancer and how it is treated. They may also a lot of worries, fears, and misconceptions. Providing them with encouragement and reasons to feel optimistic and empowered is as important as making sure they have accurate information.

> My husband died after battling brain cancer for 2 years. My older son was in remission from osteosarcoma when my 16-year-old son was also diagnosed with osteosarcoma. It made telling my younger son about his cancer especially difficult

and complicated. I decided to have the orthopedic oncology surgeon tell him while I was in the room. The surgeon then took the time to build him up and give him the confidence to move forward by telling him that he "could see the fight in his eyes." My son held on to that for his entire treatment.

Children will have many questions throughout their treatment. Parents must assure their child that this is normal and that they will always answer the child's questions honestly. Gentle and honest communication is essential for the child to feel loved, supported, and encouraged.

Will was 13 when he was diagnosed with osteosarcoma. When we were called into the doctor's office to go over the MRI, Will and I were together and the doctor spoke to both of us at the same time. I was impressed that the doctor looked at both of us while speaking. I don't remember exactly how much he spoke directly to Will, but he did listen to both of us and answer the questions we had. He did not in any way ignore Will. The most important thing to Will was the truth. He wanted to know everything: the good, the bad, and the ugly. Not all of the information was given at one time, but was shared as questions came up. We never sugarcoated anything and we didn't try to stop Will from reading anything. I don't honestly know how much he read or researched on his own; I've never asked. Will and I were inseparable from the moment we got to the hospital, so it was only natural that we would hear things at the same time.

When your child asks a question, take a moment to be sure you heard and understood it correctly, and then formulate a thoughtful answer your child will understand. Parents are under tremendous stress and have many things on their minds. In this distracted state, it is easy to toss off a superficial answer or answer a question the child did not ask; but doing so can increase the child's confusion and undermine their trust in the parent as a source of information. Barbara Sourkes, PhD, explains the importance of understanding the child's question before responding:

Coping with the trauma of illness can be facilitated by a cognitive understanding of the disease and its treatment. For this reason, the presentation of accurate information in developmentally meaningful terms is crucial. A general guideline is to follow the child's lead: he or she questions facts or implications only when ready, and that readiness must be respected. It is the adult's responsibility to clarify the precise intent of any question and then to proceed with a step-by-step response, thereby granting the child options at each juncture. He or she may choose to continue listening, to ask for clarification, or to terminate the discussion. Offering less information with the explicit invitation to ask for more affords a safety gauge of control for the child. When these guidelines are not followed, serious miscommunications may ensue. For example, an adult who hears "What is going to happen to me?" and does not clarify the intent of the query may launch into a long statement of plans or elaborate

reassurances. The child may respond with irritation, "I only wanted to know what tests I am going to have tomorrow."

Telling the siblings

The diagnosis of cancer is traumatic for siblings. Family life is disrupted, their time with parents decreases, and the ill child receives a lot of attention. Older children and teens who understand the seriousness of a cancer diagnosis will be worried and fearful, but may hesitate to burden their parents with their concerns. Brothers and sisters need as much knowledge about what is going on as their sick sibling does. Information provided should be age-appropriate, and all questions should be answered honestly. Healthcare providers (physicians, physician assistants, nurse practitioners, child life specialists, and social workers) can help parents educate the siblings. Siblings can be extremely cooperative if they understand the changes that will occur in the family, and their role in helping the family cope. Maintaining open communication and respecting their feelings helps siblings feel loved and secure.

> *We always, always explained everything that was happening to Brian's older brother Zack (8 years old). He never asked questions, but always listened intently. He would say, "Okay. I understand. Everything's all right." We tried to get him to talk about it, but through all these years, he just never has. So we just kept explaining things at a level that he could understand, and he has done very well through the whole ordeal. The times that he seemed sad, we would take him out of school and let him stay at the Ronald McDonald House for a few days, and that seemed to help him.*

· · · · ·

> *We have tried to spend one-on-one time with each of the other kids. These are some other things that have been good for us:*
>
> - *The kids have been going to the hospital with Ethan one at a time, and getting a sense that this is no picnic, what he is going through.*
>
> - *If one of us is out of town and Ethan is in the hospital, I have hired a babysitter to be with him in the evening and have done something special with the other kids for one of the nights. This works great if you live close enough to the hospital where your child is being treated.*
>
> - *My husband and I have each taken the older kids on the traditional summer trips. This has been hard on Ethan, but none of this is perfect.*
>
> - *My husband and I have each taken one school subject for the kids and have really spent time with them on it. I did reading with Tucker (I read everything he does and we talk about it), French with Abe, and Spanish with Jake. My husband has different topics, and we do something every day. We were too dysfunctional to be able to do more than one subject, so we decided to focus, and it has been a lot of fun for us.*

We talk about lots of things as a family and help the kids as needed, but these are "special" things. This has been a long year for us, but I think these things helped.

Even with good communication and support, parents may see siblings struggling with tough emotions that may lead to behavioral changes, such as regression, school problems, and trouble sleeping. Chapter 19, *Siblings*, explores sibling issues in detail and includes many suggestions from both parents and siblings who have gone through this experience.

Notifying the family

Notifying relatives is one of the first painful jobs for the parents of a child newly diagnosed with cancer. Depending on the family dynamic, the family may be a refuge or a source of additional stress.

I called my mother and asked her to tell everyone on my side of the family. My husband called his sister and asked her to tell everyone. We asked that they not call us for a few days because we needed a little time to feel less fragile and didn't want to cry in front of Christine too much.

Family members often react in surprising ways, with unexpected help coming from some people and a disappointing lack of support from others. Parents must be prepared for these unexpected responses and try not to take them personally. Usually, the other person is struggling to process this difficult news in his or her own way and may be trying to spare the parent from more stress by not asking too many questions.

My dad had always been my rock, but when I told him about my son's illness, he basically didn't say anything and he never came to the hospital. I was furious with him. It took me a long time to realize that he needed me to be strong for him, too. He was just devastated by the thought that his only grandchild might be taken from him and that there was nothing he could do to stop it.

Notifying friends and neighbors

The easiest way to notify friends and neighbors is to delegate one person to do the job. Calling only one neighbor or close friend prevents you from having numerous tearful conversations. Most parents are at their child's bedside and want to avoid more emotional upheaval, especially in front of their child. Parents need to recognize that friends' emotions will mirror their own: shock, fear, worry, helplessness. Because most friends want to help but don't know what to do or say, they will welcome any suggestions you can give about what might be helpful.

Tell a trusted friend exactly what information you want him or her to pass on and, most importantly, whether you would welcome visits, phone calls, or cards. The more clarity you can provide, the less stress you will experience and the better your friends can support you. If you want visitors, for example, let people know when visiting hours are and whether there are any restrictions set by the hospital (or by you or your child) about who can come and how long they can stay.

> There were many days I wanted to hide in bed and pull the covers over my head. I know everyone meant well and genuinely cared, but the constant stream of people through the house and phone ringing added to the stress we were already under. We already had a home care nurse coming 5 days a week, a physical therapist coming 3 days a week, in addition to constant phone calls to follow up on blood work and tests, appointments to schedule, and family members to keep track of. Bubba, our dog, loved all the commotion, but the rest of us tired quickly.

Not everyone you know will want or need the same level of detailed information. You may wish to encourage hospital or home visits from your closest friends, but ask others to wait for phone or email updates. However, think twice before leaving anyone off the notification list. Many parents report that individuals they barely knew ended up being some of their most helpful and supportive resources.

It can be helpful to choose a trusted friend or family member to provide information via email, text messages, or social media so that you are not exhausted with repeated phone calls and messages and can focus on your child. You may want to create a dedicated Facebook page that you and your "social director" control, where either of you can post updates and photos. This makes sharing information simple and quick. Consider making it a private page that can only be read and commented on by people you allow, giving you more control over your family's privacy. There are also dedicated online services such as *www.CaringBridge.com, www.CarePages.com, www.LotsaHelpingHands.com,* and *www.CareCalendar.com* that you can use to update friends, family, and supporters, and enlist help with meals, sibling child care, fundraisers, and other tasks. More information is available in Chapter 20, *Family and Friends*.

Notifying your child's school

You should notify the principal as soon as possible about your child's diagnosis. It is a good idea to do this in writing (either by email or letter), in part because it is a less emotional way to convey the news, but also because it helps ensure you pass along all the relevant information, including:

- The diagnosis and a brief description in non-technical language of what it means.

- A very brief outline of what is expected to happen next and the impact it will have on your child's ability to attend school.

- The address, email address, and phone number where you can be reached.

- A brief description of the educational resources available at the hospital or any other educational information you received from the hospital social worker or school liaison.

- How your child's teacher or classmates can reach your child in the hospital.

You can also express your hope that you, the school, and the hospital will work together to ensure that your child's education sustains as few interruptions as possible. You can ask the principal to share your letter with the teacher (or teachers) or you can send them separate emails or notes.

When notifying students at the school, the wishes of your child (especially if a teenager) about contacting the school and friends should be respected. If you and your child want to ask the teachers and students to stay in touch, inform them that he may sometimes feel too tired to answer right away. Personal visits may not be feasible or welcome, at least at first, but cards, letters, pictures, classroom videos, or other updates will make your child feel less isolated and will remind her that there are people who care for her outside of her family and the hospital staff. In some schools it may be possible to attend school virtually—when it is feasible and the technology is available. More information is available in Chapter 22, *School*.

As Joseph was getting cleaned up after biopsy surgery, we met the oncologist who had explained that our sweet, green-eyed 4-year-old had orbital rhabdomyosarcoma, and he gave us information about the tests that would need to be done in the days ahead. The next morning, Joseph and I woke up in the hospital room together for the very first time. We had been up a lot in the night getting him comfortable. With the early morning sun up, Joseph and I had some quiet time. I sat down on his bed next to him and told him in fairly simple words that the doctors had found out he had a sickness called cancer behind his eye. We would have to stay at the hospital for a few more days because cancer can travel around in your body and make you sick in other places, and we had to do different kinds of tests to make sure it hadn't gone anywhere else inside him. I promised that I would be right with him for everything— we would do it all together. I meant it fiercely, with every bone in my body. I would do everything I could to make sure he wasn't hurt or afraid and that he would get better. At that moment, my husband was home with our 7-year-old, telling him his little brother had cancer. Later I found out that Nate went to school that morning and cried with his teacher. I wish we had all been together to talk about it, but we did the best we could at the time.

Chapter 9

Choosing a Treatment

THE FIRST FEW weeks after diagnosis are utterly overwhelming. In the midst of confusion, fear, and fatigue, you might need to make an important and sometimes difficult decision: whether to choose the best-known treatment (standard treatment) or enroll your child in an experimental treatment (clinical trial). This chapter explains helpful things to know before deciding on a treatment for your child, including the difference between standard treatment and clinical trials. It also covers questions to ask about proposed treatments, informed consent, the pros and cons of selecting a clinical trial, and stories from parents about the decisions they made.

Treatment basics

To receive the best available treatment, it is essential that a child with a solid tumor be treated at a pediatric medical center by board-certified pediatric oncologists and pediatric surgeons with extensive experience treating the type of tumor the child has. For most children, treatment begins within days of diagnosis and requires aggressive supportive care. The goal of treatment is to achieve complete remission by killing all cancer cells as quickly as possible.

Treatment of childhood solid tumors includes one or more of the following:

- Surgery (see Chapter 14)
- Chemotherapy (see Chapter 15)
- Radiation therapy (see Chapter 17)
- Stem cell transplantation (see Chapter 18)

Standard treatment

The standard treatment (or standard of care) for each type and stage of tumor is the treatment that has worked best for the most children up to that point in time. The current standards of care are the result of decades of clinical research studies. As researchers analyze the results from ongoing or completed clinical trials, they accumulate knowledge and make changes in standard treatments. For example, in the first decade of the

21st century, most children with high-risk neuroblastoma received a standard treatment that included chemotherapy, surgery, radiation therapy, stem cell transplantation, and a 6-month course of 13-cis-retinoic acid. Carefully controlled clinical trials during that time demonstrated that the overall survival rate increased dramatically by adding courses of immunotherapy drugs at the end of treatment. As a result, the standard of care for children with high-risk neuroblastoma was changed.

To learn about the standard of care for your child's type and stage of tumor, contact the National Cancer Institute's (NCI) Physician Data Query (PDQ) by calling (800) 422-6237 (800-4-CANCER) or by going to the pediatric section of its website at *www.cancer. gov/cancertopics/pdq/pediatrictreatment*. PDQ provides information about pediatric solid tumors, state-of-the-art treatments, and ongoing clinical trials. Two versions are available online:

- One for families—uses simple language and contains no statistics; and

- One for professionals—is technical, thorough, and includes citations to scientific literature.

> *The study that our institution was participating in at the time of my daughter's diagnosis was attempting to lessen the treatment to reduce toxicity yet still cure the disease. My family began a massive research effort on the issue, and we had several family friends who were physicians discuss the case with the heads of pediatric oncology at their institutions. The consensus was that since my daughter was at the high end of the high-risk description, it was advisable to choose the standard treatment, which was more aggressive than one of the parts of the proposed clinical trial.*

If a cancer is very rare, extensive research may not have been done to determine a standard treatment. If your child is diagnosed with one of these tumors, the medical team will consult with other experts to create a treatment plan best suited to the type, stage, and location of your child's cancer.

The protocol

If your child receives the standard treatment, you will be given a written copy of the treatment plan, called a protocol. Just like a recipe for baking a cake, a protocol has a list of ingredients, the amounts to use, and the order to use them for the best chance for success. The protocol lists the treatments, drugs, dosages, and tests for each segment of treatment and for follow-up care.

The portion of the protocol devoted to the schedule for treatments and tests may be quite long. The family may also be given an abbreviated version (one to two pages) for quick reference on a daily basis. This abbreviated part of the protocol is frequently

called the "roadmap." Parents and teenage patients should review these documents carefully with the treatment team to be certain they understand them.

> *It took me a long time to get over my hang-up that things needed to go exactly as per protocol. Any deviations on dose or days were a major stress for me. It took talking to many parents, as well as doctors and nurses, to realize and feel comfortable with the fact that no one ever goes along perfectly and that the protocol is meant as the broad guideline. There will always be times when your child will be off drugs or on half dose because of illness or low counts or whatever. It took a long time to realize that this is not going to ruin the effectiveness, that the child gets what she can handle without causing undue harm.*

Clinical trials

If a clinical trial is open for your child's particular type and stage of tumor, within days of diagnosis you will be asked to consider enrolling your child in it. You then must choose between the standard treatment and the clinical trial.

Clinical trials are carefully controlled research experiments that use human volunteers to develop better ways to prevent or cure diseases. Pediatric clinical trials attempt to improve upon existing treatments. A clinical trial can involve a totally new approach that seems promising, or it may fine-tune existing treatments by reducing their toxicity or developing new ways to assess responses to treatments. Many children are needed in each clinical trial for the results to be statistically meaningful.

In some cases, such as when a young child has Wilms tumor with favorable histology, the standard treatment has a high likelihood of resulting in complete and lasting cure. For other types of tumors, the prognosis may be poor on the standard treatment, and parents may be more motivated to choose a clinical trial. Occasionally, parents choose to enroll their child in a clinical trial because they want to contribute to better treatments in the future. Other parents may be wary of participating in an experimental program and may opt for standard treatment. There is no right choice. Obtain all the information you can, weigh the pros and cons, and make a decision based on your values and comfort level.

Your treatment team may also tell you about studies that are sponsored by pharmaceutical companies, especially those designed to support patients through the effects of treatment. Such supportive care trials evaluate antibiotics, antinausea drugs, and new agents to raise blood counts, minimize pain, or control other symptoms. The oversight and control of these trials is entirely different than the oncology treatment studies discussed in this chapter. Ask your doctor or nurse to discuss these studies with you if your child is invited to participate in one.

You also may be asked for permission to allow biological studies of your child's tumor. These studies involve performing specific tests on pieces of your child's tumor to help develop better treatments. The pediatric surgeon or pediatric oncologist may ask your permission to send any tumor left over after diagnosis to a tumor bank for research. Because solid tumors can have subtle differences (called subtypes), biological studies help researchers better identify and understand the subtypes. Scientists are also using banked tumor cells to test responses to new medications and immunotherapy.

Types of clinical trials

The three main types of clinical trials for children with solid tumors are described below.

- **Phase I.** Drug studies begin in laboratories, where the drugs are evaluated using chemical or biological models, tissue samples, and other methods to see whether there is a chance the drug might be effective at treating disease. If laboratory evidence suggests a drug may work in humans, it is first tested in a Phase I study. These studies examine how the body processes (metabolizes) the drug, establish the highest dose that can safely be given to a patient (the maximum tolerated dose, or MTD), and evaluate the side effects.

  In pediatric Phase I trials, the dose of a new drug is gradually increased in small groups of children until it becomes too toxic; essentially, one small group of children gets a low dose, the next small group gets a slightly higher dose, and so on, until an unacceptable number of children experience unacceptable side effects.

  Phase I studies are experiments, and their purpose is not to cure the participants. The true beneficiaries of Phase I studies are future patients. In most cases, parents are not asked to enroll their child in a Phase I study unless all other treatment options have failed. Parents often enroll their children in these trials in the hope that a new and untried drug will be effective against their child's disease, but they need to recognize that the chances of achieving remission are low. Because they require careful monitoring, Phase I studies are only conducted in a select few hospitals.

- **Phase II.** Phase II trials refine the safety parameters and evaluate new drugs' effects on specific tumors. This is the stage at which many drugs fail—meaning they are not as effective as originally predicted or they have unexpected or serious side effects. Occasionally, Phase II trials are designed to test an exceptionally promising agent against a tumor for which no effective therapies exist.

- **Phase III trials.** These clinical trials determine whether a new treatment is better than the standard therapy. Some Phase III trials are designed solely to improve survival; others are done to try to maintain survival rates while lowering the toxicity of treatment. In pediatric Phase III studies, some children will receive the standard therapy,

while others receive a modified version. Modifications include higher or lower doses of medication or radiation, different combinations of drugs, or different types of surgery. Some children will derive direct benefit if a new treatment is superior to the standard therapy. Other children will receive the same therapy they would have received if not enrolled on the study (the standard arm). To ensure the results are accurate, Phase III studies require thousands of participants and take several years to complete.

The National Cancer Institute (NCI) offers several resources to help parents understand the clinical trial process. You can call the NCI at (800) 422-6237 or visit its clinical trials website at *www.cancer.gov/clinical_trials*.

The information in the rest of this chapter pertains to Phase III trials that are reviewed and funded by the NCI. Enrolling in Phase I and Phase II trials is very different, as is enrolling in trials sponsored by pharmaceutical companies.

Design of clinical trials

In 2000, four pediatric cancer research groups merged to form a single pediatric cancer research organization called the Children's Oncology Group (COG), which is supported by NCI. Approximately 200 institutions that treat children with cancer are members of COG (*www.childrensoncologygroup.org*). Researchers from these institutions contribute to the design of new clinical trials for children with cancer. In addition, the NCI and some large children's hospitals design their own clinical trials for children. When designing pediatric clinical trials, the first priority is to protect the children from harm. Researchers are ethically bound to offer treatments they think will be at least as safe and effective as the standard of care.

Study arms

Phase III clinical trials sort participants into different groups (called arms) that receive different treatments. Every Phase III trial has one arm that is the current standard of care, called the standard arm. Each of the other arms contains one or more experimental components, such as the following:

- New drugs

- Old drugs used in a new way (e.g., different dose or new combinations of old drugs)

- Duration of treatment that is shorter or longer than standard care

- The addition, deletion, or change in dose of certain treatments (e.g., radiation therapy or surgery)

- The use of new supportive care interventions (e.g., preventative antibiotics or new drugs to control nausea)

Once the trial is complete, the effectiveness of each experimental arm is compared to the standard arm.

> *Sean missed the deadline for enrolling in a clinical trial when he was diagnosed. However, when his tumor regrew we did enroll him on a trial. The particular trial he was in was a randomized computer trial that decided if he was getting one or two chemotherapy agents. We felt if we enrolled him in the trial, maybe the results would help other children.*

Randomization

Phase III trials require a process called randomization, meaning that after parents agree to enroll their child in a clinical trial, a computer randomly assigns the child to one arm of the study. The parents will not know which treatment their child will receive until the computer assigns one. The purpose of computer assignment is to ensure that children are evenly assigned to each arm without bias from physicians or families. One group of children (the control group) always receives the standard treatment to provide a basis for comparison to the experimental arms. At the time the clinical trial is designed, there is no conclusive evidence to indicate which arm will be superior. As a result, it is impossible to predict whether your child will benefit from participating in the study.

> *We had a hard time deciding whether to go with the standard treatment or to participate in the study. The "B" arm of the study seemed, on intuition, to be too harsh for her because she was so weak at the time. We finally did opt for the study, hoping we wouldn't be randomized to "B." We chose the study basically so that the computer could choose and we wouldn't ever have to think "we should have gone with the study." As it turned out, we were randomized to the standard arm, so we got what we wanted while still participating in the study.*

Researchers closely monitor each ongoing clinical trial and modify it if one arm is identified as superior during the course of the trial or if an arm has unacceptable side effects.

Supervision of clinical trials

The ethical and legal codes governing medical practice also apply to clinical trials. In addition, most research is federally funded or regulated and has rules that protect patients. For example, all COG trials are federally funded and have review boards that meet at prearranged dates for the duration of each trial to ensure the risks of the trial are acceptable relative to the benefits.

The treating institution is required to report all adverse side effects to COG, which reports them to the U.S. Food and Drug Administration. If concerns are raised, the

study may be put on hold while an independent Data Safety and Monitoring Board and the study committee review the situation. If one arm of the trial is causing unacceptable side effects, that arm is stopped, and the children enrolled are given the better treatment.

All institutions that conduct clinical trials also have an Institutional Review Board (IRB) that reviews and approves all research taking place there. The purpose of the IRB—made up of scientists, doctors, nurses, and citizens from the community—is to protect patients. Funding agencies (e.g., National Cancer Institute) also review and approve trials before children are enrolled.

Questions to ask about clinical trials

To fully understand the clinical trial proposed for your child, here are some important questions to ask the oncologist:

• What is the purpose of the study?

• Who is sponsoring the study? Who reviews it? How often is it reviewed? Who monitors patient safety?

• What tests and treatments will be done during the study? How do these differ from standard treatment?

• What are the possible benefits?

• What are all possible disadvantages?

• What are the possible side effects or risks of the study? What are the side effects of the study compared to those of standard treatment?

• How will the study affect my child's daily life?

• What are the possible long-term impacts of the study compared with the standard treatment?

• How long will the study last? Is this shorter or longer than standard treatment?

• Will the study require more hospitalizations than standard treatment?

• Does the study include long-term follow-up care?

• Will you compare the study versus standard treatment in terms of possible outcomes, side effects, time involved, costs, and quality of life?

• Will our insurance cover the costs of the clinical trial?

After discussing the clinical trial with the oncologist, you will need a copy of the information to review later. Many parents record the coversation or bring a friend to take notes; others write down all the doctor's answers for later reference.

A clinical trial involving very high-dose chemotherapy followed by stem cell transplant was proposed for our 2-year-old daughter. We asked numerous questions, and I wrote down all the answers in my notebook. The two primary questions were: How many kids die during and after this treatment? Are her chances of long-term survival worth the pain we were going to put her through? We struggled with the concept of hurting her if it wasn't going to do any good. We also asked about the specific drugs, their side effects, and what to expect from each treatment. It was a very difficult process and decision.

Things to consider about clinical trials

Deciding whether to enroll your child in a clinical trial is often difficult. The following lists describe why some families choose to enroll and why others choose not to enroll. These lists may help clarify your feelings about this important decision.

Why some families choose to enroll:

- Children receive either state-of-the-art investigational therapy or the best standard therapy available.

- Clinical trials can provide an opportunity to benefit from a new therapy before it is widely available.

- Children enrolled in clinical trials may be monitored more frequently throughout treatment.

- Review boards of scientists oversee clinical trials.

- Participating in a clinical trial often makes parents feel they did everything medically possible for their child.

- Information gained from clinical trials will benefit children with cancer in the future.

Reasons why families choose not to enroll:

- The experimental arm may not provide treatment that is as effective as the standard, or it may cause additional side effects or risks.

- Some families do not like the feeling of not having control over choosing the child's treatment.

- Some clinical trials require more hospitalizations, treatments, clinic visits, or tests that may be more painful than the standard treatment.

- Some families feel additional stress about which arm is the best treatment for their child.

- Insurance may not cover investigational studies. Parents need to carefully explore this issue prior to signing the consent form.

Informed consent process

Before a child is enrolled in a clinical trial, the parents need to sign an informed consent form. True informed consent is a process, not merely an explanation and signing of documents. Informed consent requires that:

• All treatments available to the child have been explained—not just the treatment available at your hospital or through your doctor, but all the treatments that could be beneficial, wherever they are given.

• The parents and, to the extent possible, the child, have discussed these options and chosent the treatment they want.

• The option selected is thoroughly discussed, with all its benefits and risks clearly explained.

• Aspects of the study that are considered experimental and those that are standard are clearly described.

An informed medical decision is one that weighs the relative merits of a therapy after full disclosure of benefits, risks, and alternatives. During the discussions between the doctor(s) and family, all questions should be answered in language that is clearly understood by the parents and child or teen, and there should be no pressure on parents to enroll their child in a study. The objective of the informed consent process is that all family members are comfortable with their choice and can comply with it. Studies show that the more questions parents ask during the informed consent process, the better they understand what they are agreeing to.

> We had many discussions with the staff prior to signing the informed consent to participate in the clinical trial. We asked innumerable questions, all of which were answered in a frank and honest manner. We felt that participating gave our child the best chance for a cure, and we felt good about increasing the knowledge that would help other children later.

Informed consent is a process that occurs over several meetings. During the meetings, the pediatric oncologist provides information and the parents ask questions (and get answers). However, the informed consent process does not always work as it should for a variety of reasons, including the parents' state of mind, the communication style of the doctor, and the system in place to discuss treatment options. Usually, this situation is the result of miscommunication arising from some combination of the following:

• No formal meeting times were established in advance to discuss treatment options, so parents did not understand the importance of the discussion they were having with the doctor and the treatment team.

• Parents, who are tired, confused, and mentally numb, appear to understand things they are barely hearing.

- The doctor does not recognize that the parents are not following what he is saying and that they need more guidance and time to absorb the choices.

- The doctor is unconsciously promoting the choice she believes is the best one and she interprets the lack of questions as agreement.

- There is no one in the room except the doctor and the parents; therefore, there is no one to help with communication.

It is a good idea to ask the treatment team immediately after diagnosis when and how the treatment decision will be made and to ask for specific meeting dates and times to discuss treatment, even if it means a slight delay before starting treatment. Parents may want to invite a trusted friend or their child's pediatrician to attend this meeting to ensure they understand their options.

> When my son was diagnosed, we were told we had two options: a clinical trial or standard treatment. We decided to get a second opinion before making our decision. Our pediatrician, my husband, and I met in the pediatrician's office for a telephone conference with a pediatric oncologist from a major treatment center. We each presented our concerns. Our pediatrician thought of some issues neither my husband nor I had considered. I think we all came away better informed of our options.

Some families seek a second opinion to help sort out their options. It is most useful to get a second opinion from a center that treats significant numbers of patients with your child's diagnosis. Most pediatric oncologists are willing to arrange the second opinion for you.

Studies have shown that when treatment team members who are not doctors are present during the informed consent meetings, parents have a better understanding of their choices. You may want to ask for a nurse or a social worker to be present during the meetings.

> Two days after my child was diagnosed, the oncologist told me it was time to begin treatment. I do remember him talking a lot, but I swear it actually sounded like "Wah, wah, wah, protocol, wah, wah, wah, very successful, wah, wah, wah, sign here." And I did. It was several days before it sank in that I had authorized an experimental treatment protocol and not the standard of care. The irony is that I worked in clinical research. I knew how this was supposed to go. But I was alone and tired and frightened and went along like a sheep. Did he railroad me? Maybe; but I don't think he meant to and in the end it was my responsibility to hold it together and ask what needed to be asked. But it just wasn't in me at the time. Later, I told the doctor this and he was astonished to learn that I hadn't heard a word he said.

Assent

Assent means that children and adolescents are involved in decisions about their treatment. Children younger than age 18 do not have the legal right to refuse standard treatment for their cancer. They do, however, have the right to accept or reject experimental treatments. All clinical trials are considered to be experimental treatments. Regardless of whether children will receive the standard treatment or an experimental treatment, they have the right to have the disease, treatment, and procedures explained to them at an age-appropriate level.

Doctors and parents are required to allow children to make their wishes known about their treatment. According to the American Academy of Pediatrics (AAP), assent means that the child:

• Is aware of the nature of his or her disease.

• Understands what to expect from tests and treatments.

• Has had his or her understanding assessed.

• Has had an opportunity to accept or reject the proposed treatment.

Parents can read or download a copy of the AAP policy statement ("Informed Consent, Parental Permission, and Assent in Pediatric Practice") from the APP website. In part, the policy states, "In situations in which the patient will have to receive medical care despite his or her objection, the patient should be told that fact and should not be deceived." This policy applies to standard treatment.

Clinical trials, however, are research, and Internal Review Boards (IRBs) decide whether the child's assent is necessary. If parents and the child or teen disagree about treatment, discussions are usually held with a mediator (for example, a social worker or pediatric psychologist) to try to reach an agreement. If parents and their child or teen still disagree, an advocate for the child is appointed and a decision about treatment is made by the hospital ethics committee.

In short, parents can legally make decisions about standard care, but both parents and children have decision-making rights about whether or not to participate in clinical trials.

Making a decision

As soon as possible after diagnosis, parents sit down with the medical team to discuss treatment options. If your child is being treated at a COG hospital, the first discussion is usually about standard treatment and a clinical trial (if a trial is open and your child qualifies). Parents are often very conflicted about choosing a treatment.

Paige (age 4) took part in a clinical trial to treat her stage IV neuroblastoma. Her oncologist was the principal investigator, and he presented it to us as the best treatment plan for her. I have a stepsister who is a pediatric oncology nurse/researcher, and we discussed the treatment plan with her. Once all our questions were answered to our satisfaction, we decided to agree to the clinical trial.

The choice to opt for standard treatment or a clinical trial is a strictly personal one, but parents should only make it after they are certain they understand the implications of each path. The doctor is legally and ethically bound to inform parents of the full range of appropriate treatment options available to their child, and to help them understand what each option entails before asking them for written consent to begin a particular treatment plan. The doctor may recommend the treatment option that he believes to be best for the child, but he may not coerce or deceive the parents into approving a treatment. Once the parents have consented to standard treatment or a clinical trial, the doctor must abide by their decision.

Saying no to a clinical trial

Parents, children, and teens have the legal right to decide whether or not to participate in a clinical trial. If the family chooses for the child not to participate in the proposed clinical trial, or if their insurance refuses to pay for the treatments given in the clinical trial, the child or teen is given the best-known treatment (standard treatment) for his type of tumor.

We just were not comfortable with the concept of a clinical trial. It seemed like gambling to us. We also felt totally overwhelmed about making decisions on important subjects that we didn't understand. Even though we asked many, many questions, we just couldn't come to grips with the whole idea in the 2 days after our daughter was diagnosed. So, we declined the trial and had the best known treatment. We are happy with our decision.

Saying yes to a clinical trial

If you decide to enroll your child in a clinical trial, the form you sign will have language similar to the following: "The study described above has been explained to me, and I voluntarily agree to have my child participate in this study. I have had all of my questions answered, and understand that all future questions that I have about this research will be answered by the investigators listed above." It is a good idea to keep a copy of the signed form.

The entire clinical trial document

If your child is enrolled in a clinical trial, the roadmap described earlier is actually a very small portion of a lengthy document describing all aspects of the study. The entire document usually exceeds 100 pages and covers the following topics: study hypothesis, experimental design, scientific background and rationale with relevant references from the scientific literature, patient eligibility and randomization, therapy for each arm of the study, required observations, pathology guidelines, radiation therapy guidelines (if applicable), supportive care guidelines, specific information about each drug, relapse therapy guidelines, statistical considerations, study committee members, record-keeping requirements, reporting of adverse drug reactions, and a consent form.

The full protocol is intended for use by specialists in oncology. It is highly technical and may be confusing or overwhelming for some parents.

However, some parents are medical professionals or people who want to better understand their child's illness and treatment. These parents may want to have a copy of the full study document for several reasons. First, it provides a description of some previous clinical trials and explains the reasons the investigators designed this particular study. Second, it provides detailed descriptions of drug reactions, which may comfort parents who worry that their child is the only one exhibiting extreme responses to some drugs. Third, motivated parents who have only one protocol to keep track of occasionally prevent errors in treatment. Finally, for parents who are adrift in the world of cancer treatment, it can give them a bit of control over their child's life.

> Since knowledge is comfort for me, I really wanted to have the entire clinical trial document, despite its technical language. Whereas the brief protocol that I had listed day, drug, and dose, the expanded version listed the potential side effects for each drug, and what actions should be taken should any occur. I needed all of that information.

Other parents may find that reading hundreds of pages of technical information is overwhelming or not helpful. As with almost every topic discussed in this book, families need to make choices based on what works best for their unique situation.

If your child is enrolled in a clincial trial and you would like a copy of the entire document, ask your child's oncologist for a copy. If the oncologist will not provide it, call COG (626-447-0064) and ask for a copy. Informed consent documents for COG trials specifically state that families will receive a copy of the full protocol upon request. After reading the document, it may be helpful to schedule an appointment with your child's oncologist, nurse practitioner, or research nurse to discuss any questions or concerns.

The full clinical trial document is not for general distribution, because it is unethical to use these protocols outside a controlled research setting. Parents who obtain a copy should not circulate it.

Removing your child from a clinical trial

Parents have the legal right to withdraw their child from a clinical trial at any time, for any reason. But before doing so, it's a good idea to discuss questions or concerns with your child's oncologist. The decision to withdraw from a trial should not be held against the parent, and the child will still receive the best available care for his type of cancer. On the consent form signed by the parent, there will be language similar to this: "You are free not to have your child participate in this research or to withdraw your child at any time without penalty or jeopardizing future care."

> Jesse was enrolled in a clinical trial to assess long-term consequences of radiation. The testing was free, and we were glad to participate. Unfortunately, the billing department of the hospital continually billed us in error. We tried to correct the problem, but it became such a hassle that we withdrew from the study.

Protocol changes

Many parents express anguish when their child's doses or schedules for chemotherapy change during treatment. It is very common for doses to be lowered or treatment to be delayed while a child recovers from low blood counts, infection, or toxic reactions to the treatment. In fact, almost every child has dose reductions or delays in treatment. The protocol is a guideline that will be modified, depending on your child's response to treatment.

> When we were struggling with the decision of whether to join the study, I asked the oncologist how would we ever know if we made the right decision. He said something very wise, "You will never know and you should never second guess yourself, no matter how the study turns out. Statistics are about large groups of kids, not your child. Your child might respond no matter which arm she is on or she might show no benefit from a treatment arm where most other kids do well. Statistics for you will be either 100 percent or 0 because your child will either live or die. I can't tell you which will be the better treatment—that is why we are conducting the study. But no matter what, we will be doing absolutely the best we can."

Chapter 10

Coping with Procedures

THE PURPOSE OF THIS chapter is to prepare children and parents for several common procedures by providing detailed descriptions of each. Because many procedures are repeated frequently during treatment for childhood cancer, it is important to establish a routine that is comfortable for you and your child. The procedure itself may cause discomfort, but a well-prepared, calm child fares far better than a frightened one.

Planning for procedures

Procedures are needed to make diagnoses, check for spread of disease, give treatments, and monitor responses to treatment. Some procedures are pain-free and easy to tolerate when the parents and child know what to expect. Other procedures can cause both physical and psychological distress, which can be amplified if the child or parents are taken by surprise.

The best way to prepare the child is for parents to prepare themselves, intellectually and emotionally, to provide the support and comfort their child needs during procedures. In most cases, although the procedure itself is non-negotiable, options are available to lessen the pain or stress. Parents need to know what these choices are to be effective advocates for their child.

A family-centered approach works best when planning and implementing procedures. Most children's hospitals have a child life program. These programs exist to minimize psychological trauma and maintain, as much as possible, normal living patterns for hospitalized children. The American Academy of Pediatrics considers child life programs the standard of care for hospitalized children. As soon as possible after admission, find out whether your hospital has a child life program or an equivalent support team.

> *Matthew was in sixth grade when he was diagnosed, and he was worried about the surgery for implanting the port. The child life specialist came in and really helped. She showed him what a port looked like; then they explored the pre-op area, the*

actual surgery room, and post-op. She showed him on a cloth doll exactly where the incision would be and how the scar would look. Then she introduced him to "Fred," the IV pump. She said that Fred would be going places with him, and that Fred would keep him from getting so many pokes. She told Matthew that he could bring something from home to hang on Fred. Of course, he brought in a really ugly stuffed animal. Throughout treatment, she really helped his fears and my feelings about losing control over my child's daily life.

Child life specialists or other team members may provide support before and during procedures. They establish relationships with children based on warmth, respect, and empathy. They also communicate with the other members of the treatment team about the psychosocial needs of children and their families.

One way to help child life specialists do their job is to communicate openly with them from the beginning. In particular, it is helpful to share insights about your child's temperament and history to help the specialist understand how to approach your child.

You can do quite a bit to prepare your child for procedures. Discuss with the child life professional or social worker when and how to prepare for upcoming procedures. Although it may not always be possible, try to schedule procedures so the same person does the same procedure each time. Call ahead to check for unexpected changes to prevent any surprises for your child. Repetition can provide comfort and reassurance to children. Ritual can also be important. A child may prefer a precise sequence of steps or the use of certain cue words to signal the start of a procedure. If staff members know the child and comply with her wishes, the child is usually calmer and more cooperative.

I started giving my 4-year-old daughter 2 days' notice before procedures. But she began to wake up every day worried that "something bad was going to happen soon." So we talked it over and decided to look at the calendar together every Sunday to review what would happen that week. She was a much happier child after that.

Parents should have a choice whether or not to be present during a medical procedure. If your child does better when you are not in the room, ask the child life specialist or another member of the treatment team to be present solely to comfort your child. Teens often want to handle the procedure on their own and it is normally best to respect their wishes.

During procedures, a parent's role is to be supportive and loving. In most cases, the best place to position yourself is at your child's head, at eye level. Speak calmly and positively to your child. You can tell stories, sing songs, or read a favorite book. It helps to praise your child for good behavior, but don't reprimand or demean your child if problems occur.

We decided from the very beginning that, even though it's no fun to have procedures, we were going to make something positive out of it. So we made it a party. We'd bring pizza, popcorn, or ice cream to the hospital. We helped Kristin think of the nurses as her friends. We'd celebrate after a procedure by going out to eat at one of the neat little restaurants near the hospital.

Giving children some control over what happens helps tremendously, but only give choices when they truly exist.

Oncology clinics usually have a special box full of toys or a selection of rewards for children who have had a procedure. It sometimes helps for the child to have a treat to look forward to afterward. Some parents bring a special gift to sneak into the box for their child to find.

Pain management

The goal of pediatric pain management should be to minimize discomfort while performing the procedure. The two methods used to achieve this goal are psychological (using the mind) and pharmacological (using drugs). These two methods can be used together to provide an integrated mind/body approach.

Psychological methods

It is essential to prepare for every procedure, because unexpected stress is more difficult to cope with than anticipated stress. If parents and children understand what is going to happen, where it will happen, who will be there, and what it will feel like, they will be less anxious and better able to cope. Here are some ways to prepare your child:

- Verbally explain each step in the procedure

- Meet the person who will perform the procedure, if possible

- Tour the room where the procedure will take place

- Let small children use dolls to play-act the procedure

- Let older children observe a demonstration on a doll

- Let adolescents watch a video that demonstrates the procedure

- Encourage discussion and answer all questions

For my daughter, playing about procedures helped release many feelings. Parents can buy medical kits at the store or simply stock their own from clinic castoffs and the pharmacy. We had IV bottles made from empty shampoo containers, complete with tubing and plastic needles. Katy's younger sister even ran around sometimes with her own pretend port taped onto her chest.

My daughter (3 years old) took an old stuffed animal to the clinic with her. Having the nurse and doctor perform the procedure first on "bear" helped her immensely.

Children and teens can learn mindfulness-based stress reduction techniques, using thoughtful awareness to help manage anxiety. A psychologist or other specialist who is experienced in mindfulness meditation can teach specific techniques that help children cope with difficult situations. This can be very helpful for your child during and after their cancer treatment. You can ask the psychologist at your treatment center to provide a referral to an experienced practitioner (e.g., psychologist or counselor who has training in mindfulness work), preferably one who is covered by your medical insurance.

Guided imagery is another technique children can learn to help manage pain. It is an active process that helps children feel as if they are actually entering the imagined place. Focusing on pleasant images allows the child to shift attention from the pain. Ask if the hospital has someone to teach your child this very effective technique.

A 17-year-old wrote the following description of using imagery during procedures. It is reprinted with permission from the *Free to Be Yourself* newsletter of Cancer Services of Allen County, Indiana.

My Special Place

Many people had a special place when they were young—a special place that they still remember. This place could be an area that has a special meaning for them, or a place where they used to go when they wanted to be alone. My special place location is over the rainbow.

I discovered this place when I was 12 years old, during a relaxation session. These sessions were designed to reduce pain and stress brought on by chemotherapy. This was a place that I could visualize in my mind so that I could go there any time that I wanted to—not only for pain, but when I was happy, mad, or sad.

It is surrounded by sand and tall, fanning palm trees. The blue sky is always clear, and the bright sun shines every day. It is usually quiet because I am alone, but often I can hear the sounds of birds flying by.

Every time I come to this place, I like to lie down in the sand. As I lie there, I can feel the gritty sand beneath me. Once in a while I get up and go looking for seashells. I usually find some different shapes and sizes. The ones I like the best are the ones that you can hear the sound of the ocean in. After a while I get up and start to walk around. As I walk, I can feel the breeze going right through me, and I can smell the salt water. It reminds me of being at a beach in Florida. Whenever I start to feel sad or alone or if I am in pain, I usually go jump in the water because it is a soothing

place for me. I like to float around in the water because it gives me a refreshing feeling that nobody can hurt me here. I could stay in this place all day because I do not worry about anything while I am here.

To me this place is like a home away from home. It is like heaven because you can do anything you want to do here. Even though this place may seem imaginary or like a fantasy world to some people, it is not to me. I think it is real because it is a place where I can go and be myself.

Distraction can be used successfully with all age groups, but it should never be used as a substitute for preparation. Babies can be distracted by colorful, moving objects. Parents can help distract preschoolers by showing them picture books or videos, telling stories, singing songs, or blowing bubbles. Many youngsters are comforted and distracted from pain by hugging a favorite stuffed animal. School-aged children can watch videos or TV, or listen to music. Some institutions use interactive video games on tablets to help distract older children or teens.

Relaxation, biofeedback, massage, acupuncture, Reiki (Japanese energy healing), and accupressure are all also used successfully to manage pain. Ask the hospital's child life specialist, psychologist, or nurse to discuss and practice different methods of pain management with you and your child.

Pharmacological methods

Most pediatric oncology clinics sedate or anesthetize children for procedures that are painful or that require them to lie completely still. If your clinic does not offer this option, strongly advocate for it. Sedation and anesthesia have the advantage of calming children, reducing pain, and, in many cases, removing all memory of the procedure.

Three types of drugs are used for pain management during procedures:

- **Sedatives,** which depress the central nervous system and result in relaxation. The child or teen may fall asleep, but will remain conscious.

- **General anesthetics,** which induce a loss of consciousness to prevent the child or teen from experiencing pain or remembering a procedure.

- **Local anesthetics,** which temporarily interrupt nerve transmission at a specific site on the body to lessen pain.

Sedatives and general anesthetics

Sedatives and general anesthetics are given intravenously in the operating room (OR) or in a preoperating area or clinic sedation room. Certain drugs must be administered

by an anesthesiologist (a doctor specializing in anesthesia) in a hospital setting. Drugs commonly used during procedures include:

- **Valium® (diazepam) or Versed® (midazolam), plus morphine or fentanyl.** Valium® and Versed® are sedatives that are used with pain relievers such as morphine or fentanyl. These drugs can be given in the clinic, but the possibility of slowed breathing requires expert monitoring and the availability of emergency equipment. The combination of a sedative and a pain reliever will result in your child being awake but sedated. Your child may move or cry, but he will not remember the procedure. Often, EMLA® or lidocaine are also used to ensure the procedure is pain-free.

> My son was treated from ages 14 to 17. During his spinal taps he would get Versed® once he was positioned on the table. I would always sit at his head and keep his shoulders forward while his head rested on my arm. (Kind of a hug.) As the Versed® took effect, he would look up at me with huge eyes and give me a grin a mile wide, then he would say something off the wall. He had to spend an hour flat after the spinal tap. He'd be groggy the whole time, constantly asking me what time it was and how soon we could leave. He'd forget he asked and ask me again 5 minutes later. This continued for the whole hour. Later, we'd laugh about it. He never remembered anything from the spinal taps.

- **Propofol.** Propofol is a general anesthetic that will cause your child to lose consciousness. It must be administered in a hospital by an anesthesiologist. It is given intravenously and has the benefit of acting almost immediately with little recovery time. At low doses, propofol prevents memory of the procedure but may not relieve all the pain, so it is often used with EMLA® or lidocaine.

> Patrick (12 years old) hates the lack of control involved when having a procedure and getting propofol. He attempts to regain some control by verbally explaining to the doctors just exactly how he wants it done each time. He has his own little routine—tells them jokes, sings "I Want to Be Sedated" (you know, the Ramones song), etc. Patrick's biggest problem is the taste from the propofol. We have tried so many different things when he wakes up to mask the taste—Skittles®, gum, Gatorade®. We now have a supply of Atomic Fireballs®. I give him one as soon as they bring him out, and he says that really helps cover the taste.

· · · · ·

> Let's face it, kids don't care about lab work or protocols, they just want to know if they are going to be hurt again. I think that one of our most important jobs is to advocate, strongly if necessary, for adequate pain control. If the dose doesn't work and the doctor just shrugs her shoulders, say you want a different dosage or drug used. If you encounter resistance, ask that an anesthesiologist be consulted. Remember that good pain control and/or amnesia will make a big difference in your child's state of mind during and after treatment.

Emotions may run high after a difficult procedure. Instead of immediately having a discussion about what went wrong, schedule an appointment with the doctor well in advance of the next scheduled procedure to explain your concerns and problem-solve.

Because treatment for solid tumors may take months or years, some children build up a tolerance for sedatives and pain relievers. Over time, doses may need to be increased or drugs may need to be changed. If your child remembers the procedure, advocate for a change in the drugs or dosage. It is reasonable to request the services of an anesthesiologist to ensure the best outcome for your child.

A new anesthesiologist suggested nitrous oxide before general anesthesia for my young daughter's MRIs. Life around MRIs has never been the same. She is actually excited about scans now as if it is some kind of holiday! The first time with laughing gas she started to go "Wheeeee!!!!" I asked her if she was feeling like she was on a roller coaster, and she said, "No, I feel like I'm on the TILT-A-WHIRL!" The next day she said, "Mommy, I don't want to go to school today, I want to have ANOTHER SCAN!" I can't say I share her anticipation of a scan, but I am thankful for a good attitude and experience.

Your child will not be allowed to eat or drink for several hours before procedures that require sedation or anesthesia. After a procedure, your child may eat or drink when she is alert and able to swallow.

Local anesthetics

There are several types of local anesthetics used to prevent discomfort or pain during procedures.

- **EMLA®.** This anesthetic cream, which contains lidocaine and prilocaine, is put on the skin 1 to 2 hours before a painful procedure. It is held in place on the skin by an adhesive patch or sticky cling wrap.

- **Synera®.** This anesthetic patch contains lidocaine and tetracaine and is placed on the skin 20 to 30 minutes before a needle poke or other painful procedure for children age 3 or older.

- **Ethyl chloride spray.** This anesthetic spray can be used immediately before a procedure to anesthetize the surface of the skin.

For more information about these local anesthetics, see the section called "Topical anesthetics to prevent pain" in Chapter 15, *Chemotherapy*.

Danica was age 5 at diagnosis and she learned quickly how to be comfortable with getting her port accessed. She would pop into the chair, pull up her shirt, and be ready to go. The first time her port was accessed, it was still bruised from the

insertion of the port, and they didn't tell me to put the EMLA® patch on it an hour before. That really hurt. After we learned about EMLA®, she did fine and would even remind me to put it on her.

There is also a non-drug option called Buzzy® that parents can purchase without a prescription. It is popular for children who either don't like or have an allergy to topical anesthetics. Buzzy® uses cold and vibration to block the pain of needle pokes. Parents can carry the cute bee-shaped plastic Buzzy® with them and use it for 30 to 60 seconds to numb the area before a shot, blood draw, or port access is done.

Working with the team

There are many types of drugs and several methods used to administer them. Sometimes 10 minutes of mild sedation is all your child needs; for other procedures, the best option might be full general anesthesia in the operating room. Talk to your oncologist and anesthesiologist about the options and note that it may take some experimentation to determine which techniques and medications work best for your child.

Some treatment centers have a rotating team of anesthesiologists, so you may be working with several different doctors who provide anesthesia or sedation to your child. You can request that the anesthesiologist assigned to your child be experienced in dealing with children and able to communicate well with them.

Holden at age 2 had to be under anesthesia for radiotherapy every day. It was hard because the anesthesiologists didn't always have a good bedside manner, and we got a different one pretty much every time over 28 treatments. They had a new computer system and they were always having trouble finding the notes from the last sedation. Some of them wouldn't listen to me about what would work best for him, so it often took longer than it should. When he was stressed he screamed, and I had a lot of anxiety.

• • • • •

Joseph (age 5) had a good experience with the anesthesiologists who came to sedate him before each of his 6 weeks of daily radiation treatments. They were kind and gentle, and explained each step of what would happen. They kept good records so once we figured out the medications and dosages that would allow him to go down and come back up quickly and cheerfully, they made sure to do that each day. It could have been a scary experience, but they smiled at him, encouraged him, and told him he was a champ. He was always happy to see them even when he felt pretty crummy.

Procedures

Knowing what to expect will lay the foundation for months or years of tolerable tests. Because hospitals and practitioners have their own guidelines and preferences, the descriptions of procedures in the rest of this chapter may not exactly mirror your experience, but the fundamentals are the same everywhere. Reading the rest of this chapter may lessen your fears and help you to calm and prepare your child.

Questions to ask before procedures

You need information prior to procedures to prepare yourself and your child. Consider asking your doctor these questions:

- Why is this procedure necessary and how will it affect my child's treatment?
- What information will the procedure provide?
- Who will perform the procedure?
- Will it be an inpatient or outpatient procedure?
- Would you explain the procedure in detail?
- Is there any literature available that describes it?
- Is there a child life specialist on staff who will help prepare my child for the procedure? If not, are there nurses, social workers, or parents who can talk to me about how to prepare my child?
- Is the procedure painful?
- How long will it take?
- What type of anesthetic or sedation is used?
- What are the risks, if any?
- What are the possible side effects?
- When will we get the results?

Accessing catheters

The procedure that occurs most often during treatment is accessing your child's central venous catheter. This procedure is described in detail in Chapter 13, *Venous Catheters*.

> *My daughter had a terrible time having her port accessed. She would scream and cry (probably terrifying the other kids waiting outside the room for their turn!) and I became an expert at holding her down. I'd lie down next to her, holding down her*

hands, pressing my knee on her legs to keep her from kicking, and with my head on her forehead. It was horrible. I don't think it was particularly painful, just a terrible invasion for her, and she knew she'd feel badly after her treatment. We ended up meeting with the neuropsychologist on staff at the hem-onc office. The doctor was wonderful and warm, she talked to my daughter about why having her port accessed bothered her so much, and we talked about ways that she might cope. The doc made some good suggestions: listening to music, looking at a book, dreaming herself somewhere else. The neuropsychologist then accompanied her into the procedure room. My daughter was calm and completely still through the whole procedure, and never made a fuss again about having her port accessed. I'm very grateful.

Audiogram

Some of the chemotherapy drugs that children receive for treatment of solid tumors can cause hearing loss. In addition, some children with these tumors experience hearing loss as a result of injury to nerves caused by the tumor itself, or from surgery or radiation. Your child's doctor may order a hearing test, called an audiogram, to check for possible hearing problems.

> *They tested my 5-month-old daughter's hearing after the first two rounds of chemo and it was normal. After the third round, she had fluid in her ears so she couldn't be tested. So, they are going to test it again after her surgery when she is in the PICU [pediatric intensive care unit]. They said they can do a more thorough test when she is under anesthesia.*

During the audiogram, your child is tested in a soundproof room to prevent outside noises from interfering. You can remain with your child during this procedure. Earphones are placed on your child's ears, through which sounds (such as beeps and tones) are relayed. Your child will be asked to signal when he hears a sound by either raising his hand or pressing a button. Each ear is tested separately. The results of the audiogram are usually displayed in the form of a graph, and the amount of hearing loss is measured in decibels.

Audiograms are repeated throughout therapy to monitor your child's hearing if he is taking drugs that place him at risk.

> *Matthew experienced some high-frequency hearing loss from the cisplatin he received as part of his treatment for neuroblastoma. He had periodic audiograms performed at various stages of his treatment protocol. They were never a big deal for him, and in fact, he found them to be fun in many ways. The audiologist had a knack for making him feel comfortable. I think to Matthew, stepping into the soundproof booth and putting on his headset was somewhat like a game. The first few audiograms were done with me sitting in the booth beside him. Eventually, he reached a point where he*

felt he could do this test on his own, and so I would sit with the audiologist, watching him through the window. I think I might have messed the test up a few times with all those funny faces I was making at him. Fortunately for us, the audiologist had a sense of humor!

A different type of hearing test, called a brainstem auditory evoked response, is described later in this chapter.

Blood draws

Frequent blood samples are a part of life during treatment for a solid tumor. Blood samples are primarily used for three purposes: to obtain a complete blood count (CBC), to evaluate blood chemistries, or to culture the blood to check for infection. A CBC measures the types and numbers of cells in the blood. Blood chemistries measure substances in the blood plasma to determine whether the liver and kidneys are functioning properly. Blood cultures help evaluate whether a child is developing a bacterial or fungal infection. For a list of normal blood counts, see Appendix A, *Blood Tests and What They Mean*.

A finger poke provides enough blood for a CBC, but blood chemistries or cultures require one or more vials of blood. Children with catheters usually have blood drawn from the catheter rather than the arm or finger. If the child does not have a catheter, blood is usually drawn from the large vein on the inside of the elbow. The procedures for a blood draw are similar to those for placing an IV, which are described later in this chapter. The only difference is that with a blood draw, the needle is removed as soon as the blood is obtained.

Bone growth test

A bone growth test is an x-ray of your child's nondominant hand and wrist; for example, if your child is right-handed, the left hand and wrist will be x-rayed. It is performed to determine whether your child's growth is appropriate for her age. Your child's x-ray film will be compared with a series of photographs of wrist films of children of all ages so the radiologist can define your child's "bone age" compared to her chronological age. The results help determine the need for endocrine testing. This test takes only a few moments to perform and is not painful.

Bone marrow aspiration

Bone marrow aspirations or biopsies are done as part of the diagnostic workup for several types of solid tumors to see whether the tumor has spread to the bone. They are also done prior to stem cell transplantation.

During a bone marrow aspiration, bone marrow is extracted from bones with a needle. Bone marrow biopsies remove a small piece of bone marrow with a special biopsy needle. Without sedation, bone marrow aspirations are very painful, so almost all hospitals anesthetize children for this procedure. Do not hesitate to advocate for this at your treatment center.

Doctors usually take a sample of the marrow from the iliac crest of the hip (the top of the hip bone in back or front). This bone is right under the skin and contains a large amount of marrow. The child lies face down on a table, sometimes on a pillow to elevate the hip. The doctor puts on sterile gloves, finds the site, and then wipes it several times with an antiseptic to eliminate any germs. The nurse places sterile paper around the site, then an anesthetic (usually xylocaine) may be injected into the skin and a small area of bone. The doctor then pushes a hollow needle (with a plug inside) through the skin into the bone, withdraws the plug, and attaches a syringe. She then aspirates (sucks out) the liquid marrow through the syringe. Finally, she removes the needle and bandages the area.

> Melissa (age 5) has had several bone marrow aspirations since her diagnosis. We always use propofol (which I refer to as the "milk of human kindness," because of its milky appearance) before the procedure. After the aspiration is over, Melissa wakes up from a very deep sleep and has felt no pain whatsoever. She's usually hungry and ready to go ASAP. Propofol has worked exceptionally well for her.

Bone scan

A bone scan is a test performed in the nuclear medicine department to assess the status of a particular bone or the entire skeletal system. It is often used when the oncologist suspects there is cancer present in the bones—either in the form of a primary bone sarcoma or metastatic disease.

Your child will be given an injection of a radioactive material, called technetium, which will travel through the blood to the bones. Approximately 2 hours later, the scan will be performed. You should be allowed to stay with your child during this procedure.

> Mikey (age 4) had numerous full body bone scans that would pinpoint hot spots after injection of radioactive isotopes. He also had MRIs of his legs, as well as CT scans and x-rays, but the bone scans were the scary ones for me. I suppose it was because it would outline his whole skeleton, and I could see those glowing areas.

Brainstem auditory evoked response (BAER)

A brainstem auditory evoked response (BAER) test uses clicking sounds to evaluate a child's hearing when a standard audiogram is not possible, either because of a child's

age or inability to respond. During the test, clicking noises or tone bursts are delivered through earphones. Your child's brain waves are then measured by electrodes placed on the scalp and each earlobe. The test is not painful and takes about 30 minutes.

> BAER was very easy, quick, and painless. They attached leads to my daughter's head, very gently, and they didn't get tangled up in her hair or anything. Then they put earphones on, and the doctor told her she would hear a series of clicks in one ear, and a whooshing sound in the other, and to just sit still. So she did, and the little lines came out on the computer screen. The doctor duly recorded all the highest humps in the lines, and switched ears. Then they did the TV part, which I think is called VAER. She stared at a small American flag in the center of a TV screen. The rest of the screen is small black and white squares, and they move around as the child stares at the flag in the center. I would say the test took about 5 minutes of sitting and staring.

Computerized tomography (CT) scan

Computerized tomography (CT) is a complex, computer-enhanced procedure for obtaining x-ray images of the body. The machine looks like a big donut, and your child will be placed in the hole in the middle. Instead of having a fixed x-ray directed at one part of the body, the donut-shaped x-ray tube rotates around the body during the CT scan, generating hundreds of images as it moves. These images are called slices.

> Rachel, unfortunately, is very familiar with CT scans. From the beginning we've looked for ways to get her to lie still. The way we accomplished this was by me standing next to her and holding her hand. The parent must wear a shield in order to do this. The CT scanner at our hospital does not make that much noise, but they had a music player and I would always bring her favorite music and set it up right next to her during the whole thing. Also, they would let her have her blankie and baby with her. They were very accommodating.

Before the procedure begins, your child may need to receive a liquid dye, called a contrast agent, which is given intravenously. If your child requires a CT scan of the abdomen, oral contrast will also be given. The technologist will position your child so the area being imaged is inside the opening of the CT machine. The technologist will not stay in the room while the images are taken.

> When we first went in and Luke was going to get a CT scan, I was told he could just drink the contrast in a bottle. Um, that's great, but, he didn't take a bottle...ever. So, their solution was to insert an NG [nasogastric] tube and squirt the stuff directly into his tummy. I felt horrible. I felt like he was being punished because I breastfed him. The next time he had to have a CT, I worried about them having to pin him down and sticking the NG tube in him. I told the nurse that I really, really didn't

want that to happen and asked if there was any other way we could get the contrast in. She asked if he'd drink from a cup (nope, not yet) but I told her that he did take medicine from a syringe and I asked if I could use a syringe to squirt the contrast in him. That's what I did. It took me half an hour of filling and squirting nonstop but I was less stressed and Luke, while not too thrilled, took it anyway and it was okay.

If you plan to remain with your child, you will need to wear a lead apron to protect your body from unnecessary exposure to radiation. Sometimes, if the site being imaged is the chest area, your child may be asked to breathe in and hold her breath for several seconds. It is important that your child remain still during the CT scanning process. Small children who are unable to remain motionless for several minutes at a time are sedated before the procedure. You are usually asked to stay in the department until the images have been reviewed by the technologist to ensure they are adequate and do not need to be repeated.

My son handled CT scans like a little trooper. Even at the age of 3, he never needed sedation to help him remain perfectly still. He had so many of them, he was able to lip-sync along with the recording that was asking him to "breathe in and hold your breath." The only part he strongly disliked was having to drink the contrast material before the scan. We experimented with this until we found something that was palatable for him. We mixed the contrast with orange juice, which made it much easier for him to drink.

Conventional x-ray

X-rays, a type of electromagnetic radiation, provide the doctor with a quick and simple way to view organs and structures inside your child's body. X-rays are performed for many reasons during a child's treatment for a solid tumor. Some of the most common reasons for taking x-rays are because they are:

- Needed before operations.
- Needed after your child's central venous catheter is placed to confirm it is in the proper location.
- Used to determine whether your feverish child has pneumonia.

For chest x-rays, your child may be asked to breathe in, hold his breath, and remain perfectly still for a few seconds. The technologist leaves the room during the time the x-rays are taken. If you are planning to stay with your child, you need to wear a lead apron to protect you from radiation. Your child may also have to wear a lead apron or lead shield to protect specific areas of his body. Pregnant women should not be in the room when x-rays are taken.

Echocardiogram

Several drugs used to fight cancer can damage the muscle of the heart, decreasing its ability to contract effectively. Many protocols require a baseline echocardiogram to measure the heart's ability to pump before any chemotherapy drugs are given. Echocardiograms are then given periodically during and after treatment to check for heart muscle damage.

An echocardiogram uses ultrasound waves to measure the amount of blood that leaves the heart each time it contracts. The percentage of blood ejected during a contraction compared to blood in the heart when it is relaxed is called the ejection fraction.

The echocardiogram is performed by a technician, nurse, or doctor. The child or teen lies on a table and has conductive jelly applied to the chest. Then the technician puts a transducer (which emits the ultrasound waves) on the jelly and moves the device around on the chest to obtain different views of the heart. Pressure is applied on the transducer and can sometimes cause discomfort. The test results are displayed on a videotape and photographed for later interpretation.

> Meagan used to watch a video during the echocardiogram. Sometimes she would eat a sucker or a popsicle. She found it to be boring, not painful.

Finger pokes

Finger pokes are different from blood draws because they only require a quick puncture of the skin to obtain a few drops of blood. The technician will hold the finger and quickly prick it with a small sharp instrument. Blood will be collected in narrow tubes or a small container. It is usually necessary for the technician to squeeze the fingertip to get enough blood. If a Buzzy® or EMLA® is not used, the squeezing part is uncomfortable and the finger may ache for a while.

One way to minimize the discomfort of a finger poke is to put a blob of EMLA® on the tip of the middle finger, cover the fingertip with plastic cling wrap, and then use tape or a bandage to hold it in place. Another method is to buy long, thin balloons with a diameter a bit wider than your child's finger. Cut off the open end, leaving only enough balloon to cover the finger up to the first knuckle. Fill the tip of the balloon with EMLA® and slide it on the fingertip. EMLA® needs to be applied an hour before a finger poke to be effective. When it is time for the poke, remove the plastic wrap or balloon, wipe off the EMLA®, and ask for a warm pack. Wrapping this heated pack around the finger for a few minutes opens the capillaries to allow the blood to flow out more readily. Now your child is ready for a pain-free finger poke.

Even though we use EMLA®, Katy (5 years old) still becomes angry when she has to have a finger poke. I asked her why it was upsetting if there was no pain, and she replied, "It doesn't hurt my body anymore, but it still hurts my feelings."

Some children are more anxious about the anticipation of a poke than the actual poke itself, so the use of EMLA® may cause them to worry. As you try various methods, you and your child will learn what works best. Children who choose their own routines for pain control may feel more comfortable and secure.

Gallium scan

Gallium scans are performed in the nuclear medicine department and help doctors identify sites of tumors and infections. Prior to the scan, your child will be injected with a radiopharmaceutical, called gallium citrate, though the venous catheter or a IV. Usually, the scan is performed 24 to 48 hours after the injection. The procedure takes about 30 minutes. Your child needs to lie flat on an examination table while the machine scans above her. The machine makes noise but the procedure is not painful. You can stay with your child during this procedure.

Gastrostomy

A gastrostomy is the creation of an external opening in the abdominal wall through which a feeding tube (usually called a G-tube) is placed in the child's stomach. This is appropriate for children who cannot eat normally because of chronic swallowing problems or long-term pain in the mouth or throat, or for children who have lost their appetite for a prolonged period because of disease or treatment. The stomach end of the feeding tube has a small balloon on it that prevents it from being accidentally pulled out.

A skilled gastroenterologist or surgeon can perform the procedure in about 10 minutes. Most children have general anesthesia for the procedure and remain in the hospital for 1 to 2 days after the operation to receive pain medication and make sure they can tolerate tube feedings. After 2 to 3 months, the tube may be replaced with an unobtrusive skin-level device called a button. After a short recovery, children may play, bathe, and swim normally.

The G-tube is used for liquid feedings and medications for as long as the child needs it. If a child no longer requires the tube, it is removed and a bandage is placed over the site. The wound closes spontaneously in a day or two.

My daughter was diagnosed with hepatoblastoma when she was 3 months old. During her second round of chemo, I told them that the sound of her crying had changed, and she was coughing a lot while nursing. It turns out her vocal cords were paralyzed from the vincristine. She was in a lot of pain and needed to be on

a continuous drip for that. I couldn't nurse her anymore so they put a G-tube in because they were afraid she might aspirate and get pneumonia. We had the same surgeon who had put in her Hickman® and did the biopsy. She needed a way to get nutrition, but it was very hard not to be able to nurse her.

Intravenous pyelogram (IVP)

Your child's doctor may order an IVP if he feels there is an abnormality involving the urinary tract. Your child may need to fast before the procedure. Prior to the IVP, your child will have a contrast material injected into the bloodstream through an IV or venous catheter. X-rays are taken as the contrast material is collected and excreted by the kidneys. The process usually takes about an hour and you can stay with your child while the IVP is being performed. Children with an allergy to iodine should not have this test.

Magnetic resonance imaging (MRI)

MRI uses a magnetic field to create two-dimensional images of a cross section of an area of the body. Your child may need to receive a liquid dye, called a contrast agent, prior to or during the scan. The dye can be administered through your child's central venous catheter or via a peripheral IV. For the MRI, your child lies on a platform that slides into a long tube. Inside the tube is a donut-shaped magnet. A special device, called a surface coil, is placed around the area of the body that is to be imaged.

> *During the first year of getting scans, Cassandra (age 5) would have to be anesthetized to have the MRI done, since it scared her to be in that tube for so long. It was difficult for her to come out of the anesthesia and she would be crabby for the rest of the day. One day she decided, at my prodding, that she would try to do it without being asleep if I would stay with her and hold her hand. She has done it this way ever since. She listens to music and usually falls asleep, while I am stretched out, holding her hand inside the tube for up to an hour. To celebrate having the scans finished, Cassandra and I go shopping for something special afterwards—for a while it was different-colored Converse high tops. On those evenings, my husband, the girls, and I go out for a special dinner to celebrate the cancer still being gone!*

The technologist does not stay in the room during the MRI. The MRI machine makes a loud knocking noise as the images are taken. Your child may need to wear special earplugs to help block out this sound. Young children, or any child with a fear of closed-in spaces (claustrophobia), may need to be sedated for the MRI procedure. MRI takes longer to perform than CT scans and requires that your child lie perfectly still. Although some centers now have open MRI scanners, they are not currently available in the majority of hospitals.

We don't run around trying to get copies of scans after the fact (the ones made then aren't as clear anyway and cost money). We ask the technician for a second set of MRI scans to be made the same day it's taken. That way we always have sets to pull out for consults and other doctor visits. We've also learned that it appears to help with interpreting MRIs to use the same MRI machine, and we also try to get the same technician.

I-metaiodobenzylguanidine (mIBG) scan

Children who have neuroblastoma may require a special nuclear medicine scan called I-metaiodobenzylguanidine (mIBG) that can identify tumor cells in the bone or soft tissues. This procedure uses a radioactive substance—either iodine 123 metaiodobenzylguanidine or iodine 131 metaiodobenzylguanidine—that is injected in a vein 24, 48, or 72 hours prior to having the scan. The injected substance accumulates in neuroblastoma tumor cells, which then appear on the scan as a "hot spot." Prior to the injection, and for 3 to 5 days after, your child will need to take an oral medication, called potassium iodide (also known by the brand name SSKI®), to protect the thyroid gland.

The scan takes place in a machine that is similar to a CT scanner. During the scan, the technician will place your child on a scanning bed, and two special cameras, one above and one below the bed, take images from head to foot. You should be permitted to stay with your child during this procedure. A mIBG scan usually takes much longer than other imaging techniques, and the child must remain very still during the procedure. Some young children will need to be sedated while the test is being done.

One of the scans that Matthew disliked most of all was the mIBG scan. Not because there was anything painful involved, but because he found it to be so incredibly boring. He knew if we were making a visit to nuclear medicine for that particular test, it meant spending the next few hours lying motionless on the scanning bed. Fortunately, Matthew developed a very good relationship with the technicians who performed the procedure. They were wonderful to him, and he came to love them all very much. It certainly made things a lot easier for both of us. He never once needed to be sedated for his many mIBG scans—very impressive for a child diagnosed at the age of 3 with neuroblastoma. I think this was because of his attitude and because of how he was treated by the technicians.

Parents often notice obvious hot spots during the mIBG scan. It is important to bear in mind that mIBG is excreted in the urine, and rare false positive results can appear in the groin area (for example, urine-soaked diapers or underwear). False positive results are also possible if the radioactive substance leaks around the central line or IV used for injection of the material.

Needle aspiration biopsy

Needle aspiration biopsies are sometimes used to obtain a sample of cells from a mass in an accessible area. Prior to the biopsy, children need to fast for several hours. The pediatric surgeon will first use ultrasound or CT images to determine the exact location of the mass. Once your child has been anesthetized, a needle is guided through the skin and into the mass; then a sample is removed. The sample is then sent to a pathologist, who will view the cells under a microscope. Your child will need to stay in bed for the next several hours with vital signs closely monitored to ensure there is no bleeding.

> Eric (age 16) had a fine-needle biopsy of some lesions appearing on his brain. His oncologist thought that his osteosarcoma had metastasized. I was with him as he was sedated in the CT room, standing right beside him, holding his hand when he fell asleep. The biopsy was guided by the CT pictures and a metal frame that had been "screwed" into his skull. Because of the sedation, Eric didn't feel any pain.

Using a thin, flexible tube called an endoscope, doctors can perform a needle aspiration biopsy in parts of the gastrointestinal (GI) tract. While your child is sedated, a gastroenterologist guides the endoscope through the mouth and into the stomach and duodenum. The tip of the endoscope contains a miniature ultrasound probe that creates visual images of the GI system. During the endoscopic ultrasound, a biopsy can be done of any tumor tissue seen via a needle that comes out of the end of the endoscope.

Positron emission tomography (PET) scan

Positron emission tomography (PET) is a type of imaging scan used to identify biochemical changes in the body's tissues. MRI and CT scans provide information about structure and anatomy, but PET scans provide additional information about metabolism. This information helps more clearly identify location and extent of tumor and, after treatment, whether masses showing up on CT or MRI are scar tissue, dead tissue, or new growth of disease.

The PET scan involves injection of a radioactive drug (tracer) prior to scanning. The most common drug used is fluorine 18, also known as FDG-18, which is a radioactive version of glucose. The amount of radiation is very small, about the same as a conventional x-ray. After the injection, your child will wait for an hour or so until the tracer has spread throughout the body, and then the scan is done. No anesthesia is used and the entire procedure takes about 2 hours.

Usually, parents are told to not let their child consume any caffeine (e.g., soda, tea, chocolate) for 24 hours before the PET scan. Other than water, your child should not have any food or fluids for 4 hours before the scan. Your child should be told that the scan will not hurt and that he will have to remain very still while in the scanning machine.

Pulmonary function test

Some of the chemotherapy drugs children receive can damage the lungs. Your child's doctor may order a pulmonary function test to evaluate your child's respiratory status. The basic pulmonary function test is called a spirogram. Your child will blow into the machine to measure the amount of air she can inhale and exhale. The respiratory technician who administers the test will coach and instruct your child throughout the procedure to ensure she is giving her maximum effort. The test is administered at least three times to ensure the results are reliable. You can stay with your child while this test is done.

Your child cannot take this test if she is agitated, in pain, or too young to cooperate with the procedure. Your child should not take any bronchodilators or use an inhaler for 6 hours prior to the procedure. Also, be sure to have a list of medications your child is currently taking with you, because this is necessary for proper test interpretation.

> Our son didn't like having pulmonary function tests. On the outside, it looks so simple. But blowing into the spirogram was hard for him. He was usually a little tired after the test was complete. We would always make a trip to the hospital gift shop afterwards, because we felt he deserved a special treat for working so hard.

Spinal tap (lumbar puncture or LP)

Due to the blood-brain barrier, systemic chemotherapy sometimes cannot destroy cancer cells present in the central nervous system (brain and spinal cord). Chemotherapy drugs may have to be directly injected into the cerebrospinal fluid (CSF) to kill any cancer cells present. For certain diseases, spinal taps are used to monitor a child's response to treatment.

Most hospitals sedate children for spinal taps. If a child is not sedated, EMLA® cream is usually prescribed to lessen the pain. Even with sedation, EMLA® may be applied to minimize the sting of the topical anesthetic. To perform a spinal tap, the doctor or nurse practitioner first asks the child to lie on his side with his head tucked close to the chest and knees drawn up. A nurse usually helps hold the child in this position. The doctor, wearing sterile gloves, finds the designated spot in the lower back, swabs it with antiseptic several times, and administers one or two shots of an anesthetic (usually xylocaine) into the skin and deeper tissues. It is necessary to wait a few moments to ensure the area is fully anesthetized.

The doctor will push a needle between two vertebrae and into the space where CSF is found. The CSF will begin to drip out of the hollow needle into a container. After collecting a small amount of CSF, the doctor removes the needle, bandages the spot, and sends the CSF to the laboratory to see whether any cancer cells are present.

It is important to lie extremely flat for at least 30 minutes after a spinal tap to reduce pressure changes in the CSF. Sitting or standing up too soon can cause severe headaches. If your child develops a persistent severe headache following the procedure that lessens while he lies flat but throbs when he sits up, notify the doctor or nurse. The nurse will likely have your child lie flat and will offer him a high-caffeine beverage (such as Mountain Dew®) to drink. If the headache persists, an anesthesiologist sometimes does a procedure called a "blood patch," during which your child lies in the same position as for the spinal tap. The anesthesiologist will draw a small amount of blood from your child's arm or central line. She will then inject the blood at the site of the prior spinal tap where CSF may be slowly leaking into the tissues. If this is the cause of the headache, the relief is immediate. You can stay with your child during the procedure.

Starting an intravenous (IV) drip

Most children with cancer have a permanent venous catheter implanted in their chest within a week of diagnosis to avoid the pain of multiple IV sticks (see Chapter 13, *Venous Catheters*). However, there may be instances when your child will need an IV line started, as well.

Most children's hospitals have teams of technicians who specialize in starting IVs and drawing blood. The IV technician will generally use a vein in the lower arm or hand. First, a constricting band is put above the site to make the veins larger and easier to see and feel. The technician feels for the vein, cleans the area, and inserts the needle. Sometimes she leaves the needle in place and sometimes she withdraws it, leaving only a thin plastic tube in the vein. The technician will make sure the needle (or tube) is in the proper place, then will cover the site with a clear dressing and secure it with tape.

Here are a few ways to make this procedure a bit easier:

- **Stay calm.** The body reacts to fear by constricting the blood vessels near the skin's surface. Small children are usually more calm with a parent present, but teenagers may prefer privacy. Listening to music, visualizing a tranquil scene (such as floating in a pool or watching snow fall in the mountains), or using the same technician each time can help.

- **Use a topical anesthetic or a Buzzy®.** Using a topical anesthetic (e.g., EMLA®) or a Buzzy® (described earlier in the chapter) can be very helpful when starting an IV.

- **Keep warm.** Cold temperatures cause the surface blood vessels to constrict. Wrapping the child in a blanket and putting a warm pack or heating pad on his arm can enlarge the veins.

- **Drink lots of fluids.** Dehydration decreases fluid in the veins, making them harder to find.

- **Let gravity help.** If your child is lying in bed, she can hang her arm down over the side to increase the size of the vessels in her arm and hand.

- **Let your child have control, as appropriate.** If your child has a preference, let him pick the arm to be stuck. If he is a veteran of many IVs, let him point out the best vein.

- **Stop if problems develop.** The art of treating children requires spending lots of time on preparation and not much time on procedures. If a conflict arises, take a time-out and regroup. Children can be remarkably cooperative if they feel you are respecting their needs and if they are given some control over the situation.

> You'll think I'm crazy, but I'll tell you this story anyway. After getting stuck constantly for a year, my daughter (5 years old) lost it one day when she needed an IV. She started screaming and crying, just flew into a rage. I told the tech, "Let's let her calm down. Why don't you stick me for a change?" She was a sport and started a line in my arm. I told my daughter that I had forgotten how much it hurt and I could understand why she was upset. I told her to let us know when she was ready. She just walked over and held out her arm.

Traditionally, infants and young children have been restrained on their backs to insert IVs. This technique minimizes the risk of misplacing the IV, but it can cause significant fear and distress. Many treatment centers now allow parents to hold children upright in their laps to minimize stress. Child life specialists can teach parents ways to hold a young child to help him feel secure while undergoing procedures.

Subcutaneous injections

Some children require medications given by subcutaneous (under the skin) injection during their treatment. For example, Neupogen® (filgrastim) is a granulocyte colony-stimulating factor (G-CSF) that is often used to boost the white blood cell count. It is usually given by subcutaneous injection. If you are required to give shots at home, make sure a nurse has trained you to do it and ask her to write down any tips she may have for making the shot as easy for your child as possible.

> We found that giving 4-year-old Joseph as much power in the process as possible really helped. The shots themselves are non-negotiable, but there are many parts of the process where the child can have some control (where to put the EMLA® cream, where to be sitting for the cream and/or the shot, who holds him, what toy to hold during the procedure, etc.). We also made sure to have a consistent little treat available afterwards, although this became unnecessary after a while. Even at 4, Joseph loved money, so for a long time he kept a pint jar, which would travel to the hospital and back home again, and he'd get to drop in a nickel for each pill successfully swallowed (a huge chore for him) and a quarter for each shot. Of course, adults would

look very surprised when we told them we gave Joseph "quarter shots." Something
tells me the bar scene will be very confusing to him when gets to college.

To minimize pain caused by subcutaneous injections, apply EMLA® cream 1 to 2 hours before the shot, and then cover it with a Tegaderm® patch or plastic cling wrap. Parents can also reduce pain by numbing the site prior to the injection by using a Buzzy® device for 30 to 60 seconds or by rubbing ice over the skin.

We always used EMLA® cream before our son needed a subcutaneous injection. I
think part of the benefit to him was pharmacological, and part of it was psychologi-
cal. He just seemed to be more at ease with the injections when he knew the EMLA®
was applied a few hours before the needle was given.

Taking oral medications

As the parent of a child with a cancer, one of your most important jobs is to administer each dose of all oral medications to your child on time—every day. To accomplish this, it is essential to get off to a good start and establish cooperation early in the process. Pill swallowing is an essential skill for children and teens to master, and having a cancer diagnosis means they will need to learn how to do it in a short span of time. Many pills can be chewed or swallowed whole without leaving a bad taste in the mouth, but some medications should not be chewed because they have a bitter aftertaste and may cause your child to develop an aversion to all oral medications.

To teach Brent (6 years old) to swallow pills, when we were eating corn for dinner I
encouraged him to swallow one kernel whole. Luckily, it went right down and he got
over his fear of pills.

Children and teens can learn how to swallow pills by practicing with candy. One method, developed by the Child Study Center at New York University Langone Medical Center, starts with a child swallowing a tiny candy such as Nerds®. When the child is able to easily do this five times, he practices swallowing a slightly larger candy. The size of the candies is gradually increased (e.g., mini M&Ms®, Tic Tacs®, and then full-sized M&Ms®). This method allows your child or teen to practice swallowing in a relaxed setting at home with as much repetition as needed. With lots of encouragement from parents, the stress is minimal. If this method does not work for your child, a more gradual way to learn to swallow pills is described online at *http://research4kids.ucalgary. ca/pill-study* and listed in Appendix C, *Books, Websites, and Support Groups.*

I wanted Katy (3 years old) to feel like we were a team right from the first night. So
I made a big deal out of tasting each of her medications and pronouncing it good.
Thank goodness I tasted the prednisone first. It was nauseating—bitter, metallic,
with a lingering aftertaste. I asked the nurse for some small gel caps, and packed

them with the pills which I had broken in half. I gave Katy her choice of drinks to take her pills with and taught her to swallow gel caps with a large sip of liquid. Since I gave her more than 3,000 pills and 1,100 teaspoons of liquid medication during treatment, I'm very glad we got off to such a good start.

Empty gel caps come in many sizes, and you can purchase them at a pharmacy or ask a nurse for them if your child is in the hospital. Many parents put pills inside gel caps to mask the taste and make them more slippery and easier to swallow. Number 4s are small enough for a 3- or 4-year-old child to swallow. Children develop different taste preferences and aversions to medications, and gel caps are useful for any medication that bothers them.

After much trial and error with medications, Meagan's method became chewing up pills with chocolate chips. She's kept this up for the long haul.

. . . . .

I always give choices such as, "Do you want the white pill or the six yellow pills first?" It gives him a little control in his chaotic world.

For younger children who are not able to swallow pills, many parents crush the pills into a small amount of pudding, applesauce, jam, frozen juice concentrate, or another favorite food. However, your child may develop a lifelong aversion to these foods after treatment is over. Before mixing pills with food, check with the doctor or pharmacist, because some foods can negate the effects of medications.

Jeremy was 4 when he was diagnosed, and we used to crush up the pills and mix them with ice cream. This worked well for us.

. . . . .

Our son was 2 ½ years old when diagnosed. We put the med in an oral syringe and put very hot water in a tiny glass. Then we would draw a wee bit of the hot water into the oral syringe and then we would cap it. Then you gently shake the syringe and turn it back and forth while the med completely dissolves. Then we would take off the cap and fill it the rest of the way with nice cold Kool-Aid®. Alexander would get to choose the flavor of Kool-Aid® each day and we would just mix up a couple different batches of flavors and keep them in the fridge. He felt like he was in control because he chose the flavor, and it covered up the lousy taste of the medication. We asked our oncologist about this at the very beginning, and he said it was a great way to do it because neither the water nor the Kool-Aid® had any unwanted effects on the medication. Anyway, we never once had any problem with this method.

. . . . .

The method we used for getting my son to take his foul-tasting chemo/meds was the mixing agent Syrpalta®. This is a grape-flavored syrup available from the pharmacy. It doesn't react with most meds and the flavor can hide almost anything.

We used quite a bit of the stuff. First, we crushed his pills with a pill crusher/cutter, then we mixed them in a cup before putting them in a syringe to squirt in his mouth. (Keep in mind he was only about 15 months old when he got sick.) We had to make sure he got every drop though, since some of the pills were really small and a little bit of syrup could hide a significant portion of the dose.

You should make sure that any med you do this with is safe to crush or mix with Syrpalta® (or chocolate, or anything else for that matter). Meds with time-release or slow-release agents should never be crushed.

Pharmacists can flavor oral medications with a product called FlavorX®, allowing your child to choose from a variety of flavors such as banana, strawberry, mango, watermelon, and chocolate. The pharmacist can advise you about which flavors will work best to cover up the taste of each medication. You can find a local pharmacy that offers FlavorX® by visiting the website *www.flavorx.com*.

Whenever my son had to take a liquid medicine, such as antibiotics, he enjoyed taking it from a syringe. I would draw up the proper amount, then he would put it in his mouth and push the plunger.

Teens and medication

Teenagers usually have completely different issues around taking pills than do young children. Most problems with teens revolve around autonomy, control, and feelings of invulnerability. It is normal for teenagers to be noncompliant, and they cannot be forced to take pills if they choose not to cooperate. Trying to coerce teens fuels conflict and frustrates everyone. If you need help, ask the psychosocial team at the hospital to work out a plan for treatment adherence. Everyone will need to be flexible to reach a favorable outcome.

I think the main problem with teens is making sure that they take the meds. Joel (15 years old) has been very responsible about taking his nightly pills. I've tried to make it easy for him by having an index card for the week, and he marks off the med as he takes it. I also put a list of the meds on a dry erase board on the fridge as a reminder. As he takes the med, he erases it. That way it's easy for him (and me) to see at a glance if he's taken his stuff. The index card alone wasn't working because sometimes he couldn't find a pen or forgot to mark it off.

Taking a temperature

Fever is the enemy during treatment because it signals infection, and children on chemotherapy cannot fight infection effectively if their white blood cell counts are depressed. Parents take hundreds of temperatures, especially when their child is not feeling well.

Temperatures can be taken under the tongue, under the arm, on the forehead, or in the ear using a special type of thermometer. Rectal temperatures are not recommended due to the risk of tears and infection. Here are a few suggestions that might help:

- Use an infrared thermometer on the forehead.

- Use a digital thermometer under the tongue or arm. Some have an alarm that beeps when it is time to remove the thermometer.

> We bought a digital thermometer that we only use under his arm. It has worked well for us because he likes the beep.

- Tympanic (ear) thermometers are very easy to use.

> When my in-laws asked at diagnosis if there was anything that we needed, I asked them to try to buy a tympanic thermometer. The device cost over 100 dollars then, but it worked beautifully. It takes only 1 second to obtain a temperature. I can even use it when she is asleep without waking her. They are now sold at pharmacies and drug stores, and cost much less.

Before you leave the hospital, you should know when to call the clinic because of fever. Usually, parents are told not to give any medication for fever and to call if the fever goes above 101° F (38.5° C). It is particularly important for parents of children with implanted catheters to know when to call the clinic, as an untreated infection can be life-threatening. It is also helpful to have a copy of your child's most recent blood cell counts when you call to notify the doctor about fever.

Transfusions (blood)

Cancer treatment can cause severe anemia (a low number of oxygen-carrying red blood cells). This is because the normal lifespan of a red blood cell is 3 to 4 months, and as old cells die, the chemo-stressed marrow cannot replace them. Many children require transfusions of red blood cells when they are first admitted to the hospital and periodically throughout treatment.

> Whenever my son needed a transfusion, I brought along bags of coloring books, food, and toys. The number of video players at the clinic was limited, so I tried to make arrangements for one ahead of time. When anemic (hematocrit below 20%), he didn't have much energy, but by the end of the transfusion, his cheeks were rosy and he had tremendous vitality. It was hard to keep him still. After one unit (bag) of red cells, his hematocrit usually jumped up to around 30.

One bag (called a "unit") of red cells takes 2 to 4 hours to administer and is given through an IV or catheter. Mild allergic reactions are common. If your child is prone to allergies or experiences an allergic reaction, it may be necessary to premedicate her

with an antihistamine such as Benadryl® (diphenhydramine). Acute allergic reactions are rare, but they do happen. If your child develops chills and/or fever or any difficulty breathing during a transfusion, notify the nurse immediately so the transfusion can be stopped.

There are some risks of infection from red blood cell transfusions. Excellent tests are used to detect the most serious viruses in donated blood. The risk of exposure to the HIV virus from a blood transfusion is now less than 1 in 2 million. The risk of acquiring hepatitis B is 1 in 800,000, and hepatitis C is 1 in 1.6 million. Exposure to cytomegalovirus is also a small possibility. These very small risks are the reason transfusions are given only when absolutely necessary.

> *My daughter received several transfusions at the clinic in Children's Hospital with no problems. After we traveled back to our home, she needed her first transfusion at the local hospital. Our pediatrician said to expect to be in the hospital at least 8 hours. I asked why it would take so long when it only took 4 hours at Children's. He said he had worked out a formula and determined that she needed two units of packed cells. I mentioned that she only was given one unit each time at Children's. He called the oncologist, who said it was better to give only one unit. We went to the hospital, where a unit of red cells was given. Then a nurse came in with another unit. I questioned why he was doing that and he said, "Doctor's orders." I asked him to verify that order, as we had already discussed it with the doctor. He went into another room to call the doctor, and came back and said the pediatrician thought my daughter needed 30 cc more packed cells. I called Children's and they said she didn't need more, so I refused to let them administer any more blood. It just wasn't worth the risk of hepatitis to get 30 cc of blood. Even though I was pleasant, the nurses were angry at me for questioning the pediatrician.*

Transfusions (platelets)

Platelets are an important component of blood. They help form clots and stop bleeding by repairing breaks in the walls of blood vessels. A normal platelet count for a healthy child is 160,000 to 450,000/mm^3. Chemotherapy can severely depress the platelet count. If a child's platelet count is very low, it may be necessary to transfuse platelets so uncontrollable bleeding does not occur. Many centers require a transfusion when a child's platelet count goes below 10,000 to 20,000/mm^3, and sometimes repeat transfusions are required every 2 or 3 days until the marrow recovers. Platelet transfusions usually take less than an hour.

As with other blood products, an allergic reaction is possible and platelets are capable of transmitting infections such as hepatitis, cytomegalovirus, and HIV. Even though the chance of contracting these viruses is extremely low, platelets are transfused only when necessary.

Three-year-old Matthew had countless platelet transfusions, and only once did he have a reaction. It was an awful thing to watch, but the nurse who was monitoring him was very calm and professional, which helped both of us. Matthew was always premedicated for his platelet transfusions with Benadryl®, which made him very drowsy. Most often he would sleep through the entire transfusion.

Ultrasound imaging

Ultrasound provides the doctor with a quick and radiation-free tool for imaging internal organs. The ultrasound involves placing a small device called a transducer against the skin in the area that needs to be examined. The transducer sends inaudible sound waves into the body, which bounce off the internal organ and return to the transducer. The ultrasound machine uses these sound waves to form an image of the organ.

Before the procedure begins, your child may have to remove some items of clothing or jewelry that could interfere with the ultrasound. Sometimes your child will be asked to wear a hospital gown. The technologist will position your child on the examination table, and a clear gel will be applied to the area to be imaged. The technologist will move the transducer over the surface of the skin while the child remains still and relaxed. After the images have been taken, you may need to wait until they are reviewed before you can leave the department.

Urine specimens

Children taking chemotherapy often need to provide urine specimens. One way to help obtain a sample is to encourage your child to drink lots of liquids the hour before. If your child has an IV, you can also ask the nurse to increase the drip rate. Explain to the child why the test is necessary. Ask the nurse to show how the dip sticks work. (They change color, so they are quite popular with preschoolers.) You can use a shallow plastic bucket (called a hat) under the toilet seat to catch urine.

Turn on the water while the child sits on the toilet. I don't know why it works, but it does.

As all parents learn, eating and elimination are functions that the child controls. If she just can't or won't urinate in the hat, go out, buy her the largest drink you can find, and wait.

It may be necessary to obtain a sterile specimen of urine, or "clean catch," if infection is suspected. You or your child will need to cleanse the perineal area with soap or an antiseptic towelette, and she will need to urinate into a small sterile container.

If your child is not yet toilet trained, if a clean catch is impossible, or if your child is unable to urinate, it may be necessary to insert a Foley catheter. This procedure can be quite stressful because it involves placing a sterile rubber tube up the urethra and into the bladder. It is definitely appropriate to ask that your child be given a mild sedative or muscle relaxant before the procedure if he is anxious, and to request that the most skilled person available perform the procedure. In skilled nursing hands, the procedure takes less than 5 minutes to perform.

Six-year-old Ethan's introduction to procedures started the day he was diagnosed. The MRI that afternoon was no problem for him because he was nearly comatose. Getting through that scan was difficult only for my peace of mind. His next scan was a day later; he lay still, occasionally giggling, because he was watching Men in Black *through special MRI-safe video goggles. Scans became a not-so-hard routine. Reminded to lie still, he often fell asleep through the jackhammer-like din of the MRI magnet.*

Getting to Ethan's blood was, at first, a bit more challenging. After his port was placed, we at first had to hold Ethan down while accessing it. We were told it shouldn't hurt after being anesthetized with EMLA®, but the sight of the needle was scary. The breakthrough came when a child life specialist (what a great addition to pediatrics!) distracted him and he found that it really did not hurt.

Since that time, with my suggestions, he has devised (often-changing) routines; for accessing the port, he is sitting semi-upright, clutching his left ear with his left hand and holding a parent with his right. For receiving daily G-CSF shots, the special Band-Aid® that looks like a tattoo needs to be open on the table; the appropriate site (left or right thigh) agreed upon, pinched, and alcohol-swabbed; a sibling holding one hand and he pinching an ear with the other; on the count of three the QUICK injection, followed as nearly instantaneously as possible by the Band-Aid®. Simple, really, when you know how. No fear and no tears. Now if we can only get by the hurdle of the eye-drops which sting like the devil.

Chapter 11

Forming a Partnership with the Medical Team

IT IS VITALLY IMPORTANT that parents and the medical team establish and maintain a relationship based on excellent medical care, good communication, and caring. In this partnership, trust is paramount. Doctors rely on parents to make and keep appointments, give the proper medicines at the appropriate times, prepare the child for procedures, and monitor the child for signs of illness or side effects. Parents rely on doctors for medical knowledge, expertise in performing procedures, good judgment, compassion, and clear communication. It is a delicate balance that spans years of trauma and emotional upheaval. A climate of cooperation and respect between the healthcare team and parents allows children to thrive. This chapter explores ways to create and maintain that environment.

Choosing a hospital

At diagnosis, if your family is not initially referred to a specific hospital, or if there are several excellent pediatric hospitals in the area to choose from, you may be able to choose where you would like your child to be treated. Parents can obtain a free referral to an accredited center from the National Cancer Institute (800) 422-6237 or:

Children's Oncology Group
(626) 447-0064
https://childrensoncologygroup.org/index.php/locations

In recent years, the way health care has been planned and delivered to children has transformed. It is now based on the concept of family-centered care, which fosters healthy relationships among healthcare providers, parents, and children. At most children's hospitals, a family-centered team is assigned to each family with a newly diagnosed child. This team—composed of physicians, nurses, child life specialists, psychologists, social workers, physical and occupational therapists, and others—strives to ensure that the emotional, social, and developmental needs of every member of the family are addressed, in addition to the medical care of the child. The core concepts of

family-centered care are respect, dignity, information sharing, participation, and collaboration. Members of your child's team will be there to answer questions, provide emotional support, and recognize that you are the expert about your child.

> The day my 3-month-old daughter, Estele, was diagnosed with hepatoblastoma, we met the team—oncologist, nurse, nurse practitioner, child life specialist, and social worker. They are the ones who take care of us during Estele's frequent hospitalizations; they provide consistency and much, much more. The nurses just get it. They understand why sometimes I burst into tears when they say, "How are you doing?" They have been our family in the darkest of hours. They are the only thing I am going to miss when this is all over.

The doctors

At large children's hospitals, there are doctors at all levels of training, from first-year medical students to experienced professors of medicine. It is often hard to sort them all out in the early days after diagnosis. This section describes each type of doctor you might meet at a training hospital.

A **medical student** is a college graduate who is attending medical school. Medical students often wear white coats, but they do not have MD after the name on their name tags. They are not doctors.

An **intern** (also called a first-year resident) is a graduate of medical school who is in the first year of postgraduate training. Interns are doctors who are just beginning their clinical training.

A **resident** is a graduate of medical school in the second or third year of postgraduate training. Most residents at pediatric hospitals will be pediatricians when they complete their residencies. Residents are temporary: they rotate into different services (e.g., cardiology, neurology, oncology) every 4 weeks.

A **fellow** is a doctor pursuing postresidency study in a particular specialty. Most fellows you encounter will be specializing in pediatric oncology. Not all teaching hospitals have fellowship programs.

Attending doctors (or simply, **attendings**) are highly trained doctors hired by the hospital to provide and oversee medical care and to train interns, residents, and fellows. Many of them also teach at a medical school.

Consulting doctors are doctors from other services who are brought in to provide advice or treatment to a child in the oncology unit. The attending may ask for consults with other specialists, who may appear in your child's hospital room unexpectedly. If

questions arise about who these doctors are and what role they play, you should ask the fellow or attending assigned to your child or any member of your family-centered team.

Each child in a teaching hospital is assigned an attending, who is responsible for that child's care. This doctor should be "board certified" or have equivalent medical credentials. This means the doctor has taken rigorous written and oral tests given by a board of examiners in his or her specialty and meets a high standard of competence. You can call the American Board of Medical Specialties at (866) ASK-ABMS (275-2267) or visit *www.certificationmatters.org/is-your-doctor-board-certified.aspx* to find out whether your child's attending is board certified.

> *Our medical team was wonderful. They always answered our questions and spent the time with us that we needed. We had a group of doctors who were all working together for the patients. I always felt that we were known by each doctor, and that they were on top of Paige's treatment.*

If your family is insured by a health maintenance organization (HMO), or an insurance company that maintains a list of preferred hospitals, you probably will be sent to an affiliated hospital, which will have one or more pediatric oncologists on staff. If this hospital is not a regional pediatric hospital, you can go elsewhere to get state-of-the-art care (see the "Choosing a hospital" section later in this chapter). However, make sure your insurance will cover care at the institution you want to use.

The nurses

An essential part of the hospital hierarchy is the nursing staff. The following explanations will help you understand which type of nurse is caring for your child.

An **LPN** is a licensed practical nurse. LPNs complete certificate training and must pass a licensing exam. In some medical facilities, LPNs are allowed to perform most nursing functions, except those involving administration of medications. Many pediatric oncology services limit the involvement of LPNs to personal care, such as patient hygiene and monitoring fluid input and output.

An **RN** is a registered nurse who obtained an associate's degree or higher in nursing and then passed a licensing examination. RNs who have a bachelor's degree in nursing are also referred to as BSNs. RNs supervise all other nursing and patient care staff (such as nurses aides or nursing assistants), give medicines, take vital signs (e.g., heart rate, breathing rate, blood pressure), monitor IV machines, change bandages, and care for patients in hospitals, clinics, and doctors' offices. Many RNs in the pediatric oncology service have received specialized training in pediatric oncology nursing and have taken an examination to receive the credential of Certified Pediatric Hematology/Oncology Nurse (CPHON®).

A **nurse practitioner** or **clinical nurse specialist** is a registered nurse who has completed an educational program (generally a master's or doctoral degree) that teaches advanced skills. For example, in some hospitals and clinics, nurse practitioners perform procedures such as spinal taps. Nurse practitioners or clinical nurse specialists are often the liaison between the medical teams and patients and their families. They often coordinate a child's care, answer parent calls, help parents keep all the different multidisciplinary team members straight, and interpret medical jargon.

The **head** or **charge nurse** is an RN who supervises all the nurses on the hospital floor for one shift. If you have any problems with a nurse in the inpatient unit, your first step in resolving the issue should be to talk to the nurse involved. If this does not resolve the problem, a discussion with the charge nurse is your next step.

The **clinical nurse manager** is the administrator for an entire unit, such as a surgical or medical floor or outpatient clinic. The clinical nurse manager is in charge of all nurses in the unit.

> At our hospital, each of our nurses is different, but each is wonderful. They simply love the kids. They throw parties, set up dream trips, act as counselors, best friends, and stern parents. They hug moms and dads. They cry. I have come to respect them so much because they have such a hard job to do, and they do it so well.

The tumor board

Many hospitals have a committee to review surgery, pathology, and radiology findings and discuss potential treatment plans for patients. This committee is called the tumor board. Members consist of representatives from the child's multidisciplinary team, a pathologist, a radiologist, and other senior specialists who deal with solid tumors. Often, the consensus opinion from the tumor board is the treatment offered to the family. Many centers present individual cases to the tumor board at various times during treatment, such as after each imaging study or when the effects of treatment need to be assessed as per the protocol.

Finding an oncologist

Parents do not have the luxury of time in choosing a pediatric oncologist. At diagnosis, the family is usually sent to the nearest children's hospital. The child will be assigned a pediatric oncologist (attending) or fellow who is in charge of all treatment. Often the assigned oncologist is a good match, and the family finds the doctor to be competent,

caring, and easy to communicate with. If the medical facility allows you to choose your child's oncologist, here are several traits to look for:

- Board certified in the field of pediatric oncology

- Establishes good rapport with your child

- Communicates clearly and compassionately

- Performs procedures skillfully

- Answers all questions

- Consults with other doctors on complex problems

- Uses language that is easy to understand

- Makes the results of all tests available

- Acknowledges parents' right to make decisions

- Respects parents' values

- Able to deliver the truth with hope

> I've been very lucky that our doctors have been very open with us. When Samantha was first diagnosed, our doctor spent two hours explaining and answering our questions, and it has never stopped. Even if we haven't asked, but the doctors notice concern in our faces, they sit and take the time to find out our worries. They've all been great—the nurses, hospital, and support staff.

If you don't develop a good rapport with the oncologist assigned to your child, you can ask to be assigned to a different oncologist you may have met on rounds or during clinic visits. Most parent requests are accommodated, as hospitals realize the importance of good communication between family members and doctors. Your child will, however, still be seen by several different doctors, because most institutions have rotating doctors on call.

Types of relationships

Three types of relationships tend to develop between doctors and parents.

- **Paternal.** In a paternal relationship, the parent is submissive, and the doctor assumes a parental role. This dynamic may seem desirable to parents who are uncomfortable or inexperienced in dealing with medical issues, but it places all the responsibility for decisions and monitoring on the doctor. Doctors are human. If your child's doctor makes a mistake and you are not monitoring drugs and treatments, these mistakes may go unnoticed. You are the expert when it comes to your child, and you know best how to gauge his reactions to drugs and treatments.

> *I once asked a fellow about my daughter's blood work. She literally patted me on the head and said it was her job to worry about that, not mine. I said in a nice voice that I thought it was a reasonable question and that I would appreciate an answer.*

Some parents are intimidated by doctors and fear that if they question the doctors their child will suffer. This type of behavior robs the child of an adult advocate who speaks up when something seems wrong.

- **Adversarial.** Some parents adopt an "us against them" attitude, which is counterproductive. They seem to feel the disease and treatment are the fault of the medical staff, and they blame staff for any setbacks that occur. This attitude undermines the child's confidence in her doctor.

> *I knew one family that just hated the Children's Hospital. They called it the "House of Horrors" or the "torture chamber" in front of their children. Small wonder that their children were terrified.*

If you or someone in your family has had negative interactions with medical professionals in the past, it can be difficult to get past those feelings and work comfortably with doctors and nurses. It is helpful to really get to know how the pediatric oncology world works, because it is often more collaborative and open to patient and family input than other arenas of medical care. Find out which people are responsible for various parts of your child's tests and treatments, and try to get to know each of them. That way you can feel more comfortable asking them questions. You will also have a better sense of when care is being handled well, and if something goes wrong you will have good relationships with the people you need to call on to correct it.

- **Collegial.** This is a true partnership in which parents and doctors are all on the same footing and they respect each other's domains and expertise. The doctor recognizes that the parents are the experts about their child and are essential in ensuring that the protocol is followed. The parents respect the doctor's expertise and feel comfortable discussing various treatment options or concerns that arise. Honest communication is necessary for this partnership to work, but the effort is well worth it. The child has confidence in his doctor, the parents have lessened their stress by creating a supportive relationship with the doctor, and the doctor feels comfortable that the family will comply with the treatment plan, giving the child the best chance for a cure.

> *We had a wonderful relationship with our daughter's oncologist. He perfectly blended the science and the art of medicine. His manner with our daughter was warm, he was extremely well-qualified professionally, and he was very easy to talk to. I could bring in articles to discuss with him, and he welcomed the discussion. Although he was busy, he never rushed us. I laughed when I saw that he had written in the chart, "Mother asks innumerable appropriate questions."*

Another mother relates a different experience:

We tried very hard to form a partnership with the medical team but failed. The staff seemed very guarded and distant, almost wary of a parent wanting to participate in the decisions made for the child. I learned to use the medical library and took research reports in to them to get some help for side effects and get some drug dosages reduced. Things improved, but I was never considered a partner in the health-care team; I was viewed as a problem.

A pediatric oncologist shares her perspective:

All parents are different and have different coping styles. Some deal best with a lot of information (lab results, meds, study options) up front, while others are over-whelmed and want the information a little bit at a time. There is no way for the doctor to know the parents' coping styles at the beginning. (Even the parents may not yet know!) So if they let the doctor know how much information they want or don't want, it is very helpful.

Communication

Clear and frequent communication is the foundation of a positive doctor/parent relationship. Doctors need to be able to explain clearly and listen well, and parents need to feel comfortable asking questions and expressing concerns before they grow into grievances. Nurses and doctors cannot read parents' minds, nor can parents prepare their child for a procedure unless it has been explained well. The following are parent suggestions about how to establish and maintain good communication with your child's healthcare team.

• Tell the staff how much you want to know.

I told them the first day to treat me like a medical student. I asked them to share all information, current studies, lab results, everything, with me. I told them, in advance, that I hoped they wouldn't be offended by lots of questions, because knowledge was comfort to me.

• • • • •

If the doctors at Children's told me to do something, I didn't question it because I trusted them.

• Inform the staff of your child's temperament, likes, and dislikes. You know your child better than anyone, so don't hesitate to tell the clinic staff about what works best.

Whenever my daughter was hospitalized, I made a point of kindly reminding doctors and nurses that she was extremely sensitive, and would benefit from quiet voices and

soothing explanations of anything that was about to occur, such as taking temperatures, vital signs, or adjustments to her IV.

- Encourage a close relationship between doctor, nurse, and child. Insist that all medical personnel respect your child's dignity. Do not let anyone talk in front of your child as if she is not there. If a problem persists, you have the right to ask the offending person to leave. Marina Rozen observes in *Advice to Doctors and Other Big People*:

  The best part about the doctor is when he gives me bubble gum. The worst part is when he's in the room with me and my mom and he only talks to my mom. I've told him I don't like that, but he doesn't listen.

- Most children's hospitals assign each child a family-centered team, including a primary nurse. Try to form a close relationship with your child's nurse. Nurses usually possess vast knowledge and experience about both medical and practical aspects of cancer treatment. Often, the nurse can rectify misunderstandings between doctors and parents.

- Children and teenagers should be included as part of the team. They should be consulted about treatments and procedures and be given age-appropriate choices.

  Leeann's doctor has been great. She knows how to talk to kids without talking down to them. She would take the time during her hospital rounds to help Leeann with her homework and laugh at all of our stupid jokes. A good sense of humor was a must for all of us.

- Coordinate communication. If your hometown pediatrician will handle bloodwork or other routine testing, find ways to facilitate communication between the oncologist and pediatrician.

  We had a problem with the pediatrician's office not calling me with the results of my daughter's blood work in time for me to call the hospital ped onc clinic. This would result in worry for me and a delay in changes to her chemotherapy doses. I told the pediatrician's nurse that I knew how busy they were and I hated having to keep calling to get the results. I asked her if it was possible for them to give the lab authorization to call me with the results. They thought it was a great idea, and it worked for years. The lab would fax the doctor the results, but call me. Then I would call the hospital clinic and get the dose changes. The clinic would then fax that information to the pediatrician's office. It was a win/win situation: the pediatrician's office received no interruptions, they got copies of everything in writing, and I got quick responses from the clinic on how to adjust her meds to her wildly swinging blood counts.

- Go to all appointments with a written list of questions. This prevents you from forgetting something important and saves the staff from numerous follow-up phone calls.

- Ask for definitions of unfamiliar terms. Repeat back the information to ensure you understood it correctly. Writing down answers or recording meetings are both common practices.

- Some parents want to read their child's medical chart to get more details about their child's condition and to help in formulating questions for the medical team. Sometimes the doctor or nurse will let the parents read the chart in the child's hospital room or in the waiting room at the clinic, but some hospitals have policies that prohibit this. As access to online medical records becomes more common, you may be able to log in to the chart from home to read the physicians' notes, and keep track of blood counts and other test results. Most states and provinces have laws that allow patient access to all records. If you want a copy of your child's chart, you may have to write to the doctor asking to review the chart and pay any duplication costs. Keep in mind that some medical systems now restrict parental access to the full medical record if the child is a teen; this is done to protect your child's confidential medical discussions with his physician. You teen can choose (or not) to sign a form allowing you complete access to the records.

- If you have questions or concerns, discuss them with the nurses or residents. If they are unable to provide a satisfactory answer, ask the fellow or attending doctor assigned to your child.

> We found that sitting down and talking things over with the nurses helped immensely. They were very familiar with each drug and its side effects. They told us many stories about children who had been through the same thing and were doing well years later. They always seemed to have time to give encouragement, a smile, or a hug.

- The medical team includes many specialists: doctors, nurses, child life specialists, social workers, physical therapists, nutritionists, x-ray technicians, radiation therapists, and more. At training hospitals, many of these people will be in the early stages of their training. If a procedure is not going well, you have the right to tell the person to stop and to request that a more skilled person do the job.

> While I truly supported the teaching hospital concept, it was difficult to deal with a first-year resident who couldn't do a spinal tap or insert an IV. We had a tendency to lose patience rather quickly when our child was screaming and the doctor was getting impatient. More than once we requested a replacement and had someone else do the test.

- Know your rights—and the hospital's. Legally, your child cannot be treated without your permission. If the doctor suggests a procedure you do not feel comfortable with, keep asking questions until you feel fully informed. You have the legal right to refuse the procedure if you do not think it is necessary.

One day in the hospital, a group of fellows came in and announced that they were going to do a lung biopsy on Jesse. I told them that I hadn't heard anything about it from her attending, and I just didn't think it was the right thing to do. They said, "We have to do it," and I repeated that I just didn't think it needed to be done until we talked to the attending. They seemed angry, but we stood our ground. When the attending came later, he said that they were not supposed to do a biopsy because the surgeon said it was too risky of an area in the lung to get to.

However, if the hospital staff feels you are endangering the health of your child by withholding permission for treatment, they can take you to court. All parties must remember that the most important person in this circumstance is the child.

- Use "I" statements. For example, "I feel upset when you won't answer my questions," rather than, "You never listen to me."

- If it helps you feel more comfortable, keep track of your child's treatments to check for mistakes.

> *Few children were on the same protocol at the time my daughter was being treated. The attendings always knew exactly what was supposed to be done, but the fellows sometimes made mistakes. I was embarrassed to correct them, but I just kept reminding myself that they had dozens of protocols to keep track of, and I had only one.*

- Be specific and diplomatic when describing problems. For example, "My son gets very nervous if we have to wait a long time for our appointment, which makes him less compliant with the doctor. Could we call ahead next time to see whether the doctor is on schedule?" rather than, "Do you think your time is more valuable than mine?"

> *Noah was 5 months old and receiving radiation treatment for a small tumor (retinoblastoma) located adjacent to the optic nerve. I felt very strongly that an infant should be able to wake up to his mother (and that not having the mother present was emotionally damaging to the baby). I was upset that the anesthesia team was not honoring this concern, and I was simply told, "He won't remember." I made the point that "He may not remember here," pointing to my head, but that "He does remember here," pointing to my heart. I arranged to be called to the treatment room shortly before he awakened from anesthesia.*

- If you have something to discuss with the doctor that will take some time, request a conference or a family meeting. These are routinely scheduled between parents and doctors and should be scheduled to allow enough time for a thorough discussion. Grabbing the attention of a busy doctor in the hallway is not fair to her and may not result in a satisfactory answer for you.

> *One technique I use to keep from forgetting what I want to say at the doctor's appointment is to type out an agenda for the appointment. I also make a copy for the*

doctor. This helps me stay calm and focused on the agenda, and it gives me and my doctor a written record of what our concerns were, and what was discussed during the appointment.

- Do not be afraid to make waves if you are right or to apologize if you are wrong.

  When my daughter was in the hospital one time, the nurse came in with two syringes. I asked what they were, and she said immunizations. I said that it must be a mistake, and the nurse said that the orders were in the chart. So I checked my daughter's chart, and the orders were there, but they had another child's name on them.

- Show appreciation.

  I sent thank-you notes to three residents after my daughter's first hospitalization. The notes were short but sweet. I wanted them to know how much we appreciated their many kindnesses.

  • • • • •

  I always try to thank the nurse or doctor when they apologize for being late and give the reason. I don't mind waiting if it is for a good cause, and I feel they show respect when they apologize.

Getting a second opinion

There are times during your child's treatment when a second opinion may be advisable. Parents are sometimes reluctant to request a second opinion because they are afraid of offending their child's doctor or creating antagonism. Conscientious doctors will not resent a parent for seeking a second opinion. If your child's doctor does resist, ask why. Second opinions are a common and accepted practice, and they are sometimes required by insurance companies.

There are two ways to get a second opinion: see another specialist or ask your child's doctor to arrange a multidisciplinary second opinion. Many parents seek a second opinion at the time of diagnosis, but it is better not to do this in secret. Explain to your child's pediatric oncologist or surgeon that, before proceeding, you would like an additional viewpoint. To allow for a thorough analysis, arrange to have copies of all records, scans, and pathology slides sent ahead to the doctor who will give the additional opinion.

  Personally, I feel there is nothing wrong with getting a second opinion from another major center. If you like and feel comfortable with your current team, that's great, but I definitely do not like when a doctor tells us there's "no reason" to go elsewhere, that "they can't do anything we don't do," and so forth. Many people choose to go elsewhere and have great results when a first doctor may have told them "no surgery,"

"it's hopeless," whatever the case may be. Many people travel great distances to get treatment at another facility whose treatment philosophy they prefer. And, granted, that is their choice. Now, your second opinion doctor may look at your child's MRIs and say, "Your team is doing exactly the right things; stick with them," or he may tell you something totally different and then you can make your own decision on what to do.

Multidisciplinary second opinions incorporate the views of several different specialists. Parents who would like to get various viewpoints can ask to have their child's case discussed at a tumor board, which usually meets weekly at major medical centers. These boards include medical, surgical, and radiation oncologists, as well as fellows and residents. Your child's oncologist will present the facts of your child's case for discussion. Ask him to tell you what was said at the meeting.

Doctors informally seek second opinions all the time. Residents confer with their fellows about complicated situations; fellows might confer with the attending when unusual drug reactions or responses to treatment occur. Attendings call colleagues at other institutions. Thus, parents should feel free to ask their child's physician whether he has conferred with other staff members to gain additional viewpoints.

Brent developed a seizure disorder after a rare drug reaction, so he was on anticonvulsants as well as chemotherapy for 2 years. We worried about the interaction of all the drugs, as well as the advisability of his continuing on the more aggressive arm of the protocol. We asked the fellow to arrange a care conference, and she met with the clinic director as well as Brent's neurologist to discuss how best to manage his case.

Conflict resolution

Conflict is a part of life. In a situation where a child's life is at risk, the heightened emotions and constant involvement with medical bureaucracy guarantee conflict. Because clashes are inevitable, resolving them is of utmost importance. A speedy resolution may result if you adopt Henry Ford's motto, "Don't find fault; find a remedy."

Following are some suggestions from parents about how to resolve problems:

• Treat the doctors with respect, and expect respect from them.

I always wanted to be treated as an intelligent adult, not someone of lesser status. So I would ask each medical person what they wished to be called. We would either both go by first names or both go by titles. I did not want to be called mom.

• Expect a reasonable amount of sensitivity from the staff.

One of the things that I didn't appreciate was constantly being told that we were lucky and Elizabeth had the "good cancer." One nurse actually told me that they call Wilms the "spit and rub" cancer because it is so easy to get rid of.

- Treat the staff with sensitivity. Recognize that you are under enormous stress, and so are the doctors and nurses. Do not blame them for the disease or explode in anger. Be an advocate, not an adversary.

- If a problem develops, state the issue clearly, without accusations, and then suggest a solution.

I found out late in my daughter's treatment that short-acting, safe sedatives were being used for some children at the clinic to prevent pain and anxiety during procedures. Only parents who knew about it and requested it received this service. I felt that my daughter's life would have been incredibly improved if we had been able to remove the trauma of procedures. I was angry. But I also realized that although I thought that they were wrong not to offer the service, I was partially at fault for not expressing more clearly how much difficulty she had the week before and after a procedure. I called the director of the clinic and carefully explained that I thought that poor staff/parent communication was creating hardships for the children. I suggested that the entire staff meet with a panel of parents to try to improve communication and to educate the doctors on the impact of pain on the children's daily lives. They were supportive and scheduled the conference. After the conference, they changed the policy so all children were sedated for painful procedures. This is a classic example of how something good can come out of a disagreement, if both parties are receptive to solving the problem.

- Recognize that although it is hard to speak up, especially if you are not naturally assertive, it is very important to solve the problem before it grows and poisons the relationship.

- Most large medical centers have social workers and psychologists on staff to help families. One of their major duties is to serve as mediators between staff and parents. You can ask for their advice about problem solving.

- Monitor your own feelings of anger and fear. Be careful not to dump on staff inappropriately. On the other hand, do not let a doctor or nurse behave unprofessionally toward you or your child. Parents and staff members all have bad days, but they should not take it out on each other.

During our little boy's first MRI, I was very emotional, and wondered out loud if he could feel or hear what was going on even though he was sedated. The MRI nurse caught me completely off-guard by banging loudly on the side of the transport bed without getting any reaction from him. "See, he's out," she said. I was too startled then, but I wished I had told her how much that bothered me.

- Do not fear reprisal for speaking up. It is possible to be assertive without being aggressive or argumentative. If you are worried, you can practice what you have to say with a trusted listener before approaching the treatment team.

- There are times when no resolution is possible, but expressing one's feelings can be a great release.

> *My son and I waited in an exam room for over an hour for a painful procedure. When I went out to ask the receptionist what had caused the delay, she said that a parent had brought in a child without an appointment. This parent frequently failed to bring in her child for treatment, and consequently, whenever she appeared, the doctors dropped everything to take care of the child. When the doctor finally came in, an hour and a half later, my son was in tears. The doctor did not explain the delay or apologize, he just silently started the procedure. After it was finished, I went out of the room, found the doctor, and said, "This makes me so angry. You just left us in here for hours and traumatized my son." He told me that I should have more compassion for the other mother because her life was very difficult. I replied that he encouraged her to not make appointments by dropping everything whenever she appeared. I added that it wasn't fair to those parents who played by the rules; she was being rewarded for her irresponsibility. After we had each stated our position, we left without resolution.*

Changing doctors

Facing childhood cancer is one of life's greatest struggles. A skilled doctor you trust, who communicates easily and honestly with you, can greatly ease this struggle. If the doctor adds to your family's discomfort rather than reducing it, you may have to change doctors. Changing doctors is not a step to be taken lightly, but it can be a great relief if the relationship has deteriorated beyond repair. It is a good policy to exhaust all possible remedies before separating and to examine your own role in the relationship to prevent the same problems from arising with the new doctor. Mediation by social service staff and improved communication can often resolve the issues and prevent the disruption of changing doctors.

Although there are many valid reasons for changing doctors, some of the most common are:

- Lack of qualifications.

- Grave medical errors being made.

- Poor communication skills or refusal to answer questions.

- Serious clash of philosophy or personality; for example, a paternalistic doctor and a parent who wishes to be informed and share in decision making.

Many parents, fearing reprisal, choose to continue with a doctor in whom they have no confidence. Such reprisals rarely happen at large children's hospitals. Although there may be lingering bitterness or anger between parents and doctors, the child will continue to benefit from the best-known treatment. Children may actually suffer more from the additional family stress caused by a poor doctor–parent relationship than from changing doctors.

> *Early in my daughter's treatment, we changed doctors. The first was aloof and patronizing, and the second was smart, warm, funny, and caring. He was a constant bright spot in our lives through some dark times. So every year during my daughter's treatment, she and her younger sister put on their Santa hats and brought homemade cookies to her doctor and nurse. This year was the first time she was able to walk in, and she looked them in the eye and sang, "We Wish You a Merry Christmas." Her nurse went in the back room and cried, and her doctor got misty-eyed. I'll always be thankful for their care.*

Once the decision is made to change doctors, parents must be candid. They should give an explanation for the change, either verbally or in writing, and make a formal request to transfer records to the new doctor. Doctors are legally required to transfer all records upon written request.

> *We've had wonderful docs, mediocre docs, and one who made a terrible mistake. We've had warm, compassionate docs, ho-hum docs (on a good day they're nice, on a bad day they're neutral), and we've met a couple of world-class jerks. Sounds pretty much like a slice of humanity, right?*
>
> *Parents hold doctors to a different standard because the stakes are so high—our kids' lives. But the reality is they are usually overworked, exhausted, and deal with newly diagnosed families on an almost daily basis, day after day, week after week, year after year. I can't even begin to imagine the emotional toll that must take.*
>
> *I tell my kids all human relationships are like a goodwill bank. If you make lots of deposits, an occasional withdrawal won't be so noticeable. I tell my docs and my kids' docs whenever things go right. I like to write, so I send many thank-you notes. When our pediatrician went on sabbatical, he took me into his office and showed me every mushy Christmas card I'd sent him lined up on the back of his messy desk.*
>
> *I also have been known to bring in brownies for the office staff. We did this on my daughter's last day of radiation and several people brushed away tears when they saw the thank-you note she drew—a picture of herself holding a Snow White and the Seven Dwarves audiotape. She listened to that during every radiation session because I'd promised that day's radiation treatment would be over before the dwarves appeared.*

I recently asked one of my favorite doctors (a pediatric oncologist who has incredible compassion) how many thank-you notes she had received from parents over the years. She said she could count them on two hands. I asked how many complaints, and she said, "You wouldn't want to know."

So, while I think docs should be called out for bad behavior and bad medicine, I also think we should continually acknowledge good medicine and good behavior. I'd like to encourage the good ones to stick around—new little innocents keep getting cancer every day.

Chapter 12

Hospitalization

THERE ARE FEW THINGS in life more uncomfortable than rising from a lumpy pull-out couch to face another day of your child's hospitalization for cancer. Hospitals are noisy bureaucracies that run on a time schedule all their own. Staff members wake children in the middle of the night to draw blood or check temperature, pulse, and blood pressure.

For a child, being hospitalized means being separated from parents, brothers, sisters, friends, classmates, pets, and the comfort and familiarity of home. A child's hospitalization can rob both parent and child of a sense of control, leaving them feeling helpless. With a little ingenuity, however, you can make the most of the facilities, liven up the atmosphere, and even have some fun.

The room

Because kids on chemotherapy are at increased risk of infection, many hospitals give them private rooms. This means more space for the child, the parents, and visitors; it also means much more freedom to personalize and decorate the room. Covering the walls with big, bright posters of interest to your child can brighten up the room immensely.

> The first thing we put up in Meagan's room was a huge poster of The Little Engine That Could saying, "I think I can, I think I can."

Cards can be displayed on the walls, hanging from strings like a mobile, or taped around the windowsills. You can display pictures of your child engaged in her favorite activities, and add photos of her friends. Most hospitals do not allow flowers on oncology floors because they can grow a fungus that can make children sick; but it's fun to have bouquets of mylar balloons bobbing in the corners (hospitals do not allow latex balloons). Younger children may be greatly comforted by having a favorite stuffed animal, blanket, or quilt on their bed. If your child likes certain scents, you can make the room smell good with aromatherapy oils.

I went and bought a travel bag on wheels. It is so much easier than trying to carry several handle bags when Zach is admitted. It has several pockets to carry stuff. I love it and wished I had done it 2 years ago when we started this!

I take these things to the hospital: flavored creamer for my coffee (a little treat for me); a book for us to read together so I don't go crazy from Cartoon Network (we are reading the Narnia series, and Zach begs me to read to him. I snuggle up with him in his bed while we read); his favorite pillow from home; little airplanes and parachuters to drop from the third floor at night when the lobby is empty (if he's feeling well enough); my thermometer so I can check his temp any time I want to; lots of Legos®; phone numbers of friends; canned ravioli; toaster strudels; audio books (Adventures in Odyssey®); and music CDs with earphones.

To personalize visits, some parents bring a guestbook for people to sign. Others put up a medical staff sign-in poster, which must be signed before examinations begin or vital signs are taken. Another variation of the sign-in poster is to have each staff member or visitor outline his or her hand and write his or her name within the handprint. Children can use a digital camera or smartphone to take pictures of the many staff members who come into the room.

In my position as a parent consultant, I suggest that a journal (possible titles are Book of Hope, Book of Sharing, My Cancer Experience, *and* Friends Indeed*) be kept in the child's room for any visitor, family member, or medical caregiver to write in at any time. Leaving a message if the child is sleeping or out of the room for procedures can be a nice surprise. Later, a surviving child and her family, or the family of a child who has died, have a memory book of those who have touched their lives.*

Bringing music and a portable music player with small speakers will help block out some of the hospital noise and can help everyone relax. A portable sound machine that has relaxing sounds such as ocean waves, falling rain, or white noise can be played while the child sleeps. An iPod® or other portable audio device with headphones and the child's favorite music or audio books also make the time pass more quickly.

My daughter's preschool teacher sent a care package. She made a felt board with dozens of cutout characters and designs that provided hours of quiet entertainment. She also included games, drawings from each classmate, coloring books, markers, get well cards, and a child's tape player with earphones. Because we had run out of our house with just the clothes on our backs, all of these toys were very, very welcome.

Many children's hospitals have in-room or portable DVD players available. You can check out DVDs from the hospital media library or bring a favorite funny movie or DVD of a television show. Humor helps, so joke books and things that make kids laugh (such as Silly String®) are great items to pack. Most hospitals have wireless Internet,

so children and teens can use social media, play games online, and stream movies and television shows.

A friend brought in a bag from the local dollar store. He included a water pistol (good for unwelcome visitors or unfriendly interns), Play-Doh®, a Slinky®, checkers, dominos, bubbles, a book of corny jokes, and puzzles.

The floor

Ask for a floor tour as soon as possible after admission. During the tour, you will find out whether a microwave and refrigerator are available, what the approved parent sleeping arrangements are, and whether showers are available for parents. You can also ask about a hospital handbook. These booklets often include information about billing, parking, discounts, and other helpful items.

Either my husband or I stayed with Delaney the entire time she was in the hospital. To improve the comfort of the fold-out chair that the hospital provides for the sleep-in parent, we used a self-inflating camping mat. When it is rolled out, it self-inflates with a one-way valve. The straps can be used to secure it to the vinyl chair. It makes the chair much more comfortable and allows your muscles to relax. When it is not in use, it can be rolled up with straps and set in the corner.

Although many hospitals provide colorful smocks for young patients, some children and teens prefer to wear their own clothing. This can pose a laundry problem, so find out whether the hospital has laundry facilities for families to use.

Food

Buying meals day after day in the hospital cafeteria is expensive. Check with the hospital social worker to find out whether the hospital has food discount cards or free meals for parents. Some hospitals deliver meals to families via a meal cart or provide sandwiches in a family lounge at meal times. Get directions to a grocery store near the hospital to purchase fresh food and healthy snacks if you are comfortable leaving for a short amount of time. Check to see whether the floor has a refrigerator for parents' food and stock it with your favorite items. Remember to put your name in a prominent place on your containers.

Our hospital provides vouchers for the cafeteria that can be used instead of ordering food for the room. For us, they have been a godsend. The food on the tray is much worse than what is in the cafeteria. Also, oncology patients have no spending cap on the vouchers, so we can get a few extras. When our son is not able to go to the cafeteria, we go down and bring the food back to his room.

Many hospitals have cooking facilities for families where they can cook or microwave favorite meals brought from home. Family and friends can bring food when they visit, and some parents order extra items for their child's tray. Ordering out for dinner can also be a nice change of pace for you and your child. As long as there are no medical restrictions, food from local restaurants can be delivered to your child's hospital room. You can check with the nurses to see whether they have menus from local restaurants or recommendations.

> *Just the smell of food nauseated my daughter. I'll never forget taking the tray out in the hall and gobbling the food down myself. I always felt so guilty, and thought that the staff viewed me as that parent who ate her kid's food. But it saved money and prevented her meals from going to waste. I also did not want to leave her side for the few minutes it took to go to the cafeteria although, in hindsight, the walk would have done me some good.*

Parking

Many parents of children with cancer have unpleasant memories of driving around in endless loops looking for a parking space while their child was throwing up in a bucket in the back seat (or even worse when the bucket was left at home). Some hospitals charge patients to park and some do not. The hospital might have both long-term and short-term parking arrangements. If your hospital charges for parking, the nurses or the patient advocate can tell you whether parking passes are available or where the cheapest parking is located. Some hospitals have valet parking, which may be as inexpensive as self-parking for a short appointment.

> *I had no idea that the hospital gave out free parking passes to their frequent customers. Now I tell every new parent to check as soon as possible to see if they can get a parking pass. It will save them lots of money that they would have spent on meters and parking tickets, and time that they would have spent running out to move the car out of the emergency parking spot.*

The endless waiting

Everything seems to take forever in the hospital, so parents must learn the art of waiting patiently or they will go nuts. For example, the nurse might tell you not to go to the playroom because someone will be "right up" to take your child for an echocardiogram. "Right up" can easily mean 2 hours or more. Many parents find themselves getting nervous or angry while waiting for the doctors to appear during rounds each morning (when the attending physicians, fellows, residents, and interns move from room to room in a large group), then feeling let down when the visit lasts only a few moments. If

you have questions to ask the doctors, write them down and tell the doctors when they come in that you would like a moment to discuss concerns or ask questions.

You don't have to go too crazy. Make sure you watch the videos or eat the popcorn or flirt with the nurses or taunt the residents or leave notes for the cleaning lady or chat with the security guard or make coffee for all the parents or pretend you like puking or show the nurses how to hack into the hospital mainframe or paint your face with butt paste. Or, all of the above, if you like. Just do something.

It helps for both the parent and child to be prepared for long waits each time they come to the hospital. Some well-supported institutions have iPads®, DVDs, video games, and toys available, but you might need to bring your own entertainment such as favorite card games, board games, computer games, drawing materials, and books. Some children will take comfort from having a favorite blanket or pillow along with them for a day in the clinic or during a lengthy hospitalization. If your child is scheduled for surgery, you can bring a good book, a model airplane project, your holiday card list, or a jigsaw puzzle that several people can work on together.

Our emergency bag had two sides. The most important was mine, because our hospital provided nothing for parents. I would pack deodorant (plus an extra set of clothes), a book I had not read (I survived on romance novels that I bought at the used bookstore, four for a dollar), decent lighting, a soft sweatshirt top and bottom to wear at night, paper and pen for taking notes, and clean socks. You might laugh, but I can deal with a scared, irritable kid for a L-O-N-G time as long as I have clean, soft socks!

On the kids' side was an art kit with Play-Doh®, crayons, pencils, markers, scissors, glue, finger paints, clay, and reams of paper. It also had plastic cutlery, and some cookie cutters for the Play-Doh®. I always brought the game Trouble®, since it's self-contained and the dice are enclosed in the little bubble. The pieces fit nicely in a plastic sandwich bag (or medication bag). The lifesaver was video games. They provided hours of enjoyment. We also brought a Lego® table with blocks. Since Matthew is usually neutropenic, or in isolation for some mysterious complication, we bring our own games. Monopoly® and Battleship® are both games that can take an entire morning to play.

We also made it a habit to always bring Matthew's special blanket on any clinic or ER visits. I cannot imagine trying to have him in the hospital without it. He does not carry it around, but it is always there at bedtime.

I also kept a box of stuff for me to do in case of incarceration at Club Children's. In particular, the box had pictures and photo albums. One nurse remarked how organized I was, but I pointed out that the album I was putting together was of Matthew's first birthday. He was almost 6 at the time.

Working with the staff

There are wonderful and not-so-wonderful people employed by hospitals. It helps to remember that working in the pediatric oncology field is extremely stressful and that most of the staff are working hard on behalf of the children. Even the tiniest effort on your part to ease their burden or empathize with their circumstances will go a very long way toward establishing a cooperative and friendly relationship. For example, if parents help change soiled bedding, take out food trays, and give their child baths, it can free up overworked nurses to take care of medicines and IVs. If you are making a run to the coffee shop, ask whether you can bring them something, too. Simply remembering to thank them every day will make a big difference. Chapter 11, *Forming a Partnership with the Medical Team*, contains suggestions for how to enhance your relationship with the staff.

> *I always made a point of introducing myself to my daughter's nurse and resident for each shift. I told them my child's name and which room we were in. I told them that I would be there the whole time and that I would help as much as I could. I tried to talk to them about non-hospital matters to give them a break from their routine, as well as to get to know them. I thanked them for any kindnesses and told them I appreciated how hard their jobs were. Although I wasn't angling for favors, I found that they soon came to like me and helped me out whenever any difficulty arose. Although there were a few that I didn't care for, on the whole I found the staff members to be warm, caring, dedicated people.*

Having cancer strips children of control over their bodies. To help reverse this process, parents can take over some of the nursing care. Children may prefer to have their parents help them to the bathroom or clean up their diarrhea or vomit. Making the bed, keeping the room tidy, changing dressings, and giving back rubs helps your child feel more comfortable and lightens the burden on the nurses. However, some children and teens may feel better if the nurses provide these services.

> *Parents should not have to worry about helping the staff or whether the staff is stressed. They have enough on their plate to worry about. But families often feel like they're so helpless, and they think, "What can I do, how can I get in control of this situation?" Many parents find comfort in changing the bed; they very often feel so completely overwhelmed, because they can't give the medicines, and they can't make the cancer go away. So they do what they can do for their child. Look at the staff as a team. You are part of that team. But no one can be your child's parent but you.*

It helps to learn about the shift changes on the oncology floor. If you need to leave during the day or night, do not leave a request with one nurse if another will be coming on duty soon. If you have a request or reminder, you can post it on your child's door, on the wall above the bed, or on the chart.

In addition, parents and staff can help children regain some control by encouraging choices whenever possible. Older children should be involved in discussions about their treatments, while younger children can decide when to take a bath, which arm to use for an IV, what to order for meals, what position their body will be in for procedures, what clothes to wear, and how to decorate the room. Some children request a hug or a handshake after all treatments or procedures.

> Our son is almost 6. He prefers to talk first with the nurse or technician about fun stuff, like his trains, before he allows any kind of IV or blood draw. Most good techs don't mind; they try to do that anyway. He definitely prefers it when I step back, stay quiet, and let him lead.

It also helps to find out whether there are support groups for parents, the child with cancer, and siblings. These groups help family members of newly diagnosed children understand the diagnosis and treatment, as well as provide much needed support.

Staying with your child

Hospitals can be frightening places for children. Fear can be prevented or lessened if parents are there to provide comfort, protection, and advocacy for their child. Most pediatric hospitals are quite aware of how much better children do when a parent is allowed to sleep in the room. Some rooms contain small couches convert into beds, or parents can use a cot provided by the hospital.

> Whenever my husband couldn't be at the hospital at bedtime, he would bring in homemade tapes of him reading bedtime stories. Our son would drift off to sleep hearing his daddy's voice.

Of course, sometimes it isn't possible to stay with your child if you are a single parent or if both parents work full-time. Many families have grandparents, older siblings (older than age 18), or close friends who stay with the hospitalized child when the parents cannot be present. Older children and teenagers may not want a parent in the room at night, but they may need an advocate there during the day just as much as the preschoolers.

> Our hospital did not allow parents into the MRI suite. We worked with the head of that department, and being with your child during the MRI now it is permitted for all families. This avoided the use of general anesthesia, so it was good for everyone involved. You don't need to take "no" for an answer.

Some families find staying at the hospital day and night to be too stressful. An oncologist made the following suggestion:

> When people are subject to stress, some people cope by focusing on all the details. For these people, being there all the time reduces their stress level. In other words, they would be more stressed if they were at home or work because they would be worrying all the time. Other people cope with stress by blocking out the details and trying to make life normal. I think that you need to think about how your family can best cope with this process and make your decisions based on that. Have a family meeting to sort out these issues, and don't feel bad if you decide what is best for your family is different from what other people say you should do.

Preventing mistakes

Everyone makes mistakes and hospital workers are no exception. You can help by checking before any medications or blood transfusions are given. For instance, check that the name of the drug and the dose match what the protocol says should be given; if you were not given a copy of the protocol (sometimes called the roadmap), you can ask your nurse or doctor for a copy. You should feel free to ask questions or point out any deviations from prescribed treatment. Parents are the last line of defense against mistakes.

> In the beginning I didn't feel comfortable voicing my opinion, but I got over that, thank goodness. I used to be a people pleaser and worried about stepping on people's toes. But now, I recommend trusting your instincts and never doubting that you know your child best. For instance, when a nurse was putting a new dressing on my daughter's line, I saw a hole in the dressing right over the site. It felt like an out of body experience. I pointed out the hole and the nurse said, "Oh, my goodness!" and she fixed it. I've learned not to second guess myself about things that bothered me. I've always been naive thinking that doctors and nurses always know what they are doing. But, now I realize it's been empowering for me as a mom that I know when things are wrong. Although I wish I was learning that lesson in a different way.

Whenever a family member is not present, children who are old enough should have a cell phone or be taught to use the telephone in the room. Tape a phone number nearby where a parent can be reached and tell your child to call if anyone tries to do procedures that are unexpected. The hospital staff should be informed that any changes in treatment (except emergencies) need to be authorized by a parent.

> Brian was 12 and could have stayed alone, but we never left him for more than 5 minutes to run down the hall for coffee, bathroom, etc. Someone—my husband, me, a grandparent, an aunt or uncle—was always there. If we had needed them, church members and friends had also volunteered, as Kevin (the younger brother) was only 2 at the time. With my husband rotating days at work and the hospital,

and me rotating home and hospital, somehow we managed. A caring employer is essential.

Also, Brian became very familiar with all his drugs, allergies, reactions, and doses. Several times he corrected the staff even before I could. We also had errors and near-errors, as I'm sure everyone does, but many fewer, I'm sure, because of the constant presence and watchful eyes. Operating room doctors and nurses accessed his line without first swabbing with alcohol. Someone wanted to give ibuprofen for fever. Non-oncology nurses were working the pediatric oncology floor and knew less than we did. Our hospital is now greatly improved, but things like this happen everywhere.

• • • • •

Know every drug your child takes. Write down the name of the drug and the dosage. Watch that the name on the drug matches what YOU are expecting your child to get, and ask if it isn't something you recognize. Watch that the name on the unit of blood is your child's name. Watch everything.

Playing

Children need to play, especially when hospitalized. The hospital probably has a recreation therapy or child life department that has toys, books, dolls, and crafts. The specialists really know how to play with children and also provide many therapeutic activities, such as medical play with dolls, which helps children express fears or concerns about what is happening to them. By encouraging contact with other children in similar circumstances, recreation therapy helps children feel less alone and less different from their peers.

Sometimes you can create your own fun with just a little imagination. On one particular occasion, Matthew was feeling especially bored. With a little ingenuity, we soon discovered that four unused IV poles and as many blankets as we could "steal" from the linen cart made for one pretty cool tent. We then used the mattress from a roll-away cot, and spent the night "camping" in his hospital room. He had a wonderful time.

The fun-filled activities and smiling staff people in the child life department are a cheerful change from lying in a hospital bed. If your child is too ill or if her counts are too low to go to the play area, arrangements can be made for a recreational therapist to bring a bundle of toys, games, and books to the room. Some hospitals host bingo games and silly variety shows on closed circuit TV so children who aren't able to go to the playroom can be included in the fun. Music and art therapists may also come to the bedside. This can give the parent time to go out to eat or take a walk.

When I wanted to have a conference with the oncologist about Katy's protocol, I called recreation therapy and they sent two wonderful ladies to the clinic. The doctor and I were able to talk privately for an hour, and Katy had a great time making herself a gold crown and decorating her wheelchair with streamers and jewels.

Exercise is important, too. For kids strong enough to walk, exploring the hospital can be fun. Even if they can't walk, you can wheel them around or pull them in a wagon if they feel up to it. (This is also a great workout for you.) Plan a daily excursion to the gift shop or the cafeteria. Go outside and walk the entire perimeter of the hospital if weather and the neighborhood permit. Do not feel limited by an IV pole; it can be pushed or pulled and will feel normal after a while. Many children stand on the base of the IV pole with a parent pushing them down the hall at a good clip. Physical and occupational therapists can help your child incorporate exercise into the daily routine.

At our hospital, there was a large metal tricycle with a huge metal basket on the back. I would heplock Kenny, toss him in the back, then we would pedal all over the hospital. There is one part of the hospital called "the tunnel" that connects the children's hospital with Emory Hospital. It is about a mile-long tunnel—all downhill. Man, we would fly—laughing and screaming. Of course, coming back up was pure hell.

Any action that parents, family members, and friends take to support and advocate for the child with cancer buoys the spirit. Courage is contagious.

In our hospital photos, I have several of a grinning 4 year old, hooked up to an IV, in a hospital bed, with the head raised waaaaaaayyyy up, as she'd slide down to the bottom. Of course I was doing guard duty at the door, to alert the happy child when a nurse was coming and she needed to "cease this unsafe behavior immediately!" Sometimes you have to make memories while you can, wherever you are.

Chapter 13

Venous Catheters

MOST CHILDREN WITH SOLID TUMORS require intensive treatment, including surgery, chemotherapy, intravenous (IV) fluids, IV antibiotics, blood and platelet transfusions, frequent blood sampling, and sometimes IV nutrition. Venous catheters provide a very effective method for allowing entry into the large veins for intensive therapy. They eliminate the difficulty of finding veins for IVs and allow drugs to be put directly into the heart, where they are rapidly diluted and spread throughout the body. They also reduce stress and discomfort for the child by eliminating the need for hundreds of needle sticks.

The three types of venous catheters are external catheters, subcutaneous ports, and peripherally inserted central catheters (PICC). Other names for a venous catheter include venous access device, right atrial catheter, implanted catheter, indwelling catheter, central line, Hickman®, Broviac®, PORT-A-CATH®, and Medi-port®.

This chapter first describes external, implanted, and PICC catheters—what they look like, how they are placed, the care they need, and their risks. It then compares the costs of venous cathers and the various types of adhesives that can be used to secure the lines in place. The final part of the chapter offers information to help families decide which catheter to choose.

External catheter

An external catheter is a long, flexible tube with one end located in the right atrium of the heart and the other end outside the skin of the chest. The tube tunnels under the skin of the chest, enters a large vein near the collarbone, and threads inside the vein to the heart (see Figure 13-1). The tube that channels the fluid is called a lumen. Some external catheters have double lumens in case two drugs need to be given at the same time.

Because chemotherapy drugs, transfusions, and IV fluids are put in the end of the tube hanging outside the body, the child feels no pain. Blood for complete blood counts (CBC) or chemistry tests can also be drawn from the end of the catheter. With daily care, the external catheter can be left in place for years.

How it's put in

External catheters are usually put in while the child is under general anesthesia. Once the child is anesthetized, the surgeon makes two small incisions. One incision is near the collarbone over the spot where the catheter will enter the vein, and the other is in the area on the chest where the catheter exits the body. To prevent the catheter from slipping out, it is stitched to the skin where it comes out of the chest (see Figure 13-1). There is a plastic cuff around the catheter right above the exit site (under the skin) into which body tissue grows. This tissue growth further anchors the catheter and helps prevent infection. Some surgeons also place a small antibiotic-infused disk around the catheter at the exit site. After healing is complete, the child can resume normal activities.

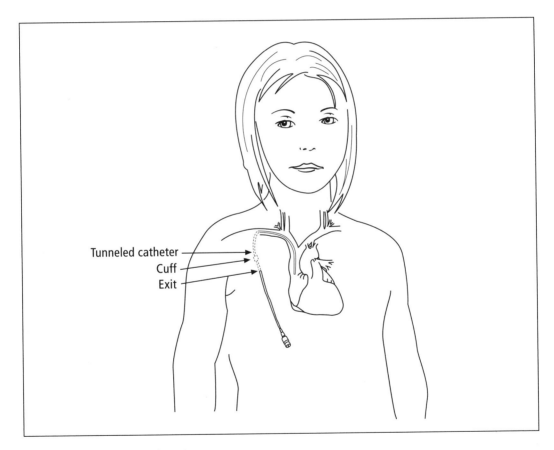

Figure 13-1: External catheter

Daily care

An external catheter requires careful maintenance to prevent infection or the formation of blood or drug clots. The site where the catheter exits the body needs to be frequently cleaned and bandaged (schedules range from daily to weekly). Procedures and schedules for cleaning and bandaging vary from one institution to another. No matter what the care schedule is, the site should be checked daily for redness, swelling, and drainage.

To prevent clots, parents or older children are taught to flush the line with a medication called heparin that prevents blood from clotting. Each institution uses its own flushing schedule, and nurses at the hospital teach parents and children how to care for the catheter. Both parent and child should be given lots of time to practice with supervision and should not be discharged until they are comfortable with the entire procedure. At discharge, parents can arrange for home nursing visits to provide further help, if needed.

> *We were very grateful for Matthew's Hickman® line. Like a lot of children, he was terribly afraid of needles. The maintenance that was necessary to keep his line working properly became second nature to me. After his diagnosis, and again after his relapse, he had a Hickman® implanted. In total, he had his external catheter for more than 4 years.*

Risks

The major complications of using an external catheter are infections—either in the blood or at the insertion site—and the formation of clots in the line. Rare complications include kinking of the catheter, the catheter moving out of place, or breakage of the external part of the catheter.

Infections

Even with the best care, infections are common in children with external catheters. Children who have low white blood cell counts for long periods of time are at risk for developing infections anyway, and each time the line is flushed or cleaned there is a chance of contamination. Usually, it is a bacterium called staphylococcus epidermidis—which lives on the skin—that is the culprit, although a host of other organisms can cause infections in children receiving chemotherapy.

> *After my son Trevor (4 years old) was diagnosed with Wilms tumor, he had a nephrectomy (kidney removal) and an 18-week course of chemotherapy. During the nephrectomy, the surgeons also inserted a tube—called a Broviac®—into Trevor's chest. This enabled Trevor to receive his chemotherapy treatment without getting a new IV put in each week. My husband and I were responsible for cleaning and flushing the Broviac® tube daily.*

Throughout the whole thing, Trevor was so strong and brave. After he had completed all his treatments, we were told that the catheter needed to stay in for a few more weeks. However, soon after treatment ended, Trevor was admitted back to the hospital when his catheter became infected. The doctors treated him with antibiotics and decided to remove the Broviac® a little early. The Broviac® prevented a lot of unnecessary pain, and we were grateful that he had it.

If your child develops a fever higher than 101° F (38.5° C), redness or swelling at the insertion site, or pain in the catheter area, you should suspect an infection. This is a life-threatening situation, so call the doctor immediately. To determine whether bacteria are present, blood will be drawn from the catheter to culture (i.e., grow in a laboratory for 24 to 48 hours). Treatment with antibiotics will start whenever an infection is suspected and will end if the culture comes back negative. If the culture is positive, treatment usually continues for 10 to 14 days. Some physicians require that the child be hospitalized for antibiotic treatment, while others allow the child to receive treatment at home. If the infection does not respond to treatment, the catheter will need to be removed.

When my daughter had a line infection, I wanted to use the antibiotic pump at home. It was hard, though. It took 2 hours per dose, three doses per day, for 14 days. I would get up at 5 a.m. to hook her up, so that she would sleep through the first dose. The second dose I would give while she watched a TV show in the early afternoon. Then I would hook her up at bedtime so she would sleep through it. I had to wait up to flush and disconnect, so I was very tired by the end of the 2 weeks.

• • • • •

We used the IV infusion ball when Joseph needed a vancomycin infusion because he didn't have to sit chained to a pump. The IV infusion ball is cool because if you have a sweatshirt with front pockets, you can make a tiny hole in the back of the sweatshirt to put the tubing through and stash the ball in the pocket so you can go about your business while your IV is infusing and no one has to know a thing! It's handy for pain meds, too. He even used it at school, as long as I was there with him. An awesome invention—brilliantly simple. Here's the website that describes it: www.halyardhealth.com/solutions/iv-therapy/homepump-infusion-systems.aspx.

Clots

Even with excellent daily care, some external catheters develop blockages or clots. If the catheter becomes blocked with a blood clot, it will be flushed with a drug that dissolves the clot, such as alteplase, urokinase, or streptokinase. These agents are given in the clinic or hospital, and the child usually needs to remain nearby for 1 to 2 hours. On rare occasions, the catheter becomes blocked by solidified medications, which can occur if two incompatible drugs are administered simultaneously. In those cases, a diluted hydrochloric acid solution may be used to dissolve the blockage.

Two months before the end of Kristin's treatment, her line plugged up. We tried several maneuvers at home unsuccessfully. We had to bring her in for the IV team to work on it. I think the bumpy ride to the hospital loosened it because at the hospital they were able to dislodge the clot just by flushing it with saline.

Kinks

Rarely, a kink develops in the catheter due to a sharp angle where the catheter enters the neck vein. In such cases, the fluids may go in the catheter but it is hard to get blood out. Parents and nurses are often able to work around this problem by experimenting with different positions for the child when blood is drawn. The nurse may ask your child to bear down as if having a bowel movement, take a deep breath, cough, stretch, or laugh.

My son is 16, and his Hickman® was giving the nurses problems, so they planned to do a dye study. They didn't even have to inject the dye; the x-ray showed the line had come out and was clear across the opposite side of his chest and kinked! I don't think it had been out long. But it was a little scary to think that chemo may be going everywhere. They did a procedure where they go in and pull the catheter back into place. It was still attached to the vein, so the chemo hadn't been going amok. We are all so happy they got it fixed without surgery.

Catheter breakage

Breaks in the line do happen, but they are extremely rare. If a break or rupture of the line inside the body occurs when the line is not in use, only heparin will leak into surrounding tissues (which is not a major problem). If the break occurs when harsh chemotherapy drugs are flowing through the catheter, they may leak and cause damage to surrounding tissue. However, the risk of an internal line leaking is far lower than the chance of leakage from an IV in a vein of the hand or arm.

The external portion of the catheter can also break. If this occurs, clamp the line between the point of breakage and the chest wall, cover the break in the line with a sterile gauze pad, and notify the doctor immediately. In most cases, the line can be repaired. Many treatment centers send a catheter repair kit home with parents so they can put on a temporary patch until a new line can be inserted.

I think it is important for parents to obtain clamps from the treating institution to carry with them. The preschool or school the child attends should also have one, in case something happens to the external line above the clamps that exist on the catheter. Younger children should wear a snug tank top that helps hold the catheter in place. Pinning it to the shirt is not the best solution for an active or young child.

Other factors to consider

The proper care and maintenance of an external catheter requires motivation and organization. The site needs to be cleaned and dressed frequently, and heparin must be injected using sterile techniques. If your child's skin is quite sensitive, or if he cries when tape or Band-Aids® are removed from his skin, the external line may not be the best choice because the dressing must be taped to the skin.

> One of my most difficult times was learning to change the dressing for Ben's catheter. I am totally freaked out by syringes, and anything like that, and we were given a 10-minute demonstration in the hospital and an instruction book and that was it. I was petrified of doing something wrong to hurt my son. My husband tried, but he does not have very good balance, and he could not get the sterile gloves on without contaminating them. I went into panic mode the first week home from the hospital. I felt like the most inadequate mother in the whole world. Since neither of us could do what had to be done, my husband called a home health agency and they sent a nurse.

> Kathy was the most wonderful person on earth. She told me that even though she had been a nurse for 20 years, she didn't think she could change the dressing on her own child, and she perfectly understood my fears. She had me watch her over and over again until I was comfortable enough to do it with her watching, and then finally on my own. She also talked to our insurance company numerous times to explain why she had to change the dressing instead of the family, and they ended up paying for her services! It was totally amazing. In addition, she helped my mental mood immensely, always telling me how good Ben was doing and sharing stories with me. I could tell her anything and she always understood. After I no longer needed her, she still stopped by about once a month to see how Ben was doing. She was my guardian angel.

The external line is a constant reminder of cancer treatment and can cause changes in body image. Both parent and child need to be comfortable with the idea of seeing and handling a tube that emerges from the chest. It is noticeable under lightweight clothing and bathing suits, but not under heavier clothing such as sweaters or coats. If a younger sibling might pull or yank on the catheter, the Hickman® or Broviac® might not be the appropriate choice.

On the other hand, the reason external lines are chosen so frequently is that there are no needles and no pain. This is a very important consideration for any child or teen who is scared of needles and/or pain. Some treatment protocols require double lumen access, and the external catheter is the only option for this. For instance, children who need a stem cell transplant use double-lumen external venous catheters. But in most cases, families have a choice of which type of catheter to use.

> Ben had a double-lumen catheter, a long tube with two ends that came out of his chest just above his right nipple. When not in use, it was curled and taped against

his skin. I hated this thing. It made him Borg-like. I had to clean it every day for more than a year, and flush both ends of the tube. This hated thing, however, was what kept Ben from having to be stuck with needles several times a week. It was direct access to his blood supply, for tests, medication administration, and chemotherapy. One day Ben told me he had "made friends with his tubies." They had names, "The red one was Ralph, and the white one was Henry." He liked his tubies, he said, because they kept him from getting "ouchies." I was speechless. His matter-of-fact example showed me that the sooner I made friends with Ralph and Henry, the better off I'd be.

Children with external catheters sometimes have restrictions about playing contact sports, swimming, using hot tubs, bathing, and showering.

Subcutaneous port

Several types of subcutaneous (under the skin) ports are available. The subcutaneous port differs from the external catheter in that it is completely under the skin. A small metal chamber (1.5 inches in diameter) with a rubber top is implanted under the skin of the chest. A catheter threads from the metal chamber (portal) under the skin to a large vein near the collarbone, and then inside the vein to the right atrium of the heart (see Figure 13-2). Whenever the catheter is needed for a blood draw or infusion of drugs or fluid, a needle is inserted by a nurse through the skin and into the rubber top of the portal. Usually a topical numbing agent such as EMLA® is used to make the needle insertion less painful.

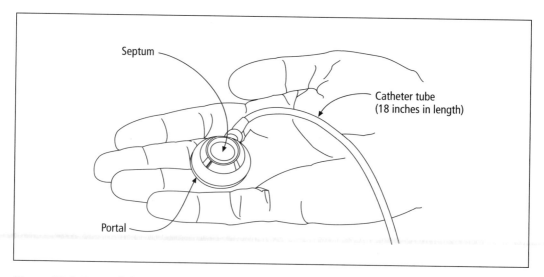

Figure 13-2: Parts of the subcutaneous port

How it's put in

The subcutaneous port is implanted under general anesthesia; the procedure generally takes less than an hour. The surgeon makes two small incisions: one in the chest where the portal will be placed, and the other near the collarbone where the catheter will enter a vein in the lower part of the neck. First, one end of the catheter is placed in the large blood vessel of the neck and threaded into the right atrium of the heart. The other end of the catheter is tunneled under the skin where it is attached to the portal. Fluid is injected into the portal to ensure the device works properly. The portal is then placed under the skin of the chest and stitched to the underlying muscle. Both incisions are then stitched closed. The only evidence that a catheter has been implanted are two small scars and a bump under the skin where the portal rests.

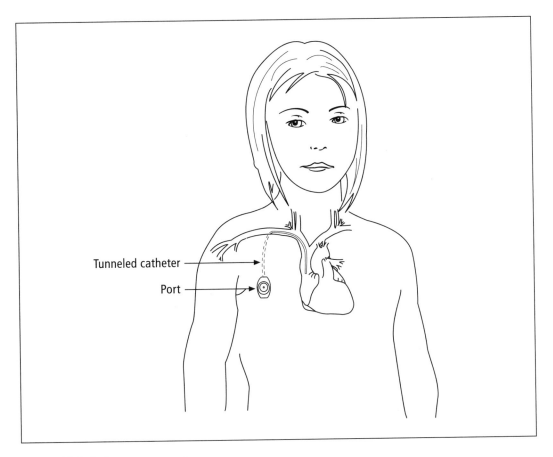

Figure 13-3: Subcutaneous port

Before my child's surgery to have a port implanted, I saw other children being wheeled into the operating room screaming and trying to climb off the gurney to return to the parents. It broke my heart. When it was Jennifer's turn, I asked them to give her enough premedication so that she was relaxed and happy to go. I also insisted that I be in the recovery room when she awoke.

• • • • •

Christine had her port surgery late at night. The resident gave her some premedication, then the chief resident ordered him to give her more. She felt so silly that she looked at me, giggled, and said "Mommy has a nose as long as an elephant's." I asked the surgeon if I could be in the recovery room before she awoke, and he said, "Sure." When I told the nurse that I had permission to go in recovery, she refused. When I persisted, she became angry. I told her that my child was expecting to wake up seeing my face, and I wanted to be there. I suggested that she go in and ask the surgeon to resolve the impasse. When she came out, she let me in the recovery room.

How it works

Because the entire subcutaneous port is under the skin, a needle is used to access it. The skin is thoroughly cleansed with antiseptic, and then a special needle is inserted through the skin and the rubber top of the portal. The needle is attached to a short length of tubing that hangs down the front of the chest. A topical anesthetic cream (see Chapter 10, *Coping with Procedures*) can be applied 1 hour before the needle poke to anesthetize the skin, or ethyl chloride ("freezy spray") can be sprayed on right before the poke. Subcutaneous ports have a rubber top (septum) that reseals after the needle is removed. It is designed to withstand years of needle insertions, as long as a special "non-coring" needle is used each time. Fluid will leak into the tissues if the wrong needle is used.

If the child is in a part of treatment that requires using the line every day, the nurse will attach the tubing to IV fluids or will close the end off with a sterile cap after flushing the line with saline solution. A transparent dressing will be put over the site where the needle enters the port. The port can remain accessed in this way for up to 7 days. After that time, to avoid the risk of infection, the needle should be removed and the port reaccessed when necessary. If the needle and tubing are to be left in place, it is important to tape them securely to the chest to avoid accidents.

Molly (3 years old) hated tape removal, so we did not secure the IV tubing to her stomach or chest. On one of her many trips to the potty, we accidentally tugged on the tubing and caused a very small tear in the skin around the needle. It became infected. We did home antibiotics on the pump and felt very fortunate that we were able to clear the line with antibiotics. We were glad our doctor was not too quick to remove the line, but it did require 2 weeks off chemotherapy.

If the port is only needed infrequently, the sequence of events is: clean the site, put in the needle, rinse the line with saline, give the drug or draw blood, rinse the line with saline, add heparin to the line, withdraw the needle, and place an adhesive bandage over the site.

Care of the port

The entire port and catheter are under the skin and therefore require no daily care. The skin over the port can be washed just like the rest of the body. Frequent visual inspections are needed to check for swelling, redness, or drainage. Signs of infection include redness, swelling, pain, drainage, or warmth around the port. Fever, chills, tiredness, and dizziness may also indicate that the line has become infected. You should notify the doctor immediately if any of these signs are present or if your child has a fever above 101° F (38.5° C).

> *My son had a PORT-A-CATH® for 3 years, from age 14 to 17. During that time, he played basketball, football, softball, and threw the shot put in track. His port was placed on his left side just below his armpit. For football, I worked with the trainer and we developed a special pad that went into a pocket I sewed into some T-shirts. That way the port had a little extra padding. We also found shoulder pads that had a sidepiece that covered the area. He never had any problems or soreness from the port.*

The subcutaneous port must be accessed and flushed with saline and heparin at least once every 30 days, which might coincide with clinic visits or blood draws. This procedure is done by a nurse or technician. Ports don't require maintenance by a parent.

> *My 3-year-old had a port inserted for a period of about a year and a half. His port survived all kinds of normal kid wear and tear. I remember that kids with external lines were discouraged from swimming, but with a subcutaneous port, there weren't any restrictions in activity or special precautions, which meant one less thing for us to worry about.*

Risks

The risks for a subcutaneous port are similar to those for an external catheter: infection, clots, and, rarely, kinks or rupture. If the needle is not properly inserted through the rubber septum, or if the wrong kind of needle is used, fluids can leak into the tissue around the portal.

> *My son (8 years old) has had a PORT-A-CATH® for 33 months with absolutely no problems. He uses EMLA® to anesthetize it prior to accessing. He hates finger pokes so much that he has his port accessed every time he needs blood drawn.*

We had a few unusual problems in the beginning with the catheter. It was a bit kinked where the catheter went under the collarbone and would not easily draw. This caused more stress than anything in the hospital, because their middle-of-the-night blood draws were always an ordeal for our daughter. They needed to wake her up and try multiple manipulations. Once we were familiar with its idiosyncrasies and were outpatient, we worked it out much better. Then about halfway through treatment, her catheter broke at the kink and travelled into her heart. To make a long story short, it was retrieved by a cardiologist without major surgery, and she got a new one placed, this time with the catheter going down from her neck. It works like a dream.

Infection

Most studies show that the infection rate for subcutaneous ports is lower than that of external catheters. If the subcutaneous port does become infected, it is treated the same way an infected external catheter is treated.

Katy had two infections in her PORT-A-CATH® during treatment. One occurred when the tape loosened during a blood transfusion. She developed a fever the next day and required 14 days of vancomycin. Eighteen months later, we went in for her monthly chemo, and she became ill in the car on the way home. Her skin became white and clammy, and she felt faint and nauseated. She spiked a 102° temperature, which only lasted for 2 hours. The blood culture both times grew staphylococcus epi.

Kinks, clots, and ruptures

These events rarely occur with a subcutaneous port. If they do occur, they are treated as described in the external catheter section.

My son had a very bad blood clot in his PORT-A-CATH®. In fact, he had two. He was put on Lovenox® (low molecular weight heparin) for 3 months (twice a day). We went for an ultrasound last week and it showed that the clots are mostly gone now.

• • • • •

When we got to the clinic for weekly chemo, no matter what gravity-defying positions we tried (raising arms, lying down, standing up), our nurse couldn't get the line to flush. Adrienne's port was clogged. Luckily, they were able to clear the line with an injection of streptokinase, although it meant entertaining her in the clinic for more than an hour while we waited for it to work. They did tell us that if this didn't work we'd have to go in overnight for slow infusion of chemo, but the line cleared, and we did chemo outpatient.

Peripherally inserted central catheter

A peripherally inserted central catheter is also referred to as a PICC line. This type of catheter is placed in the antecubital vein (a large vein in the inner elbow area) and is threaded into a large vein above the right atrium of the heart (see Figure 13-4). Unlike other catheters, a PICC line can be inserted by an IV nurse rather than a surgeon.

The PICC line can remain in place for many weeks or months, avoiding the need for a new IV every few days. It can be used to deliver chemotherapy, antibiotics, blood products, other medications, and IV nutrition. When the PICC line needs to be accessed, an IV line is connected to the end of the catheter. When it is not in use, the IV is disconnected and the catheter is flushed and capped.

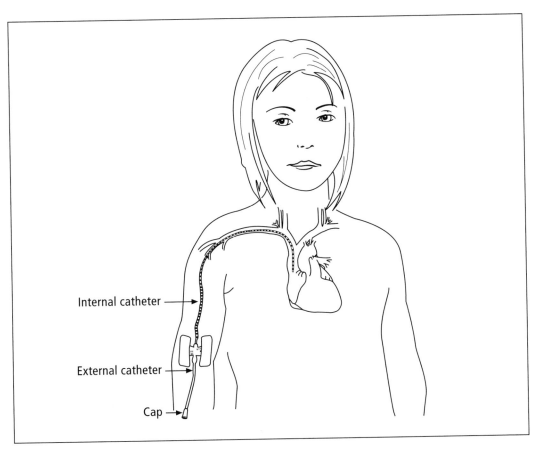

Figure 13-4: Peripherally inserted central catheter (PICC) line

How it's put in

The PICC line can be inserted in your child's hospital room by a nurse or doctor. Your child will be positioned on a flat surface, and he will need to keep his arm straight and motionless during the procedure. An injection to numb the area is given to decrease discomfort during insertion. A special needle is used to place the PICC line into the arm vein. The catheter is then threaded through the needle. Once the line is in place, a chest x-ray is taken to ensure it is positioned properly. Some children may require light sedation during the procedure.

Care of the PICC line

The PICC line, like the external catheter, requires care to prevent problems. A nurse will teach you how to change the dressing, flush the line, change the injection cap, and inspect the site for possible signs of infection. The dressing covering the exit site is changed once a week, or if it becomes wet. The line must be flushed after every use, or at least every day. You should get plenty of practice under the supervision of a nurse until both you and your child are comfortable with caring for the line. The care required for your child's PICC line may be slightly different from what has been described in this section, because institutional preferences vary.

> Kelsey had a PICC line in her right arm, and she would not straighten it out, but kept it a little bent. I definitely think she was protecting it, and also I think when she tried to straighten it, it pulled on the suture and on the dressing in an uncomfortable way that could have been painful, so she just wouldn't try. I had to do a heparin flush every day and change the dressing twice a week. She could not tolerate Tegaderm®, so we used another kind of porous adhesive bandage, and doused it with Detachol®, which dissolved the adhesive within a few minutes, allowing us to get the bandage off quite easily. The Detachol® was a godsend for her, as removing the adhesive was like pulling teeth and a source of unnecessary pain. (For more information about Detachol®, see the section "Adhesives" later in this chapter.)

Risks

The problems associated with a PICC line are similar to those of any external catheter. Veins may become irritated, infection can occur, or the line can be accidentally torn or moved.

Irritated veins

Within the first few days of insertion, the vein where the catheter is located may become irritated. Signs of irritation include swelling or pain in the area. Often, the discomfort can be alleviated by placing a warm, moist cloth or a carefully monitored heating pad on the vein. Elevating the arm on a pillow is also sometimes helpful.

Infection

Meticulous care using sterile techniques is extremely important to reduce the risk of infection. The dressing over the exit site should be changed every week, or if it becomes wet. Injection caps must also be regularly changed using sterile techniques when the line is not in use, and the line must be flushed on a regular basis. Signs of infection include redness, swelling, pain, drainage, or warmth around the exit site. Fever, chills, tiredness, and dizziness may also indicate that the line has become infected. You should notify the doctor immediately if any of these signs are present or if your child has a fever above 101° F (38.5° C).

Torn catheter

Accidents sometimes happen, and a hole or tear in the line can occur. Careful handling of the catheter can help prevent these accidents. You should suspect a torn catheter if fluid leaks out of the line, especially during an injection. If a tear is found, you should find the hole, fold the line above the tear, tape it together, cover it with sterile gauze, and immediately notify your child's doctor.

Displaced catheter

As with other external catheters, a PICC line must be securely taped to the exit site to prevent movement. Signs of a displaced catheter include chest pain, burning or swelling in the arm above the exit site or in the chest, fluid leaking around the catheter, or pain when fluid is injected into the line. If you suspect the line has moved, tape the catheter in place and immediately notify your child's doctor.

Cost

External catheters and PICC lines require supplies for cleaning, dressing, and irrigating the line, but a subcutaneous port does not. The port itself, however, is usually more costly than the external catheter and PICC line. The external catheter and the subcutaneous port require operating room time and the services of a surgeon and an anesthesiologist to insert them, but PICC lines are usually inserted in the hospital room by a doctor or nurse. External catheters can be removed in the clinic with only IV sedation, but subcutaneous ports can only be removed in the operating room. PICC lines are removed in the hospital room and require no sedation. A good rule of thumb to consider is that if an external catheter or subcutaneous port stays in place at least 6 months, the overall costs are almost equal (see comparison chart on next page).

Most insurance plans will cover the placement of any central venous catheter and the services of the surgeon, anesthesiologist, and operating room. Many plans, however, will not cover the cost of the supplies to maintain the line, and this can be an additional financial hardship for families.

Things to Consider	External Catheter	Subcutaneous Port	Peripherally Inserted Central Catheter
Infection rate	Higher	Lower	Higher
Maintenance	Daily	Monthly	Daily
Visability	Tube outside body	Small lump under skin	Tube outside body
Pain	Frequent dressing changes	Needle poke to access (use EMLA®); infrequent dressing changes— only when accessed	Needle poke to insert the line; frequent dressing changes
Anxiety	Low to high	Low to high	Low to high
Cost	Insertion cost: moderate Maintenance cost: high	Insertion cost: highest Maintenance cost: low	Insertion cost: lowest Maintenance cost: high
Risk of drugs leaking into tissues	Lowest	Low	Low

Choosing not to use a catheter

Many doctors automatically schedule surgery for catheter implantation as soon as a child is diagnosed with a solid tumor. A few, however, do not recommend using implanted catheters in their pediatric patients. If your child's doctor recommends not using one, ask why and and discuss it thoroughly if you are uncomfortable with the options presented.

> Stephan (6 years old) has no catheter. Sometimes I wish he had one. It seems like it would be easier. We were told he didn't need it. He is running out of usable veins and it is getting harder and harder.

Some children and teens prefer IVs to an implanted catheter.

> My son had a port for a very short time, and due to frequent fevers (with no evidence of infection) and because he had a blood clot form in his heart, they pulled the port. He had IVs for the remainder of treatment and was much happier with the IVs than with what he called "that foreign object in my chest."

To help you make the best decision for your particular situation, the chart on the previous page compares the various catheters. There is no right or wrong choice; different options are available because each child, parent, and family is unique.

Making a decision

After getting information about your options, talk with the doctor about the merits of each type of catheter and ask for his opinion. Talk about the pros and cons with your child if she is old enough. Then make the rounds on the oncology unit, asking both parents and children which type of catheter they chose and why. You will probably hear many opinions about the benefits and drawbacks of each type of catheter.

The nurses in the clinic and on the unit are another source of valuable information. They will have seen dozens (or hundreds) of children with catheters, and they can give excellent advice. There is no right or wrong choice, just different options for each unique child.

> When we asked one of the young children on the ward which catheter she had, she pulled up her shirt with a big grin to show us her Hickman®. She had a coil of white tubing neatly taped to her chest. My husband's face turned as white as her tubing.
>
> • • • • •
>
> My 4-year-old daughter Christine loved ballet and was extremely interested in her appearance. Her younger sister was very physical, and we were worried that if we chose the Hickman® her toddler sister would grab and pull on the tubing. We chose the PORT-A-CATH® so that Christine could wear her tutus without reminders of cancer, and so the children could play together without mishap.
>
> • • • • •
>
> We chose the Hickman® for Shawn because we didn't want any needles coming at him. He spent almost the whole first year in the hospital, so it saved him from so many pokes. The line was a blessing. He went 3 years and 3 months with no infections. We thought it was just a beautiful thing.
>
> • • • • •
>
> We didn't get a choice when my daughter needed a stem cell transplant. They needed to put in two Broviac® lines to accommodate all of the meds, fluids, and TPN [total parenteral nutrition] she needed for the procedure. I remember seeing six bags hanging up at once. I did the dressing changes, and we didn't have any trouble with the lines throughout her recuperation.

Adhesives

Whether your child has a subcutaneous port, external catheter, or PICC line, dressing changes will be necessary. Some children don't mind having the Tegaderm® or tape pulled off. For others, it is traumatic every time. Parents have many suggestions for ways to make it easier for children and teens. These suggestions also work for removing the tape used to hold plastic wrap over EMLA®:

• Don't use Tegaderm® if it bothers your child or reddens the skin. Try plastic wrap cut into a square and use paper tape or tape with perforations.

• Try Hypafix®, a dressing retention material that looks like gauze with a sticky side. Usually, several sterile 2x2 gauze pads are put over the needle entry site, and then Hypafix® is applied to hold them in place.

> I like Hypafix® because when it's time to take it off, you can use the adhesive dissolver where it's stuck to the skin, and even without the dissolver, it comes off more easily and gently than the Tegaderm®. The nurses at our oncology clinic use this all the time. Our local clinic and hospital do not use Hypafix®, so I bought a roll and take it with me whenever we have to go locally for a port access so we don't have to use the Tegaderm®.

• When it is tape removal time, use an effective adhesive remover such as Detachol® (an orange-colored product made by Eloquest Healthcare®—*www.eloquesthealthcare.com/detachol*). If you douse the paper tape with adhesive remover and wait a couple of minutes, it will usually pull right off with no pain.

• Ask for expert advice.

> Apryl has had skin tears and reactions from the adhesives as a result of using Tegaderm®. We were using Primapore® dressings for a while, but after a year she started having the same reaction. When she had her line replaced, I asked for a consultation with the skincare nurse. She recommended All-Dress®. It is a waterproof dressing with non-stick gauze in the center surrounded by Hypafix® tape. Apryl changes hers once every 3 days, whether it gets wet or not. She also has this pink tape that has zinc oxide in the adhesive to protect the skin. These two materials have worked out great.

• Once you find a routine that works well, negotiate with the nurses to remove the tape yourself or to have them follow your system.

> Using adhesive dissolver (or peeling off tape or Tegaderm® millimeter by millimeter) takes a bit of time—it's not just a swipe—but it works. It has to sort of soak in and takes some time to dissolve the sticky stuff. I know the nurses are really busy and under pressure to keep on time schedules, so it's probably a conflict for them. I deal

with this by always being the one to get the Tegaderm® off. This took some "muscling in" with nurses who were used to doing it, but it works much, much better. I try to make a joke of it: "I have a deal with my kid that I'm taking off the Tegaderm®. It might take a while and I wouldn't want you to fall asleep waiting on us—how about if I holler out the door when it's off and we're ready?" That way they don't have to stand around and wait, and you don't feel like you need to hurry your child.

Catheters are usually removed as soon as treatment ends; this process is explained in Chapter 26, *End of Treatment and Beyond*.

When Scott (age 3) was diagnosed, his doctor gave us a choice of which central line we could use. He showed us a mannequin with a Broviac® and a PORT-A-CATH®. He also told us the pros and cons of each type, then asked us to decide. We chose the Broviac®, and feel it was the best decision for Scott. The day it was installed was the end of a lot of unnecessary pain (from needle sticks) for Scott.

Scott finished all his treatments 3 months ago, and yesterday he had his Broviac® removed. It went extremely smoothly. And to think I fretted and worried about the removal all week!

He has lots and lots of energy. His hair is coming back in and he actually has color in his face. He looks so healthy! I love it!

Chapter 14

Surgery

SURGERY HAS A CENTRAL ROLE in the treatment of solid tumors. At each new treatment stage, surgery is considered as an option. Surgery is used to take a sample of a tumor (called a biopsy), remove all or part of a tumor, amputate a limb, salvage a limb, or insert a venous catheter.

This chapter describes the importance of using an experienced pediatric surgeon and the types of surgeries children with solid tumors sometimes need. It then lists the questions you can ask during the discussions with the pediatric surgeon and the anesthesiologist. Finally, the surgery, discharge from the hospital, and rehabilitation services are described.

Pediatric surgeons

If your child does not require emergency surgery, you have time to locate a board-certified pediatric surgeon with lots of experience operating on children with solid tumors. Surgeons who devote the majority of their practice to children usually provide the most appropriate surgical approach to try to cure the child. A pediatric surgeon suggests:

> The most important advice I would offer to a family is logical but not necessarily widely accepted. Quite simply, be certain that your child is cared for by a surgeon who is experienced in caring for children. Children are not simply "little adults." There is no rationale in assuming that the surgeon who cares largely for adults is equally qualified to look after a newborn baby or young child. This has nothing to do with intelligence, but is simply a logical extension of the meaning of experience in any facet of life. A carpenter who builds bookshelves will probably do it better than a carpenter that has spent his life building houses. A pilot of a space shuttle is not trained to be an airline pilot.

Surgical treatment is only one aspect of overall care. Therefore, when a major surgical procedure is planned, it is essential that it be carried out in a children's hospital that uses a team approach. With a team approach, pediatric oncologists, pediatric anesthesiologists, pediatric radiologists, pediatric nurses, child life specialists, and social workers are all part of an integrated group that is devoted to a single goal: the recovery of your child.

Types of surgery

Surgery is performed at different times during treatment. This section describes (in alphabetical order) several of the most common types of surgery used to treat children with solid tumors.

Amputation and enucleation

For some children with retinoblastoma and sarcomas, surgery includes the removal of all or a portion of a body part. With the advances being made in childhood cancer treatment, amputation and enucleation (removal of the eye) are done less frequently than in the past. Researchers continue to look for better methods to treat these diseases—methods that will provide the best possibility of a cure while saving the affected limbs and eyes. These surgeries are discussed in Chapter 2, *Bone Sarcomas,* and Chapter 5, *Retinoblastoma.*

Biopsy

A biopsy involves taking a sample of tissue from a tumor. An area that looks abnormal on a magnetic resonance imaging (MRI) scan is not always a tumor, so a biopsy is usually necessary before major surgery or other treatment begins. Biopsies of possible tumors should be done at a pediatric cancer center. This is especially important if the tumor is one that requires surgery as part of the treatment, because poor biopsy technique can affect the success of future surgeries. Before a biopsy is performed:

- The risks, benefits, options, and outcomes of the procedure are discussed with the child (if old enough) and the parents.

- The oncologist, pathologist, radiologist, and pediatric surgeon all meet to decide on the best procedure to use and how much tissue needs to be removed.

- The biopsy route and site are chosen based on which will have the least impact on future surgeries.

- The multidisciplinary team discusses whether more than one procedure should be done while the child is anesthetized for the biopsy (e.g., put in the catheter).

The tissue removed during the biopsy is sent to a pathologist to determine whether the mass is a tumor and, if so, what type of tumor it is. Three types of biopsies are described below: excisional biopsy, incisional biopsy, and fine-needle aspiration biopsy.

Excisional biopsy

A surgical procedure that removes an entire tumor is called an excisional biopsy. This technique is used when the surgeon feels he can safely remove the entire mass. The

surgeon will also remove the tissue around the mass. The healthy tissue removed from around the tumor is called the "margin." The pathologist carefully checks this tissue to see whether any microscopic disease remains.

Courtney's original laparotomy (abdominal surgery) was to stage her disease and hopefully remove her tumor, but that wasn't possible because of its size. She had four rounds of chemo to shrink it, then surgery was performed to remove the remainder of her tumor.

Incisional biopsy

A surgical procedure that removes only a portion of a tumor is called an incisional biopsy. This technique is used when removal of the entire mass isn't possible. It is most commonly done when the mass is located in an area that is difficult to reach, when the tumor is too large to remove safely, or when it surrounds vital structures that can be saved if the tumor is first treated with chemotherapy.

Duncan was diagnosed with a large liver tumor at 15 months old, which we came to find out was stage IV hepatoblastoma with metastases in his lungs. His biopsy surgery was very difficult. They hit a wrong spot and Duncan lost a lot of blood. He needed blood transfusions and blood products, and they put him into a medically induced coma. He went to the pediatric ICU on a ventilator. A special nurse prepped us for what we would see. There were pumps and beeps and IV lines and a ventilator, but he looked beautiful. He was on the ventilator for 2 weeks. Chemo started a week after the surgery while he was still in the PICU. He responded very well to chemotherapy and he is now a healthy survivor.

• • • • •

Jessica was 2 years old when she had her biopsy. The surgeon removed a chunk of her tumor to see what it was, and that's when the word "neuroblastoma" first entered our lives.

Fine needle aspiration biopsy

Fine needle aspiration (FNA) is another way to get a sample of a suspicious mass. FNA can be performed under local anesthesia in the operating room, in the treatment room of the clinic, or in the radiology department. A needle is inserted into the tumor and a small sample of cells is removed. To obtain more tissue, a core needle biopsy may be performed. A core needle biopsy uses the same technique, but the needle is slightly larger so it can remove more tissue. A surgeon or interventional radiologist may use an ultrasound, fluoroscopy, or computerized tomography (CT) scan to pinpoint the exact area to be biopsied.

Computer-guided surgery

Until recently, surgeons had only an MRI picture to refer to during surgery. Now it is possible to use the MRI along with a computer in the operating room to help the surgeon find and remove the tumor. For this procedure, an MRI is performed before the surgery. The information from the MRI is then transmitted to a computer in the operating room, which serves as a navigational system. The surgeon uses a pointer aimed at various reference points on the child's body and the computer generates a three-dimensional picture of the tumor location. This technology allows removal of the tumor through a much smaller incision.

Debulking

Sometimes a tumor is too large or too close to vital structures for the surgeon to remove it safely. Debulking the mass (which means removing as much of the tumor as possible without removing it entirely) can have several benefits. The child is often more comfortable after the mass has been debulked, and chemotherapy and radiation are sometimes more effective on a smaller tumor.

Enteral access

Adequate nutrition plays an important role in children's overall well-being and prognosis. Children who are unable to eat sometimes need enteral access so nutrients can be delivered directly to the gastrointestinal tract. Enteral access can be accomplished in several ways, including the insertion of a nasogastric tube (a tube passed down the nose to the stomach) or the surgical installation of a gastrostomy tube (a tube placed through the abdominal wall into the stomach). For more information, see Chapter 24, *Nutrition*.

Palliative care

Palliative care is a type of health care that focuses on relieving or preventing suffering. If tumors that do not respond to radiation or chemotherapy continue to grow and cause painful pressure, surgeons can remove parts of the tumor that are causing the pain.

> *Surgery was the only thing that made Laura feel better. She wanted to have the tumor operated on each time it came back. Before the last operation, she spoke to the surgeon and asked him to take it out one more time so that she could enjoy her summer.*

Resection of a primary tumor

Surgical removal (called resection) of the primary tumor offers the best chance of a cure for most children diagnosed with a solid tumor. Resection of the primary tumor may happen before or after chemotherapy. In a few instances, complete resection may be the

only treatment required. Resection of a primary tumor usually involves major surgery performed under general anesthesia. The surgeon will remove the affected organ or all of the mass, along with a margin of tissue (the area immediately around the mass).

Second-look procedures

Second-look procedures allow the surgeon to visually inspect the area to check for recurrence and to biopsy surrounding tissue. Some children with solid tumors have a second-look procedure 3 to 6 months after the tumor is removed.

Vascular access

Children with solid tumors have to endure months or years of treatment. To avoid the pain of repeated needle sticks, most children receive a surgically implanted catheter. Direct access to a blood vessel allows the administration of chemotherapy, antibiotics, blood products, and hyperalimentation (IV nutrition) and avoids the pain of repeated needle sticks for the child. For more information, see Chapter 13, *Venous Catheters*.

Presurgical evaluation

Soon after the diagnosis of a solid tumor, parents meet with the pediatric surgeon to discuss the child's upcoming surgery. The consultation is important because it provides the surgeon with background information about your child, including your family's medical history. It is also important for the family, because the surgeon will explain the procedure, answer questions, and address any concerns you have. Only an experienced, board-certified pediatric surgeon is equipped to handle the intricacies of treating a pediatric solid tumor.

> *My son had several surgeries at different points in his treatment. Each time we had a long discussion with his surgeon to review the procedure and to talk about the possible complications. It made me feel scared when I thought about my little boy lying on an operating table being cut with a knife. Still, I'm glad that the surgeon was so thorough in explaining everything to us. I think that if I didn't know what was going to happen, my imagination would have really given me a hard time.*

Following is a list of questions you can ask the pediatric surgeon before signing a consent form for surgery:

- What percentage of your practice is pediatrics?
- How many other children with this type of tumor have you operated on?
- What is the purpose of the surgery? What are the expected findings?

- What are the common and not-so-common side effects that my child might develop after surgery?
- How much of the tumor do you expect to remove?
- Where will the incision be?
- How large will the incision be?
- How long will the operation take?

> Our son was admitted for surgery to have his tumor resected early on a Monday morning. The surgery took 5 hours. We stuck close by in a waiting room, although the hospital provided beepers to call us if we wanted to leave the area. It was an unbearable wait, but we were given updates every hour or so.

- What are the possible complications of the surgery?
- What types of tubes will my child have after surgery (e.g., number of IV lines, naso-gastric tube, catheter in bladder, or drain)?
- Will blood transfusions or blood products be required?
- Will my child remain on a ventilator (breathing tube) afterwards? For how long?

> When my child had surgery, the doctor said that there was a possibility that he would need to stay on the ventilator for a few days. Thankfully, that never happened, and he came from the recovery room breathing completely on his own.

- How long will my child need to stay in the pediatric intensive care unit (PICU) after the surgery? How long will my child need to stay in the hospital after leaving the PICU?
- How much pain will my child have after the surgery? How will it be controlled?

> An epidural [a catheter inserted into the space just outside the spinal cord to deliver pain control medications] was in place for 3 days for pain control after Hunter had surgery. It helped to make him very comfortable. He also had a catheter to take out the urine. This was quite uncomfortable for him, but he only needed it for a day or so.

- When will my child be able to eat?
- How long will it take my child to recover?

> Zachary had two surgeries to resect an abdominal tumor. He recovered from the first fairly quickly, but the second wasn't so easy. It was a horrible 3-week-long recovery period involving painful bladder spasms, extreme diarrhea, infections, and weight loss. But the good news was that his tumor was completely removed the second time around without losing any of his organs.

- Will I need to learn how to care for her operation site after my child is discharged?

- How long do the stitches or staples stay in?

- What are the possible long-term effects of this procedure?

- Will the scar be very noticeable?

> *Logan, who had hepatoblastoma at age 1, has many scars. He has a two-inch scar from his port. He has a big scar from his G-tube. It's deep and quite large and it looks just like another belly button. He has two drainage tube scars. Logan always says that he had boo-boos in his stomach and the doctors had to cut them out. His doctors always called his scar the Mercedes cut: an upside-down V with a two-inch cut in the center going up the breast bone. Every time we were near a wishing well, we would rub money on Logan's belly and wish that his tumor would never come back. So now every time Logan has a coin, he pulls up his shirt and rubs the money all over his scar. I tell him they're just his battle scars, and he has a special tummy (since he does have two belly buttons). But I hope they'll fade out some.*

Your child may undergo many tests before the operation, depending on the type of surgery and your child's medical condition. This is usually called presurgical testing. Some frequently ordered tests are blood work, urinalysis, x-rays, electrocardiogram, echocardiogram, and pulmonary function tests. If computer-assisted surgery is planned, an MRI is done a few hours before the surgery. Your child's pediatric surgeon should explain what tests are necessary.

It is important that the preoperative preparation includes explaining the upcoming surgery to the child. Most large centers have a child life specialist, child psychologist, or nurse practitioner who can help you prepare your child for surgery. A simple, age-appropriate explanation can be given to the child during the preoperative testing or, in some cases, just prior to surgery.

> *The psychologist on our team suggested that we think up age-appropriate, honest descriptions about what was going to happen. The idea was to give our 5-year-old son some vocabulary so he could think about his situation and maybe process things without being afraid of the unknown. The day before his surgery, we told him that he needed an operation. We explained, "An operation is where they open the skin to fix something. This time, they will be taking the tumor out. A special doctor will give you medicine that puts you to sleep, but it's really more than sleep; while the medicine is working, you can't feel anything. After the surgery, you'll feel very sleepy. If you have a headache, a nurse will give you medicine to make it go away." We reassured him that we would stay in the hospital with him, and we were clear about the whereabouts of each family member. "Mommy will be here when you wake up, but Daddy will sleep on the couch in the room with you."*

The older the child, the more detailed the explanation should be. However, follow your child's lead and give brief but clear answers for each question. Then ask if there is anything else he would like to know. If you don't know the answers, write down the questions and ask the surgeon or nurse practitioner at the next appointment. Make sure you and your child have all of your questions answered prior to surgery.

Anesthesia

The anesthesiologist is a key member of the surgical team. It is his responsibility to ensure your child is properly anesthetized and monitored during the operation. Prior to surgery, you will have a consultation with the anesthesiologist, during which he will ask you about your child's medical history and any medication allergies. Take this opportunity to ask any questions you have or to express concerns. For instance, if your child is very frightened, ask the anesthesiologist if he could prescribe a presurgical sedative.

Here's a list of questions you can ask the anesthesiologist before the surgery:

- Will my child be sedated prior to the operation?

- How will my child be anesthetized (mask or intravenous medication)?

- What are the common side effects of the anesthesia drugs?

> Surgery was a scary time for me. My mother and sister don't do very well under anesthesia, and we were afraid that Sean might react badly to it also. Sean did very well and came through the procedure without any complications.

- Will I be able to stay with my child until he is anesthetized?

> For our son's surgery, we weren't able to attend the hospital's children's tour for surgery, and he wasn't that well-prepared. But we had a great experience for his port insertion at our local tertiary care center. We were invited to attend an evening tour of an operating room by Maureen, from Child Life. Our son sat in a circle with other kids while the whole anesthesia process was explained. They all tried on masks and practiced breathing deeply. On the day of surgery, the anesthesiologist spent time talking to our son. My husband suited up in scrubs, our son was pre-sedated, and they went off together down the hall to the operating room chatting with the anesthesiologist.

You will be asked to sign a consent form prior to the administration of any anesthesia. The anesthesiologist will answer any questions or concerns you might have and may explain some of the ways children react when coming out of anesthesia.

The surgery

The surgical technique used to remove your child's tumor depends on several factors, including the type and location of the tumor, your child's general medical condition, and the type of procedure needed. However, some principles apply to all operations requiring a general anesthetic. Children are usually given anesthesia through a breathing mask, an intravenous injection, or both. A breathing tube is placed in the trachea (windpipe) and connected to a ventilator that will breathe for the child every few seconds. Your child will be anesthetized before the breathing tube is inserted.

During the operation, your child will be connected to many different monitors to ensure there is an adequate supply of oxygen in the blood and that fluids are maintained at proper levels. Blood pressure, heart rate, and other functions are also carefully monitored.

> The surgery was handled very well. Paige was prepared and treated with kindness, so she wasn't too scared. We were informed of her progress while surgery was taking place, and the surgeon explained the outcome as soon as he could.

Once your child awakens from the anesthesia, clear liquids are given first and solid foods are offered after the surgeon feels it is safe. Some children are not able to drink and/or eat for several days, depending on the surgery. These children are given nutrition through an intravenous line or through a nasogastric tube (NG) tube through the nose to the stomach.

> Michelle had a number of major surgeries and more minor ones than I can remember. She hated waking up to a liquid diet of Popsicles®, Jell-O®, and juice. One day she pleaded with the doctor to have something else. The doctor replied, "If you can think of anything else that's clear, you can have it." Michelle thought and thought, and she finally came up with jelly, no seeds. So on her next liquid diet tray were little packets of clear grape jelly.

Some children with abdominal tumors undergo surgeries that are complex and last for several hours. Parents and siblings can become exhausted while waiting, and it is helpful to have a calm, comforting friend or family member sit with you. Bring or ask someone to deliver a supply of healthy snacks and water. Stretch and take short walks while you wait. Many surgeons will arrange for you to be contacted every hour or so with updates, either on your cell phone or by hospital pager, so you don't have to remain in one place for the duration of the surgery.

> Tala was diagnosed with bilateral Wilms tumor at 9 months old, and after 6 weeks of chemotherapy to shrink the tumors, she had surgery to remove as much of them as

possible. Tala's surgery was the longest day of my life. We went to the pediatric ICU because she would have to stay there a few days after surgery. They came for her at 7 a.m. and gave us a little pager to give us updates throughout the day. They said it would take 6 to 8 hours but it took almost 10 hours. The doctor had a hard time removing one of the tumors. They said not to be alarmed when she comes back, that she would be filled with tubes and wires, but it's still such a shock to see.

After that, Tala slept for 3 days in the PICU. It was hard to see her like that, but you just have to get through it. You just want her to be alive and grow with you and you'll do anything it takes to see her through that. She did very well, and she continues to do very well.

Most children do not experience serious complications after surgery. Many children are awake and hungry by the evening of surgery and are out of bed and walking the next day. The risk of complications in children is usually lower than in adults, because children recover from postoperative symptoms and weakness at a much faster rate than adults.

My son was anxious to start moving about a few hours after he had his surgery to remove his tumor. He really amazed me. His mobility was limited for a few days, but he didn't let the operation stop him from trying to do most activities.

· · · · ·

I think one of the hardest things about Sean's abdominal surgery was forcing him to follow the doctor's orders and be up and about. He would cry when we would try to make him walk. I felt like such a bad mom, even though I knew it would help him heal faster.

Discharge

When your child is discharged from the hospital after surgery, you are given written instructions about home care. These should include instructions for care of the incision or directions about dressing changes. The most important thing to remember when caring for the operation site is to wash your hands thoroughly with soap and water before changing dressings. All supplies used should be sterile, including gloves and bandages.

At discharge, you will be scheduled for a follow-up appointment with your child's pediatric surgeon to have any staples or stitches removed. Your surgeon should let you know the next step in the treatment process and which member of the multidisciplinary team is in charge of that phase of treatment.

Rehabilitation

Rehabilitation services are necessary for some children with solid tumors. The tumor itself, or the effects of treatments, may impair use of parts of the body. If these problems occur while your child is hospitalized, she should see a pediatric physiatrist—a medical doctor who evaluates children's physical function and then writes the orders for physical, occupational, and/or speech therapy.

The initial evaluation occurs soon after surgery, and periodic evaluations focus on revising the long- and short-term goals of therapy. After discharge from the hospital, most children receive rehabilitation services on an outpatient basis. Physical, occupational, recreational, and speech therapy are all components of rehabilitation, and they are discussed in Chapter 16, *Common Side Effects of Treatment*.

Luke's (age 2) surgery occurred 4 days after diagnosis, so we were still in shock when it happened. There hadn't been any indication that he had cancer except for a fever and partial leg paralysis that gave rise to the diagnosis. He looked sick, but relatively normal, which made it hard for us to accept that he had a cancerous tumor inside of him. His surgery was initially for biopsy only, but once his doctor was in, she decided to do a partial resection. A short operation turned into 6 hours. We were given updates throughout, which alternately buoyed our spirits (she thought there was a single, encapsulated tumor that she could remove) and dashed them (she found more).

The hard part was seeing him in the recovery room. Our baby, who looked physically perfect and cheerful going into surgery, came out bruised, full of tubes, and miserable. I felt like I had inflicted this on him, even though intellectually I knew that it had to be done. I also felt the first pangs of guilt over not being able to "do something" about his illness. After the surgery, he was so hungry and he couldn't understand why I wouldn't feed him. This went against every motherly instinct in me—a mother feeds her child, right? So surgery was an emotional roller coaster ride for me.

More than a year has passed and today Lucas is a happy, energetic little boy. We do all we can to hear his laughter, and enjoy every precious minute of life.

Chapter 15

Chemotherapy

THE WORD CHEMOTHERAPY IS DERIVED from a combination of the words "chemical" and "therapy" (meaning treatment). During chemotherapy, drugs are used individually or in combination to destroy or disrupt the growth of tumor cells. This chapter explains how chemotherapy drugs work, how they are given, and how dosages for children and teens are determined. It then describes the most common drugs used for solid tumors, as well as medications used to prevent nausea and treat pain. Numerous stories are included that show the range of responses to different chemotherapy drugs. A brief discussion of complementary and alternative treatments is also included.

Reading about chemotherapy's potential side effects can be disturbing. However, by learning what to expect from the various drugs, you may be able to recognize symptoms early and report them to the doctor so swift action can be taken to make your child more comfortable. On rare occasions, side effects may be life-threatening and some can persist throughout life. However, most side effects are merely unpleasant and subside soon after treatment ends.

Not all children respond to these drugs in the same way. Some children develop serious side effects from certain drugs, but others are unaffected. In most cases, it is impossible to predict how an individual child will tolerate chemotherapy.

How chemotherapy drugs work

Normal, healthy cells divide and grow in a well-established pattern. When these cells divide, an identical copy is produced. The body only makes the number of normal cells it needs at any given time. As each normal cell matures, it loses its ability to reproduce. Normal cells are also preprogrammed to die at specific times. In contrast, tumor cells reproduce uncontrollably and grow in unpredictable ways. They invade surrounding tissue and disrupt normal body functions.

All chemotherapy drugs work in some way to interfere with the cancer cells' ability to live, divide, and multiply. Here are some of the types of drugs used to treat solid tumors:

- **Alkaloids.** These drugs are derived from plants and interrupt cell division through a variety of mechanisms, including interfering with DNA and specific enzyme activities.

They also disrupt the membrane (outer wall) of the cancer cell, causing cell damage or cell death.

- **Alkylating agents.** All cells contain DNA and RNA, which contain the instructions cells need to make exact copies of themselves. Alkylating agents poison cancer cells by interacting with DNA or RNA to prevent cell reproduction.

- **Antibiotics.** This type of drug prevents cell growth by blocking reproduction, weakening the outer wall of the cell, or interfering with certain cell enzymes.

- **Antimetabolites.** These drugs starve cancer cells by replacing essential cell nutrients when cells are preparing to divide.

- **Immunotherapeutic agents.** These substances, usually used in targeted therapies, either encourage the cancerous cells to die or help the body destroy them. One category of immunotherapy drugs being used to treat cancer are anti-angiogenesis agents. These drugs disrupt the blood supply to the tumor, depriving it of nutrients it needs to grow.

How chemotherapy drugs are given

The five most common ways to give chemotherapy drugs during treatment for childhood cancer are as follows:

- **Intravenous (IV).** Drugs are delivered directly into the bloodstream through a venous catheter in the chest or an IV in the arm or hand. IV medicines can be administered in a few minutes or as an infusion over a number of hours.

- **Oral (PO).** Drugs, taken by mouth in liquid, capsule, or tablet form, are absorbed into the blood through the lining of the stomach and intestines.

- **Intracavitary/Interstitial/Implanted.** Drugs are delivered directly into a body cavity through a catheter, or they are placed in a tumor bed in a form that will slowly dissolve.

- **Intramuscular (IM).** Drugs that need to seep slowly into the bloodstream are injected into a large muscle such as the thigh or buttocks.

- **Subcutaneous (Sub-Q).** Drugs are injected into the soft tissues under the skin of the upper arm, thigh, or abdomen.

- **Sublingual (SL).** Some drugs are available as lozenges that dissolve quickly when placed under the tongue.

Dosages

Dosages vary by protocol, but most are based on your child's weight or body surface area (BSA). BSA is calculated from your child's weight and height, and it is measured in meters squared (m^2). Your child's doses should be recalculated by the doctor at the beginning of each new phase of treatment. Recalculating doses more frequently is necessary if your child experiences significant weight gain or loss (more than 10% of initial weight).

> My son's protocol required that his height and weight be measured each time chemotherapy was to start. When we would arrive in clinic, the nurses would take his measurements, then calculate his body surface area using those figures. His weight fluctuated considerably over the course of his treatment, so the actual dosage of the drugs that he received was never quite the same.

You do not need to do the calculations, but it is important to know the appropriate dosage for each drug given at home and how you should give it to your child. Many parents write the dosages for each drug on a calendar and cross them out after each dose has been given to make sure they don't forget a dose or accidentally repeat a dose.

Different responses to medications

Children's bodies have a wide range of responses to medications, some of which are due to their genes. Some children inherit genes that do not allow them to break down (metabolize) certain drugs, or that allow them to break the drugs down very slowly. If a child cannot metabolize a drug or metabolizes it slowly, the drug can build up in the blood stream and cause excessive toxicity.

In addition, the tumor cells in individual children also vary dramatically in how they respond to different chemotherapy drugs. The tumor cells in one child's body might be extraordinarily sensitive to a specific chemotherapy drug, while the tumor cells in another child's body might be very resistant to that same drug.

Therefore, the combination of variability in children's ability to metabolize drugs and variability in how sensitive their tumor cells are to certain drugs causes a big range in the effectiveness of standard doses of medications. How much of this variability is due to genetics is not well understood. However, researchers are identifying ways to test children's ability to metabolize certain drugs and are tailoring treatments based on that genetic information. This area of science is called pharmacogenetics. Following are two examples of genetic characteristics that are used by doctors to tailor treatments to a child's unique genetic makeup.

CYP2D6. A genetic variation currently being investigated concerns the *CYP2D6* gene, which affects the metabolism of codeine. Approximately 10 percent of people do not get pain relief from codeine, because they are genetically unable to metabolize the codeine into morphine. Because codeine products are often used for painful side effects of treatment (e.g., vincristine neuropathy), some institutions test all children with cancer for this genetic variation so appropriate pain medications can be prescribed.

Methlyenetetrahydrofolate reductase (MTHFR). The chemotherapy drug methotrexate is used to treat some children with solid tumors. A common genetic variation (called *MTHFR C677T*) increases some children's sensitivity to methotrexate, resulting in liver toxicity, excessively low blood cell counts, and other side effects. Children who have these reactions while receiving methotrexate are sometimes tested for this genetic variation.

Questions to ask the doctor

Before giving your child any drug, you should be given answers to the following questions:

- What is the dosage? How many times a day should it be given?
- Should the drug be given at a particular time of day or under specific conditions (e.g., on an empty stomach or before bed)?
- What are the common and rare side effects?
- What should I do if my child experiences any of the side effects?
- Will the drug interact with any over-the-counter drugs (e.g., Tylenol®), foods, or vitamins?
- What should I do if I forget to give my child a dose?
- What are both the brand and generic names of the drug?
- Is it okay to use the generic version?
- Will you counsel my teen about the risks associated with drinking alcohol, smoking cigarettes or marijuana, or getting pregnant while using this drug?

Guidelines for calling the doctor

Sometimes parents are reluctant to call their child's oncologist with questions or concerns, so here are some general guidelines about when you should call:

- A temperature above 101° F (38.5° C)

- Shaking or chills

- Shortness of breath

- Severe nausea or vomiting

- Unusual bleeding, bruising, or cuts that will not heal

- Pain or swelling at a chemotherapy injection site

- Pain, swelling, or redness around the central line site

- Any severe pain that cannot be explained

- Exposure to chicken pox or measles

- Severe headache or blurred vision

- Constipation lasting more than 2 days

- Severe diarrhea

- Severe headaches

- Painful urination or bowel movements

- Blood in urine

Parents should not hesitate to bring their child to the hospital if she is ill and her blood cell counts are low, as this can be a life-threatening emergency. Any time your child is sick and you are concerned, call the oncologist or nurse practitioner.

Chemotherapy drug list

Drugs used to treat children with solid tumors are known by various names, which can get very confusing. You may hear the same drug referred to by its generic name, an abbreviation, or one of several brand names, depending on which doctor, nurse, or pharmacist you talk to. The table on the next page provides the generic names of the most commonly used chemotherapy drugs and some of the most common brand names.

Drug Names	Brand Names
Actinomycin D Dactinomycin	Cosmegen®
Busulfan	Busulfex®
Carboplatin	Paraplatin®
Cisplatin	Platinol®, Platinol®-AQ
Cyclophosphamide	Cytoxan®, Cytoxan Lyophilized®, Neosar®
Doxorubicin	Adriamycin®
Etoposide VP-16	VePesid®, Toposar®
Fluorouracil 5-FU	Carac®, Efudex®, Adrucil®
Ifosfamide	Ifex®
Irinotecan	Camptosar®
Melphalan	Alkeran®
Methotrexate MTX	Trexall®
Topotecan	Vesanoid®, Hycamptin®
Vincristine	Oncovin®, Vincasar PFS®

Chemotherapy drugs and their possible side effects

This section describes common and infrequent side effects of anticancer drugs, which may be overwhelming to read. Please remember, each child is unique and will handle most drugs without major problems. Most side effects are unpleasant, but not serious, and subside when the medication stops. The experiences of parents included here may provide insight, comfort, and suggestions should your child have an unusual side effect. If you have any concerns after reading these descriptions, consult with your child's oncologist.

> The chemotherapy made Rachel's tastes change, so we adapted to what she liked or would eat. She lived on bland or very salty foods, like pickles and bacon. Basically, we gave her whatever she wanted to eat, whenever she wanted it.

Remember to keep all chemotherapy drugs in a locked cabinet away from children and pets.

Side effects terminology

Many of the side effects caused by the drugs described in this chapter have medical names that may be unfamiliar to you. The following table defines these terms. This way, you can understand what the members of your child's treatment team mean when they discuss side effects or when they write these terms in your child's chart or electronic medical record.

Medical Name	Description
Alopecia	Hair loss
Amenorrhea	Absence of a menstrual period
Anemia	Low red blood cell count, which causes weakness, fatigue, and paleness
Dyspnea	Shortness of breath; breathing difficulties
Dysuria	Painful urination
Hematuria	Blood in the urine
Hemorrhagic cystitis	Inflammation of the bladder; characterized by pus or blood in urine, pain with urination, and decreased urine flow
Hyperpigmentation	Darkening of the skin
Hypertension	High blood pressure
Hypotension	Low blood pressure
Jaundice	Yellowish discoloration of the skin or eyes, caused by too much bilirubin in the blood; jaundice may indicate liver toxicity
Myelosuppression	Decreased bone marrow activity, resulting in lowered counts of all blood components (red blood cells, white blood cells, and platelets)
Neutropenia	Not enough neutrophils (white blood cells that fight infection); this condition increases the risk of infection
Pancytopenia	Reduction in the number of all kinds of blood cells (red blood cells, white blood cells, and platelets)
Peripheral neuropathy	Pain, numbness, tingling, swelling, or weakness, usually in the hands, feet, or lower legs; caused by damage to the nerves that transmit to the extremities; usually temporary
Petechiae	Small red spots under the skin caused by bleeding in tiny blood vessels
Photosensitivity	Sensitivity to the sun; can cause sunburn, rash, skin discoloration, hives, and itching
Stomatitis	Inflammation or irritation of the membranes of the mouth; mouth sores
Thrombocytopenia	Not enough platelets, resulting in poor blood clotting, bleeding, bruising, and petechiae

Chemotherapy drugs

This section lists drugs commonly used to treat children newly diagnosed with solid tumors.

Actinomycin-D (ack-tin-o-MY-sin) or Dactinomycin (dack-tin-o-MY-sin)

How given: Intravenous (IV)

How it works: Interferes with DNA and RNA

Precaution: Burning pain and swelling can occur if any of the drug leaks into tissues.

Common side effects:

- Low blood cell counts, which may increase risk of infection or bleeding and cause weakness, fatigue, and paleness

- Loss of appetite

- Nausea and vomiting

- Hair loss

- Potentiates (makes stronger) the effect of radiation in the body. This drug is normally not given while the child is undergoing radiation therapy. After radiation, doses of actinomycin D/dactinomycin may cause the tissues in the radiation field to become inflamed (called radiation recall).

Infrequent side effects:

- Mouth sores

- Diarrhea

- Fever and chills

- Rash

- Difficulty swallowing

- Liver damage

Busulfan (byoo-SUL-fan)

How given: Pills by mouth (PO)

How it works: Alkylating agent that interferes with DNA to prevent cell division

Precaution: The child should have lung function tests for early detection of possible toxicities.

Common side effects:

- Low blood counts, which may increase risk of infection or bleeding, and cause weakness, fatigue, and paleness
- Patchy darkening of the skin
- Nausea, vomiting, and diarrhea (usually mild)
- Fever
- Loss of appetite
- Mouth sores
- Dry mouth
- Liver damage

Infrequent side effects:

- Lung toxicity (sometimes permanent)
- Cataracts (with long-term use)
- Blurred vision
- Mental confusion
- Seizures

Hints for parents: Giving your child busulfan at bedtime often decreases nausea and vomiting. Promptly report any respiratory, visual, or neurological symptoms to your child's doctor or nurse. Schedule your child's pulmonary function tests the week before starting a new cycle of therapy so test results will be available for your child's doctor to review.

Carboplatin (car-bo-PLAT-un)

How given: Intravenous (IV)

How it works: Inhibits DNA replication, RNA transcription, and protein synthesis

Precautions: The child may be given extra fluids to prevent possible kidney toxicity. A diuretic drug, called mannitol, may also be given to decrease the risk of kidney damage. Children are also usually given a baseline hearing test and then another hearing test before each dose.

Common side effects:

- Low blood counts, which may increase risk of infection or bleeding and cause weakness, fatigue, and paleness
- Nausea and vomiting
- Altered taste

Infrequent side effects:

- Ringing in the ears
- Hearing loss
- Problems with coordination
- Numbness or tingling in fingers and toes
- Kidney damage

Hints for parents: Make sure that you have adequate antinausea medication at home after your child receives this drug. Taste distortion may alter your child's food preferences. Promptly report to the doctor any hearing problems, such as ringing in the ears, problems hearing in the classroom, or background noise interference. Also report any fine motor coordination problems, such as difficulty buttoning clothes, writing, or picking up small objects.

> Our son did experience ringing in his ears and had some questionable hearing tests during treatment with carboplatin, but a recent thorough hearing test after we finished showed his hearing is near perfect.

Cisplatin (sis-PLAT-un)

How given: Intravenous (IV)

How it works: Inhibits DNA replication, RNA transcription, and protein synthesis

Precautions: The child should be given large amounts of IV fluids while receiving cisplatin to prevent kidney damage. A diuretic drug, called mannitol, may also be given to decrease the risk of kidney damage. All urine output should be measured during the infusion. The child should be given a baseline hearing test before cisplatin is given and be monitored for possible hearing loss.

Common side effects:

- Nausea and vomiting
- Low blood counts, which may increase risk of infection or bleeding and cause weakness, fatigue, and paleness
- Loss of appetite
- Taste distortion
- Hearing loss
- Ringing in the ears
- Abnormal sodium, potassium, calcium, or magnesium levels
- Kidney damage
- Tingling and weakness in the hands and feet
- Temporary hair loss

Infrequent side effects:

- Low blood pressure
- Allergic reactions
- Rapid or slow heart rate
- Liver damage
- Dizziness, agitation, paranoia
- Temporary blindness, color blindness, or blurred vision

> *Missy's protocol required her to have both cisplatin as well as carboplatin (for her stem cell transplant). Both of these drugs, over the course of her treatment, damaged her high-pitch frequency hearing so much that her speech development took a turn for the worse. She needed hearing aids to help correct the problem.*

Hints for parents: Administering IV fluids for several days after receiving cisplatin can help eliminate the drug from your child's system. Because elimination of this drug is much slower than many other agents, make sure you have adequate antinausea medication on hand at home. Promptly report any hearing or neurological symptoms to your child's doctor or nurse.

Cyclophosphamide (sye-kloe-FOSS-fa-mide)

How given: Intravenous (IV)

How it works: Alkylating agent that disrupts DNA in cancer cells, preventing reproduction

Precaution: The child should drink lots of water or be given large amounts of IV fluids while taking cyclophosphamide to prevent bladder damage. A drug called mesna is also given to prevent bladder damage. Antinausea drugs should be given before and for several hours after this drug is administered.

Common side effects:

- Low blood counts, which may increase risk of infection or bleeding and cause weakness, fatigue, and paleness
- Nausea, vomiting, and diarrhea
- Loss of appetite
- Temporary hair loss
- Mouth sores

Infrequent side effects:

- Blood in urine
- Cough or shortness of breath
- Skin rash, dryness, and darkening
- Metallic taste during injection of the drug
- Blurred vision
- Irregular or absent menstrual periods in postpubertal girls (temporary)
- Permanent sterility in postpubertal boys (rare at routine doses, more common at doses given for transplants or for high-risk or relapse treatment)

> *Christine breezed through the Cytoxan® infusions. She would go to Children's in the afternoon, they would give her lots of IV fluids, and then ondansetron [Zofran®] a half hour before the Cytoxan®. She would sleep through the night with absolutely no nausea, because they were so good about giving her the ondansetron all night and the next morning. It was hard on me because I had to wake up every 2 hours to change her diaper so that the nurse could weigh it to make sure she was passing enough urine.*

Doxorubicin (Dox-o-ROO-bi-sin)

How given: Intravenous (IV)

How it works: Antibiotic that prevents DNA from forming, thus preventing cancer cells from multiplying

Precautions: Doxorubicin is a red color, and urine will turn red for a day or two after each dose. This is normal. Burning pain and swelling can occur if the drug leaks into tissues.

Common side effects:

- Low blood cell counts, which may increase risk of infection or bleeding and cause weakness, fatigue, and paleness
- Nausea and vomiting
- Temporary hair loss
- Mouth sores

Infrequent side effects:

- Loss of appetite
- Diarrhea
- Burning pain and swelling if any drug leaks into tissues
- Heart damage
- Shortness of breath
- Fever and chills
- Abdominal pains

> The Adriamycin® just burned right through my son. He never got mouth sores, but he sure had problems at the other end. They had him lie on his stomach with the heat lamp on his bare bottom. His whole bottom was blistered so badly that it looked like he'd been in a fire. They used to mix up what they called "Magic Butt Paste," and I'll never forget the recipe: one tube Nystatin® cream, one tube Desitin®, and Nystatin® powder. It was like spackle that they would just slather on. He had a lot of gastrointestinal bleeding, too, so he was continuously getting platelets.

· · · · ·

> Other than red urine and the expected low counts, hair loss, and nausea, Christine had no problems from her many doses of Adriamycin®. We check her heart function every 2 years, though, because that problem can develop years later.

Etoposide (e-TOE-poe-side)

How given: Intravenous (IV) injection or infusion; pills by mouth (PO)

How it works: Prevents DNA from reproducing and causes cells to die

Precautions: No live vaccines should be given while taking etoposide. It also interacts with several common drugs and herbs, such as aspirin, cyclosporine, glucosomide, and St. John's wort. Etoposide may cause birth defects if taken during pregnancy. Burning pain, swelling, and tissue damage can occur if any drug leaks into tissues.

Common side effects:

- Low blood counts, which may increase risk of infection or bleeding and cause weakness, fatigue, and paleness
- Loss of appetite
- Nausea and vomiting
- Temporary hair loss
- Temporary changes in menstrual cycle in girls

Infrequent side effects:

- Low blood pressure
- Shortness of breath
- Numbing of fingers and toes
- Fever with or without chills

Fluorouracil (Floor-ROAR-ah-sill)

How given: Intravenous (IV)

How it works: Antimetabolite that prevents DNA synthesis and blocks RNA translation

Precaution: Children should be monitored for possible liver toxicity.

Common side effects:

- Low blood cell counts, which may increase risk of infection or bleeding and cause weakness, fatigue, and paleness
- Nausea and vomiting
- Mouth sores

- Diarrhea
- Blurred vision
- Darkening of the skin

Infrequent side effects:

- Temporary hair loss
- Brittle nails
- Extreme sensitivity to the sun
- Rash
- Itching
- Watery eyes
- Soreness and redness of the soles of the feet and palms of the hands

> *Coley received several different chemotherapy drugs to treat her hepatoblastoma, including 5-FU. She lost a lot of weight and her hair fell out. She also had a lot of vomiting, but the antinausea drugs helped a great deal.*

Ifosfamide (eye-FOSS-fah-mide)

How given: Intravenous (IV)

How it works: Alkylating agent that disrupts DNA in cancer cells, preventing reproduction

Precautions: The child should be given extra fluids by mouth or intravenously during infusion. Mesna, a drug that protects the bladder, should also be given. Your child must urinate every 1 to 2 hours during the treatment, and her urine will be tested for blood. Grapefruit or grapefruit juice may affect the effectiveness of this drug, so parents should check with the doctor about whether their child should avoid these while taking vincristine.

Common side effects:

- Low blood counts, which may increase risk of infection or bleeding and cause weakness, fatigue, and paleness
- Temporary hair loss
- Nausea and vomiting
- Dizziness

- Excessive sleepiness and mental confusion

Infrequent side effects:

- Kidney damage that may be permanent
- Bladder irritation and bleeding
- Liver damage
- Irritation to veins used for administration

Hints for parents: Have your child drink plenty of fluid, if possible, prior to treatment. This drug is usually given over 3 to 5 consecutive days, so make sure you have an adequate supply of antinausea medicine at home for your child. This drug may cause the kidneys to lose important substances, such as calcium and phosphorus, and it may be necessary for your child to take oral supplements.

Irinotecan (eye-rin-oh-TEE-can)

How given: Intravenous (IV)

How it works: Plant alkaloid that disrupts the structure of DNA, preventing cell reproduction

Precaution: Seizure medications may affect the metabolism of irinotecan

Common side effects:

- Low blood counts, which may increase risk of infection or bleeding and cause weakness, fatigue, and paleness
- Loss of appetite
- Nausea and vomiting
- Abdominal cramping and diarrhea
- Excessive sweating, salivation, and facial flushing during administration
- Temporary hair loss
- Fatigue

Infrequent side effects:

- Mouth sores
- Muscle cramps
- Temporary liver damage

- Skin rash
- Sugar in the urine
- Dizziness
- Numbness and tingling of hands and feet

Hint for parents: Many of the side effects that occur while, or immediately after, your child receives this drug may be controlled by the administration of a drug called atropine.

> *The big side effect that comes along with irinotecan is diarrhea. There are two forms: early and late. Early diarrhea could happen even during the infusion (we had this problem during the second dose). Late diarrhea is every bit as much irinotecan's fault but might not be so obvious, because it can take 4 to 11 days post-infusion to show up. I guess I should say that there are really two other forms: the kind you can tolerate as a mild inconvenience and the more potent kind. Most doctors suggest that Imodium A-D® (over the counter) be given per label instructions, and if that doesn't control the diarrhea, you should call them for something more. Our second-line drug was Lomotil® by prescription (we gave that and Imodium® and still had no luck). Use common sense with any diarrhea. Call in if it seems out of line, and hydrate, hydrate, hydrate to replace the fluids.*

Melphalan (MEL-fa-lan)

How given: Pills by mouth (PO)

How it works: Alkylating agent that interferes with DNA, RNA, and nucleic acid function

Precaution: The child should drink lots of water or be given large amounts of IV fluids while receiving melphalan.

Common side effects:

- Low blood cell counts, which may increase risk of infection or bleeding and cause weakness, fatigue, and paleness
- Temporary hair loss
- Menstrual irregularities

Infrequent side effects:

- Nausea and vomiting
- Skin rashes

- Shortness of breath
- Mouth sores
- Lung scarring

Methotrexate (meth-o-TREX-ate)

How given: Intravenous (IV) infusion

How it works: Antimetabolite that replaces nutrients in the cancer cells, causing cell death

Precautions: Children should not be given extra folic acid in vitamins or the methotrexate will not be effective. Several drugs can cause methotrexate to stay in the system too long or worsen its side effects. Some of these drugs include aspirin, non-steroidal anti-inflammatory drugs, penicillin, bactrim, septra, and several anti-seizure drugs. Children taking methotrexate are very sensitive to the sun and should always wear protective clothing and sunscreen.

Common side effects:

- Low blood counts, which may increase risk of infection or bleeding and cause weakness, fatigue, and paleness
- Extreme sun sensitivity
- Diarrhea
- Skin rashes

Infrequent side effects:

- Mouth sores
- Temporary hair loss
- Nausea and vomiting
- Loss of appetite
- Fever, with or without chills
- Temporary liver damage
- Temporary kidney damage
- Shortness of breath and dry cough
- Nervous system damage (can be temporary or permanent)

- Neurotoxicity that can cause learning disabilities
- Redness at the site of previous radiation (called radiation recall)

> *My daughter had serious problems with rashes during treatment with methotrexate. The doctors thought that she had developed an allergy. She often would be covered with rashes that looked like small, red circles with tan, flaky skin inside. They were extremely itchy.*

Topotecan (toe-poe-TEE-can)

How given: Intravenous (IV)

How it works: Plant alkaloid that interferes with an enzyme involved in maintaining the structure of DNA

Precaution: Dosing may need to be adjusted for children with kidney damage.

Common side effects:
- Low blood counts, which may increase risk of infection or bleeding and cause weakness, fatigue, and paleness
- Nausea and vomiting
- Diarrhea
- Loss of appetite
- Temporary hair loss
- Headache during the infusion
- Dizziness and light-headedness during the infusion
- Fever
- Fatigue

Infrequent side effects:
- Mouth sores
- Skin rashes
- Kidney damage
- Elevated blood pressure and heart rate
- Blood in the urine

Hint for parents: Your child may have diarrhea during treatment with this drug. It can persist for several days after therapy is completed.

> *Matthew tolerated the topotecan very well. He had the usual nausea and vomiting that he experienced with other chemotherapy drugs, though. He wouldn't eat much during the treatments, but within a day or two he was usually back to his old self again.*

Vincristine (Vin-CRIS-teen)

How given: Intravenous (IV) injection or infusion

How it works: Alkaloid (derived from the periwinkle plant) that causes cells to stop dividing

Precautions: Care should be taken to prevent vincristine from leaking at the IV site because it will damage tissue. Before taking the first dose of vincristine, your child should be started on a program to prevent constipation. Vincristine interacts with several other chemotherapy drugs, so care should be taken in planning the dosing schedule. Grapefruit or grapefruit juice may affect the effectiveness of this drug, so parents should check with the doctor about whether their child should avoid these while taking vincristine.

Common side effects:

- Severe constipation
- Pain (may be severe) in jaw, face, back, joints, and/or bones
- Foot drop (child has trouble lifting front part of foot)
- Numbness, tingling, or pain (may be severe) in fingers and toes
- Extreme weakness and loss of muscle mass
- Drooping eyelids
- Temporary hair loss
- Pain, blisters, and skin loss if drug leaks during administration

Infrequent side effects:

- Headaches
- Dizziness and light-headedness
- Seizures
- Paralysis, including vocal cord paralysis

Hints for parents: Start your child on a stool softener at the beginning of treatment with this drug (do not wait!) and give it consistently. Joint pain (in the jaw, wrists, elbows, and knees) is a temporary side effect, but it is often severe enough to warrant an oral narcotic. Watch your child's gait and strength, especially going up and down stairs and performing fine-motor activities, such as coloring, writing, or buttoning clothes. Report problems in these areas promptly because your child's doctor may choose to alter the dose. Sometimes medications (e.g., gabapentin, also known by the brand name Neurontin®) and physical therapy are necessary to counteract the side effects of this drug.

> *My daughter was diagnosed with hepatoblastoma when she was 3 months old. Her chemo included vincristine, 5-FU, cisplatin, and doxorubicin. She had really bad mucositis and nausea/vomiting during the first two rounds of chemo. I told them that the sound of her crying had changed, and she was coughing a lot during feedings. It turns out her vocal cords were paralyzed from the vincristine. She was in a lot of pain and needed to be on a continuous drip for that. They removed vincristine from the next two chemo rounds. I couldn't nurse her anymore so they put a G-tube in because they were afraid she might aspirate and get pneumonia.*

• • • • •

> *Preston (diagnosed age 10) had an awful time from vincristine. He would develop cramping in his lower legs, and would just curl up in bed, in great pain. It would start a couple of days after he received the vincristine, and would last a week. I would massage his legs, use hot packs, and give him Tylenol®. I would have to carry him into the clinic, because he couldn't walk. I did some research and discovered that when the bilirubin is high, the child can't excrete the vincristine and therefore the toxicity is increased. We lowered his vincristine dose and got him into physical therapy.*

• • • • •

> *Soon after diagnosis at age 5½, Robby became so weak that he stopped walking. He did not walk for at least a week, maybe more. When Robby did walk, he was up on his toes. I kept asking the doctors about it, and they poohpoohed it, saying it was just the vincristine. Finally, I took Robby to the pediatrician, who was horrified at how bad his feet had gotten. We immediately started daily physical therapy and major exercises and got traction boots to wear at night.*

Prophylactic antibiotics

Many children and teens on chemotherapy take antibiotics 2 to 3 days each week to prevent pneumocystis pneumonia (PCP). They usually continue taking the antibiotics a few months to a year after treatment ends. The antibiotic of choice for PCP prevention is a combination drug containing sulfamethoxazole and trimethoprim (SMZ-TMP); it is sold under the brand names Bactrim® and Septra®. This antibiotic can cause

gastrointestinal upset, skin rashes, sun sensitivity, and low blood counts. If a substitute is needed, one of the following is used:

- Pentamidine is administered by IV once a month, as an aerosol, or through a nebulizer. Use of the nebulizer can be difficult for children because it takes 20 minutes to administer and it smells and tastes bad.

- Dapsone® are pills given once a day.

> We just started the Dapsone® because Katie was starting to buck the nebulizer treatment. (It smells and tastes horrible.) The Bactrim® costs about $3/month, the dapsone about $7/month, and the pentamidine nebulizer treatment is about $300/ month!

Colony-stimulating factors

Colony-stimulating factors (CSFs) are often used for children with solid tumors. High-dose chemotherapy reduces the number of white blood cells needed by the body to fight infections. The administration of CSFs, such as granulocyte colony-stimulating factor (G-CSF, also known by the brand name Neupogen®) and granulocyte-macrophage colony-stimulating factor (GM-CSF, also known as sargramostim, or by the brand name Leukine®), can reduce the severity and duration of low white blood counts, lessening the chance of infection. G-CSF may be administered by IV or by subcutaneous injection. GM-CSF must be administered by subcutaneous injection.

> Kenny was only 2 years old when he was receiving G-CSF, so he was too young to understand why he needed the shots. He would cry and beg us not to hurt him—that he was sorry. My heart would break, but I would have to give him the shot. We finally developed a really good system. Right before being discharged after a round of chemo, we would put EMLA® on Kenny's arm and then have the nurse place an insulflon. It was a small catheter that Kenny didn't even notice was in his arm. It was good for 7 to 10 days, which was the duration of his G-CSF for the entire month. We would draw up the amount needed for injection, then place it in the insulflon and inject it very slowly. Kenny never felt it and no longer begged us not to do the G-CSF. Oh, how I wished we had done this from the beginning! Kenny's counts would usually start to decline about 4 days after his chemo. At about Day 10 the G-CSF would kick in, and his counts would skyrocket.

> • • • • •

> Katie had no side effects from Neupogen® that I can recall. The worst thing about it for us was giving the shots at home. They're subcutaneous, so the needle is short, but Katie still said they hurt, even with EMLA®.

Antinausea drugs used during chemotherapy

Antinausea drugs, also referred to as antiemetics, make chemotherapy treatments more bearable, but they sometimes cause side effects. This section lists the most commonly used antinausea drugs. Other less commonly used drugs to prevent nausea are not described here (e.g., Marinol®, Reglan®, scopolamine patch, and Atarax®).

Antinausea drug list

As with chemotherapy drugs, several different names can be used to refer to each antinausea drug. The list below will help you find detailed information about each drug on the following pages.

Drug name	Brand name(s)
Aprepitant	Emend®
Diphenhydramine	Benadryl®
Granisetron	Granisol®, Kytril®, Sancuso®
Lorazepam	Ativan®
Ondansetron	Zofran®
Prochlorperazine	Compazine®
Promethazine	Phenergan®

Aprepitant (a-PREP-it-ant)

How given: Capsule by mouth (PO) or intravenous (IV) infusion

When given: Capsule is taken 1 hour before chemotherapy. IV infusion is given over a 15-minute span, starting 30 minutes before chemotherapy.

Precaution: This drug interacts with many drugs, so make sure the pharmacist knows about every drug your child takes.

Common side effects:

- Fatigue
- Dizziness
- Constipation
- Diarrhea
- Hiccups

- Heartburn
- Itchiness
- Loss of appetite

Diphenhydramine (die-fen-HIGH-dra-meen)

How given: Liquid, pills, or capsules by mouth (PO), or intravenous (IV) injection

When given: Usually given every 6 to 8 hours

Common side effects:

- Drowsiness
- Dizziness
- Impaired coordination
- Dry mouth
- Excitability (in young children)
- Low blood pressure

> *Our go-to drugs for nausea and vomiting are Zofran® and Benadryl®. But, 9-month-old Wyatt was hospitalized when he couldn't stop throwing up even on those two meds, so they also gave him Ativan® and Reglan® while he was inpatient. We just had a 3-week break from treatment and he gained a pound a week. It was depressing to go back in, but they didn't want to stop treatment for longer than 3 weeks.*

Granisetron (gran-ISS-eh-tron)

How given: Intravenous (IV) injection, pills by mouth (PO), or a patch on the skin

When given: Granisetron is usually given 30 minutes before the start of chemotherapy infusion. Doses may be repeated every 12 to 24 hours.

Common side effects:

- Headaches
- Diarrhea
- Constipation

Infrequent side effects:

- High blood pressure
- Fatigue
- Fever
- Allergic reaction
- Abnormal heart rhythms

> *Sarah got Zofran® at first, then the clinic switched to liquid Kytril®. Sarah usually hates liquid meds (she much prefers pills), but she loves Kytril®. She thinks it's really yummy. And it works, too!*

· · · · ·

> *Kytril® is an antinausea pill. It is incredibly expensive but brilliant in treating chemo-related sickness. It sometimes takes a bit of juggling to get the timing right; Michael used to take it an hour before taking the pills at bedtime. None of the other antiemetics worked for him nearly as well.*

Lorazepam (lor-AZ-a-pam)

How given: Pills or liquid by mouth (PO), sublingually (pill dissolved under the tongue), or subcutaneous (Sub-Q), intravenous (IV), or intramuscular (IM) injection

When given: This tranquilizer is generally given in combination with other antinausea drugs.

Precaution: This drug interacts with several other drugs, so parents should tell the doctor about everything else their child is taking, including over-the-counter drugs.

Common side effects:

- Drowsiness and sleepiness
- Poor short-term memory
- Impaired coordination
- Low blood pressure
- Excitability (in young children)

Ondansetron (on-DAN-se-tron)

How given: Intravenous (IV) injection, liquid or pills by mouth (PO), or sublingual (pill dissolved under the tongue)

When given: Usually given 30 minutes prior to chemotherapy drugs, then every 4 to 8 hours until nausea ends. Can be given in a higher dose once a day.

Note: Ondansetron comes in flavored oral solutions; 1 teaspoon = 4 mg. You can mix the dose in a small amount of a drink your child likes.

Common side effects:

- Headache with rapid IV administration

- Diarrhea

- Constipation

Infrequent side effects:

- Serious allergic reaction

- Abnormal heart rhythm

> *After Jeremy had his first outpatient chemo, every couple hours he would vomit. The next morning, when his oncologist asked him how it had gone, Jeremy was hesitant to tell him about the vomiting. When he did, the doctor asked us if the Zofran® hadn't helped. I gave him a confused look and asked him what a Zofran® was. I can laugh about it now, but it was an oversight. Everyone thought someone else had taken care of it! We rarely had any problems with nausea after that.*

· · · · ·

> *The absolute best for me were the Zofran® lozenges: simply dissolve on or under the tongue for instant relief. The prescription must state lozenges. You'll love those "melty pills."*

· · · · ·

> *Ondansetron works great for Ethan. He does have late nausea after chemo, so he takes it once a day for 10 days afterwards, and hasn't vomited or felt nauseated.*

Prochlorperazine (pro-chlor-PAIR-a-zeen)

How given: Pills, long-acting capsule, or liquid by mouth (PO); rectal suppository; or intramuscular (IM) or intravenous (IV) injection

When given: Used when mild nausea is expected.

Common side effects:

- Drowsiness
- Low blood pressure
- Nervousness and restlessness
- Uncontrollable muscle spasms, especially of the jaw, face, and hands
- Blurred vision

Promethazine (pro-METH-ah-zeen)

How given: Pills or liquid by mouth (PO), rectal suppository, or intramuscular (IM) or intravenous (IV) injection

When given: Usually given every 4 to 6 hours.

Common side effects:

- Drowsiness
- Dizziness
- Impaired coordination
- Fatigue
- Blurred vision
- Euphoria
- Insomnia

Drugs used to relieve pain

As with other medicines, drugs used for pain relief can be given by various methods and can cause side effects. This section lists some drugs commonly used to relieve pain. Additional medications sometimes used to relieve pain in children are acetaminophen, nalbuphine, fentanyl, hydrocodone, and others.

Pain medication list

Several different names can be used to refer to each of the pain medications. You may hear the same drug referred to by its generic name, an abbreviation, or one of several brand names, depending on which doctor, nurse, or pharmacist you talk to. The following list provides the generic name of several commonly used pain medications and some of the most common brand names.

Drug name	Brand names
Codeine	Codrix®
Hydromorphone	Dilaudid®
Meperidine	Demerol®, Mepergan®
Methadone	Methadose®, Dolophine®
Morphine	Astramorph PF®, Avinza®, Duramorph®, Infumorph®, Kadian®, MS Contin®, Oramorph SR®, Roxanol®
Oxycodone	Percocet®, Percodan®, Oxycontin®, Roxicet®, Roxilox®, Roxycodone®, M-Oxy®, Oxyfast®, OxyIR®, ETH-Oxydose®, Tylox®

Codeine

How given: Intramuscular (IM) injection, intravenous (IV) injection or infusion, subcutaneous (Sub-Q) injection, or pills or liquid by mouth (PO)

How it works: Codeine is an opiate that reduces pain.

Note: This drug is added to numerous other non-narcotic pain relievers. See earlier section in this chapter called "Different responses to medications."

Common side effects:

• Light-headedness

• Dizziness

- Sedation
- Euphoria
- Constipation

Infrequent side effects:
- Nausea
- Vomiting
- Allergic reaction
- Slowed heart rate

Hydromorphone

How given: Intravenous (IV) injection or infusion, pill by mouth (PO), rectal suppository, or subcutaneous (Sub-Q) injection

How it works: Hydromorphone is a narcotic pain reliever.

Precaution: It can cause slowed breathing.

Common side effects:
- Dizziness and light-headedness
- Sedation
- Nausea and vomiting
- Excessive sweating
- Euphoria and other mood alterations
- Headaches
- Constipation
- Slowed breathing

Infrequent side effects:
- Hallucination and disorientation
- Diminished circulation
- Shock
- Cardiac arrest

Meperidine

How given: Intravenous (IV), intramuscular (IM), or subcutaneous (Sub-Q) injection; or liquid or pill by mouth (PO). It is not as effective if taken by mouth.

How it works: Meperidine is a narcotic that works similarly to morphine.

Common side effects:

- Sedation
- Constipation
- Dizziness
- Nausea and vomiting
- Dry mouth
- Flushing or sweating

Infrequent side effects:

- Slowed breathing
- Decreased blood pressure
- Seizures
- Headaches
- Visual disturbances
- Mood changes
- Slowed heart rate

Methadone

How given: Intravenous (IV), intramuscular (IM), or subcutaneous (Sub-Q) injection; or liquid or pill by mouth (PO)

How it works: Methadone is a narcotic pain reliever.

Common side effects:

- Light-headedness and dizziness
- Sedation
- Nausea and vomiting

- Excessive sweating
- Euphoria
- Constipation
- Loss of appetite

Infrequent side effects:
- Slowed breathing
- Decreased circulation
- Depression or euphoria
- Confusion
- Shock

Morphine

How given: Intravenous (IV) injection or infusion, short- or long-acting pill by mouth (PO), liquid by mouth (PO), or suppository

How it works: Morphine is a narcotic derived from the opium plant.

Common side effects:
- Euphoria
- Nausea and vomiting
- Sedation
- Dry mouth
- Headaches
- Drowsiness
- Constipation

Infrequent side effects:
- Reduced body temperature
- Slowed breathing
- Allergic reactions, including hives and itching
- Seizures

Zachary's first surgery was fairly easy to recover from. His second, however, had a horrible 3-week recovery period, involving painful bladder spasms, extreme diarrhea, an infection in his Hickman® line, and massive weight loss. It took a lot of morphine to help him feel comfortable.

Oxycodone

How given: Pills or liquid by mouth (PO)

How it works: Oxycodone is a narcotic derived from opium.

Common side effects:

- Light-headedness
- Dizziness
- Sedation
- Constipation
- Nausea and vomiting

Infrequent side effects:

- Slowed breathing
- Skin rash
- Mood changes
- Headaches
- Insomnia
- Low blood pressure
- Slowed heart rate
- Delayed digestion
- Allergic reactions

Topical anesthetics to prevent pain

Several products are commonly used to prevent pain from injections, finger pricks, intravenous (IV) insertions, and spinal taps. Most of these drugs fall into two categories (creams and sprays), which are described below. Use of these drugs is also discussed in Chapter 10, *Coping with Procedures*.

Topical anesthetizing creams

Examples: EMLA®, ELA-Max®, and many other brand names

How given: Each product has slightly different instructions. In general, they are applied to the skin between 30 to 90 minutes before a procedure. Some must be covered with an airtight dressing.

How they work: These creams contain the topical anesthetic lidocaine. ELA-Max® uses lidocaine alone; EMLA® uses lidocaine in combination with prilocaine.

Note: It may take longer than an hour to achieve effective anesthesia in dark-skinned children. When using EMLA®, sometimes the blood vessels constrict, making it harder to find a vein. To prevent this problem, it helps to apply a warm, damp cloth immediately before the injection.

> We use EMLA® for everything: finger pokes, accessing port, shots, spinal taps. I even let her sister use it for shots because it lets her get a bit of attention, too. Both of my children have sensitive skin that turns red when they pull off tape, so I cover the EMLA® with plastic wrap held in place with paper tape. I also fold back the edge of each piece of tape to make a pull tab so the kids don't have to peel each edge back from their skin.

Vapocoolant sprays

Examples: Fluori-Methane Spray® and Fast Freeze®

How given: These aerosol sprays are applied to the sterilized target area immediately before the procedure. They can also be applied by spraying the solution into a medicine cup for 10 seconds, then dipping a cotton ball into the solution and holding it on the site for 15 seconds immediately before the procedure.

How they work: Most vapocoolant sprays use the refrigerant ethyl chloride to numb the area before an injection or infusion.

Note: If the spray is applied too long, it can cause frostbite. Spray just until skin begins to turn white (3 to 10 seconds). The spray can should be held between 3 to 9 inches away from the skin.

Complementary treatments

In recent years, increasing research has been done on mind–body medicine and its effect on coping with the side effects of illness. Complementary (also called adjunctive) therapies are those that can be expected to add something beneficial to the treatment. For example, visualization and music therapy are widely used to help children and teens prepare for or cope with medical procedures. Other helpful complementary therapies are acupuncture, aromatherapy, biofeedback, relaxation, massage, mindfulness meditation, prayer, and Reiki.

> Christine was terrified of needles, and it was a nightmare every time we went in to get her port accessed or blood drawn. We went to a psychologist who specialized in methods to cope with pain. She taught my daughter visualization. They made an audiotape of an underwater snorkeling trip. It included watching all of the colorful fish and feeling the soothing warm water. She would listen to it in the clinic, or visualize the trip without the tape. It really helped her develop a technique to cope with accessing the port.

Alternative treatments

Alternative treatments are defined as either treatments that are used in place of conventional medical treatments or treatments that may have unknown or adverse effects when used in addition to conventional treatments. Sometimes alternative treatments are illegal or unavailable in the United States or Canada, and families travel to other countries to obtain them.

Alternative treatments are usually based on word-of-mouth endorsements, called anecdotal evidence. Medical treatments are based on scientific studies using data collected from large groups of patients. In treating childhood cancer, these large clinical trials have resulted in dramatic increases in survival rates over the past 3 decades.

It is extremely important that any alternative therapy that involves ingestion or injection into the body (e.g., herbs, vitamins, oils, special diets, enemas) only be given with the oncologist's knowledge. The oncologist's involvement is necessary to prevent you from giving something to your child that could lessen the effectiveness of the conventional chemotherapy or cause additional toxicity. For instance, folic acid (a type of B vitamin) replaces methotrexate in cells and reduces or eliminates its effectiveness,

allowing cancer cells to flourish. The oncologist will be much more knowledgeable about these potential conflicts than a parent, herbalist, or health food store salesperson.

Never inject any alternative product into a central line. Children have developed life-threatening infections and have died from this.

If you want to evaluate claims made about alternative treatments, here are two ways to collect information from reliable sources:

- Check the National Institutes of Health's National Center for Complementary and Alternative Medicine to see whether any scientific evidence or warnings exist about the treatment that interests you. This information is available online at *http://nccam.nih.gov.*

- Contact your local American Cancer Society or Canadian Cancer Society's division office and ask for information about the therapy you are considering. These organizations have compiled information about many therapies that describe the treatment, its known risks, side effects, opinions of the medical establishment, and any lawsuits that have been filed in relation to the therapy. The American Cancer Society has an online database with information about many alternative treatments.

- Take all the information you gather to your child's oncologist to discuss any positive or negative impacts the alternative treatment may have on your child's current medical treatment. Do not give any alternative treatment or over-the-counter drugs to your child in secret. Some treatments prevent chemotherapy from killing cancer cells, and other substances, such as those containing aspirin or related compounds, can cause uncontrollable bleeding in children with low platelet counts. If the alternative treatment is made from plant materials, it may contain bacteria or fungi that could make a child with low blood cell counts very ill.

> At one point, we decided to try some alternative therapies with our son. Our plan was to use it in conjunction with his conventional treatment. I scheduled a meeting with his oncologist and discussed the alternatives with him. I wouldn't dare attempt to start anything, not even vitamin supplements, without first talking it over with the doctor, because I was scared that I would cause my child more harm than good. I was grateful that the oncologist was willing to listen to what I had to say and offer his opinion.
>
> We both agreed that the alternative therapy we had in mind wouldn't do any damage or interfere with the chemotherapy my son was receiving. Two months later, we decided that it was doing absolutely nothing for him, so we stopped. I figured the money would be better spent at the toy store than on a useless therapy. I learned a valuable lesson from that experience. I'm much more skeptical now than I used to be. My new motto is "show me the proof."

I gave my son echinacea when he received chemotherapy. I checked with his doctor first. He didn't think it would hurt but didn't think it would help, either. Still, all the nurses in emergency swore by the stuff. We got good results, too. We started the echinacea after lots of treatment, and it was the first time that he didn't have to be readmitted 3 days after chemo for febrile neutropenia. I'm convinced that it helped him during the recovery period when his counts would bottom out.

If, after thorough investigation, you feel strongly in favor of using an alternative treatment in addition to conventional treatment and your child's oncologist opposes it, listen to her reasons. If you disagree, get a second opinion from another oncology specialist. Remember, your child's health should be everyone's priority.

When Zack (age 6) was treated, he always developed a fever after chemotherapy. I could tell when his counts were dropping because the fever would start off low and go up to around 102°. When his fever went over 101°, the doctor would put him on IV antibiotics and draw blood cultures every day. His fevers usually started about 7 days after the first day of chemo. His counts would drop real fast. For us, it became normal. He'd also always need platelet and red blood cell transfusions after chemotherapy. It was a scary time but we became used to it.

Chapter 16

Common Side Effects of Treatment

CHEMOTHERAPY DRUGS AND RADIATION THERAPY INTERFERE with tumor cells' ability to grow and reproduce. Because tumor cells divide frequently, they are more susceptible to chemotherapy and radiation than most normal cells. Unfortunately, normal, healthy cells that multiply rapidly can also be damaged by chemotherapy and radiation. These normal cells include those of the brain, bone marrow, mouth, stomach, intestines, hair follicles, and skin.

This chapter explains the most common side effects of treatment for childhood cancer and explores ways to deal with them effectively. It also covers different types of rehabilitation services and questions about owning pets when your child is receiving chemotherapy. Chemotherapy and radiation therapy side effects that prevent good nutrition are discussed in Chapter 24, *Nutrition*. Side effects of treatment are listed in alphabetical order below.

Bed wetting

Bed wetting can be a very upsetting side effect of cancer treatment, particularly for older children and teens who are used to being able to control their bladder. It might happen because:

- Radiation to the bladder can cause bladder spasms or make it difficult for the muscles that hold the bladder to function properly.

- Some chemotherapy drugs increase thirst and others disrupt normal sleep patterns, both of which make bed wetting more likely.

- Intravenous (IV) fluids at night cause the bladder to fill with urine.

- Anything that disturbs sleep (e.g., anxiety, nightmares, post traumtic stress) increases the liklihood of bed wetting.

When the bed wetting is caused by drugs or IVs, time will cure the problem. If bed wetting continues beyond an expected length of time, or there is pain involved, you can

request a consultation with a urologist to rule out any ailments or damage that might require further treatment.

There are also psychological reasons for bed wetting during treatment. The trauma of cancer treatment causes many children to regress to earlier behaviors such as thumb sucking, baby talk, temper tantrums, and bed wetting. Punishment for these behaviors only adds to the child's distress and rarely solves the problem. Following are parents' suggestions:

- Adopt an attitude that lets your child know bed wetting is "no big deal." There should be no shaming or punishment.

- Use disposable, absorbent underwear.

- Put down a plastic liner covered by fitted and flat sheets, and then put another plastic liner with a fitted and flat sheet on top. During the night, simply pull off the wet top sheets and plastic and there are fresh sheets below.

- Keep a pile of extra-large or beach towels next to the bed. Cover the wet spot with towels and save the bed change for the morning.

- Give the last drink 2 hours before bedtime so your child can go to the bathroom right before bed.

- If your child is bothered by bed wetting, ask if he wants you to set the alarm for the middle of the night so he can get up and go to the bathroom.

> My teenaged son wet the bed whenever he was given antinausea medicine prior to high doses of chemotherapy. He was so embarrassed. I stayed with him every night at the hospital. He was so groggy that even if he woke up in time, I had to help him out of bed and support him while he stood, half asleep, to use the urinal.

- Change sleeping arrangements.

> During treatment, my daughter had nightmares and frequent bed wetting. I felt if she could sleep through the night, the bed wetting might stop. I told her she could sleep with me during that round of chemo, but that after that she would move back into her own bed. It calmed her to sleep with me. The nightmares and bed wetting decreased, and she moved back into her own bed without complaint when the time came.

- Give extra love and reassurance.

> When my daughter started bed wetting, I didn't think it was the drugs. I thought long and hard about any additional worries that she might have, and I realized that because her dad had emotionally withdrawn from her during her illness, she might

be worried that I would do the same. So I told her one night, "You know, I just realized that every day I tell you how much I love you. But I've never told you that no matter how hard life gets and no matter how mad we get at each other, I will always love you. I love you now as a child, I will love you as a teenager, and I will love you when you are all grown up." She started to sob and hugged and hugged me. She has never wet the bed again.

Changes in taste and smell

Chemotherapy can cause changes in the taste buds, altering the brain's perception of how food tastes. Meats often taste bitter and sweets can taste unpleasant. Even foods that children crave can taste bad. The sense of smell is also affected by chemotherapy, heightening smells that other family members do not notice and sometimes causing nausea in the child on chemotherapy.

Both the senses of smell and taste can take months to return to normal after treatment ends. During chemotherapy and radiation treatment, it is best to avoid favorite foods that do not taste the same, so that when treatment ends, these foods can be enjoyed once again.

> Once Katy begged me to make her my special double chocolate sour cream cake. Surprisingly, it smelled really good to her as it baked. She took a big bite, spit it out all over the table, and ran back to her room sobbing. She cried for a long time. She told me later that it had tasted "bitter and horrible."

Constipation

Constipation means a decrease in a child's normal number of bowel movements or dry, hard stool that is painful to pass. Some drugs, such as vincristine, slow the movement of stool through the intestines, resulting in constipation. Pain medication, decreased activity, decreased eating and drinking, and vomiting can all affect the normal rhythm of the intestines.

Following are parents' suggestions for preventing and/or coping with constipation:

- Encourage your child to be as physically active as possible.
- Encourage your child to drink plenty of liquids every day. Prune juice is especially helpful.
- Serve high-fiber foods such as raw vegetables, beans, bran, graham crackers, whole-wheat breads, whole-grain cereals, dried fruits (especially prunes, dates, and raisins), and nuts.

- Check with the doctor before using any medications for constipation. He may recommend a stool softener such as Colace®. If the doctor suggests liquid Docusate®, be aware that many children don't like the taste. Senokot®, another frequently prescribed stool softener, comes in a tablet, chocolate-flavored liquid, and granules that can be mixed into yogurt or ice cream. Metamucil® and Citrucel® increase the volume of the stool, which stimulates the intestines. Milk of Magnesia®, magnesium citrate, and MiraLAX® help the stool retain fluid and remain soft.

> Vincristine constipation resulted in horrible screaming, bottom itching, and constant trips to the bathroom with no luck, for days at a time. It is absolutely frustrating! We now have a preventative routine so that never happens again. Beginning the morning of a vincristine injection, I give one Peri-Colace® (stool softener plus laxative) each morning and evening until things improve—which is usually after about a week or so. Then, I taper down to one a day until things seem to be getting on the too soft side, then stop. The Peri-Colace® is manufactured in a brown "soft-gel" thing, and the liquid inside it tastes horrible. If at any time during our Peri-Colace® phase there are 2 consecutive days with no bowel movements, I give bisacodyl in the evening of the second day, and things usually get straightened out the next morning. Unfortunately, if it's a school day, I have to keep him home until mid-morning, as the laxatives lead to a very busy morning in the bathroom.

- Do not give enemas or rectal suppositories. These can cause anal tears that can be dangerous for a child with a weakened immune system.
- When your child feels the need to have a bowel movement, sipping a warm drink can help the feces come out.

> My 4-year-old daughter either had diarrhea or severe constipation for months. When constipated, she would just sob and try to hold it in. This made her stool even harder and more painful. One time she cried, "Why is my anus round and my poop square?" We ended up just putting her in a bathtub full of warm water, gave her warm drinks, and let her go in the bathtub.

Dental problems

Both radiation and chemotherapy can cause changes in the mouth, teeth, and ability to salivate. Awareness of the potential problems, coupled with good preventive care, can help maintain oral health during treatment.

During treatment, plaque can build up rapidly on your child's teeth, increasing the likelihood of cavities and gum infections. Take your child to the dentist for a cleaning and check-up every 3 to 4 months, as long as her blood counts are high (an ANC of

more than 1,000 and platelets of more than 100,000). Children with a central venous catheter should be given antibiotics before and after each visit to the dentist.

> When Kevin turned 2, I asked our oncologists if they thought he should see a dentist, that I was worried about his teeth. They tried to take a peek at his teeth, but Kevin was like Fort Knox. They both said that he shouldn't have any problems because of his illness and that we could bring him to our regular dentist when he turned 3. When Kevin was a little over 2 ½, I suspected that he had a few cavities. I brought him to a local pediatric dentist. After a horrible exam with three people holding him down, the dentist said he had four cavities. He wanted to fill them all without putting Kevin under anesthesia.

> After talking to our pediatrician, she said, "Why don't you go to a Children's Hospital dentist?" So we did, and the exam was much better. Anyway, they thought he had more than four cavities and that two of his teeth would have to be removed. They wouldn't know for sure until they did an x-ray during surgery. He was put under for his surgery and they removed two teeth and filled five cavities. After his cavities were filled, the Children's dentist wanted to see him every 3 months for a cleaning and checkup.

Ask your child's oncologist and dentist for advice about tooth care when white blood cell counts are very low. Often parents are advised to use a sponge or damp gauze to gently wipe off their child's teeth after meals instead of brushing.

> My daughter had problems with thick yellow saliva during the entire time she was treated. It coated her teeth and formed a lot of plaque. I brought her to an excellent pediatric dentist every 3 months to have the plaque removed. She took antibiotics half an hour before treatment and then again 6 hours afterward. He also put sealants on all of her molars and, even though there were many weeks when her teeth could not be brushed, she never got a cavity.

Some parents report delays in the arrival of their child's permanent teeth. Children who receive chemotherapy or radiation therapy near the mouth may also have poorly developed or absent permanent teeth and blunted tooth roots.

Diarrhea

Because chemotherapy destroys cells that are produced at a rapid rate, such as those that line the mouth, stomach, and intestines, it can cause diarrhea, ranging from mild (frequent, soft stools) to severe (abundant quantities of liquid stool). Diarrhea during treatment can also be caused by some antinausea drugs, antibiotics, and intestinal infections. After chemotherapy ends and immune function returns to normal, the lining of the digestive tract heals and the diarrhea ends.

The following suggestions for coping with diarrhea come from parents:

- Do not give any over-the-counter drug to your child without approval from the oncologist. She might want to test your child's stool for infection prior to treating the diarrhea. Frequently recommended drugs for diarrhea are Kaopectate®, Lomotil®, and Immodium®.

- It is very important that your child drink plenty of liquids. The liquids will not increase the diarrhea, but they will replace the lost fluids.

   My 3-year-old daughter had stopped drinking from bottles long before her diagnosis. When she first began her intensive chemotherapy, she had uncontrollable, frequent diarrhea. Liquid would just gush out without warning. It was hard for her to drink from a cup, so one night she said in a small voice, "Mommy, would it be okay if I drank from a bottle again?" I said, "Of course, honey." It was a great comfort to her, and she took in a lot more fluids that way.

- Hot or cold liquids can increase intestinal contractions, so give your child lots of room-temperature clear liquids or mild juices such as water, Gatorade®, ginger ale, peach juice, or apricot nectar.

- Diarrhea depletes the body's supply of potassium, so give your child foods high in potassium, such as bananas, orange juice, baked or mashed potatoes without the skin, leafy greens, fish, tomato juice, and milk or yogurt (if tolerated).

- Low potassium can cause irregular heartbeats and leg cramps. If these occur, call the doctor.

- Do not serve greasy, fatty, spicy, or sweet foods.

- Do not serve foods high in fiber, such as bran, fruits (dried or fresh), nuts, beans, or raw vegetables.

- Serve bland, low-fiber foods such as bananas, white rice, plain noodles, applesauce, unbuttered white toast, creamed cereals, cottage cheese, fish, and chicken or turkey without the skin.

   During treatment, my son had severe diarrhea for a week. He had large amounts of liquid stool 20 times a day. I felt so sorry for him. The doctor cultured a stool specimen, but they never identified a cause. It cleared up after a week of the BRAT diet (bananas, rice, applesauce, toast).

- Keep a record of the number of bowel movements and their volume to keep the doctor informed. Call the doctor if you notice any blood in the stool, or if your child has any signs of dehydration such as dry skin, dry mouth, sunken eyes, decreased urination, or dizziness.

- Keep the area around the anus clean and dry. Wash with warm water and mild soap after every bowel movement, and then gently pat the area dry.

- If your child's anus is sore, check with the doctor before using any non-prescription medicine. She may recommend using Desitin®, A&D ointment®, or Bag Balm® after each bowel movement.

> During treatment, my daughter had a terribly sore rectum, which was a big problem.
> It hurt to have bowel movements, she'd cry and have to squeeze our hands to go,
> then the urine would run back and burn. She was very itchy. We carried around bags
> with Q-tips® and every known brand of rectal ointment—A&D®, Preparation H®,
> Desitin®, and Benadryl® cream.

- Call the doctor if your child has significant pain with bowel movements, especially if your child has low blood cell counts.

Fatigue and weakness

Fatigue, a feeling of extreme tiredness, is an almost universal side effect of cancer treatments. General weakness, although different from fatigue, is also caused by cancer treatment. Fatigue and weakness may be constant throughout therapy or intermittent. They can be minor annoyances or totally debilitating. Fatigue and weakness are usually caused by one, or a combination, of the following things:

- Radiation therapy
- Your child's body working overtime to heal tissues damaged by treatment and to rid itself of dead and dying tumor cells
- Medications to treat nausea or pain
- Mineral imbalances caused by chemotherapy, diarrhea, or vomiting
- Malnutrition caused by nausea, vomiting, loss of appetite, or taste aversions
- Anemia (low red blood cell count)
- Infections
- Emotional factors such as anxiety, fear, sadness, depression, or frustration
- Disruption of normal sleep patterns (common when hospitalized or when taking some drugs)

Following are suggestions from parents about ways to deal with fatigue and weakness:

- Make sure your child gets plenty of rest. Naps or quiet times spaced throughout the day help.

Erica took a 2 ½ hour nap every afternoon throughout therapy. She's 4 now and off treatment, but her endurance is low and she still tires easily.

- Limit visitors if your child is weak or fatigued.

  While in the hospital, my daughter was very weak. She had too many visitors, yet didn't want to hurt anyone's feelings. We worked out a signal that solved the problem. When she was too tired to continue a visit, she would place a damp washcloth on her forehead. I would then politely end the visit.

- Serve your child well-balanced meals and snacks, but don't get upset if he doesn't eat them (see next point about stress).

- Parents and children should try to avoid physical and emotional stress, whenever possible.

- Encourage your child to pursue hobbies or interests, if able. For example, if your child is too weak to play on an athletic team, let her go cheer the team on.

  My eighth-grade daughter was a fabulous athlete prior to her diagnosis. When she went back to school after missing a year, she wasn't very competitive, but she managed the softball team and dressed for basketball. So she was still part of the social scene and was able to do things with the teams.

- Help your child make a prioritized list of activities. If he feels strongly that he wants to attend a certain event and you think he may run out of energy, throw a wheelchair or stroller into the car and go.

- Encourage your child to attend a kid or teen support group, and go to the parent group yourself. Seeing that others have the same problems and talking about how you are feeling can lighten the load.

Some children go through treatment without fatigue or weakness, but other children are not so lucky. The following stories describe two common experiences.

Before Brent was diagnosed at age 6, he was exceptionally well coordinated and a very fast runner. During treatment, he slowed down to about average. He played soccer and T-ball throughout, and was very competitive.

• • • • •

Jeremy has had some major, persistent problems with weakness and loss of coordination. When he was 9 years old, a year off therapy, he still could not catch a ball. When he ran, he was like a robot, and the trunk of his body stayed straight. Some kids made fun of him, and he got very frustrated with himself. He had lots of

physical therapy, and now, 3 years off treatment, his skills have improved, but he still has to work harder than the other kids. We put him into martial arts in hopes of further increasing his motor skills and his confidence.

Hair loss

Because hair follicle cells reproduce quickly, chemotherapy causes some or all body hair to fall out. The hair on the scalp, eyebrows, eyelashes, underarms, and pubic area may slowly thin out or fall out in big clumps.

Hair regrowth usually starts 1 to 3 months after chemotherapy ends. The color and texture may be different from the original hair. Straight hair may regrow curly; blond hair may become brown.

The following suggestions for dealing with hair loss come from parents:

- When hair is thin or breaking, use a brush with very soft bristles. When hair is wet, use a wide-toothed comb, not a brush.

- Avoid bleaches, curlers, blow dryers, and hair gels, as these may cause additional damage.

- If hair is thin, use a mild shampoo specifically designed for overtreated or damaged hair.

- A flannel blanket placed on the pillow at night will help collect hair that falls out.

- Once hair loss begins, consider a very short hair cut to ease the transition to complete hair loss.

- Recognize that coping with hair loss is difficult for almost all children, but it is especially hard on teenagers.

- Emphasize to your child that the hair loss is temporary and that it will grow back.

    During the first year after Belle was diagnosed (and lost her hair), her brother and I found some Barbie® hats/bandanas with wigs attached at the local dollar store. So the Barbies® whose heads were shaved had something to wear while their hair grew out! Belle also made numerous outfits for "chemo Barbie®" out of supplies at the hospital: napkins, masks, various kinds of tape.

- Try to have your child meet children off therapy so she can see for herself that hair will regrow soon.

- Allow your child to choose a collection of hats, scarves, or cotton turbans to wear. These are tax-deductible medical expenses and may be covered by insurance.

- To order several styles of reversible, all-cotton headwear for girls and teens, contact Just in Time Soft Hats® at (215) 247-8777 or online at *www.softhats.com*. Another company called Hip Hats with Hair® sells hats with human hair, which are soft, comfortable, and fun to wear. Visit its website at *www.hatswithhair.com*.

- If your child expresses an interest in wearing a wig, take pictures of her hairstyle prior to hair loss. Also, cut snippets of hair to take in to allow a good match of original color and texture. The cost of the wig may be covered by insurance if the doctor writes a prescription for a "wig prosthesis" and includes the medical reason for the wig, such as "alopecia due to cancer chemotherapy." The American Cancer Society, (800) ACS-2345, and some local cancer service organizations offer free wigs in some areas.

- Advocate that school-aged children be permitted to wear hats or other head coverings in school. Use a 504 Plan, described in Chapter 22, *School*, if necessary.

- Separate your feelings about baldness from your child's feelings. Many parents rush out to buy wigs and hats without discussing with their child how he or she wants to deal with baldness. Allow your child to choose whether to wear head coverings or not. Let it be okay to be bald. An oncologist comments:

> *Consider whether hair loss bothers your child. If it bothers him, then you should pursue things to hide or resolve the problem. If it bothers you but not him, then focus your efforts on trying to deal with your concern and anxiety. Think of this as an opportunity to teach him that it is what is on the inside that counts. In today's culture that places so much emphasis on outward appearance and conformity, this is a valuable lesson. It has been my experience that kids who have visible late effects after cancer treatment can adjust quite well to external differences if they are given a lot of support at home. As a parent, if you let him know he is a great kid, he will believe it.*

The amount of hair loss varies among children being treated for cancer. Some children lose some of their hair, some have hair that thins out, and some quickly lose every hair on their head.

> *Preston never completely lost his hair, but it became extremely thin and wispy. When he was first diagnosed, a friend bought him a fly-fishing tying kit, and he became very good at tying flies. He even began selling them at a local fishing shop. When his hair began to fall out, we would gather it up and put it in a plastic bag. He started tying flies out of his hair, and they were displayed in the shop window as "Preston's Human Hair Flies." He was only 11, but the shop owner hired him to help around the shop. He became very popular with the clientele, because everyone wanted to meet the boy who tied flies from his own hair. He really turned losing his hair into something positive.*

· · · · ·

Three-year-old Christine's hair started to fall out within 3 weeks of starting chemo. She had beautiful curly hair, but she never talked about losing it, and I thought it didn't bother her. Occasionally she would wear a hat or the hood of a sweatshirt, but most of the time she went bald. One day, I learned how she really felt. We were talking about the different colors of hair in our family, and she began shouting, "I don't have brown hair! I'm bald, just like a baby."

· · · · ·

My 11-year-old daughter cut and dyed her hair bright fuchsia as soon as she learned she had cancer. It made her hair seem less hers than something to play with. Then, when she started receiving chemo, she asked that it be cut and shaved really short like some of her boy friends in her class. Our local coach came over and shaved it for her. It was only about a quarter of an inch long at that point. Then when it fell out a week later, it was no big deal for her, because she had already taken it off. That was her way of controlling the situation.

Now we celebrate her baldness by painting henna designs on her head and using face paints to paint fancy designs whenever we go somewhere special or visit the hospital. On July 4th, we painted stars and rockets in red, white, and blue. On our last visit to the hospital, we painted a floral vine with flowers and lightning bolts above her ears to show she's hot stuff. She even had her sisters add two eyes at the back of her head—to watch the doctors and nurses when her back is turned. Everyone loves to check out her head when she comes in the hospital, and she receives tons of attention as a result of it. Also, now she's beginning to play with rub-on tattoos and is placing them where the doctors like to inspect, just to surprise them when they pull up her shirt.

She also loves to dress up her head with funny wigs and masks. Last week she was dancing in the front yard with a black/blue fright wig, monster ears, a Grateful Deadhead shirt and black platform heels. She literally stopped traffic! It was a riot. She absolutely refuses to talk to most of her doctors and nurses, and is extremely shy, but this is her silly way of poking fun at them and the whole situation with her cancer.

· · · · ·

TJ was almost 3 when he was diagnosed. He was very upset about losing his hair. They told us it was unusual for a child his age to care about his hair, but he asked us to have it back over and over. He cried when clumps started to come out and said "Mommy! Fix it! Fix it!" He was so sad when he looked in the mirror and it was gone. After a while I asked him if he wanted to paint his head with face paints and he liked that idea. He would paint it or let me paint it. Sometimes he would want something painted on his head before we went to clinic. He would say, "Paint a snowman on my head" and then show it to everyone when we got there.

Learning disabilities

Some children who have been treated for cancer are at risk of developing learning disabilities as a consequence of their treatment. Those at highest risk include children younger than age 5 who receive radiation to the head and certain chemotherapy drugs, especially high-dose methotrexate. There is considerable research on the types of learning difficulties caused by treatment for childhood cancer. This subject is covered in Chapter 22, *School*.

Low blood cell counts

Bone marrow—the spongy material that fills the inside of the bones—produces red blood cells, white blood cells, and platelets. Chemotherapy drugs can damage or destroy the cells inside the bone marrow and can dramatically lower the number of cells circulating in the blood. Frequent blood tests will be done to determine whether your child needs a transfusion. Many children treated for cancer require transfusions of red blood cells and sometimes platelets. When the number of infection-fighting white blood cells is low, your child is in danger of developing serious infections.

Absolute neutrophil count (ANC)

The absolute neutrophil count (ANC) provides an indication of a child's ability to fight infection. Generally, an ANC of 500 to 1,000 provides children with enough protective neutrophils to fight off infection caused by bacteria and viruses. When your child's ANC is this high, you can usually allow her to attend all normal functions such as school, athletic events, and parties. However, it is wise to keep close track of the pattern of the rise and fall of your child's ANC. If you know the ANC is 1,000, but is on the way down, it will affect which activities are appropriate for your child. The reality is that the activities of families of children with cancer often revolve around the sick child's white blood cell (WBC) count and, specifically, the ANC.

When your child has an abnormally low level of neutrophils (white blood cells) in the blood, it is called neutropenia. Your child will be deemed neutropenic when he has a low ANC (below 500).

When a child has blood drawn for a complete blood count (CBC), one section of the lab report will state the total WBC count and a "differential." The differential lists each type

of WBC as a percentage of the total. For example, if the total WBC count is 1500 mm³, the differential might look like this:

White Blood Cell Type	Percentage of Total WBC
Segmented neutrophils (also called polys or segs)	49%
Band neutrophils (also called bands)	1%
Basophils (also called basos)	1%
Eosinophils (also called eos)	1%
Lymphocytes (also called lymphs)	38%
Monocytes (also called monos)	10%

To calculate the ANC, add the percentages of segmented and band neutrophils, and then multiply by the total WBC. Using the example above, the ANC is 49% + 1% = 50%; 50% of 1,500 (.50 x 1500) = 750; so the ANC is 750.

> Erica ran a fever whenever her counts were low, but nothing ever grew in her cultures. They would hospitalize her for 48 hours as a precaution. She was never on a full dose of medicine because of her chronically low counts. She's 2 years off treatment now and doing great.

How to protect a child with a low ANC

Each hospital has different guidelines concerning activities for children with low ANCs, but here are parents' suggestions for ways to prevent and detect infections:

- Insist on frequent, lengthy (at least 1 to 2 minutes), and thorough hand washing for every member of the family. Use plenty of soap and warm water, lather well, and rub all portions of the hands, including between all the fingers and under the fingernails. Children and parents need to wash before preparing meals, before eating, after playing outdoors, and after using the bathroom.

> We always had antibacterial baby wipes in our car. We washed Justin's hands, and our own, after going to any public places such as parks, museums, or restaurants. They can also be used to wipe off tables or high chairs at restaurants.

- Make sure all medical personnel at the hospital or doctor's office thoroughly wash their hands before touching your child.

> Nurses and doctors frequently come into the room and don't wash their hands. I make them wash their hands, change their gloves, or squirt Purell® on them. I always had a bottle of Purell® with me. They would say that they washed their

hands before they came into the room. Well, you just touched the doorknob and you have to wash them again. I had a situation like this with our oncologist. He washed his hands, and then right before starting my daughter's spinal, his cell phone rang and he answered it. He started to proceed, and I stopped him and told him to wash his hands again because he touched the cell phone. He was taken aback for a second, and then agreed.

- Keep your young child's diaper area and skin creases clean and dry.

- Whenever your child needs a needle stick, make sure the technician cleans your child's skin thoroughly with both betadine and alcohol.

- If your child gets a small cut, wash it with soap and water, rinse it with hydrogen peroxide, and cover it with a small bandage.

- When your child is ill, take his temperature every 2 to 3 hours. Call the doctor if your child's temperature is 101° F (38.5° C) or above.

- Do not permit anyone to take your child's temperature rectally (in the anus) or use rectal suppositories, as these may cause anal tears and increase the risk of infection and bleeding.

    Believe it or not, we once stopped the nursing assistant from doing a rectal temp during an inpatient admission. When we had a room on the pediatric oncology side, this never happened. But for that admission those rooms were full, and we were on the other side of the floor.

- Do not use a humidifier, as the stagnant water can become a reservoir for contamination.

- Apply sunscreen whenever your child plays outdoors. The skin of children taking certain chemotherapy drugs or who have recently received radiation therapy is sensitive to the sun, and a bad sunburn can easily become infected.

- Your child should not receive routine immunizations while on chemotherapy. Your child's doctor or nurse can complete medical exemption forms for your child's school.

- Siblings should not be given the live polio virus (OPV); they should get the killed polio virus (IPV). Verify that your pediatrician is using the appropriate vaccine for the siblings.

    Christine was diagnosed just a week after her younger sister, Alison, had been given the live polio vaccine. Because there was a small risk that Alison could infect any immunosuppressed child with polio, she was not allowed to visit the oncology floor of the hospital.

- If your child's ANC is low, an infected site may not become red or painful.

  My daughter kept getting ear infections while on chemotherapy. They would find them during routine exams. I felt guilty because she never told me her ears were hurting. I told her doctor that I was worried because she didn't complain of pain, and he reassured me by telling me that she probably felt no pain because she didn't have enough white cells to cause swelling inside her ear.

  $\bullet\ \ \bullet\ \ \bullet\ \ \bullet\ \ \bullet$

  Shawn had continual ear infections while on treatment. He had two sets of tubes surgically implanted while on chemotherapy.

- Never give aspirin for fever, because aspirin and drugs containing aspirin interfere with blood clotting. Aspirin is not recommended for children in general. Ibuprofen may be given if approved by your child's oncologist. If your child has a fever, call the doctor before giving any medication.

- Ask your child's oncologist about using a stool softener if your child has problems with constipation. Stool softeners can help prevent anal tears.

- Call the doctor if any of the following symptoms appear: fever above 101° F (38.5° C), chills, cough, shortness of breath, sore throat, severe diarrhea, bloody urine or stool, and pain or burning while urinating. Bring your child immediately to the hospital if there is a fever and you know your child is neutropenic (low ANC) because, if not treated immediately, this could be a life-threatening situation.

  Some people choose to keep their kids away from everything and everyone during treatment, while others restrict their activities when they're neutropenic or receiving a particularly heavy dose of chemo. You will learn how to trust your instincts and your doctor's advice, and also learn how to take your cues from your child. For us, we try to walk a fine line between keeping Hunter's life as normal and stimulating as possible, while not taking any foolish risks with his health. When he's neutropenic (ANC below 500), when he's in a particularly heavy round of chemo, or when there's chicken pox going around we keep him at home. When he's doing well then we take him out a bit more, but sensibly: no shopping malls on Saturdays, no contact with anyone who's sick, and limited contact with other kids. During the week, I will take him with me to the grocery store, or to see his grandparents or cousins, provided everyone is healthy. When he's feeling well, we also go to the park, ride our bikes, and do normal kid stuff. I carry around antibacterial hand wipes with me so I can keep him clean after playgrounds.

Mouth and throat sores

The mouth, throat, and intestines are lined with cells that divide rapidly and can be severely damaged by chemotherapy drugs. This damage is more common for children on very intensive protocols and for those having stem cell transplants. The sores that develop in the mouth, throat, and intestines are extremely painful and can prevent eating and drinking. Check your child's mouth periodically for sores, and if any are present ask the oncologist for advice. Following are some suggestions from parents:

- To prevent infection, the mouth needs to be kept as clean and free of bacteria as possible. After eating, have your child gently brush teeth, gums, and tongue with a soft, clean toothbrush.

- If your child is old enough, the doctor may recommend a rinse to decrease the amount of bacteria in your child's mouth, which helps prevent mouth sores.

> When David was told to use Peridex®, I asked the doctor if we could substitute 0.63% stannous fluoride rinse. He said yes. As a dentist, I knew Peridex® kills bacteria and lasts up to 8 hours, but it tastes terrible and stains teeth. Children do not like using it. The 0.63% stannous fluoride has the same bacteria-killing properties and also lasts up to 8 hours, but has a better taste and does not stain as badly. The fluoride also helps prevent cavities and makes the teeth less sensitive. It comes in a variety of flavors like mint, tropical, and cinnamon. It is a prescription drug that a lot of dentists dispense.
>
> Mix 1/8 ounce of concentrate with warm water, making 1 ounce. A measuring cup comes with the bottle. I have David swish with half the mixture for 1 minute. (Time it, because it's longer than you think!) This rinse can only be used by kids who are old enough not to accidentally swallow it. Six-year-old David has no problem taking this once a day before he goes to bed. If and when he starts developing mouth sores, he will take it morning and evening. It's important not to eat or drink for 30 minutes after rinsing. That is why David rinses before bedtime, after he has taken his meds and brushed his teeth.

- Serve bland food, baby food, or meals put through the blender.
- Use a straw with drinks or blender-processed foods.

> My son got bad mouth sores every time he was on methotrexate. He could not swallow, but we were supposed to be forcing fluids to flush the drugs out. The only thing that felt good on his throat was guava nectar. It was very expensive and hard to find, and he would drink several quarts a day through a straw. Unfortunately, my daughter and husband both developed a liking for it, too. At one point, we cornered the market on guava nectar at three grocery stores in our neighborhood.

- Several prescription products are available to treat mouth sores. One common product is called "magic mouthwash," which contains an antibiotic, an antihistimine, an antifungal, and an antacid. Some formulations add dexamethasone. More information about this product is available at *www.mayoclinic.com/health/magic-mouthwash/AN02024*. If your child has painful mouth sores, ask the oncologist for a prescription. Because large amounts of lidocaine can numb the back of the throat and cause difficulty swallowing, this medication should be used at a dose recommended by the oncologist.

- Glutamine, a nutritional supplement available at most drug and health food stores, may help prevent or minimize mouth sores in some children. If your child is receiving chemotherapy with a high probability of causing mouth sores, you may want to try glutamine as a preventive measure. The powder can be mixed in juice and should be started 1 or 2 days before your child starts a cycle of chemotherapy. Be sure to get your oncologist's approval before giving glutamine.

> Roger just began his second round of chemo. He is on lomustine, procarbazine, and some intravenous chemo. He seemed to be tolerating it fairly well until he started breaking out in terrible sores all through his mouth and under his tongue. They were very painful for him. He couldn't even eat. I decided to get him to gargle and swish 100% pure aloe vera juice all through his mouth. He held the aloe vera in his mouth for 5 minutes before swallowing it that night before he went to bed and then 3 or 4 times a day for the next few days until he felt better. Strangely enough, the sores were almost all gone by morning. Roger woke up the next morning and said, "Wow that stuff works fast!"

Nausea and vomiting

The effects of anticancer drugs vary from person to person and dose to dose. A drug that makes some children violently ill often has no effect on other children. Some drugs produce no nausea until several doses have been given, but others cause nausea after a single dose. There is no relationship between the amount of nausea and the effectiveness of the medicine. Because the effects of chemotherapy are so variable, each child's treatment for nausea must be tailored to her individual needs.

The development of newer antinausea medications has made a significant impact on the amount of nausea and vomiting associated with chemotherapy. Many childen eat normally and never exhibit any signs of nausea while on chemotherapy because of the effectiveness of the antinausea medications. For a discussion of drugs used to prevent nausea and vomiting, see Chapter 15, *Chemotherapy*.

Following is a list of suggestions for helping children and teenagers cope with nausea and vomiting:

- Give your child antinausea medications as prescribed. Nausea is easier to keep under control than to get control of, so never miss a dose.

- Ask your doctor whether a drug that blocks gastric secretions, such as famotidine (Pepcid®) or ranitidine (Zantac®), would be helpful.

- Have your child wear loose clothing, because it is both more comfortable and easier to remove if soiled.

- Try to have at least one change of clothes for your child in the car.

- Keep large zip-lock plastic bags in the car. They are an easy-to-use and highly effective container if your child gets sick. They can be sealed and disposed of quickly and neatly, ridding the car of unpleasant odors that could make your child's nausea worse.

- Carry a bucket, towels, and baby wipes in the car in case of vomiting.

- Try to keep your child in a quiet, well-ventilated room after chemotherapy.

- Try not to cook in the house when your child feels nauseated. If possible, open windows to provide plenty of fresh air. Smells can trigger nausea.

- Use a covered cup with a straw for liquids if your child is nauseated by smells.

- Do not serve hot foods if the odor aggravates your child's nausea.

- Serve dry foods such as toast, pretzels, cereal, or crackers in the morning or whenever your child is feeling nauseated.

- Serve several small meals rather than three large ones.

- Have your child keep his head elevated after eating. Lying flat can induce nausea.

- Provide plenty of clear liquids such as water, juice, Gatorade®, and ginger ale.

- Avoid serving sweet, fried, or very spicy foods. Instead, stick with bland foods such as potatoes, cottage cheese, soup, bananas, applesauce, rice, or toast when your child feels nauseated.

- Watch for any signs of dehydration, including loose or dry skin, dry mouth, sunken eyes, dizziness, and decreased urination. Call the doctor if your child appears dehydrated.

- Use distractions such as TV, movies, music, games, or reading aloud to divert attention from nausea.

- Have your child rinse her mouth with water or a mixture of water and lemon juice after she vomits to help remove the taste.

- Let your child chew gum or suck on popsicles if he develops a metallic taste in his mouth; it may help alleviate the taste of metal.

- Consider trying acupuncture, aromatherapy, massage, or meditation to help alleviate symptoms.

A friend whose wife had undergone radiation for breast cancer recommended acupuncture to us as being good for energy and mood and lessening nausea. So, Ezra went to the acupuncturist every week while he did radiation and the doctors were impressed with his energy level. The fact that he managed to pull off his bar mitzvah on the last day of 6 weeks of radiation speaks well of his stamina.

Another reason we liked the acupuncture was this: because cancer treatment is so grueling, it seems everything we do for the kids harms them in some overt way. Since diagnosis, Ezra's life has been a series of painful, damaging, exhausting, and nauseating treatments. Acupuncture was something that was only there to make him feel better, no bad effects. He likes the warm room, the soft table, the soothing music. There is a trickling fountain in the room which he loves. Because it's hard to fit this treatment into a school week, he didn't go to the acupuncturist during the 6-week rest period or the first 6-week round of chemotherapy, but at that point he was so miserable, had been vomiting every morning and basically had no good days for 6 weeks, so we sent him back to the acupuncturist and he went weekly during the second 6-week round. Maybe it was a coincidence, but his mood has been wonderful and the nausea almost nonexistent over this period. He likes and looks forward to his sessions.

If antinausea medications do not work well for your child, investigate the Food and Drug Administration-approved Relief Band®. This wrist band gives an electrical stimulation (too faint to feel) to an acupuncture point on the wrist that affects the portion of the brain that controls nausea. Information about this band is available at *www.reliefband.com.*

During Megan's treatment, nausea was a big problem at first. I made a point to work with the staff to address this, and this is the plan we came up with: Megan would be given the maximum tolerated dose of Zofran® the first time chemo was administered, then 4 hours later she'd get the regular dose, then we would give the regular dose every 6 hours.

Rehabilitation needs

Rehabilitation services include physical therapy, occupational therapy, and recreational therapy. Children and teens who need rehabilitation services often start receiving them while they are in the hospital (e.g., after surgery). Then, at discharge, the oncologist will write orders for home services. Various rehabilitation services are available either privately (paid for by insurance, if covered) or through the school system.

Rehab has been difficult at times. Tyler was diagnosed at age 7 with osteosarcoma and has had three leg surgeries. One to remove half of the femur with osteosarcoma, another because his bone wasn't grafting to the donor bone, and his latest surgery was another attempt to get his bone to graft to his donor bone and fix the bowed out area of his leg. After each surgery, Tyler has had to be non-weight bearing for at least 6 months. He's spent a tremendous amount of time in a wheelchair over the last 4 years. He has yet to be able to walk freely without assistance. Depending on his daily activities, he uses either crutches or a wheelchair. Anyone who knows the energy a young boy has, knows what a challenge this presents.

Physical therapy is a challenge. He doesn't mind going, but to get through a session is a lot of hard work. Thankfully, he has two amazing physical therapists who work hard to make PT fun so Tyler will try his hardest to get through the session. He has PT exercises to do at home, which is a huge struggle. Being so young, it is a challenge for him to really understand that he has to put a lot of work in to regain strength in his leg. But, at the end of the day, he's still a happy child and doesn't let his leg disability get in the way of him enjoying life.

Physical therapy

Physical therapy involves using exercise and motion to improve the body's strength and movement. If an arm or leg is not moving at all, the physical therapist moves the limb through the entire range of motion to prevent the muscles from tightening during recovery. When the arm or leg begins to recover, the physical therapist devises strengthening exercises for the affected limb. Physical therapy uses equipment such as tilt tables, stationary bicycles, and treadmills. Therapy in a pool (also called aquatic therapy) is another form of physical therapy used to strengthen affected limbs.

Once Hunter was home from his operation to remove his primary tumor, he was back to himself in less than 2 weeks. However, it did take his left side many months to recover its strength. Physical therapy was provided once a week.

Occupational and recreational therapy

Occupational therapy focuses on recovering or maintaining the ability to participate in activities of daily life. For example, occupational therapists help children regain the fine motor skills needed to tie shoes, hold a pencil, eat, and dress themselves. They also evaluate the child's need for any special equipment to maximize independence, such as an adaptive holder to help the child write with a pencil or a computer if writing by hand is not a realistic goal.

Recreational therapy also works on activities of daily living, as well as working on social and cognitive functioning, developing coping skills, and integrating children back into

community settings. Examples of methods used by recreational therapists are creative arts (e.g., painting, dance, drama), sports, and leisure activities.

Accessing therapies in school

Rehabilitation helps many children make a full, or near full, recovery. These children will have the rehabilitation services slowly phased out. Other children have disabilities that require long-term rehabilitation to maximize and maintain function. Once a child re-enters the school environment, your child may be able to get rehabilitative services within the school. Schools are required to provide educationally relevant therapies (e.g., speech therapy and occupational therapy). For information about therapies provided by schools, see Chapter 22, *School*.

> *Our son had some physical therapy as soon as he could tolerate it in the hospital. He was under 3 and eligible for early intervention services (which are available to all children younger than school age who have the potential for delayed development) because of his diagnosis, so we asked for and received some physical therapy from them for a period of time after he was discharged from the hospital.*

Therapeutic activities in the community

Formal rehabilitation in the outpatient or school setting is frequently enhanced by recreational activities. Community and school athletic teams are excellent therapy for children who can participate in them. The arts, such as music, painting, drama, and dance, are also very helpful.

Many communities have formal or informal therapeutic (also called adaptive) activities. Some have sports teams for children and teens with disabilities, and many communities have therapeutic riding programs for children with medical challenges.

Serious illnesses

Two illnesses that are especially dangerous for children during treatment are pneumonia and chicken pox.

Pneumonia

Pneumonia is inflammation of the lungs caused by bacteria, viruses, or other organisms. The symptoms of pneumonia are rapid breathing, trouble getting a breath, chills, fever, chest pain, cough, and bloody sputum. Children with low blood cell counts can rapidly develop a fatal infection and must be treated quickly and aggressively. Most cancer centers recommend an annual influenza (flu) shot to help prevent pneumonia.

My son received chemotherapy just days before he was scheduled to go to the camp for kids with cancer. His ANC was 1,200 and he looked so sick, but he begged to go and I let him. It was early in his treatment, and I didn't realize the pattern of his blood counts. They called me from camp on Friday to say he had a temperature of 103° and needed to go to the hospital. He was very weak and feverish; his WBC was 140, and his ANC was 0. Both lungs were full of pneumonia. I was furious at the doctor for giving him permission to go to camp and at myself for not paying closer attention to how quickly his counts dropped. I'm sure he had the pneumonia before he even went to camp. They started him on five different antibiotics, and his fever went up to 106° that night. We didn't know if he would live or die. He started to improve the next morning and was completely recovered in a week.

• • • • •

Erica complained that her back hurt for 2 days. Then she woke up in the night crying, and she couldn't move because it hurt her too badly. She was blazing with fever, and screamed if I touched her. Her x-ray showed that her left lung was half full of fluid. They put her on antibiotics, and within 24 hours she was on the mend.

Chicken pox

Chicken pox is a common childhood disease (although less so than it used to be because of the vaccine) caused by a virus called varicella zoster. The symptoms are headache, fever, and tiredness, followed by eruptions of pimple-like red bumps that typically start on the stomach, chest, or back. The bumps rapidly develop into blister-like sores that break open and then scab over in 3 to 5 days. Any contact with the sores can spread the disease. Children are contagious up to 48 hours before breaking out.

Chicken pox can be fatal for immunosuppressed children, so extreme care must be taken to prevent exposure. You will need to educate all teachers and friends so they will vigilantly report any outbreaks. Your child should not go to school or preschool until an outbreak is over.

Chicken pox can be transmitted through the air or by touch. Exposure is considered to have occurred if a child is in direct contact or in a room for as little as 10 minutes with an infected person. If an immunosuppressed child is exposed to chicken pox, call the oncologist immediately. If the child gets a shot called VZIG (varicella zoster immune globulin) within 72 hours of exposure, it may prevent the disease from occurring or minimize its effects.

We knew when Jeremy was exposed, so he was able to get VZIG. He did get chicken pox, but only developed a few spots. He didn't get sick; he got bored. He spent 2 weeks in the hospital in isolation. We asked for a pass, and we were able to go outside for some fresh air between doses of acyclovir.

If a child develops chicken pox while on chemotherapy, the current treatment is hospitalization or, if possible, home therapy for IV administration of acyclovir, a potent antiviral medication that has dramatically lowered the complication rate of chicken pox.

> *Kristin broke out with chicken pox on the Fourth of July weekend. Our hospital room was the best seat in the house for watching the city fireworks. She did get covered with pox, though, from the soles of her feet to the very top of her scalp. We'd just give her gauze pads soaked in calamine lotion and let her hermetically seal herself. They kept her in the hospital for 6 days of IV acyclovir; then she was at home on the pump [a small computerized machine that administered the drug in small amounts for several hours] for 4 more days of acyclovir. She had no complications.*

A child who has already had chicken pox may develop herpes zoster (shingles). If your child develops eruptions of sores similar to chicken pox that are in lines (along nerves), call the doctor. The treatment for shingles is identical to that for chicken pox.

> *Kristin also got a herpes zoster infection, this time on Thanksgiving. It looked like a mild case of chicken pox, limited to her upper right arm, her upper right chest, and her right leg. They kept her overnight on IV acyclovir and then let her go home for 9 more days on the pump.*

Untreated chicken pox or shingles can result in life-threatening complications including pneumonia, hepatitis, and encephalitis. Parents must make every effort to prevent exposure and watch for signs of these diseases while their child is on treatment.

Skin and nail problems

Minor skin problems frequently occur while on chemotherapy. The most common problems are rashes, redness, itching, peeling, dryness, and acne. Following are suggestions for preventing and treating skin problems:

- Avoid hot showers or baths, as these can dry the skin.

- Use moisturizing soap.

- Apply a water-based moisturizer after bathing, and once or twice daily, depending on the level of skin dryness.

- Avoid scratchy materials such as wool. Your child may feel more comfortable in loose, cotton clothing.

- Have your child use sunscreen with a sun protection factor of at least SPF 30. This is especially important for areas that have been irradiated.

- Insist on head coverings or sunscreen every time your child goes outdoors if she is bald, especially if she had radiation to the head or neck.

- Buy your child lip balm with sunscreen.

> *Matthew's lips would get very dry and eventually start to peel. It irritated him, and he developed a habit of biting on his lips. To minimize the problem, I learned that wiping a cool, wet cloth over his mouth many times a day worked well. I would then apply a light coating of Vaseline® to his lips to keep them moist.*

- Rub cornstarch on itchy skin to help soothe it.

If your child has chemotherapy drugs injected into the veins (rather than a central venous catheter), you may notice a darkening along the veins; this will fade after treatment ends. However, skin and underlying tissues can be damaged or destroyed by drugs that leak out of a vein. If your child feels a stinging or burning sensation, or if you notice swelling at the IV site, call a nurse immediately.

Call the doctor anytime your child gets a severe rash or is very itchy. Scratching rashes can cause infections, so you need to get medications to control the itching.

Chemotherapy also affects the growing portion of nails located under the cuticle. After chemotherapy, you may notice a white band or ridge across the nail as it grows out. These brittle bands are sometimes elevated and feel bumpy. As the white ridge grows out toward the end of the finger, the nail may break.

Can pets transmit diseases?

Some oncologists recommend that parents rehome pets while their child is being treated for cancer. Although it is very unlikely that your child will be harmed by living with a household pet, several common sense precautions can help protect a child with a low ANC from disease, worms, or infection:

- Make sure your pet is vaccinated against all possible diseases.
- Have your pets checked for worms as soon as possible after your child is diagnosed, and then every year thereafter (more often for puppies). Give preventive treatments to your pets as directed by your veterinarian.
- Do not let pets eat off plates or lick your child's face.
- Keep children away from the cat litter box and any animal feces outdoors.
- Have all of your children wash their hands after playing with the pet.
- Make sure your pet has no ticks or fleas.
- If you have a pet that bites or scratches, consider finding another home for it. But if you have a gentle, well-loved pet, it may be a source of great comfort.

I think parents should know that you should not automatically get rid of your dog because your child has a low ANC. We went through a small crisis trying to decide whether to give away our large but beloved mongrel. The doctors wouldn't really give us a straight answer, but a parent in the support group said, "DO NOT get rid of your dog. Your son will need that dog's love and company in the years ahead." She was right. The dog was a tremendous comfort to our son.

If at all possible, try to delay getting a new pet until your child has finished treatment. If your child wants a pet while undergoing cancer treatment and the family is in a position to take care of it, follow these guidelines:

- Do not get a puppy. All puppies bite while teething, increasing the chance that your child may contract an infection.

- Do not get a parrot or parakeet, as these species can transmit an infection called psittacosis to humans.

We had an odd situation when Christopher (age 3) was diagnosed with neuroblastoma. Our oncologist told us about not letting Christopher around any birds or animals with a lot of fur. The problem was I am a farmer. Not just cattle, but I also raise turkeys. When the houses are full, we hold about 60,000 at a time.

Even before Christopher could walk he would go to work with me. He especially enjoyed helping me feed baby birds. Christopher had a huge plastic dump truck he would put feed in and push around while I fed with a wheelbarrow. We would take our shirts off and be silly together—a very special time. When Christopher was diagnosed, I told the doctors I had no problem selling or shutting the farm down if it gave Christopher a better chance of surviving or would reduce the chance of infection. They told us to keep Christopher away from the animals and especially the turkeys and to keep him inside when his ANC was low, which we did. Every time I got baby turkeys in, I would move his truck to that house. Sometimes I would cry, sometimes I wouldn't. But I absolutely hated taking care of the little birds.

In late June when Christopher was declared in remission, we happened to get a house full of baby turkeys in. This time, Christopher didn't want his truck, but he pushed my wheelbarrow and we got silly again. I had really missed that.

- Do not get a turtle or other reptile (e.g., snake, iguana) as they sometimes carry salmonella.

- Get an animal that is unlikely to bite or scratch.

We bought Sarah a young adult dog. We were very selective about the breeder and the breed. The dog has given my little girl back to me. After she got the dog, she started to want to walk again. She started to laugh. She had reason to think beyond herself and how terrible this illness is. She had someone who needed her. Someone

who was delighted to see her and made her feel special in a way no human can. It literally transformed my child.

The dog's name is Libbe, and after having Libbe for about a week, Sarah started asking when Libbe was going to die. She knew Libbe was young, but she really was asking about herself. We were able to tell her that Libbe will be around when she is a teenager and she can take Libbe with her on those big-girl sleepovers. Heck, she could take Libbe in the car for a ride, if she wanted. She beamed. It put the death and dying issue to rest.

If you have any concerns or questions about pets you already own or are thinking about purchasing, ask your oncologist and veterinarian for advice.

There were times during my son's protocol that I felt he suffered more from the side effects of treatment than from the disease. It was emotionally painful for me to watch him go through so much. I think one of the hardest moments for me was the day he lost all his hair. Up until that point I had been living in a semi-state of denial. His bald head was more proof of our reality—he really did have cancer.

I had to learn how to accept our situation, because I needed to be strong for my child. To get through, I reminded myself every day that the treatments were necessary, and that without them he would die. It was a struggle, but the unpleasant side effects soon passed, and he was able to resume his normal activities. I was constantly amazed at his resilience.

Chapter 17

Radiation Therapy

RADIATION THERAPY IS ONE of the oldest and most effective therapies for many children with solid tumors. It can be used to shrink a tumor, delay tumor growth, prevent a tumor from returning, or treat symptoms associated with tumor growth, such as pain.

Radiation therapy can cause acute (short-term) side effects and permanent damage that may not be evident until months or years after treatment. The younger the child when treated, the greater the risk for side effects from radiation. For this reason, radiation treatment is sometimes avoided or postponed for very young children, and the benefits and risks of treatment with radiation must be carefully weighed by both doctors and parents.

This chapter explains what radiation is, when and how it is used, and its potential side effects. It clearly explains what you and your child can expect from radiation treatment.

Children who need radiation therapy

Your child's oncologist may recommend radiation treatment, based on your child's type and stage of cancer. Some solid tumors do not respond to radiation, but others are very radiosensitive. Childhood solid tumors that usually respond to radiation include neuroblastoma, Wilms tumor, Ewing sarcoma, and soft tissue sarcomas. Children or teens with tumors in weight-bearing bones are sometimes treated with radiation to prevent fractures.

> Brinley was diagnosed at age 3 with stage III Wilms tumor with favorable histology. Her treatment plan was surgery to remove the kidney, followed by 25 weeks of chemotherapy and 7 days of radiation therapy. She started radiation the Monday after she was released from the hospital after surgery. She tolerated it very well.

Radiation is not used to treat osteosarcoma, and it is not commonly used to treat liver tumors, except to treat disease that has spread to other sites.

Types of radiation therapy

Radiation therapy directs high-energy x-rays at targeted areas of the body to destroy tumor cells or interfere with their ability to grow. Because tumor cells may remain after surgery, radiation is used to help kill remaining tumor cells after a biopsy or after a total or partial surgical removal of a tumor. Radiation is also used to relieve symptoms, such as pain. When used for pain relief, the treatment is called palliative radiation. Radiation can be given internally (called brachytherapy) or externally (called external beam radiation).

> *I was very proud of my 6-year-old son for handling his radiation treatments so well. In total, he had 10 days of external radiation to destroy cancerous lesions in his skull. He never required sedation and was always cooperative. I'm convinced that it was partly because of his personality, and partly because of how the staff treated him. Every day that he received radiation, his favorite stuffed toy, Mr. Bear, was radiated, too.*

External beam radiation

External beam radiation uses high-energy x-rays called photons, or high-energy positively charged atoms called protons, to kill tumor cells. For photon radiation therapy, a large machine called a linear accelerator directs x-rays to the precise portion of the body where the tumor is located. The treatment is usually given in doses measured in units called gray (Gy).

Radiation oncologists create an individualized treatment plan for each child using computers that combine images from magnetic resonance imaging (MRI), computerized tomography (CT), and positron emission tomography (PET) scans of the tumor and surrounding areas. This plan allows the radiation oncologist to aim the radiation directly at the tumor or surgical cavity and spare as much healthy tissue as possible.

Radiation is usually given every day for a specific number of days, excluding weekends. This process is called standard or conventional fractionation, and it is the most common way radiation is given to children and teens with solid tumors. Radiation given more than once a day is called accelerated fractionation, or hyperfractionation. It uses smaller amounts of radiation for each treatment. Hyperfractionation may reduce long-term side effects, but short-term side effects are sometimes worse.

Specific types of external beam radiation therapy are:

- **3D conformal radiation therapy.** This type of therapy delivers high-dose photon radiation tailored to the precise area of the tumor, while delivering a lower dose to the normal tissue surrounding the tumor. It uses 3D images from CT, MRI, and PET scans to identify the margins of the tumor and their relationship to surrounding structures.

Multiple radiation beams are delivered from several different directions so they overlap at the tumor. By using this technology, the tumor receives the high-dose radiation and the normal tissues surrounding it receive a lower dose.

- **Intensity modulated radiation therapy (IMRT).** This type of 3D conformal photon radiation therapy can spare surrounding tissue by varying the intensity of the radiation beams. IMRT is the most advanced form of photon (x-ray) radiation available. A disadvantage of this type of radiation is that a lower dose of radiation is given to a larger amount of normal tissue.

- **Proton beam radiation.** With this type of radiation, a machine called a synchrotron or a cyclotron accelerates (speeds up) the protons. Proton therapy delivers radiation to the tumor while limiting damage to surrounding healthy tissue, because the protons travel to a specific depth in the tissues based on their energy and deliver very little radiation to tissues beyond the specified depth. This advanced technique may result in fewer short- and long-term side effects than conventional x-ray radiation therapy. It is sometimes used in children with retinoblastoma to reduce the radiation dose to the orbit around the eye, or in children with soft tissue sarcomas in the head and neck. Children or teens with pelvic sarcomas sometimes get proton radiation to decrease the amount of radiation to the ovaries and pelvic bones. Proton beam therapy is only available at a few specialized centers, but it will soon be available at some major pediatric centers.

> *Kasey was diagnosed at 13 with stage 2, intermediate risk, alveolar rhabdomyosarcoma of the maxillary sinus cavity. Her treatment protocol was 42 weeks of chemotherapy, but surgery was not an option. She was set up for proton radiation within that first week. The radiation oncologists walked into her hospital room with a confident smile—they had a plan and made us feel really great. She had 6 weeks of daily proton radiation that went smoothly. We are fortunate that our local children's hospital offers proton radiation so we didn't have to travel to another city like many people do.*

Children do not become radioactive from these types of radiation treatments, and no specific precautions or activity restrictions are necessary.

Internal radiation

Internal radiation—also called brachytherapy, implant therapy, or interstitial therapy—uses radioactive materials (called seeds or implants) placed directly into the tumor (interstitial implants) or applied to the surface of the tumor (plaques). It differs from external beam radiation because it typically provides a continuous low dose of radiation to the tumor over a predetermined time period rather than requiring weeks of daily treatments.

Your child is radioactive while receiving the internal radiation. He will need to stay in a special isolation room with a private bathroom during treatment. The room has plastic covers on all fixtures, and disposable serving plates and utensils are used. Parents are allowed to spend a limited amount of time with their child; the time allowed depends on the type of internal radiation the child receives. The rest of the time you can sit outside your child's room to talk or read to him. Children and pregnant women cannot visit when your child is radioactive.

Other forms of radiation

Other ways radiation is used to treat children with solid tumors are described below.

- Intraoperative radiation uses external beam radiation applied directly to a tumor site during a surgical procedure. The major advantage to intraoperative radiation is that it allows the doctor to give a very high dose of radiation to a single area while minimizing radiation exposure and damage to normal surrounding tissue.

- Radioactive iodine meta-iodobenzylguanidine (I-131 mIBG) is administered intravenously to some children with neuroblastoma. Cancer cells absorb the radioactive material after it is injected into the body. The treatment is given in specially-built hospital rooms that have lead shielding. The child must stay in the room until the radioactive materials in the body have been excreted.

Experimental treatments used with radiation

In some clinical trials, radioimmunotherapy and chemical modifiers are used in conjunction with radiation to treat children with solid tumors.

Radioimmunotherapy uses radiolabeled antibodies as radiation carriers. The antibodies are attached (labeled) to a radioactive material and then injected into the body through a venous catheter or IV. Once injected, the antibodies begin a "seek and destroy" mission, searching for specific tumor cells. Radiolabeled antibodies lessen the chance of radiation damage to normal cells. Experience with this method of radiation in children is limited.

Chemical modifiers are compounds used at the same time as radiation therapy. Two classes of compounds are currently under study in children: radiation sensitizers and radioprotectors. Radiation sensitizers increase delivery of oxygen to tumor cells, making them more sensitive to the effects of radiation. Radioprotectors are drugs given with the radiation treatments; they are designed to shield normal cells from radiation damage by using substances absorbed by healthy normal cells but not by tumor cells. Studies using these compounds are ongoing or under development in the Children's Oncology Group.

Questions to ask about radiation treatment

If radiation has been recommended as a treatment for your child, some questions you can ask the radiation oncologist include:

- Why does my child need radiation?

- What type of radiation does my child need?

- What type of radiation treatments do other facilities offer?

- What part of my child's body will be treated with radiation?

- What is the total dose of radiation my child will receive?

- How many treatments of radiation will my child get?

- How much experience does this institution have in administering this type of radiation to children?

- How will my child be positioned on the table?

- Will any restraints be used?

- Will anesthesia or sedation be needed?

- How long will each treatment take?

- What are the possible short-term and long-term side effects?

- Are there alternatives to radiation?

- Will any precautionary procedures be done prior to radiation therapy (e.g., move ovaries out of the radiation field)?

Where should your child go for radiation treatment?

For optimal treatment, children should receive radiation therapy only at major medical centers with extensive experience treating children with solid tumors. Doctors who are experienced in pediatric radiation oncology should supervise all treatments. State-of-the-art equipment, expert personnel, and vast experience with many types of childhood tumors are what you should look for when choosing a center. Pediatric anesthesiologists should administer sedation or general anesthesia to young children who require it during radiation.

Radiation oncologist

A radiation oncologist is a medical doctor with years of specialized training in using radiation to treat cancer. In partnership with the other members of the treatment team, the radiation oncologist develops a treatment plan specifically tailored to your child.

The radiation oncologist will explain to you and your child what radiation is, how it will be administered, and any possible side effects. She will also answer all your questions about the proposed treatment. You will be given a consent form to review prior to the first treatment. Take the consent form home if you need extra time to read it. Parents should not sign the consent form until they thoroughly understand all benefits, risks, alternatives to, and possible side effects of the radiation. During the radiation treatment, the radiation oncologist will meet at least weekly with you and your child to discuss how the treatment is going and to address concerns or answer questions.

Radiation therapist

Radiation therapists are specially trained technologists who operate the machine that delivers the dose of radiation prescribed by the radiation oncologist. This member of the medical team will give your child a tour of the radiation room, explain the equipment, and position your child for treatment. The technologist will operate the machine and will monitor your child via a TV and a two-way intercom.

Immobilization devices

Different institutions use a variety of devices to immobilize children or teens to ensure the radiation beam is directed with precision. Custom fitting the devices on a child who has already undergone numerous procedures requires skill and patience. This is especially true for children being fitted for a mask (device to hold the head still during treatment) in preparation for radiation to the head or spine. Great care should be taken to ensure that making the mask is not traumatic. This can often be accomplished by using play therapy to demonstrate the procedure.

> When 3-year-old Katy was being given the tour of the radiation room by her technologist, Brian, he was just wonderful with her. He gave her a white, stuffed bear that he used to demonstrate the machine. He immobilized the bear on the table using Katy's mask, then moved the machine all around it so that she could hear the sounds made by the equipment. He then took a Polaroid picture of the bear on the table, in the mask, for Katy to take home with her.

Masks are made from a lightweight, porous, mesh material. First, the technologist should explain and demonstrate the entire mask-making process to the child. The child then lies down on a table. The technologist places a sheet of the mask material in warm water to soften it. This warm mesh sheet is placed over the child's face and quickly molded to his features. The child can breathe the entire time through the mesh material, but must hold still for several minutes as the mask hardens. The mask is lifted off the child's face, and the technologist cuts holes in it for the eyes, nostrils, and mouth.

> *The cancer center staff had scheduled 2 hours to make a mask for my 3-year-old daughter. I asked them to very quietly explain every step in the process. I told her that I would be holding her hand, and I promised that it would not hurt, but it would feel warm. I asked her to choose a story for me to recite as they molded the warm material to her face to make the time go faster. She picked "Curious George Goes to the Hospital." She held perfectly still; I recited the story; the staff were gentle and quick; and the entire procedure took less than 20 minutes.*

For children having radiation to the spine or abdomen, immobilization devices can be as simple as Velcro straps to hold the body in place. Some children will lie in special foam or "bean-bag like" molds made to allow greater accuracy when directing the radiation.

> *My 4-year-old son needed 6 weeks of radiation just weeks after his stem cell transplant. His immune system was still low, although he was starting to recover from the month-long ordeal. The technicians thought he would lay face down quietly in a tub of warm plaster so that they could make his mold. I don't think so! He was scared, and kicked and screamed, so we went home. We came back the next day, they sedated him with propofol, and then it took just a few minutes to make the mold.*

Immobilization devices can be fitted on well-prepared, calm children or sedated children. The following are parent suggestions for preparing a child for the fitting of an immobilization device:

- Give the child a tour of the room where the fitting will take place.

- Explain each step of the process in clear language.

- Be honest in describing any discomfort the child may experience.

- For small children, fit the device onto a mannequin or stuffed animal to demonstrate the process.

- For older children or teenagers, show a video or read a booklet describing the procedure.

Spending ample time on preparation generally means less time will be needed to fit a device. At many hospitals, child life specialists help prepare children before an immobilization device is fitted. If the fitting goes well, it establishes trust and good feelings that will help make the radiation treatments proceed smoothly.

> *Seventeen-month-old Rachel was fitted with two immobilization devices. They made a mask to hold her head in position, as well as a body mold from her neck to her thighs.*

Sedation

All infants, most preschoolers, and some school-aged children require sedation or a short-acting anesthesia (most commonly propofol given intravenously) to ensure they remain perfectly still during radiation therapy. Parents will receive written instructions about when their child should stop eating and drinking before sedation or anesthesia.

> *About 1 month after he was diagnosed, Sam started a course of 30 daily radiation treatments. In some ways, this was the easiest part. Each day we woke up at the same time we always had, got dressed and went directly to the hospital. Because of Sam's young age, he received anesthesia so that he would lie still for the radiation session. He had a Hickman® catheter in his chest, so that made getting the anesthesia into him a quick process. The anesthesia acted very quickly, and the technicians and nurse would place him in position and the treatment would start. Each session lasted about 15 minutes. He'd then be moved into a recovery area where I'd wait while he awoke. He usually came out of it happy, but hungry. I learned to pack lots of easy snacks, like cheerios, crackers, and juice boxes. Once he was fully awake, I'd wheel him to the car in the baby stroller. Most days we were home by 9:30 am. One of the blessings of daily radiation is seeing nurses and technicians every day. I was very touched by the caring and comfort of the staff in the radiation department. Another benefit of the daily radiation was being able to change the dressing on Sam's Hickman® while he was under anesthesia.*

Anesthesia is given through a small plastic mask or through the child's catheter or intravenous line (IV). Sometimes the parent can hold or comfort the child while anesthesia is administered, but the parent must leave the room before radiation treatment begins. Once your child is awake and can swallow, you can take her home. The entire procedure generally takes 30 to 90 minutes.

> *Kenny had 24 cycles of radiation under anesthesia to treat his rhabdomyosarcoma. At first it was really horrible for me to leave him in that big, dark room. I would hold his anesthesia mask over his face until he was asleep, and then I would leave.*

I was the last and first face he saw every time. Kenny was so brave. Towards the end of the 24 treatments, he would stand in front of the big doors yelling, "Hurry up in there! It's my turn to go night-night!" The only request he had was that a Coke and a green Popsicle® be waiting for him when he woke up.

Nausea and vomiting are occasional side effects of anesthesia, but they can usually be controlled by antinausea drugs such as ondansetron (Zofran®). Over time, your child may become comfortable with the treatment and not require anesthesia.

Each time my young son came in for radiation, part of the routine was to place the hard plastic mesh mask over his face while he was awake, just for an instant, to get him used to the idea of trying to wear it for treatments without sedation. No pressure was ever put on him about it, it was just mentioned as a possibility of something he could try, something that would let him keep eating and drinking all through the day, instead of having to fast for a few hours before each sedation, which was very hard for such a small boy who was getting sedation twice a day.

They left the mask on him for a tiny bit longer each time, until he was tolerating it for several seconds, and by the end of the third week, close to a minute. His fifth birthday was at the exact middle of treatment, and he decided that since he was such a big boy now, he would try to do it without sedation. I know he was trying to please and impress all these kind people. He worked it out quietly with a favorite technician, asked the "sleepy medicine doctor" to wait outside the treatment room, let them screw the mask down to the table and did the whole thing awake.

I've never been more proud in my life. Everyone cheered and hugged him. He finished the last three weeks of treatments without sedation, sometimes eating and drinking on his way in the door just to show off that he could!

What to expect during a radiation treatment

Radiation treatments can be very stressful for both children and parents, but knowledge and preparation can make the entire process much easier. This section describes radiation simulation and the various types of radiation therapy.

Matthew had his own calendar outside the radiation treatment room. For every treatment he received, he picked a sticker to place on his calendar. It was a wonderful way to show him how far he had come and how much farther he had to go before he would be finished. Matthew loved rummaging through the sticker box for the perfect addition to his calendar. When the last treatment had been given, he was allowed to remove the calendar from the wall and bring it home as a keepsake. We still have our son's calendar. It now has a special place in his scrapbook of memories.

Radiation simulation

Prior to receiving any external beam radiation therapy, measurements and a CT scan are performed to map the precise area to be treated. This preparation for therapy is called the "simulation" or "planning session." The simulation will take longer than any other appointment—from 30 minutes to 2 hours. Because simulation does not involve any high-energy radiation, parents may be allowed to remain in the treatment room to help and comfort their child. Young or active children require sedation for the simulation.

During simulation, the radiation oncologist and technologist use a specialized x-ray machine or a CT scanner to outline the treatment area. They will adjust the table that the child lies on, the angle of the machine, and the width of the x-ray beam needed to give the exact dosage in the proper place. Ink marks or permanent tattoos are placed on the skin or the immobilization device to ensure accuracy of treatment. After the simulation is completed, the child can leave while the radiation oncologist carefully evaluates the developed x-ray film and measurements to design the treatment field.

External beam radiation treatment

To receive external beam radiation, children are given appointments to visit the radiation clinic for a specific number of days, usually at the same time each day. If a child will have anesthesia for treatment, the sessions are usually scheduled early in the morning, because the child will not be able to eat or drink before coming in for treatments. Older children who require anesthesia may be treated later in the day, such as late afternoon, so they can continue to attend school, if possible. Radiation is given 5 days a week for 2 to 7 weeks (weekends off); the duration of the radiation treatment varies, depending on the type of cancer being treated. At some institutions and for some protocols, children go more than once a day to receive hyperfractionated dosing.

When the parent and child arrive, they must check in at the front desk. The technologist or nurse then comes out to take the child into the treatment room. Often, parents accompany young children into the room. If the child requires anesthesia, it is usually given in the treatment room.

> I desperately wanted my 4 year old to be able to receive the radiation without anesthesia. I asked the center staff what I could do to make her comfortable. They said, "Anything, as long as you leave the room during the treatment." So I explained to my daughter that we had to find ways for her to hold very still for a short time. I said, "It's such a short time, that if I played your Snow White tape, the treatment would be over before Snow White met the dwarves." Katy agreed that was a short time, and asked that I bring the tape for her to listen to. She also wanted a sticker (a different one every day) stuck on the machine for her to look at. I brought her pink blanket to wrap her in because the table was hard and the room cold. Each day, she chose a different

comfort animal or doll to hold during treatment. So we'd arrive every day with tapes, blanket, stickers, and animals. She felt safe, and all treatments went extremely well.

The technologist will secure children or teens in place with an immobilization device. Measurements are taken to verify that the child's body is perfectly positioned. Frequently, the technologist will shine a light on the area to be irradiated to ensure that the machine is properly aligned. The technologist and parents leave the room, closing the door behind them.

At some institutions, parents are allowed to stay and watch the TV monitor and talk to their child via the speaker system. If this is the case, the parent should be careful not to distract the technologist as he administers the radiation. At other institutions, parents are asked to wait in the waiting room. It's important that parents understand the department's policies; they should ask the radiation therapist if anything is unclear.

The treatment takes only a few minutes and can be stopped at any time if the child experiences any difficulty. When the treatment is finished, the technologist turns off the machine, removes the immobilization device, and the parents and child can go home. If the child received anesthesia, she will need to recover from the anesthesia before she can go home. There is no pain at all when receiving external beam radiation treatment, but some children report seeing flashing lights or noticing a burning smell. Both of these are normal experiences, but it is important to let the radiation oncologist know if your child mentions either of them.

> *There was something about the radiation or the anesthesia that frightened Shawn terribly. He would scream in the car all the way to the hospital. It was a scream as if he was in pain. He had nightmares while he was undergoing radiation and every night after it was over. We decided a month after radiation ended to bring a box of candy to the staff who had been so nice. Shawn asked, "Do I have to go in that room?" When I explained that it was over and he didn't need to go in the room anymore, he asked if he could go in to look at it once more. He stood for a long time and just looked and looked at the equipment. Somehow he made his peace with it, because he never had any more nightmares.*

Because external beam radiation therapy is usually given at short, daily appointments for several weeks, families who do not live within an hour or so of their treatment center often have to arrange to stay near the hospital. Your social worker can help you arrange to stay at a Ronald McDonald House or other similar facility, at a hotel, or at a short-stay apartment near the hospital. If the hospital you will go to for radiation is different than your child's regular hospital, your oncologist will work closely with an oncologist from the radiation center who will make sure she receives any blood tests, chemotherapy, or other care that is required during that time.

Charlie was diagnosed with rhabdomyosarcoma of the prostate at 16 months old. The radiation oncologist at our hospital in Pennsylvania referred him for proton radiation, and they sent us to Boston. I was terrified of the whole prospect. Our older son was in school and I had put him to bed every night of his life, and I would have to leave him. My husband still had to work. It ended up being just a wonderful experience. My mom came with us to Boston. She cooked and did laundry and cared for me while I cared for Charlie. We had never been to Boston and we loved it. We go every year because it's a celebration and he is enrolled in a study so he has to go back for 5 years. We rented an apartment right across the street from the hospital from a list provided by the social worker. We would go downstairs, go across the street, and get his treatment. He had no hesitation. He would sit in the crib and say "Whee!" as we went down the hall. He was sedated for every treatment. He fell asleep in my arms, and I would walk out of the room. After Charlie woke up from anesthesia, we had the rest of the day to do whatever we wanted. He had no radiation burns, and one day of diarrhea. He had no black skin, no problems at all.

Internal radiation treatment

Internal radiation therapy, also called brachytherapy or seed implantation, involves the placement of radioactive materials inside the affected area. This form of therapy delivers a high dose of radiation directly to the cancerous area. Children are admitted to the hospital to receive internal radiation. A catheter is inserted into the child in the radiology department or in the operating room, and radioactive materials are placed via the catheter.

The child is then transported to a hospital room specially designed for children undergoing this type of treatment. The walls may contain lead (to keep the radiation in the room), and often items such as sheets and eating utensils are disposable. The child will remain there until he is no longer radioactive. The radioactive materials, also called interstitial implants, will generally remain in place for several days. Once they are removed, your child may resume normal activities and will no longer require isolation.

Children and pregnant women cannot visit while a child is receiving internal radiation. Parents and nursing staff can spend a limited amount of time in the child's room. This may be distressing for very small children who are unable to understand why people must maintain a safe distance. It may be possible to keep the door to your child's hospital room open. In these instances, you can sit in the hall and talk to your child to help alleviate fears or boredom. You can ask the nursing staff and the child life specialist if they have suggestions about how to make your child as comfortable as possible.

Our son was 5 years old when he was admitted for his internal radiation. The biggest issue we had to deal with was boredom. It was hard for him to understand that I wasn't allowed to spend all my time at his bedside. The door to his room was open at all times, so I moved a reclining chair into the hall, and that was where I stayed for 4 days. I would read him stories, stopping from time to time to hold up the book so he could see the pictures. He had computer games and a DVD player in his room, and that helped to keep him entertained.

Possible short-term side effects

Generally, radiation therapy given to children with solid tumors takes place over 2 to 7 weeks. If side effects occur, it is often hard to differentiate those caused by radiation from those caused by the chemotherapy, which is sometimes given at the same time. The severity of the side effects depends on the area being irradiated, the dose of radiation, and the sensitivity of the tissues in the area being treated. The radiation oncologist is familiar with all possible side effects and is responsible for their treatment.

Possible short-term side effects include the following:

• Loss of appetite

> *Calories are most important; nutrition can come after treatment. We use whole milk, and put butter on everything: Ethan would eat any time, anything. When Ethan completely lost his appetite during radiation, we used Megace®, a prescription appetite stimulant. It has fairly few side effects and did seem to work for him.*

• Nausea and vomiting

• Diarrhea

• Mouth and throat sores (making it painful to eat or swallow)

> *There are several concoctions that radiation oncologists prescribe, sometimes called "Miracle Mouthwash," that often work wonders for mouth and throat sores.*

• Fatigue

• Temporary hair loss

• Reddened, itchy, peeling, or burned skin

> *Where the beams entered at two places, his scalp was burned like a sunburn, and aloe vera gel helped to keep that soft.*

· · · · ·

Radiation was the most difficult part of treatment. The burns appeared after about 2 weeks. Aquaphor® and Neosporin® creams were the only things that helped. My son said the prescription cream made it itchy. The pain was very bad. It has been 2 months since his radiation ended, and it still itches and hurts.

- Low blood counts
- Changes in taste and smell (sometimes occurring during treatment sessions)
- Increased or decreased saliva or dry mouth (ask your physician about saliva substitutes such as Moi-Stir® or Salivant®)

My daughter Mandy (age 4) had a problem with thick saliva while she was being treated. We started to give her about 200 ml of extra water each day through her G-tube. This seemed to help although she would still have the problem some days, just not as much.

Whether your child will develop any side effects depends on the part of the body being radiated and the dose of radiation. Side effects also vary from child to child. For additional methods of coping with many of the above side effects, see Chapter 16, *Common Side Effects of Treatment*.

When Sean (age 18) was diagnosed with rhabdomyosarcoma, part of his treatment included 25 days of radiation therapy to the chest and shoulder area. For the first few weeks his only side effects were low white blood cell counts. However, by the sixteenth treatment, he developed bad burns under his arm and in his throat. This caused him to stop eating and drinking, which led to a hospitalization because he was dehydrated.

Sean has had radiation recall [a skin reaction resembling a severe sunburn that occurs when certain chemotherapy drugs are given during or soon after radiation treatment] twice since his radiation treatments have ended. It seems that each new type of chemotherapy causes it to come back. The recall makes him lose his appetite, so when he feels good I make sure he eats everything his heart desires to build him back up—just in case it happens again.

· · · · ·

Radiation was the hardest part of the treatment for us. Holden was 2 and received photon radiation to his bladder and prostate. Huge, thick pieces of skin peeled off, and there was some bleeding. The burns were painful. The internal inflammation was so bad, and he was on so many strong pain medications that he sometimes became very violent; hitting, kicking, and biting. We were afraid he would hurt himself, so they put him on an antipsychotic. Radiotherapy was in February and March and the burns lasted 6 weeks. He has really done amazingly well since treatment. He's off all meds; it's like it never happened. You would never guess he had ever been sick.

One side effect uniquely associated with radiation to the head is somnolence syndrome. This is characterized by drowsiness, prolonged periods of sleep (up to 20 hours a day), low-grade fever, headaches, poor appetite, nausea, vomiting, and irritability. It may occur during radiation or as late as 12 weeks after radiation treatment ends; it can last from a few days to several weeks.

> *Hunter developed somnolence syndrome and it caused him to sleep often during the day, sometimes for as much as 20 hours. Luckily, his doctors were just a phone call away. They reassured me that his symptoms were a result of the syndrome. His doctors really listened to me and put my mind at ease. I had been worried because he was experiencing many of the same symptoms that he'd had at diagnosis.*

Possible long-term side effects

While short-term effects appear and subside, long-term side effects may not become apparent for months or years after treatment ends. Specific late effects depend on the age of the child, the dose of radiation, the part of the body treated with radiation, and the vulnerability of each child. When treatment is complete, you should be given a summary of your child's care, including type of radiation, location, and dose. You also should be given a clear plan for all necessary follow-up care. More information is available in Chapter 26, *End of Treatment and Beyond.*

The effects of radiation on the heart, lungs, brain, bones, teeth, and fertility range from no late effects to severe, life-long impacts. Second tumors in the radiation field occasionally develop years after treatment. Detailed information about possible late effects are described in *Childhood Cancer Survivors: A Practical Guide to Your Future*, 3rd edition by Nancy Keene, Wendy Hobbie, and Kathy Ruccione.

> *As I carried my unconscious son back to the waiting room after radiation treatment, a woman there stared intently. On impulse, I took the seat next to her. As I arranged Ben into a bear hug with my arms wrapped around him, she whispered to me, "I'm so jealous." I was taken aback by the heat in her voice. She told me she was making these daily treks with her son, too. Only, he was 21 years old, and wouldn't let her hold him or hug him. It broke her heart to see Ben and I wrapped up in ourselves in that unique mom-child world of clinging hugs, multiple kisses, and rubby-faces. Her son was a brave, valiant, independent young man, and she was proud of him. But what she really wanted to do was wrap herself around him, tuck his head under her chin, and make everything all better like she used to.*

Chapter 18

Stem Cell Transplantation

PERIPHERAL BLOOD STEM CELL TRANSPLANTATION (PBSCT) is a complicated procedure used to treat some cancers and blood diseases that were once considered incurable. In this procedure, stem cells in the blood are collected and the child is given high-dose chemotherapy to kill as many cancer cells as possible. After the chemotherapy, the stem cells that were collected earlier are infused into the child's veins. The stem cells migrate to the cavities inside the bones where new, healthy blood cells are then produced.

Stem cell transplants are expensive, technically complex, and potentially life-threatening. Understanding the procedure and its ramifications at a time of crisis can be tremendously difficult. This chapter explains the type of PBSCT currently used to treat a small number of children with solid tumors, and it shares the experiences of several families.

What is a peripheral blood stem cell transplant?

Bone marrow is the spongy material inside bones. It is full of the youngest type of blood cells—called stem cells—from which all other blood cell types develop (white blood cells, red blood cells, and platelets). Stem cells are also found in circulating (also called peripheral) blood, although in a much less concentrated form.

There are different types of stem cell transplants. When peripheral blood is used as a source of stem cells for a transplant, it is called a peripheral blood stem cell transplant or PBSCT. If the child does not have cancer cells in the bone marrow, as is usually the case for children with solid tumors, the child usually is able to donate his own stem cells for a transplant. This type of transplant is called an autologous PBSCT, and this chapter deals specifically with this type of stem cell transplant.

In an autologous PBSCT, the number of stem cells in the blood are increased by giving children a drug called granulocyte colony-stimulating factor (G-CSF). The G-CSF is given as a shot under the skin. It is typically started 24 hours after chemotherapy, and continued until the stem cell collection has been completed.

The stem cells are collected in a procedure called apheresis. These cells can be stored for months or even years. When a child is admitted to the hospital for the transplant procedure, high doses of chemotherapy drugs that are known to be effective against the type of tumor they have are administered. These very high doses kill more tumor cells, but they also prevent the bone marrow from producing stem cells. The child's own stem cells are then given back to the child via a central venous catheter (e.g., Hickman® catheter). See the section titled "Stem cell harvest and storage" later in this chapter for a description of the collection and storage process.

The transplant can be done one or more times, allowing doctors to expose the tumor cells to high doses of chemotherapy while limiting toxicity and the risk of life-threatening infections. When this process is done more than once, it is called tandem PBSCT, serial PBSCT, or sequential PBSCT.

> Hunter's high-risk neuroblastoma was treated with a tandem stem cell transplant. His own stem cells were harvested previously. He had enough cells collected to do three transplants. The third deposit of cells is still frozen in case it's needed. The doctor told me that they could be frozen for a very long time. It has been over a year, and he continues to do extremely well.

When are transplants necessary?

The current standard of care for children with high-risk neuroblastoma includes PBSCT. A recent study suggested that using tandem transplants might improve outcomes, so it is possible your oncologist will recommend this approach. Children with high-risk neuroblastoma usually have stem cells collected and frozen early in treatment, and then infused during the consolidation phase of treatment. In some clinical trials for other solid tumors, tandem PBSCTs are also used. Although preliminary data from some of these trials are encouraging, tandem transplants are still considered experimental in treating most, but not all, solid tumors.

If a PBSCT has been recommended for your child or teenager, you may want to get a second opinion before proceeding. In addition, you may want to ask the oncologist and transplant physician some or all of the following questions:

- What are all the treatment options for my child's tumor?
- For my child's type of tumor, history, and physical condition, what chance for survival does she have with a transplant? What are her chances with other treatments?
- What are the risks and the benefits of this type of transplant?
- What will be my child's likely short-term and long-term quality of life after the transplant?

- Where would my child receive this type of transplant?

- What portion of the procedure will be outpatient versus inpatient?

- What is the average length of stay in the hospital for children undergoing this procedure?

- What are the anticipated and the rare complications of this type of transplant?

- Will my child have to take medicines after the transplant? For how long?

- What are the side effects of these medicines?

- Is this transplant considered to be experimental, or is it the current standard of care?

- Do insurance companies usually pay for this type of transplant?

Choosing a transplant center

If the institution where you child is treated is also an accredited transplant center, you will not need to travel for this part of your child's treatment. However, if you need to choose a transplant center, it is an important and often difficult decision. Institutions may just be starting a stem cell transplant program, or they may have vast experience. Some centers may be excellent for adults, but have limited pediatric experience. Some may allow you to stay overnight with your child; others may restrict access.

The center closest to your home may not provide the best medical care available for your child or allow the necessary quality of life (social workers, child life services) that you need. In addition, your insurance plan may require your child to have the PBSCT at a specific center. To see a list of transplant centers, visit *www.bmtinfonet.org/before/ choosingtransplantcenter.* Asking the following questions can help you learn about the policies of different transplant centers:

- Is your center accredited by the Foundation for Accreditation of Cellular Therapy (*www.factwebsite.org/AboutFACT*)? This agency inspects transplant programs and certifies programs that provide high-quality care.

- What are your program's 1-, 2-, and 5-year survival rates? (Remember that some institutions accept very-high-risk patients, and their statistics will not compare to a center that performs less-risky transplants.)

- What is the nurse-to-patient ratio? Do all staff members have pediatric training and experience?

- What support staff is available (e.g., educators, social workers, child life specialists, clergy, support groups, volunteers)?

- Will my child be on a pediatric or combined adult–pediatric unit?

- What are the institution's rules about parents staying in the child's hospital room?

- Are children allowed to visit?

- What kinds of temporary and long-term housing are available near the center? What are the costs for this housing?

- What infection control measures does this center use for transplant patients? Isolation? Gown and gloves? Washing hands?

- What kinds of activities are available for children during their hospital stay?

- What is the average length of time before a child leaves the hospital? For a child who has been discharged from the hospital but whose home is far away, how long before he can leave the area to go home?

- What long-term follow-up is available? Does the center have post-transplant clinics that focus on late effects?

- How does the center stay in contact with the child's primary doctor?

- Explain the waiting list requirements, if any.

- How much will this procedure cost? How much will my insurance cover?

Many transplant centers have videos and booklets for patients and their families that explain services and describe what to expect before, during, and after transplant. Call any transplant center that you are considering and ask that all available materials be sent to you.

> The head of oncology from a major transplant center comes to our city every 2 months to follow up with the kids who have been treated there. It was a big draw for us to have post-transplant follow-up at home, rather than having to travel a great distance to get back to the center. The families weren't required to cap and gown, only scrub their hands. Since I'm allergic to those hospital gloves, this allowed me to stay with my daughter throughout. We did, however, call around to several centers to compare facilities, costs, and insurance coverage.

Making an informed consent is a serious decision when considering a life-threatening procedure such as a PBSCT. It is very important to work closely with your child's oncologist and treatment team when making this decision. Do not hesitate to keep asking questions until you fully understand what is being proposed. Ask the doctor to use simpler language if she has lapsed into medical jargon. Record the conversation to review later, or take along a family member or friend to take notes. You do not need to sign the consent form until you feel comfortable that you understand the procedure and have had every question answered. Even after you sign the consent form, you can still change your mind up until your child is admitted for transplant.

Stem cell harvest and storage

Stem cells are collected through a process called apheresis. The stem cells are usually collected ("harvested") at your children's hospital or at the transplant center as your child's bone marrow recovers from an intensive cycle of chemotherapy. A medication called granulocyte colony stimulating factor (G-CSF) is given to your child after the chemotherapy to further increase the number of stem cells in the blood.

When your child's peripheral blood cell counts rise, blood is removed through your child's central venous catheter or a special temporary catheter placed in a vein (usually in the neck or groin area). If a temporary catheter is required, the child is given anesthesia or deep sedation to keep him comfortable during the procedure. For older children with large veins, the arms may sometimes be used for the PBSC collection. One side of the catheter (or an IV inserted into one arm) collects blood, which then goes into a machine that filters out the stem cells. The filtered blood is returned to the body through the other side of the catheter (or an IV inserted into the other arm). Each apheresis procedure takes 3 to 6 hours.

> Sean had an autologous stem cell transplant. His cells were collected in a process called apheresis. He was connected to a machine that was a lot like what is used for kidney dialysis. He had a catheter installed in his groin area that was used to connect him to the apheresis machine. His blood was removed through the catheter and run through a centrifuge that removed his stem cells and returned the remaining blood components back to his body. His stem cells were given back to him on transplant day.

The number of sessions required varies. Infants may need only one session, but older children may need two, or occasionally three, sessions. In rare cases, it is impossible to get enough stem cells from the blood of children who have recently undergone extensive chemotherapy and/or radiation. In these rare instances, stem cells from the bone marrow are used.

> Six-year-old Ethan had a stem cell harvest after his recovery from the first Cytoxan® doses he got. He was on Neupogen® (G-CSF), which was a piece of cake for him. Once he had enough of the stem cells in his bloodstream, he had a femoral PICC line placed because they needed a larger catheter to do this. The only downside was that he had to lay completely flat for about 6 hours, and collection took 2 days, so he had limited movement the night between collections. Plan a lot of quiet activities! Videos, recorded books, handheld games, cards. He hated the no bathroom privileges and refused to use a urinal at all.

Possible complications of peripheral blood stem cell apheresis include:

- **Hypocalcemia (low calcium in the blood).** Your child may experience muscle cramps, chills, tremors, tingling of the fingers and toes, dizziness, and chest pain. She will be closely monitored during the procedure, and IV or oral calcium supplements will be given to try to prevent this problem.

- **Thrombocytopenia (low platelets).** Sometimes platelets stick to the inside of the apheresis machine. Your child's platelet count will be checked before and after the apheresis, and a platelet transfusion will be given if needed.

- **Hypovolemia (low blood volume).** This can occur at any time during the procedure and is more common in small children. Symptoms can include low blood pressure, rapid heart rate, lightheadedness, and sweating. To prevent this problem, the apheresis machine may be "primed" with a unit of blood (from a blood donor) prior to the procedure.

- **Infection.** If your child develops fever, chills, or low blood pressure, blood cultures will be obtained and IV antibiotics given.

After collection, the child's stem cells are treated, frozen, and stored until they are used. Various compounds (e.g., dimethyl sulfoxide [DMSO]) are used to protect the stem cells during storage.

Most apheresis procedures are safely performed on an outpatient or short-stay basis, so you and your child can go home each evening. Some transplant centers, however, do require hospitalization throughout the procedure. Hospitalization is generally needed when a special apheresis catheter has to be used for the procedure and the PBSC collection cannot be completed in 1 day.

The transplant

Prior to the stem cell transplant, the child's bone marrow is suppressed using high-dose chemotherapy (radiation is generally not used for to prepare a child with a solid tumor for a PBSCT). This portion of treatment, called conditioning, kills tumor cells and makes room in the bone marrow for new stem cells.

> Tanner was 17 months old when he had a single transplant to treat his stage 4 neuroblastoma. My husband and I split time with him at the hospital. I was there the first part of the week, and he took off Fridays and came to the hospital so I could go home. When you have a little one and he's connected to all those IVs, it's so hard. I learned to block off a space in the hospital room so he had an area he could move around in, but keep the IV safe. Because we were worried about germs, neither of his brothers could visit. Video chat made a big difference. People from child life

would come and play with him so I could get out, walk to a nearby park, and clear my head. Child life was awesome. Tanner came home on day 23, but he was still on TPN [total parenteral nutrition] and oral pain meds. He was on the TPN for about 3 weeks after he came home. Even after his mouth sores were gone, he just didn't seem to feel like eating. He is doing very well now and is an energetic and happy little boy!

Conditioning regimens vary according to institution and protocol; they also depend on the medical condition and history of the child. For tandem transplants, the chemotherapy is given for 2 to 6 days. Sometimes all or part of the therapy is given in an outpatient setting.

If your child receives conditioning chemotherapy as an outpatient, he will need to go to the transplant unit no later than the evening before the procedure for hydration. Your child also may need IV fluids at night to provide hydration.

Leah was feeling very good and very healthy when she went in for her transplant. We lived near the transplant center, and she had a least 20 visitors a day. I think the visits and the nonstop telephone conversations really kept her spirits up.

The transplant itself consists of infusing the stem cells through a central venous catheter into the child, just like a blood transfusion. The stem cells travel through the blood vessels, eventually settling in the bone marrow.

I cannot say enough good things about the transplant center. They were very family-oriented, allowed us in the room 24 hours a day. I was allowed to sleep in bed with her (I just told the nurses to make sure to poke her and not me). The nurses were wonderful, and I still think of them as family.

A transplant doctor will monitor your child during the infusion of stem cells. A variety of minor to major complications might occur, including:

- Abdominal cramps
- Difficulty breathing
- Slow heartbeat
- Tightness in the chest
- Chills
- Cough
- Diarrhea
- Skin rash
- Fever

- Flushing

- Headache

- Changes in blood pressure

- Nausea and vomiting

- Unpleasant taste in the mouth

- Kidney failure

The complications that occur are typically due to the DMSO used to keep the stem cells alive during the storage process. Washing the stem cells prior to infusion minimizes the risk of these complications, but is not standard practice for all transplant centers.

Emotional responses

PBSCT can take a heavy emotional toll on the child, the siblings, and the parents. It can be a physically and mentally grueling procedure, with the possibility of late effects. Most transplant team members are extensively trained to meet the needs of the child and family during the transplant itself and throughout the recovery period that follows. The team usually includes doctors, nurses, social workers, educators, nutritionists, child life specialists, and physical, occupational, and speech therapists.

> Levi's transplant experience was like watching someone wake up from a deep sleep. For 2 weeks he was flat on his back, suffering greatly from mucositis and a tummy bug that caused diarrhea for days straight. It was a real horror. Then one evening he sat up and said, "What's all that stuff?" He was referring to all the gifts that had piled up in the corner of his room. He opened every toy, got down on the floor, and drew pictures of all the foods he was craving, and he never looked back. It was like an instant transformation. I think my own recovery was longer. I believe part of me froze in order to survive the transplant, and it took a long time to thaw.

• • • • •

> What helped me the most were the decorations and having a positive attitude. My mom decorated the area outside the transplant room with balloons, cards, and posters. It was hard to take the medicine, so my mom made a huge poster to mark off how well I did. Every time I took my medicine, I got a sticker. When I got one hundred stickers, I got some roller blades.

Often so much time and energy is focused on the child who needs the transplant that the needs of the siblings are overlooked. Siblings need to be prepared for what will happen to their brother or sister.

All their questions should be answered and all their concerns addressed. For more information about siblings, read Chapter 19, *Siblings*. Organizations that offer emotional support to families during the transplant are listed in Appendix B, *Resource Organizations*.

Paying for the transplant

PBSCTs are expensive. Some transplants are considered the standard of care, so insurers cover the procedure without problems. However, you will need to carefully research whether your insurance company considers the type of transplant proposed for your child to be experimental, and therefore not covered. Most insurance plans have a lifetime cap on benefits, and many only pay 80 percent of the costs of the transplant up to the cap. Often, transplant centers will not perform the procedure without all of the money guaranteed. With time being of the essence, this can cause great anguish for families who struggle to raise funds or need to take out a second mortgage to pay for a PBSCT.

> *Our first quote from the transplant center was $350,000, but we were able to negotiate a lower price.*

Most insurance companies will assign your child's care to a transplant coordinator or case manager who is responsible for making arrangements with the transplant center and handling financial issues. Coordinators can be valuable resources during this stressful time, especially if you get to know them and share you needs and concerns. If the insurance company does not assign a case manager, you can request to have one assigned or you can speak with a benefits manager about coverage and costs.

> *Right at the beginning, our doctor explained the different treatment options, including a double stem cell transplant. The insurance company denied coverage for the double transplant because they considered it experimental, even though our oncologist wrote several appeals. The insurance company did not even cover the full costs of the single transplant, and the hospital wrote off the rest of the costs. Social workers and the doctor dealt with the insurance company but we felt the stress of it. You shouldn't have to stress over that when your kid is so sick! Because the insurance company denied it, we couldn't afford the second transplant. Even though I'm worried he didn't have it, I'm also sort of glad he didn't need to go through it again because he got so sick during the first one.*

If you do not have health insurance, check *www.healthcare.gov* to see whether you are eligible for government-sponsored insurance plans. Another option is the National Cancer Institute (*https://ccr.cancer.gov*), which offers transplants free of charge to children who qualify for one of its research studies.

In Canada, each province and territory has a provincial health plan that usually covers the medical costs of transplantation. However, many other expenses will need to be covered by the family. Children often have to travel long distances to facilities that can perform a transplant. Travel, accommodations, and related costs have to be paid by parents.

Complications after transplant

Some children have a smooth journey through the transplant process, but others bounce from one life-threatening complication to another. There is no way to predict which children or teens will develop problems, nor is there any way to anticipate whether the new development will be a mere inconvenience or a major health crisis.

> *The transplant center was very clear about all of the potential problems. That was good because it prepared me. My attitude is watch for them, hope they don't happen, if they do, then live with them. She had an easy time with the transplant. She's a happy third grader, she's alive, and we feel so, so very lucky.*

This section presents some of the major complications that can develop post-transplant (in alphabetical order) and the experiences of several families who coped with these problems.

Bleeding

Bleeding can occur in different ways while your child is recovering from a PBSCT, including the following:

- Bruising
- Bleeding from the gums, or the urinary or gastrointestinal tract
- Nosebleeds

These common problems are usually managed with platelet transfusions. Serious bleeding can also occur in the lungs, stomach, intestines, or brain. Most transplant centers strive to keep children's platelet counts at a safe level until blood cell recovery has occurred. In general, platelets are the last type of blood cell to fully recover after a PBSCT.

Eating difficulties

Almost all children undergoing PBSCT require nutrition support during their recovery. Some centers feed children using tubes inserted through the nose to the stomach or small intestine. This is a good choice if your child is not experiencing nausea and

vomiting. Other children require IV nutrition (see Chapter 24, *Nutrition*). Most transplant centers start IV or tube feeding promptly after transplant and continue until the child's appetite and ability to take in adequate calories by mouth have returned.

A variety of factors contribute to eating difficulties, including pre-existing nutritional problems, side effects of conditioning chemotherapy, anticipatory nausea and vomiting, mouth sores, and infections of the gastrointestinal tract.

Your child may require ulcer medications to coat the lining of the stomach or to decrease the amount of stomach acid produced. He may experience ongoing nausea, in spite of the fact that he is long past his conditioning chemotherapy. Ask to speak to the transplant unit dietitian and keep accurate records of what your child eats and drinks. Your child's ability to eat and drink more normally is closely correlated with improved blood cell counts.

Hemorrhagic cystitis

Hemorrhagic cystitis (bleeding from the bladder) may result from certain chemotherapy drugs used in your child's conditioning regimen. If your child receives a chemotherapy drug that has the potential to cause this problem (e.g., cyclophosphamide), she will probably also receive IV hydration and the drug mesna to help coat the bladder lining to prevent damage. Occasionally, hemorrhagic cystitis is caused by a bacterial or viral bladder infection. Signs of infection include blood in the urine (which may be obvious to the eye or microscopic), blood clots in the urine, pain when urinating, and bladder discomfort. If your child develops hemorrhagic cystitis or a urinary tract infection, she may receive antibiotics or antiviral agents, IV fluids, and pain medication as needed.

Infections

The immune system of healthy children quickly destroys any foreign invaders; this is not the case for children who have undergone a transplant. The immune systems of children undergoing PBSCT have been temporarily impaired by chemotherapy. Until the new stem cells begin to produce large numbers of white blood cells (2 to 4 weeks after the transplant), children are at risk of developing serious infections.

> *After Hunter's double stem cell transplant, we had to follow many precautions. We had to be careful when we took him out, avoiding large crowds or public places (especially those indoors). He needed to wear a mask when we took him to his doctor's visits. We would take him to plenty of outdoor places for fun. I found the precautions easy to follow.*

To help prevent bacterial infections, children receive prophylactic antibiotics during the first weeks after transplant when their white blood cell count is low. Intravenous

antibiotics are started if the child has a fever. Fungal infections can also occur after transplant. The risk of fungal infections can be reduced by use of prophylactic medications such as fluconazole, and bone marrow growth factors such as G-CSF, that stimulate and accelerate white blood cell recovery. Your child will begin receiving prophylactic medications 1 to 2 days after the transplant. In addition, your child will be carefully evaluated each day for signs and symptoms of infection. Potential sites for problems include the skin, mouth, anus, and central venous catheter exit site. Report any new symptoms, such as cough, shortness of breath, abdominal pain, diarrhea, pain on urination, vaginal discharge, or mental confusion to the nurses promptly.

After transplant, children are susceptible to serious viral infections; the most common are herpes simplex virus, influenza, respiratory syncytial virus (RSV) parainfluenza virus (the virus that causes croup), and varicella zoster virus (which causes chickenpox and shingles). Viral infections are very hard to treat, so many centers use prophylactic medications, such as acyclovir, to prevent them. An organism that can cause a severe form of pneumonia is Pneumocystis jirovecii. Fortunately, the risk of Pneumocystis infection can be greatly decreased by using prophylactic antibiotics such as trimethoprim/sulfamethoxazole (Bactrim) or IV pentamidine.

> Our daughter (age 9) had a peripheral blood stem cell transplant. It's been several months and her white blood cell count is still low, but we have come to the conclusion that we can't make her live in a bubble anymore. We are careful to avoid potential risks, though, such as being around large crowds of people.

During recovery, children must redevelop immunity to common organisms, which may require redoing the usual childhood immunizations. You should discuss the transplant center's re-immunization policy with the transplant physician.

Preventing infection is the best policy for children who have had a stem cell transplant. The following are suggestions to minimize exposure to bacteria, viruses, and fungi:

- Have medical staff members and all family members thoroughly wash their hands before touching your child.
- Keep your child away from crowds and people with infections.
- Do not let your child receive live virus inoculations until the immune system has fully recovered; your child's oncologist will determine the appropriate date for getting immunizations.
- Keep your child away from anyone who has recently been given a live virus (e.g., chicken pox, polio, FluMist®).
- Keep your child away from barnyard animals and all animal feces.
- Avoid remodeling your home while your child is recovering.

- Avoid areas of active construction where ground digging is occurring.

- Shampoo all home carpets and rugs before your child returns home from transplant.

- Bathe and shampoo all family pets prior to your child's return home from transplant.

- Thoroughly wash fruits and vegetables prior to eating and completely cook all meat, poultry, and fish.

- Do not allow your child to share utensils, dishware, or drinks with other people.

- Call the doctor at the first sign of a fever or infection.

Mucositis

Mucositis (inflammation of the mucous membranes lining the mouth and gastrointestinal tract) and stomatitis (mouth sores) are common complications following PBSCT. Symptoms include reddened, discolored, or ulcerated membranes of the mouth; pain; difficulty swallowing; taste alterations; and difficulty speaking. The majority of children undergoing transplants experience this problem.

Your child will require frequent mouth care, changes in diet, and pain medications. To make daily mouth care less painful, try to ensure that it happens after pain medicine has been given. Likewise, it helps to make sure your child receives pain medication before eating. When the bone marrow starts making white blood cells again, your child's mouth will heal.

> High-dose chemo kills your taste buds, and I wanted to only eat sweet or spicy food, anything else tasted like cardboard. I'd eat ribs with BBQ sauce. KFC® mashed potatoes and gravy was great. Drinking was hard. I used to suck on ice cubes. It's gross when the lining of your mouth comes out. It just pulls out, it's white, but it doesn't hurt. It comes out during bowel movements, too, but you don't realize it. But, you can't swallow because of the sores, so you have to spit a lot.

Pulmonary edema

Pulmonary edema (collection of fluid in lung tissue) is sometimes seen in children who have had a PBSCT. Symptoms may include rapid breathing, shortness of breath, cough, and bloody sputum. Children may also experience swelling of the hands and feet because of too much fluid in their body. Your child may require oxygen, diuretic medications (to help him urinate), corticosteroids, and temporary fluid restriction until the problem resolves.

Veno-occlusive disease

Veno-occlusive disease (VOD), also known as sinusoidal obstruction syndrome (SOS), is a complication in which the flow of blood through the liver becomes obstructed. Children who have had more than one transplant, previous liver problems, or past exposure to intensive chemotherapy are more at risk of developing VOD. It can occur gradually or very quickly. Symptoms of VOD include jaundice (yellowing of the eyes and skin), enlarged liver, pain in the upper right abdomen, fluid in the abdomen, unexplained weight gain, and poor response to platelet transfusions. Treatment includes fluid restriction, diuretics (such as Lasix®), anti-clotting medications, and removal of all but the most essential amino acids from IV nutrition.

Long-term side effects

Increasing numbers of children are being cured of their disease and surviving years after a single or tandem PBSCT. The intensity of the treatment prior to, during, and after transplant can cause major effects that are not apparent for months or even years. This section describes a few of the possible long-term side effects that sometimes develop after transplant.

Dental development

Certain chemotherapy drugs, administered in high doses prior to transplant, may result in improper tooth development and blunted or absent tooth roots in children who had a transplant when they were younger than age 5. Your child should have a comprehensive dental exam prior to the transplant and a dental follow-up every 6 to 12 months after recovery from the PBSCT.

Thyroid function

Children who receive only chemotherapy before transplant do not usually develop thyroid deficiency. If, however, your child receives radiation therapy to the head, neck, or chest, either before or after a transplant, she should have lifelong monitoring for thyroid deficiency. Tablets containing thyroid hormone are effective in treating the problem if it develops.

Puberty and fertility

The risk of puberty or fertility problems is not well known for transplants in which the marrow is not completely destroyed (e.g., tandem transplants). For this reason, boys who have gone through puberty should bank sperm, if possible, before treatment begins. You may also consider experimental protocols that are attempting to preserve

fertility in girls. Any child or teen who had a transplant should be followed closely by a pediatric endocrinologist who can prescribe hormones if necessary (testosterone for boys, estrogen and progesterone for girls) to assist in normal pubertal development and who can assess fertility in older survivors.

Second cancers

Children who receive a PBSCT have a small risk of developing a second cancer. The risk depends on the chemotherapy drugs given and whether any radiation treatment was given.

Because transplants are relatively new treatments for children and teens with solid tumors, the overall impact and long-term effects are not yet clear. Your child's oncologist can explain known risks given your child's disease and treatment. You can also read about late effects in *Childhood Cancer Survivors: A Practical Guide to Your Future, 3rd ed.* by Nancy Keene, Wendy Hobbie, and Kathy Ruccione. It is very important that any child who had a transplant be followed for life by an expert in the late effects of treatment for childhood cancer. Many of these late effects, if found early, are treatable.

The road of chemotherapy treatment was long and harsh, but transplant was a test of faith and patience. Knowing that Mia's immune system would be zapped to the point of no return was scary. However, it felt like the last step in killing off any sign of cancer in my little girl's body and a step closer to the end of this nightmare. Isolation was tough on both of us but once again the staff, the programs, the volunteers, and everyone in the hospital were amazing. Mia's room was personalized and decorated just for her. She only asked to leave the room the day before we left for good, day 38! The nurses and doctors did everything in their power to make the whole transplant process go as smoothly as possible for all of us. They kept us informed, called us on their days off, helped me clean Mia up when she was sick, and even played dress up to help get her out of bed and to the shower. We survived, and Mia was discharged on day 39. She walked out dressed like a princess.

Chapter 19
Siblings

CHILDHOOD CANCER TOUCHES all members of the family, with especially long-lasting effects on siblings. The diagnosis creates an array of conflicting emotions in siblings. Not only are the they concerned about their ill brother or sister, but they usually resent the turmoil that the family has been thrown into. They feel jealous of the gifts and attention showered on the sick child, yet feel guilty for having these emotions. The days, months, and years after diagnosis can be extremely difficult for the sibling of a child with cancer.

Ways to explain the diagnosis to siblings are discussed in Chapter 8, *Telling Your Child and Others*. This chapter focuses on common emotions and behaviors of siblings and provides insights into how to cope from parents and siblings who have been through this experience.

Emotional responses of the siblings

Brothers and sisters are shaken to the very core by cancer in the family. Parents, the leaders of the family clan, sometimes have no time, and little energy, to focus on the siblings. During this major crisis, siblings sometimes feel they have no one to turn to for help. They may feel concerned, worried, fearful, guilty, angry, sad, abandoned, or other powerful emotions. If you understand these ever-changing emotions are normal, you will be better able to help your children talk about and cope with their strong feelings.

Although the months or years of treatment are emotionally potent for every member of the family, research has shown that siblings have good psychological outcomes, particularly if they have been assured they are valuable, contributing members of the family whose thoughts and feelings matter. In the years afterwards, siblings frequently report the experience as life-changing in many positive ways. Following are descriptions and stories about the emotions felt by siblings.

Concern for sick brother or sister

Children really worry about their sick brother or sister. It is difficult for them to watch someone they love be hurt by needles and sickened by medicines. It is scary to see a

brother or sister lose weight and go bald. It is hard to feel so healthy and energetic when the brother or sister has to stay indoors because of weakness or low blood counts. The siblings may be old enough to know that death is a possibility. There are plenty of reasons for concern.

I'm the mother of three children. Logan was 19 months old when diagnosed. It was very hard on all of us. Kathryn (5½ at the time of diagnosis) felt that she had to take so much on herself. She was there with us the entire time Logan was in the hospital. She had a cot right next to Logan's bed, and only she and I were the ones who could take care of "our Logan."

She used to love to visit the other kids on the hospital floor and entertain them. She hated to go home. She would get so involved with the other kids and didn't want to leave them. She actually got very close to two little girls that lost the battle, so here she was at 6, dealing with the loss of two friends.

Fear and worry

It is extremely common for young siblings of children with cancer to think the disease is contagious—that they can "catch it." Many also worry that one or both parents may get cancer. The diagnosis of cancer changes children's view that the world is a safe place. They feel vulnerable, and they are afraid. Many siblings worry that their brother or sister may get sicker or may die.

When my infant daughter was diagnosed with hepatoblastoma, I had two older daughters—5 and 3 years old. They are having a hard time because my husband and I have been gone most of the last 3 months staying in the hospital. Our oldest is very worried. She's been talking to her counselor at school once a week, and she's expressed that she is making us sad and that the doctor's aren't taking good enough care of her sister. She said that she was worried that her sister is going to die. We think she understands our explanations that her sister needs to stay in the hospital to get medicine to make the tumor smaller so they can take it out. It's been hard.

Fears of things other than cancer may emerge: fear of being hit by a car, fear of dogs, fear of strangers. Many fears can be quieted by accurate and age-appropriate explanations from parents or medical staff.

My 3-year-old daughter vacillated between fear of catching cancer ("I don't ever want those pokes") to wishing she was ill so that she would get the gifts and attention ("I want to get sick and go to the hospital with Mommy"). She developed many fears and had frequent nightmares. We did lots of medical play, which seemed to help her. I let her direct the action, using puppets or dolls, and I discovered that she thought there was lots of violence during her sister's treatments. She continues to ask questions, and we are still explaining things to her, 4 years later.

· · · · ·

It's almost midnight, which means that it will be exactly 36 hours before my sister goes for her first MRI after radiation. I don't know what to expect, but I would really love to hear some positive words coming from the oncologist's mouth when we meet up with him to receive the results. I can hardly sleep because, although I am always hoping for a miracle, I constantly worry, to the extent of having nightmares, about hearing something that I don't want to hear.

Jealousy

Despite feeling concern for the ill brother or sister, almost all siblings also feel jealous. Presents and cards flood in for the sick child. Mom and Dad stay at the hospital with the ill sibling, and most conversations revolve around that child. When the siblings go out to play, the neighbors ask about the sick child. Even at school, the teachers are concerned about their ill sibling. Is it any wonder brothers and sisters feel jealous?

The siblings' lives are in turmoil and they sometimes feel a need to blame someone. It's natural for them to feel it is the sick sibling's fault that family life has changed, or for taking all the adults' attention, or to feel angry and blame the parents for daily life being disrupted. Some siblings even develop symptoms of illness in an attempt to regain attention from the parents.

Our 9-year-old son seemed to be dealing with things so well until one evening as I was tucking him in, he confided that he had tried to break his leg at school by jumping out of the swing. He began to cry and told me he doesn't want his brother to be sick anymore; that he needs some attention, too. As parents, we were always so concerned with our sick child that we didn't realize how much our healthy child was suffering.

Guilt

Young children are egocentric; they are not yet able to see the world from any viewpoint but their own. Some children believe they caused their brother or sister to get cancer. They may have said in anger, "I hope you get sick and die," and then their sibling got sick. Any such fears should be dispelled right after diagnosis. Children need to be told, many times, that cancer just happens, and no one in the family caused it. They need to understand that no one can make something happen just by thinking or talking about it.

Many siblings feel guilt about their normal responses to cancer, such as anger and jealousy. They think, "How can I feel this way about my brother when he's so sick?" Assure them that the many conflicting feelings they are experiencing are normal and expected.

As a parent, share some of your conflicting feelings (such as anger at the behavior of a child due to a treatment side effect, and then feeling guilty about being angry).

It is also common for some children (and parents) to feel guilt about being healthy. It is important for parents to frequently remind their healthy children that there is no connection between their health and their sibling's illness and that no one, including the sick brother or sister, wants them to feel bad about feeling good.

Abandonment

If parental attention revolves around the sick child, siblings may feel isolated and resentful. Even when parents make a conscious effort not to be so preoccupied with the ill child, siblings sometimes still perceive that they are not getting their fair share of attention and may feel rejected or abandoned.

Sometimes it is necessary to have the siblings stay with relatives, friends, or babysitters. Parents may have to miss activities, such as soccer games or school events, they would otherwise have attended. Vacation plans may be scrapped. The reasons may seem obvious to parents, but the siblings may interpret these changes as evidence that they are not as well-loved as the sick child. Parents should explain in detail the reasons for any alterations in routines, solicit feelings about the changes from the siblings, and try to find solutions that work for everyone in the family.

> When Jeremy was very sick and hospitalized, we sent his older brother Jason to his grandparents for long periods of time. We thought that he understood the reasons, but a year after Jeremy finished treatment, Jason (9 years old) said, "Of course, I know that you love Jeremy more than me anyway. You were always sending me away so that you could spend time with him." It just broke my heart that every time he made that long drive over the mountains with his grandparents, he was thinking that he was being sent away.

Sadness

Siblings have many very good reasons to be sad. They miss their parents and the time they used to spend with them. They miss the life they used to have—the one they were comfortable with. They miss their sick sibling. They worry that he or she may die. Some children show their sadness by crying often; others withdraw and become depressed. Sometimes children confide in relatives or friends that they think their parents don't love them anymore.

> We always, always explained everything that was happening to Brent's older brother Zac (8 years old). He never asked questions, but always listened intently. He would say, "Okay. I understand. Everything's all right." We tried to get him to talk about it,

but through all these years, he just never has. So we just kept explaining things at a level that he could understand, and he has done very well through the whole ordeal. The times that he seemed sad, we would take him out of school and let him stay at the Ronald McDonald House for a few days, and that seemed to help him.

• • • • •

Megan and her twin sister Melissa went to a small, Catholic high school. We got Meg's diagnosis in September just before school started, and her first treatment was on the first day of school. Melissa had to go off to the first day of their senior year alone, without her sister by her side. She was surrounded by friends who loved her, but it was devastating for her. Melissa took the semester off after Meg passed, but she made up the credits and will graduate on time. Melissa has said that everything she does, she does for Meg.

Anger

Children's lives are disrupted by the diagnosis of a sister or brother with cancer, and siblings often feel very angry. Questions such as "Why did this happen to us?" or "Why can't things be the way they used to be?" are common. Children's anger may be directed at their sick sibling, their parents, relatives, friends, or doctors.

Children's anger may have a variety of causes. They may resent being left with babysitters so often or having additional responsibilities at home, or they may notice that the sick child is not always held to the same standards of behavior as the other children. Because each member of the family may have frayed nerves, explosions of temper can occur.

As we were driving home from school one day, Annie was talking, and I was only half listening. All of a sudden I realized that she was yelling at me. She screamed, "See, this is what I mean. You never listen, your mind is always on Preston." I pulled the car over, stopped, and said, "You're right. I was thinking about Preston." I told her that from now on I would try to give her my full attention. I realized that I would really have to make an effort to focus on what she was saying and not be so distracted. This conversation helped to clear the air for a while. I tried to take her out frequently for coffee or ice cream to just sit, listen, and concentrate on what she was saying.

Worry about what happens at the hospital

Children have vivid imaginations, and when they are fueled by disrupted households and whispered conversations between teary parents, children can imagine truly horrible things. Seeing how their ill sibling looks upon returning from a hospital stay can reinforce their fears that awful things happen at the clinic or hospital. Or the sibling

may think they are missing some grand parties when they see their sister or brother and parent come home from the hospital with presents and balloons.

> *My son is only in kindergarten. He has separation anxiety worse than a 6 month old. He doesn't want to go to bed alone. The last time Karissa had the flu, I thought he was going to die from worrying so much. He cried himself to sleep every night and woke up crying. He was so worried. He hasn't gotten much better since she has started feeling better, either. He doesn't even want to go near the hospital with his sister.*

Age-appropriate explanations can help children be more realistic about what they think happens at the hospital, but nothing is as powerful as a visit. Of course the effectiveness of a visit depends on your child's age and temperament, but many parents say that bringing the siblings along helps everyone. The sibling gains an accurate understanding of hospital procedures, the sick child is comforted by the presence of the sibling(s), and the parents get to spend more time with all the children.

> *Alissa's older brother Nicholas is her best friend. We are at the hospital for appointments and therapy three nights a week, every week. Nicholas helps Alissa with "hospital homework" and he also helps with her therapy. Nicholas is doing great at school. We include him on everything.*

Another way to help a worried sibling is to read age-appropriate books together. Many children's hospitals have coloring books for preschoolers that explain hospital procedures with pictures and clear language. School-age children may benefit from reading books with a parent (see Appendix C, *Books, Websites, and Support Groups*). Adolescents might be helped by watching videos, reading books, or joining a sibling support group.

Several parents suggested that another way to reduce siblings' worries is to allow even the youngest children to help the family in some way. When children have clear explanations about the situation and concrete jobs to do that will benefit the family, they tend to rise to the occasion. Make them feel they are a necessary and integral part of the family's effort to face cancer together.

> *My younger kids have never known 11-year-old Zach when he was healthy. He had his first surgery at 5 years old; Emily was 3 and Sarah was barely 1. All Zach's life, they treated him normally. No one ever let him win at games or anything (although I tried to make them). When we found out about the relapse, something got back to Emily in third grade. She got off the bus one day and asked if Zach was dying. I was shocked! I told her that his tumor was back but we were taking him to the best tumor doctor and we would do everything we could so he wouldn't die. That seemed to totally satisfy her.*

There was only one time that I remember Emily's and Sarah's teachers both telling me at parent conferences that the girls had been chatting a lot and not listening much. At the time, we were going through more surgery with Zach, so I think that is why. They also seem to reach out more to others. The oldest two belong to Chemo Angels where they volunteer to send out small cards or packages twice a week to a child with cancer.

Concern about parents

Exhausted parents are sometimes not aware of the strong feelings their healthy children are experiencing. They may assume children understand they are loved and that they would be getting the same attention if they were the one who had cancer. Siblings frequently do not share their powerful feelings of anger, jealousy, or worry because they love their parents and do not want to place more burdens on them. It is all too common to hear siblings say, "I have to be the strong one. I don't want to cause my parents any more pain." But burdens are lighter if shared. Parents can help themselves and the siblings by talking about their own feelings and encouraging children to share their feelings, especially the difficult ones. Try to listen without becoming defensive, and use those moments as a chance to grow together and strengthen each other.

Ethan had been sharing a room with his eldest brother, Jake, prior to his diagnosis, but after the first surgery either my spouse or I slept in the room with Ethan. Ethan gradually improved over the first couple of months to the point where he was more independently mobile and Jake said he wanted to sleep in Ethan's room again so that my spouse and I could go back to sleeping together. Jake has always been calm, thoughtful, and responsible, and he really seemed to handle Ethan's illness the best of the boys. When he and I participated in a survey to evaluate Post Traumatic Stress Disorder (PTSD) in siblings, I found out that he was much more distressed than I had imagined. We took some time to talk about how the stress affected each of us, and I was really grateful that we had agreed to do the research project.

Sibling experiences

Simply understanding the pain and fears of your healthy children eases their journey. Being available to listen and say, "I hear how painful this is for you," or "You sound scared. I am, too," reminds siblings they are still valued members of the family. They need to understand that even though their brother or sister is absorbing the lion's share of their parents' time and care, they are still cherished. Siblings need to hear that what they feel matters, especially if parents do not have a lot of time to spend with them. If parents understand that overwhelming emotions are normal, expected, and healthy, they can provide solace to all their children.

Brothers and sisters of children with cancer shared the following stories about some of the difficulties they faced.

Silent hurting heart

Dayna E. wrote the following poem when she was 13 years old. Two of Dayna's brothers had cancer—one lived and one died.

"Oh, nothing's wrong," she smiled,
grinning from ear to ear.
The frown that just was on her face
just seemed to disappear.

But deep down where secrets are kept,
the pain began to swell.
All the hurt inside of her
just seemed to stay and dwell.

All the pain in her heart
was too much for her to take.
Pretending everything's OK
is much too hard to fake.

She'd duck into the bathrooms
and hide inside the stalls.
Because no one could see her tears,
behind those dirty walls.

She was sick and tired of losing
and things never turning out right.
She had no hope left in her.
She was ready to give up the fight.

But she wiped away the teardrops,
put a smile back on her face,
pulled herself together, and
walked out of that place.

Life went on and things got better.
She thought that was a start.
But still, no one could see inside
her silent hurting heart.

Alana's story

Alana F. (11 years old) remembers how family life changed when her sister, Laura, had cancer.

My sister was in fifth grade and had been sick for the last week or so. Laura always seemed to be my hero. Although we got into arguments, all siblings get into fights, so I didn't worry. I didn't know what was about to happen, but neither did anyone else.

I don't quite remember how my parents told me she had cancer, but I do remember a lot of tears.

As time progressed, my life changed. I lived with my best friend and her parents, Catherine and Bill, but that changed too. Kelsie (my friend) and I got into a lot of arguments, but we still do. I don't know if that is why my grandmother and grandfather moved up to live in our house so that they could take care of me. Living with them was different. My grandmother had different expectations of me than my mother did.

My parents would each take turns staying at the hospital. Some nights I would live with my mom, grammy, and grandpy; and the next it would be with my dad and them.

Of course going through this dilemma I felt left out. Here I was living with my grandparents, and my sister got to live with our parents. She got lots of flowers, cards, and gifts, and all I got was the feeling of love from my relatives. I know that love is better than material things, but when you are 6 years old, you don't think so.

Things stayed the same for a long time. Then my sister went into remission and started living at home. I had to get used to my parents again and missed my grandparents.

My sister was spoiled at home, too. They bought her a waterbed, so she wouldn't get cold. What did I get? A heating blanket; a used heating blanket.

Having a sister with cancer

Alison L. (6 years old) describes the experience of having a sister with cancer.

I think having a sister with cancer is not fun. My mom paid more attention to Kathryn, my sister. I had to stay with Daddy. Mommy picked Kathryn up and not me. I wanted my sister's PJs. Guess what? I did not get them! Although my mommy wanted to stay with me, she did not want to leave my sister alone. Sometimes I felt like I was going to throw up. But now it has been 2 years since she has stopped having medicine, and she is completely better. To celebrate we are going to Disneyland.

My brother's a legend

To Erin H. (18 years old), her brother has become a legend by surviving childhood cancer.

I'm really proud of my brother Judson for handling everything so well. During those years, there were times when I was jealous of him, not only for the attention he received, but for his courage as well. This little boy was going through so much, and I still cowered at getting my finger pricked. As I look back, I wonder if I would have been able to make it through, not only physically, but emotionally as well.

According to some people, a person needs to be dead in order to be a legend, or to have been famous, or well liked. A legend to me, though, is someone who has accomplished something incredible, enduring many hardships and pains, and still comes out of it smiling.

Judd is a legend to me because he didn't give up in a time that he might have. He is a legend because he survived an illness that many do not. Now I look at him after being in remission for almost 5 years, and I hope that someday if I am ever faced with a challenge like his, I will have the same strength and courage he had.

When my brother got cancer

Annie W. (15 years old) relates some ways she benefited from her brother's battle with childhood cancer.

One experience in my life that was in no way comfortable for my family or myself and caused me a lot of confusion and grief was when my brother had cancer. Along with the disruption of this event, it also caused me to grow tremendously as a person. The Thanksgiving of my third-grade year, Preston, my brother, became very ill and was diagnosed a few weeks later with having cancer.

This event helped me to grow to become a better person in many ways. When my brother had very little hair or was puffed out from certain drugs, I learned to respect people's differences and to stick up for them when they're made fun of. Also, when Preston was in the hospital, I was taught to deal with a great amount of jealousy that I had. He received many gifts, cards, flowers, candy, games, and so many other material things that I envied. Most of all though, he received all the attention and care of my mother, father, relatives, and friends. This is what I was jealous of the most. As I look back now, I can't believe that I was that insensitive and self-centered to be mad at my brother at a time like that.

The thing that made this a "graced" experience was the fact that it enabled me to be very close to my brother as we grew up. My brother and I are now good friends and are able to talk and share our experiences with each other. I don't think that we would have this same relationship if he never had cancer, and I think that has been a very positive outcome. Another thing that has been a positive outcome of this event

is the people I've been able to meet. Through all the support groups, camps, and events for children with cancer and their siblings, I have met some people with more courage and more heart than anyone could imagine. In no way am I saying that I'm glad my brother had cancer, but I will say I'm very glad with some of the outcomes from it.

My sister had cancer

Eleven-year-old Jeff P. explains what happened when "My Sister Had Cancer." (Reprinted with permission from Candlelighters Childhood Cancer Foundation Canada's *CONTACT* newsletter.)

My sister Jamie got cancer when she was 23 months old. I was 8, and my two other sisters were 6 and 4.

My sisters and I were scared that Jamie was going to die. We weren't able to go to public places and also weren't allowed to have friends in our house. We missed a lot of school when there was chicken pox in our school. I got teased in school sometimes because my sister had no hair. Once an older kid called my sister a freak. My mom was sad most of the time. It was very hard.

We are all pleased that Jamie is doing well, and our lives are getting back to normal. It was an experience I'll never forget, and I hope it has made me a stronger person.

From a sibling

Fifteen-year-old Sara M. won first prize in a Candlelighters Creative Arts Contest with her essay, "From a Sibling." Her work is reprinted with permission.

Childhood cancer—a topic most teens don't think much about. I know I didn't until it invaded our home.

Childhood cancer totally disrupts lives, not only of the patient, but also of those closest to him/her, including the siblings. First, I was numbed with unbelieving shock. "This can't be happening to me and my family." Along with this came a whole dictionary full of incomprehensible words and a total restructuring of our (up to that time) fairly normal lifestyle.

One day I was waiting for my parents to pick me up from summer camp and anticipating the start of our family vacation to Canada. When they arrived, they informed me that my older brother Danny was very sick, and we wouldn't be taking that trip after all. The following day, the call came that confirmed the diagnosis. Instead of packing for vacation, we packed our bags and headed for Children's Hospital in Denver, 200 miles away, where Danny was scheduled for surgery and chemotherapy.

I developed my own disease (perhaps from fear I would "catch" what Danny had) with symptoms similar to my brother's:

Sympathy pains. I asked, "Why him?" when he came home from the hospital, exhausted from throwing up a life-saving drug for three days.

Fear. "How much sicker is Danny going to get before he gets well? He is going to get well, isn't he?"

Resentment. My parents seemed so worried about him all the time. They didn't seem to have time for me anymore.

Confusion. Why couldn't Danny and I wrestle around like we used to? Why couldn't I slug him when he made me mad?

Jealousy. I felt insignificant when I was holding down the fort at home.

The parts I hated the most were: not understanding what was being done to him, answering endless worried phone calls, and hearing the answers to my own questions when my parents talked to other people.

I was helped to sort out these feelings and identify with other siblings when I attended a program held just for teens who had siblings with cancer. We got together, tried to learn how to cross-country ski, and talked about our siblings and ourselves.

Perhaps you remember this story: "US [speed skating] star Dan Jansen, 22, carrying a winning time into the back straightaway of the 1,000 meter race, inexplicably fell. Two days earlier, after receiving word that his older sister, Jane, had died of leukemia, Dan crashed in the 500 meter" (Life Magazine). Having a sibling with cancer can immobilize even an Olympic athlete. Dan was expected to bring home two gold medals, but cancer in a sibling intervened. He became, instead, the most famous cancer sibling of all time. He shared his grief before a television audience of two billion people. Dan later went on to win the World Cup in Norway and Germany, and capture the gold at the Olympics. He is the first to tell you the real champions can be found in the oncology wards of children's hospitals across our nation, and the siblings who are fighting the battle right along beside them.

Siblings: Having our say

A group of siblings at a national conference gave advice to parents and siblings of children with cancer.

Twelve young people aged 7 to 29 met at the 25th Anniversary Candlelighters Childhood Cancer Foundation Conference to talk about what it is like having a sibling with cancer in the family. We talked about our families, our anger, jealousy, worries, and fears, and thought about what we wanted to tell others about our experiences. In fact, we made lists of things we wanted other people to know: one for parents, one for other children or young adults in our position, and one for the child who has been diagnosed with cancer.

Some parts of these lists reflect anger and bitterness, but that was not the overriding feeling in the session. I hope it isn't the only message you take away. If nothing else, the issues raised here may provide you with a good starting point for discussions in your own family.

To parents:

- We know you are burdened and trying to be fair. But try harder.
- Give us equal time.
- Be tough on disciplining the child with cancer. No free rides.
- Put yourself in our shoes once in a while.
- If you are away from home a lot, at least call and tell us, "I love you."
- Tell us what is going on. Don't just sit us in front of a video (about cancer); talk with us about it.
- Keep special time with us like lunch once a week or something. Time for just us. And if you can't be with us, find someone who can.
- When you talk to family members, say how everyone is doing—what we are doing is important, too.
- Ask how we are feeling. Don't assume you know.

To siblings of newly diagnosed kids:

- Keep a diary if you don't want to talk to your parents.
- Expect to not get as much attention.
- Expect that your parents are going to be extra cautious about what your brother/ sister does, who he/she hangs out with, etc.
- Hang in there. You're all you've got for now.
- Don't feel like you have to think about the illness all the time.
- Be understanding of your parents and stay involved.
- Tell someone how you are feeling—don't bottle it up.
- Go to the hospital to visit when you can.
- Make as many friends as possible at school.

To our siblings who struggled or are struggling with cancer:

- The world does not revolve around you.
- Stop feeling sorry for yourself.
- Not everything is related to cancer. Stop using that as an excuse for everything

- *I'm jealous of you sometimes, but I'm not mad. I know it sometimes seems like I'm mad, but I'm not.*

- *Don't take advantage of all the extra attention you get.*

- *Tell mom and dad to pay attention to me sometimes, too.*

- *Now that you are feeling better, where's the gratitude for all those chores that I did?*

- *I really admire your strength and courage. I wouldn't have gotten through your illness without you.*

Helping siblings cope

The following are suggestions from several families about ways to help brothers and sisters cope.

- Make sure you explain the tumor and its treatment to the siblings in terms they understand. Create a climate of openness so they can ask questions and know they will get answers. If you don't know the answer to a question, write it on your list to ask the doctor at the next appointment, or ask your child if he would like to go to the appointment with you and ask the question himself.

- Make sure all the children clearly understand that cancer is not contagious. They cannot catch it, nor can their ill brother or sister give it to anyone else. Impress upon them that nothing the parents or brothers and sisters did caused the cancer.

- Bring home a picture of the brother or sister in the hospital, and encourage the children to talk on the phone or send e-mails or text messages when their sibling is hospitalized.

  My daughter was 18 months old when her 3-year-old sister was diagnosed. Each member of the family flew in to stay at the house for 2-week shifts, so she had a lot of caregivers. A friend of mine gave her a big key chain that held eight pictures. We put a picture of each member of the family (including pets) on her key chain, and she carried it around whenever we were away. It seemed to comfort her.

- Try to spend time individually with each sibling.

  We began a tradition during chemotherapy that really helped each member of our family. Every Saturday each parent would take one child for a 2-hour special time. We scheduled it ahead of time to allow excitement and anticipation to grow. Each child picked what to do on their special day—such as going to the park, eating lunch at a restaurant, riding bikes. We tried to put aside our worries, have fun, and really listen.

- If people only comment about the sick child, try to bring the conversation back to include the sibling. For example, if someone exclaims, "Oh look how good Lisa looks," you could say, "Yes, and Martha has a new haircut, too. Don't you think she looks great?"

- Share your feelings about the illness and its impact on the family. Say, "I'm sad that I have to bring your sister to the hospital a lot. I miss you when I'm gone." This allows the sibling an opportunity to tell you how she feels. Try to make the illness a family project by expressing how the family will stick together to beat it.

> I never kept my feelings secret from Shawn's two older brothers (5 and 7 years old). If I was scared, I talked about it. Once when we thought he was relapsing, my stomach was so knotted up that I could barely walk. Kevin said, "Mom, I'm really worried about Shawn." I told him that I was, too, and then we both just hugged and cried together. They really opened up when we didn't hide our feelings.

- Include siblings in decision-making, such as giving them choices about how extra chores will be divided up or devising a schedule for parent time with the healthy children.

> We always gave the boys choices about where they would stay when Shawn had to be in the hospital. I felt like it gave them a sense of control to choose babysitters. They usually stayed at a close neighbor's house where there were younger children. It allowed them to ride the same bus to school and play with their neighborhood friends. Their lives were not too disrupted. They also really pitched in and helped with the younger kids. I think it helped them to help others.

· · · · ·

> Sometimes I think that my mom does not treat us equally. For example, if I left my snack garbage on the floor I would not get a snack the next night but Zach would get a snack if he left his garbage on the floor. I know he cannot walk but he could ask someone to take it out for him or he could say, "I need to take my garbage out so can somebody help me walk out so I can throw my garbage away."

- Allow siblings to be involved in the medical aspects of their brother or sister's illness, if they want to be. Often the reality of clinic visits and overnight stays is easier than what siblings imagine. Many siblings are a true comfort when they hold their brother or sister's hand during procedures.

> Just yesterday, Spencer out of the blue said "Mom, I wish I could have donated my marrow to Travis." And he's 5! He also donated money to plant a tree in Israel today at Sunday school and asked us to write that it was "In honor of God and my brother, Travis." Oh man, we can never forget how this experience is seared in the memory of

our children who don't have cancer. I am convinced that for Spencer, too, we will be seeing effects of this entire experience in many ways, long into the future.

• Give lots of hugs and kisses.

> *We assumed everything was fine with Erin because she had her grandma, who adored her, staying with her. We made a conscious decision to spend lots of time with her and include her in everything. But we realized later that she felt very left out. My advice is to give triple the affection that you think they need, including lots of physical affection such as hugs and kisses. For years, Erin felt jealous. She thought her brother got more of everything: material things, time with parents, opportunities to do things she was not allowed to do. She finally worked it out while she was in college.*

• Be sure to alert teachers of siblings about the tremendous stress at home. Many children respond to the worries about cancer by developing behavior or academic problems at school. Teachers should be vigilant for the warning signals and provide extra support or tutoring for the stressed child or teen. Continue to communicate frequently with the teachers of the siblings to make sure you are aware of any developing problems.

• Expect your other children to have some behavior problems as part of living with cancer in the family. This is a normal response.

> *When my 4-year-old healthy child screams and sobs over a minor skinned knee, she gets as much sympathy as my child with cancer does when having her port accessed. I put a bandage on the knee, rock her, sing a song, and get her an ice pack. The injuries are not equal, but the needs of each child are. They both need to be loved and cared for; they both need to know that mom will help, regardless of the severity of the problem. I even let her use EMLA® for routine shots. My pediatrician laughs at me, but I just tell him, "Sibs need perks, too."*

> • • • • •

> *When Matt was in treatment and his older brother Joey was 5, we knew Joey needed some support, too. He would hide behind the couch with his blanket and suck his thumb when home health nurses, equipment company personnel, or respiratory therapists came to our home. We were fortunate that a reputable counselor was near our home and, under our challenging and chaotic circumstances, we could take him for a few sessions without adding further commotion to our life. The support gave Joey the benefit of knowing he had a helper, too, and that he felt cared for as much as his brother did.*

• The child with cancer receives many toys and gifts, which can result in hurt feelings or jealousy in the siblings. Provide gifts and tokens of appreciation to the siblings for helping out during hard times, and encourage your sick child to share.

My daughter Jacqueline is 7 years old. We have three other children, ages 14, 8½, and 3. We found (through trial and error) that letting them know as much as they were able to handle, and making sure they felt comfortable asking any questions they might have, helped a great deal. We also made sure we called them two or three times a day from the hospital, and talked to them about how THEIR day was. We let them come to the hospital any time they wanted, after checking that it was okay with the docs. The second time around, we made sure that anyone coming to visit, or sending her something through the mail, either brought something small for the other three kids, or didn't bring anything at all. We also kept a small stock of wrapped presents for those who didn't remember our rule.

- Encourage a close relationship between an adult relative or neighbor and your other children. Having a "someone special" when the parents are frequently absent can help your child feel cared for and loved.

We tried very hard to attend to the feelings of Ethan's siblings ourselves, but we realized early on that we were going to need help. We have a friend who is a children's librarian. She and her husband took the boys out every week and spent the evening with them. The kids picked out books at the library with her help and input, talked about the things they were doing at school, what was going on in their lives, got an ice cream, and were made to feel wanted and special. When Ethan had to go to the hospital for chemotherapy, the children's music teacher would have a sleep over for the boys at her house. She made them a favorite meal, rented a movie, made popcorn, and had a pajama party at her house so that they felt there was something special for them.

- You can also take advantage of any workshops, support groups, or camps for siblings. These can be of tremendous value for siblings, providing fun and friendships with others who truly understand their feelings.

Positive outcomes for the siblings

After reading about all the difficult emotions your children might experience, it is important to note that many siblings exhibit great warmth and active caretaking while their brother or sister is being treated for cancer. Their empathy and compassion seem to grow with the crisis.

Some brothers and sisters of children with cancer feel they have benefited from the stressful experience in many ways, such as increased knowledge about disease, increased empathy for the sick or disabled, increased sense of responsibility, enhanced self-esteem, greater maturity and coping ability, and increased family closeness. Many of these siblings mature into adults interested in the caring professions, such as medicine,

social work, or teaching. Character can grow from confronting a personal crisis, and many parents speak of their healthy children with admiration and pride.

Brothers and sisters of those with cancer go through much adversity, as we parents do. At times, much is overlooked, unintentionally of course, because of the many changes in our lives that we experience at such a difficult time. Well, today, I want to pay a small tribute to Tommy's 15-year-old brother, Matt. From the time Tommy was diagnosed, Matt has been by his side. The first night Matt wouldn't go to bed, just so he could stand by Tommy's bedside and be close to him. When we got back home, Matt took over and made sure Tommy would get his "daily laugh." Every evening, even when Tommy felt too sick to sit up, Matt would be there and always made us smile and laugh. As we all know, the siblings sacrifice much of their own lives during this time. Whether it be their social activities or school work, much of their "normal" lifestyle is changed. They even show their courage through the wide range of emotions, including much sorrow, that they experience. It is said, "Angels shine their light on us that we may see more clearly." So as our angel on earth, thank you Matt for shining your light on your brother Tommy, and may you also be blessed with the light of angels.

Chapter 20

Family and Friends

THE INTERACTIONS BETWEEN the parents of a child with cancer and their family members and friends are complex. Potential exists for loving support and generous help, as well as for bitter disappointment and disputes. The diagnosis of childhood cancer creates a ripple effect, first touching the immediate family, then reaching extended family, friends, coworkers, neighbors, schoolmates, members of religious groups, and, sometimes, the entire community.

This chapter begins with how family life can be restructured to cope with treatment. It then provides many practical ideas about helpful things that extended family members and friends can do to support the family of a child with cancer. To prevent possible misunderstandings, parents of children with cancer also share their thoughts about things that are not helpful.

Restructuring family life

Every family of a child with cancer needs assistance. Many people have difficulty asking for, and accepting, help from others. However, learning to ask for help when it is needed and accepting help gracefully will ensure you get the support your family needs. Many family members, friends, and neighbors will want to help, but they need direction from you about what is helpful, but not intrusive.

Jobs

In families where both parents are employed, decisions must be made about their jobs. Single parents who are employed full time also need to make tough decisions about whether to take a leave of absence from work or cut back on hours to care for their child. It is better, if possible, to use all available sick leave and vacation days before deciding whether one parent needs to terminate employment. Parents need to be able to evaluate their financial situation and insurance availability; this requires time and clarity of thought—both of which are in short supply in the weeks following diagnosis.

> *When Garrett got sick, I used up all of my vacation. At that time, our head of Human Resources called me in and informed me that I now had to take unpaid*

leave if I wanted to stay out of the office any longer. He then added that in order to continue my benefits, I had to pay "my share" of all benefits costs during this leave. This included insurance, retirement, and other contributions. The weekly outlay was not insignificant. I was dismayed to say the least.

Fortunately, our senior management and common sense prevailed. We came to an informal arrangement where I "made up" lost time by working weekends and extended days when Garrett was home and doing okay. When he was inpatient (most of the first year and the first 3 months of the second), I would stay with him in the hospital on the weekends (Friday night through Sunday evening) and on Tuesday night and all day Wednesday. This would give my wife a break from the hospital and let me spend time with my son.

It worked very well. Pam later calculated that I worked more hours in make-up than I missed for Garrett. The company came out ahead. Every situation is different and every solution will be different in these circumstances. There is only one constant: You will never ever regret the precious time you spent with your child.

In August 1993, the Family and Medical Leave Act (FMLA) became federal law in the United States. FMLA protects the job security of employees of large companies who:

- Take a leave of absence to care for a seriously ill child.

- Take medical leave because the employee is unable to work because of his or her own medical condition.

- Take leave after the birth or adoption of a child.

The FMLA:

- Applies to all public employers (federal, state, county and local, including schools) and private employers with 50 or more employees within a 75-mile radius.

- Applies to employees who have worked at a qualified place of employment for at least 12 months, and who have worked at least 1,250 hours during those 12 months.

- Provides 12 weeks of unpaid leave during any 12-month period to care for a seriously ill spouse, child, or parent, or to care for oneself. In certain instances, the employee may take intermittent leave, such as reducing his or her normal work schedule.

- Requires employers to continue providing benefits, including health insurance, during the leave period.

- Requires employers to return employees to the same or equivalent positions upon return from the leave. Some benefits, such as seniority, need not accrue during periods of unpaid FMLA leave.

- Requires employees to give 30-day notice of the need to take FMLA leave, when the need is foreseeable.

- Is enforced by the Wage and Hour Division, U.S. Department of Labor, or by private lawsuit. You can locate the nearest office of the Wage and Hour Division by calling (866)-4-USWAGE (487-9243).

- Your state government may provide for family leave benefits broader than what is mandated by the federal government. For example, California, New Jersey, and Rhode Island have a paid family leave benefit as part of their state disability insurance programs. Other states do not provide for paid leave, but do require certain employers to allow more unpaid family leave than the federal minimum. Visit the website of your state's employment department to find out what rights and benefits you may be legally entitled to.

In Canada, a parent may be entitled to benefits under the Employment Insurance Act. Consideration is provided in the act for a parent having to leave work to care for an ill child. Entitlement to benefits is made on a case-by-case basis. Should a parent qualify, benefits are determined by the number of hours the parent has worked prior to making the claim. For more information, parents should contact the nearest Employment and Social Development Canada office, listed in the Government of Canada pages of the telephone directory.

Marriage and partnerships

Diagnosis and treatment place enormous pressure on marriages and partnerships. Couples may be separated for long periods of time, emotions run high, and coping styles and skills may differ. Initially, family life may be shattered; couples then must work together to rearrange the pieces into a new pattern. Following are parents' suggestions and stories about how they managed.

- Share medical decisions.

> My husband and I shared decision-making by keeping a joint medical journal. The days that my husband stayed at the hospital, he would write down all medicines given, side effects, fever, vital signs, food consumed, sleep patterns, and any questions that needed to be asked at the next rounds. This way, I knew exactly what had been happening. Decisions were made as we traded shifts at our son's bedside.

• • • • •

> I made most of the medical decisions. My husband did not know what a protocol was, nor did he ever learn the names of the medicines. He came with me to medical conferences, however, and his presence gave me strength.

. . . . .

Curt and I discuss every detail of the medical issues. It is so helpful to hash things over together to get a clearer idea of what our main concerns are.

• Take turns staying in the hospital with your child.

We took turns going in with our son for painful procedures. The doctors loved to see my husband come in because he's a friendly, easygoing person who never asked them any medical questions. We shared hospital duty, also. I would be there during any crisis because I was the person better able to be a strong advocate, but he went when our son was feeling better and needed entertaining company. It worked out well.

. . . . .

My husband fell apart emotionally when our daughter was diagnosed, and he never really recovered. He stayed with her once in the hospital and cried almost the whole time. She never wanted him there again, so I did all of the hospital duty.

. . . . .

Whenever Brian was in the hospital, we both wanted to be there. We were able to be there most of the time because our children have a wonderful aunt and uncle who stayed with them when needed. During Brian's second extended stay in the hospital, we both let go a little, and we each took turns sleeping at the Ronald McDonald House. That way we each got a decent night's sleep (or some sleep) every other night.

. . . . .

My wife took care of most of the medical information gathering because she had a scientific background. But my work schedule was more flexible, so I took my son for almost all of his treatments and hospitalizations. I cherish my memories of those long hours in the car and waiting room.

. . . . .

My husband does about 75 percent of the hospital/clinic/radiation visits. In fact, he does all of them when he is in town. I take care of the rest of the children and float in when I get a chance. I keep in touch with the doctors via email.

• Share responsibility for home care.

We had a traditional relationship in which I took care of the kids and he worked. I didn't expect him to cook or clean when I was staying at the hospital—it was all he could do to ferry our daughter to her various activities and go to work.

· · · · ·

We both worked full-time, so we staggered our shifts. He worked 7 to 3 during the day; I worked 3 to 11 at night. He did every single dressing change for the Hickman® catheter—584 changes, we counted them up. Wherever I left off during the day, he took over. He was great, and it really worked out well for us. We shared it all.

· · · · ·

My husband really didn't help at all. I couldn't even go out because he wouldn't give the pills. He kept saying that he was afraid he would make a mistake.

- Accept differences in coping styles.

  We both coped differently, but we learned to work around it. I didn't want to deal with "what if" questions, but he was a pessimist and constantly asked the fellow questions about things that might happen. I felt that it was a waste of energy to worry about things that might never happen. I didn't want to hear it and felt that it just added to my burden. It was all I could do to survive every day. We worked it out by going to conferences together, but I would ask my questions and then leave. He stayed behind to ask all of his questions.

  · · · · ·

  My husband didn't have the desire to read as much as I did. However, whenever I read something that I felt he should read, he always took the time to do so and then we discussed it.

  · · · · ·

  My husband and I have always been a team. We complement the strengths and weaknesses of each other and I think that was the reason we managed to hold everything together. When I was down, he would bring me up. When he was down, I would do the same for him. With the exception of the initial trauma when our son was diagnosed, we handled things in that manner throughout treatment.

- Seek counseling.

  I went for counseling because I couldn't sleep. At night, I got stuck thinking the same things over and over and worrying. I ended up spending 2 years on antidepressants, which I think really saved my life. They helped me sleep and kept me on an even keel. I'm off them now, my son is off treatment, and everything is looking up.

  · · · · ·

  My husband and I went to counseling to try to work out a way to split up the child rearing and household duties because I was overwhelmed and resenting it. I guess it helped a little bit, but the best thing that came out of it was that I kept seeing the

counselor by myself. My son wanted to go to a "feelings doctor," too. I received a lot of very helpful, practical advice on the many behavior problems my son developed. And my son had an objective, safe person to talk things over with.

Most marriages and partnerships survive, but some do not. Relationships that deteriorate oftne have serious pre-exisiting problems that are further strained by cancer treatment.

My husband had a lot of problems that really brought my daughter and me down. The cancer really opened my eyes to what was important in life. We stayed together through treatment, but we divorced after the transplant. I just realized that life is too short to spend it in a bad relationship.

• • • • •

My husband went to work rather than go with us to Children's when our son was diagnosed. It went downhill from there. He started using drugs and mistreating us, so we divorced.

Blended families

Many children diagnosed with cancer live in blended families. Parents may be separated or divorced, remarried, or living as single parents. There may be foster parents, biological parents, step parents, or legal guardians. Communication between involved adults may be open and amiable or it may be strained. It is best for the child when all parents/guardians involved put their differences aside and work together to provide an environment focused on curing and supporting the ill child. Counseling is also helpful.

My son's dad and I are divorced and we are both remarried with kids. We found it to be helpful and important to have all four parents at all of the meetings that discussed treatments and options, as well as any follow-up meeting where decisions needed to be made. While the forms that needed to be signed for treatments and protocols only needed to be signed by my ex-husband and me, we found it to be especially important that all four of us signed the paperwork. On one hand, it provided a way for stepparents to take part in and feel included in something that was so important to a child who they, too, loved, but it also alleviated the potential of someone casting blame later on if treatment didn't work out in our favor. The doctors gladly added two more signature lines underneath the two signatures that were required.

If the child with cancer has two homes due to a blended family, it often helps to have a journal that goes with the child to each family. It keeps everyone involved up to date. It can contain information about medications given, dose changes, doctor's appointments, blood test results, and current symptoms.

Unfortunately, the diagnosis of cancer in a child can make strained family relations even worse. It is important that all parents/guardians with a legal right to information about all aspects of the illness receive that information and are able to participate in the decision-making process. In some situations, a social worker, nurse practitioner, primary care physician, or psychologist will work with all parties to set up family meetings (together as a group or separately, depending on family dynamics) with healthcare providers to make this possible.

Single parents

Some parents are single and do not share parenting with an former spouse or partner (e.g., widows, widowers, single parents who adopted children, parents whose former partner is no longer involved). Experiencing a crisis of this magnitude with no one to talk to or help with daily tasks can leave a single parent feeling isolated, helpless, lonely, and overwhelmed. In addition, many single parents are both the sole breadwinner for the family and the sole caretaker of the child with cancer and the siblings. Single parents shared the following suggestions on ways to cope:

- Involve a best friend in making the medical decisions and providing care

- Ask a family member to stay with you at the hospital for support

- Have a friend bring you changes of clothes or relieve you for an hour while you take a walk

- Talk with a therapist or other single parent about medical choices and feelings

> It's really difficult being a single parent when your child is in the hospital, as there is no other parent to take turns sitting with your child, run errands, help you make medical decisions, or support you emotionally as you are watching your child suffer. It can feel incredibly lonely! That is when friends become your lifeline. One day we rushed to the ER for what I thought would be a quick visit, and my daughter ended up being admitted for a week's stay. I had no extra clothes, laptop, no cell phone charger, none of her comfort items, nothing! And my dog was home alone with no food or way to get outside. Before my phone died, I sent out some texts and a Facebook post to friends, coworkers, and church members. Then I dissolved into tears, feeling totally sad and overwhelmed. Next thing I knew, church members had arranged to pick up our dog; my best friend went to my home and brought me a change of clothes, my laptop and chargers, my daughter's favorite CDs and movies, and warm food. Then a food delivery guy showed up at the door of the hospital room with a bunch of Italian food that my coworkers had ordered for me. And by day's end I had more than 100 Facebook comments from friends, sending their love, prayers, and hopes. At that moment, I realized that though I did not have a partner to share my burdens, I was not alone and never would be. Through my daughter's entire

illness, I was supported by friends and church members. It taught me that it is okay to ask for help; it doesn't mean you are weak or incapable of parenting alone. Quite simply, being a single parent, full-time worker, and full-time caregiver is incredibly hard, and you cannot do it alone. Don't be afraid to ask for help! People can be incredibly compassionate and generous when you give them a chance.

The extended family

Extended family—grandparents, aunts, uncles, cousins—can cushion the shock of diagnosis and treatment with loving words and actions. Extended family members sometimes drop their own lives to rush to the side of the newly diagnosed child, and often remain steadfast throughout the months or years of treatment. Regrettably, some family members are not helpful, either out of ignorance about what your family needs or simply because they are frightened by the diagnosis or overwhelmed by events in their own lives.

> *The first day Zach was diagnosed, my sister and sister-in-law met us near the hospital and walked in with us so they could be with us. They brought their laptops so we could set up a CaringBridge page and connect with the outside world by email right after we first met with the oncologist. My sister took detailed notes for me at every meeting and would ask question to clarify what she was writing down so we could talk about it and ask questions later. A few days later, she could not come to meet the radiology team so she made sure another family member was there to take notes. With a 2-year-old to watch, having someone to be an extra set of ears was always helpful.*

Some extended families, and even entire communities, rally around the family; for other families, support never materializes. Several factors affect the strength of support that is offered including well-established community ties, good communication within the extended family, physical proximity to the extended family, and clear exchange of information about the needs of the affected family. If any of these elements is missing, support may dissipate or never appear.

> *We had just moved 3,000 miles away from family and friends for my husband to accept a new job. We had no family close by, no friends. Each family member and some close friends used their vacations to fly out and take 2-week shifts at our new house to help out. Thankfully, they got us through the first months, but the rest of treatment was lonely.*

· · · · ·

> *We spent almost 9 months in the children's hospital. Without my parents, my husband and I couldn't have done it. My parents were at the hospital every single day (other than when my mom got the flu). My parents even had to stay with Chad at*

the hospital for 2 weeks with us, because I had to have surgery. They went to every single appointment with us. They were there for us 100% of the time. I also lost contact with a lot of family and friends during that time. People said "they couldn't handle it." But we gained new friends among the parents of kids with cancer.

Families with strong community ties often receive support throughout treatment.

My son was diagnosed with osteosarcoma at age 11. During his treatment, various members of my family came from the Midwest to the east coast and stayed to help out with everything. My 81-year-old mother spent more than 3 months helping clean the house, cook, do laundry, get groceries, take care of my kids, go to the hospital, do clinic visits, do surgery visits, take care of the garden—pretty much anything that needed doing so that I could continue working at least part time since I was the insurance holder and sole income provider. My two sisters also came out for weeks at a time to spell my mom. One sister even took unpaid leave to come and help. When she couldn't come out one week, her 20-year-old daughter, my niece, came to help us during her college spring break. My 24-year-old nephew loaned me his car and came by whenever he could get off base (he's in the military). I don't think I would have made it through my son's treatment without my extended family.

Grandparents

Grandparents grieve deeply when a grandchild has cancer. They are concerned not only for their grandchild, but also for their own child (the parent). Cancer wreaks havoc with grandparents' expectations, reversing the natural order of life and death. Grandparents frequently say, "Why not me? I'm the one who is old." A cancer diagnosis in a grandchild is a major shock to bear.

Many parents reported that the grandparents responded to the crisis with tremendous emotional, physical, and financial support.

My mother was a rock. She lived far away, but she put her busy life on hold to come help. She took care of the baby and kept the household running when I was living at the hospital with my very ill child. She was strong, and it gave me strength.

Some parents express tremendous gratitude for the role played by the grandparents in providing much-needed stability to the family rocked by cancer. When grandparents are able to care for the siblings or help with meals and other home chores, the parents can focus on the most urgent needs, such as caring for the sick child or putting in necessary time at work.

My son JJ was diagnosed with cancer at 24 months old, and at the time I also had an infant who was 5 months old. I knew that JJ's young age meant that I would need to be by his side the entire time, from start to finish. My in-laws came down,

packed up the baby, and took him back to their house, an hour and a half away. My father-in-law, who was off work at the time, had never had children of his own (he was a stepfather), but he stepped up and took care of my baby like he was his flesh and blood. He did all the middle of the night feedings (and actually enjoyed it!). He fed him his first solid foods and showed him off all around their small, country town, just like a proud grandpa should! As much as it pains me that I missed those 6 months of my baby's life, I was able to focus my undivided attention on my newly diagnosed son. I knew my baby was being exceptionally well-cared for and it was one fewer thing that I needed to worry about.

• • • • •

John is Grampa's only grandchild. He's always there to play a board game, tell jokes, or watch his favorite video with him for the 1,000th time. I wish he'd hide his fears a little better, but that may be too much to expect from a truly loving grandfather.

Other families are not as fortunate. Many grandparents are too old, too ill, or simply unable to cope with a crisis of this magnitude. Some simply fall apart.

My mother-in-law became hysterical when my daughter was diagnosed. She called every day, sobbing. Luckily, she lived far away, and this minimized the disruption. We had to ask her not to come, because we just couldn't handle the catastrophe at home and her neediness too. It hurt her feelings, but we just couldn't cope with it.

Other grandparents allow pre-existing problems with their adult child to color their perceptions of what the family needs or what role they should take on during the crisis. For example, sometimes cancer allows grandparents to renew criticism of the way grandchildren are being raised.

While we stayed at the hospital, the grandparents moved into our house to care for our 8-year-old daughter. They decided that this was their chance to "whip her into shape, teach her some manners, and get her room cleaned up." Our daughter was in tears, and we ended up saying, "We appreciate your help, but we will take over."

It is hard to predict how anyone will react to the diagnosis of childhood cancer; grandparents are no exception. Some respond with the wisdom gleaned from decades of living, others become needy or overbearing, and some withdraw. It is natural in a time of grave crisis to look to your parents for support and help, but it is important to remember that grandparents' ability to respond also depends on events in their own lives. If problems between family members develop, help can be obtained from hospital social workers or through individual counseling.

Helpful things for extended family members to do

Families differ in what is truly helpful for them. The suggestions in this chapter are snapshots of what some families appreciated. Connections can be made in many different and personally meaningful ways. Extended family members should try to support the family of the child with cancer in ways that respect their wishes, while also honoring their privacy.

Parents of the ill child may want to share the following suggestions with their extended family and friends so they have a better idea of how to help.

- Be sensitive to the emotional state of both the sick child and the parents. Sometimes parents want to talk about the illness; sometimes they just need a hand to hold. The same is true for the child or teen with cancer. Some will want to share their feelings, but others will prefer to be distracted and do "normal" fun things with you to whatever extent they can.

- Encourage all members of the extended family to keep in touch through visits, calls, video chats, mail, e-mail, text messages, and social media. When visits are welcome, make them brief and cheerful. Not only do long visits sometimes distress sick children and teens, but they can also overtax a tired parent.

  Our relatives who lived close to the hospital had teenagers. One was a candy striper at Children's on Saturdays. The aunts, uncles, and cousins came to visit several times a week any time he was in the hospital during his years of treatment. They were all very supportive, very positive, and fun to be around.

- Be understanding if the parents do not want phone calls while in the hospital. Remember that parents often have to stay very close to their sick child, and the child can hear what is being said in phone conversations, so text or voicemail messages are sometimes better.

- A cheerful hospital room really boosts a child's spirits. Encourage sending balloon bouquets, funny cards, posters, signs with messages on them, toys, or humorous books. Most hospitals do not allow latex balloons, so only send mylar balloons. Flowers are usually not allowed in children's rooms.

  We plastered the walls with pictures of family and friends, and so many people sent balloons that the ceiling was covered. It was a lovely sight.

- Laughter helps heal the mind and body, so send funny videos or arrive with a good joke if you think it is appropriate.

My brother Bill and his wonderful girlfriend, Cathleen, created an exciting "trip" for my 4-year-old daughter. She was bald, big-bellied from prednisone, and her counts were too low to leave the house, but her interest in fashion was as sharp as ever. Bill and Cathleen bought 10 outfits, rigged up a dressing room, and with Cathleen as saleswoman, turned Katy's bedroom into a fashion salon. She tried on outfits, discussed all of their merits and shortcomings, and had a fabulous time. It was a real high point for her.

- Distraction is the name of the game. Puzzles, card games, picture books, coloring books, age-appropriate video games, new movies, and craft kits are welcome. For a child who cannot get out of bed, a remote control car or a foam dart launcher can be a fun way to extend their reach and have more active play while they are stuck in one spot.

  A friend who was a nurse came to my son's room shortly before Christmas and brought an entire gingerbread house kit, including confectioner's sugar for the icing. We had a very good time putting it together.

- Offer to give the parent(s) a break from the hospital room. A walk outside, shopping trip, haircut, dinner out, or just a long shower can be very refreshing.

- Bring a fresh, home-cooked meal to the hospital for the parents. This can be a wonderful respite from hospital food for parents who are staying with their child.

  My coworkers had Italian food from a nice restaurant delivered to me while my daughter was in the hospital and it made my week!

- Donate frequent flyer miles to distant family members who have the time but not the money to help.

  A close friend (who lived 3,000 miles away) had just lost her job and wished she could be there for us. My parents gave her their frequent flyer miles. She flew in for 3 weeks during a hard part of treatment and helped enormously.

- Donate blood. Your blood may not be used specifically for the ill child, but it will replenish the general supply, which is depleted by children with cancer.

  Our family friend John is terrified of needles. John always avoided giving blood. John doesn't like going to the doctor. But John showed up to donate platelets once, early on, and we found that he was a great platelet match for Deli. So he kept returning to that awful two-needle machine that you stay hooked onto for 3 hours at a time, probably a couple dozen times, because we needed him. Then we had Beth, who was one of my professional acquaintances. Beth was always pretty nice to us, but she found out that she too was a good "sticky" platelet donor. Probably at least a dozen times she took hours out of her work day and donated platelets whenever Deli needed some.

We concentrated on the few "star" friends and relatives, the one or two people whose attitude, abilities, and circumstances allowed them to be the most helpful.

Friends

Like family, friends can cushion the shock of diagnosis and ease the difficulties of treatment with their words and actions.

Helpful things for friends to do

Mother Theresa once said, "We can do no great things—only small things with great love." The family of a child being treated for cancer is overwhelmed. The list of helpful things to do is endless, but following are some suggestions from parents who have traveled this hard road.

It is very helpful if a friend creates an online task calendar. These free programs allow the family to list tasks they need help with (e.g., meals, pet care) on certain dates such as scheduled hospitalizations or clinic days. Then, helpers can sign up to take care of chores or be on call for tasks such as snow shoveling or lawn mowing. You can find a list of online calendars used for providing help to families of children with cancer in Appendix C, *Books, Websites, and Support Groups*.

Household

- Provide meals. It is helpful to find out whether anyone in the family has food allergies or whether there are types of food the family prefers to eat—or prefers to avoid. It is best to be thoughtful when delivering meals, as the family may feel too tired or the child too ill to welcome friends in for an extended chat.

> *Friends and family delivered home-cooked meals to our house 5 nights a week. My sister-in-law organized it online through Care Calendar. We left a cooler outside because Meg's counts were so low and we were so exhausted. We had talked to people all day long. We don't want to chat, we just want to plop down on the couch and heat up that meal. We made a sign for the front door that said, "If there's a cooler out, please leave food in the cooler and ring the doorbell." We had one friend who plugged herself into the calendar and cooked for us every Friday night. She loves to do gourmet cooking, and she wrote a little menu for us and brought appetizers, dinner, and dessert.*

> • • • • •

> *One of the biggest ways our extended family helped us was by setting up a Care Calendar online for the entire 48 weeks of treatment and procedures. Then they*

would provide meals based on the specific need. For example, if we were inpatient, it would be gift cards and hospital-delivered meals. Big chemo weeks would be several meals delivered to our home the next couple of days. Full-day infusions meant someone would bring a meal that evening. They worked to anticipate what our needs would be. I was also able to add photos and updates on how she was doing for the volunteers.

- Take care of pets or livestock.

- Mow grass, shovel snow, rake leaves, water plants, and weed gardens.

  We came home from the hospital one evening right before Christmas, and found a freshly cut, fragrant Christmas tree leaning next to our door. I'll never forget that kindness.

- Clean the house or hire a cleaning service.

  My husband's cousin sent her cleaning lady over to our house. It was so neat and such a luxury to come home to find the stove and windows sparkling clean.

- Grocery shop (especially when the family is due home from the hospital).

- Do laundry or drop off and pick up dry cleaning.

- Provide a place to stay near the hospital.

  One of the ladies from the school where I worked came up to the ICU (intensive care unit) waiting room where we were sleeping and pressed her house key into my hand. She lived 5 minutes from the hospital. She said, "My basement is made up, there's a futon, there's a TV; you are coming and staying at my house." I hardly knew her, but we accepted. Every day when we came in from the hospital there was some cute little treat waiting for us like a bowl of cookies, or two packages of hot chocolate and a thermos of hot milk.

A child life specialist shared the following suggestion:

For many of the families I work with, allowing acquaintances into the home to clean and cook is just too personal and uncomfortable during such a private time in their lives. It's just too intrusive. However, these families have shared many stories of anonymous giving. For instance, the following items, mysteriously left at the doorstep, were very welcome: restaurant/fast food certificate, baskets of beauty products, a journal, and gas card. The anonymity helped prevent the family from feeling indebted.

Siblings

An entire chapter of this book is devoted to the complex feelings that siblings experience when their brother or sister has cancer. Chapter 19, *Siblings*, provides an in-depth examination of the issues from the perspective of both siblings and parents. Below is a list of suggestions about how family and friends can help the siblings.

- Babysit younger siblings whenever parents go to the clinic or emergency room, or need to be with their child for a prolonged hospital stay.

- When parents are home with a sick child, take siblings somewhere fun to get their minds off of the stresses at home. Find out what they would enjoy, and spend special time with them going to the park, a sports event, minature golfing, bowling, the zoo, or a movie.

- Invite siblings over for meals.

- If you bring a gift for the sick child, bring something for the siblings, too.

> *Friends from home sent boxes of art supplies to us when the whole family spent those first 10 weeks at a Ronald McDonald house far from our home. They sent scissors, paints, paper, and colored pens. It was a great help for Carrie Beth and her two sisters. One friend even sent an Easter package with straw hats for each girl, and flowers, ribbons, and glue to decorate them with.*

· · · · ·

> *We got a lot of care packages, not just for our child with cancer but also for her siblings. It really lifted their spirits too. Cancer is a family battle and the whole family needs to be supported!*

- Offer to help siblings with homework.

- Drive siblings to lessons, games, or school.

- Listen to how they are feeling and coping. Siblings' lives have been disrupted; they have limited time with their parents, and they need support, attention, and care.

Psychological support

There is much that can be done to help the family maintain an even emotional keel.

- Call frequently, and be open to listening if the parents want to talk about their feelings. Also, talk about non-cancer related topics (e.g., neighborhood or school news) to help them feel less isolated.

> *What I wished for most was that friends and family had been able to call more often to see how we were doing; that someone could have handled my confidence on*

the good days and my tears on the bad days. It somehow took too much emotional energy to make a call myself, but I valued any phone call I received.

- Visit the hospital and bring fun stuff such as bubbles, silly string, water pistols, joke books, funny movies, rub-on tattoos, and board games.

- If a parent has to leave work to stay in the hospital with the sick child, coworkers can send messages by mail, e-mail, or social media.

- If you think the family might be interested, ask the social worker at the hospital whether there are support groups for parents and/or kids in your area.

- Offer to take the children to the support groups or go with the parents. For most families, the parent support group becomes a second family with ties of shared experience as deep and strong as blood relations.

- Drive the parent and child to clinic visits.

- Buy books for the family if they enjoy reading.

- Send e-mail, cards, or letters.

> *Word got around my parents' hometown, and I received cards from many high school acquaintances who still cared enough to call or write and say we're praying for you, please let us know how things are going. It was so neat to get so many cards out of the blue that said, "I'm thinking about you."*

- Babysit the sick child, and any siblings, so the parents can go out to eat, exercise, take a walk, or just get out of the hospital or house.

> *Joseph's kindergarten teacher would come to play with him so we could get out of the hospital and eat and take a break for an hour or so. She just seemed to understand how much we needed that and how hard it would be for us to do it otherwise.*

- Ask what needs to be done, and then do it.

> *A close friend asked what I needed the day after Michelle was diagnosed. I asked if she could drive our second car the 100 miles to the hospital so my husband could return in it to work. She came with her family to the Ronald McDonald House with two big bags containing snack foods, a large box of stationery, envelopes, stamps, books to read, a book handmade by her 3-year-old daughter containing dozens of cut-out pictures of children's clothing pasted on construction paper (which my daughter adored looking at), and a beautiful, new, handmade, lace-trimmed dress for my daughter. It was full-length and baggy enough to cover all bandages and tubing. She wore it almost every day for a year. It was a wonderful thing for my friend to do.*

- Give lots of hugs.

Financial support

Helping families avoid financial difficulties can be a very important form of support. In the United States, medical bills are the top cause of personal bankruptcy. It is estimated that even fully insured families spend 25 percent or more of their income on co-payments, travel, motels, car maintenance, meals, childcare for siblings, and other expenses that aren't covered by insurance. Uninsured or underinsured families may struggle to pay even the most basic household bills while trying to keep up with medical bills, and some are forced to lose their car or home when they cannot keep up with payments.

At the same time, families can face a substantial loss of income while caring for their critically ill child. Caring for a child or teen with cancer is complex and intensive, and one parent often needs to leave work for the entire duration of treatment. A single parent usually has no other source of employment income, but may need to reduce hours or take FMLA to care for the child—often causing financial distress. Most families need financial assistance, and there are a variety of ways to help.

- **Start a support fund.** There are many ways to start a support fund, but certain guidelines should be followed to protect everyone involved. Always check with the parents first. It is important to respect any privacy concerns they may have, and to allow them to have a say over anything organized in their child's name. Some people are embarrassed to have their personal financial situation or sensitive medical information shared with others in the community, while others are comfortable freely sharing that with anyone. Also, the parents may need to work with the hospital social worker to ensure that any bank account created to assist the family is set up in such a way that it does not endanger any state or federal benefits the child is receiving. Volunteers should not have access to the account, though the parents can designate someone to pay bills for them directly out of the fund,

In a smaller community, a fundraising drive can be as simple as leaving jars at local stores for contributions or sending an email to family, friends, and the local newspaper that includes the address of a bank account where contributions can be dropped off or mailed. A newer method of collecting donations for a family in need is to use an online resource such as *www.youcaring.com* or *www.gofundme.com*. You can create a fundraising site with photos and stories from the family and share a link to the site on social media to reach family and friends all over the world. These companies charge fees to host your fundraising page and process the donations, so it is important to carefully read the fine print. Find out more about online fundraising sites in Appendix C, *Books, Websites, and Support Groups*.

> A friend of mine called and asked very tentatively if we would mind if she started a support fund. We felt awkward, but we needed help, so we said okay. She did everything herself, and the money she raised was very, very helpful. We did ask her to stop

the fund when people started calling us to ask if they could use giving to the fund as an advertisement for their business.

- **Share leave with a coworker.** Governments and some companies have leave banks that permit people who are ill, or taking care of someone who is ill, to use coworkers' leave so they will not have their pay docked for taking time off work.

  My husband's coworkers didn't collect money, they did something even more valuable. They donated sick leave hours so he was able to be at the hospital frequently during those first few months without losing a paycheck.

- **Job share.** Some companies allow job-share arrangements in which a coworker donates time to perform part of the parent's job so the parent can spend extra time at the hospital. Job sharing allows the job to get done, keeps peace at the job site, and prevents financial losses for the family. Another possibility is for one or more friends with similar skills (e.g., word processing, filing, sales) to rotate through the job on a volunteer basis to cover for the parent of the ill child.

- **Collect money at work.**

  The day my daughter was diagnosed, my husband's coworkers passed the hat and gave us over $250. I was embarrassed, but it paid for gas, meals, and the motel until there was an opening in the Ronald McDonald House.

  $\bullet \quad \bullet \quad \bullet \quad \bullet \quad \bullet$

  Finances were a main concern for us because I wanted to cut back on work to be at home with Meagan. Sometimes my coworkers would pool money and present it with a card saying, "Here's a couple of days work that you won't have to worry about."

- **Organize a fundraising event.** Collect money by organizing a bake sale, dance, spaghetti supper, silent auction, or raffle. Find a vendor to make t-shirts with a supportive message for the child or teen on them and sell them in the community or at the fundrasing event.

  Coworkers of my husband held a Halloween party and charged admission, which they donated to us. We were very uncomfortable with the idea at first, but they were looking for an excuse to have a party, and it helped us out.

- **Offer to help keep track of medical bills.** Keeping track of these bills is time-consuming, frustrating, and exhausting for the parents. If you are a close relative or friend, you could offer to review, organize, and file (either on paper or into a computer spreadsheet) all the stacks of paperwork. Making the calls and writing the letters over contested claims or errors in billing can also be very helpful.

Help from schoolmates

The friendships and social lives of children often revolve around school. Trying to maintain ties with teachers and friends, and keeping up as much as possible with schoolwork and school activities will help your child make a smooth transition back to the classroom.

- Encourage visits (if appropriate), cards, e-mails, text messages, and phone calls from classmates.

> *Our son had a rough time with fever and seizures during chemo, and he was really missing his routine. His preschool teachers, Kate and Ellie, surprised him one time with a homemade book. They had all the kids pose for a photo for the cover, and each one drew a picture for the inside. He loved it.*

- Ask the teacher to send the school newspaper and other news along with assignments.

- Classmates can sign a brightly colored banner or poster to send to the hospital.

> *Brent's kindergarten class sent a packet containing a picture drawn for him by each child in the class. They also made him a book. Another time they sent him a letter written on huge poster board. He couldn't wait to get back to school.*

- School friends and civic groups can show their support by doing volunteer work at their local hospital or by participating in, or organizing, cancer- awareness events.

> *Ethan's school read* Sadako and the Thousand Paper Cranes, *which is a story about a Japanese girl from Hiroshima who contracted leukemia after World War II. The crane is the sign of health, good fortune, and long life in Japan. There is a legend that if you fold a thousand origami cranes, you will be granted one wish. Sadako's wish was that she live a long and healthy life, but she died of cancer 386 cranes short of her goal. Her classmates finished her cranes for her, and paper cranes subsequently became a symbol of peace.*

> *So, the kids at Ethan's school began to fold cranes for him. Each crane has a wish written on the wing (things like "Cancer Be Gone" and "Ethan, I love your spirit"). Some are the size of a robin, and some are smaller than a dime.*

> *They reached their goal of a thousand last week and they are now hanging (on strands, from one to 10 cranes per strand) on the ceiling over Ethan's bed. They are absolutely magical to look at, all rotating and casting shadows; and you can actually read each one's wish on the lower hanging ones. I thought it was a beautiful thing to do.*

Religious support

Following are a few suggestions for families who have religious affiliations:

- Arrange for church/synagogue/mosque members and clergy to visit the hospital, if that is what the family wants.

- Arrange prayer services for the sick child.

> The day our son was diagnosed, we raced next door to ask our wonderful neighbors to take care of our dog. The news of our son's diagnosis quickly spread, and we found out later that five neighborhood families gathered that very night to pray for Brent.

- Have your child's religious education class send pictures, posters, letters, balloons, or audio or video tapes.

Accepting help (for parents)

As a parent of a child with cancer, one of the kindest things you can do for your friends is to let them help you. Let them channel their time and worry into things that will make your life easier. Think of the many times you have visited a sick friend, made a meal for a new mom, babysat someone else's child in an emergency, or just pitched in to do what needed to be done. These actions probably made you feel great and provided a good example for your children. When your child is diagnosed with cancer, both you and your friends will benefit immensely if you let them help you and if you give them guidance about what you need.

One father's thoughts about accepting help:

> Fathers have a deep-seated need to protect their family. Yet here I was with a child with cancer, and there wasn't a single thing that I could do about it. The loss of control really bothered me. The very hardest thing I had to learn was to let go enough to let people help us.

One mother's thoughts about accepting help:

> The most important advice I received as the parent of a child newly diagnosed with cancer came from a hospital nurse whom I turned to when I was overwhelmed with all the advice being offered by family and friends. This wise nurse said, "Don't discount anything. You're going to need all the help you can get." I think it is very important for families to remain open and accept the help that is offered. It often comes when least expected and from unlikely sources. I was totally unprepared at diagnosis for how much help I would need, and I'm glad that I remained open to offers of kindness. This is not the time to show the world how strong you are.

What to say (for friends)

Following are some suggestions for friends about what to say and how to offer help. Of course, much depends on the type of relationship that already exists between you and the family you want to help; but a specific offer can always be accepted or graciously declined.

- "Our family would like do your yardwork. It will make us feel as if we are helping in a small way."

- "We want to clean your house for you once a week. What day would be convenient?"

- "Would it help if we took care of your dog (or cat, or bird)? We would love to do it."

- "I walk my dog three times a day. May I walk yours, too?"

- "The church is setting up a system to deliver meals to your house. When is the best time to drop them off?"

- "I will take care of Jimmy whenever you need to take John to the hospital. Call us anytime, day or night, and we will come pick Jimmy up."

Things that do not help

Sometimes people say things to parents of children with cancer that are not helpful and can even be hurtful. If you are a family member or friend of a parent in this situation, please do not say any of the following:

- "God only gives people what they can handle." (Some people cannot handle the stress of childhood cancer, and it is painful to be told that your child was singled out to have cancer because they or you are strong.)

- "I know just how you feel." (Unless you have a child with cancer, you simply don't know.)

- "You are so brave," or "so strong." (Parents are not heroes; they are normal people struggling with extraordinary stress.)

> Whenever someone says: "You're so strong" or "I don't know how you do it," answer: "I don't do it alone," or "With lots of help" or (if it's true) "I'm pretty close to losing it completely." There's a thin line between being honest about your situation and being oppressive, for want of a better word. In my more cynical moments, I am convinced the world wants us (i.e., the cancer kids/families) to valiantly triumph over hardship with the Movie-of-the-Week-attitude. Well if that gets them to wash my floors, it's a small price!

> I think some of the most supported families I've seen on treatment had a knack at keeping people informed about the current situation. I updated the outgoing message

on our answering machine every couple of days and people could call our home for current news (a hospice nurse/neighbor gave me that idea). Other friends from the hospital used newsletters, phone chains, announcements in church, etc. Again, my cynical side recognizes that you're opening up your most personal moments to the public (anyone who called my house and heard the message the day after my son's stroke probably felt like an intruder) but it's a way to help people feel invested in your family.

- "They are doing such wonderful things to save children with cancer these days." (The prognosis might be good, but what parents and children are going through is not wonderful.)

- "Chemo killed my aunt/grandma/sister. That stuff is terrible. Those doctors can't really cure cancer." (Cancer is no longer a death sentence. Many people don't understand that cancer treatments for both adults and children have improved a great deal over the years.)

- "All those chemicals are unnatural! I learned about a guy whose cousin's daughter used kale juice/essential oils/shark cartilage/ground apricot pits/exotic spices instead." (Most people are well-meaning, but undermining a family's decision to seek evidence-based medical care for a child with a life-threatening illness is not supportive.)

- "Well, we're all going to die one day." (True, but parents do not need to be reminded of this fact.)

- "It's God's will" or "Everything happens for a reason." (These are just not helpful things to hear.)

- "At least you have other kids," or "Thank goodness you are still young enough to have other children." (A child cannot be replaced.)

> *A woman whom I worked with, but did not know well, came up to me one day and out of the blue said, "When Erica gets to heaven to be with Jesus, He will love her." All I could think to say was, "Well, I'm sorry, but Jesus can't have her right now."*

Parents also suggest the following things:

- Rather than say, "Let us know if there is anything we can do," make a specific suggestion.

> *Many well-wishing friends always said, "Let me know what I can do." I wish they had just "done," instead of asking for direction. It took too much energy to decide, call them, make arrangements, etc. I wish someone would have said, "When is your clinic day? I'll bring dinner," or "I'll baby-sit Sunday afternoon so you two can go out to lunch."*

- Do not make personal comments about sick children in front of them, such as, "When will his hair grow back in?" "He's lost so much weight." or "She's so pale."

> When in the mall or other public place, strangers had no qualms about staring at Ayla (age 3) who had an eye patch, tubes that sometimes snuck out from under her shirt, and no hair. We combated this by telling her that she was so absolutely stunningly beautiful that people just could not help but stare at her. We really played this up and tied it in to her belief in Snow White, Cinderella, etc. Many times we let her and her sister Jasmine wear their princess costumes out in public. Then they really got a kick out of people staring. I also did not hesitate to tell people that she had cancer when they asked what was wrong with her. I never minimized what she was going through. We talk about cancer freely and how doctors are there to fix you up if you get this.

- Do not do things that require the parents to support you, such as repeatedly calling them up and crying about their child's illness.
- Do not ask "what if" questions: "What if he can't go to school?" "What if your insurance won't cover it?" Or, "What if she dies?" The present is really all the parents can deal with.

Losing friends

It is an unfortunate reality that most parents of children with cancer lose some of their friends. For a variety of reasons, some friends just cannot cope and either suddenly disappear or gradually fade away.

> We had friends and family we thought would be the greatest sources of support in the world. Yet, they pulled away from us and provided nothing in the way of help, emotional or otherwise. We also had friends that we never expected to understand step up in surprising ways. My wife's friend, Leslie, a busy single woman who we would never expect to do such a thing, actually negotiated time off with a new employer so she could fly from her home in Tampa and help out after Garrett's transplant. She stayed with us for over a week, then came back a few months later to do it again.

> A couple of my SCUBA diving buddies who we liked, but didn't know well, have since become our best friends. They would visit us in the hospital, bringing gifts for both of our kids, and giving us a much-needed break. They were the only folks who regularly came by when Garrett was home after the transplant and who always followed our strict rules without complaint. Of course, the best support we had was from other parents of kids with serious illnesses or problems.

Telling your friends about cancer is difficult, but it's not as hard as keeping it a secret would be. Fighting this cancer has been a family effort and, frequently, an effort involving our larger circle of friends. The more people we've been able to call on for support, the better. We've had to keep in mind that we've had an opportunity to adjust. But, the news is brand new to our friends, and it can be a shock. People often don't know what to do or say when they've been told that someone they care about has cancer.

After we've given them some time, and when they ask what they can do, we tell them something constructive: mow the lawn, take back the recyclables, go to the store, bring over a pizza on Friday night, whatever would help.

Before my son was diagnosed, I had no idea what this experience was like, and I try to remember that my friends don't really know either, unless I tell them. They can't know the sleepless nights, the anxiety over tests, the fear when your child says he doesn't feel well, or the terror that we might lose our precious child. Some of us have found great support and others none. I hope your family and friends come to your side.

I want to say that I hope that cancer does not become your life. For us, it used to be an "elephant in the living room," and now it's maybe a "zebra in the kitchen." There are times when it demands everything you can give, no doubt, but there will be moments when there is time for the rest of your life.

Chapter 21

Communication and Behavior

UNDER THE BEST OF CIRCUMSTANCES, child rearing is a daunting task. When parenting is complicated by an overwhelming crisis such as childhood cancer, communication within the family may suffer, and both children and parents may have difficulty adjusting to the new stressors in their lives.

Prior to a cancer diagnosis, children usually know the family rules and the consequences for breaking them. After diagnosis, normal family life is disrupted, and all sorts of confusing and distressing feelings and behaviors may appear. When people are under great stress, they often behave in ways they would not under normal circumstances. In response, parenting styles may need to adjust to the frequently shifting needs and behaviors of the ill child and affected siblings.

This chapter discusses feelings that many children have about their disease and some emotional and behavioral changes that may arise in both children and parents. It also offers suggestions for maintaining effective communication and appropriate behavior within the family. Parents share stories about what they experienced and how they coped with their and their ill child's powerful, and sometimes overwhelming, emotions. For more stories about the emotions of siblings, please see Chapter 19, *Siblings*.

Communication

Chapter 1, *Diagnosis*, lists many of the feelings parents may experience after their child's diagnosis of a solid tumor. It is helpful to remember that children, both the ill child and siblings, are also overwhelmed by strong feelings, and they generally have fewer coping skills than adults. At different times and to varying degrees, children and teens may feel fearful, angry, resentful, powerless, violated, lonely, weird, inferior, incompetent, or betrayed. Children have to learn ways to deal with these strong feelings to prevent "acting out" behaviors (aggression, risk taking) or "acting in" behaviors (depression, withdrawal).

Good communication is the first step toward helping your family identify how cancer is affecting behavior and family functioning, and how family members can work with each other, and with professionals, to restore order and a nurturing climate. Clear and loving communication with your children or teens is the foundation for trust. Children need to know from the very beginning that you will answer questions truthfully and take the time to talk about feelings.

Honesty

Above all else, children need to be able to trust their parents. They can face almost anything, as long as they know their parents will be at their side. Trust requires honesty. For your ill child and her siblings to feel secure, they must always know that they can depend on you to tell them the truth, be it good news or bad. This trust you build with your children reduces feelings of isolation and disconnection within the family.

> We were always very honest. We felt that if she couldn't trust us to tell her the truth, how scary that would be. I've seen a few incidents in the clinic of people with totally different styles who don't tell their kids the truth. I ran into the bathroom at the clinic crying after overhearing a mother who had deceived her child into coming to the clinic. Then he found out he needed a back poke and completely lost it. It makes me cringe. Children just have to be prepared. If they can't trust their parents, who can they trust?

Listening

Just trying to get through each day consumes most of a parent's time, attention, and energy. Thus, one of the greatest gifts parents can give their children is time—time when they are fully present in the moment and really focus on what children are saying and the feelings that generate the words. This can be difficult when you are physically and emotionally exhausted, but children notice when you are not really paying attention and are distracted by other thoughts and worries.

> When my daughter was 7 years old (3 years after her treatment ended), I realized how important it was to keep listening. She was complaining about a hangnail and I told her that I would cut it for her. She started to yell that I would hurt her. I asked her, "When have I ever hurt you?" and she said, "In the hospital." I sat down with her in my arms, rocked her, and explained what had happened in the hospital during her treatment, why we had to bring her, and how we felt about it. I asked her to tell me about her memories and feelings about being in the hospital. We cleared the air that day, and I expect we will need to talk about it many more times in the future. Then she held out her hand so I could cut off her hangnail.

Talking

If you are not in the habit of sharing your feelings with your children, it is hard to start doing so during a crisis. But now, more than ever, it is important to try. Parents can create an opening for discussion by simply stating how they are feeling, for example, "I have lots of different feelings at the same time. Sometimes I really get mad at the cancer because it is making your life so tough, but I am also happy that the medicine is working."

Telling your healthy children what you are feeling can strengthen your connection and reassure them of your love: "I really miss you when I have to take your sister to the hospital. I'll call you every night just so I can hear your voice," or "I wish the family didn't have to be separated so much, and I feel sad that you have to go through this." Such statements reassure children of your continued love for them and distress about being separated from them; they also create an opportunity for children to share with you how they feel about what is happening to the family.

> My daughter, diagnosed at 1 year old and now entering fifth grade, has three older siblings, so we have been through many developmental stages as far as communication goes. I try to answer their questions honestly, but I only tell them what I think they can understand without overwhelming them with information. I remember one of my boys, soon after my daughter's diagnosis, asked me if she was going to die, and I said "no" emphatically. I regretted it immediately, and realized that I would have to deal with my fears about the possibility of her dying, then go back and tell him the truth. So, later, I told him that I hadn't given an accurate answer because I was scared and that we didn't know if she was going to die. We hoped not, but we would have to wait and see. I have found that as their understanding deepens, they come back with more questions, needing more detailed answers. So, my motto is, be honest, but don't scare them. If you say everything is okay, but you are crying, they know something is wrong, and that they can't trust you for the truth.

It is also helpful to tell your sick child how the illness is affecting her siblings, for example, "It is very hard for Jim to stay at home with a babysitter when I bring you to the hospital. Let's think of something nice to do for him."

Common behavioral changes in children

Parenting is challenging, even when family life is going well. But when a child has cancer, parents are stressed, siblings may be angry or worried, and the ill child is scared and upset. Parents may find themselves reaching their emotional breaking points, and children may begin behaving in negative ways, making the situation unmanageable.

The first step to improving family life is to decide whether the ill child is going to be treated as if she only has a few months to live, or as if she will survive and needs to learn strategies for how to manage difficult emotions. Step two is to examine your own behavior to see whether you are modeling the conduct that you expect from your children. If your child becomes angry or destructive, step three is to develop a consistent, healthy response to the behaviors to help him learn ways to deal with his overwhelming emotions.

Barbara Sourkes, a respected child psychologist, wrote in her book *Armfuls of Time: The Psychological Experience of the Child with a Life-Threatening Illness*:

> While loss of control extends over emotional issues, and ultimately over life itself, its emergence is most vivid in the child's day-to-day experience of the illness, in the barrage of intrusive, uncomfortable, or painful procedures that he or she must endure. The child strives desperately to regain a measure of control, often expressed through resistant, noncompliant behavior or aggressive outbursts. Too often, the source of the anger—the loss of control—goes unrecognized by parents and caregivers. However, once its meaning is acknowledged, an explicit distinction may be drawn for the child between what he or she can or cannot dictate. In order to maximize the child's sense of control, the environment can be structured to allow for as much choice as is feasible. Even options that appear small or inconsequential serve as an antidote to loss, and their impact is often reflected in dramatic improvements in behavior.

In the following sections, parents share how they handled their children's range of emotions and behaviors.

Anger

Parents sometimes respond to the diagnosis of childhood cancer with anger, and so do children. Not only is the child angry at the disease, but also at the parents for bringing her in to be hurt, at having to take medicine that makes her feel terrible, at losing her hair, at losing her friends, and on and on. Children with cancer and their siblings have good reasons to be angry. The parents' task is to help the child learn to channel the anger appropriately.

> I always first acknowledged his feelings and whatever was the dominant feeling we went with. If he was angry, then I'd ask how he wanted to express the anger. "I want to punch something." "Okay, you get your poke done and then let's beat the hell out of these pillows or you can punch my hands." Always give choices.

• • • • •

> We have a case of the halo or the horns. Our son is either very defiant or an absolute angel. He argues about every single thing. I really think that it is because he has

had so little control in his life. I have very clear rules, am very firm, and put my foot down. But I also try to choose my battles wisely so we can have good times, too. My husband reminds me when I get aggravated that if he weren't this type of tough kid, he wouldn't have made it through so many setbacks. Then I am just glad to still have him with us.

· · · · ·

I was initially excited when my son finished treatment for Ewing's sarcoma. I really expected to have a normal life again. In reality, the whole family had a hard time adjusting. He has a twin brother, and both boys had a very rough transition to junior high school. They were frequently in trouble and began failing most of their subjects. It added a lot of stress to our home life to have the principal calling us two to five times a week. Although we started counseling, we still had major blow-ups at home.

Tantrums

Healthy children have tantrums when they are overwhelmed by strong feelings, and so do children with cancer. In some cases, tantrums can be predicted by parents paying close attention to what triggers the outburst (for example, a missed nap or anxiety about an upcoming procedure). This knowledge can help parents prevent tantrums by avoiding situations that create emotional overload for their child; but sometimes there is no warning of the impending tantrum. Knowledge can also help parents understand that many tantrums and behavioral changes are due to medication side effects and are out of the child's control.

> *We never knew what would set off 3-year-old Rachel, and to tell the truth, she didn't know what the problem was herself. She was very verbal and aware in many ways, but she had no idea what was bothering her and causing the anger. I would just hold her with her blanket, hug her, and rock until she calmed down. Later she would say, "I was out of control," but she still didn't know why.*

Of course, if the child is destructive, she needs help learning safer ways to vent her anger. A chapter in Larry Silver's *The Misunderstood Child* explains in detail how parents can initiate a behavior modification program at home. For a child who is frequently destructive, professional counseling is necessary.

> *My 5-year-old's behavior always intensified at clinic during treatment. He was hyperactive and defiant, to put it nicely. On his very last chemo day, he was hooked up to an infusion pump with a low battery, so his movement was limited to the bed. By the end of the session, he was so mad at being unable to move around, he was screaming at the top of his lungs, and throwing toys. First I tried to calm him, but then I got angry: I told him that he could just forget about the balloon we had in the*

car, it was gone. Of course, that just made it worse. We were both out of control, and they'll remember us there for quite some time, I'm sure.

· · · · ·

My daughter had frequent, violent rages that sometimes caused damage (toys thrown at the walls, books ripped up). She was small, but strong. I talked to her when she was calm about how the tantrums would be handled. Tantrums with no damage would be ignored; afterwards we would cuddle and talk about what prompted the anger and other ways for her to handle the anger. If she began to break things or hurt people, I would wrap her in a blanket and rock her until she relaxed. I would tell her, "I need to hold you because you are hurting people. This is so hard. I know. I love you." All of the tantrums ended after she went off treatment, but dealing with her destructive anger was one of the hardest things I have ever experienced.

· · · · ·

When my son needed to get out a good old temper tantrum just to unload, I'd let him. Then he'd fall into my reassuring arms and soak up some good ole momma lovin' and just whimper till he slept...my hand stroking his hair, and I'm whispering things like, "I know, honey, I know. It's just so wrong. I'm here, baby. I love you. I know. I know. Just sleep for now. I'll be here when you wake. I'm not moving. I'm not going anywhere. I love you. There now."

Withdrawal

Some children deal with their feelings by withdrawing rather than blowing up in anger. Like denial, withdrawal can temporarily be helpful as a way to come to grips with strong feelings. However, too much withdrawal is not good for children, and it can be a sign of depression. Parents or counselors need to find gentle ways to allow withdrawn children to express how they feel.

My daughter became very depressed and withdrawn as treatment continued. She started to talk only about a fantasy world that she created in her imagination. She seemed to be less and less in the real world. She didn't ever talk to her therapist about her feelings, but they did lots of art work together. At the beginning, she only drew pictures of herself with her body filling the whole page. With time, she began to draw her body more normal sized. As she got better, she began to draw the family again. When she drew a beautiful sun shining on the family, I cried. She just couldn't talk about it, but she worked so much out through her art.

The emotional impact of cancer is very pronounced during the teenage years, a time when appearance is particularly important. When adolescents look different from their peers, they may feel sad, angry, embarrassed, bewildered, helpless, and scared. Thus,

depression is common during and after treatment. Children and teens may go through a period of withdrawal and/or grieving; it is crucial that they receive support and counseling during these times.

> I had cancer when I was 15. I tried so hard as a freshman in college to put it all behind me and get on with my life. It just didn't work. Next to treatment, that was the worst year of my life. It showed me that if I didn't deal with it consciously, I was going to deal with it subconsciously. I had nightmares every night. I'd wake up feeling that I had needles in my arms. I decided to start taking better care of myself in a different kind of way. I do something fun every day. I try to see the positive side of situations. I read more and write a lot. I unplug from the cancer community whenever I feel overwhelmed. I try to explore my feelings with my counselor rather than shove them in the back corner. It's like garbage; if you don't take it out, it starts to stink. Once I started dealing with these feelings, things really improved.

Comfort objects

Many parents worry when, after diagnosis, children regress to using a special comfort object. Many young children ask to return to using a bottle, or cling to a favorite toy or blanket. It is reasonable to allow your child to use whatever he can to find comfort against the difficult realities of treatment. The behaviors usually stop either when the child starts feeling better or when treatment ends.

> My daughter was a hair twirler. Whenever she was nervous, she would twirl a bit of her hair around her finger. As her hair fell out, she kept grabbing at her head to find a wisp to curl. I told her that she could twirl mine until hers grew back. She spent a lot of time next to me or in my lap with her hand in my hair. It was annoying for me sometimes, but it had a great calming effect on her. When hers grew back, I would gently remind her that she had her own hair to twirl. She also went back to a bottle, although we did limit the bottle use to home or hospital. Both behaviors, hair twirling and drinking from a bottle, disappeared within 6 months of the end of treatment, when she was 6 years old.

· · · · ·

> Matthew had a special teddy bear that a friend had bought for him in Germany. Mr. Bear, as he was called, went through everything Matthew went through. When he received cranial radiation, Mr. Bear had his skull irradiated, too. If Matthew needed oxygen, they both got a mask. That little teddy bear even had surgery a few times. Each time my son was admitted to the hospital, Mr. Bear went along and got his own hospital identification bracelet. They went through a lot together. It's amazing how much comfort he received from a stuffed toy.

Talking about death

Part of effective parenting is allowing children to talk about topics that may cause feelings of discomfort in parents and children. No parent wants to talk, or even think, about the possibility of a child's death. In some cultures, the subject of death is taboo. But a diagnosis of cancer forces both parents and children to acknowledge that death is a very real possibility. Even children as young as age 3 may think about death and what it means. They need to be able to talk about their feelings, fears, or questions without their parents shutting down the conversation.

> *Eighteen months into treatment, 5-year-old Katy said, "Mommy, sometimes I think about my spirit leaving my body. I think my spirit is here (gesturing to the back of her head) and my body is here (pointing to her belly button). I just wanted you to know that I think about it sometimes."*

· · · · ·

> *Courtney's diagnosis was very difficult for her two older brothers. Especially Jay, who at the age of 10 understood the concept of death far better than Vaughn did at age 6. Both boys had to deal with our sudden departure late at night, taking with us their baby brother, Jared (age 9 weeks) and Courtney, who was 18 months old at the time. One of the hardest things I've ever done in my entire life was to answer a question Jay asked me one night. He asked me if his sister was going to die. I ached to lie to him and tell him that everything would be all right. I wanted to say, "Of course she isn't," but I couldn't do it. I had always been honest with the children, and felt that, difficult as it was, now more than ever he needed to know that he could trust that what I was saying was true. I told him his sister might die, but that we were going to do everything we could to make sure that didn't happen.*

Trusting your child

Sometimes children will tell you what they need to do to persevere through this trial. Their coping choices may not be what the parents would choose—the decisions may even make the parents nervous. But it is the child or teen's way to make peace with the day-to-day reality of diagnosis and treatment.

> *Early one summer morning, 12-year-old Preston and I left the hospital after a week-long stay for chemotherapy. He had been heavily sedated and was groggy and shaky on his feet. My husband and daughter were getting ready to go on a boat trip, and I felt Preston was too sick to go. We sadly saw them off, then returned to the car. Preston said, "Mom, I really need to go fishing. I know you don't understand, but I really need to do this."*

> *It made me very uncomfortable, but we went home to get his equipment. We then drove up to the mountains to a very deserted spot on the river, and Preston said that*

he needed to be out of my sight. So I watched him put on his waders, walk into the swift river, and disappear around a bend upstream. I went out into the river and sat on a rock. I waited for 2 hours before Preston came back. He said, "That's what I needed; I feel much better now."

There is a fine line between providing adequate protection for our children or teens and becoming overly controlling because of worry about the disease. You might ask yourself, "If she didn't have cancer, would I let her do this?"

Coping

Some children, because of both temperament and the environments in which they have lived, are blessed with good coping abilities. They understand what is required, and they do it. Many parents express great admiration for their child's strength and grace in the face of adversity. Many children and parents have difficulty coping during parts of treatment, or throughout treatment. Many resources (e.g., therapy, working with a child life specialist) are available to help if this is your situation.

> *My daughter, Lilly, did not have many coping skills due to preexisting mental issues and PTSD, and this was one of the biggest challenges during hospital visits. We were helped by a home therapist who came twice a week to the house and spent time teaching Lilly how to recognize emotions and healthy ways of dealing with them as well as healthy ways to express anger, sadness, hurt, etc., rather than hurting herself or me.*

· · · · ·

> *Stephan has not had any behavior problems while being treated for his initial diagnosis (age 5) or his relapse (age 7). He has never complained about going to the hospital and views the medical staff as his friends. He has never argued or fought about painful treatments. Unlike many of the parents in the support group, we've never had to deal with any emotional issues. We are fortunate that he has that confident personality. He just says, "We've got to do it, so let's just get it done."*

Common behavioral changes in parents

It is impossible to talk about children's behavior without discussing parental behavior. Your child's development does not occur in a vacuum; it occurs within the context of your family, and you set the tone for your home's atmosphere. At different times during their child's treatment, parents may be under enormous physical, emotional, financial, and existential stress. The crisis can cause parents to act in ways that reflect their own fear and lack of control—ways they would not behave under normal circumstances. Some of the common problem behaviors mentioned by parents follow.

Dishonesty

As stated earlier, children feel safe when their parents are honest with them. If parents start to keep secrets from a child to protect her from distressing news, she may feel isolated and fearful. She might think, "If Mom and Dad won't tell me, it must be really bad," or, "Mom won't talk about it. I guess there's nobody I can talk with about how scared I am."

Denial is a type of unconscious dishonesty. This occurs when parents say things to children such as, "Everything will be just fine," or, "It won't hurt a bit." This type of pretending just increases the distance between child and parent, leaving the child with no support. However horrible the truth, it seldom is as terrifying to a child as a half-truth upon which his imagination builds.

> I try so hard to be honest with my 5-year-old son, but blood draws, which he thinks of as "shots," are just so hard for him. Every doctor's visit, that's his first question, "Am I going to get a shot?" and I just want to say no. My husband's the one who started saying, "It'll be fine," but the anxiety that came up later at the appointment was so much worse that I put an end to that pretty quickly. Now I say, "Yes, but just once," because if I say, "I don't know," it just makes him worry.

Depression and anxiety

Parents of children with cancer often feel sad or depressed, or overwhelmingly anxious. If you are consistently experiencing any of the following symptoms, it is often helpful to speak with a counselor or psychologist:

- Changes in sleeping patterns (sleeping too much, waking up frequently during the night, early morning awakening)
- Appetite disturbances (eating too little or too much)
- Loss of sex drive
- Fatigue
- Panic attacks
- Inability to experience pleasure
- Feelings of sadness and despair
- Racing thoughts
- Poor concentration
- Social withdrawal

- Feelings of worthlessness

- Suicidal thoughts

- Drug or alcohol abuse

The above symptoms are responses to stress that can happen to anyone. If you have an underlying tendency toward anxiety or depression, the experience of having a child diagnosed with cancer can bring on more symptoms. Depression and anxiety are extremely common and very treatable, and should be dealt with early on.

> *Find a counselor you click with. Stick with that person until you truly feel some peace about your experiences and strength for dealing with the ongoing stress of treatment or whatever else might come up. I regret that I toughed it out and didn't recognize the depression I was experiencing for such a long time. I think finding sources of support in a variety of ways at the earliest moment possible can greatly mitigate long-term difficulties in coping.*

> • • • • •

> *It was 2 years after my son finished treatment that my depression became severe enough that I recognized it. I actually had a lot of suicidal thoughts and my husband urged me to see a doctor. He started me on Zoloft® and it has helped me tremendously.*

Losing your temper excessively

All parents lose their tempers sometimes. They lose their tempers with spouses, healthy children, pets, and even strangers. When you are living with the chronic stress of having a child with cancer, you may find that you lose your temper much quicker than in the past and over situations that normally would not upset you. In part, this is because chronic stress leads to prolonged, higher cortisol levels—a hormone that is released as part of our bodies our "flight or fight" response.

There are many ways to naturally lower your cortisol levels, such as exercise, yoga, meditation, eating a healthy diet, watching a funny movie, and listening to music. Also, if you start to notice when you are close to losing your temper, get away from the situation until you can respond more calmly—take a walk, listen to music, do breathing exercises, find a private place to cry or yell, pet the family dog or cat, or ask another adult to step in give you a break. Self-care is vital to preserving healthy relationships and avoiding saying or doing things you will later regret.

> *I had my share of temper tantrums. The worst was when my son was having his radiation. I tried to make him eat because it would be so many hours before he could have any more food. He always threw up all over himself and me, several times,*

every morning. It seemed like we changed clothing at least three times before we even got out of the house each day. I remember one day just screaming at him, "Can't you even learn how to throw up? Can't you just bend over to barf?" I really flunked mother of the year that day. I can't believe that I was screaming at this sick little kid, who I love so much.

Emotional and/or physical abuse of children and spouses increases at times when either or both spouses feel incompetent and powerless, and when there is chronic stress in your life. If you find yourself unable to manage your temper, seek professional counseling immediately. Counseling can help you prevent or repair any damage your outbursts may have caused to your family relationships. It takes courage and strength to seek help. But asking for help is a sign that you care deeply about your family and want your home atmosphere to be healthier and happier.

I had always taught my children that feeling anger was okay, but we had to make good choices about what to do with it. Hitting other people or breaking things was a bad choice; running around outside, or punching pillows were good choices. But, as with everything else, they learned the most from watching how I handled my anger, and during the hard months of treatment my temper was short. When I found myself thinking of hitting them, I'd say, in a very loud voice, "I'm afraid I'm going to hurt somebody so I'm going in my room for a time-out." If my husband was home, I'd take a warm shower to calm down; if he wasn't, I'd just sit on the bed and take as many deep breaths as it took to calm down.

Unequal application of household rules

You will guarantee family problems if the ill child gets a pass while the siblings are asked to step up and do extra chores. Granted, it is hard to know the right time to insist that your ill child resume making his bed or setting the table, but it must be done. Siblings need to know from the beginning that any child in the family, if sick, will be excused from chores, but that she will have do them again as soon as she is physically able.

I spoiled my sick daughter and tried to enforce the rules for my son. That didn't work, so I gave up on him and spoiled them both. He was really acting out at school. What he needed was structure and more attention, but what he got was more and more things. They both ended up thinking the whole world revolved around them, and it was my fault.

A child life specialist commented:

It's hard for parents to learn that saying "No" is okay, especially when there is only one child. One mom told me the other day that it's easier for her because there are two kids, and if it was just the child undergoing treatment, he'd get away with a lot

more, but the sister has to do "X, Y, and Z" and so her brother does, too. But it's hard to learn to say, "No, you don't get everything you want when we go to the grocery store," or "No, you don't get a new toy every single time you leave clinic."

Overindulgence of the ill child

Overindulgence is a very common behavior of parents of children with cancer. There are a variety of reasons for this: parents are trying to make up for the suffering their child is enduring or they are trying to make other parts of the child's life more enjoyable. In some cases, parents overindulge their sick child because it makes the parents feel better.

> I bought my daughter everything I saw that was pretty and lovely. I kept thinking that if she died she would die happy because she'd be surrounded by all these beautiful things. Even when I couldn't really afford it, I kept buying. I realize now that I was doing it to make me feel better, not her. She needed cuddling and loving, not clothes and dolls.

· · · · ·

> Four days into Selah's diagnosis, we were doing anything to keep her happy. Our sweet little 4 year old had turned into a demon child in that short time. Luckily, my very dear friend took me outside into the hallway, pushed me against the wall, and demanded to know exactly what I was doing. I just looked at her and said, "I have no idea." I just didn't want my daughter to die and that was my only focus. She then told me I was giving my daughter no boundaries, no behavior expectations, and she had no respect for anyone who walked into the room. Through my tears and our hugs, she assured me that the way we were going, if she didn't die from cancer, we were going to want to kill her because of the monster we were creating. I am still so grateful that she wasn't afraid to tell me what I needed to hear.

One aspect of overindulgence that is quite common is parents not expecting children to learn life skills. After years of dealing with a physically weak and sometimes emotionally demanding child, parents may forget to expect age-appropriate behaviors.

> I realized that I had formed a habit of treating my daughter as if she were still young and sick. I was still treating her like a 3 year old, and she was 7. One day, when I was pouring her juice, I thought, "Why am I doing this? She's 7. She needs to learn to make her own sandwiches and pour her own drinks. She needs to be encouraged to grow up." Boy, it has been hard. But want her to grow up to be an independent adult, not a demanding, overgrown kid.

Not spending enough time with the sibling(s)

While acknowledging that there are only so many hours in a day, parents interviewed for this book felt the most guilt about the effect that diagnosis and treatment had on the siblings. They wished they had asked family and friends to stay with the sick child more often, allowing them to spend more of their precious time with the siblings. Many expressed pain that they didn't know how severely affected the siblings had been.

> We didn't have problems with our child with cancer, but his brother (6 years old) really suffered. He would get the flu and sob all night. He would scream that he would have to go to the hospital and that he would die. He also had behavior problems at school. I ended up quitting work because my son with cancer was having trouble making it through the entire school day, and his brother needed some loving attention. Many of the sibling problems cleared up with lots of one-on-one attention.

· · · · ·

> I try to find some time in each holiday, weekend, or whenever it is just for Christopher and me. No matter how ill Michael is, someone else can cope with it for an hour or two, and nothing is allowed to interfere with that. We still go out, even if it is only Christopher and me at McDonald's®. Bottom line is that all mothers have to accept that along with the baby is delivered a large package of guilt, and whatever we do for one we will wish we had done for the other.

> But I don't think you can put one child on hold for the duration of the other's illness, because the year that Christopher has lost while Michael has been ill won't ever come again. He'll only be 11 once, just as surely as Michael will only be 14 once (or possibly forever), and we owe it to our healthy kids to allow them to be just that.

Using substances to cope

Some parents find themselves turning to alcohol or drugs to help them cope. Some parents use illegal drugs for stress relief and escape, while others overuse over-the-counter and prescription drugs. If you find yourself drinking so much that your behavior is affected, or using drugs to get through the day or night, seek professional help.

Coping

Many parents find unexpected reserves of strength and are able to ask for help from friends and family when they need it. They realize that different needs arise when there is a great stress to the family, and they alter their expectations and parenting accordingly. These families usually had strong and effective communication prior to the illness and pull together as a unit to deal with it.

The majority of families, however, have periods of calm alternating with times when nerves are frayed and tempers are short. In the end, most families survive intact and are often strengthened by the years of dealing with cancer.

> *After 12 years living with cancer, I have made my own peace with the fact that I may not be able to prevent or choose what my daughter has to deal with. I can, however, make a difference in how we go through it so she finds peace and comfort.*

> *We have been truly blessed by most of the care she has received. We have felt the compassion of those who have been willing to recognize the feelings of this process as a part of the medicine and were willing to communicate and acknowledge that to my daughter and to us. For her that makes a tremendous difference in how she responds.*

Improving communication and discipline

Parents suggest the following ways to keep the family more emotionally balanced.

- Make sure the family rules are clearly understood by all of the children. Stressed children feel safe in homes with regular, predictable routines.

> *After yet another rage by my daughter with cancer, we held a family meeting to clarify the rules and consequences for breaking them. We asked the kids (both preschoolers) to dictate a list of what they thought the rules were. The following was the result, and we posted copies of the list all over the house (which created much merriment among our friends):*
>
> 1. *No peeing on rug.*
> 2. *No jumping on bed.*
> 3. *No hitting or pinching.*
> 4. *No name calling.*
> 5. *No breaking things.*
> 6. *No writing on walls.*
>
> *If they broke a rule, we would gently lead them to the list and remind them of the house rules. It really helped.*

- Have all caretakers consistently enforce the family rules.

> *We kept the same household rules. I was determined that we needed to start with the expectation that Rachel was going to survive. I never wanted her to be treated like a "poor little sick kid," because I was afraid she would become one. We had to be careful about babysitters, because we didn't want anyone to feel sorry for her or treat her*

differently. I do feel that we avoided many long-term behavior problems by adopting this attitude early.

- Give all the kids some power by offering choices and letting them completely control some aspects of their lives, as appropriate.

  For a few months we ignored Shawn's two brothers as we struggled to get a handle on the situation. We just shuttled them around with no consideration for their feelings. When we realized how unfair we were being, we made a list of places to stay, and let them choose each time we had to go off to the hospital. We worked it out together, and things went much smoother.

  • • • • •

  My bald, angry, 4-year-old daughter asked me for some scissors one day. I asked what she was going to do, and she said "Cut off all the Barbies'® hair." I told her those were her dolls and she could cut off their hair if she chose. I asked her to consider leaving one or two with hair, because when she had long hair again, she might want dolls that looked like her then, too. But I said it was up to her. She cut off the hair (down to the plastic skull!) of all but one of the dolls. It really seemed to make her feel better. A few months later, she dismembered them. Fifteen years later, we occasionally find Barbie® legs and arms lying around the house, and we all laugh.

- Take control of the incoming gifts. Too many gifts make the ill child worry excessively ("If I'm getting all of these great presents, things must be really bad") and the siblings feel jealous. Be specific if you prefer that people not bring or send gifts, or if you prefer gifts for each child, not just the sick one.

  Paige has a sister, Chelsea, who was 5 at diagnosis, and a brother, Dan, who was 4 months old. Chelsea had a very difficult time. She didn't like it that Paige was getting so many presents, and she often felt left out. When I would try to do something special for her, she would get mad—she just wanted normalcy.

- Recognize that some problems are caused solely by treatment. It helps to remember that children with cancer are not naturally defiant or destructive. They are feeling sick, powerless, and altered by surgery, radiation, and/or drugs, and parents need to try to help by sympathizing, yet setting limits. Remember, with time, their real personalities will return.

  In the beginning, my 2-year-old daughter was incredibly angry. She would have massive temper tantrums, and I would just hold her until she changed from angry to sad. When she was on certain chemotherapy drugs, she would either be hugging me or pinching, biting, or sucking my neck. It drove me crazy. Now she's not having

*as many fits, but she still pushes her sisters off swings or the trampoline. She has a
general lack of control. Sometimes, when I can't stand it anymore, I swat her on the
bottom, and then I feel really bad.*

- If your child likes to draw, paint, knit, collage, or do other artwork or crafts, encourage it. Art is both soothing and therapeutic, and it gives children a positive outlet for feelings and creativity. This is true for kids with cancer and their brothers and sisters.

  Recently, when Cami was going through another "This-is-the-last-time-I'm-going-to-the-doctor" outburst, we spent the waiting time writing a list of all the horrible things we want to do to cancer (step on it; put needles in its eye; not let it have cake). I also draw cells—good and bad. We give lollipops to the good cells and scribble out the bad ones. It sounds simplistic, but it really helps.

- Allow your child to be totally in charge of her art. Do not make suggestions or criticisms (e.g., "stay inside the lines" or "skies need to be blue not orange"). Rather, encourage her and praise her efforts. Display the artwork in your home. Listen carefully if your child offers an explanation about the art, but do not pry if he says it is private. Above all, do not interpret it yourself or disagree with your child about what the art represents. Being supportive will allow your child to explore ways to soothe himself and clarify strong feelings.

  Jody was continually making projects. We kept him supplied with a fishing box full of materials, and he glued and taped and constructed all sorts of sculptures. He did beautiful drawings full of color, and every person he drew always had hands shaped like hearts. If we asked him what he was making, he always answered, "I'll show you when I'm done."

- If your child does artwork or likes to write, recognize that powerful emotions may surface for both child and parents.

  At my daughter's preschool, once a week each child would tell the teacher a story, which the teacher wrote down for the child to take home. Most of my daughter's pre-diagnosis stories were like this: "There was a rhinoceros. He lived in the jungle. Then he went in the pool. Then he decided to take a walk. And then he ate some strawberries. Then he visited his friend." But during treatment, she would dictate frightening stories (and this from a kid who wasn't allowed to watch TV and had never seen any violence). Two examples are: "Once there were some bees and they stung someone and this someone was allergic to them and then they got hurt by some monkeybars and the monkeybars had needles on them and the lightning came and hit the bees," and, "Once upon a time there were six stars and they twinkled at night and then the sun started to come up. And then they had a serious problem. They shot their heads and they had blood dripping down."

- Come up with acceptable ways for your child to physically release her anger. Some options are: ride a bike, run around the house, swing, play basketball or soccer, pound nails into wood, mold clay, punch pillows, yell, take a shower or bath, or draw angry pictures. In addition, teach your child to use words to express his anger, for example, "It makes me so angry when you do that," or "I am so mad I feel like hitting you." Releasing anger physically and expressing anger verbally in appropriate ways are both valuable life skills to master.

> Our kids go along okay for a while, dealing with stuff. Then suddenly (because they're tired, have reached a new point developmentally, or are not feeling well in a way they can't describe), they lose it. It seems that every kid needs something different at these times, but what works best for Cami is for us to help her find words for her frustration. We talk about how unfair cancer is, how terrible treatment is, how no one else really knows what she's going through. Sometimes she just bursts out crying with relief that someone understands!

• • • • •

> Shawn was very, very angry many times. We had clear rules that it was okay to be angry, but he couldn't hit people. We bought a punching bag, which he really pounded sometimes. Play-Doh® helped, too. We had a machine to make Play-Doh® shapes, which took a lot of effort. He would hit it, pound it, push it, roll it. Then he would press it through the machine and keep turning that handle. It seemed to really help him with his aggression.

• • • • •

> Our therapist recommended that we have our 5-year-old daughter make an "angry sheet." She should be encouraged to draw or write what she felt like doing when she was angry, and encouraged to get it all out. It was pretty scary, because she drew pictures of stamping people, gouging their eyes out, shooting them, etc. It was amazing how much better she felt afterwards. Then we went through the pictures together and discussed which ones she could really do, and which ones she could only think about doing because really doing it would hurt someone.

- Treat your ill child as normally as possible.

> When Justin was in the hospital, I could never stand to see him in those little hospital gowns. I asked if we could dress him in his own outfits, and they said yes. So even when he was in the ICU [intensive care unit] with all the tubes coming out of his body, we dressed him every day in something cute. It just felt better to see him in his clothes. Several months later my mother said she really admired us for doing that, because we were sending the message to Justin that everything was going to be okay. That even though he couldn't breathe on his own, he was still going to get up every day and get dressed. Now I think it probably did communicate to him that things were going to be normal again.

- Get professional help whenever you are concerned or run out of ideas about how to handle emotional problems. Mental health professionals (see Chapter 23, *Sources of Support*) have spent years learning how to help resolve these kinds of problems, so let them help your family.

> *My daughter and I both went to wonderful therapists throughout most of her treatment. My daughter was a very sensitive, easily overwhelmed child, who withdrew more and more into a world of fantasy as cancer treatment progressed. Her therapist was skilled at drawing out her feelings through artwork and play. My therapist helped me with very specific suggestions on parenting. For instance, when I told the therapist that my daughter thought that treatment would never end (a reasonable assumption for a preschooler), she suggested that I put two jars on my daughter's desk. One was labeled "ALL DONE," and the other was labeled "TO DO." We put a little rock for every procedure and treatment already completed in the ALL DONE jar, and one rock for every one yet to do in the TO DO jar. (Only recommended if the child is more than halfway through treatment.) Then, each time we came home from a procedure, my daughter would move a rock into the ALL DONE jar. It gave her a concrete way to visualize the approach of the end of treatment. She could see the dwindling number of pebbles left. On the last day of treatment, when she moved the last pebble over and the TO DO jar was empty, I cried, but she danced.*

- Most emotional problems resulting from cancer treatment can be resolved through professional counseling. However, some children and parents also need medications to get them through particularly rough times.

> *My daughter was doing really well throughout treatment until a combination of events occurred that was more than she could handle. Her grandmother died from cancer during the summer, one of her friends with cancer died on December 27, then another friend relapsed for the second time. She was fine during the day, but at night she constantly woke up stressed and upset. She had dreams about trapdoors, witches brewing potions to give to little children, and saw people coming into her room to take her away. She would wake up smelling smoke. She was awake 3 or 4 hours in the middle of the night, every night. Her doctor put her on sleeping pills and anti-anxiety medications, and the social worker came out to the house twice a month.*

- Teach children relaxation or visualization skills to help them cope with strong feelings. (See Appendix C, *Books, Websites, and Support Groups*, for additional information about developing such skills.)

- Have reasonable expectations. If you are expecting a sick 4 year old to act like a healthy 4 year old, or a teenager to act like an adult, you are setting your child up to fail.

> *It seemed like we spent most of the years of treatment waiting to see a doctor who was running hours behind schedule. Since my child had trouble sitting still and was*

always hungry, I came well prepared. I always carried a large bag containing an assortment of things to eat and drink, toys to play with, coloring books and markers, books to read aloud, and Play-Doh®. He stayed occupied and we avoided many problems. I saw too many parents in the waiting room expecting their bored children to sit still and be quiet for long periods of time.

• As often as possible, try to end the day on a positive note. If your child is being disruptive, or if you are having negative feelings about your child, here is an exercise you can use to end the day in a pleasant way. At bedtime, parent and child each tell one another something they did that day that made them proud of themselves, something they like about themselves, something they like about each other, and something they are looking forward to the next day. Then a hug and a sincere "I love you" bring the day to a calm and loving close.

Checklist for parenting stressed children

A group of parents compiled the following suggestions for ways to parent stressed children.

• Model the type of behavior you desire. If you talk respectfully and take time-outs when angry, you are teaching your children to do so. If you scream or hit, that is how your children will handle their anger.

• Seek professional help (for you and/or your children) for any behaviors that trouble you.

• Teach your children to talk about their feelings.

• Listen to your children with understanding and empathy.

• Be honest and admit your mistakes.

• Help your children examine why they are behaving the way they are.

• Distinguish between having feelings (always okay) and acting on strong feelings in destructive or hurtful ways (not okay).

• Have clear rules and consequences for acting on destructive feelings.

• Teach children to recognize when they are losing control.

• Discuss acceptable outlets for anger.

• Give frequent reassurances of your love.

• Provide plenty of hugs and physical affection.

• Notice and compliment your child's good behaviors.

• Recognize that the disturbing behaviors result from stress, pain, and drugs.

- Remember that with lots of structure, love, time, and sometimes professional help, the problems will become more manageable.

Every possible grouping of our family has been in therapy at one point or another. We have all done individual therapy, family therapy, and my husband and I did couples therapy. I feel that each of these sessions was a gift to our family. It helped us vent, cry, plan, and forge stronger bonds. We are all happy together many years after our daughter's cure, and every single penny we spent was worth it.

Our children look to us to learn how to handle adversity. They learn how to cope from us. Although it is extremely difficult to live through your child's diagnosis and treatment, it must be done. So we each need to reach deep into our hearts and minds to help our children have hope, endure, and grow.

I used a method with my son that I called, "Why are we here?" I used it for everything from IV pokes to taking meds. Anything we needed him to cooperate with got the "Why are we here" talk. He was 3 ½ when he was diagnosed with stage 4 neuroblastoma and parenting him and guiding/coaching him through procedures is something I'm pretty proud of.

Before a blood test, for example, I would say, "Why are we here? We can't see what is going on inside your body, but your blood tells us a story. It can tell us how you're doing and how healthy your body is and how to help you feel better. But we need to take some blood out to be able to find all this out. How do you think we should get it?" This made my son feel empowered and he would offer suggestions and make some of the decisions. Once he has chosen to cooperate on his own terms, could move on; we just need to give him the tools to do it. Many times, he still wouldn't want to, but now he understands why we have to.

There can always be choices. Do you want to use freezing cream so it hurts less? Do you want the nurse to take it from your hand or arm? Which arm, right or left? Do you want mom or dad to help you? Hold you? Do you want a treat for cooperating? (The treat box didn't work for long for us). Do you want to watch?

Explain clearly what is expected of him. Acknowledge that it will hurt. Tell him that I'll be right there with him so he doesn't have to do it alone. Sometimes we would ask him how the nurse is supposed to do it to make sure she/he did things according to his preference. Kids watch everything so they know things like cleaning the arm takes 30 seconds of wiping, or you clean the port site with three cleaning sticks and let it dry before poking. Consistency with details like that can cut down on anxiety.

Chapter 22

School

CHILDREN AND TEENS WITH SOLID TUMORS often experience disruptions in their education because of repeated hospitalizations or side effects from the disease or treatment. As their health improves and their treatment schedule allows, returning to school can be either a relief or a challenge.

For many children, school is a refuge from the world of hospitals and procedures—a place for fun, friendship, and learning. School is the defining structure of children's daily lives and returning to school can signal hope for the future and a return to normalcy. Some children and teens, however, may dread returning to school because of temporary or permanent changes to their appearance or concerns that prolonged absences may have changed their social standing with friends.

In addition, physical disabilities caused by the tumors or cancer treatment may prevent children from participating in games, physical education class, athletics, or other activities. These physical impairments sometimes require time out from the regular classroom for physical, occupational, and speech therapies. School can also become a major source of frustration for children who learn differently as a result of the tumor and/or treatment. Some survivors of solid tumors require specialized education and rehabilitation services.

Although educating children who have or had cancer can be a complex process, many challenges can be successfully managed through careful planning and good communication. This chapter covers ways to work with the school to address any educational challenges your child may encounter during and after treatment. It also includes information about avoiding communicable illnesses at school and obtaining accommodations for your child.

Keeping the school informed

A school-aged child diagnosed with cancer is usually admitted to a children's hospital (sometimes far from home) and is no longer able to attend school. To prevent your child from being dropped from school rolls due to nonattendance, you need to notify the school in writing about your child's medical situation. This notification allows

planning to begin for your child to receive hospital- or home-based schooling once he is able to resume his studies. If needed, enlist the assistance of a hospital social worker to write the letter and send to the school. Following is a sample letter, reprinted with permission from Sharon Grandinette, Exceptional Education Services.

Date

Dear [Name of Principal],

Our son, John Doe, [date of birth], a student at [name of school], was diagnosed with cancer in [month/year] and had surgery to remove the tumor. He is still hospitalized. He is unable to attend school at this time, and may undergo treatment with chemotherapy or radiation.

We are requesting that a Student Study Team meeting be scheduled with the school nurse in attendance. The purpose of the meeting is to discuss John's current medical status and how it may affect his school attendance and functioning. John may require accommodations or special education services, and we would like to discuss those options at the meeting. Depending on John's medical status, we may be able to attend the meeting in person, but if not, we request that it take place by phone.

Please send us the appropriate release forms so that we can authorize an exchange of information between the school and the medical/rehabilitation professionals treating John.

Sincerely,

[Parent/guardian name(s) and contact information]

Because treatments for solid tumors (e.g., surgery, chemotherapy, radiation, and stem cell transplantation) may cause changes in children's behavior and ability to function in school, both during and after treatment, the study team meeting can lay the foundation for any needed accommodations or interventions.

At the meeting, you may wish to distribute booklets about how to help children with cancer in the classroom, as well as age-appropriate information that can be shared with the classmates. You can formulate a communicable disease notification strategy, if necessary, and do your best to establish a rapport with the entire school staff. Take this opportunity to express appreciation for the school's help and your hopes for a close collaboration in the future to create a supportive climate for your child.

> *My daughter Julia was diagnosed when she was in second grade. We had her tutored at home by a district-sponsored, certified teacher and it was a great experience. She received the tutoring right through the end of the school year. (She started around mid-January with the tutoring, and it continued through June.) The teacher we had was fabulous, and Julia stayed caught up with (and even went ahead of) her class. Our school district has everything in place for kids who, for medical reasons, need to be tutored at home. I think it was much less stressful than trying to get into school for a day or two at a time and not being able to keep track of homework. Plus, we didn't have to worry about all the germs floating around. It was hard being home all those months, (I took a leave of absence from work) but we managed. Actually, I believe our relationship really deepened during the time home. I now have a closeness with Julia that is really special. When Julia went back to school last year, she had no adjustment problems and did very well.*

At the meeting, the school will designate a person (e.g., child's teacher, guidance counselor, special education expert) to communicate with a designated person at the hospital (e.g., school liaison). To read about how St. Jude Children's Research Hospital manages this process, visit *www.stjude.org* and enter the search term "School program."

> *I still feel unbelievable gratitude when I think of the school principal and my daughter's kindergarten teacher that first year. The principal's eyes filled with tears when I told her what was happening, and she said, "You tell us what you need and I'll move the earth to get it for you." She hand-picked a wonderful teacher for her, made sure that an illness notification plan was in place, and kept in touch with me for feedback. She recently retired, and I sent her a glowing letter, which I copied to the school superintendent and school board. Words can't express how wonderful they were.*

· · · · ·

> *We had a very difficult time with the school. They viewed my daughter as another problem they had to deal with. Her first grade teacher was impatient with her, at one point telling her she was too slow getting ready for the bus home, and closing her in the room by herself. The door was too heavy for her to open (she was weak from chemo and radiation), and another parent heard her crying, got her out, and put her on the bus. The principal and the teachers' union supported the teacher. We pulled her out to homeschool her.*

The designated liaisons will work to keep information flowing between the hospital and school and will help pave the way for a successful school reentry for your child. The liaison from the hospital should encourage questions and address any concerns the school staff have about having a seriously ill child in the school. The hospital liaison may also help school staff understand how the child's illness might affect school attendance or performance. Privacy laws prohibit liaisons from communicating unless parents sign a release form authorizing the school and hospital to share information. These forms are available at schools and hospitals.

In the months and years after diagnosis, try to maintain an open and amicable relationship with the school in the hope that your child, who may be emotionally or physically fragile, continues to be welcomed and nurtured.

Keeping the teacher and classmates involved

While your child is hospitalized, it helps to stay connected with the teacher and classmates. Parents can help by calling the teacher periodically and sending notes or taped messages from the sick child to classmates. Following are some suggestions for keeping the teacher and classmates involved with your child's life:

- Give the teacher a copy of the book *Educating the Child with Cancer* (listed in Appendix C, *Books, Websites, and Support Groups*).

- Have the hospital's school liaison give a presentation to your child's class about what is happening and how their classmate may look and feel when he returns to school. This talk should include a question and answer session to clear up misconceptions and alleviate fears. All children, especially teenagers, should be involved in deciding what information will be discussed with classmates and whether or not the child/teen wants to be present.

- Encourage your child's classmates to keep in touch. The class can make a card or banner or send a group photo. Individual students can call on the phone or send notes, emails, text messages, or pictures.

- Allow children who are old enough to establish a page on a social network to communicate with friends, express feelings and thoughts, post photos, and remain connected.

- If possible, use Skype®, FaceTime®, or a similar webcam software application to allow your child to interact "face-to-face" with classmates using a laptop, tablet, or smartphone. Use of this technology provides an opportunity for classmates to see changes in appearance as they gradually occur during treatment. This may lessen the surprise about changes in appearance when your child returns to school.

Keeping up with schoolwork

As treatment progresses, your child may return to school either part time or full time, but extended absences due to infections or complications from treatment are common. A child who is out of school longer than 2 weeks for any medical reason is entitled by law to instruction at home or in the hospital. It is a good idea to request offsite instruction as soon as you find out your child may be out of school for longer than 2 weeks. The school will require a letter from the doctor stating the reason and expected length of time offsite instruction will be needed.

If your child is hospitalized far from home, the hospital will provide onsite teachers or will make arrangements with teachers from the local community. If your child is hospitalized close to home or is at home but cannot attend school, your school district provides the teacher (called a homebound teacher). The homebound teacher is responsible for gathering materials from the school and tutoring your child.

Technology provides many ways to keep up with schoolwork. For example, some school systems provide a computer so the student can keep up via teleconferencing and online classes.

> We used Skype® and had a weekly time set up so that Patrik could see his classmates, and they could see him. If an oral presentation was due, he heard a few of theirs, and presented his. If nothing shareable was due, they just traded jokes or did a show and tell of something that had happened that week. Both Patrik and his classmates enjoyed collecting jokes all year. If he was not feeling well or was hospitalized, it was cancelled for that week. It sure helped make him still feel a part of his class, and the teacher said it really helped his classmates to see he was still okay, and still himself. He wasn't allowed to attend school at all for frontline treatment (almost 10 months).

> Patrik started the first day of 5th grade this year. He was able to walk in the building, feel welcome, and step right back into his friendships. No problems at all with that. I really thank his teacher last year for keeping him a part of his class despite not being in school.

Helping siblings

The diagnosis of cancer affects all members of the family. Siblings can be overlooked when the parents need to spend most of their time caring for the ill child. Many siblings feel frustrated, angry, frightened, neglected, or guilty, but they may try to keep their feelings bottled up to prevent placing additional burdens on their parents. Often, these complicated feelings emerge at school. Siblings may cry easily, fall behind in classwork,

do poorly on tests, cut classes, challenge teachers, withdraw from friends or school activities, or disrupt the classroom.

> *Lindsey was in kindergarten when Jesse was first diagnosed. Because we heard nothing from the kindergarten teacher, we assumed that things were going well. At the end of the year, the teacher told us that Lindsey frequently spent part of each day hiding under her desk. When I asked why we had never been told, the teacher said she thought that we already had enough to worry about dealing with Jesse's illness and treatment. She was wrong to make decisions for us, but I wish we had been more attentive. Lindsey needed help.*

To help prevent problems from developing, you can send a letter to each sibling's school principal requesting that teachers, counselors, and nurses be informed of the cancer diagnosis in the family and asking for their help with, and support for, the siblings.

If possible, try to include the siblings' teachers in some of the school discussions concerning the ill child. Teachers of siblings need to be aware that the stressors facing the family may cause the siblings' feelings to bubble to the surface during class. Chapter 19, *Siblings*, deals exclusively with siblings and contains suggestions about how to help them cope.

Returning to school

Parents may not even think about school when treatment first begins, but returning to school can help children regain a sense of normalcy and provide a lifeline of hope for the future.

> *Shoshana (16 years old) did incredibly well psychologically while being treated for osteosarcoma. She kept up with school (tutors at home and hospital for tenth and eleventh grade). She also took the SATs and went for a college interview (bald and on crutches). She wrote a research paper using a college library (she was the brains and I was her legs) that blew them over at the interview. She also helped to create a multimedia project for patient information at the hospital.*

> *Shoshana was back in school for her senior year. It was a big adjustment socially. Some kids didn't remember her; some thought she was a transfer student. She was still recovering from the side effects of chemo (lower counts, weight loss, low energy). Shosh was determined to put it all behind her and made college plans. She interned in a research lab and won an award from our community called Courage to Come Back. She won a full scholarship to our local university (Distinguished Honor Scholar).*

Preparation is the key to a successful return to school. You and the hospital school liaison may want to prepare a package for the school staff that contains the following information:

- A doctor's statement that describes your child's health status; ability to safely return to the school environment; physical restrictions, including any limits to physical education or recess; and probable attendance disruptions.

- Whether your child will attend full or half days.

- A description of any changes in physical appearance, such as weight loss or hair loss, and suggestions about how to help the other children handle them appropriately.

> Adam was not comfortable going back to school (kindergarten) when his hair fell out. His blood counts were down most of the time and he caught every cold that came around. When people asked what happened to his hair, he would simply reply, "Cancer," but he wouldn't go into detail. After 5 years, he still doesn't go into details. I think that he tries to put it behind him and go on with life. He's done a very good job with that.

- A request that your bald child be permitted to wear a wig, hat, or scarf to school.

- An explanation of possible effects medications may have on academic performance and a list of medications or other health services that will need to be provided at school (see section later in this chapter called "Individual healthcare plan").

- A list of signs and symptoms requiring parent notification (e.g., fever, nausea, vomiting, pain, swelling, bruising, or nosebleeds) and notification procedures to be followed.

- Concerns about exposure to communicable diseases, if necessary (e.g., if you live in an area with low immunization rates, you will need to know whenever students in the school have chicken pox, whooping cough, or measles).

- Any accommodations, such as extra snacks, rest periods, extra time to get from class to class, use of the nearest restroom (even if it is the staff restroom), and the need for restroom breaks without permission. This list should also include any requests for academic accommodations such as extended time for tests, reduced workload, or access to online textbooks. (These services are discussed in greater detail later in this chapter.)

> My 16-year-old son was allowed to leave each textbook in his various classrooms. This prevented him from having to carry a heavy backpack all day. They also let him out of class a few minutes early because he was slower moving from room to room.

School reentry plans require peer education and teacher education, but the guiding principle should be meeting the needs of the returning student. Therefore, frequent communication among school personnel, parents, the student, and the hospital liaison

is paramount before, during, and after school reentry. The following are parent suggestions for preventing problems through preparation and communication:

- Keep the school informed and involved from the beginning to foster a "we're all in this together" spirit.

- Bring a pediatric oncology nurse or school liaison into the classroom to talk about childhood cancer and answer questions. Make sure to ask whether your child wants to be part of the presentation. If treatment is lengthy, this should be done at the beginning of each school year to prepare new classmates. Because the sick child may be given accommodations that could cause other students to feel upset or jealous, the nurse or school liaison should explain that the student has some different rules because of the illness.

- Explain what is happening to their classmate and reassure them that cancer is not contagious.

> Elizabeth was in preschool at the time of her Wilms diagnosis. The manager did a wonderful job of integrating her back into the fold. All of the other children at the school were taught what was happening to Elizabeth and what would be happening (such as hair loss). They learned that they had to be gentle with her when playing. The manager was a former home health nurse, so I was very confident that she would be able to take care of my daughter in the event of an emergency. She was already familiar with central lines and side effects from chemotherapy. She was a gem!

- Ask the school liaison or other hospital personnel to make a PowerPoint that contains pictures of places that the child usually visits and the people she interacts with. This will help tell the story of her hospital life.

- Arrange places for your child to rest if she is too tired to participate in class.

> Robby was diagnosed in January of his kindergarten year. He returned to kindergarten the same day he got out of the hospital. His teacher was wonderful. She moved the desks around in the classroom so that if Robby got tired, she would go get his cot and put it in the center of the classroom so he could lay down and still listen. If a child had a cold, she would move him/her to the other side of the classroom. The kids washed their hands at least four times a day. The teacher's aide would sit in the rocking chair holding Robby if he was sad.

- For elementary school children, enlist the aid of the school liaison or school counselor to help select the teacher for the upcoming year. You do not have a legal right to choose a particular teacher, but you can write a letter to the principal discussing your

child's particular needs and requesting that they be considered when making assignments for the upcoming year.

> *Because my son has had such a hard third-grade year, I have really researched the fourth-grade teachers. I sat in class and observed three teachers. I sent a letter to the principal, outlining the issues, and requested a specific teacher. The principal called me and said, "You can't just request who you want. What would happen if all the parents did that? You'll have to give me three choices just like everybody else." I said, "My son has medical problems, behavior problems, and learning disabilities. Can you think of a child who has a greater need for special consideration?" My husband and I then requested a meeting with him, and at the meeting he finally agreed to honor our teacher request.*

• Prepare the teacher(s) and your child for the upcoming year.

> *I asked for a spring conference with the teacher selected for the next fall and explained what my child was going through, what his learning style was, and what type of classroom situation seemed to work best. Then, I brought my son in to meet the teacher several times, and let him explore the classroom where he would be the next year. This helped my son and the future teacher get to know to one another.*

• Have a mental health therapist talk with your child about his emotions and life both inside and outside of school.

> *My daughter went to a psychotherapist for the years of treatment. It provided a safe haven for frank discussions of what was happening, and also provided a place to practice social skills, which were a big problem for her at school.*

• Realize that teachers and other school staff can be frightened, overwhelmed, and discouraged by having a child with a life-threatening illness in their classroom. Accurate information and words of appreciation can provide much-needed support.

> *It can be so helpful for the school staff to have periodic meetings to address concerns, fears, progress, or to learn about upcoming procedures. I don't think enough parents know they can request meetings (for an Individualized Education Program [IEP] or otherwise) as they feel the need, and so can school staff. When Matt started school (elementary), I requested monthly inclusion meetings for the first semester and then every other month during the second semester with his IEP team. We wrote this in his IEP so it actually happened. I learned to do this from a parent much wiser than me!*

Avoiding communicable diseases

The dangers of communicable diseases to immunosuppressed children are discussed in Chapter 16, *Common Side Effects of Treatment*. The following information applies to children whose white blood cell counts are very low, which only occurs with some types of treatment.

Parents of children with low blood white cell counts need to work closely with the school to develop a plan for a chicken pox, whooping cough, measles, or flu outbreak if the school does not already have a communicable disease notification plan in place. If you know that children at school have these illnesses, you can keep your child at home. If your child is exposed to an illness at school, the school should notify you immediately so you can tell the oncologist.

Several methods can be used to ensure rapid reporting of outbreaks. Some parents notify all the classmates' parents by letter to ask them for prompt reports of illness. If you have a good rapport with the teacher, ask that he or she immediately report to you any cases of communicable disease.

> My daughter's preschool was very concerned and organized about the disease reporting. They noted on each child's folder whether he or she was immunized against measles, whooping cough, and chicken pox. They told each parent individually about the dangers to Katy, and then frequently reminded everyone in the monthly newsletters. The parents were absolutely great, and we always had time to keep her out of school until there were no new cases.

Other parents enlist the help of the office staff who answer the phone calls from parents of absent children.

> We asked the two ladies in the office to write down the illness of any child in Mrs. Williams' class. That way the teacher could check daily and call me if any of the kids in her class were ill.

After treatment

State-of-the-art treatment for childhood cancer has resulted in greater numbers of long-term survivors, but not without cost. Surgery, radiation, chemotherapy, and stem cell transplant can cause changes in learning abilities, motor skills, vision, hearing, and social skills (see Chapter 16, *Common Side Effects of Treatment*). Parents and educators need to remain vigilant for these issues and intervene as early as possible. Teachers and other school personnel may not be aware of how long-term effects can influence

learning potential and school performance. The hospital school liaison can provide materials to school personnel to help them understand these issues and/or attend school meetings to provide additional information.

Many of the same services and accommodations that assist students with school reentry also help students with learning problems that are related to their diagnosis and treatment. Regardless of where your child is on the treatment continuum, there are federal laws that will assist you in the process of obtaining appropriate educational services for your child.

Federal laws

Two federal laws protect the education rights of children ages 0 to 21 who have disabilities—Section 504 of the Rehabilitation Act of 1973 and the Individuals with Disabilities Education Act (IDEA). These laws guarantee every public school student the right to education regardless of physical, mental, or health impairment. Every state has a department of education website that describes state guidelines about how these laws are implemented and ways to obtain more information.

Examples of impairments affecting school performance that may develop during or after treatment for childhood solid tumors include the following:

- Motor problems after treatment for bone or soft tissue sarcomas
- Problems with small motor and gross motor skills (temporary or permanent) due to vincristine neuropathy
- Hearing loss after treatment with platinum-based chemotherapy drugs and/or aminoglycoside antibiotics
- Vision problems from treatment for retinoblastoma or orbital or nasopharyngeal rhabdomyosarcoma
- Hormonal issues
- Learning disabilities
- Post-traumatic stress, depression, and anxiety

No matter how good your relationship is with the school, any services needed by your child should be documented in a written and signed Individualized Education Program (IEP) or 504 Plan (see information below). A written plan will document your child's legal right to services and accommodations, and if your family moves, the new school will be legally required to follow the former school's plan until a new one is agreed upon and put into place.

Section 504 of the Rehabilitation Act of 1973

Some children will be eligible for services under Section 504 of the Rehabilitation Act whether on or off treatment. Commonly referred to as Section 504, this civil rights law prohibits discrimination against any individual with a physical or mental impairment that substantially limits one or more major life activity. Section 504 comes into play when a student with a disability attending a public school, or any private school, college, or university that receives federal funds, needs accommodation to access the educational opportunities available to children who are not disabled. Children who do not need special education services can be eligible for an educational plan under Section 504.

The school's Section 504 team determines whether a child is eligible for a 504 Plan based on information from a variety of sources, including the findings and recommendations of the treatment team about how the illness and treatment affect school participation. For example, a child being treated for cancer might need a Section 504 Plan that provides:

• Exemption from regular attendance/tardy policies

• A school-based health plan

• Reduced homework when ill or hospitalized

• Occupational, physical, or speech therapy

Section 504 can also be used when a student who is off treatment has disabilites that do not meet the requirements of the IDEA but do limit one or more major life activity. For example, a student who had a limb amputated might need a 504 Plan to obtain accommodations such as extra time to walk between classes, keeping a set of textbooks at home and in each classrooom to avoid carrying a heavy backpack at school, and adaptive physical education. Although schools are not required to provide a written 504 Plan, parents should request a written plan that specifically lays out all of the accommodations and educational services to be provided to the student.

Individuals with Disabilities Education Act

The cornerstone of all federal special education laws in the United States is the Individuals with Disabilities Education Act. This law, first passed in 1990, has been amended several times. It covers children and their families from birth to age 3, preschoolers, and students up to age 22 who have not received a high school diploma. Under the IDEA:

• All children, regardless of disability, are entitled to a free and appropriate public education and necessary related services provided in the least restrictive environment.

- Children are entitled to a fair evaluation to determine their need for special education services.

- Parents of a child with disabilities participate in the planning and decision-making for their child's special education.

- Parents can challenge decisions made by the school system, and disputes will be resolved by an impartial third party.

> Our son has multiple late effects from his chemotherapy, radiation, and stem cell transplant. He has an FM unit to help him hear his teacher. The school system was great about providing physical therapy, occupational therapy, and speech therapy. However, they wanted to put him in a special needs school, but I wanted him to have support in the classroom. They said they had no staff, so I put an ad in the newspaper at a university graduate school near his school. We found a second-year grad student in special ed to help him in the classroom. The school district refused to hire her, so we appealed and had a hearing. We won. The aide is wonderful and helps him stay on task, understand instructions, and keep organized. I'm an effective, but exhausted, advocate.

Several online sources provide reliable information about learning disabilities and parental rights under the IDEA and Section 504. Reputable websites include Wrightslaw (*www.wrightslaw.com*), the National Center for Learning Disabilities (*www.ncld.org*), and LD Online (*www.ldonline.org*).

Referral for services

The first step to getting educational support is to submit a written "referral for services" letter. A parent or a child's teacher can make a request for special education testing. Do not ask for a referral verbally; testing and services must be requested in writing. Obtain written, dated acknowledgement of the school's receipt of the request, because school staff are legally required to hold a meeting within 30 days of receiving the request.

> My son had problems as soon as he entered kindergarten while on treatment. He couldn't hold a pencil, and he developed difficulties with math and reading. By second grade, I asked the school for extra help, and they tested him. They did an IEP and gave him special attention in small remedial groups. The school system also provided weekly physical therapy, which really helped him.

The next steps in the special education process are evaluation, eligibility, development of an individualized education program (IEP), annual review, and 3-year assessment. You will need to become an advocate for your child as your family goes through the steps to determine what placement, modifications, and services your child is entitled to

We have had an excellent experience with the school district throughout preschool and now in kindergarten. We went to them with the first neuropsychological results, which were dismal. They retested him and suggested a special developmental preschool and occupational therapy. Both helped him enormously. He had an evaluation for special education services done and now has a full-time aide in kindergarten. He is getting the help he needs.

· · · · ·

The IEP process was more difficult, and more psychologically damaging, than my daughter's cancer treatment. Although we provided a detailed report of her neuropsychological evaluation that included specific recommendations for the type of reading instruction proven to work with children with her deficits, the school said it did not use those nationally recognized interventions. She was subjected to testing at the beginning and end of each school year, but different types of tests were used each time, so we could never make an apples-to-apples comparison of results. After 4 years, I placed her in a private school for students with learning disabilities, where she is flourishing. To this day, she dissolves into tears if pulled out of class for educational testing without prior notice, but she has no problem going back for checkups at the hospital where she was treated for cancer.

Evaluation

Once the referral is made, an evaluation is needed to determine whether the child qualifies for services as a student with a disability. Usually, a team composed of a general education teacher, special education teacher, district representative, and others (e.g., school nurse) attend the first meeting. It helps immensely to have the liaison from the hospital present to make sure the IEP team fully understands the child's illness, treatment, and impairments. The evaluation usually includes educational, medical, social, and psychological areas.

Most children treated for cancer should have a thorough neuropsychological evaluation, which is best administered by pediatric neuropsychologists experienced in testing children with cancer. The results should be shared with the school system, which must consider the findings but may also conduct its own assessment. If parents disagree with the findings from the school's evaluation, they have the legal right to request an independent educational evaluation by a third-party practitioner, which is paid for by the school district.

Children may also be evaluated to determine the need for specific therapies or services in identified areas (called "related services"). Examples of related services are physical therapy, occupation therapy, adaptive physical education, and assistive technology.

Initially, the school was reluctant to test Gina because they thought she was too young (6 years old). But she had been getting occupational therapy at the hospital for 2 years, and I wanted the school to take over. I brought in articles and spoke to the teacher, principal, nurse, and counselor. Gina had a dynamite teacher who really listened, and she helped get permission to have Gina tested. Her tests showed her to be very strong in some areas, and very weak in others. Together, we put together an IEP, which we have updated every spring. Originally, she received weekly occupational therapy and daily help from the special education teacher. She's now in fourth grade and is doing so well that she no longer needs occupational therapy; she only gets extra help during study hall.

From the time the parents agree to the evaluation, school districts have 60 days to complete the evaluation and present the findings. Parents attend a meeting with the IEP team to discuss the evaluation results and make a determination about whether a child is eligible for services. Students can be included in this meeting, although younger children most often are not.

Eligibility for special education

The IDEA requires that students meet two requirements to be eligible for special education services: 1) The child must have one (or more) of the 14 disabilities listed in the law; and 2) as a result of the disability, the child needs special education services to access the general education program. The 14 eligibility categories for special education are:

- Autism
- Deaf/blindness
- Deafness
- Developmental delay
- Emotional disturbance
- Hearing impairment
- Intellectual disability
- Multiple disabilities
- Orthopedic impairment
- Other health impairment (OHI)
- Specific learning disability
- Speech or language impairment

- Traumatic brain injury (TBI)

- Visual impairment, including blindness

Most children with effects from treatment for solid tumors qualify for services under the category of OHI and often a secondary eligibility (e.g., hearing impairment, speech or language impairment, orthopedic impairment).

> *Destiny (age 11) has some long-term effects from her treatment for stage IV neuroblastoma 9 years ago. Her treatment included high-dose chemotherapy, radiation to the head and brain, and transplantation. Her learning ability (in particular, comprehension and short-term memory) has been affected. The special ed department at the school told us she was entitled to extra help because of her "other health-impaired" status. Destiny is in a general education classroom setting, but a special education teacher comes into the room several times daily to give extra help to the kids who need it. Examples of services are: helping with problem solving (especially math), giving her extra time to do work, as well as allowing her to repeat tests that she didn't perform well on. We have found this to be a great help in Destiny's education. She is now making As and Bs as well as exhibiting a more positive attitude toward school in general.*

Individualized education program (IEP)

After eligibility is determined, a meeting is called to develop an IEP. The IEP team attending this meeting includes the parent(s), the student's regular education teacher, a special education teacher, a representative of the school district, someone who can interpret the instructional implications of the evaluation results, the student (when appropriate), and any other person with knowledge or special expertise regarding the child.

Attending an IEP meeting can be intimidating (because school personnel usually outnumber the parents) and emotional (because it can be difficult to discuss evaluation results and additional challenges facing your child). You are entitled to bring another adult with you as an advocate, to take notes, or simply to observe. This meeting is an opportunity to involve the hospital's school liaison to make sure that all meeting participants understand the child's current and past medical issues and that they use that information to write the IEP goals.

> *My daughter suffered profound high-frequency hearing loss as a result of her treatment. Our audiologist recommended she be evaluated for speech therapy because she was mispronouncing certain sounds that she could no longer hear. At the IEP meeting, I sat across the table from six school representatives who said that the speech*

deficits were just mild developmental delays, probably due to her illness, and that she would catch up without intervention. I had to explain at some length that, due to her illness, she was unlikely to "catch up" because she could no longer hear those sounds and would not be able to figure out how to make them without assistance.

The IEP should describe in detail the special education program and any other related services that need to be provided to meet the individual needs of your child. The IEP describes what your child is to be taught, how and when the school is to teach it, and any educational accommodations that will be made.

Students with disabilities need to learn the same things as other students: reading, writing, mathematics, history, and other subjects that help them prepare for jobs, vocational training, or college. The difference is that with an IEP in place, many specialized services—small classes, speech therapy, physical therapy, counseling, and instruction by special education teachers—are used.

The IEP has five parts:

1. **Present level of performance.** This section describes your child's present level of social, behavioral, and physical functioning, academic performance, learning style, and medical history.

2. **Goals and objectives.** This section lists skills and behaviors that your child is expected to master in a specific time period and how progress will be assessed. These goals should not be vague like "John will learn to write a report," but rather, "John will prepare and present an oral book report with two general education students by May 1." Each goal should answer the following questions: Who? What? How? Where? When? How often? When will the service start and end?

3. **Related services.** Many specialized services to be provided at no cost to the family can be mandated in the IEP, including the following:

   • Speech therapy

   • Physical therapy and adaptive physical education

   • Occupational therapy

   • Social skills training

   • Mental health services

   • Assistive technology assessment and training

   • Functional behavior assessment and behavior intervention plans

   • Transportation to and from school and therapy sessions

For each of these services, the IEP should list the frequency, duration, start date, end date, and whether the services will be provided in a group or individual setting, for example, "Jane will receive individual speech therapy twice a week, for 60 minutes a session, from September through December, when her needs will be reevaluated."

As discussed in Chapter 16, *Common Side Effects of Treatment*, rehabilitation services help many children make a full or near-full recovery. Children who have a long-term need for rehab can access some of these services through the school system. To obtain these services, parents should provide letters of medical necessity from individual therapists and physicians and present them as supporting documentation during the IEP meeting.

4. **Placement.** The term *placement* refers to the least restrictive setting in which the IEP goals and objectives can be met. For example, one student may be in the general education classroom all day with an aide present, and another might leave the classroom for part of each day to receive specialized instruction in a resource room. The IEP should state the amount of time (minutes or hours) the child will be in the general education program and the frequency and duration of any special services.

5. **Evaluating the IEP.** Meetings with all members of the IEP team will be held periodically to review your child's progress toward attaining the short- and long-term goals and objectives of the IEP. To determine whether the IEP is working for your child, an annual IEP meeting is required, but parents can request more meetings, if needed, to address any concerns.

If at any time communication deteriorates and you feel your child's IEP is inadequate or not being followed, here are several facts you need to know:

- The IEP cannot be changed without parental consent.

- If parents disagree about the content of the IEP, they can withdraw consent and request (in writing) a meeting to draft a new IEP; or they can consent only to the portions of the IEP with which they agree.

- Parents can request that the disagreement be settled by an independent hearing officer in an administrative law proceeding called a due process hearing. School districts generally are represented by a lawyer at such hearings, and parents are usually best served in such proceedings by hiring a lawyer or educational advocate.

- An IEP is a legal document that schools are legally required to comply with. However, if a school does not comply with an IEP, there is no governmental agency parents can call upon to enforce it—the only enforcement mechanism is a due process hearing.

The IDEA does not describe specific types of educational placements, modifications, and related services. Because options are open, an IEP should reflect those programs and services uniquely appropriate for the student's needs. Advocates, disability organizations, your child's medical team, teachers, and therapists can assist in determining which options best suit your child, although ultimately you know your child best.

> This year (third grade) has been a nightmare. My son has an IEP that focuses on problems with short-term memory, concentration, writing, and reading comprehension. The teacher, even though she is special ed qualified, has been rigid and used lots of timed tests. She told me in one conference that she thought my son's behavior problems were because he was "spoiled." The IEP required that she send a note home with my son if he has a seizure, and she has never done it. I learned that the IEP is only as valuable as the teacher who is applying it.

Hundreds of accommodations are available through an IEP. Here are a few examples:

- Preferential seating
- Study groups with discussion for learning/memory
- Recording of classes for reinforcement
- Books on tape or CD
- A copy of notes from a peer to improve listening in class and reduce the need for writing
- A copy of a teacher's planning notes prior to instruction
- Shortened assignments
- Use of a computer for written assignments
- Keyboard training (kindergartners are not too young to learn)
- Use of graphic organizers
- Use of a calculator or number line
- Extended time for tests
- Oral rather than written tests
- An assignment check-off system
- Breakdown of large assignments into steps
- Extra time to travel between classes
- Accessible locker

Nettie recently was tested for auditory processing disorder. Nettie does demonstrate a great deal of difficulty processing things presented orally. It was suggested that we try using a device called an "Easy Listener." She would wear a little box with headphones. The teacher would wear a microphone which links right to the box Nettie is wearing. That would mean that no matter what the noise level in the room, or where the teacher is, the teacher's voice will always sound only 6 inches away from Nettie's ears. We are also going to try using a computer program called Earobics® to try and retrain parts of her brain to "listen" better. Auditory processing disorder is sort of like having dyslexia of the ears. The ears hear fine, but the brain doesn't receive the message properly. So we'll see if any of these things help her.

- To learn about other accommodations used by survivors and children on treatment, visit *www.acco.org/Information/Resources/Books.aspx* to order a free copy of the book *Educating the Child with Cancer, 2nd edition.*

Transition services

Students receiving special education services receive transition planning, starting by the time the child is 16 (or younger if determined by the IEP team or required by state law). This planning helps to prepare for life after high school, in higher education, vocational training, employment appropriate to their abilities, or adult services. Your child's IEP should outline actions that will be taken to prepare your child to transition from high school to college, vocational school, or life in the community. High schools in in the United States may have a Department of Rehabilitative Services (DRS) vocational counselor on staff to help students with disabilities plan for life after high school, or as part of the student's transition services, the school can connect the student with the DRS.

The DRS can provide:

- Career guidance and counseling

- Diagnostic evaluations

- Supported employment and training

For more information about transition planning, visit *www.wrightslaw.com/info/trans. index.htm.*

> *As my son grew older, we could see he was ready to interact with a world that was bigger than his high school. With my assistance during his application, interview, and training, a local grocery store hired him as courtesy clerk. Easter Seals®*

arranged for a job coach who watched Ben on the job to make sure he was safe in the parking lot and who came to our home to teach him how to bag groceries (from the options in my kitchen pantry!) He has worked about 20 hours per week for 10 years now. He is proud of his job and his managers always say he is their hardest worker. There have been bumps along the way, though. Sometimes employees and customers do not understand that Ben is hearing impaired or is a very concrete thinker. He is inflexible and his social skills are not great. On a few occasions, I have had to facilitate conversations between him and his coworkers or help him communicate with management when he needs adjustments to his shift schedule. Despite these issues, this job had been a great thing for him.

IDEA Part C—Early intervention services

Part C of the IDEA mandates early intervention services for infants and toddlers (from birth up to age 3) with disabilities, and, in some cases, children at risk for developmental delays. These services are administered either by the school district or the state health department, with the services usually provided in the family home. You can find out which agency to contact by asking the hospital social worker or calling the special education director for your school district.

The law requires services not only for eligible infants and toddlers, but for their families, as well. Therefore, an Individualized Family Service Plan (IFSP) is developed. This plan includes:

- A description of the child's physical, cognitive, language, speech, psychosocial, and other developmental levels

- Goals and objectives for the family and child

- The description, frequency, and delivery of services to be provided, such as speech, vision, occupational, and physical therapy; health and medical services; and family training and counseling

- A caseworker who locates and coordinates all necessary services

- Steps to support transition to other programs and services

- By age 3, children are transitioned to the school district for assessment of the need for special education services. If the child is eligible, the school district provides early childhood special education services. For more information, visit *www.parentcenterhub. org/repository/preschoolers.*

	IDEA	Section 504
Type of law	A federal education law	A civil rights law
Who is covered	Students ages 3–21 in primary or secondary school whose disability affects their ability to access the general education curriculum. Part C covers infants and toddlers.	Any student with a disability in an educational setting. College students, regardless of age, have rights under Section 504.
Types of disabilities	Child must have one or more of the 14 disabilities listed in the law.	Any physical or mental disability (including cancer) that substantially limits one or more major life activity.
Person in charge	Special education director	Section 504 coordinator
Evaluation of eligibility	Several assessment tools are used to determine whether the child has a qualifying disability. A written request must be submitted for an evaluation, and consent must be obtained from a parent or guardian before evaluation begins. A reevaluation is required every 3 years.	Evaluation is conducted in the area of concern. Written consent of a parent or guardian is not required for evaluation, but notice must be provided. Yearly reevaluation or review is required.
Tools used to implement law	A written Individualized Education Program (IEP) is legally required and parents/guardians must receive and sign a copy of the final plan. If a functional behavioral analysis is conducted, a Behavior Intervention Plan can be developed for any child with a disability who also has a behavioral issue that interferes with learning.	A 504 Plan can be developed without notice to, or participation of, the parents/guardians. A written 504 Plan may be requested, but is not required by law.
Change in placement	A meeting with the parents/guardians is required before any change in placement or services is made.	Changes in placement or services can be made without notice to parents/guardians.
Due process	School districts must provide resolution sessions and due process hearings for parents/guardians who disagree with evaluation, implementation, or placement.	School districts must provide a grievance procedure for parents/guardians who disagree with evaluation, implementation, or placement; due process hearing is not required.

Individual health care plan (IHCP)

If your child has medical issues that need to be managed at school (e.g., seizures, headaches, or medication), your child's doctor should write a letter to the principal with written orders for care. The school nurse will then develop an IHCP to ensure your child's medical needs are appropriately managed at school. The IHCP is incorporated into either an IEP or Section 504 Plan, and it includes a brief medical history, medications and side effects, student health goals, clear descriptions of health services that

will be provided by the school, and contact numbers for emergencies. Parents and school personnel must sign the plan before it is implemented, and it should be updated every year.

Your legal rights (Canada)

Each Canadian province and territory has its own ministry or department of education and establishes its own laws, policies, procedures, and budgets pertaining to educational requirements and services. The Council of Ministers of Education operates on a voluntary basis to advocate for educational services, establish common goals, and improve the quality of education across the country. One of the shared goals of this group in recent years has been to improve the delivery of special education services to children across Canada.

Most provinces and territories have an evaluation process similar to the one used in the United States. Canada also employs a similar IEP process, although the specific rules vary by province. For a list of province-specific special education legislation, contacts, and resources, visit *www.cps.ca/en/issues-questions/map/provincial-special-education-legislation-and-contacts.*

The terminally ill child and school

In the sad event that a child's health continues to deteriorate, parents and school staff members should discuss ways the school can be supportive during the child's final days. Fellow students need timely and appropriate information about their ill classmate so they can deal with her declining health and prepare for her death. The following are suggestions about how to prepare classmates and school personnel for the death of a student:

- The school staff needs to be reassured that death is not likely to suddenly occur at school.

- Staff needs to be aware that going to school is vital to the child's well-being. School staff members should welcome and support the child's need to attend school for as long as possible.

- Staff can design flexible programs for the ill student.

> *Jody was lucky because he went to a private school, and there were only 16 children in his class. Whenever he could come to school, they made him welcome. Because children worked at their own pace, he never had the feeling that he was getting behind in his classwork. He really felt like he belonged there. Sometimes he could*

only manage to stay an hour, but he loved to go. Toward the end when he was in a wheelchair, the kids would fight over whose turn it was to push him. The teacher was wonderful, and the kids really helped him and supported him until the end.

- It is helpful to provide age-appropriate reading materials about death and dying for the ill child's classmates, siblings' classmates, teachers, and school staff, and opportunities for discussion.

- Extraordinary efforts should be made to keep in touch when the child can no longer attend school. Cards, banners, videos, texts, emails, telephone calls, and webcam or conference calls from the entire class or individual classmates are good ways to share thoughts and best wishes.

- Classmates can visit the hospital or child's home, if appropriate. If the child is too sick to entertain visitors, the class can come wave at the front window and drop off cards or gifts.

- The class can send books, video games, or a basket of small gifts and cards to the hospital or home.

- The class can decorate the family's front door, mailbox, and yard when the child will be returning home from the hospital.

All of the above activities encourage empathy in classmates, as well as help them adjust to the decline and imminent death of their friend. The activities also help sick children know they have not been forgotten by teachers, friends, and classmates, even if they cannot attend school.

When the child dies, a memorial service at school gives students a chance to grieve. School counselors or psychologists should be available to talk to the classmates to allow them to express their feelings. Parents usually very much appreciate receiving stories about their child from classmates.

My son Zachary has been out of school for over a year. Zachary received a stem cell transplant for his neuroblastoma, and school has not been an option for him in the months afterwards. He is taught by a teacher provided by our county for "homebound" students. She's great, and Zach is ahead of the regular second grade curriculum.

Zach is so comfortable with his teacher that he doesn't want to return to school in the fall. He feels everyone will think he's weird and will tease him. So I tell him we're all weird in our own way and everyone gets teased over something! Actually, I'm not that glib about it. I realize this is an important issue for him, so he is seeing a therapist in preparation for return to school. I feel that will help him a great deal.

Chapter 23

Sources of Support

THE DIAGNOSIS OF CANCER CAN BE a frightening and isolating experience. Every parent of a child with cancer has a story to tell of lost or strained relationships. Yet we are social creatures, reliant on a web of support from family, friends, neighbors, and religious communities. We need the presence of people who not only care for us, but who sincerely try to understand what we are feeling. Many parents of children with cancer experience deep loneliness after the first rush of visits, cards, and phone calls ends—when the rest of the world goes back to normal life.

Members of families struck by childhood cancer—parents, the child with cancer, and siblings—often turn to support groups and various other forms of psychological and emotional help. Families join support groups to dispel isolation, share suggestions for dealing with the illness and its side effects, and talk to others who are living through the same crisis. Individual and family counseling can help address shifting responsibilities within the family, explore methods to improve communication, and help find ways to channel strong feelings constructively.

This chapter offers information about resources that can help families regain a sense of control over their lives and find wonderful new friends who understand what they are going through.

Hospital social workers

Pediatric oncology social workers usually have a master's degree in social work, with additional training in oncology and pediatrics. They serve as guides through unfamiliar territory by mediating between staff and families, helping with emotional or financial problems, locating resources, and easing the child or teen back into school. Many social workers form close, long-lasting bonds with families and continue to answer questions and provide support long after treatment ends.

> Over the course of my son's treatment, I became very close to the hospital's social worker. I came to see her as not only a person who was very good at her job and providing me with wonderful support, but also as a friend. She was very much in tune

with my personality, and seemed to sense when I was having a rough day, even if I had been doing my best to hide it. So many times she would stop by my son's room and invite me to join her for coffee in the cafeteria, her treat. And we would sit and talk about anything and everything. She seemed to have a natural talent for making me laugh when I really needed to most. And she never expressed discomfort when I needed to cry or curse the unfairness of the situation we were in. She was a very good listener.

In addition to social workers, most hospitals have child life specialists, psychiatric nurses, psychiatrists, psychiatric residents, and psychologists on staff who can help you deal with problems while your child is in the hospital. Ask your child's nurse, treating physician, or the hospital social worker to help you connect with these resources.

We went to a children's hospital that was renowned in the pediatric cancer field. The medical treatment was excellent, but psychosocial support was nonexistent. The day after diagnosis, we were interviewed for 20 minutes by a psychiatric resident, and that was it. I never met a social worker, and the physicians were so busy they never asked anything other than medical questions. I didn't know any parents of a child with my daughter's diagnosis; I didn't know there was a local support group; I didn't know there was a summer camp for the kids. I felt totally isolated.

Support groups for parents

Support groups offer a special perspective for parents of children with cancer and help them feel less alone. Parents in similar circumstances can share practical information learned through personal experience, provide emotional support, give hope for the future, and truly listen and empathize.

The countless heartfelt consultations, gestures, and visits from the nurses, doctors, hospital staff, and program developers were amazing. They gave me strength and they guided me through this. I was not in control. I was lost in a world I did not know and had no experience with. But they gave me hope, they told me I could do it, and they kept me informed and made me part of their process. The parent support group was instrumental in that movement from helpless to hopeful. I was not alone and I realized that no matter how bad we had it, we were lucky that our children were alive and fighting. I had to pull myself and our lives back together. We built a life and routines around this unfortunate situation and we began to adapt.

Coping with a life-threatening illness requires a unique perspective—the ability to focus on the grave situation at hand while balancing other aspects of daily life. In support groups, many families get help finding this emotional balance. Just meeting people who have lived through the same situation is profoundly reassuring.

The group was a real lifeline for us, especially when Justin was so sick. We looked forward to the meetings and were there for every one. It was a real escape; it was a place to go where people were rooting for us. People from the group would always swing by the ICU to see us whenever they were bringing their own kids in for treatment. They always stopped by to visit and chat. We amassed a tremendous library of children's books that the group members would drop off. The support was wonderful.

· · · · ·

I felt like I was always putting up a front for my family and friends. I acted like I was strong and in control. This act was draining and counterproductive. With the other parents, though, I really felt free to laugh as well as cry. I felt like I could tell them how bad things were without causing them any pain. I just couldn't do that with my family. If I told them what was really going on, they just looked stricken, because they didn't know what to do. But the other parents did.

· · · · ·

Our Tuesday gatherings were an anchor for us. It was a time to meet with parents who truly understood what living with cancer meant. These parents had been in the trenches. They knew the midnight terrors, the frustrations of dealing with the medical establishment; after all, it was an alien world to most of us. They knew about chemo, hair loss, friend loss, and they knew the bittersweet side of cherishing a child more than one thought one could cherish anyone. We gathered to cry, to laugh, to whine, to comfort one another, to share shelter from a frightening world. It was a haven.

Cancer can be a very isolating experience. For the parents of a child with cancer, the issues that other parents in their social circles are dealing with seem light years away. But the moms and dads in the kitchen at a Ronald McDonald House or the ped-onc lounge can offer practical advice about things such as burnt skin from radiation and how long it will take to heal. They understand each other's feelings and emotions, because they are sharing the same experience. It is a bond that cuts across all social, economic, cultural, and racial differences.

My 2-year-old daughter was diagnosed 1 week after I gave birth to a new baby girl. I remember early in her treatment, I was sitting with Gina on my lap, and my husband sat next to me, holding the new baby. The doctor breezed in and said in a cheerful voice, "How are you feeling?" I burst into sobs and could not stop. He said "Just a minute" and dashed out. A few minutes later a woman came in with her 8-year-old daughter who had finished treatment and looked great. She put her arms around me and talked to me. She told me that everyone feels horrible in the beginning; and it might be hard to believe, but treatment would soon become a way of life for us. She was a great comfort, and of course, she was right.

Many wonderful national and regional organizations exist to help families of children with solid tumors. Several of them are listed in Appendix B, *Resource Organizations*. In addition to these organizations, there are many different types of support groups, ranging from those with hundreds of members and formal bylaws to three moms who meet for coffee once a week. Some groups deal only with the emotional aspects of the disease, while others may focus on education, advocacy, social opportunities, or crisis intervention. Some groups are facilitated by trained mental health practitioners, while others are self-help groups led by parents. And, naturally, as some members drop out and new families join, the needs and interests of the group may shift.

> *Our group is very informal. We do have two social workers who are considered the facilitators and are there as resource persons. We just talk about whatever anyone wants to discuss. Occasionally we have invited speakers in. I remember having a psychiatrist discuss stress management, and we also had a talk on therapeutic massage. We have formed close friendships from the group, and we still go twice a month, even though our daughter is a year off treatment and doing great. I think our presence comforts the new families.*

It is important to remember, however, that support group members are not infallible. One person may say something thoughtless or hurtful. Someone else may provide incorrect information. It is best to accept the support in the spirit in which it is given, but to always take any concerns or questions you have to your child's doctor or nurse practitioner.

Online support

Parents from small, isolated communities or who live a long distance from their treatment center may have a difficult time finding a support group in their area that fits their needs. This may also be true for single parents, parents who aren't able to attend support group meetings, or parents who prefer some anonymity. For these parents and families, finding emotional support is possible via the internet. Many online discussion groups exist for families dealing with childhood cancer. Such groups can provide parents with the understanding that only another parent of a child with cancer can give.

> *The support I have gained through online discussion groups is priceless. I have received a great deal of comfort from my participation in these groups. They have enabled me to connect with families from all over the world, many of whom are fighting the exact same disease. I have often come to my computer in the middle of the night, when everyone else in the house was asleep. I can express my fears at 3:00 a.m. and know someone will always be there to reassure me with the knowledge*

that they have felt these things, too. That's one of the most beautiful things about these groups. Someone is always there, even in the middle of the night.

• • • • •

How ironic that we subscribed to this list in a moment of panic, with a black cloud lined with despair lingering above. But now we can say we have lassoed cyberspace, and here, among new friends, we have found and we have shared love, hope, support, informative information, mutual stories, mutual questions, thoughtful and sincere answers, honesty, disagreement, pain, inspiration, fundraising, friendship, humor, and enjoyment, as well as understanding. This list reflects the roller coaster of life. Activity on this list enables individuals to place that initial black cloud in their back pocket, hold sunshine in their hand, and watch hope dance above.

• • • • •

I try not to be too active on the online support group because hearing lots of negative or scary things isn't helpful to me. I don't think people share enough of the positive. Clearly, everyone is different. But, for me, focusing on the positive is what's getting me though this. It's self-preservation for me to stay in my happy place.

• • • • •

I love the Rhabdo Kids group on Facebook, and I met a lot of parents at the very beginning. Finding other moms who understood was hugely helpful, and I was able to hear from other moms who had gone through exactly the same things as I was. I am very statistically driven and I wanted to know everything I could know as quickly as possible, and I couldn't find much else about this online.

To find online solid tumor discussion groups, parents can start by searching the lists on *www.acor.org, www.yahoogroups.com, or groups.google.com.* Parents or guardians of a child with cancer can join the popular Momcology discussion groups on Facebook by filling out an application at *www.momcology.org.* Some online discussion groups are not moderated, but many are carefully monitored by experienced peer-support leaders.

Support groups for children with cancer

Many pediatric hospitals have ongoing support groups for children with cancer. Often these groups are run by experienced pediatric social workers or psychologists who know how to balance having fun with sharing feelings. For many children, these groups are the only place where they feel completely accepted, and where most of the other kids are bald and have to take lots of medicine. The group is a place where children or adolescents can say how they really feel, without worrying that they are causing their parents more pain. Many children form wonderful and lasting friendships in peer groups.

Some support groups accommodate the whole family—the child or teen with cancer, siblings, and parents. The youngest children can play or do crafts with trained volunteers, while older kids have a chance to talk and share, and the parents can do likewise. This makes it possible for the whole family to go somewhere together and get to know other families on the childhood cancer journey.

Leah was 13 and her brother was 14 when she was diagnosed. The family support group was important for us, and they both liked talking to the parents as much as with the other teens. Having that group was Leah's main way to deal with her cancer. She was treated only with surgery, she wasn't on chemo and didn't have radiation, so she didn't look sick. But she had cancer and if it spread there wouldn't be much we could do, so we needed to be with other families.

Support groups for siblings

As part of the ongoing effort to provide family-centered care, some hospitals offer support groups to improve communication, education, and support for siblings. These groups give siblings a special place to have their voices and concerns heard and to interact with others going through the same experience. Some organizations provide support for siblings of children with cancer as part of their support groups for any child who has a family member (including a parent or grandparent) with cancer.

All four of my kids have been going to the support groups for over 7 years now. We have one group for the kids with cancer, which is run by a social worker. The siblings group is run by a woman who specializes in early childhood development. Both groups do a lot of art therapy, relaxation therapy, playing, and talking. They meet twice a month, and I will continue to take my children until they ask to stop. I think it has really helped all of them. We also have two teen nights out a year. All of the teenagers with cancer get together for an activity such as watching a hockey game or basketball game, or going bowling, to the movies, or out for pizza. They also see each other at our local camp for children surviving cancer (Camp Watcha-Wanna-Do) each year.

Parent-to-parent programs

Some pediatric hospitals, in conjunction with parent support groups, have developed parent-to-parent visitation programs. The purpose of these visits is for veteran parents to provide one-on-one support to parents of newly diagnosed children. The services provided by the visiting parent can be informational, emotional, or logistical. The visiting parent can offer many types of help, including the following:

• Empathize with the parents of newly diagnosed children

- Help notify family and friends
- Ease feelings of isolation
- Provide hospital tours
- Write down parents' questions for the medical team
- Offer advice about sources of financial aid
- Explain unfamiliar medical terms
- Be available by phone for any problems that arise
- Supply lots of smiles and hugs, and (above all) hope

Families of newly diagnosed children can ask whether the hospital has a parent-to-parent program. If not, you can ask to speak to the parent leader of the local support group. Often, this person will ask a parent to visit you at the hospital. Many parents are more than willing to visit, as they know only too well what those first weeks in the hospital are like. They are often accompanied by their child who has completed therapy and is rosy-cheeked and full of energy—a living beacon of hope.

> I am the parent consultant for our region. Among the services I provide are: meet with all newly diagnosed families; give a packet of information to each child or teen with cancer; continue to visit the families whenever they return to the hospital; educate families about the various local resources; provide moral support; stay with children during painful procedures if the parents can't; organize and present all of the school programs; liaison with schools for school reentry; organize and send out monthly reminders for parent support group meetings, child support group meetings, and sibling group meetings; send out birthday cards to kids on treatment; serve as activities director at the summer camp; and generally try to help out each family in any way possible.

Hospital resource rooms

Staff members in hospital resource rooms and libraries help families find information—electronic or print—about specific conditions.

> Patient resource rooms are wonderful places. They usually have basic information on your child's illness, listings of agencies and cancer organizations, online access, and a person available to answer questions and help get you started if you're unfamiliar with doing internet searches; it should be one of the first places you go.

Clergy and religious community

Religion is a source of strength for many people. Some parents and children find that their faith is strengthened by the cancer ordeal, while some begin to question their beliefs. Others, who have not relied on religion in the past, may now turn to it for solace.

Most hospitals have staff chaplains who are available for counseling, religious services, prayer, and other types of spiritual guidance. The chaplain often visits families soon after diagnosis and is available on an on-call basis. As with all types of emotional support, approaches that work well with one family may not be helpful for others.

> When our son was first diagnosed, we didn't feel as if we could discuss any of our fears with the hospital chaplain. I believe it was simply because our personalities didn't "click" well together, and we would feel more uncomfortable than anything else whenever he would visit. Several months into treatment, the hospital had a new chaplain, and we hit it off immediately. It was a joy to see him walking down the hall toward my son's room. He seemed to have a natural gift for making me feel better, even when things seemed to be crumbling around me.

· · · · ·

> When Shawn was first diagnosed, Father Ron came in, and we all just really bonded with him. Shawn was in the hospital most of the first year, so we had a chance to become very close. Often Shawn would ask for Father Ron before he had to have a painful procedure. Father Ron would talk to him, give him a little stuffed animal and a big hug, and then Shawn would feel better.

> When Shawn was very ill, I began to worry about the fact that he had never been baptized, and I asked Father Ron to baptize him in the chapel. We ended up going to his own little church nearby, and we had a private service with just godparents and family, because Shawn's counts were so low. It was a wonderful, special service; I'll never forget it.

Parents who were members of a church, synagogue, or mosque prior to their child's diagnosis may derive great comfort from the clergy and members of their religious community. Members of the congregation usually rally around the family, providing meals, babysitting, prayers, and support. Regular visits from clergy provide spiritual sustenance throughout the initial crisis and subsequent years of treatment.

> We belong to a religious study group that has met weekly for 8 years. In our group, during that time, there have been three cancer diagnoses and one of multiple sclerosis. We have all become an incredibly supportive family, and we share the burdens. I

cannot begin to list the many wonderful things these people have done for us. They consistently put their lives on hold to help. They fill the freezer, clean the house, support us financially, parent our children. They do the laundry covered with vomit. They quietly appear, help, then disappear. I can call any one of them at 3:00 a.m. in the depths of despair and find comfort.

Individual and family counseling

Cancer is a major crisis for even the strongest of families. Many parents find it helpful to seek out sensitive, objective mental health professionals to explore the difficult feelings—fear, anger, depression, anxiety, resentment, guilt—that cancer arouses.

Family dynamics undergo profound changes when a child is diagnosed with cancer. Seeking professional counseling for ways to adjust and manage is a sign of strength. When a child has cancer, problems may be too complex and family members may be too exhausted to manage on their own. Seeking professional help sends children a message that the parents care about what is happening to them and want to help face it together.

One of the first questions that arises is, "Who should we talk to?" There are numerous individuals in the cancer community who can make referrals and valuable recommendations, including the following:

- Other parents who have sought counseling

- Pediatricians

- Oncologists

- Nurse practitioners

- Social workers

- School psychologists or counselors

- Health department social workers

You can ask the people listed above for a short list of mental health professionals who have experience working with the issues your family is struggling with, for example, traumatized children, marital problems, stress reduction, or family conflicts. Generally, the names of the most well-respected clinicians in the community will appear on several of the lists.

The whole treatment experience put an enormous strain on our marriage. My wife has always been easy to excite, whereas I've always been very "laid back." There were moments when I was afraid that it would completely fall apart. Counseling

really helped. We managed to survive, and I think in many ways, it has even brought us closer together.

In making your decision, it helps to understand the various types of mental health professionals and their different levels of education and licensure. The following disciplines train individuals to offer psychological services:

- **Psychology (EdD, MA, PhD, PsyD).** Marriage and family psychotherapists have either a master's degree or a doctorate; clinical and research psychologists have a doctorate.

- **Social work (MSW, DSW, PhD).** Clinical social workers have either a master's degree or a doctorate in a program with a clinical emphasis.

- **Pastoral care (MA, MDiv, DMin, PhD, DDiv).** These are laypeople or clergy who receive specialized training in counseling.

- **Medicine (MD, RN, ARNP, PA).** Psychiatrists are medical doctors who completed a residency in psychiatry. Physician assistants and advanced practice nurses have the equivalent of master's level training in medicine and may have additional training in mental health. These three types of specialists are the only mental health professionals who can prescribe medications. In addition, some registered nurses (RNs) obtain postgraduate training in psychotherapy, but they cannot prescribe medications.

- **Counseling (MA).** In most states, individuals must have a master's degree and a year of internship before they can work as counselors.

You may hear all of the above professionals referred to as "counselors" or "therapists." The following designations refer to licensure by state professional boards, not academic degrees:

- LCSW (Licensed Clinical Social Worker)

- LSW (Licensed Social Worker)

- LMFCC (Licensed Marriage, Family, Child Counselor)

- LPC (Licensed Professional Counselor)

- LMFT (Licensed Marriage and Family Therapist)

These initials usually follow others that indicate an academic degree (e.g., PhD); if they do not, inquire about the therapist's academic training. Most states require licensure or certification in order for professionals to practice independently; unlicensed professionals are allowed to practice only under the supervision of a licensed professional (typically as an "intern" or "assistant" in a clinic or licensed professional's private practice).

When you are seeking a mental health professional, ask the professional how long she has been in practice. A licensed marriage and family therapist who has been seeing patients for 10 years may be a better clinician for your needs than a licensed psychologist or psychiatrist in his first year of practice.

> *Choosing to get therapy isn't easy. And going to a psychologist isn't easy. The only way to really work through the emotional pain is to look closely at it. Sometimes they ask hard questions. But it has been very beneficial for me. The best part about therapy is the person you are talking to is impartial. They aren't related to you, don't go to church with you, don't live with you, and have no connection to you or your situation. A totally unbiased perspective can be helpful when it feels like you are at the bottom of the pit, with no handholds, no ladder, but a shovel right beside you to help you dig deeper.*

> *If you decide to get counseling, do your research. I called and asked for references from a cancer help line and the social worker at the clinic. Then I talked to a couple of therapists before I decided which one to go with. She was willing to work with me on a payment schedule.*

Another method for finding a suitable counselor is to contact the American Association for Marriage and Family Therapy in Alexandria, VA, at (703) 838-9808, or online at *www.aamft.org.* This is a national professional organization of licensed/certified marriage and family therapists. It represents more than 50,000 therapists in the United States and Canada, and its membership also includes licensed clinical social workers, pastoral counselors, psychologists, and psychiatrists.

A psychiatrist who is the mother of a child with cancer offers a few thoughts:

> *Counseling helps, preferably from someone who regularly deals with parents of seriously ill children. This therapy is almost always short—although there may be some pre-cancer problems complicating the cancer issues that need to be hammered out.*

> *Antidepressants definitely have a role in the "so your child has cancer" coping strategy. They cannot make the diagnosis go away. They can improve concentration, energy, sleep, appetite, and the ability to get pleasure in life, and hope for the future—all of which you, your child with cancer, your spouse, and your other kids need you to have! They are not a magic bullet. They take 2 to 8 weeks to work, and you may need to change once before you get the right medication, but it can make all the difference.*

> *Also, nurture yourself. Take bubble baths. Buy flowers. Let people pamper you. Say yes when people offer to help. Redefine normal so things can be good again. Make time for yourself. Spend time with your spouse (even an hour to walk and talk and*

hold hands). Find time for your non-cancer kids, reveling in their accomplishments. Celebrate what is good about your life.

Pick out things that you feel are important to keep up with and do them. (For me it was laundry.) Ignore things that don't matter for the time being. (For me it was tidy rooms and cooking.) Make peace with your decisions and follow them.

To find a therapist, a good first step is to call two or three therapists who appear on several of your lists of recommendations. Following are some suggested questions to ask during your telephone interviews:

- Are you accepting new clients?

- What are your fees? Do you take insurance? Do you accept my insurance? Do you bill the insurance company directly?

- Do you charge for an initial consultation?

- What training and experience do you have working with ill or traumatized children?

- How many years have you been working with families?

- What is your approach to resolving the problems families develop from trauma? Do you use a brief or long-term approach?

- What evaluation and assessment procedures will be used to define the problem?

- How and when will treatment goals be set?

The next step is to make an appointment with one or two of the therapists you think might best address your needs. Be honest about the fact that you are interviewing several therapists prior to making a decision. The purpose of the introductory meeting is to see whether you feel comfortable with the therapist. After all, credentials do not guarantee that a given therapist is a good fit for you. Compatibility, trust, and a feeling of genuine caring are essential. It is worth the effort to continue your search until you find a good match.

I called several therapists out of desperation about my daughter's withdrawal and violent tantrums. I made appointments with two. The first I just didn't feel comfortable with at all, but the second felt like an old friend after 1 hour. I have been to see her dozens of times over the years, and she has always helped me. I wasn't interested in theory; I wanted practical suggestions about how to deal with the behavior problems. My 8-year-old daughter asked why I was going to see the therapist, and I said that Hilda was a doctor, but instead of taking care of my body, she helped care for my feelings.

. . . . .

*We went into family therapy because every member of my family experienced misdi-
rected anger. When they were angry, they aimed it at me—the nice person who took
care of them and loved them no matter what. But I was dissolving. I needed to learn
to say "ouch," and they needed to learn other ways to handle their angry feelings.*

If your child is going to go to a therapist, he needs to be prepared, just as he would be
for any appointment. Following are several parents' suggestions about how to prepare
your child:

- If you are bringing your child in for therapy, explain why you think talking to an
  objective person might benefit him.

- Older children should be involved in the process of choosing a counselor. Younger
  children's likes and dislikes should be respected. If your child does not get along well
  with one counselor, change counselors.

- Make the experience positive (e.g., describe the therapist as "the talking doctor").

- Reassure young children that the visit is for talking, drawing, or playing games, not
  for anything that is painful.

  *In the beginning of treatment, my son had terrible problems with going to sleep
  and then having nightmares, primarily about snakes. We took him to a counselor,
  who worked with him for several weeks and completely resolved the problem. The
  counselor had him befriend the snake, talk to it, and explain that it was keeping him
  awake. He would tell the snake, "I want you to stop bothering me because I need to
  go to sleep." The snake never returned.*

- Ask the therapist to explain the rules of confidentiality to both you and your child. Do
  not quiz your child after a visit to the therapist.

  *David had a very difficult time dealing with his brother's cancer. Realizing that we
  were unable to provide him with the help he needed, we sought professional help for
  him. I think the reason he feels so comfortable with his therapist is that he is aware
  of the rules of confidentiality. After his sessions, I'll always ask him how it went.
  Sometimes he'll just grin and say it was fine, and other times he might share a little
  of his conversation with me. I never push or question him about it. If it is something
  he needs to discuss, I wait until he decides to broach the subject.*

- Make sure your child does not think she is being punished; assure her that therapists
  help both adults and children understand and deal with feelings.

- Go yourself for individual or family counseling or to support group meetings. You not
  only will be taking care of yourself, but you will also be a good role model for your
  children.

Some other types of therapy used to help children with cancer, or their siblings, are music therapy (*www.musictherapy.org*), art therapy (*www.arttherapy.org*), and dance therapy (*www.adta.org*).

In *Armfuls of Time*, psychologist Barbara Sourkes quotes Jonathan, a boy with cancer, who told her, "Thank you for giving me aliveness." She discusses the importance of psychotherapy for children with a life-threatening illness:

> *Even when life itself cannot be guaranteed, psychotherapy can at least "give alive-ness" to the child for however long that life may last. Through the extraordinary challenges posed by life-threatening illness, a precocious inner wisdom of life and its fragility emerges. Yet even in the struggle for survival, the spirit of childhood shines through.*

Camps

Summer camps for children with cancer, and often their siblings, are becoming increasingly popular. These camps provide an opportunity for children with cancer and their siblings to have fun, meet friends, and talk with others in the same situation. Counselors are usually cancer survivors and siblings of children with cancer, or sometimes oncology nurses and resident physicians. At these camps, children can have their concerns addressed in a safe, supportive environment that is supervised by experts. Camps provide a carefree time away from the sadness and stress at home or from the all-too-frequent hospital visits.

> *Of all the ways to get support, I think the camp really helps the most. You are all there together for enough time to break down the barriers. Although camp does not focus on cancer, many times we really got down to talking about how we really felt. I have been a counselor at the camp for eight summers now. Most of the campers know that I relapsed three times and I'm doing great many years later. They see the many other long-term survivors who are counselors, and it gives them what they need the most—hope. The best support is meeting survivors, because nobody else truly understands.*

· · · · ·

> *Caitlin went to camp, and this was a dream come true for her. As we pulled into the parking lot, she exhaled a deep breath and said, "I made it. I am finally normal!"*

· · · · ·

> *I made Leah go to teen camp for whitewater rafting, and she found her support community there. She went every time she could after that, including a D.C. advocacy trip with her camp group that taught her to speak up for herself in so many ways.*

She likes mentoring other people because she needed other people to talk to when she was diagnosed.

Some camps are set up to accommodate not only the child who has undergone treatment, but also their siblings and parents. Many other camps offer separate weeklong camping experiences just for siblings. Appendix B, *Resource Organizations*, contains a short list of camps with contact information. To view a comprehensive list, visit *www.acor.org/ped-onc/cfissues/camps.html*.

It's like your psyche has been hit by a truck. Some days the pain is worse than others. Some days your threshold is stronger than others, but allow yourself the help that is available to get back to stable. Take it from me—it is next to impossible to pull from a dry well. Unlike children, we can't temper tantrum ourselves out of our feelings, we can't rant and scream and stomp our feet at the unfairness of it all. We can't just sit in momma's arms and have a hug and feel better. We have to handle it with an attitude and the responsibility that is expected of being adult. And we have to be a nurse, teacher, mom, emotional measuring stick for our kids, care for the marriage, pay the bills, and, oh yeah, don't forget about ourselves—all at the same time. It's just far too much. Say "Yes" to yourself, and your needs—get help when you need it. Other things that I found helpful were:

- *Saying "No," "No, thank you," and "I'll take that into consideration when I make my decision"*

- *Saying "Yes," "Yes, please, that would be a great help," and "Sure, if you could drop off a lasagna or pick up some milk on your way over that would be great"*

- *Writing in a journal*

- *Taking a retreat weekend*

- *Playing cards with the girls*

- *Counseling (on occasion with priest, psychologist, social worker)*

- *Having movie night with my sisters (usually a comedy—you are allowed to laugh)*

- *Treating myself to an inside-and-out car wash*

- *Allowing myself to "cry in my cornflakes," then getting up, splashing some cold water on my face and getting on with the day*

- *Enjoying a glass of wine, a candle, and Andrea Boccelli*

- *Gardening*

- *Having coffee with a friend*

- *Helping someone else who is in worse shape than I am*

- *Talking with other cancer kid moms about cancer kid family stuff*

- *Talking with non-cancer kid moms about non-cancer family stuff (the kids bickering, too much housework, the latest magazine, and what the women in it are wearing)*

- *Declaring the next 5 minutes as "get the crazies out" time, and tickling, dancing silly, and playing "make me laugh" (you know you're losing it when you do this, and no one else is home)*

- *Going out with my husband (Even if I had to drag him, we always enjoyed the evening in spite of ourselves)*

And anything else I deemed necessary to help me get through it.

Chapter 24

Nutrition

NOW, MORE THAN EVER, it is important for your sick child to eat balanced, healthful, and energy-packed meals. Yet the reality is that the eating habits of children with solid tumors often go haywire. Although your child's body needs added energy to metabolize medications and repair the damage to healthy cells caused by chemotherapy and radiation, those same treatments can wreak havoc on your child's appetite and taste sensations. This chapter discusses eating problems, explains good nutrition, suggests ways to pack extra calories into small servings, and offers tips about how to make food more appealing to children undergoing treatment.

How treatment affects eating

Eating is tremendously affected by chemotherapy, radiation, and stem cell transplants. Listed below are several common side effects of treatment that often prevent good eating. Other side effects that affect eating—nausea, vomiting, diarrhea, constipation, and mouth and throat sores—are covered in detail in Chapter 16, *Common Side Effects of Treatment*. In addition, radiation to the head or neck can change the way food tastes, making previously loved foods bland or undesirable.

Loss of appetite

Loss of appetite is one of the most common problems associated with cancer treatment. Children suffering from nausea and vomiting, diarrhea or constipation, altered sense of smell and taste, mouth sores, and other unpleasant side effects understandably do not feel hungry. Loss of appetite is most pronounced during the intensive periods of treatment. If your child loses more than 10 to 15 percent of her body weight, she may need to be fed intravenously or by nasogastric tube. Sometimes this can be avoided if parents learn how to increase calories in small amounts of food.

> *My son looked like a skeleton several months into his protocol. I used to dress him in "camouflage" clothes—several layers thick. This kept him warm and prevented stares.*

In addition to simple loss of appetite, your child may experience a side effect of chemotherapy called early filling. This means the child has a sense of being full after only a few bites of food. If your child is suffering from early filling and only eats when hungry, she may begin losing weight and become malnourished.

Lactose intolerance

Lactose intolerance is when the body cannot absorb the sugar (lactose) contained in milk and other dairy products. Both antibiotics and chemotherapy can cause lactose intolerance in some children. The part of children's intestines that breaks down lactose stops functioning properly, resulting in gas, abdominal pain, bloating, cramping, and diarrhea when dairy products are ingested. If your child develops lactose intolerance, it is important to talk to a nutritionist to learn about low-lactose diets and alternate sources of protein. The following are suggestions for parents of children with lactose intolerance:

- Add special enzyme tablets or drops to dairy products to make them more digestible for children with lactose intolerance. Some of these products are over-the-counter additives, but others require a prescription. Discuss these additives with the oncologist before giving them to your child.

- Children who cannot tolerate the lactose in cow's milk often can manage acidophilus milk, soy milk, rice milk, almond milk, goat's milk, or lactose-free milk. These are easier to digest and come in a variety of flavors.

- Remember that milk is a common ingredient in other foods, such as bread, candy, processed meats, and salad dressings. Read ingredient lists carefully.

- If your child cannot tolerate any dairy products, add calcium to his diet by serving canned salmon, sardines, spinach and other green leafy vegetables, or calcium-fortified fruit juices. Consult your child's oncologist and nutritionist about calcium supplements. Many children like the taste of a chewy calcium supplement called Viactiv®, which is available at most drug stores.

> My daughter Lilly is severely lactose intolerant, but she can eat hard, aged cheese and dairy-free, vegan products that taste like cheese. I buy vegetarian cheese/cream cheese, and make her grilled cheese sandwiches with Swiss cheese, as she wants to eat nothing but cheese. You can even get pizza made with vegetarian cheese, which melts like regular cheese.

Altered taste and smell

One common reason children on treatment do not eat is because, for them, food has no taste or tastes bad. If food tastes bland to your child, try serving spicy cuisines, such as Italian, Mexican, or Greek foods.

Chemotherapy often causes foods, particularly red meats, to taste bitter and metallic. If that happens, avoid using metal pots, pans, and utensils, which can magnify the metallic taste. Serve your child's food with plastic knives, forks, and spoons. You can also replace red meat with tofu, pork, chicken, turkey, eggs, and dairy products.

For some children, taste returns to normal after radiation; for others, it returns after treatment ends. And for a few children, it takes years before some foods taste pleasant again.

What kids should eat

A healthy diet includes sufficient calories to ensure a normal rate of growth; fuels the body's efforts to repair and replace healthy cells; and provides the energy the body needs to break down the various chemotherapy drugs given and excrete their byproducts. Over the time that chemotherapy is being administered, maintaining weight is a higher priority than a balanced diet. Research shows that well-nourished children can tolerate more treatment with fewer side effects, recover faster from treatment, and maintain weight better.

When the body becomes malnourished, body fat and muscle decrease. This leads to weakness, lack of energy, weight loss, a decreased ability to digest food, and a diminished ability to fight infection. These health issues sometimes require a reduction in the dose of chemotherapy drugs.

To keep your child's body well-nourished, foods from all six basic food groups are needed. The groups are (1) meat and other proteins; (2) dairy products; (3) bread and cereal; (4) fruits; (5) vegetables; and (6) fats and sweets. Children on chemotherapy also benefit from a higher than average intake of fats, which add needed calories.

Examples of foods contained in each group are listed below, with a small child's serving size in parentheses beside each food. Consult a nutritionist to determine the serving size that is appropriate for your child.

Meat and other proteins (two or three servings per day)

Meat (1 ounce)	Eggs (1)
Fish (1 ounce)	Peanut butter (2 tbsp.)
Poultry (1 ounce)	Dried beans, cooked ($1/2$ cup)
Cheese (1 ounce)	Dried peas, cooked ($1/2$ cup)

These foods provide protein, which helps build and maintain body tissues, supply energy, and form enzymes, hormones, and antibodies. Some typical 1-ounce servings of

meat and meat substitutes are: a meatball 1 inch in diameter, a 1-inch cube of meat, one slice of bologna, a 1-inch cube of cheese, or one slice of cheese.

Dairy products (two or three servings per day)

Milk ($^1/_2$ cup)	Tofu ($^1/_2$ cup)
Cheese (1 ounce)	Custard ($^1/_2$ cup)
Ice cream ($^1/_2$ cup)	Yogurt ($^1/_2$ cup)

Dairy products provide calcium, vitamin D, and protein, which are necessary for bone growth and strength.

Breads and cereals (six to 11 servings per day)

Bread ($^1/_2$ slice)	Dry cereal ($^1/_2$ cup)
Oatmeal ($^1/_2$ cup)	Granola ($^1/_2$ cup)
Cream of wheat ($^1/_2$ cup)	Cooked pasta ($^1/_2$ cup)
Graham crackers (1 square)	Saltines (3 squares)
Rice ($^1/_2$ cup)	Potatoes (1 baked)

Breads and cereals supply vitamins, minerals, fiber, and carbohydrates. Try to use only products made with whole wheat flour and limited sugar to get more nutrients per serving. One sandwich made with two slices of bread provides four servings of this food group.

Fruits (two to four servings per day)

Fresh fruit (1 medium piece)	Dried fruits ($^1/_4$ cup)
Canned fruit ($^1/_4$ cup)	Fruit juice ($^1/_2$ cup)

Fruits provide vitamins, minerals, and fiber. Fruits can be camouflaged by puréeing them with ice cream or sherbet in the blender to make a tasty milkshake or smoothie, or by adding them to cookie and muffin recipes.

Vegetables (three to five servings per day)

Raw vegetables ($^1/_4$ cup)	Cooked vegetables ($^1/_4$ cup)

Vegetables, like fruit, are excellent sources of vitamins, minerals, and fiber. If your child does not want vegetables, they can be grated or puréed and added to soups or spaghetti sauce. If you own a juicer, add a vegetable to fruits being juiced. There are also many brownie, cake, bread, and muffin recipes that use vegetables that cannot be tasted, such as zucchini bread, brownies with spinach, carrot cake, and veggie muffins.

Fats and sweets (several servings per day)

Butter or oil	Nuts
Mayonnaise	Whipped cream
Peanut butter	Avocado
Meat fat (in gravy)	Olives
Ice cream	Chocolate

Although the food pyramid calls for fats to be used sparingly, higher consumption of fats is needed for children being treated for cancer. Experiment to find the fats your child enjoys eating and serve them frequently.

Making eating fun and nutritious

In some homes, mealtimes turn into battlegrounds, with worried parents resorting to threats or bribery to get their child to eat. Parents rarely win these battles—eventually they give in, exhausted and frustrated, and serve the sick child whatever she will eat (often to the dismay of the siblings who still have to eat their vegetables). The next several sections are full of methods used successfully by many parents to make mealtimes both fun and nutritious.

How to make eating more appealing

Many children are finicky eaters at the best of times. Cancer and its treatment can make eating especially difficult. Here are some general suggestions for making eating more appealing for your child:

- Give your child small portions throughout the day rather than three large meals. Feed your child whenever she is hungry.

- Make mealtimes pleasant and leisurely.

- Rearrange eating schedules to serve the main meal at the time of day when your child feels best. If he wakes up feeling well most days, make a high-protein, high-calorie breakfast.

- Do not punish your child for not eating.

- Set a good example by eating a large variety of nutritious foods.

- Have nutritious snacks available at all times. Carry them in the car, to all appointments, and in backpacks for school.

- Serve fluids between meals, rather than with meals, to keep your child from feeling full after only a few bites of food.

- Limit the amount of less nutritious foods in the house. Potato chips, corn chips, soda, and sweets with large amounts of sugar will fill your child up with empty calories.

- If your child is interested, include her in making a grocery list, shopping for favorite foods, and food preparation.

Make mealtimes fun

Here are some suggestions for making mealtime more fun:

- Try to take the emphasis off the need to eat food "because it's good for you." Focus instead on enjoying each other's company while sharing a meal. Encourage good conversation, tell stories and jokes, and perhaps light some candles.

- Make one night a week "restaurant night." Use a nice tablecloth and candles, allow the children to order from a menu, and pretend the family is out for a night on the town.

- Because any change in setting can encourage eating, consider having a picnic on the floor occasionally. Order pizza or other takeout, spread a tablecloth on the floor, and have an in-home picnic. One parent even sent lunch out to the treehouse.

> My son enjoyed eating in different places around the house and seemed to eat more when he was having fun. I sometimes fed the kids on their own picnic table outdoors in good weather, and at the same picnic table in the garage during the winter. They were thrilled to wear their coats and hats to eat. Occasionally I would let them eat off TV trays while watching a favorite program or tape.

- Some families have theme meals, such as Mexican, Hawaiian, or Chinese. They use decorations, wear costumes, and cook foods with exotic spices.

- Some children seem to eat more if food is attractively arranged on the plate or is decorated in humorous ways. Preschoolers enjoy putting a smiley face on a casserole using strips of cheese, nuts, or raisins. Sandwiches can be cut into funny shapes using knives or cookie cutters.

> My daughter liked to have food decorated. For example, we would make pancakes look like a clown face by using blueberries for eyes, a strawberry for a nose, orange slices for ears, etc. She also enjoyed eating brightly colored food, so we would add a drop of food coloring to applesauce, yogurt, or whatever appealed to her.

How to serve more protein

Because many children cannot tolerate eating meat while on chemotherapy, below are suggestions for increasing protein consumption:

- Add 1 cup of dried milk powder to a quart of whole milk, then blend and chill. Use this extra-strength milk for drinking and cooking.

- Use extra-strength milk (above), whole milk, evaporated milk, or cream instead of water to make hot cereal, cocoa, soup, gravy, custards, or puddings.
- Add powdered milk to casseroles, meat loaf, cream soups, custards, and puddings.
- Add chopped meat to scrambled eggs, soups, and vegetables.
- Add chopped, hard-boiled eggs to soups, salads, sauces, and casseroles.
- Add grated cheese to pizza, vegetables, salads, sauces, omelets, mashed potatoes, meat loaf, and casseroles.
- Serve bagels, English muffins, hamburgers, or hot dogs with a slice of cheese melted on top.
- Spread peanut butter on toast, crackers, and sandwiches. Dip fruit or raw vegetables into peanut butter for a quick snack.
- Spread peanut butter or cream cheese onto celery sticks or carrots.
- Serve nuts for snacks, and mix nuts into salads and soups.
- Serve yogurt and granola bars for extra protein. Top pie, Jell-O®, pudding, or fruit with ice cream or whipped cream.
- Use dried beans and peas to make soups, dips, and casseroles.
- Use tofu (bean curd) in stir-fried vegetable dishes.
- Add wheat germ to hamburgers, meat loaf, breads, muffins, pancakes, waffles, and vegetables, and use it as a topping for casseroles.

Ways to boost calories

Many parents have ingrained habits about serving only low-fat meals and snacks. While your child is on chemotherapy, your mission is to find ways to add as many calories as possible to your child's food. Here are some suggestions:

- Add butter to hot cereal, eggs, pasta, rice, cooked vegetables, mashed potatoes, and soups.
- Use melted butter as a dip for raw vegetables and cooked seafood such as shrimp, crab, and lobster.
- Use sour cream to top meats, baked potatoes, and soups.
- Add mayonnaise or sour cream when making hamburgers or meat loaf.
- Use cream instead of milk over cereal, pudding, Jell-O®, and fruit.
- Make milkshakes, puddings, and custards with cream instead of milk.
- Serve your child whole milk (not 2% or skim milk).

- Sauté vegetables in butter.

- Serve bread hot so it will absorb more butter.

- Spread bagels, muffins, or crackers with cream cheese and jelly or honey.

- Make hot chocolate with cream and add marshmallows.

- Add granola to cookie, bread, and muffin batters. Sprinkle granola on ice cream, pudding, and yogurt.

- Serve meat and vegetables with sauces made with cream and pan drippings.

- Add dried fruits to recipes for cookies, breads, and muffins.

Nutritious snacks

Try to always bring a bag of nutritious snacks whenever you leave home with your child. This allows you to feed her whenever she is hungry and avoid stopping for non-nutritious junk food. Examples of healthful snacks include:

- Apples or applesauce

- Baby food

- Breakfast bars

- Buttered popcorn

- Celery sticks filled with with cheese or peanut butter

- Cookies made with wheat germ, oatmeal, granola, fruits, or nuts

- Cereal

- Crackers with cheese, peanut butter, or tuna salad

- Dips made with cheese, avocado, butter, beans, or sour cream

- Dried fruit such as apples, raisins, apricots, or prunes

- Fresh fruit

- Granola mixed with dried fruit and nuts

- Muffins

- Nuts

- Peanut butter on crackers or whole wheat bread

- Pizza

- Puddings

- Protein bars

- Sandwiches with mayonnaise or butter
- Vegetables such as carrot sticks or broccoli florets
- Snacks that you can carry in a small cooler with ice packs are:
- Ice cream made with real cream
- Yogurt, regular or frozen
- Cheese
- Chocolate milk
- Cottage cheese
- Hard-boiled and deviled eggs
- Juice made from 100 percent fruit
- Milkshakes made with whole milk or cream
- Fruit smoothies made with frozen fruit, sherbet, or ice cream

Vitamin supplements

The nutritional needs of kids with cancer are higher than other children's, yet kids on treatment often eat less food. Most children and teens being treated for cancer are unable or unwilling to eat the variety of foods necessary for good health. In addition, damage to the digestive system from chemotherapy alters the body's ability to absorb the nutrients contained in the food your child does manage to eat. As a result, vitamin supplements are usually necessary.

> I gave my teenage daughter supplements of vitamins and some minerals. I also increased her vitamin intake by using the juicer every day. She always drank a big glass of fruit or vegetable juice, and I really think it helped her do as well as she has.

Vitamin supplements should only be given after consultation with your child's oncologist and nutritionist. Oversupplementation of some vitamins, folic acid for example, can make your child's chemotherapy less effective. But providing other vitamins can make the difference between a pale and listless child and one with bright eyes and more energy.

> Halfway through treatment, my daughter just looked awful. Her new hair began to thin out and break easily and her skin felt papery. I had been giving her a multivitamin and mineral tablet every day because her appetite was so poor, but it didn't seem to be enough. I talked to her doctor, then began to give her more of the antioxidant vitamins: betacarotene, E, and C. I bought the C in powder form, which effervesced when mixed with juice. She really liked her "bubble drinks." The betacarotene and

E she swallowed along with the rest of her pills. Within a few weeks her hair stopped falling out, her skin stopped peeling, and she felt better.

What kids really eat

This chapter has listed ideas for increasing calories and making food more appealing. What follows are accounts of what several kids really ate while on chemotherapy. You will notice how varied the list is, so experiment to see what your child will eat. Remember that children's tastes and aversions may change throughout treatment.

Judd craved chicken chow mein and fried rice takeout from a Chinese restaurant. He also loved Spaghetti-Os® and hot dogs.

• • • • •

I let Preston eat whatever tasted good to him, which was usually lots of potatoes and eggs. He liked spicy food (especially Mexican).

• • • • •

Katy typically only ate one food for days or weeks at a stretch. One time, she ate pesto sauce (made from olive oil, garlic, Parmesan cheese, and basil leaves) on pasta for every meal for weeks. She also went through a spicy barbecue sauce phase, in which she wouldn't eat any food unless it was completely immersed in sauce. She ate no fruits, vegetables (except potatoes), or meat for the entire period of treatment. She ate mostly cereal and beans when she was feeling well, and mostly puréed baby food when she was really sick.

• • • • •

In the beginning, when Meagan lost so much weight, we snuck Polycose® (a powdered nutritional supplement) into everything. She finally got stuck on cans of mixed nuts. They are high calorie and were instrumental in putting back on the weight. She also craved capers and would eat them by the tablespoonful.

• • • • •

All Brent asks for are "peanut butter and jelly sandwiches, cut in fours, no crusts, with Fritos." The only fruit he has eaten for 3 years is an occasional banana, and he eats no vegetables. He always ate everything before his diagnosis at age 6.

• • • • •

The doctor told me to keep Kim on a low-salt, low-folic-acid diet. She wouldn't eat anything, so he eventually said he didn't care what she ate, as long as she ate. She liked Spaghetti-Os®, Chick-fil-A® nuggets, Chick-fil-A® soup, and McDonald's® sausage and pancakes.

All Carl ate was dry cereal, dry waffles, oatmeal, and bacon. He ate no other meat or vegetables throughout treatment, but did drink milk. I thought that he would never be healthy, but he's 15 now (diagnosed when 2), eats little junk food, never gets sick, and looks great.

Dietitian/nutritionist

It can be very helpful to consult with the hospital nutritionist to get more information and ideas about how to add more protein, calories, and vitamins/minerals to your child's diet. You can also consult with a private registered dietitian nutritionist (RDN) who has experience helping children with cancer. The Academy of Nutrition and Dietetics (*www.eatright.org*) is the country's largest group representing registered nutrition professionals; on its website, you can search for an RDN in your area.

I had two quite different experiences with hospital nutritionists. At the children's hospital, I couldn't get the doctors concerned about my daughter's dramatic weight loss. She was so weak she couldn't stand, and her muscles seemed to be wasting away. I finally asked them to please send in a nutritionist. A very young woman came in and talked to me about the major food groups. I felt my cheeks begin to flush, and my eyes glistened as I said, "I know what she is supposed to eat; I need to know how I can make her want to eat." I must have sounded a bit crazy, because she just handed me a booklet and backed out the door.

The next week when my daughter began her radiation, the radiation nurse took one look at her and called the nutritionist right down. This nutritionist was very warm and caring. She helped me understand that I needed to think fat, protein, and calories, and she gave me lots of practical suggestions on how to boost calories. I think that she probably saved my daughter from tube feedings.

Parent advice

Several parents whose children have finished treatment offer the following suggestions about how to handle the inevitable eating problems of children on therapy.

Doctors sometimes reassure parents by saying, "His appetite will return to normal." Don't be surprised if this does not happen until long after the most intensive parts of treatment are completed.

. . . . .

Let your child control what type of food and how much he wants. In the beginning, any food is good food.

. . . . .

Buy a juicer and use it every day. This was the only way we got any fruits or vegetables into our daughter. Make apple juice and sneak in a carrot. Sometimes we would make the juice, then blend it in the blender with ice cubes to make an iced drink, which we would serve with a straw.

. . . . .

I solved my daughter's salt cravings by buying sea salt and letting her dip french fries in it once a week. For some reason, that satisfied her and stopped her from begging for regular table salt at every meal.

. . . . .

One magic word: butter, butter, butter. We would make Maddie peanut butter and jelly sandwiches with a layer of butter on each side of the bread first. Milkshakes are great and Häagen Dazs® ice cream has the highest fat content. We also went to an "eat when she's hungry" mode. It was definitely more relaxing.

. . . . .

Take good care of yourself by eating well. We are all under tremendous stress and need good nutrition. I gave my daughter healthy foods and glasses of juiced fresh fruits and vegetables while I was living on lattés (a coffee drink). I now have breast cancer and wish that I had eaten well during my daughter's treatment.

. . . . .

There is reason for hope. My daughter ate almost nothing while on treatment. After treatment ended, she ate more food, but still no variety. She didn't turn the corner until a year off treatment, but now she is gradually trying new foods, including fruits and vegetables again. I'm glad I never made an issue of it.

Commercial nutritional supplements

Many children cannot tolerate solid food or can only eat small amounts each day. Liquid supplements can help provide the necessary calories. The following are some supplements that can be purchased at pharmacies or grocery stores. If you are unable to locate a particular brand, your pharmacist may be able to order it for you:

• **Boost Kids Essential®.** High in calcium and formulated for kids ages 1 to 10. Flavors are chocolate, strawberry, and vanilla. (Nestle)

- **Citrotein®**. Orange-flavored powder that is added to water or juice. (Doyle Pharmaceutical)

- **Ensure®**. Lactose-free liquid. Flavors are chocolate, vanilla, black walnut, coffee, butter pecan, banana, and strawberry. Other formulas have high protein or extra fiber. (Ross Laboratories)

- **Ensure Plus®**. Concentrated liquid. (Ross Laboratories)

- **Enrich®**. Lactose-free liquid with fiber. (Ross Laboratories)

- **Instant Breakfast®**. Powder that is added to milk. Variety of flavors. (Carnation)

- **Isocal®**. Lactose-free, vanilla-flavored liquid. (Mead Johnson)

- **Kindercal®**. Lactose-free liquid in vanilla and chocolate flavors. Formulated for children. (Mead Johnson)

- **Myoplex® Nutrition Shake**. A liquid that is added to water and a little ice and mixed in a blender. Flavors include orange, piña colada, banana cream pie, chocolate, strawberry, and vanilla. (EAS, Inc.)

- **Nutren Junior®**. Vanilla-flavored liquid formulated for children ages 1 to 10 who need nutritional support. It comes with or without added fiber. (Nestle)

- **PediaSure®**. Liquid designed for children ages 2 to 16 that can be swallowed or delivered through an NG tube. (Abbott Nutrition)

- **Polycose®**. Liquid or powder. Powder is added to milk, juice, gravy, or soups. Adds carbohydrates for extra calories. (Ross Laboratories)

- **Sustacal®**. Lactose-free liquid. Flavors are chocolate, vanilla, eggnog, and strawberry. It also comes in a high-protein or extra-fiber formula. (Mead Johnson)

- **Sustacal Pudding®**. Flavors are chocolate, vanilla, and butterscotch. (Mead Johnson)

- **Sustacal HC®**. Concentrated liquid. Flavors are vanilla, chocolate, strawberry, and eggnog. (Mead Johnson)

We tried all the high-calorie drinks: Pediasure® in three flavors, and Boost®. The one that Emily would drink is called Nutra/Shake® (tastes like melted ice cream and can also be eaten frozen). Of course Pediasure® and Boost® are available over the counter. We had to get Scandi-shake® (a powder that you mix with milk) at the hospital. I had to do some research to find the Nutra/Shake®. It comes frozen, and Kroger grocery stores carry it.

· · · · ·

We tried Ensure®, Sustacal®, and Carnation Instant Breakfast®. All were basically the same, with Carnation® being much more palatable. The other two have a bit of a

medicinal smell and taste to them. You can add calories by throwing it in a blender with ice cream, bananas, or strawberries. My other two non-cancer kids loved this stuff. Mandy would "sip" a tiny bit but would rather eat the spicy food: bologna, Polish sausage, or tomatoes drowning in Catalina dressing. Reese's® peanut butter cups were breakfast for a long time (7 grams of protein!).

Feeding by tube and IV

Sometimes, it becomes necessary to feed children intravenously or through a gastric (G-tube) or nasogastric (NG) tube. Although intravenous (IV) feeding and feeding by tube may require additional hospitalization, it helps if parents understand the benefits. As appetite and weight decrease, the child's ability to tolerate and recover from chemotherapy diminishes. The child becomes progressively weaker and his resistance to infection decreases. Infections and weakness may require interruptions in treatment. To prevent this scenario, most protocols require tube or IV feeding after 10 percent of body weight is lost. The two types of supplemental feeding are described below.

Total parenteral nutrition (TPN)

TPN, also known as hyperalimentation, is a form of IV feeding used to prevent or treat malnutrition in children who cannot eat enough to meet basic nutritional needs. Below are some of the many reasons why your child may require TPN:

- Severe mouth and throat sores that prevent swallowing

- Severe nausea and vomiting

- Severe diarrhea

- Inability to chew or swallow normally

- Loss of more than 10 percent of body weight

TPN ensures that your child receives all the protein, carbohydrates, fats, vitamins, and minerals she needs. TPN is administered through a central venous catheter, but children receiving TPN can also eat solids and drink fluids.

My daughter needed TPN for 2 weeks after her stem cell transplant. They told us ahead of time that it would be necessary, and they were right. She got terrible sores throughout her GI tract and couldn't drink or eat. They just hooked the TPN bag up to her Broviac®. After a couple of weeks, she started gingerly sipping small amounts of water and apple juice. For some reason, I just didn't worry about her eating. I assumed that when she could eat, she would. She was a robust eater before her illness, so I thought that would help. Before we left for home, she asked for a hospital pizza (yuck!) and ate a few bites. Her eating at home quickly went back to normal, although it took some time to regain the weight she lost.

In most cases, TPN is started in the hospital. Each day the concentrations of glucose, protein, and fat will be increased, and doctors will assess your child's tolerance for the mixture. Generally, TPN is given 8 to 12 hours per day, depending on your child's situation. The infusion may be delivered over the hours that work best for your family. For example, if your child attends school, overnight infusions will probably work best.

You can request a small portable infusion pump and backpack from a home care company so your child can go about his daily activities as usual. Your child's oncologist may need to write a letter to your insurance company to verify your child's malnutrition so this therapy will be covered.

Enteral nutrition

The doctor may recommend enteral feeding if your child requires supplemental nutrition and her bowel and intestines are still functioning well. Enteral feedings are preferred over IV, whenever possible. Enteral nutrition is feeding via a tube placed through the nose and into the stomach or small intestine (NG tube) or via a tube surgically placed directly into the stomach through the abdominal wall (G-tube). Nutritionally complete liquid formulas are delivered through the tube. Infrequent side effects of enteral nutrition are irritated throat, nausea, diarrhea, or constipation.

> Rachel (age 14) used a backpack to carry a G-tube pump and her bag of Ensure® with her when she went out. When chemo was over, she worked for about a month with a psychiatrist who used hypnotherapy to get her to start eating normally again. After about 3 months, she was eating everything she used to. The tube was removed, and the hole closed on its own.

· · · · ·

> My daughter found it almost impossible to eat. She said that apart from her stomach feeling sick, everything tasted bad, and she didn't want to put that food in her mouth because the taste made her feel worse. As an adult you can say to yourself, this is for my own good, and force yourself to eat, but not kids.

> When she had to get a nasogastric (NG) tube after she'd lost a third of her body weight, I felt nearly as bad as when she was first diagnosed. I believed that because she wasn't eating she had given up the will to live. I was a mess! The ward social worker gently pointed out to me that it was not my daughter's choice about whether to eat or not—it was entirely the fault of the chemo. When she got the NG tube, it was wonderful! She was able to get nutrition without forcing herself to eat when she really couldn't. And sure enough, once we got over the hurdle of that part of the treatment, she slowly regained her appetite again and we were able to wean her off the NG feeds. Four years later, she is still a very fussy eater—but I can live with that.

I feel good nutrition is very important to good health, but the reality of the situation with our child was that he hated anything nutritious when he was on chemotherapy. I could doctor it up, add the best toppings, make it look terrific, season it just right, and it would still be rejected. So I decided that since my son wasn't allowed to make any decisions in regard to the pills, treatments, tests, or hospital stays, he wouldn't be forced to eat everything nutritious if he didn't want to. Whether this was a right or wrong decision, I don't know. I just know that I served him a lot of processed foods during those years, and he's a healthy and happy boy 10 years later. After he was finished with chemotherapy, however, we did require that he eat healthier foods.

Chapter 25

Medical and Financial Record-keeping

KEEPING TRACK OF paper work—both medical and financial—is a trial for every parent of a child with cancer. But having accurate records can help prevent medical errors and reduce insurance overbillings. Having easy access to medical reports and properly organizing bills can also mean less time spent in conflicts with insurance companies and collection agencies. This chapter suggests a few ways for keeping both medical and financial records.

Keeping medical records

Think of yourself as someone with two sets of books, the hospital's and yours. If the hospital loses your child's chart or misplaces lab results, you will still have a copy. If your child's paper chart becomes a foot thick (or hundreds of pages in an electronic chart), you will still have your simple system that makes it easy to spot trends and retrieve dosage information. The following are suggested items that you should record:

- Dates and results of all lab work
- Dates and reports of all scans (e.g., CAT, MRI)
- Dates of chemotherapy, drugs given, and doses
- All changes in dosages of medicine
- Any side effects from drugs
- Any fevers or illnesses
- Dates of all scheduled and unscheduled hospitalizations
- Dates of all medical appointments and name(s) of the doctor(s) seen
- Dates for any procedures performed (both surgical and non-surgical)
- Dates of radiation therapy, including total dose delivered and areas treated
- Dates of diagnosis, completion of therapy, and recurrences (if any)

Keeping daily records of your child's health for months or years is hard work. But remember that your child will be seen by pediatricians, oncologists, residents, radiation therapists, lab technicians, nutritionists, psychologists, social workers, and physical, occupational, and speech therapists. Your records will help keep it all straight and help pull all the information together. Your records also will help you remember questions to ask, prevent mistakes, and notice trends. In short, your records will help the entire team provide your child with the best possible care.

I am the one handling all of the administrative duties for the family. We have learned when Kevin gets his MRI to ask the techs to make a copy for us right then and there. I have to keep copies of everything regarding Kevin's treatment and surgery, including pathology reports, second opinion consults, lab reports, etc. I now have copies of all MRI films, all of the hospital records, every report that was ever written, and all of the radiological reports.

The following sections describe several record-keeping methods parents have used successfully.

Journal

Keeping a journal in a notebook works extremely well for people who like to write. Parents make entries every day about all pertinent medical information and often include personal information such as their own feelings or memorable things their child said or did. Journals are easy to carry back and forth to the clinic, and journal entries can be written while waiting for appointments. One disadvantage is that journals can be misplaced.

Stephan's oncologist is kind of hard to communicate with. I learned early on to keep a journal of Stephan's appointments, drugs given, side effects, and blood counts. That way if I ever had to call the doctor I would have it right in front of me. I also recorded Stephan's temperature when his counts were low to keep track of infections.

In *You Don't Have To Die*, Geralyn Gaes writes of the value of keeping a journal:

*Some days my entries consisted of only a few words: "Good day. No problems."
Other times I had so many notes and questions to jot down that my handwriting spilled over into the next day's space. I must confess that I probably went overboard, documenting every minute detail of Jason's life down to what he ate for each meal. If he gets over this disease, I thought, maybe this information will be useful for cancer research.*

I'm not so sure I was wrong. Jason went 2 years without a blood transfusion, unusual for a child receiving such aggressive chemotherapy. Studying my journal, one of his

physicians remarked, "This kid eats more oatmeal than anybody I've ever seen."
Which was true. Jason wolfed it down for breakfast, after school, and before bedtime.
The doctor speculated, "Maybe that's why Jason's blood is so rich in iron and builds
back up so fast."

Many institutions give families a notebook that contains information about their child's cancer and treatment plan. Often, these notebooks have blank pages for recording blood cell counts.

Record-keeping—very important! My father came to the hospital soon after diag-
nosis and brought a three-ring binder and a three-hole punch. I would punch lab
reports, protocols, consent forms, drug information sheets, etc., and keep them in my
binder. A mother at the clinic showed me her weekly calendar book, and I adopted
her idea for recording blood counts and medications. Frequently the clinic's records
disagreed with mine as to medications and where we were on the protocol. I was very
glad that I kept good records.

Calendar

Many parents report great success with the calendar system. They buy a new calendar each year and hang it in a convenient place, such as next to the telephone. You can record counts on the calendar while talking on the phone to the nurse or lab technician and take the calendar with you to all appointments.

Each year I purchase a new calendar with large spaces on it. I write all lab results,
any symptoms or side effects, colds, fevers, and anything else that happens. I bring
it with me to the clinic each visit, as it helps immensely when trying to relate some
events or watch trends. I also use it like a mini-journal, recording our activities and
quotes from Meagan. Now that she's off treatment, I'm superstitious enough to still
bring it to our monthly checkups.

· · · · ·

I wrote the counts on a calendar or on little pieces of paper that got lost. But, to be
honest, I didn't keep the medical records very well. I'm upset with myself when I
think of it now.

· · · · ·

For a long time I was unorganized, which is very unlike the way I usually am. I
found that my usual excellent memory just wasn't working well. It all seemed to run
together, and I began to forget if I had given her all of her pills. Then I began using
a calendar for both counts and medications. I wrote every med on the correct days,
then checked them off as I gave them.

Blood cell count charts

Many hospitals supply folders containing photocopied sheets for record-keeping. Typically, they have spaces for the date, white blood cell count, absolute neutrophil count, hematocrit, platelet level, chemotherapy given, and side effects.

My record-keeping system was given to me by the hospital on the first day. We were given a notebook with information about the illness and treatment. Also included were charts that we could use to keep all the information about my child's blood work, progress, reactions to drugs, etc. While we were at the hospital we were able to get the information off one of the computers on our floor each afternoon. My notebook holds records and notes for 3 years. Perhaps I was being compulsive with my record-keeping, but it made me feel that I was part of the team working on bringing my boy back to health.

Tape or digital recorder

For parents who keep track of more information than a calendar can hold, and who find writing in a journal too time consuming, using a voice recording device works well. Small recording machines are inexpensive and can be carried in a pocket or purse. Most smartphones also can record. Digital devices can be downloaded to a flash drive or computer for storage. If you want to transcribe the recordings to a written record, there are programs such as Dragon Speak® that you can train to understand your voice, and that can be used to change your spoken word into a written document.

I started keeping a journal in the hospital, but I was just too upset and exhausted to write in it faithfully. A good friend who was a writer told me to use a tape recorder. It was a great idea and saved a lot of time. I could say everything that had happened in just a few minutes every day. I kept a separate notebook just for blood counts so I could check them at a glance.

Computer

For some parents, saving all medical records on the computer hard drive is a good option. Parents can print out bar graphs of the blood counts in relation to chemotherapy and quickly spot trends. You can also keep a running narrative of your thoughts, feelings, and concerns during your child's treatment. As with all other computer records, keep a backup copy on a flash drive or external hard drive.

At our hospital, the summary of counts for a given child can be formatted to print out as a "trend review," with each date printed out on the left side of the page and the various lab values in columns down the page. The system permits printouts from the very first blood draw if that is desired. Periodically, on slow days, I'll ask if I can have a trend review. Then I put it in my binder of records.

Keeping financial records

You will not need a calendar or journal for financial records, just a big, well-organized file cabinet. It is essential to keep track of bills and payments. Dealing with financial records is a major headache for many parents, but keeping good records can prevent financial catastrophe. Financial record-keeping is most important when families are covered by private medical insurance. The following are ideas about how to organize financial records:

- Have hanging files for hospital bills, doctor bills, all other medical bills, insurance explanation of benefits (EOBs), prescription receipts, tax-deductible receipts (e.g., tolls, parking, motels, meals), and correspondence.

- Whenever you open an envelope related to your child's medical care, file the contents immediately. Don't leave it on the desk or throw it in a drawer.

- Keep a notebook with a running log of all tax-deductible medical expenses, including the service, charge, bill paid, date paid, and check number.

- Do not pay a bill unless you have checked over each item listed to make sure the charge is correct.

- Start new files every year.

> To be honest, the paper trail really gets me down. I can only deal with the stacks every few months. I open things and make sure the insurance company is doing its part, and then I try to sort through and pay our part.
>
> • • • • •
>
> I started out organized, and I'm glad I did because the hospital billing was confusing and full of errors. I cleared out a file cabinet and put in folders for each type of bill and insurance papers. I filed each bill chronologically so I could always find the one I needed. I made copies of all letters sent to the insurance company and hospital billing department. I wrote on the back of each EOB [Explanation of Benefits] any phone calls I had to make about that bill. I wrote down the date of the call, the person's name who I spoke to, and what she said. It saved me a lot of grief.

Deductible medical expenses

It is estimated that families of children with cancer spend 25 percent or more of their income on items not covered by insurance. Examples of these expenses are gas, car repairs, motels, food away from home, health insurance deductibles, prescriptions, and dental work. Many of these items can be deducted from federal income tax. Often parents are too fatigued to go through stacks of bills at the end of the year to calculate their deductions. If a monthly total is kept in a notebook, then all that needs to be done at tax time is to add up the monthly totals.

The Internal Revenue Service (IRS) generally allows you to deduct any reasonable cost for procedures or expenses that are deemed by a doctor to be medically necessary. You may also deduct certain other expenses with proper documentation; some of the costs that are currently deductible include wheelchairs, wigs, acupuncture, psychotherapy and counseling, HMO fees, special education or tutoring costs for sick children, meals at the hospital, parking at the hospital, and transportation and lodging costs while your child is in the hospital.

To find out what can be deducted while your child is undergoing treatment, get IRS Publication 502 for the relevant tax year. You can download this publication from the IRS website at *www.irs.gov* or make a copy from a master form at your local library (ask a reference librarian where the IRS forms are kept). You can contact an IRS representative at (800) 829-1040, Monday through Friday.

Canadian families are able to deduct many of the same medical expenses as U.S. families. To find out what can be deducted in Canada, visit the Revenue Canada website at *www.cra-arc.gc.ca* and type in the search term "deductible medical expenses," or call (800) 959-8281.

If you keep a calendar, an easy way to keep track of tax-deductible items is to glue an envelope to the inside cover. Whenever you incur an expense that may be tax deductible (e.g., parking at the hospital), put the receipt in the envelope and file it when you get home.

Dealing with hospital billing

Unfortunately, problems with billing are common for parents of children with cancer. Here are two typical experiences:

> *Insurance was an absolute nightmare. It almost gave me a nervous breakdown. After all we go through with our children, to have to deal with the messed-up hospital billing was just too much.*

> *We would stack the bills up and try to go through them every 2 or 3 months. Our insurance was supposed to pay 100%, but the billing was so confusing that they refused to cover some things because it wasn't clear what they were being billed for. The hospital frequently double billed, especially for prescriptions. We just stopped getting our prescriptions there.*

> *We would call them to try to get the mess straightened out, but the billing department was just as confused as we were. They kept sending our account to collections. We did everything in our power to get it straight, but we never did.*

• • • • •

We had two distinctly different experiences at the two institutions we dealt with. The university hospital where my daughter received her radiation gave me a folder the first day. It included, among other things, a sheet from a financial counselor giving all the information needed for preventing and solving billing problems. I never needed to call her because the hospital billing was clear, prompt, and organized.

The children's hospital where my daughter was a frequent inpatient and clinic patient was another story altogether. They billed from three different departments, put charges from the same visit on different bills, frequently over-billed, continuously made errors, and constantly threatened to send the account to collections. I never spoke to the same billing clerk twice. It was a never-ending grind and a constant frustration.

It is impossible to prevent billing errors, but it is necessary to deal with them. Here are step-by-step suggestions for solving billing problems:

• Keep all records filed in an organized fashion.

• Check every bill from the hospital to make sure there are no charges for treatments not given or errors such as double billing.

• Check to see whether the hospital has financial counselors. If so, make contact early in your child's hospitalization. Counselors provide services in many areas, including help with understanding the hospital's billing system, understanding explanations of benefits, managing hospital/insurance correspondence, dealing with Medicaid, working out a payment plan, designing a ledger system for tracking insurance claims, and resolving disputes.

• If you find a billing error, immediately call the hospital billing department. Write down the date, the name of the person you talk to, and the plan of action.

I often couldn't even get through to the billing representative; I was just put on hold forever. Then I tried to discuss the problems with the director of billing, but she was never in. After about 20 phone calls, I finally said to her secretary, "You know, I have a desperately sick child here, and I've been as patient and polite as I can. What else can I do?" She said, "Honey, get irate. It works every time." I told her to put me through to somebody, anybody, and I would. She connected me to the person who mediates disputes, I got irate, and we went through all the bills line by line.

• If the error is not corrected on your next bill, call and talk to the billing supervisor. Explain the steps you have already taken and how you would like the problem fixed.

The hospital billing was so bad, and I had to call so often, that I developed a telephone relationship with the supervisor. I always tried to be upbeat, we laughed a lot, and it worked out. She stopped investigating every problem and would just delete the erroneous charge.

- If the problem is still not corrected, write a brief letter to the billing supervisor explaining the steps you have taken and requesting immediate action. Keep a copy of each letter that you write and all written responses.

- Every time you receive an Explanation of Benefits (EOB) from your insurance company, compare it to the hospital bill. Track down discrepancies.

- If you are inundated with a constant stream of bills and there are major discrepancies between the hospital charges and what is being paid for by your insurance, ask both the hospital billing department and your insurance company, in writing, to audit the account. Insist on a line-by-line explanation for each charge.

   Within 5 months of my daughter's diagnosis, the billing was so messed up that I despaired of ever getting it straight. When the hospital threatened to send the account to a collection agency, I took action. I wrote letters to the hospital and the insurance company demanding an audit. When both audits arrived, they were $9,000 apart. I met with our insurance representative, and she called the hospital, and we had a three-way showdown. We straightened it out that time, but every bill that I received for the duration of treatment had one or more errors, always in the hospital's favor.

- If you are too tired or overwhelmed to deal with the bills, ask a family member or friend to help. That person could come every other week, open and file all bills and insurance papers, make phone calls, write all necessary letters, and even scan your records into your computer for storage.

- Do not let billing problems accumulate. Your account may end up at a collection agency, which can quickly become a nightmare.

   Our insurance was constantly months behind in paying our bills to the Children's Hospital. The hospital sent our account to collections, despite my assurances that I was doing everything I could to get the insurance to pay. We were hounded on the phone constantly by the collection people, often until we were in tears. We finally just took out a second mortgage and paid off the hospital, but now I don't know if we will be reimbursed by insurance.

Not all stories are so grim. People who are in a single payer healthcare system, in some managed care systems, or on public assistance may never see bills. Many people with insurance encounter no problems throughout their child's treatment.

Our insurance paid 80% of everything, no questions asked, and always paid us within a month. People shouldn't have to worry about finances or their insurance program at a difficult time like this.

· · · · ·

We have a low income, so we are on the state plan. They give us coupons for each child, and we just hand over a coupon at each visit. I have never seen a bill.

· · · · ·

Although hospital billing was not ever perfect anywhere we went, we did have an absolutely great relationship with our regional HMO for 4 years. Whenever an out-of-area appointment was needed, I called the pediatrician to start their paperwork, then immediately let our insurance nurse coordinators know. We also kept in touch through phone calls and cards.

Coping with insurance

Finding one's way through the insurance maze can be a difficult task. However, understanding the benefits and claims procedures can help you get the bills paid without undue stress. The following sections outline some steps to help prevent problems with insurance.

Understand your policy

As soon as possible after diagnosis, read your entire insurance policy. Make a list of any questions you have about terms or benefits.

- Learn who the "participating providers" are under the plan and what happens if you see a non-participating provider. It is possible you will be penalized financially or that your claims may be denied if you go outside the network.

- Determine whether your physician needs to document specific requirements to obtain coverage for expensive or extended services.

  With our insurance, neuropsychological tests, outpatient occupational therapy, speech therapy, and physical therapy are covered, but the phrasing must be that it is a "medical necessity" due to diagnosis and treatments.

- Find out what your insurance copays are for different levels of service (e.g., office visit, outpatient surgery, outpatient testing).

- Find out what your outpatient prescription drug benefits are for generic and nongeneric drugs.

- Find out what your deductible is.

- Find out whether there is a point at which coverage increases to 100 percent.

- Determine whether there is a lifetime limit on benefits.

- Find out when a second opinion is required.

- Learn when you have to precertify a hospitalization or specialty consultation. Many insurance companies require precertification, even for emergencies.

- Determine whether your policy has benefits for counseling. If so, find out how many visits are covered and how much of the cost is covered.

- Find out the names of approved providers for home infusion supplies (e.g., IV medications, central venous catheter supplies, and home nutrition) and home nursing care. These are often separate companies. Determine policy coverage for these services.

> *We changed to a new pediatrician, and he asked me if I thought it would be easier on my son to have visiting nurses come to our home to do the chemotherapy injections and some blood work. Since my son had very low counts, it made a lot of sense not to have to go out. It also lessened his fears to be able to stay at home and have the same nurse come to do the procedures. It was a pleasant surprise to find these services covered by our insurance.*

Find a contact person

As soon as possible after diagnosis, call your insurance company and ask who will be handling your claims. Explain that there will be years of bills with frequent hospitalizations, and it would be helpful to deal with the same person each time. Some insurance companies may assign your child's account to a case manager who will review your child's plan of care in detail and make suggestions designed to make proper use of your policy benefits. Try to develop a cooperative relationship with your case manager, because she can really make your life easier. Also, your employer may have a benefits person who can operate as a liaison with the insurer.

> *My employee benefits representative was Bobbi. She was just wonderful. The hospital would send her copies of the bills at the same time they sent mine. Since I found so many errors, she would hold the bills a week until I called to tell her that they were correct before she paid them. She was very pleasant to deal with.*

Negotiate

Do not be afraid to negotiate with the insurance company over benefits. Often, your case manager may be able to redefine a service your child needs to allow it to be covered.

> *My husband works for a small city that contracts out health insurance. A year into our child's treatment, the contract was being renegotiated. He brought home a copy of the proposed contract, and I was horrified to see that they had halved the benefit for transplants, from $200,000 to $100,000. I called the members of the committee negotiating the contract, the union representative, the city insurance liaison, and the city attorney. I was very polite, but I told them that if my child needed a transplant, the new contract would bankrupt us. We would lose our home and have to sell all of our belongings to pay our part of the procedure. Then I called two transplant centers, and had them fax me the estimated cost of a routine transplant (about $220,000). I sent copies of the fax to everyone that I could think of, and followed it up with phone calls. They changed the transplant coverage in the new contract back to $200,000. One person can make a big difference.*

Challenging a claim

The key to obtaining the maximum benefit from your insurance policy is to keep accurate records and challenge any denied claims, sometimes more than once. Here are some tips for record-keeping.

- Make photocopies of everything you send to your insurance company, including claims and letters.

- Pay bills by check or credit card, and keep all your canceled checks and/or credit card monthly summaries of charges.

- Keep all correspondence you receive from billing companies and insurance.

- Write down the date, name of person contacted, and content of all phone calls concerning insurance.

- Keep accurate records of all medical expenses and claims submitted.

> *Talking to insurance people really hits a sore spot with me; right from the beginning of the call, there is a menu with many options to choose from, and it can take 10 minutes if you are lucky to get a real live person on the phone. I have, many times, asked for supervisors, demanded and insisted that expediency is necessary. I have learned to take the person's name, their title, and write down time and date on every conversation I have. It is a time-consuming job.*

Policy holders have the right to appeal a claim denied by their insurance company. The following are suggested steps to contest a claim:

- Keep original documents in your files and send photocopies to the insurance company with a letter outlining why the claim should be covered. Make sure to request a written reply and keep a copy of the letter for your records.

> We were making inquiries into hospice care, feeling it was time to explore that option. I found out that the only pediatric hospice provider in the state of Georgia was not on the preferred provider list. Our insurance company would pay for benefits, but at a reduced rate; not a good thing since the lifetime maximum for hospice care was $7,500. I felt like my only options were reduced pediatric care or full benefits using adult services. I wrote a letter of appeal stating that medically and ethically, neither of these were good choices. Well, we got a better outcome than I asked for. Not only will they cover the pediatric provider, but they have waived the lifetime maximum!

- Contact your elected representative to the U.S. Congress. All Senators and members of the House of Representatives have staff members who help constituents with problems. You can also contact your state insurance board with concerns and complaints.

> When I ran into insurance company problems, I wrote a letter to the insurance company detailing the facts, the decisions the insurance company made, and a logical explanation about why the procedure needed to happen. I also noted in the letter that a copy was going to our state insurance commissioner, and I sent both letters by certified mail. Within 2 days, the insurance company all of a sudden decided to cover the procedure. I later found out that the insurance commissioner's office started an investigation against them. Letters help, especially when sent by certified mail.

- If none of the above steps resolves the dispute, take your claim to small claims court (which does not require you to hire an attorney). You could also find an attorney who will represent you for free (called pro bono), or hire an attorney skilled in insurance matters to sue the insurance company.

It may not feel comfortable being so persistent, but sometimes it is necessary to ensure you get the support to which you and your child are entitled.

> When I finally got an advocate assigned for my child within our insurance company, I fretted to her one day that every single claim was initially rejected. She replied that the agents were trained to reject all claims the first two times they were submitted as a cost-saving strategy. She said, "Very few subscribers are tenacious enough to come back three times, so we save millions of dollars each year just because they give up."

Sources of financial assistance

Sources of financial assistance vary from state to state and town to town. To begin tracking down possible sources, ask the hospital social worker for assistance. In addition, some hospitals have community outreach nurses or case workers who may point out potential sources of assistance.

Hospital policy

If you are unable to pay your hospital bills, do not sell your house or let your account go to collections. Ask the hospital social worker to set up an appointment for you with the appropriate person to discuss the hospital policy for financial assistance. Many hospitals write off a percentage of the cost of care if the patient is uninsured or underinsured. You can also talk to the hospital about setting up a monthly payment plan.

Supplemental Security Income (SSI)

SSI is an entitlement program of the U.S. government that is based on family income and administered by the Social Security Administration. Recipients must be blind or disabled and have a low family income and few assets. Children with cancer qualify as disabled for this program, making some of them eligible for monthly aid if the family income and assets are low enough. To find out whether your child qualifies for SSI, contact your nearest Social Security field office.

> Our Katie was approved for SSI right away. It did take a large amount of preparation with the required paperwork. I researched and when I found a roadblock, I asked the social security people what I needed to overcome these obstacles. In our case, we had too much money in the bank, so we "spent down" by prepaying bills. I made sure I had all our birth certificates, that Katie's medical records were complete, etc. Since I found this so cumbersome, you can't imagine how happy I was when our income and Katie's health excluded us from SSI and we became self-sufficient again. That said, I sure was glad it was there when needed.

In addition, if you need legal help appealing a denial for SSI, there is a professional organization of attorneys and paralegals called the National Organization for Social Security Claimants' Representatives (NOSSCR). NOSSCR can refer you to a member in your geographic location. You can contact NOSSCR by phone at (800) 431-2804, or online at *www.nosscr.org*.

Medicaid

Medicaid is a program that pays for medical services needed by low-income citizens. Medicaid is administered by state governments, and the federal government pays a portion of the entitlement. Rules about eligibility vary, but families with private insurance sometimes are eligible if huge hospital bills are only partially covered by their insurance company. Some states cover children younger than age 21 if they are hospitalized for more than 30 days, regardless of parental income. In addition to medical bills, Medicaid sometimes also pays for transportation and prescriptions.

Free medicine programs

Children with cancer, and survivors of cancer, often need expensive medications, and sometimes families cannot afford them. Most major U.S. drug companies have patient-assistance programs, and you can apply to obtain free or low-cost prescription drugs. Although each company has its own criteria for qualification, in general, you must fit the following criteria:

- Be a U.S. citizen or legal resident
- Have a prescription for the medication you are applying to get
- Have no prescription drug coverage for the medication
- Meet income requirements

You may qualify even if you have health insurance, if it does not cover the medication prescribed for your child. For expensive medications, the income cut-off is high, so it is worth investigating whether or not you qualify. Several organizations that can help you find and apply to patient-assistance programs are listed in Appendix B, *Resource Organizations*. Because the application process takes time and includes obtaining information from your child's doctor(s), plan ahead so you do not run out of medication.

> *Our insurance does not cover the growth hormone that my daughter needs. Her physician cannot believe that our insurance company denied coverage for a survivor with a history of radiation to the brain and multiple late effects to the endocrine system, but that's our situation. The medication is incredibly expensive. We applied to a patient-assistance program and were thrilled to find out that we qualified if our adjusted gross income was less than $100,000 a year. The application process the first year was hard and took a few months, but now we just fill in a form and send in our tax return every year, and she is requalified. We get a shipment of growth hormone every 3 months and keep it in the fridge.*

Although the cost of in-hospital treatment in Canada is covered by provincial governments, families have to pay for some medications. For families without private insurance, this often creates financial hardship. In many instances, the Department of Social Services can help pay for medications. The qualifications vary in each province and the decision is based on financial need. Canadian parents should contact their provincial Department of Social Services for further information.

State-sponsored supplemental insurance

Most states have supplemental insurance programs for families with children who are living with chronic conditions. These programs often help cover services, prescriptions, and co-payments that your primary insurance will not. You can get more information about the specific programs in your state from your medical team or hospital social worker, or by calling your state's department that regulates insurance (e.g., State Insurance Commission).

> In Michigan, besides my husband's insurance, we also have what is called Children's Special Health Care Services (CSHCS). It is a secondary insurance that pays for what our primary insurance doesn't—co-pays and prescriptions, trips back and forth to the hospital, doctor appointment and prescription co-pays for my husband and me, our stay at the Ronald McDonald House. Any expenses related to treatment that our primary insurance won't cover, this will. The amount you pay for this coverage is based on family income. It has been a lifesaver for us.

Service organizations

Numerous service organizations help families in need, providing aid such as transportation, wigs, special wheelchairs, and food. Often, all a family has to do is describe its plight, and good Samaritans appear. Some organizations that may exist in your community are: American Legion; Elks Club; fraternal organizations such as the Masons, Jaycees, Kiwanis Club, Knights of Columbus, Lions, and Rotary; United Way; and religious groups of all denominations. In addition, local philanthropic organizations exist in many communities. To locate them, call your local health department, ask to speak with a social worker, and ask for help.

Organized fund raising

Many communities rally around a child with cancer by organizing a fundraiser. Help is given in various ways, ranging from donation jars in local stores to an organized drive using all the local media. There are many pitfalls to avoid in fund raising, and great care must be taken to protect the sick child's privacy to the fullest extent possible. Because there have been some unfortunate scams in which generous people were bilked out of

contributions for sick children who did not exist, if you decide to try fundraising, it is best to obtain legal assistance and to establish a trust fund for the express purpose of paying the child's medical expenses.

If your child is on or seeking Social Security or Medicaid eligibility, funds must be held in a special needs trust and paid directly to providers. If the family receives the money, or the child's Social Security number is used to open the bank account, the child can lose funding from both Social Security and Medicaid.

Miscellaneous insurance issues

Loss of insurance coverage is every parent's worst nightmare. If you lose your job, change jobs, or move while your child is on treatment, speak to your employer's benefits manager promptly. You can continue insurance coverage with your previous employer through a Consolidated Omnibus Budget Reconciliation Act (COBRA) plan until you are certain your new insurance coverage is in effect, or you can look for coverage under the Affordable Care Act (ACA). Although using COBRA may impose some financial strain on your family for several months, it will ensure your child's coverage without interruption.

> We just switched to an ACA plan from COBRA, as did a friend of mine with cancer. I am saving $300 per month and she is saving $400. ACA covers preexisting conditions, and you can get a special tax credit that is not available with COBRA if your income level is within certain limits.

Speak to your employer about whether participation in a Section 125 Plan (sometimes called a cafeteria plan, flexible spending account, or health savings account) is an option at your place of employment. These plans generally allow you to have your employer withhold pre-tax dollars from your pay for expenses such as childcare costs and non-reimbursed medical expenses. However, you will need to fill out reimbursement forms and submit them by year's end, otherwise you might lose the money.

> We had excellent insurance coverage, so we never experienced any major financial difficulties during my son's treatment. However, insurance company literature can be so complicated that I felt I almost needed an advanced degree in rocket science to decipher our coverage. Our hospital has a financial counselor available for families that need help. Given the enormous stress that parents are under, I think it's an invaluable service.

Chapter 26

End of Treatment and Beyond

THE LAST DAY OF TREATMENT is a time for both celebration and fear. Most families are thrilled that the days of pills and procedures have ended, but some fear a future without drugs to keep the disease away. Concerns about relapse are an almost universal parental response at the end of treatment; but for many families, the months and years roll by without recurrence of the tumor.

However, many children and teens have lingering or permanent effects from treatment for solid tumors. This chapter covers the emotional and physical aspects of ending treatment, the need for excellent medical follow-up, and employment and health insurance issues.

Emotions

Parents should anticipate that, after many months or years spent watching their child go through the rigors of active treatment, they may have lost the feeling of a normal life. They may experience relapse scares and may frequently need to call the doctor to describe the symptoms and be reassured.

> Every time Sean sneezed, I was there with a thermometer. I was constantly on the lookout for "bad germs." It took about a year before I was finally able to relax and stop feeling so paranoid.

With diagnosis came an acute awareness that life can be cruel and unpredictable. Many parents feel safe during treatment and feel that therapy is keeping the cancer from coming back. The end of treatment leaves many parents and children feeling exposed and vulnerable. When treatment ends, parents must find a way to live with uncertainty—to find a balance between hope and reasonable worry.

> I had a lot of anticipatory worry—it started about 6 months before ending treatment. By the last day of treatment I had been worrying for months, so it was just a relief to quit.

We were thrilled when treatment ended. I knew many people who felt that celebrating would jinx them; they just didn't feel safe. Well, I felt that we had won a big battle—getting through treatment—and we were going to celebrate that. If, heaven forbid, in the future we had another battle to fight, we'd deal with it. But on the last day of treatment, we were delighted.

Last treatment

The last treatment usually includes a physical examination, blood work, a magnetic resonance imaging (MRI) scan, and a discussion with the oncologist. The doctor should review the treatment that was given, outline the schedule for scans and blood tests for the future, and sensitively discuss the potential for long-term side effects. If you do not already have a detailed summary of your child's treatment, it should be provided as your child is completing the last round of treatment.

The nurses at our clinic really made a big deal on the last day of treatment. They brought out a cake and balloons, and sang "Going off Chemo" to the tune of "Happy Birthday to You." They made Gina a banner and bought her a present. I sat in a corner and cried, because I was scared to death of the future. A nurse came over, hugged me, and said, "This must be so hard; we're taking away your security blanket." She was exactly right.

When treatment was finally over, we felt like we had been cut adrift at sea. Suddenly, our hospital safety net was gone. This was the day that we had been waiting for— and now we were terrified.

Catheter removal

Children and teens usually cannot wait to have the catheter removed, as it symbolizes that treatment has truly ended. Venous catheters are usually removed soon after treatment ends.

During Elizabeth's last treatment, her doctor told me he was going to schedule her for surgery to remove her central line. I was so ecstatic! To me, Elizabeth wasn't really in remission as long as the central line was still there. I know it was irrational, but part of me felt as if there were cancer cells dangling at the end of that central line. If we didn't get it out right away, Elizabeth would still have cancer. I wanted it out "right now."

Removal of an external catheter is usually an outpatient procedure. The child is given a mild sedative, then the oncologist gently pulls the catheter out of the child's body by hand.

> Kristin's Broviac® removal wasn't too bad. They gave her fentanyl ahead of time, so she was fairly relaxed. I wish they had offered me a sedative as well! One of the nurses had her hand on Kristin's shoulder and quietly talked to her to try to keep her focused elsewhere. I held her legs, and my wife held her hand. The doctor put one hand on her chest, and pulled on the tubing with the other. It only took about 2 seconds to come out. There was little blood; they just put a Band-Aid® on the site and sent us home.

Implanted catheters such as the PORT-A-CATH® are removed surgically in the operating room. Children are usually given general anesthesia, and the operation takes less than half an hour. Only one incision is made, generally just above the port at the same place as the scar from the implantation surgery. The sutures holding the port to the underlying muscle are cut, and the port with tubing is pulled out. The small incision is then stitched and bandaged. When the child begins to awaken, he is brought to the recovery room where his parents can join him. The family then waits until the surgeon approves their departure. Often, the wait is short, because as soon as the child is awake enough to take a small drink or eat a popsicle, he is released. However, if your child becomes nauseated from the anesthesia, the wait can be several hours; he will not be released until he is feeling better.

> Brent had a very easy time with his port-removal surgery. We scheduled him to be the first patient early in the morning, so there was no delay getting in. Then the anesthesiologist asked him what flavor of gas he wanted, which he liked. They brought him out to us while he was still groggy, and he woke up feeling goofy and happy. We went home soon thereafter. It felt more like the ending than did the last day of treatment.

· · · · ·

> Our docs said that my son's port could come out after the next MRI, which was just after treatment ended. It was a short procedure under general anesthesia, and he actually woke up without thrashing or crying this time. He was so happy to have it gone. He was just barely 5. We talked a little before about the "button" and the tubing coming out, just so he understood it wasn't part of his body that was being taken out.

Ceremonies

Some families enjoy having ceremonies to celebrate the end of cancer treatment. For younger children who have spent much of their lives taking pills and having procedures, ceremonies really help them grasp that treatment is truly over. Here are ideas from many families about how to commemorate this important occasion:

- Take "last day of treatment" pictures of the hospital and staff
- Take a picture of your child taking her last pill
- Give trophies to your child and siblings
- Ask the clinic to present your child with a certificate
- Go on a trip or vacation to celebrate
- Throw a big party for friends and family

> *Erica ended treatment in December, and we threw a big party at the church. We called it a "Celebration of Life." We invited all of the families that we had become so close to through the support group. We especially wanted the families who had lost their children to cancer, and they all came. My normally even-tempered husband gave a talk about Club Goodtimes (the support group) and how it was a club that no one ever wanted to join. When he talked about the many wonderful people we met there, his voice shook with emotion. Then the preacher prayed for the children who weren't with us. We ate a huge cake, and the children were entertained by a clown. It was both moving and fun.*

- Throw a big party at school.

> *Joseph finished treatment when he was in kindergarten. The kids had gone through almost an entire year with him. They had known all about his treatments and frequent hospitalizations and had talked as a group about it when we made a presentation to the class, and at other times as well. It seemed appropriate to have an "all done with treatment" celebration. We even had his two best friends who go to different schools come over to join us; and his big brother, Nate, came down from his class to share in the fun.*
>
> *It was a very joyous occasion, and we made it as much like a birthday party as we could. I brought cupcakes and juice and we played games. A friend who leads the story hour at our children's bookstore came and did some songs and stories with the kids; and I even sent each classmate home with a treat bag. At the end, right before time to go home, Joseph pulled out several cans of his favorite hospital discovery, and the kids took turns blasting a shower of Silly String® on everyone else! We all clapped and cheered, and Joseph's wonderful teacher and I had a chance to have a*

good celebratory cry while the kids put on their things to go home. Clean-up wasn't too darn bad, and it meant a lot to all of us.

There's still a tiny remnant of green Silly String® on one of the fluorescent light fixtures, and my big second-grader likes to go down and admire it when he visits his old kindergarten teacher.

- If your child has been seeing a counselor, schedule a visit to talk about the accomplishment.

- Have friends and family send congratulations cards.

- If consistent with your beliefs, have a religious ceremony of thanksgiving.

  I preached the sermon at church after Kristin ended treatment. It was the first Sunday of Lent, and I related our experience to that. Other than that, we didn't celebrate, because it's still not over. We still have to be vigilant. Ending treatment was a big milestone, but it paled in comparison to having the line pulled. We all have so much more freedom: no more lines to flush, changing bandages, or wrapping up for baths and swimming.

- Some parents do not feel comfortable celebrating the end of treatment. One mother described her feelings this way:

  Finishing treatment was very difficult. I thought that I would feel like celebrating and cheering—but all I felt was fear. Treatment was over, but cancer was still a part of our lives. I think we will always live with the fear of relapse. It has taken me some time to come to grips with that reality.

As you have read so often in this book, every child, brother, sister, parent, and relative reacts differently to treatment—and to the end of treatment. The differences do not matter. What is important is that you feel free to express your feelings, whatever they may be. You may feel joyful, relieved, fearful, or terrified, but the end of treatment is emotionally charged for every member of the family.

What is normal?

After years of treatment, families grapple with the idea of returning to normal. Unfortunately, most parents no longer really know what "normal" is. Parents realize that returning to the carefree pre-tumor days is unrealistic, that life has changed. The constant interaction with medical personnel is ending, and a new phase is beginning in which routines do not revolve around caring for a sick child, giving medicines, coping with hospitalizations, and keeping clinic appointments. Although it is true that the

blissful ignorance of the days prior to cancer are gone forever, a different life—one often enriched by friends and experiences from the cancer years—begins.

> We're a year off treatment, and I really don't think about relapse very often. I do occasionally find myself studying her to see if she looks pale, or I worry when she seems tired or her behavior is bad. Usually, I'm feeling safer. But honestly, I don't think any of us will ever go back to the days when we just assumed that our kids would grow up, that the parents would die first; that sense of security is probably gone forever.

· · · · ·

> Shawn is 6 months off treatment, and he's just like a flower beginning to bloom. He's so happy, and I try to be happy with him. I try very hard to put worries about the future out of my mind, because I feel that those thoughts will rob me of just being able to enjoy Shawn.

· · · · ·

> Chemo is such a horrible thing for your child to endure, but at least you are actively fighting the beast; so when it ends you feel a bit like you're flying without a net. You get so used to this bizarre new "normal" of treatments and blood tests and doctor visits, and then suddenly you stop, but you don't get the old normal back.

> I think it's probably best to approach the end of treatment as a chance to see your child get his healthy color and energy back, and an opportunity to create and explore a new "normal" for your family that is richer and more meaningful than the one you left behind. It's also really nice to finally have the chance to reconnect with your spouse (and other children) and heal all the relationships that have taken a beating during the stressful treatment period.

> As for me, for perhaps a year after Joseph's treatment, I existed in a dazed mix of emotions and thoughts. I was fearful of relapse, thrilled that Joseph had survived the cancer and the treatment, concerned about what late effects lay around the corner, all tempered with a warm and thankful feeling that I knew I would never, EVER take my kids or my good life for granted anymore, or sweat the small stuff the way I used to. There were days I felt like I didn't want to crawl out from under the bed, and other days I couldn't stop singing and being silly. I think off treatment is a lot like on treatment—you just have to take it one day at a time.

"Normal" is a moving target—different for every person and family. No one can tell you what your normal will be. Normal is what keeps the family alive and planning and moving together to face their individual and collective futures.

For many people, helping others is a satisfying way to reach out or bring closure to the active phase of cancer treatment. Serving others can create something enormously

meaningful out of personal challenges, which is why many parents and children like to give back to the cancer community in some way. Some examples of ways people have given back include the following:

> I requested that the clinic and local pediatricians refer newly diagnosed families to me if the parents wanted someone to talk with. I remembered how impossible it was to go to meetings in the first few months, and how desperately I needed to talk to someone who had already traveled the same road.

> We started a Boy Scout project to keep the toy box full at the clinic.

> My children are counselors at the camp for kids with cancer.

> We organized a walk to raise funds for the Ronald McDonald House.

> We (a group of parents of children with cancer) requested and were granted a conference with the oncology staff to share our thoughts about ways to improve pain management and communication between parents and staff. It was very well received.

> We circulated a petition among parents to request increased hospital funding for psychosocial support staff. We presented it to the director of the hematology/oncology service.

> I give platelets and blood regularly.

> I took all of our leftover catheter line supplies to camp and gave them to a family that needed them.

The possibilities are endless. Parents and children can use whatever talents they have to help others—from designing head coverings to writing newsletters for families struggling with childhood cancer.

> I have administered several online support groups for parents of children with cancer over the past decade. Many of these groups have over 500 participants who live all over the world. Some of the members' children have been cancer free for years, some are newly diagnosed, and some are parents of children who have died. These online communities are an important way to find comfort, support, and information. Parents who are far out from treatment remain involved in order to help those who are newly diagnosed. When my son was first diagnosed, I was so reassured that people survive the ordeal. After treatment ended, I wanted to be there to help others.

An equally healthy response to ending treatment is to put it behind you. Many families, after years of struggles, just want to move on. They don't want constant reminders of cancer and feel it's not good for children to be reminded of those hard times.

I realized that it was time to put it behind us when I watched my two children play-ing house one day. There was only one adult and one child in the family. I asked what happened to the rest of the family and they both said, "Cancer; they died." I didn't want them to have any more cancer in their lives. They had had enough. I know people who worry all the time about the cancer returning, and it is not healthy for them or their children. I decided to get out of the cancer mode and back to being my usual upbeat self. I feel that we are finally back to normal, and it's a good place to be.

Parents and children need to talk with one another, examine their emotions, decide what course they want to chart, and work together toward creating a healthy life after cancer.

Shawn is a year off treatment and I find myself letting go of the bad memories more and more. They are just fading away. What I am left with is awe, admiration, and amazement that my son handled all of the hardships of treatment and survived. He's very determined and strong-willed, and I'm so proud of him. When people say to me, "Oh, you were so strong to make it through that," I respond, "All I did was drive him to the appointments; he did the rest."

This experience has really changed me and my entire family. My marriage is much better, my other sons are stronger and closer to us, and Shawn has shown us all how tough a little kid can be. We take each precious day, one at a time, and try to get the most out of it. I so appreciate life and my family.

Initial follow-up care

Protocols for clinical trials require specific follow-up schedules for 3 to 5 years after treatment ends. For instance, your child may require follow-up every 3 months for a period of time (usually 1 to 2 years), then every 4 to 6 months for a while, and then annually. Follow-up might include:

- Physical exams by a pediatric oncologist and sometimes a radiation oncologist
- MRI scans
- Blood tests
- Eye examination under anesthesia (for children who had retinoblastoma)
- Echocardiograms
- Audiograms

Clinical trial documents outline the follow-up schedule. If your child was not on a clinical trial, find out from the oncologist what the required schedule will be and where the appointments will take place. Make sure your child understands that after treatment ends, doctor appointments, scans, and blood draws will still be an occasional necessity.

Long-term follow-up care

In the past, most survivors of childhood cancer were sent back to their local doctors after follow-up for the recurrence of the cancer was complete. But as the population of long-term survivors grew, it became apparent that these young men and women often faced complex medical, psychological, and social effects from their years of treatment. As a result, some institutions started survivorship clinics to provide a multidisciplinary team to monitor and support survivors. The nucleus of the team is usually a nurse coordinator, pediatric oncologist, pediatric nurse practitioner, social worker, and psychologist. The team also includes specialists such as endocrinologists and cardiologists.

Yearly appointments with follow-up programs usually include a review of treatments received, counseling about potential health risks (or lack thereof), and treatment-specific diagnostic tests (e.g., echocardiograms or hearing tests). Follow-up clinics not only provide comprehensive care for survivors, they also participate in research projects that track the effectiveness of and side effects from various clinical trials. In addition, the follow-up clinics act as advocates for survivors with schools, insurance companies, and employers.

If your institution does not provide comprehensive, long-term, survivorship care, you can find a list of survivor programs at *www.acor.org/ped-onc/treatment/surclinics.html*. Many survivors travel to comprehensive programs for their yearly follow-up visits.

Possible late effects

At diagnosis, parents do not know the price their child will ultimately pay for reprieve from the tumor. Short-term effects are many, but they come and then go. Long-term effects range from none to severe. These can include physical disabilities, learning disabilities, an impaired endocrine system, hearing loss, altered bone growth, infertility, and an increased risk of second cancers.

It is important to know the possible risks based on the treatment your child received. You can then store this knowledge in the back of your mind. As one mother said, "I hope for the best and I deal with the rest." For detailed information about possible late effects from childhood cancer, read *Childhood Cancer Survivors: A Practical Guide to the Future, 3rd edition,* by Nancy Keene, Wendy Hobbie, and Kathy Ruccione.

Healthy choices

An essential aspect of survivorship is making healthy choices. Good health habits and regular medical care help protect survivors' health and lessen the likelihood of late effects from cancer treatment. A sizable number of adult cancers are linked to life-style choices. Eating a healthy diet, staying physically active, using sunscreen, avoiding excessive alcohol consumption, maintaining a healthy weight, and not smoking all help keep survivors healthy and cancer-free. To protect survivors from injury, it is also important to wear bike or motorcycle helmets, use seat belts, and call a cab if the person driving has had too much to drink. Survivors have little or no control over their genetic make-up or the environment in which they live, but making healthy choices about how to live the rest of their lives gives them some control over their future.

Immunizations

If your child was diagnosed before she received all her immunizations, ask the oncologist when she should resume the regular schedule for immunizations. If your child had one or more stem cell transplants, then all immunizations may need to be repeated.

Risks of smoking

Teens need continuing counseling about problems associated with smoking cigarettes or engaging in other high-risk behaviors. The combination of effects from treatment and smoking increases the chance of heart disease; heart attack; congestive heart failure; stroke; cancer of the mouth, throat, and lungs; and death from sudden cardiac failure. An article about survivors and smoking in a youth newsletter ends with these words:

> If you've had cancer and your friends haven't, they don't face the same risks from smoking that you do. You've fought hard for your life. Don't put it out in an ashtray.

Safe sex

Every teen and young adult who has survived cancer should be counseled about safe sexual practices. Despite the prevalence of sexual messages in our culture, most teens and young adults are woefully underinformed about the facts. Even though some chemotherapy drugs may cause infertility, many babies have been born to long-term survivors of solid tumors. Survivors should not assume that they are infertile.

In addition, sexually transmitted diseases are of concern for anyone engaging in sexual activity. All sorts of diseases, some potentially fatal (e.g., hepatitis C, HIV/AIDS) and

some not (e.g., genital herpes, genital warts, gonorrhea), can be transmitted through sexual intercourse and oral sex. One nurse practitioner at a large follow-up clinic stated:

> *I tell every teenager who comes through the door, regardless of their medical background, that I think he or she is too young to have sex, and I explain why. But then I say, in the event that you do choose to become sexually active, you always need to use a condom, and not just any condom. I tell them to only use a latex condom with a spermicide, which is the most barrier-protective. I explain that no sex is the only guarantee to avoid the many diseases out there, but a latex condom with spermicide offers the next best protection. And I really stress that this should be done whoever the partner is, and for whatever type of sex. So many teenagers think that diseases only happen to other kinds of kids.*

Treatment summaries

Once treatment and follow-up for recurrence of disease are completed, many children and young adults will no longer be cared for by pediatric oncologists who are familiar with their history. A transition back to their local doctor often occurs. Moreover, many primary care doctors—pediatricians, family practice doctors, internists, gynecologists—are not fully aware of all the different treatments used for the multitude of childhood cancers, or of the late effects they can cause.

In addition, when treatment ends, patients and parents are not always given adequate information about the risks of developing late effects in the months, years, or decades after treatment. The risks of delayed effects are real, and it is imperative that survivors become informed advocates for their own health care. They need to be educated, in a supportive and responsible way, about the risk of late effects; then if a problem does arise, it will be recognized early and receive prompt attention. Young adults who have survived childhood cancer need to be fully informed of their unique medical history and be able to share this information with all doctors who care for them in the future.

A few months before the end of treatment, ask the oncologist to fill out the treatment summary form that can be found at *www.childhoodcancerguides.org/treatment-record*. Make several copies of the completed form, because this health history will become an indispensable part of your child's medical records for the rest of her life. The hard copy version should be kept in a safe place, and a copy should be given to each medical caregiver. You can also scan the health history and store a copy on your computer, which makes it simple to print out new copies in the future and provides a backup in case the hard copy is ever misplaced or lost. When your child leaves home to begin her adult life, this treatment summary should go with her, and you should keep a copy in a safe place. If you have the history on computer, you can easily put it onto a portable device (e.g., thumb drive, flash drive, memory stick) for your child to take with her.

Employment

The number of adults who have survived childhood cancer is growing at a rapid rate. It is estimated that 420,000 survivors of childhood cancer live in the United States. Thousands of survivors are staying well, growing up, and successfully entering the workforce.

Despite their numbers, some survivors still face job discrimination. Under federal law and many state laws, an employer cannot treat a survivor differently from other employees because of a history of cancer. The Americans with Disabilities Act of 1990 (ADA) prohibits many types of job discrimination by employers, employment agencies, state and local governments, and labor unions. In addition, most states have laws that prohibit discrimination based on disabilities, although what these laws cover varies widely.

The ADA prohibits discrimination based on actual disability, perceived disability, or history of a disability. Any employer with 15 or more workers is covered by the ADA. The ADA requires the following:

- Employers cannot make medical inquiries of an applicant, unless the applicant has a visible disability (e.g., uses a wheelchair), or the applicant has voluntarily disclosed her cancer history. Such questions must be limited to asking the applicant to describe or demonstrate how she would perform essential job functions. Medical inquiries are allowed after a job offer has been made or during a pre-employment medical exam.

- Employers must provide reasonable accommodations unless it causes undue hardship.

- Employers may not discriminate because of family illness.

The U.S. Equal Employment Opportunity Commission (EEOC) enforces Title 1 (employment) for the ADA. Visit *www.eeoc.gov* or call (800) 669-4000 (voice) or (800) 669-6820 (TTY) for enforcement publications. Other sections are enforced or have their enforcement coordinated by the U.S. Department of Justice (Civil Rights Division, Public Access Section), which can be contacted online at *www.ada.gov* or by calling (800) 514-0301.

The Job Accommodation Network (JAN) is a service provided by the U.S. Department of Labor's Office of Disability Employment Policy. JAN supports the employment, including self-employment and small business ownership, of people with disabilities. JAN can be reached at www.askjan.org or by calling (800) 526-7234 (voice) or (877) 781-9403 (TTY).

In Canada, the Canadian Human Rights Act provides essentially the same rights as the ADA. The Act is administered by the Canadian Human Rights Commission. You can get more information by visiting the national office's website at *www.chrc-ccdp.ca.*

Health insurance

Job discrimination can spell economic catastrophe for cancer survivors in the United States because most health insurance is obtained through one's place of employment. The Patient Protection and Affordable Care Act (often abbreviated as ACA or referred to by the nickname "Obamacare") of 2010 and its companion amendments allow access to healthcare for survivors, who in the past could often not get healthcare due to pre-existing conditions. You can find up-to-date information about the law at *www. healthcare.gov.*

The ACA includes the following provisions that are relevant to childhood cancer survivors:

- Young adults are allowed to stay on their parents' insurance plan until they turn 26 years old, whether or not they are in college.

- Certain preventive services are covered, including services that are important aspects of survivorship care.

- If a survivor is unemployed or has a limited income—up to about $15,000 per year for a single person—he may be eligible for health coverage through Medicaid.

- If an employer does not offer health insurance, survivors can buy it through the Health Insurance Marketplace (sometimes called an "exchange"), which offer a choice of health plans. To learn about the options in your state, visit *https://www.healthcare.gov/ quick-guide.*

- You may get tax credits to help pay for insurance if your income is less than about $43,000 for a single individual and your job does not offer affordable coverage.

- Health plans can no longer limit or deny coverage to anyone with a "pre-existing" medical condition.

Following are some legal remedies for insurance discrimination.

- **COBRA.** The Comprehensive Omnibus Budget Reconciliation Act (COBRA) is a federal law that requires public and private companies employing more than 20 workers to provide continuation of group coverage to employees if they quit, are fired, or work reduced hours. Coverage must extend to surviving, divorced, or separated spouses, and to dependent children. You must pay for your continued coverage, but it must not exceed by more than 2 percent the rate set for the company's full-time employees. By purchasing continued coverage, you have time to seek other long-term insurance. The U.S. Department of Labor provides a COBRA fact sheet at *www.dol.gov/ebsa/faqs/ faq-consumer-cobra.html.*

- **ERISA.** The Employee Retirement and Income Security Act (ERISA) is a federal law that protects workers from being fired because of the cancer history of the employee or beneficiaries (spouse and children). ERISA also prohibits employers from encouraging a person with a cancer history to retire as a "disabled" employee. ERISA does not apply to job discrimination (denial of new job due to cancer history), discrimination that does not affect benefits, or to employees whose compensation does not include benefits.

- **Health Insurance Portability and Accountability Act of 1996 (HIPAA).** This law allows individuals to change employers without losing coverage, if they have been insured for at least 12 months. It also increases portability if you change from a group to an individual plan. For additional information, a HIPAA fact sheet with frequently asked questions is available by visiting *http://www.dol.gov/ebsa/faqs/faq_consumer_hipaa.html*.

Appendix B, *Resource Organizations*, lists organizations that can help if you or your child faces job discrimination or problems with insurance due to treatment for cancer.

Well, we finally did it. We took a deep breath, a heavy sigh, and we packed up the medical supplies. While this step may seem insignificant for some, those who have dealt with a chronic/life-threatening illness in their family know that the disposal of your arsenal of medical supplies is a symbolic rite of passage. It can only mean two things: your loved one has passed on, or you simply don't need the supplies anymore. We thank God every day that we ended up with the latter reason.

Katy's medical "tower" was stored in our hallway, and included various bins and drawers full of central line supplies, a mini IV pump, masks and gloves, hypodermics, and sharps containers. It was very conspicuous. You simply couldn't miss it if you walked through the house. It was our constant reminder that we had a sick child, and at times, for me, a crutch. I think I felt that as long as the tower was there and properly stocked and arranged, I was somehow in control of Katy's illness. I feared disposing of, or putting anything away, thinking that if I did, she would most assuredly relapse and I'd need it again.

However, as the months passed, the tower gathered dust, and soon, I couldn't remember the last time we'd even used any of the supplies. A few more months passed, and I began to realize what an eyesore this bunch of junk was! So, after my husband brought some big boxes home from work, it was time. We did it together.

Into the boxes went the tubing and syringes, the masks and dressing change kits for the kids' oncology camp. Into the garbage went all the expired meds, heparin, and saline. It was so liberating! I can't imagine why we kept that stuff around for so long. It felt like the end of an era. And in a way it was.

Chapter 27

Recurrence

PARENTS FREQUENTLY DESCRIBE the return of their child's cancer as more devastating than the original diagnosis. They sometimes feel betrayed, guilty, and/or angry. They worry that if the previous treatments did not work, what will? Mostly, they are afraid. And their often unspoken but most crushing fear is: What if my child dies?

If your child's cancer has returned, it is worth remembering that you now have several strengths you didn't have before. You have already done this. You know the language, and you have a relationship with the medical team. You probably have friendships with other parents of children with cancer and you know they will be there for you. You can also hope that during the time your child's cancer was in remission, researchers were able to develop newer and more effective treatments. You know that something that seems insurmountable can be endured, one day at a time.

This chapter describes signs and symptoms of recurrence, what emotional responses you might experience, and how to set goals and decide on a treatment plan. In addition, several parents and survivors share their stories about how they managed to cope.

Signs and symptoms

Recurrence can happen at any time during treatment or after therapy is completed. Occasionally the child has no symptoms, but an MRI scan shows the cancer has returned. More frequently, however, signs and symptoms appear that include some or all of the indicators that were present at diagnosis:

- Discomfort

- A lump or mass

- Shortness of breath

- Pain

- Loss of appetite

- Fatigue

- Enlarged abdomen

- Changes in behavior
- Dizziness
- Headaches
- Limping

Remember that many of these symptoms are also seen with normal childhood illnesses. However, persistent loss of appetite, fatigue, or unusual symptoms require a call to your oncologist.

> Zack (age 6) was in remission after 13 rounds of chemo for stage IV neuroblastoma. He had scans every 3 months and everything was looking good. Nine months later, Zack started to complain that his hair hurt. "Hair pain" seemed weird to me, so we went to the doctor. Blood test results came back abnormal, and the worry intensified. We admitted Zack to the hospital feeling fine, with the exception of his sore hair! The doctor ordered a bunch of tests and scans which came back fine, but when the bone marrow aspiration was done, the news was not good. His cancer had come back.

In some cases, parents have no warning. After they bring their child in for a routine examination, they receive a totally unexpected telephone call from the doctor with the news.

> I am a long-term survivor (30 years old), who first was diagnosed with cancer at age 8 and subsequently relapsed three times, at ages 13, 15, and 16. The first relapse was by far the worst to deal with emotionally. I had been off treatment with good counts for 2 years. My mother and I didn't even wait for the test results; we went out to lunch and went shopping. Later that day, I called the clinic, and my doctor told me she needed to talk to my mother. I heard my mother say, "No, no, oh no," and she started to cry. I just stood there feeling numb, knowing the news was bad. The cancer had returned. We held each other and cried.

The site of recurrence depends on the type of solid tumor. The disease can recur in the area of the original tumor, or it may develop elsewhere.

> Jody was complaining about pain and a feeling of pressure in his leg bones. I kept bringing him back to the oncologist, saying that something was wrong, that he was in great pain, but the doctor kept insisting that it was just growing pains. He didn't even examine his legs for a month. When he did, he could feel parts of the bone radiating heat. The bone scan showed the cancer in the exact spots that Jody had pointed out.

Emotional responses

Parents whose children are in remission think or speak of regrowth of the tumor with an almost palpable dread. Just the thought can cause an eruption of the same emotions that surged in them at diagnosis. Parents, their child, and the siblings may feel a wide array of emotions at recurrence: numbness, guilt, dread, anger, fear, confusion, denial, and grief. For parents whose child has had many years of stable MRI scans with no tumor growth, the scan that confirms their worst nightmare feels overwhelming.

> I found that relapse was far worse than the original diagnosis. At diagnosis, after a certain period of adjustment, you think that treatment has a beginning, a middle, and an end. But relapse creates a bigger burden to accept. You begin to feel that maybe the disease is more powerful than the medicine. I found that for a while I just stopped functioning and thinking rationally. I felt like I was on a runaway freight train, hurtling toward an end that didn't look so good anymore.

Parents often experience physical symptoms such as dizziness, nausea, fainting, and shortness of breath. They wonder how they can ask their child to endure treatment again. They wonder how they will survive it themselves. They may oscillate between optimism and panic.

> My first relapse was the worst emotionally. Neither my parents nor I ever thought that after 5 years it would be back. I also had been so young when I was first treated that I didn't understand that I could die from it. But at 13, I remembered clearly what I had been through, and all I could think was that it hadn't worked. I told my parents that I wouldn't do it again. My father sat me down and gave me a reality check. He explained that I would die if I didn't get treatment. He said, "If you don't do it for yourself, please do it for me and your mom." The next morning I went into the clinic and started all over again.

Goal setting and treatment planning

A difficult but necessary step in making plans is discussing and deciding on your and your child's goals. Health Canada's publication, *This Battle Which I Must Fight: Cancer in Canada's Children and Teenagers*, states:

> This [recurrence] is a time of crisis and ambivalence. The decision to be made is whether to continue to try to achieve a remission or to replace this hope with the hope for comfort for the child and a special time together. Each parent, and the child who is old enough to understand, requires differing amounts of time to reach a decision about how to proceed. Careful and frequent discussions with the medical team, as well as with trusted friends and relatives, may help clarify issues and bring some peace of mind.

In a newsletter for parents of children with cancer, Arthur Ablin, MD, (Professor Emeritus of Pediatric Clinical Oncology at the University of California, San Francisco), wrote of the importance of goal setting in the decision-making process after recurrence:

> Before determining which treatment is to be chosen, a decision must be made to determine the goal of treatment—in other words, what is it that we are trying to achieve. This crucial first step is the basis upon which any decision concerning treatment must be made. But it is too often omitted from consideration and/or discussion, even by the most experienced. The frustrations accompanying the previous failure of treatment, the fear of the loss of the hope for cure, the pressure of urgency to find solutions, the new awareness of the possibility or probability of death, lead us all to want to consider treatments first rather than these more difficult considerations involved in establishing goals. These also force us to deal with reality earlier, which could mean the almost intolerable confrontation with the death of a very-much-loved child, a tragedy to be avoided at all costs.

If after discussion of goals your family decides to pursue aggressive treatment, there may be more than one option available. Therefore, it is important to understand the treatment avenues that are open to you. Treatment plans for a first recurrence may be specified in the standard treatment or clinical trial protocol document, or your child's oncologist may suggest a different approach. Suggestions for treatment may include surgery, radiation, stem cell transplantion, more intensive chemotherapy, immunotherapy, a clinical trial, or a combination of several treatments. You may need to weigh traveling to a different treatment center to gain access to therapies that are not available at your child's home hospital.

Do not rush into treatment if you or your family feel uncomfortable about the plan. There is always time to obtain answers to all of your questions and to get a second opinion. Doctors make recommendations based on knowledge, experience, and consultations with other experts in the field. Do not hesitate to ask your child's oncologist why she has suggested a certain treatment approach. Ask the doctor about treatment goals, methods, and possible side effects. Also ask if she has consulted with others in the decision-making process, and if so, with whom. Be certain older children and teens are involved in decisions about their care and treatment choices.

> Making the decision as to what treatment to choose was much more difficult when my son relapsed. The stakes were higher. While I had faith in the skills and judgment of my son's oncologists, I could not rest easy unless I had educated myself on the options available for relapse treatment. His relapse had been suspected for weeks, so

I had time to investigate possible treatment choices. His relapse site was rare, which made the usual channels less effective in our case. I started with the online NCI-PDQ and a PubMed search. I asked friends to search for me. From there I contacted a physician from a leading children's oncology research group and asked what type of treatment protocol they had to offer for my son's type of relapse. I learned that the options were few in terms of protocols addressing my son's type of relapse.

When we sat down with the treatment team, I already had some background and knew what was available in terms of treatment. When they presented their choice of protocol, I asked for and was given a copy of the protocol. Reading the rationale and background of the study they were proposing helped me to understand why this protocol was suggested. As a result, I was able to make a difficult decision and enroll my son in a clinical trial with confidence that he was getting the best treatment available. Since it was a very difficult and intense treatment protocol, it also helped my teenaged son to understand why this was the path we were following. Once begun, neither of us had any serious doubts that we'd made the best choice. Now, almost 3 years later, I am still very pleased that I was able to make a fully informed decision.

Making a decision about treatment

Treatment for children with solid tumors is evolving. The information gleaned from second opinions or your own research may reinforce what your doctor recommended, or it might provide you with additional treatment options. Either way, the information may increase your comfort level during the treatment planning process. You might want to ask your child's treatment team the following questions about the suggested treatment plan:

- Why do you think this treatment is the best option? What are the other choices, and why are you recommending this one?

- Have you consulted with other doctors? If so, with whom? Did you all agree on this treatment or were other options suggested?

- Is there a standard treatment for this type of relapse? If so, what is it?

- Are any clinical trials available?

- What are the potential benefits and possible side effects of the proposed treatment?

- How long is the proposed treatment?

- If radiation is to be included, what type and dose are you recommending?

- What are the known or potential risks of the treatment?

- How often will my child need to be hospitalized?

- If the treatment is investigational, is there scientific evidence that it works for my child's type of tumor?

- If we need to transfer to another treatment center for some or all of the proposed treatment, who will help us manage that process?

- Does insurance cover this type of treatment?

- What supportive services are available? How do we contact the people responsible for these services? (Contacts might include a hospital school coordinator, social worker, psychologist, and physical therapist.)

- What is the goal of this treatment? Remission? Comfort?

When older children and parents disagree about how to proceed, you can ask the primary nurse practitioner, social worker, or psychologist to help your family talk about the options. These discussions will help clarify each family member's thoughts and feelings and will allow the child's emotional and physical well-being to be part of the equation.

> After my son relapsed, we set immediately back to work trying to determine what the best treatment option for him should be. His oncologist was very committed to making him well again. As it turned out, the best option was a phase II study drug that wasn't yet available in our area. The hospital social worker helped us with travel arrangements and accommodations, and within a day we were on a plane headed for another hospital. Meanwhile, the oncologist completed all the necessary paperwork so that by the time the next course of chemotherapy was due, it could be administered at our own hospital. It was obvious to us from the very beginning of relapse that we had a wonderful medical team that was dedicated to helping our son get well again.

> Unfortunately, after two courses of chemotherapy, it was clear that the drug wasn't getting rid of the cancer. Once again, we all rolled up our sleeves and tried to find another treatment that might help him. I would gather the information and then his oncologist and I would sit and review all the data. As long as the therapy was reasonable and had the potential to help without further diminishing his quality of life, it was worth considering. One of the most comforting things that my son's oncologist ever said to me was, "I will always be in your corner."

After you have set goals, received answers to all of your questions, obtained a second opinion if desired, and decided on a treatment plan, it is time to proceed. Your knowledge and experience may prove to be a double-edged sword. You have no illusions about the difficulties ahead because you have done it before, but you also will be strengthened by your ties to the cancer community, your comfort with your doctors and hospital routines, and your ability to work with the system to get what your child

needs. Many parents shared how their child took the lead with relapse treatment. While the parents agonized, their child simply said, "Let's just do it." And they did.

I encourage people to try to keep things in perspective. Attitude is a big part of survival. As difficult as it is, try to maintain a good attitude and keep focused on the future. I always thought, "I have cancer, this is a bad thing, but I am going to beat it." My analogy was a boxing match. When I relapsed, I was knocked down. But I always got up and kept fighting.

I had a total of three relapses, two of which were on treatment. Every time we relapse, statistics say our chances of survival are less likely. But I survived those three relapses, and now I live a life as normal as if cancer never touched it. After cancer, I finished high school and went to college. I gave birth to a beautiful, healthy baby girl. My daughter (still beautiful) is now 7 years old. For me, life does go on after cancer.

Chapter 28

Death and Bereavement

THE DEATH OF A CHILD causes almost unendurable pain and anguish for the loved ones left behind. Death from childhood cancer comes after months or years of debilitating treatment, emotional swings, and financial difficulties. The family begins the years of grief already exhausted from the cancer treatment. It is truly every parent's worst nightmare.

In this chapter, many parents share their innermost thoughts and feelings about their decisions to transition from active treatment, to involve hospice, and to choose death at home or in the hospital, and their experiences with grief. It made no difference whether parents had recently lost a child or whether it happened years before—tears flowed when talking about their family's experience. Because family members and friends can be strong sources of support, or casualties of the grieving process, parents describe words and actions that help, and they offer suggestions about what words and actions to avoid. Grief has as many facets as there are grieving parents; what follows are the experiences of a few.

Transitioning from active treatment

For children or teenagers whose disease is progressing, medical caregivers and parents at some point need to decide when to end active treatment and begin to work toward making the child comfortable for his remaining days. This is an intensely personal decision. Some families want to try every available treatment and exhaust all possible remedies. Others reach a point where they feel they have done all they can and want to transition to a time of sharing memories, expressing love, and preparing for death. What all families share in common is a desire to continue to guide and nurture their children, parenting them even through these most difficult circumstances, up to and through the process of death itself.

When Cienna's tumors metastasized to her brain, I knew that I was not so desperate for her to live that I would sacrifice the last bit of quality life she had left, dragging her from doctor to doctor, putting her through treatment after treatment, so that I could hope to have one more day with her. Doing that would not have been for her, but for me. If Cienna had been older and able to choose for herself it would have been one thing, but she could not. I struggle with the "quantity versus quality" issue and usually keep it to myself. A lot of people, including some doctors, think quantity is more important. I believe it's not how much time you have, but what you do with it that matters most. I loved her so much that I wanted the remainder of her life to be happy and not filled with more suffering than she was already enduring from her cancer.

· · · · ·

This has been a very difficult weekend with many tears. We have had so many wonderful years beyond what we ever thought was possible with such a good quality of life for Jen and us. In spite of everything, we have no regrets. We selfishly want every moment we can have, but we have come to the crossroad where we are asking at what cost to Jen. While we have not made the commitment to hospice yet, we are all feeling that we are not far from that place unless there is a dramatic change in Jen soon. She has really fought hard. She made this damn tumor work really hard to slow her down. She is very, very tired and while my head understands this, my heart is breaking.

Dr. Arthur Ablin, Professor Emeritus of Clinical Pediatrics, University of California San Francisco, wrote about the difficulties of deciding to end active treatment:

All too often, the decision to abandon the goal for cure and, reluctantly, accept the reality of inevitable death of a child is too painful and, therefore, never made. This paralyzing pain occurs with equal frequency, perhaps, for the family and the doctor. We of the medical profession have no equal in our ability to prolong dying. We have a powerful array of mechanical, electronic, pharmaceutical, and biotechnical interventions at our command. We can keep people dying for months and even years. Applying or withholding this armamentarium is an awesome responsibility, and it requires infinite wisdom to know how to manage wisely and correctly. We can do great good by applying these tools correctly, but can also do incalculable harm through over-utilization. Physicians and families alike must work together to avoid the possible pitfalls. When cure is beyond all of us, then the challenge is to make the rest of life as worthwhile and rich as possible. There is much to do for the terminally and critically ill child and his or her family. They have that right, we have the privilege, to be of service.

One of the more difficult tasks a parent will face is sharing the news with their child that treatments have stopped working. Children and teenagers need to be an integral part of the subsequent discussions with the healthcare team. Their thoughts and feelings are crucial during the decision-making process. Honest, thorough communication between the ill child or teen, family members, and involved professionals helps everyone work together.

> My niece was diagnosed right after her third birthday and died 2½ months short of her fifth birthday. We told her about the tumor, and she knew that was what was causing all the symptoms she was experiencing. She knew she was sick and wasn't getting better, but we never told her specifically that she would die until after we had stopped all treatment and the outcome was inevitable, probably a month or so before she died.

> When we told her, we sat down with her and her 2½ year old brother and told them. She acted exactly as though she had already known what was going to happen to her, that we were telling her nothing new.

> About 2 months before we told her, the movie "Little Women" came out on video. We had previously taken her to see it in the theatre. We got the video right away, and she watched it probably three times a week or more. She would always tell me, when I watched it with her, that her favorite part was the part where Jo died. It wasn't like she got any pleasure out of that part, but it was like she knew what would happen to her and she could identify very closely with Jo.

> In retrospect, I think she had known for some time, long before we told her, but she did not speak of it because she had already come to terms with it, and she was not fearful. I think she desperately wanted to live and be cured, but she somehow knew that if a cure could not be found, she would die.

When it is clear that death is inevitable, parents struggle with the thought of how to discuss it with the ill child and siblings. All too often in our culture, children are perceived as having to be protected from death, as if this somehow makes their last days better. On the contrary, children, often as young as age 4, know they are dying. If the parents are trying to spare the child from knowing, a difficult situation develops. The child might pretend that everything is okay to please the parents, and the parents might try to mask their deep grief with false smiles.

> When my 6-year-old son Greg was in the hospital in intensive relapse treatment, he would repeat over and over again, "I want to go home." When he was finally well enough to come home for a while, he kept saying, "I want to go home." In frustration, I said, "Greg, you are home, why do you keep saying that?" He looked up

and quietly said, "I want to go to my heavenly home. I want to go to God." I said, "Honey, please don't say that," and, knowing how much we loved him, he replied, "Okay, Mom, I'll fight, I won't go." And he did fight hard for several more months. But he was way ahead of us in acceptance, he was at peace, and he knew it was time to let go.

Denial sometimes prevents children and parents from finishing up business—distributing belongings, telling each other how much they love one another, and saying good-bye. It also strips parents of their ability to prepare their child for the journey from life to death. Children need to know what to expect about dying. They need to know that they will be surrounded by people they love and that their parents will be holding them as they pass on. They also need to know the family's beliefs about what happens after death.

Jennifer contracted a respiratory fungal infection that resulted in her being hospitalized on a ventilator. She was given lots of morphine so that she wouldn't feel air hungry. She was alert off and on for a few days. We read to her and played tapes. After 1 week on the respirator, she took a turn for the worse. She didn't respond to me after that. Her kidneys were ceasing to function, and she started to get puffy. Her liver was deteriorating, and her painful pancreatitis had come back. After 10 days on the respirator, I couldn't bear it any longer. I lay down in her bed, took her in my arms, and kissed her at least 200 times. I talked to her for a long time, and told her that we would take care of her cats, and that I was sorry that she had to suffer so much, and how beautiful Heaven is. I told her to go be with Jesus, her Grandpa, and her dog. I also told her how much we all loved her and how proud we were of her. I got off the bed to change positions, and the nurse rushed in. Her heart had suddenly stopped the second I got up. I believe she heard me and just needed to know it was okay to go. She didn't want to leave until she knew her mommy was ready.

Jennifer had told me that she wasn't afraid to die, and this has been a great source of comfort to us. I believe that she was preparing for her death, even as we hoped for her remission. Before she went to the hospital, she spent all her money, gave away some of her possessions to her sisters, and said a final good-bye to her home, cats, teachers, and friends.

When it becomes clear that further treatment will not result in a cure, parents need to discuss with the child or teen what his or her goals and wishes are, and use that as a guide for medical and personal choices.

Meg was diagnosed just before the beginning of her senior year in high school, and finished treatment the next fall after her friends and twin sister had gone off to college. She had clean scans, and in January we went out to dinner with her best girlfriends just before they were all going to head out for their spring semester of

college. Meg went to the restaurant bathroom and found a lump in her groin. We got the relapse confirmation on January 20. The PET scans lit up and showed the cancer was everywhere. The doctor told her that there was nothing they could do other than give her chemo to keep her quality of life good for as long as it worked. He told her she would not live; it was treatable but not curable.

She said she didn't want to lose her hair again. "You have to take everything off the table that will take my hair." She wound up on oral etoposide every 3 weeks, and went in for an IV push of another drug. Her first question after we all cried was, "Can I go to college?" This would be her one semester at college. That was her dream, and her boyfriend had been there a semester already. She was on fentanyl patches on a college campus! We got a lockbox for her pain meds, and she was able to stay for about 8 weeks, before the pain just got to be too great and she came home.

She and her boyfriend decided they didn't want to get married, but she wanted a honeymoon. The doctors said certain locations were off limits as there wasn't good medical care in many of the places they wanted to go. The doctors agreed to Puerto Rico. Our friends and my husband's coworkers donated frequent flyer miles and hotel points to send them with first class airfare and to stay in a fancy hotel. They left on the trip on June 18. She died August 18.

Supportive care

In the United States, there are very active and effective hospice home care services for children. Hospice organizations ease the transition from hospital to home and provide support for the entire family. Hospice personnel ensure adequate pain control, allow children to control their last days or weeks of life, and provide active bereavement support to the family after the child's death.

If the family wishes for the child to die at home, a smooth transition usually occurs from the oncology ward to home hospice care. Unfortunately, sometimes children are not referred to hospice, and the parents are left to deal with their child's last days at home with no experienced help and no clear idea of what is to come. Your nurse practitioner, case manager, or hospital social worker can refer you to, or help you find, a pediatric hospice organization in your area. Before you leave the hospital, it is wise to find out the name of a contact person at the agency who will be taking over the home care of your child.

When Jody came home, he was assigned both a pediatric visiting nurse and a hospice nurse. On their first visits, I was handed a great deal of literature to read, including a whole notebook from hospice. I lacked both the desire and energy to read the literature and learn a whole new medical system—let alone two. I just wanted one phone number to call for help, with two or three consistent people to answer.

In actuality, the care we received was wonderful. The primary nurse would call, offer to visit if we wanted it, assess Jody's condition over the phone, handle any questions we had, and would ask if we wanted a call the next day. She would tell us who would be calling if she was not working at the appointed time. Interestingly, the service that I found most beneficial at that time was the nurse running interference for us with the doctor. The pain medications needed to be adjusted and changed at times; advice was needed about his intake, his mouth sores, and his hand and foot inflammation. As I, along with Jody, became quieter and more removed from outside activities, even the thought of calling the clinic and being made directly aware of the bustle and demands of that world was very unappealing.

• • • • •

When our children were babies and learning, I always used the principle of reinforcing things I wanted them to learn or understand with all their senses: hearing, seeing, touch, smell, and taste. During Jen's last days, we kept her room filled with light the way she liked it, and even a soft low light at night so whenever her eyes opened so she knew one of us was right there. We played her favorite music continuously, more upbeat during the day and softer choices at night, and we talked with her and then to her when she could no longer respond with her voice, although the squeeze of her hand and her big blue eyes spoke volumes.

We touched her constantly, sometimes just sitting next to her holding her hand and not moving, other times stroking her head, rubbing "udder" cream on her elbows and heels so she didn't get bedsores. She had lost quite a bit of her sense of smell, but we kept everything very fresh and all the flowers that came to the house were all around her because she visually could remember their wonderful scent. We learned to use the great swabs that hospice provided with very cool water and a bit of mint Listerine so her mouth felt clean and fresh, especially as she became less able to take care of herself and even more so when she was no longer able to take in water and then food. One of the nurses told us to take ice chips and put them in a very worn piece of cloth and make it tiny so she wouldn't gag and let it rest in her mouth for a few minutes at a time so she had some moisture, and when that became impossible because she could hardly open her mouth, we swabbed her lips and the gums outside of her closed teeth. All this was meant to convey the message you are loved and cared for and we will be right here for you every step of the way.

Hospice not only provides assistance in physically caring for your child, it can also provide emotional support for your child, you and your spouse, and any other children in your home. If you have questions about hospice or what support is available, you can contact Children's Hospice International online at *www.chionline.org* or by phone at (800) 242-4453.

We were very fortunate in our hospice experience, which lasted a mere 8 days. On the first day, a nurse arrived to meet all of us. She came in with a big smile and introduced herself. The nurse began by taking a very complete medical history, and I remember being surprised by the depth of information she wanted. It was like she wanted to fully understand the entire journey and what he had been through, while I suppose I had expected her to laugh off with disinterest everything that had happened before "the end," as if it wouldn't matter anymore. She listened intently, reacted appropriately at incidents that had been a bit unusual, and wrote down a great deal. Then she did a brief exam, just blood pressure, pulse, and general appearance, and assured him that she wouldn't bother him anymore. He relaxed when he realized that she wouldn't be poking him as so many others had already done. We had been apprehensive before her arrival, but afterward, it felt like the night crew had arrived after a very long day shift.

Dying in the hospital

Some children die in the hospital suddenly, while others slowly decline for weeks or months. If your child is slowly dying, you may have choices about where he will spend his last days. There are no right or wrong choices. Much depends on the number of people available to provide care at home and how comfortable they are doing so. Many parents ask their child where she would prefer to be. Some children and teens want to be with the nurses in a hospital environment, but others want to stay at home with brothers, sisters, friends, and pets.

Parents, children, and staff should talk honestly to decide on the appropriate place for the child and then obtain the support (e.g., hospice care, private nurses in the hospital, family members) needed to make the choice a comfortable reality. Remain flexible so that as the situation changes, options remain open. If the choice is made to die in the hospital, most hospitals have a palliative care team that can help families make choices that emphasize comfort.

Although we had been advised that it didn't look good for Greg, we were trying one last time to get him to transplant. He was sleeping quietly in his hospital bed. He had been complaining of severe head pain, and was on a low morphine drip. The afternoon nurse woke him to take vitals, and he chatted with her. He told me, "Mom, I'm going to go back to sleep, I love you." Two hours later the night nurse tried to wake him up to give him some medicine, and she couldn't wake him. They called the doctor in from his home, and he ordered a CAT scan. When the film came up to the floor, the doctor took me out in the hall and said, "He's not going to live through the night." He held up the film showing a massive cerebral infarction; Greg was bleeding

into the brain. He quietly died less than an hour later. Family and staff were in total shock. Nobody expected it. But, looking back, Greg had decided he had had enough; he was ready to go. I am grateful that he didn't die on a transplant floor in a strange city. We were able to call in friends and family, and we were surrounded and supported by the wonderful nurses whom we knew so intimately. I couldn't leave him until three nurses promised to stay with him and escort him to the morgue. They are still dear friends.

Parents of children who died in the hospital stressed the importance of clear communication. Parents need to be strong advocates for adequate pain control, and they need to clearly tell the staff their wishes for their child's end of life. For example, in most hospitals, if a child's heart stops or if he stops breathing, the staff immediately begins cardiopulmonary resuscitation (CPR) and electric shocks to the heart—this is called a "code." If the parents have decided they are ready to let their child die naturally, they need to discuss their wishes with the oncologist and ensure that an order of "No Code" is put in the chart and on the child's door. A No Code order is also called a "DNR," or "Do Not Resuscitate" order. Family members should understand that a DNR does not mean "Do not care for my child." On the contrary, the medical team will provide comfort measures, such as:

- Allowing the child to sleep during the night without interruptions to check temperature and blood pressure.

- Providing adequate pain medication.

- Allowing family and friends open visitation without restrictions as to length and time of stay and the number of people allowed in the room.

- A private room.

> *Alannah was medicated at any indication of discomfort, and after a week of semiconsciousness followed by a week of coma, we finally got up the guts to have her taken off the respirator, to let her go. She opened her mouth a couple of times, as if trying to breathe, and that was it. With her mother and I holding her, the staff just left us alone. Fifteen minutes later, the attending doc came back and declared time of death. She left very peacefully. We were told to expect that she might seem to be struggling or gasping, and that it would just be reflex, that she wouldn't really be struggling. It didn't happen.*

• • • • •

> *I felt bad for my daughter, because like any good child, she wanted permission, even to die. My husband had promised her that he would never give up. He kept on saying, "Fight. Fight. Don't give up, don't leave me. We'll do another transplant, we'll try different medicine. It's too early to give up." I looked at him and said, "She's not*

going anywhere until you tell her that it's okay." Then he told her, and she took her last breath. He still feels guilty to this day because of his promises. He just didn't understand that it was time; that she needed to know that it was okay with us.

Parents also should discuss whether they want nurses or doctors present when their child dies. Many families feel very close to the hospital staff and feel supported by their presence, while others prefer to have only family and close friends at the child's bedside. Advance planning helps to ensure that, as death approaches, the family's wishes are understood and respected.

Dying at home

A child's death at home, and the time just before, can be a peaceful experience, depending on the extent of preparation and the quality of support available to the family.

Four weeks before my daughter died, she called us into her room. One by one, she proclaimed her love for each of us, and thanked us for being the best family a girl could ever have. She told us not to worry, that she was going to be all right, and that one day, we would all be together again. On Memorial Day, she died in her mother's arms, with all of us at her side.

· · · · ·

We decided to bring Jody home to die for several reasons. First of all, the medical profession was offering no more realistic hope. Secondly, Jody was young enough and small enough to be easily held, carried, cared for by us. Thirdly, nothing violent or terrifying happened to make us seriously debate whether to go back in the hospital with him.

I saw many life values in a new way from the experience of Jody dying at home. What comes to my mind is a sunny, breezy afternoon, September 13. Only Jody and I were home. I held him outside under the plum tree for perhaps an hour and a half or longer. I couldn't support him well and read to him at the same time, so we didn't do anything. I spoke to him some, but mostly just held him quietly. I was aware as I looked up into the sky that my normal reaction on such a day would be to want to be hiking, biking, "doing" something. A surprise recognition burst and spread gently through my consciousness: I was exactly where I wanted to be and no doing of anything could mean as much as being there with Jody.

Jody's last day, September 16, was peaceful. A spiritual healer, whom Jody had known for 2 years, came and spent time with him. A massage therapist/healer/ friend, who had visited him several times during the 5 weeks he was home, gave him a long, gentle massage. My husband Tom stayed home from teaching that day (by chance?). Jody lay in his arms or on my lap most of the day. The visiting home nurse

came by briefly, offered to stay, but we preferred to be alone. I was holding Jody; Tom was next to me holding his feet. His breathing became labored and irregular. His eyes were unblinking long before he took his last breath, then a heartbeat, then another, then silence.

Involving siblings

Whether your child is dying at home or in the hospital, siblings should be included in the family response. Being part of things and having jobs to do help brothers and sisters remain involved, contributing members of the family. Young children can answer the door or choose music to play for the sibling. Older children can help with meals, stay with the ill child to give parents a break, answer the phone, or help make funeral arrangements. These jobs should not be "make-work"—children should truly be helping. This helps them to prepare for the death, as well as have an opportunity to say good-bye.

> *We gave our children free rein to pick out the clothes that Jesse would be buried in. They made very thoughtful choices: her favorite, very comfortable pajamas with little tea cups on them, and her teddy bear.*

For teens, the presence of their siblings and friends can be very significant in the final weeks.

> *When Megan first came home after her last hospital stay to manage the pain, she stayed on the couch and her twin sister slept on an air mattress next to her. We carried her upstairs to her bed in their shared room in a wheelchair. She lasted 2 to 3 nights in her own bed, then she needed a hospital bed. The pain pump worked well most of the time, but we had to work with hospice and her pain management team to get the right level of pain control. Her older brother in Florida took off a couple of months to come home and be with her before she died. Her friends were great with her, spending a lot of time at the house. They put her makeup on her and did her hair 2 days before she became unconscious.*

> *Megan worried about how her twin sister Melissa would cope without her. While she could still speak, Megan asked me, "For our first birthday that we're not together, will you give her this 'fearless' bracelet?" It was a leather band with metal letters spelling out fearless. "Tell her she was the fearless one." I framed it and gave it to Melissa with a card saying exactly what Megan asked her mom to share with her twin. She's studying in Rome at the moment and it's one of the few things she took with her.*

The funeral

Funerals and related rituals (e.g., memorial services, wakes, shiva, burial) are important not only as a time to say good-bye and to begin to accept the reality of death, but also to provide an opportunity to recognize the relationships and impact the child or teen had on others. Funerals allow friends and family to gather together to share memories and show support for the remaining family members. A funeral is a tangible demonstration of love.

> *We wanted to plan a perfect memorial service for Michael. Nick and I had some ideas, but we also asked Michael what he would like at his memorial service. One point he made quite clear was that he wanted balloons instead of flowers since "flowers are for girls." He also told me exactly what he wanted to wear—his 101 Dalmatians shirt with his favorite black sweat pants and Batman socks. He even helped with an idea for his gravestone. He was familiar with them since we had visited his Grampa's grave a lot. In fact, they're buried beside each other. He was very mature in the way he handled his impending death, even though he was only 4 years old. Never did he fear it, nor dwell on it, nor become angry about it. The way Michael put it was, "Well, Mom. Some people die and some people don't."*

Children of all ages should be allowed to attend the funeral if they wish, but only after they have been prepared for what to expect. They need an explanation of what the event is for, where they will be going, and what will happen. They need to know what death is, what type of room they are going to, whether the casket will be there, whether it will be open, whether there will be flowers, who will be there, how the mourners will behave, who will stay with them, what they will be expected to say or do, how long they will be there, and what will happen after the service (e.g., burial, reception). All questions should be answered honestly and the children's feelings respected. Many siblings benefit from giving one last gift to the departed, such as writing a private note and placing it in the casket, or bringing some of their sister's favorite flowers to put in her hands.

> *We celebrated our 3-year-old son Kevin's life today. The past week has been a whirlwind. All of Kevin's favorite women worked nonstop for 48 hours leading up to last night. The funeral home was beautiful. There were pictures everywhere—on pedestals, in photo albums, collages, and frames.*
>
> *There were children's books throughout the funeral home as well as red balloons, Kev's favorite color. We had patchwork squares out to create a memorial quilt for his younger sisters, Courtney and Katie. People wrote special messages and drawings on them to capture their feelings: "Kevin, Sending you love and kisses and one BIG scoop of mashed potatoes!"*
>
> *We also had sheets of paper to write stories and memories of Kevin to make a memorial book for the girls. Kevin's favorite things were on a memorial table: his*

green blankie with the hole in it, his books, his Buzz Lightyear®, his green bike, his catcher's mitt, his baseball and yellow bat, golf clubs, and more.

We rented a 6' projector screen and a big screen TV to display a 20-minute video in both rooms at the funeral home. It showed Kevin's life over the past year. And it was a pretty good life too: putting candles on Grammy's cake with Matthew, gymnastics with Grampie, wrestling with Courtney, reading with Daddy, playing football with Nana, kissing Auntie JoJo and Auntie Karin, playing golf in the yard, laying on the floor laughing, telling knock knock jokes, riding bikes in the house, at the beach at the Cape.

What does a mom do? She loves, cherishes, teaches, protects, and lets go. For one brief, shining moment, we had Kevin. For happily ever after we have our memories of him.

For families that are involved in a spiritual community, their clergy have a unique opportunity to provide support, love, and comfort to the grieving family and friends. They usually know the family well and can evoke poignant memories of the deceased child or teen during the service. Members of the clergy often have excellent counseling skills and can visit the family after the funeral to provide ongoing help during mourning.

One of our pastors was a very close personal friend who stayed with us for the last 3 days in the hospital at Jesse's bedside. When she died, we were physically and emotionally weary; we just couldn't think. He and the other pastors planned the whole service and walked us through it.

There were hundreds of people there—Jesse had touched so many lives. The pastors had known Jesse her whole life and they loved her, truly loved her. They told personal stories, reminisced about the last hugs they had shared with her. They told the story of her faith and of her death, which comforted many of those who attended. Each family member walked up during the service and brought some of her favorite flowers.

The role of family and friends

Family members and friends can be a wellspring of deep comfort and solace during grieving. Some people seem to know just when a hug is needed or when silence is most welcome. Unfortunately, in our society there are few guidelines for handling the social aspects of grief. Sometimes well-meaning people voice opinions concerning the time it is taking to "get over it" or question the parents' decision to not give away their child's clothing or other belongings. Others do not know what to say, so they are silent, pretending that life's greatest catastrophe did not occur. Many friends never again mention

the deceased child's name, not knowing that this silence, as if the cherished child never existed, only adds to parents' pain. Holidays can become uncomfortable, because they bring sadness as well as joy.

In an attempt to alleviate these difficulties, bereaved parents helped compile the following lists of what helps and what does not, in the hope that it may guide those family members and friends who deeply care, but just don't know how to help. Parents or family members can copy these lists to share with people who want to help.

These suggestions are offered with the understanding that what works for one family may not work for another. Family members and friends should use their knowledge of the bereaved family to choose options that they think will be most helpful. If in doubt, they should ask the parents. As Mother Teresa said, "Kind words can be short and easy to say, but their echoes are truly endless."

Things that help

The long lists of things that help from Chapter 20, *Family and Friends* (e.g., keeping the household running, feeding the family, and helping with bills), are still appropriate here. The following lists are specific suggestions for support with grieving.

Helpful things to say:

- I am so sorry.
- I cannot imagine the pain you are feeling, but I am thinking about you.
- I really care about you.
- You and your family are in our thoughts and prayers.
- We would like to hold a memorial service at the school for your child if you think that it would be appropriate.
- I will never forget John's sunny smile.
- I will never forget Jane's gentle way with children and animals.

Parents also offer a list of helpful things to do:

- Go to the funeral or memorial service.

  We were overwhelmed and touched by all of the people who came to the funeral. Even people that I had not seen in years—like some of my college professors— attended. Her oncologist and nurse drove 100 miles to be there.

- Show genuine concern and caring by listening.

What has helped me the most is for people to just listen. Finding time to remember and reminisce is sometimes very difficult and painful, yet other times I feel much pride and happiness. Friends whose children also have cancer have been the greatest help to me during my daughter's illness and after her death.

- Help the siblings.

  We had friends just call and say, "We will pick up Nick on Saturday and take him to Water World, then to our house for dinner. We were hoping he could spend the night. Will that be all right?" They did this many times, and it not only was fun for him, but gave us a chance to be alone with each other and our grief.

- Write the parents a note instead of sending a preprinted sympathy card with your signature. Include special things you remember about their child or your feelings about their child. Letters, poems, or drawings from classmates and friends allow children to share their feelings with the family of the deceased, as well as provide poignant testimonials that the family will cherish.

- Talk about the child who has died. Parents forever carry cherished memories of their child and enjoy hearing others' favorite recollections.

  Months after the funeral, we gathered family members and some close friends to share memories on tape. We did a lot of laughing as well as shed a few tears. But I will always cherish those tapes.

  · · · · ·

  I think most of all parents want their child to be remembered. It really comforts me to go to Greg's grave and find flowers, notes, or toys left by others.

- When parents express guilt over what they did or did not do, reassure them that they did everything they could. Remind them that they provided their child with the best medicine had to offer.

- Remember anniversaries. Call or send a card or flowers on the anniversary of the child's death.

- Respect the family's method of grieving.

- Give donations in the child's name to a favorite charity of the child or parents, for example, the child's school library, the local children's camp, or U.S. Children's Hospice International.

  Every year we still get a card saying that Caitlin's occupational therapist donated money to Camp Goodtimes. It makes me feel good that she is remembered so fondly and that the money will help other kids with cancer and their brothers and sisters.

- Commemorate the child's life in some tangible way. Examples of this are planting trees, shrubs, or flowers; erecting a memorial or plaque; or displaying a picture of the child.

  The spring after Matthew's death, his school contacted me and said they wanted to do something special in his honor. They planted a little leaf linden tree in front of the building and built a wonderful seat around its base. They picked this particular tree because of its wonderful fragrance, and because the leaves were shaped like little hearts. A plaque beside the tree proclaims that this is Matthew's Friendship Tree. In addition to his name and the date of his birth and death, it reads: "When you remember me, please have a smile and cherish the good times we shared. And in these memories I will live with you forever."

- Be patient. Acute grief from the loss of a child lasts a long, long time. Expectations of a rapid recovery are unrealistic and hurtful to parents.

- Encourage follow-up from medical personnel.

  Caitlin had a very kind, very gentle radiation oncologist. I went back to see her after Caitlin died; she said, "We were so happy when we saw the progress that Caitlin made, from a stretcher to sitting to talking and walking again; and then our hearts broke when she relapsed. I wept." It was so human and so wonderful for her to let me know that she cared.

The Compassionate Friends (see Appendix B, *Resource Organizations*) has dozens of resources to help friends and all members of the family.

What not to say

Please do not say the following to grieving parents:

- I know exactly how you feel.
- It's a blessing her suffering has ended.
- Thank goodness you are young enough to have another child.
- At least you have your other children.
- Be brave.
- Time will heal.
- God doesn't give anyone more than they can bear.
- It was God's will.
- He's in a better place now.

Every time someone approached me at the funeral home with the words, "He's gone to a better place," I felt as if I would scream. Matthew's place was with me, his mother. Seven-year-old boys need their mother. It also really angered me when people repeatedly said, "Oh, with all he suffered, you wouldn't wish him back if you could." Well, yes, I would wish my child back! I would wish him back healthy and well. To this very day I would wish my child back, even if I could hold him for just a moment or hear the sound of his laughter one more time.

- God must have needed another angel.
- It's lucky this happened to someone as strong as you.
- Don't worry, in time you'll get over it.
- Why did you decide to cremate him?
- How is your marriage holding up?
- You need to be strong for your other children.

Please do not say to the siblings:

- You need to be strong for your mom and dad.
- Don't cry; it upsets your parents.
- How does it feel to be the big sister now?

Even if bereaved parents have deep religious faith, it is often tested by their child's death. Parents are not comforted by well-meaning friends who assume faith is making the grief bearable; indeed, many parents find it to be infuriating. It is better to just say "I'm sorry."

In the months and years following the child's death, any of the following are unlikely to be appreciated and may, in fact, be hurtful:

- Don't you think it's time to get over it?
- It's been 6 months; it's time to put the past behind you.
- Life goes on.
- You need to get on with your life.
- You shouldn't be feeling that way.
- Don't you think you should give away all her clothes?
- Don't cry.
- Doesn't it bother you to have his pictures around?
- Please don't talk about Johnnie, it just stirs up all those memories.

- It's not good to just sit around, you need to get out and have some fun.

Don't let your own sense of helplessness keep you from reaching out, even if you are unsure about what to say or do. It hurts the grieving family members when others stay away or pretend nothing is wrong or avoid (or refuse) to talk about the child who has died.

What not to do

The following are suggestions from parents about what not to do:

- Don't remove anything that belonged to the child who died, unless specifically asked to by the parents.

    One family member took my son's toothbrush out of the bathroom and threw it away. I missed it immediately. She probably felt that she was doing me a favor, but it made me so angry. I needed to keep things. I have his hair from the second time it fell out, because he wanted to save it, and I've kept his teeth which had to be pulled during treatment. I just need to have those things, and I resent people who insist you must clear out a child's things. Parents should be able to keep things or get rid of them— whichever is comfortable—regardless of others' opinions.

- Don't offer advice.

    Christie's room is still her room. We still refer to it as Christie's room. People just don't have the right to say you shouldn't leave that room empty: it's not empty, it's full of her life. I know that they are not trying to hurt us. It just bothers them to see that room. Sometimes it is just a reminder of death; yet, there are times when being in there and surrounded by all her things brings us closer to her and her time with us.

- Don't say anything that in any way suggests that the child's medical care was inadequate.

    I can't tell you how many people said things like "If only you had gone to a different treatment facility," or "If only you had used this or that treatment." What people need most is support for what they are doing or did do.

- Don't look on the bright side or find silver linings.

    I became unexpectedly pregnant the month after my daughter died. I can't tell you how many people said things like "The circle of life is complete," or "God is taking one and giving you another," or "God is replacing her." She can never be replaced. It was horrible to hear those things, and I felt it was unfair to both the unborn baby and to my daughter who died.

- Don't make comments about the parents' strength.

People would say things to me like "You're so strong," or "I just couldn't live through what you have." It makes me want to scream. Do they mean I loved my child less than they love theirs because I have physically survived?

Sibling grief

Siblings are sometimes called the forgotten grievers because attention is typically focused on the parents. Children and teens sometimes hesitate to express their own strong feelings in an attempt to prevent causing their parents additional distress. Indeed, adult family members and friends may advise the brothers and sisters to "be strong" for their parents or to "help your parents by being good." These requests place a terribly unfair burden on children who have already endured months or years of stress and family disruption. Siblings need continual reinforcement that each of them is an irreplaceable member of the family and that the entire family has suffered a loss. They have the right, and need, to mourn openly and in their own way.

> *The family requires such reorganization after a child's death, and there is nowhere to look for an example. Each person in the family constellation has different feelings and different ways of grieving; there is just no way to reconcile all of this when the supposed leaders of the group are totally out of it. Not to mention the fact that both my husband and I wanted more understanding and compassion from each other than we were possibly able to give.*

Children express grief in many ways. Some children develop physical manifestations, such as stomach aches, a loss of appetite or voracious eating, or changes in sleeping or toileting habits. Many younger children regress; they may revert to diapers or baby talk, stop walking, or stop talking. Fears and phobias, such as a fear of the dark or of being alone, are common responses to loss. Children may develop unpredictable or disruptive behaviors, such as tantrums, crying, sadness, anxiety, withdrawal, or depression. Older children and teens may appear nonchalant, angry, withdrawn, or engage in risky behaviors, such as sexual promiscuity, alcohol abuse, and drug use.

Parents need to engage siblings of different ages at their appropriate developmental levels. Private time together, or individual outings with the parents, can be very helpful for siblings.

Families can pull apart when individuals within the family have incompatible ways of expressing grief. Men and women tend to express grief in different ways, which may seem intolerable or inexplicable to one another. In these situations, family therapy or some other form of counseling can help.

Some parents worry that if they start talking about their feelings, they will break down in front of the children. But the children know their parents are grieving and it hurts them to feel excluded. They are grieving, too, and if they see their parents pulling away from them, they are likely to feel that their parents do not love them as much as they loved the child they lost. Here are suggestions from families about ways to pull together while mourning:

- Let the siblings go to the funeral. They have suffered a loss and they need to say good-bye. They need support for their grief just as much as adults.

- Children and teens experience the same feelings as adults. By sharing your own feelings, you can encourage them to identify their own. (For example, "I'm really feeling sad today. How do you feel?")

- Some families establish a regular meeting time to talk about their feelings. Both tears and laughter erupt when family members talk about funny or touching memories of the departed child.

- Jointly discuss how holidays and anniversaries should be observed. Each family devises different ways to handle holidays, the child's birthday, and the anniversary of her death.

> Last year we marked our first Christmas since Matthew's death. It was so incredibly hard for me to open the boxes of decorations knowing that inside I would find treasures he had made for me over the years with his own two little hands. I cried when I found his stocking, because I didn't know what to do with it. Somehow it didn't seem right to not hang it as usual.
>
> I decided that I would continue to place Matthew's stocking beside David's and Kristina's. Instead of Santa filling it with treats, I asked my family to fill it for me. A few weeks before every Christmas, I ask members of my family to write a memory of Matthew on a piece of paper. The only stipulation is that it must be a happy memory. On Christmas morning, I look forward most of all to the gifts my children have made for me in school, and the memories that fill Matthew's stocking. Matthew will always be included in our Christmas. That's because he will always be an important member of our family.

Parental grief

Losing a child is one of life's most horrific and painful events. There is no right way to grieve. There is no timetable, no appropriate progression from one stage to the next, and no specific time when parents should "be over it." The death of a child shatters the very order of the universe—children are not supposed to die before their parents; it seems unnatural and incomprehensible. Losing a child, especially after such a long

and grueling battle to save him or her, feels cruel and unjust. When a child dies, parents mourn not only the child, but all of the hopes, dreams, wishes, and needs relating to their child. When you lose a child, you lose part of yourself and an important part of your future. Below, parents themselves share their thoughts about grief.

I truly think that it is the worst thing in the entire world. Nothing worse can happen than losing your child. There is no reprieve. None.

. . . . .

My life is void of the very essential magic of Elena, the stories, the brightness of her being. Her giggles, her sweet kisses, her calling me cupcake and giving me the nosie uggamuggums. She would be in fourth grade Tuesday, and instead she is dead! The school planted flowers by the memorial that they gave last year on her birthday. Yes, it was hard to shop for two instead of three of my kids. I miss the games and the playing school and the calls between her friends. I miss sitting with her on my lap, I miss touching her smooth skin, touching her curly hair, and smelling her scent. I miss looking at her long fingers. But I feel that I was blessed with her life, her love of life, her friends and passions, and her beauty. I will carry her life with honor in my heart for my lifetime.

. . . . .

I was having a very hard time grieving when a wonderful therapist that I was seeing said to me, "When you enter marriage, what are you called? A wife. When your spouse dies, what are you called? A widow. When you don't have a home and you are living on the street, what is the name for that? A homeless person. When you lose a child, what's it called, what's the name?" I said, "I don't know." She said, "Exactly. There is not even a word in our vocabulary. That's how terrible it is. It doesn't even have a name."

. . . . .

Every day when I walk out of my house I tell myself to grab the mask. I feel like I walk different than everybody and talk different than everybody and look different than everybody. It's the worst part of bereavement, the isolation caused by people who just don't know how to talk to you, when really all they need to do is listen and remember with you.

. . . . .

I found myself getting busier and busier, thinking that I could outrun the pain. I realized that I couldn't avoid the hurt; I just had to grit my teeth, cry, and live through it.

. . . . .

I felt like our sick daughter was the center of our universe for so long, that now I need to start feeling some responsibility for my other kids whom I've been away from

for so long, both physically and emotionally. I told my husband the other night that I didn't even know if I loved the three kids anymore. I cannot feel a thing. Pinch me, I don't feel it. Hug me, I don't feel it. I'm numb.

・ ・ ・ ・ ・

It's hard to admit, but there was an element of relief when my daughter died. Not relief for myself, but for her. I was almost glad that she wouldn't face a life full of disabilities, that she wouldn't face the numerous surgeries that would have been required to repair the damage from treatment, that she wouldn't face the pain of not having children of her own. I just felt relief that she would no longer feel any pain.

・ ・ ・ ・ ・

At first we didn't feel like a family anymore. Now it's better, but it's still not the family that I was used to, that I want. I still feel like the mother of four children, not three. I find it very hard to answer when someone asks me how many children I have. I also can't sign cards like I used to, with all of our names, so now I just write "from the gang." I guess that's not fair to the boys, but I just can't bear to leave her name off.

・ ・ ・ ・ ・

I had always heard that time heals all things. I was afraid of healing, because I didn't want to feel any farther away than I felt when he died. It's been 7 years, and he still feels really close—a presence. But I still ache to touch his body so, that little back and fat tummy.

・ ・ ・ ・ ・

Birthdays are hard for us. Greg's birthday was June 10, and his brother's is June 9. So it's pretty hard to ignore. On Greg's birthday and the anniversary of his death, we blow up balloons, one for every year he would have been alive, write messages on them with markers, and release them at his grave.

・ ・ ・ ・ ・

It seems like just about every holiday has some difficult memory attached to it now. He was diagnosed on Easter, and then relapsed the next year on Valentine's Day. I hate them both now. Christmas is always hard. And Halloween is tough because he so loved to dress up. I see all those little ones in their costumes and I'm just flooded with pain.

・ ・ ・ ・ ・

This evening my heart was so saddened. I paced up and down in front of the mantel pausing to look at each picture of my daughter. Something that I cannot describe catches in my chest, and I can't breathe right. I look at her face and try to will it to life for a kiss and a touch, for softly spoken endearments at night. How we love all of our children, yet one missing leaves such a stabbing pain.

· · · · ·

The "firsts" are going to be the hardest, going to the park, going food shopping, going to the Maine house, driving by the library and not popping in to pick up a book for Kev. I find that I don't want to spend time with anyone who didn't know Kevin. I'm not sure if it's because they won't know of how big the loss is or because I need to have people around who can talk about him and the things he used to say and do. So when people say, "How are you doing," I say, "We're doing." We're doing a lot of thinking, a lot of laughing, and a lot of crying.

· · · · ·

It's hard when people I have just met ask, "How many children do you have?" In the beginning I always felt that I had to explain that I had two but one died. Now, I just say one. I don't want their sympathy, I don't want their pity, but most of all I just don't want to have to explain. After 2 years or so, I started to feel uncomfortable giving out my life history and then having to deal with other people's discomfort. So now I just say one, and yet it still feels like I'm betraying him every time I do it.

· · · · ·

That 1-year rule, when you are supposed to start feeling better, I've found to be true. Not that any of the pain is lessened, but I realized I had managed to live through a year of holidays and anniversaries. I knew it was possible to do it a second, then a third time. One year isn't magic, but it does prove to you that you can survive.

· · · · ·

On the anniversary of my son's death we all went to the cemetery, and his girlfriend's parents planted a cherry tree at the foot of his grave. That was on a Sunday. I woke up on Monday feeling just as bad as I did the day before. All I could think was, "Oh hell, I have to go through that whole cycle again." The first year did not bring me any peace.

· · · · ·

This morning was the 4-year anniversary of my daughter's death. While I was at church I wanted to write in the intentions book, "I want my daughter back," but then I didn't because nobody would understand. I guess I'm pretty unreal in my thoughts a lot of the time.

· · · · ·

At church, we always sit with the same group of close friends who helped us through Jesse's illness and are helping us grieve her death. If they begin to sing a hymn that reminds one of us of Jesse, we all start to cry, and someone produces a box of tissues, which gets passed down the aisles. People must wonder at the group that sobs

through services. But it has helped me so much to have a community of grievers; it's been a very cleansing thing. It has spread out the tears.

• • • • •

I think parents need to know that it hurts like hell and they will feel crazy. But it is a normal craziness. If they talk to other bereaved parents, they will know that pain, guilt, rage, and craziness are how normal human beings feel when their child dies.

Bereaved parents are frequently reassured that "time will ease the pain." Most find that this is not the case. Time helps them understand the pain; the passage of time reassures them that they can adjust and they will survive. The acute pain becomes more quiescent, but it still erupts when parents go to what would have been their child's graduation, hear their child's favorite song, or just go to the grocery store. Grief is a long, difficult journey, with many ups and downs. But, with time, parents report that laughter and joy do return. They acknowledge that life will never be the same, but that it can be good again.

I just wish that I had armfuls of time.

— Four year old with cancer
Armfuls of Time

Appendix A

Blood Tests and What They Mean

KEEPING TRACK OF THEIR CHILD'S BLOOD cell counts becomes a way of life for parents of children with solid tumors. Unfortunately, misunderstandings about the implications of certain changes in blood values can cause unnecessary worry and fear. To help prevent these concerns, and to better enable parents to spot trends in the blood cell values of their child, this appendix explains the blood cell counts of healthy children, the blood cell counts of children being treated for solid tumors, and what each blood cell count value means. It also briefly describes other blood tests commonly needed in children with solid tumors.

Values for healthy children

Each laboratory and lab handbook has slightly different reference values for each type of blood test. There is also variation in values for children of different ages. For instance, in children ranging in age from newborn to 4 years, granulocytes are lower and lymphocytes are higher than the numbers listed below. The following table lists blood tests and blood count values for healthy children older than 4 years old.

Blood Test Type	Values for Healthy Children
Hemoglobin (Hgb)	11.5 to 13.5 g/100 mL
Hematocrit (HCT)	34 to 40%
Red blood count (RBC)	3.9 to 5.3 million/cm^3 or 3.9 to 5.3 x 10^{12}/L
Platelets	160,000 to 380,000/mm^3
White blood count (WBC)	5,000 to 15,000/mm^3 or 5 to 15 K/uL
WBC differential:	
Segmented neutrophils	40 to 70%
Band neutrophils	1.5 to 8%
Basophils	<0.3%

Blood Test Type	Values for Healthy Children
Eosinophils	<0.5%
Lymphocytes	20 to 50%
Monocytes	2 to 10%
Liver function tests	
ALT (sometimes called SGPT)	0 to 48 IU/L
AST (sometimes called SGOT)	0 to 36 IU/L
Bilirubin (total)	0.3 to 1.3 mg/dL
Direct (conjugated)	0.1 to 0.4 mg/dL
Indirect (unconjugated)	0.2 to 1.88 mg/dL
Kidney function tests	
Blood urea nitrogen (BUN)	6 to 20 mg/dL
Creatinine	0.5 to 1.5 mg/dL
Electrolytes	
Glucose	70 to 115 mEq/L
Potassium	3.5 to 5.0 mEq/L
Sodium	135 to 145 mEq/L
Minerals	
Calcium	8.5 to 10.5 mg/dL
Magnesium	1.5 to 2.9 mg/dL

Values for children on chemotherapy

Blood test results of children being treated for solid tumors often fluctuate wildly. WBCs can go down to zero or be above normal. RBCs may go down periodically during treatment, necessitating transfusions of packed red cells. Platelet levels may also decrease, sometimes requiring platelet transfusions. Absolute neutrophil counts (ANC) are closely watched, as they give the oncologist an idea of the child's ability to fight infections; ANCs range from zero into the thousands.

Pediatric oncologists consider all of the blood test results to get the total picture of a child's reaction to illness, chemotherapy, radiation, or infection. Trends are more important than any single value. For instance, if the values were 5.0, 4.7, and 4.9, then the second result (4.7) was insignificant. If, on the other hand, the values were 5.0, 4.7, and 4.3, then the trend would indicate a decrease in the cell line.

Children with solid tumors who are on chemotherapy can have changes in kidney and liver function, along with changes in electrolytes and mineral levels in the blood. The section below describes the most common blood tests given to children with solid tumors. If you have any questions about your child's blood test results, ask the oncologist or nurse practitioner for a clear explanation.

Common blood tests

The following sections explain each blood test listed in the table in section "Values for healthy children."

Hemoglobin (Hgb)

Red cells contain Hgb, the molecules that carry oxygen and carbon dioxide in the blood. Measuring Hgb gives doctors an exact picture of the ability of the child's blood to carry oxygen. Children may have low Hgb levels at diagnosis and during the intensive parts of treatment. This is because chemotherapy decreases the bone marrow's ability to produce new red cells. Signs and symptoms of anemia—paleness, shortness of breath, fatigue—may occur if the Hgb gets very low.

Hematocrit (HCT)

The HCT is sometimes called the packed cell volume. The purpose of the HCT test is to determine the ratio of plasma (the clear liquid part of blood) to red cells in the blood. For this test, blood is drawn from a vein, a finger prick, or central catheter and is spun in a centrifuge to separate the red cells from the plasma. The HCT is the percentage of red cells in the blood. For example, if the child has a HCT of 30 percent, it means that 30 percent of the amount of blood drawn was red cells and the rest was plasma.

When a child is on chemotherapy, the bone marrow does not make many red cells and the HCT goes down. When the HCT is low, less oxygen is carried in the blood, so your child will have less energy. Your child may be given a transfusion of packed red cells if the HCT goes below 18 or 19 percent.

Red blood cell count (RBC)

Red blood cells are produced by the bone marrow continuously in healthy children and adults. These cells contain hemoglobin, which carries oxygen throughout the body. To determine the RBC, an automated electronic device is used to count the number of red cells in a blood sample.

White blood cell count (WBC)

The total WBC indicates the body's ability to fight infection. Some treatments for solid tumor cancers kill healthy white cells or decrease the ability of the bone marrow to make new ones. To determine the WBC, an automated electronic device counts the number of white cells in a blood sample.

White blood cell differential

When a child has blood drawn for a complete blood count (CBC), one section of the lab report will state the total WBC and a "differential," meaning that each type of white blood cell will be listed as a percentage of the total. For example, if the total WBC count is 1,500 mm³, the differential might appear as in the following table:

White Blood Cell Type	Percentage of Total WBC
Segmented neutrophils (also called polys or segs)	49%
Band neutrophils (also called bands)	1%
Basophils (also called basos)	1%
Eosinophils (also called eos)	1%
Lymphocytes (also called lymphs)	38%
Monocytes (also called monos)	10%

The differential is obtained by microscopic analysis of a blood sample on a slide.

Absolute neutrophil count (ANC)

The ANC (also called the absolute granulocyte count or AGC) is a measure of the body's ability to withstand infection. Generally, an ANC above 1,000 means the child's infection-fighting ability is near normal.

To calculate the ANC, add the percentages of neutrophils (both segmented and band) and multiply by the total WBC. Using the example above, the ANC is 49 percent + 1 percent = 50 percent, and 50 percent of 1,500 (.50 x 1,500) = 750, so the ANC is 750.

Platelet count

Platelets are needed to repair the body and stop bleeding by forming clots. Because platelets are produced by bone marrow, platelet counts often decrease when a child or teen is on chemotherapy. Signs of low platelet counts are bruises and bleeding from the gums or nose. Platelet transfusions are sometimes given when the platelet count is

lower than 20,000 or when there is bleeding. Platelets are counted by passing a blood sample through an electronic device.

Alanine aminotransferase (ALT)

ALT is also called serum glutamic pyruvic transaminase (SGPT). When doctors talk about liver functions, they are usually referring to blood tests that measure liver damage. If chemotherapy is causing liver damage, the liver cells release an enzyme called ALT into the blood serum. ALT levels can go up into the hundreds, or even thousands, in some children on chemotherapy. Each institution and protocol has different points at which chemotherapy drug dosages are decreased or stopped to allow the child's liver to recover.

Aspartate aminotransferase (AST)

AST is also called serum glutamic oxaloacetic transaminase (SGOT). AST is an enzyme present in high concentrations in tissues with high metabolic activity, such as the liver. Severely damaged or killed cells release AST into the blood. The amount of AST in the blood is directly related to the amount of tissue damage. Therefore, if your child's liver is being damaged by chemotherapy, the AST count can rise into the thousands. Viral infections or reactions to an anesthetic can also cause an elevated AST.

Bilirubin

The liver converts hemoglobin released from damaged red cells into bilirubin. The liver then removes bilirubin from the blood and excretes it into bile, which is a fluid released into the small intestine to aid digestion. If too much bilirubin is present in the body, it causes a yellow color in the skin and whites of the eyes that is called jaundice.

The two types of bilirubin are indirect (also called unconjugated) and direct (also called conjugated). An increase in indirect bilirubin is seen when destruction of red cells has occurred, and an increase of direct bilirubin is seen when there is a dysfunction or blockage of the liver.

Blood urea nitrogen (BUN)

The BUN blood test is used to assess kidney function. It is also used to detect liver disease, dehydration, congestive heart failure, gastrointestinal bleeding, or shock. The test measures the amount of an end product of protein metabolism, called urea nitrogen, in the blood. For children with kidney or liver damage, BUN is often at abnormal levels.

Creatinine

Creatinine is a breakdown product of protein metabolism found in the urine and the blood. In children with solid tumors, creatinine is measured to assess kidney function. An elevated blood creatinine level is often seen in children with kidney insufficiency or failure.

Glucose

The amount of glucose (sugar) in blood changes throughout the day, depending on when, what, and how much people eat, and whether or not they have exercised. A normal fasting (no food for 8 hours) blood glucose level is between 70 and 99 mg/dL. A normal blood sugar level 2 hours after eating is less than 140 mg/dL.

Potassium

Potassium is important for the proper functioning of the nerves and muscles, particularly the heartbeat. Too much or too little potassium increases the chance of irregular heartbeats. Potassium levels can be altered by chemotherapy or other treatments for children with solid tumors.

Sodium

The amount of sodium (salt) in the body is regulated by the brain, kidneys, and adrenal glands. In addition to frequent blood tests for sodium levels, a careful record of urine output is necessary for children with abnormalities in sodium regulation. High blood sodium is associated with excessive urination, and low sodium levels result in low urine output.

Calcium and magnesium

Calcium and magnesium are minerals that can be compared to the spark plugs in your car—they spark the chemical reactions in your body needed to make it function properly. Calcium and magnesium also help to develop and maintain the strength of bones. In addition, magnesium is necessary for the development of muscle and for nerve conduction throughout the body. Many chemotherapy drugs given to children with solid tumors decrease the calcium and magnesium levels in the blood.

Your child's pattern

Each child develops a unique pattern of blood counts during treatment, and some parents like to track the changes. You can put lab sheets in a binder or enter blood test results into a computer program that shows trends over time. Doctors consider all of the laboratory results before deciding on a course of action. They should be willing to explain their plan so you can better understand what is happening and worry less.

If your child is participating in a clinical trial and you have obtained the entire clinical trial protocol (discussed in Chapter 9, *Choosing a Treatment*), it will contain a section that clearly outlines the actions that should be taken by the pediatric oncologist if certain changes in blood counts occur. For example, most protocols list each drug and when the dosage should be modified. The following is an example from a protocol for the drug vincristine.

Vincristine

1.5 mg/m^2 (2 mg maximum) IV push weekly x 4 doses days 0, 7, 14, 21.

Seizures

Hold one dose, then reinstitute.

Severe foot drop, paresis, or ilius

Hold dose(s): when symptoms abate, resume at 1.0 mg/m^2; escalate to full dose as tolerated.

Jaw pain

Treat with analgesics; do not modify vincristine dose.

Bilirubin

Withhold if total bilirubin is >1.9 mg/dL.

Administer 1/2 dose if total bilirubin is 1.5–1.9 mg/dL.

Appendix B

Resource Organizations

THE RESOURCE ORGANIZATIONS LISTED in this appendix are starting points for finding the information or help you need. The organizations are listed in the following order:

Solid tumor organizations (United States): Pages 498–499

Solid tumor organizations (Canada): Page 499

Solid tumor organizations (Australia): Page 499

Solid tumor organization (Germany): Page 500

Other service organizations (United States): Pages 500–503

Other service organizations (Canada): Page 503

Other service organizations (Australia): Pages 504–505

Camps: Page 505

Educational and legal support: Pages 505–506

Financial help: Page 507

Free air services (United States): Pages 507–508

Free air service (Canada): Page 509

Free air service (Australia): Page 509

Insurance: Page 509

Medications (low-cost or free): Pages 509–510

Sports: Page 510

Stem cell transplantation: Pages 510–511

Wish fulfillment organizations (United States): Pages 511–512

Solid tumor organizations (United States)

Children's Neuroblastoma Cancer Foundation (CNCF)
(866) 671-2623
www.cncfhope.org

The CNCF is a national organization committed to finding a cure for neuroblastoma through research, education, awareness, and advocacy. CNCF holds an annual education conference for parents and funds research.

The Eye Cancer Foundation
(212) 832-8170
www.eyecancer.com

The foundation offers information about the diagnosis and treatment of eye cancers, including retinoblastoma.

Rhabdomyosarcoma Advocacy Group
www.focusonrhabdo.org

This advocacy group works hand-in-hand with leading rhabdo researchers and clinicians from around the world. It offers information about treatments and research on rhabdomyosarcoma and a talk forum for members.

Sarcoma Foundation of America (SFA)
(301) 253-8687
www.curesarcoma.org

The mission of the SFA is to advocate for sarcoma patients by funding research and increasing awareness about the disease. The organization raises money to privately fund grants for sarcoma researchers and conducts education and advocacy efforts on behalf of sarcoma patients.

Neuroblastoma Children's Cancer Society
(800) 532-5162
www.neuroblastomacancer.org

The organization raises funds for neuroblastoma research and provides information to families of children with neuroblastoma.

Solid tumor organizations (Canada)

Neuroblastoma Canada
http://neuroblastoma.ca

This organization provides information for families on neuroblastoma treatment, along with research, peer support for parents, and an online discussion forum.

Sarcoma Cancer Foundation of Canada (SCFC)
http://sarcomacancer.ca

SCFC provides patient support and education, and it works with Canada's leading research institutions to eradicate the disease.

Solid tumor organizations (Australia)

Australian Sarcoma Study Group (ASSG)
www.australiansarcomagroup.org

ASSG provides information about sarcoma diagnosis, treatment, and links to current research studies.

Neuroblastoma Australia
www.neuroblastoma.org.au

This group funds neuroblastoma research, raises community awareness, and provides families with information.

Solid tumor organization (Germany)

German Children's Eye Cancer Foundation
www.kinderaugenkrebsstiftung.de/english-version

The website of the German Children's Eye Cancer Foundation, which has extensive materials about retinoblastoma, is available in English, German, and Spanish. You can order Elli the Elephant, a stuffed toy that has a removable eye prosthesis, designed to provide comfort and familiarity to children who have had an eye removed.

Other service organizations (United States)

Alex's Lemonade Stand Foundation (ALSF)
(610) 649-3034
www.alexslemonade.org

ALSF raises money to fund innovative research for better treatments and cures for pediatric cancer. It also offer financial assistance for travel to and from specific treatment centers, and a SuperSibs program providing emotional support to siblings of kids with cancer.

American Society for Deaf Children
www.deafchildren.org

This national information and support organization was founded and is governed by parents of deaf children.

American Speech-Language-Hearing Association (ASHA)
(800) 638-8255
www.asha.org

ASHA provides referrals to local speech/language/hearing specialists.

Amputee Coalition
(888) 267-5669
www.amputee-coalition.org

The Amputee Coalition empowers people affected by limb loss through education, advocacy, practical information, and mutual support.

Cancer Care

(800) 813-HOPE / (800) 813-4673

www.cancercare.org

Cancer Care provides referrals, one-on-one counseling, specialized support groups, and educational programs.

Chai Lifeline/Camp Simcha

(877) CHAI-LIFE / (877) 242-4543

www.chailifeline.org

Chai Lifeline offers support service programs for Jewish children and their families, including medical referrals, support groups, visits to hospitalized and housebound children, financial aid, transportation, and a camp for kids with cancer.

Children's Organ Transplant Association (COTA)

(800) 366-2682

http://cota.org/learn-more

COTA provides fundraising assistance to families facing a life-saving organ, stem cell, or bone marrow transplant. Funds raised in a COTA campaign can be used for any expenses related to the transplant.

Flashes of Hope

(440) 442-9700

www.flashesofhope.org

This organization matches professional photographers with families to create powerful, uplifting photographic portraits of children fighting cancer and other life-threatening illnesses.

Gabe's Chemo Duck Program

www.chemoduck.org

This unique educational program offers a Chemo Duck to children with cancer. This soft, cuddly companion provides huggable hope and alleviates fear and anxiety. Developed with the help of child life specialists and medical professionals, the Chemo Duck Program helps introduce children and families to their new life and encourages healing through the power of play therapy.

Hearing Loss Association of America
www.hearingloss.org

This organization provides education, advocacy, and direct support for individuals with hearing loss. It hosts an online parent-to-parent community for parents of children with hearing loss and has a network of state and local chapters.

Monkey in My Chair
(513) 772-4888
www.monkeyinmychair.org

Monkey in My Chair provides a child with cancer a "monkey kit" that includes a big stuffed monkey that takes their place in school when they are unable to be there. The kit contains a book to help teachers explain childhood cancer and its treatment to classmates to help them gain insight and empathy.

National Association for Parents of Children with Visual Impairments
(800) 562-6265
www.familyconnect.org

This association maintains a national support network via telephone and mail correspondence; provides publications, information, referrals, conferences, outreach programs; and publishes a quarterly newsletter.

National Center for Complementary and Alternative Medicine (NCCAM)
(888) 644-6226
http://nccam.nih.gov

NCCAM is dedicated to exploring complementary and alternative healing practices in the context of rigorous science, training researchers, and disseminating authoritative information.

National Organization of Parents of Blind Children
(410) 659-9314
http://nopbc.org

This division of the National Federation of the Blind connects parents to peer support and provides information and resources.

Physician Data Query (PDQ)
(800) 4-CANCER / (800) 422-6237
www.cancer.gov/publications/pdq/information-summaries/pediatric-treatment

PDQ is the National Cancer Institute's computerized listing of accurate and up-to-date information for patients and health professionals about cancer treatments, research studies, and clinical trials.

Ronald McDonald House Charities (RMC)
(630) 623-7048
http://rmhc.org

RMC is committed to helping families of seriously ill children by providing Ronald McDonald Houses, the Ronald McDonald Learning Program, and Ronald McDonald Family Rooms within hospitals.

Songs of Love Foundation
(800) 960-SONG / (800) 960-7664
www.songsoflove.org

This volunteer group has more than 200 artists who produce personalized musical portraits for children with chronic or life-threatening diseases.

Other service organizations (Canada)

Childhood Cancer Canada Foundation (CCCF)
(800) 363-1062
www.childhoodcancer.ca

CCCF invests in collaborative cancer research and provides support programs for families, such as *a teen connector* website, scholarships for survivors, and financial assistance.

Kids Cancer Care of Alberta
(403) 216-9210
www.kidscancercare.ab.ca

This foundation helps Alberta children with cancer and their families by providing camps, direct service programs for children and families, research funding, hospital programs, and student scholarships.

Other service organizations (Australia)

Cancer Australia – Children's Cancer website
http://childrenscancer.canceraustralia.gov.au

This government cancer program brings together a range of evidence-based information on children's cancers for families, health professionals, and researchers. The site includes links to support organizations and clinical trials.

CanTeen, The Australian Organization for Young People Living with Cancer
www.canteen.org.au

CanTeen provides support services for young people ages 12 to 24 through programs that include face-to-face counseling, phone support, peer mentors, and printed resources.

Challenge Foundation
www.challenge.org.au

The Challenge Foundation offers services for families of children with cancer, including camps, hospital support, respite and holiday accommodations, parent support, and family activity days.

Childhood Cancer Association
www.childhoodcancer.asn.au

This South Australian organization provides emotional, practical, and financial support to families. Programs include peer, family, and sibling support; accommodations for families from rural areas; respite support; educational assistance; and bereavement services.

Country Care Link
www.sistersofcharityoutreach.com.au

Country Care Link provides support and hospitality to people visiting Sydney for medical purposes.

Redkite
www.redkite.org.au

This organization serves children with cancer and their families through financial assistance, emotional support, and educational assistance.

Ronald McDonald House Charities Australia (RMC)
www.rmhc.org.au

RMC is committed to helping families of seriously ill children by providing Ronald McDonald Houses, the Ronald McDonald Learning Program, Ronald McDonald Family Rooms within hospitals, and the Ronald McDonald Family Retreat (free holiday accommodations).

Camps

For a comprehensive list of camps for children with cancer, visit *www.ped-onc.org/cfis-sues/camps.html.*

Camp Simcha
(877) CHAI-LIFE / (877) 242-4543
www.campsimcha.org

A camp run by the national, nonprofit Jewish organization Chai Lifeline.

Children's Oncology Camping Association International
(404) 661-5723
www.cocai.org

Umbrella organization of groups that provide camps for children with cancer.

Camp Quality (Australia)
www.campquality.org.au

Organization that provides fun therapy for children and families of children with cancer, including camps for ill children and their siblings, family camps, fun days, pamper days for moms and daughters, and fishing weekends for fathers and sons.

Educational and legal support

The Disability Rights Education and Defense Fund
(800) 348-4232
www.dredf.org

This organization trains and educates people with disabilities and parents of children with disabilities about their rights under state and federal disability rights laws.

Federation for Children with Special Needs

(617) 236-7210

www.fcsn.org

Federally funded organization with representation in every state. FCSN provides information about special education rights and laws, conferences, referrals for services, parent training workshops, publications, and advocacy information.

Job Accommodation Network (JAN)

(800) 526-7234

www.jan.wvu.edu

JAN facilitates the employment and retention of workers with disabilities by providing employers, employment providers, people with disabilities, their family members, and other interested parties with information about job accommodations, entrepreneurship, and related subjects.

Learning Disabilities Associaton of America (LDA)

(412) 341-1515

www.ldaamerica.org

LDA serves parents, professionals, and individuals with learning disabilities; has local chapters; and provides educational materials.

National Center for Learning Disabilities

(888) 575-7373

www.ncld.org

This center offers extensive resources, referral services, and educational programs about learning disabilities. It also promotes public awareness and advocates for effective legislation to help people with learning disabilities.

U.S. Department of Justice ADA Information Line

(800) 514-0301 / TTY: (800) 514-0383

www.ada.gov

Staff members answer questions about the Americans with Disabilities Act (ADA), explain how to file a complaint, and provide dispute resolution.

Financial help

Compass to Care
(773) 657-3269
http://compasstocare.org

Compass to Care schedules and pays for travel and lodging arrangements to a hospital more than 60 miles from a child's home. Child must be younger than 18 with a demonstrated financial need and on active treatment for cancer.

First Hand Foundation
(816) 201-1569
www.firsthandfoundation.org

This foundation assists children who have health-related needs when insurance and other sources of financial resources have been exhausted.

National Children's Cancer Society (NCCS)
(800) 532-6459
www.nationalchildrenscancersociety.org

NCCS serves as a financial, emotional, and educational resource for families that cannot make ends meet when their child is diagnosed with cancer.

Free air services (United States)

Air Charity Network
(877) 621-7177
http://aircharitynetwork.org

The network is made up of independent member organizations identified by specific geographical service areas. These organizations are groups of volunteer pilots or groups that coordinate free airline tickets or reduced-price ambulatory services.

Air Care Alliance
(888) 260-9707
www.aircarealliance.org

Nationwide association of humanitarian flying organizations that provide flights for medical treatment.

Angel Flight Midatlantic

(800) 296-3797

www.angelflightmidatlantic.org

Provides free transportation to medical treatment for people who cannot afford public transportation or who cannot tolerate it for health reasons. It serves patients departing from the District of Columbia, Delaware, Kentucky, Maryland, Michigan, Ohio, Pennsylvania, Virginia, and West Virginia. (A member of Air Charity Network.)

Corporate Angel Network, Inc.

(866) 328-1313

www.corpangelnetwork.org

This network gives patients with cancer available seats on corporate aircraft to get to and from recognized cancer treatment centers. Patients must be able to walk and travel without life-support systems or medical attention. A child may be accompanied by up to two adults. There is no cost or financial-need requirement.

Miles for Kids in Need

www.aa.com/kids

American Airlines provides free travel for ill children and their families. A third party, such as a charitable organization, hospital, or other tax-exempt organization, must submit travel requests.

Miracle Flights for Kids

(800) 359-1711 or (702) 261-0494

www.miracleflights.org

This organization purchases commercial airline tickets, uses private aircraft, and combines resources from individual donors to provide free transportation to medical treatment centers all across America.

National Patient Travel Center

24-hour hot line: (800) 296-1217

www.patienttravel.org

This organization refers callers to the most appropriate and cost-effective charitable or commercial services, including volunteer pilot organizations and special airline transport programs. (A member of Air Charity Network.)

Free air service (Canada)

Hope Air
(877) 346-HOPE / (877) 346-4673
www.hopeair.ca

Hope Air provides free air transport to Canadians in financial need who must travel from their communities to recognized facilities for medical care.

Free air service (Australia)

Angel Flight Australia
www.angelflight.org.au

Angel Flight coordinates free, non-emergency flights to help people dealing with bad health, poor finances, and daunting distances.

Insurance

Patient Advocate Foundation (PAF)
(800) 532-5274
www.patientadvocate.org

PAF offers a network of attorneys who provide pro bono (free) advice; helps mediate disputes with insurance companies by acting as a liaison; and provides publications about managed care and health insurance appeals.

Medications (low-cost or free)

NeedyMeds, Inc.
www.needymeds.org

This nonprofit organization helps people who cannot afford medicine or healthcare costs. Anyone can contact NeedyMeds anonymously and all assistance provided is free of charge.

Partnership for Prescription Assistance (PPA)
(888) 477-2669
www.pparx.org

PPA helps find companies and agencies that provide prescription medicines free of charge to physicians whose patients might not otherwise have access to necessary medicines.

RxHope
(877) 267-0517
www.rxhope.com

RxHope lists patient-assistance programs that are offered by federal, state, and charitable organizations.

Sports organizations

Disabled Sports USA
(301) 217-0960
www.disabledsportsusa.org

This organization provides adaptive sports opportunities for people with disabilities to develop independence, confidence, and fitness through sports.

First Descents
(303) 945-2490
http://firstdescents.org

First Descents provides life-changing outdoor adventures for young adults (age 18–39) affected by cancer.

Stem cell transplantation

Bone and Blood Marrow Transplant Information Network (BMT InfoNet)
(888) 597-7674
www.bmtinfonet.org

BMT InfoNet supplies high-quality, easy-to-understand information about bone marrow, peripheral blood stem cell, and cord blood transplants.

Children's Organ Transplant Association (COTA)

(800) 366-2682

www.cota.org

COTA provides fundraising help for families of children who need transplants (including stem cell transplants).

HelpHopeLive

(800) 642-8399

www.helphopelive.org

This organization provides fundraising assistance and donor awareness materials to transplant and catastrophic injury patients nationwide.

Wish fulfillment organizations (United States)

In addition to the large organizations listed below, many smaller and local organizations grant wishes to seriously ill children. A comprehensive list of wish fulfillment organizations can be found online at *www.ped-onc.org/cfissues/maw.html*.

Children's Wish Foundation International

(800) 323-WISH / (800) 323-9474

www.childrenswish.org

Fulfills the wishes of children with life-threatening illnesses in the United States and Europe.

Clayton Dabney Foundation for Kids with Cancer

(214) 361-2600

http://claytondabney.org

Provides last wishes and financial assistance to families of terminally ill children.

The Dream Factory, Inc.

(800) 456-7556

www.dreamfactoryinc.org

Grants the wishes of children ages 3 to 18 who are critically or chronically ill (has chapters in 30 states).

Make-a-Wish Foundation of America

(800) 722-WISH / (800) 722-9474

www.wish.org

Grants wishes to children younger than age 18 with life-threatening illnesses (has U.S. and international chapters and affiliates), regardless of financial need.

Sunshine Foundation
(215) 396-4770
www.sunshinefoundation.org

Grants wishes to chronically or terminally ill children ages 3 to 18 (no geographic boundaries).

Wish fulfillment organizations (Canada)

The Children's Wish Foundation of Canada
(905) 427-5353
www.childrenswish.ca

Provides a once-in-a-lifetime experience for children ages 3 to 18 with high-risk, life-threatening diseases (has chapters throughout Canada).

Make-A-Wish Canada
(888) 822-9474
https://makeawish.ca

The national office and eight regional chapters grant magical wishes to children with life-threatening illnesses who are ages 3 through 17, without regard to family income.

Wish fulfillment organizations (Australia)

Make-A-Wish Foundation of Australia National Office
www.makeawish.org.au

Grants seriously ill children in Australia their most-cherished wish.

Starlight Children's Foundation Australia
www.starlight.org.au

Brightens the lives of seriously ill and hospitalized children and their families through-out Australia by granting wishes, providing vans that travel to remote hospitals, and offering activities, entertainment, and social engagement in hospital Starlight Rooms.

Hospice and bereavement (United States)

Children's Hospice International (CHI)
(703) 684-0330
www.chionline.org

CHI provides resources and referrals for children and families of children with life-threatening conditions.

The Compassionate Friends National Office
(877) 969-0010
www.compassionatefriends.org

Compassionate Friends offers understanding and friendship to bereaved families through support meetings at local chapters and telephone support (they match people with similar losses). It also publishes a newsletter for parents and one for siblings.

Hospice and bereavement (Canada)

Canadian Network of Pediatric Hospices (CNPH)
http://cnph.ca

CNPH fosters collaboration and sharing among pediatric residential hospices in Canada.

Hospice and bereavement (Australia)

Bear Cottage
www.bearcottage.chw.edu.au

New South Wales's only children's hospice is located on the grounds of St. Patrick's Estate, near Sydney. It offers both respite and palliative care to children and young people with life-limiting illnesses and their families.

The Compassionate Friends New South Wales
www.tcfnsw.org.au

Compassionate Friends assists families in the positive resolution of grief following the death of a child and provides information to help others be supportive.

Hummingbird House

http://hummingbirdhouse.org.au

Queensland's only children's hospice is located in a north suburb of Brisbane. It provides respite and palliative care to children and teens with life-limiting illness, with a family-centered approach.

Palliative Care Australia (PCA)

www.palliativecare.org.au

PCA provides information, resources, and referrals.

Books, Websites, and Support Groups

A WEALTH OF INFORMATION about childhood solid tumors is available through libraries and online. This appendix briefly describes how to find the information you need. It also lists books, webistes, and support groups you might find helpful when seeking information about or support for your child's medical condition or treatment.

How to find the information you need

Libraries have a computerized database of all materials available in their various branches. If you need help learning how to use these book-locating systems, ask a librarian. You can also learn how to request a book from another branch, and how to put a book on hold if it is currently checked out. Some libraries have access to a digital library service that will allow you to check out the electronic version of a book or journal and read it on your own computer or other device.

If a book is not in your library's collection, ask a reference librarian if it can be obtained from another library via interlibrary loan. This is common practice, and you might be able to get medical texts from university or medical school libraries. Some local libraries also have online databases that list all publications available at regional libraries so you can request that a book be sent to your local library for pick up.

If you want to read medical journal articles, you can access them through your local library. The librarian can show you how to use the database to search for articles and where to find the periodicals. Public libraries often subscribe to only the most popular medical journals, such as the *New England Journal of Medicine* and *Journal of the American Medical Association*. If you are able to visit a university or medical school library, you will find many more print medical journals available. If you do not live close to one of these libraries, ask your local librarian to help you obtain copies of the articles you want.

An astonishing amount of information is available through the internet. Libraries from all over the world can be accessed, and you can download information in minutes from huge databases such as MedLine or Cancerlit. Obtaining information from respected organizations, large medical databases, reputable journals, or large libraries is exceedingly helpful for parents at home with sick children. However, the huge numbers of people using the internet has spawned websites, chat rooms, and social media sites that may or may not contain accurate information. You may want to read information only from reliable sources and adopt the motto: "Let the buyer beware."

If you do not have a home computer, many libraries provide internet access. Ask the librarian to help you connect to MedLine, Physician Data Query (PDQ), or other databases you wish to search.

Books

Below are some print books (many are also available as ebooks) that parents of children with solid tumors have found helpful. You might find there are some print books you wish to own. If they are not in stock at your local or online bookstore, ask if they can be special-ordered for you—most bookstores are happy to do this for customers. Copies of out-of-print books can often be located through the internet from used bookstores or private sellers on sites such as Amazon.com. Ebooks are available in many different formats and from many online booksellers (e.g., *www.amazon.com*, *www.barnesandnoble. com*) or from local libraries.

General reading (for adults)

Bracken, Jean Munn. *Children with Cancer: A Comprehensive Reference Guide for Parents.* (2010). Comprehensive coverage of childhood cancers, written by a librarian who is the parent of a survivor of childhood cancer.

Cochran, Lizzie. *Singing Away: Stories of Faith, Hope & Love in the Fight Against Childhood Cancer.* (2013). True stories written by families of children with cancer.

Jampolsky, Gerald G. *Advice to Doctors and Other Big People from Kids.* (1991). This book is full of stories from children with catastrophic illnesses that remind us how perceptive and aware children of all ages are, and how necessary it is to involve them in medical decisions. Available at *www.healingcenter.org/library.html*.

Kushner, Harold. *When Bad Things Happen to Good People, revised ed.* (2004). Rabbi Kushner wrote this comforting book about how people of faith cope with catastrophic events.

National Cancer Institute. *Young People with Cancer: A Handbook for Parents*. This booklet describes the different types of childhood cancer, medical procedures, dealing with the diagnosis, family issues, and sources of information. To obtain a free copy, call (800) 4-CANCER / (800) 422-6237, or read it at *www.cancer.gov/cancertopics/youngpeople*.

Sourkes, Barbara M. *Armfuls of Time: The Psychological Experience of the Child with a Life-Threatening Illness*. (1996). Written by a psychologist, this eloquent book features the voices and artwork of children with cancer. It clearly describes the psychological effects of cancer on children and explains the power of the therapeutic process.

Woznick, Leigh; Goodheart, Carol. *Living With Childhood Cancer: A Practical Guide to Help Families Cope*. (2002). Written by a mother–daughter team, this book draws on the authors' experiences with cancer, as well as their professional expertise and stories from others to help families address the psychological impact of childhood cancer.

General reading (for children)

Bourgeois, Paulette. *Franklin Goes to the Hospital*. (2011). Franklin the turtle goes to the hospital for an operation to repair his broken shell, and everyone thinks he's being very brave. But Franklin is only pretending to be fearless. He's worried that his x-rays will show just how frightened he is inside. (For young children.)

Crary, Elizabeth. *Dealing with Feelings. I'm Frustrated; I'm Mad; I'm Sad Series*. (1992). Fun, game-like books to teach young children how to handle feelings and solve problems.

Diaz, Jonathan and others. *True Heroes: A Treasury of Modern-day Fairly Tales Written by Best-selling Authors*. (2015). Gorgeous photographs and stories written by best-selling authors make children with cancer the heroes of their own modern-day fairy tales.

Gaynor, Kate. *The Famous Hat: A Story book*. (2008). This book helps children with cancer prepare for hospitalization, chemotherapy, and hair loss.

Keene, Nancy; Romain, Trevor. *Chemo, Craziness & Comfort: My Book About Childhood Cancer*. (2002). A 200-page resource that provides practical information for children diagnosed with cancer between 6 and 12 years of age. Warm and funny illustrations and easy-to-read text help the child (and parents) make sense of cancer and its treatment. Available free from *www.acco.org/Information/Resources/Books.aspx*.

Krisher, Trudy. *Kathy's Hats: A Story of Hope*. (1992). A charming book, for children ages 5 to 10, about a girl whose love of hats comes in handy when chemotherapy makes her hair fall out.

Paul, Trisha. *Chronicling Childhood Cancer: A Collection of Personal Stories by Children and Teens with Cancer.* (2014). Ten children and teens describe the cancer experience in their own words and pictures.

Richmond, Christina. *Chemo Girl: Saving the World One Treatment at a Time.* (1996). Written by a 12-year-old girl with rhabdomyosarcoma, this book describes a superhero who shares hope and encouragement.

Skole, Gary; Skole, Jarrod. *Imagine What's Possible: Using the Power of Your Mind to Help Take Control of Your Life During Cancer.* (2011). Techniques using visualization and guided imagery to help children ages 9 to 12 cope with fear, pain, anxiety, and other challenges.

General reading (for teens)

Gravelle, Karen. *Teenagers Face to Face With Cancer.* (2000). Sixteen teenagers talk openly about their experiences with cancer—from the physical difficulties of coping with treatment to the emotional trauma, which can be as painful as the illness itself. A heartfelt, honest book that demonstrates clearly how having cancer changes young people and how strength can emerge from struggles.

General reading (for siblings)

Dodd, Mike. *Oliver's Story.* (2004). A 40-page illustrated book for 3- to 8-year old siblings of children diagnosed with cancer. Order a free copy in English or Spanish from *www.acco.org/Information/Resources/Books.aspx.*

Loughridge, Sally. *Daniel and His Starry Night Blanket: A Story of Illness and Sibling Love.* (2015). With lovely images and comforting words, this book explores the many emotions felt by Daniel over the course of his sister's treatment for cancer.

National Cancer Insitute. *When Your Brother or Sister Has Cancer: A Guide for Teens.* (2012). This 100-page book helps siblings of a child with cancer prepare and cope with some of the challenges they face. Available free at *www.cancer.gov/Publications/ patient-education/sibling-has-cancer.*

O'Toole, Donna. *Aarvy Aardvark Finds Hope: A Read Aloud Story for People of All Ages About Loving and Losing, Friendship and Hope.* (1988). Aarvy Aardvark and his friend Ralphie Rabbit show how a family member or friend can help another in distress.

Hospitalization

Keene, Nancy. *Your Child in the Hospital: A Practical Guide for Parents, 3rd ed.* (2015). A pocket guide full of parent stories to help others prepare their children for short- or long-term hospitalization.

Memoirs

MacLellan, Scott. *Amanda's Gift.* (1998). A review of the emotional and financial impact of a child's 7-year fight with cancer, including a liver transplant. It covers the complexities of insurance coverage and all areas of life as a caregiver, including the impact on faith and marriage.

Scott, Bar. *The Present Giver: A Memoir.* (2011). Passionate and beautiful story by singer/songwriter Bar Scott about her 2-year-old son Forrest's journey through treatment for and death from stage IV liver cancer.

Soukup, Kathy; Soukup, Joel. *Standing Tall: On One Leg.* (2013). Short, inspirational memoir about a young man, age 16, diagnosed with osteosarcoma.

Strumpf, Katie. *I Never Signed Up for This! An Upfront Guide to Dealing with Cancer at a Young Age.* (2006). Written by a 25-year-old survivor with an upbeat attitude, this book covers returning to school, dealing with parents and doctors, losing your hair, and coping with the fear of death.

Neuroblastoma

Children's Neuroblastoma Cancer Foundation. *The CNCF Handbook for Parents of Children with Neuroblastoma.* (2009). A handbook covering medical tests, tumor pathology, clinical trials, and coping with treatments. Available for free download from Children's Neuroblastoma Cancer Foundation at *www.cncfhope.org/CNCF_Neuroblastoma_Parent_Handbook*.

Parenting

Faber, Adle; Mazlish, Elaine. *How to Talk so Kids will Listen…and Listen so Kids Will Talk.* (2012). A book about how to effectively communicate with your child.

Nelson, Jane. *Positive Discipline.* (2006). This parenting book explains how to focus on solutions while being kind and firm.

Radiation

National Cancer Institute. *Radiation Therapy and You: Support for People With Cancer.* (2007). A 60-page booklet that explains conventional radiation, what to expect, possible side effects, and follow-up care. Available online at *www.cancer.gov/publications/patient-education/radiation-therapy-and-you*.

Retinoblastoma

Talusan, Grace. *Joey's Special Eye.* (2008). A coloring book that tells the story of Joey, who has his eye removed due to retinoblastoma and receives a prosthetic eye. Available at *www.eyecancer.com/foundation/retinoblastoma-posters-and-coloring-books*.

Chernus-Mansfield, Nancy. *My Fake Eye: The Story of My Prosthesis.* (1991). A 3-year-old's experience with enucleation and the subsequent fitting of prosthesis is reassuring to both the child and the family. Available in English and Spanish from the Institute for Families, which provides support for families of children with vision loss. Available at *www.instituteforfamilies.org/books-and-dvds*.

School

Hoffman, Ruth (editor). *Educating the Child With Cancer: A Guide for Parents and Teachers, 2nd ed.* (2011). A book written by top researchers in the field that includes parents' personal experiences. Order a free copy from *www.acco.org/Information/Resources/Books.aspx*.

Leukemia and Lymphoma Society. *Living and Learning with Cancer.* (2013). Booklet about returning to school and obtaining accommodations (appropriate for children with any type of cancer). Available at *www.lls.org/content/nationalcontent/resource-center/freeeducationmaterials/childhoodbloodcancer/pdf/learninglivingwithcancer.pdf*.

Princeton Review. *K&W Guide to College Programs and Services for Students with Learning Disabilities or Attention Deficit/Hyperactivity Disorder, 12th ed.* (2014). Excellent reference book that is available at most large libraries.

Silver, Larry. *The Misunderstood Child: Understanding and Coping with Your Child's Learning Disabilities, 4th ed.* (2006). Comprehensive discussion about positive strategies that can be implemented at home and in school to help children with learning disabilities.

Siblings

Faber, Adele; Mazlish, Elaine. *Siblings Without Rivalry: How to Help Your Children Live Together So You Can Live Too, revised edition.* (2012). Offers dozens of simple and effective methods to reduce conflict and foster a cooperative spirit. Helpful information for all stressed parents.

Greves, Julie; Tenhulzen, Katy; Wilkinson, Fred. *Upside Down and Backwards: A Sibling's Journey Through Childhood Cancer.* (2014). Child life specialists and social workers from Seattle Children's Hospital describe the effect of cancer on siblings.

Survivorship

Keene, Nancy; Hobbie, Wendy; Ruccione, Kathy. *Childhood Cancer Survivors: A Practical Guide to Your Future, 3rd ed.* (2012). A user-friendly, comprehensive guide about late effects of treatment for childhood cancer. Full of stories from survivors of all types of childhood cancer. Also covers emotional issues, insurance, jobs, relationships, and ways to stay healthy.

Technical reading

Medical textbooks are very expensive. If you'd like to read one, you can usually obtain it through interlibrary loan (ask your local reference librarian).

Bleyer, Archie; Barr, Ronald. *Cancer in Adolescents and Young Adults.* (2007). Medical textbook.

Francis, Jasmine H; Abramson, David H. (editors). *Recent Advances in Retinoblastoma Treatment.* (2015). Medical textbook.

Hayat, M.A. (editor). *Neuroblastoma.* (2011). Medical textbook.

Institute of Medicine. *Comprehensive Cancer Care for Children and Their Families.* (2015). Summarizes needed improvements in research, treatments, and outcomes. Available as full text online or as a paperback at *www.nap.edu/catalog/21754/ comprehensive-cancer-care-for-children-and-their-families-summary-of.*

Kleinerman, Eugenie. (editor). *Current Advances in Osteosarcoma.* (2014). Medical textbook.

Pizzo, Philip A.; Poplack, David. (editors). *Principles and Practice of Pediatric Oncology, 6th ed.* (2010). Medical textbook.

Pritchard-Jones, Kathy; Dome, Jeffrey. *Renal Tumors of Childhood: Biology and Therapy.* (2015). Medical textbook.

Treatment journals

Alex's Lemonade Stand Treatment Journal. Alex's Lemonade Stand Foundation provides a free treatment journal to help parents of children with cancer keep track of important information. Parents can request a hard copy of the journal or can create their own online journal at *www.alexslemonade.org/childhood-cancer-treatment-journal.*

Crawford, Bonnie; Lazar, Linda. *In My World.* (1999). Journal for teens coping with life-threatening illnesses. Includes chapters called "Things Accomplished in My Life," "I've Been Thinking," and "Questions I'd Like Answered." Available by calling (866) 218-0101 or visiting *www.centering.org.*

Terminal illness and bereavement

Callanan, Maggie; Kelley, Patricia. *Final Gifts: Understanding the Special Awareness, Needs, and Communications of the Dying.* (2012). Written by two hospice nurses with decades of experience, this book helps families understand and communicate with terminally ill people. Compassionate, comforting, and insightful, *it* movingly teaches how to listen to and comfort the dying.

Bereavement: A Magazine of Hope and Healing. For a free copy or to subscribe, call (888) 604-4673 or visit *www.bereavementmag.com.*

Bernstein, Judith R. *When the Bough Breaks: Forever After the Death of a Son or Daughter.* (1998). A serious and sensitive book about how to cope with the loss of a child.

Gilbert, Laynee. *I Remember You: A Grief Journal, 2nd ed.* (2000). A journal for recording written and photographic memories during the first year of mourning. Beautiful book filled with quotes and comfort.

Kübler-Ross, Elisabeth. *On Children and Death: How Children and Their Parents Can and Do Cope With Death.* (1997). In this comforting book, Dr. Kübler-Ross offers practical help for living through the terminal period of a child's life with love and understanding. Discusses children's knowledge about death, visualization, letting go, funerals, help from friends, and spirituality.

Mitchell, Ellen, and others. *Beyond Tears: Living After Losing a Child.* (2009). Comforting book written by nine mothers who each lost a child. Includes a chapter written from the perspective of surviving siblings.

Orloff, Stacy; Huff, Susan. (editors). *Home Care for Seriously Ill Children: A Manual for Parents.* (2003). Helps parents explore the possibility of home care for the dying child. Contains practical information about what to expect, methods of pain relief, and management of medical problems. Available from Children's Hospice International by emailing info@chionline.org or online at *http://75.103.82.45/ publication-order-form.*

Wolfelt, Alan. *Healing a Parent's Grieving Heart: 100 Practical Ideas After Your Child Dies.* (2002). A list of practical actions a parent can take to memorialize their child's life and to cope and heal in the months and years that follow.

Sibling grief (adult reading)

Grollman, Earl. *Talking About Death: A Dialogue Between Parent and Child, 4th ed.* (2011). A classic guide for helping children cope with grief. Contains a children's read-along section to explain and explore children's feelings. In very comforting language, the book teaches parents how to explain death, understand children's emotions, learn how children react to specific types of death, and know when to seek professional help.

Schaefer, Dan; Lyons, Christine. *How Do We Tell the Children? A Step-by-Step Guide for Helping Children and Teens Cope When Someone Dies, 4th ed.* (2010). If your terminally ill child has siblings, read this book. In straightforward, uncomplicated language, the authors describe how to explain the facts of death to children and teens, and show how to include children in the family support network, laying the

foundation for the healing process to begin. Also includes a crisis section with quick references for what to do in a variety of situations.

White, P. Gill. *Sibling Grief: Healing After the Death of a Sister or Brother.* (2008). This book explains the emotional significance of sibling loss, drawing on clinical experience, research, and wisdom from hundreds of bereaved siblings to explain the five healing tasks specific to sibling grief.

Sibling grief (young child)

Buscaglia, Leo. *The Fall of Freddy the Leaf: A Story of Life for All Ages.* (1982). This wise yet simple story about a leaf named Freddy explains death as a necessary part of the cycle of life.

Hanson, Warren. *The Next Place.* (2002). A book of warm and peaceful images that helps young children think about the continuity and beauty of all lives, and provides comfort to teens and adults, as well.

Hickman, Martha. *Last Week My Brother Anthony Died.* (1984). A touching story of a preschooler's feelings when her infant brother dies. The family's minister (a bereaved parent himself) comforts her by comparing feelings to clouds—always there but ever changing.

Karst, Patrice. *The Invisible String.* (2000). This gentle, sweet book explains the connections between family members and helps children cope with fear of separation and loss, whether through absence or death.

Mellonie, Bryan; Ingpen, Robert. *Lifetimes: The Beautiful Way to Explain Death to Children.* (1983). Beautiful paintings and simple text explain that dying is as much a part of life as being born.

Varley, Susan. *Badger's Parting Gifts.* (1992). Badger's friends share the memories he left them and learn to accept his death. (For grades K to 3.)

Sibling grief (school-aged children)

Romain, Trevor. *What on Earth Do You Do When Someone Dies?* (1999). Warm, honest words and beautiful illustrations help children understand and cope with grief.

Rosen, Michael. *Michael Rosen's Sad Book.* (2011). Written to document the author's grief after the sudden death of his teen son. The moving illustrations can help children and adults both understand grief and loss, and feel understood.

Temes, Roberta. *The Empty Place: A Child's Guide Through Grief.* (1992). Explains and describes feelings after the death of a sibling, such as the empty place in the house, at the table, and in a sibling's heart.

Sibling grief (teenagers)

Gravelle, Karen; Haskins, Charles. *Teenagers Face to Face with Bereavement*. (2000). The perspectives and experiences of 17 teenagers comprise the heart of this book, which focuses on teens coping with grief.

Grollman, Earl. *Straight Talk About Death for Teenagers: How to Cope with Losing Someone You Love*. (1993). Wonderful book that discusses denial, pain, anger, sadness, physical symptoms, and depression. Charts methods to help teens work through their feelings at their own pace.

Hyatt, Erica Goldblatt. *Grieving for the Sibling You Lost: A Teen's Guide to Coping with Grief and Finding Meaning After Loss*. (2015). Helps teens understand grief, the symptoms that accompany it, various ways to cope, creating meaning out of loss and suffering, and when and how to ask for help.

Websites

This section lists websites that are not included in Appendix B, *Resource Organizations*, but that many parents find helpful. As with any resource, check with your child's treatment team about the accuracy of any information found on websites.

Calendars and practical help

CareCalendar
www.carecalendar.org

CareCalendar is a free service to organize meals and other help for families in need. The coordinator can upload photos and status updates to these password-protected sites.

CaringBridge
www.caringbridge.org

CaringBridge allows people who are ill or injured to create a website to share medical updates and personal photos with those who care about them. This website also provides users with the ability to post a simple task calendar to let supporters help with meals and chores.

Lotsa Helping Hands
www.lotsahelpinghands.com

Online task scheduling and information-sharing websites for families that need support from friends and family. The site allows the site manager to sign up new members, schedule tasks, communicate needs, and post messages and photos to members

of the community. Supporters can sign up to help with tasks and send messages of encouragement.

My Med Schedule App
http://mymedschedule.com

A software application to help you keep track of medication schedules, dosages, and any other important information, with reminder timers. You can record lab results and track them over time. The app is password protected and can be used from a computer, smartphone, or other device.

Dictionary

National Cancer Institute Dictionary of Cancer Terms
www.cancer.gov/dictionary

Education

Wrightslaw
www.wrightslaw.com

Accurate, up-to-date information about special education laws for parents, advocates, and attorneys.

Employment and family leave

National Conference of State Legislatures
www.ncsl.org/research/labor-and-employment/state-family-and-medical-leave-laws.aspx

State family medical leave and parental leave laws for all 50 states.

U.S. Department of Labor
www.dol.gov/whd/fmla

The Wage and Hour Division of the Department of Labor provides detailed information about employees' rights under the Family and Medical Leave Act.

Fundraising

YouCaring
www.youcaring.com

YouCaring allows individuals to create a webpage to raise money for medical expenses or other pressing bills. The link to your page can be shared by email and on social media so friends, family, and community members can help to spread the word widely

and donate to you directly. Several versions of these personal fundraising sites are available, including *www.gofundme.com* and *www.crowdrise.com*. Fundraising sites charge varying fees for processing the money donated, so read the fine print very carefully.

General online medical resources

Medline Plus
www.nlm.nih.gov/medlineplus/druginformation.html

A service of the National Institutes of Health, this site provides accurate information about drugs, including precautions and side effects.

National Cancer Institute
www.cancer.gov

A huge, reliable site that provides accurate information about cancer, treatments, and clinical trials.

Pediatric Oncology Resource Center
www.ped-onc.org

Excellent source of information about pediatric cancers created and managed by a mother of a long-term survivor. Contains detailed and accurate material about diseases, treatment, family issues, activism, bereavement, and survivorship. Also provides links to other helpful cancer sites.

PubMed
www.ncbi.nlm.nih.gov/PubMed

The National Library of Medicine's free search service provides access to more than 25 million citations in MEDLINE and PREMEDLINE (with links to participating online journals) and other related databases.

Quackwatch
www.quackwatch.com

International network of people who post information about health-related frauds, myths, fads, fallacies, and misconduct.

Rx List—The Internet Drug Index
www.rxlist.com

Accurate information about prescription medications. Also contains a medical dictionary.

Survivorship

Ped-Onc Resource Center Survivor Issues
www.ped-onc.org/survivors

Collection of information for families of survivors, including resources, technical and nontechnical articles, accurate information about late effects, sources of scholarships for survivors, list of survivorship clinics, and much more.

Children's Oncology Group Long-term Follow-up Guidelines
www.survivorshipguidelines.org

Downloadable document that details current knowledge about the late effects of childhood cancer. The late effects are listed by treatment (chemotherapy drug or radiation dose/site) and guidelines for needed diagnostic tests are provided. Includes individual "Health Links" with information about dozens of specific late effects.

Online support groups

Be sure to check the accuracy of any medical information obtained from an online support group with members of your child's treatment team.

The Association of Cancer Online Resources, Inc. (ACOR)
www.acor.org

ACOR is a unique collection of 142 online cancer communities that is designed to provide timely and accurate information in a supportive environment. It hosts several pediatric cancer discussion groups, including ones on Wilms tumor, Ewing sarcoma, retinoblastoma, and rhabdomyosarcoma.

Group Loop
www.grouploop.org

Online cancer support for teens through the Cancer Support Community/Gilda's Club network.

Imerman Angels
www.imermanangels.org

One-on-one mentoring for adolescents and young adults with cancer patients.

Momcology
www.momcology.org

Momcology is a non-profit support organization that connects primary caregivers of children with cancer for peer support and information sharing. Momcology provides real-time connections via peer moderated social networking groups where caregivers can find each other in a safe, secure and responsible environment to discuss protocols, side effects, treatment outcomes, and personal experiences. Momcology connections empower patient families to become educated contributors to their child's medical care team while providing a compassionate environment of support and healing.

Stupid Cancer
www.stupidcancer.org

An online resource for and by adolescents and young adults with cancer. Includes medical information, links to scholarships and grants, regional and national conferences, a talk radio podcast, and an active peer support community, including a one-on-one peer support smartphone app.

Index

American Speech-Language-Hearing Association (ASHA), 500

Americans with Disabilities Act (ADA), 452, 506

Amputation, 16–17, 19, 85, 200

Anaplasia, 92, 94

ANC (absolute neutrophil count), 258, 428, 490, 492

Anemia, 217
    and fatigue, 253
    and kidney tumors, 89
    and transfusions, 150

Anesthesia, 129–132, 206, 242. *See also* Sedation

Anesthesiologists, 132, 199, 277

Anger
    conflict resolution and, 166–168
    diagnosis, response to, 6–7, 350
    of children with tumors, 104, 350
    professional therapy for, 358
    releasing anger, 364
    of siblings, 309

Animals, 270–272, 301

Aniridia, 89–90

Anniversaries
    of child's death, 478, 483

Anti-angiogenesis agents, 212

Antibiotics, 212
    and lactose intolerance, 410
    and stem cell transplants, 294, 299
    dental procedures, 251
    diarrhea from, 251
    pneumonia, to prevent, 231
    with external catheters, 184

Antidepressants, 327, 403

Antimetabolites, 212

Antinausea drugs
    with chemotherapy, 264
    diarrhea from, 251
    list of, 233

Anus, protecting, 253, 260

Anxiety, 6, 101, 128, 195, 356–357, 401

Apheresis, 290, 294

Appealing insurance claim denials, 432, 435–436

Appetite changes, 409
    radiation, 285, 287
    stem cell transplants, 298
    as symptom, 29, 35, 457

Aprepitant, 233

Armfuls of Time: the Psychological Experience of the Child with a Life-Threatening Illness (Sourkes), 350, 406, 487

Aromatherapy, 171, 244, 265

Art therapy, 398, 406

Askin's tumor, 11, 21

Aspirin
    blood clotting, 245, 261
    interactions with, 224, 228

Assent to clinical trials, 121

AST (aspartate aminotransferase), 493

Astramorph PF. *See* Morphine

Ativan. *See* Lorazepam

Atropine, 227

Attending doctors, 156–158, 166

Audiograms, 134–135,

Auditing hospital accounts, 432

Autologous stem cell transplants, 289–303

Avinza. *See* Morphine

B

Back pain
    as symptom, 22, 44

Bactrim, 228, 231, 300

Bag Balm, 253

Balanced diet, 411

Baldness. *See* Hair loss

Balloons, 139, 171, 310, 333

Bathing/showering with catheter, 187

G

Gallium citrate, 140

Gallium scans, 140

Gastrostomy, 140, 202

Gel caps, 147

Genetic factors
  ESFT, and, 22
  neuroblastoma, and, 43
  osteosarcoma, and, 12
  retinoblastoma, and, 57
  rhabdomyosarcoma, and, 76
  soft tissue sarcoma, and, 84
  Wilms tumor, and, 89

Genital herpes, 451

Genital warts, 451

Gifts, 320, 362, 392

Glaucoma, 62, 64

Glutamine, 263

GM-CSF, 232

Goal setting, 459

Gonorrhea, 451

Granisol. *See* Granisetron

Grandparents, 330–332

Granisetron, 233, 234

Granulocyte colony-stimulating factor (G-CSF), 289, 293, 300

Granulocyte-macrophage colony-stimulating factor (GM-CSF), 232

Grief, 8, 482–487

Growth problems, 449
  bone growth x-rays, 135

Growth plates, 11

Guilt
  at diagnosis, 4
  on death of child, 478
  of parents, 360, 401
  of siblings, 307, 373

H

Hair loss, 217, 255–257
  chemotherapy side effect, 218, 221–230
  radiation side effect, 285

Hand washing, 259

Headaches
  from spinal taps, 145
  medication side effect, 230, 234, 239–242
  radiation therapy and, 287
  reason to call doctor, 215

Health history, keeping, 451

Health Insurance Portability and Accountability Act of 1996 (HIPAA), 454

Hearing/hearing loss
  audiogram, 134
  eligibility for special education, 379
  medication side effect, 220–221, 449

Hemangiopericytoma, 83

Hematocrit (HCT), 428, 489, 491

Hematopoietic stem cell transplant. *See* Stem cell transplant

Hematuria, 217

Hemoglobin (Hgb), 29, 489, 491

Hemorrhagic cystitis, 217, 299

Heparin, 183, 185, 186, 190

Hepatitis
  chicken pox complication, 269
  from transfusions, 151
  liver cancers, 29, 34, 36
  survivors and, 450

Hepatoblastoma, 30–34
  diagnosis of, 29
  staging, 31
  treatment, 32
  who gets, 30

Hepatocellular carcinoma, 34–36
  diagnosis of, 29
  staging, 35

Leukocoria, 60
Licensed Clinical Social Worker (LCSW), 402
Licensed Marriage and Family Child Counselor (LMFCC), 402
Licensed Marriage and Family Therapist (LMFT), 402
Licensed Practical Nurse (LPN), 157
Licensed Professional Counselor (LPC), 402
Licensed Social Worker (LSW), 402
Lidocaine, 243
    for mouth sores, 263
    in EMLA cream, 131
    in procedures, 130
Li-Fraumeni syndrome, 13, 76
Ligaments, 11, 71, 72
Liposarcoma, 83
Listening to children, 348
Liver cancers
    choriocarcinoma of the liver, 37
    diagnosis, 29
    hepatoblastoma, 30
    hepatocellular carcinoma, 34
    signs and symptoms, 29
    transplantation for, 37
    undifferentiated embryonal sarcoma, 36
Liver, functions of, 28
Lomotil, 227, 252
Lorazepam, 233, 235
Loss of appetite. See Appetite changes
Low blood cell counts, 258
Lumbar puncture, 144–145
Lumen, 181, 186

M

Magnesium citrate, 250
Magnetic resonance imaging (MRI), 141
Malignant fibrous histiocytoma, 83
Malignant peripheral nerve sheath tumor, 83
Malignant schwannoma, 83

Mannitol, 219, 220
Marriage and partnerships, 325
    coping styles in, 327
    counseling, 327
Masks in radiation therapy, 278
Mealtimes, suggestions for, 413–417
Measles, 215, 375, 378
Meat, 249, 411
Medicaid, 431, 438
    fund raising and, 440
Medical records
    calendar system, 427
    computers, 428
    journals for, 426
    tape or digital recorder, 428
    treatment summary, 451
Medical students, 156
Medical team. See Treatment team
Medi-port, 181
Meditation, 128, 244, 265, 357
Megace, 285
Melphalan, 216, 227
Memorial services, 475
    at school, 392
Mepergan. See Meperidine
Meperidine, 238, 240
Mesna
    hemorrhagic cystitis and, 299
    with cyclophosphamide, 222
    with ifosfamide, 225
Meta-iodobenzylguanidine (mIBG) scan, 142
    neuroblastoma and, 46, 276
Metamucil, 250
Methadone, 238, 240
Methadose. See Methadone
Methotrexate, 216, 228
    folic acid with, 228, 244
    learning disabilities, 258
    MTHFR, 214
    sun sensitivity, 228

Methlyenetetrahydrofolate reductase (MTHFR), 214

mIBG scan. *See* Meta-iodobenzylguanidine (mIBG) scan

Milk of Magnesia, 250

Milk products
    diarrhea, and, 252
    intolerance, 410
    servings of, 410

Mindfulness meditation, 128, 244, 265, 357

Minimal residual disease (MRD), 50, 53

Ministers. *See* Clergy

Morphine, 214, 238, 241
    for procedures, 130

Monoclonal antibody, 53

M-Oxy. *See* Oxycodone

Mouth/throat sores, 262
    glutamine for, 263
    as radiation side effect, 301
    rinses for, 263

MRD. *See* Minimal residual disease

MS Contin. *See* Morphine

MTHFR (methlyenetetrahydrofolate reductase), 214

MTX. *See* Methotrexate

Mucositis, 301

Multidisciplinary second opinions, 120, 165

Music therapy, 244, 406

Mutations of genes
    neuroblastoma, in 43
    retinoblastoma, in 57–58
    Wilms tumor, in 89–90

MYCN amplification, 48–50

N

Nail problems and chemotherapy, 269

Nanoparticles, 54

Nasogastric tubes, 422–423

National Cancer Institute (NCI)
    clinical trials, 115

    contact information, 155
    hospitals, choosing, 155
    stem cell transplants, 297

National Center for Complementary and Alternative Medicine, National Institutes of Health, 245

Nausea and vomiting, 263
    acupuncture for, 265
    Relief Band, 265

Neck
    cranial nerves, 73

Needle aspiration biopsy, 143

Nephrectomy
    partial, 93
    radical, 93

Nephroblastomatosis, 90

Neosar. *See* Cyclophosphamide

Nervous system
    peripheral, 41
    sympathetic, 41

Neupogen, 146, 232

Neuroblastoma
    diagnosis of, 45
    differentiation therapy, 53
    prognosis, 48
    signs and symptoms, 44
    staging, 47
    treatment, 49
    who gets, 42

Neurofibromatosis (NF1), 43, 76, 83

Neurofibrosarcoma, 83

Neuropsychological testing, 382

Neuroradiologist, 69

Neutropenia, 217, 258

No Code orders, 472

Non-rhabdomyosarcoma soft tissue sarcomas, 82–85

Nuclear bone scan, 136

Nurse practitioners, 107, 158

Nurses, 103, 120, 155, 157, 161, 162

R

Radiation oncologists, 274, 278
Radiation recall, 95, 218
Radiation sensitizers, 276
Radiation therapists, 278, 426
Radiation therapy, 273–287
    external, 274
    facilities giving, 277
    hyperfractionation, 274
    immobilization devices, 278
    intensity modulated radiation therapy
      (IMRT), 275
    internal, 275
    long-term side effects, 287
    masks, use of, 279
    photon beam radiation, 274
    proton beam radiation, 275
    questions about, 277
    sedation during, 280
    short-term side effects, 285
    simulation, 282
Radioimmunotherapy, 276
Radiolabeled antibodies, 276
Radioprotectors, 276
Randomization, 116
Record-keeping. *See* Financial records;
  Medical records
Recreation therapy, 179
Rectal temperatures, 150
Recurrence, 457–461
    emotional responses, 459
    goal setting and treatment plan, 459
    making a decision about treatment, 461
    signs and symptoms, 457
Red blood cell count (RBC), 253, 491
Regression, 108
Rehabilitation Act. *See* 504 plans
Rehabilitation services, 209, 265
    occupational therapy, 266

    physical therapy, 266
    school services, 267
Reiki, 129, 244
Relaxation, 365
Relief Band, 265
Religious community, 400
Renal cell carcinoma, 96
Research. *See* Clinical trials
Resection, 202
Residents, 156
Respiratory problems, 44, 73, 130, 151, 217,
  295, 301
Retina, 55, 56, 62
Retinoblastoma, 55–63
    diagnosis of, 61
    signs and symptoms, 60
    staging, 61
    treatment, 63
    who gets, 57
Retinoblasts, 56, 58
Retinoids, 43, 53
Rhabdoid tumor of the kidney, 98
Rhabdomyosarcoma, 75–82
RNs (registered nurses), 157, 402
Rotationplasty, 17
Rothmund-Thomson syndrome, 13
Roxanol. *See* Morphine
Roxicet. *See* Oxycodone
Roxilox. *See* Oxycodone
Roxycodone. *See* Oxycodone
Ruccione, Kathy, 287, 303, 449

S

Saliva, radiation and, 250, 286
Sancuso. *See* Granisitron
Sarcomas
    bone sarcomas, 11–26
    soft tissue sarcomas, 71–85
Sargramostim, 232

Treatment summaries, 451

Trexall. *See* Methotrexate

Trilateral retinoblastoma, 57

Trophies at end of treatment, 444

Trust
    in children, 348
    of parents by child, 106
    of therapist, 404
    of medical team, 104

Tube feeding. *See* Nasogastric tubes;
  Gastrostomy tubes

Tuberous sclerosis, 96

Tumor board, 158

Tylox. *See* Oxycodone

Tyrosinemia, 34

U

Ulcer medications, 299

Ultrasonography, 152

Undifferentiated embryonal sarcoma, 36

Urine
    blood in, 90, 97, 98
    specimens, 152

Urokinase, 184

V

Vaginal tumor, 73

Valium, 130

Vapocoolant sprays, 243

Varicella zoster, 268, 300

Varicella Zoster Immune Globulin (VZIG)
  injection, 268

Vasoactive intestinal peptide (VIP)
  syndrome, 45

Veno-occlusive disease (VOD), 302

Venous catheters
    adhesives used with, 197
    comparison chart, 195
    cost, 194
    external, 181
    PICC, 192
    subcutaneous port, 187

VePesid. *See* Etoposide

Versed, 130

Vesanoid. *See* Topotecan

Vincasar PFS. *See* Vincristine

Vincristine, 216, 230

Vision, loss of, 60, 63
    accommodations for, 387
    early intervention for, 389
    radiation therapy and, 67

Visualization, 244, 365

Vitamin supplements, 417

Vitreous, 55–56, 62, 64, 68

Vomiting, 263–264
    antinausea medications, 233
    from anesthesia, 281
    from chemotherapy, 218–231
    from stem cell transplant, 296
    radiation side effect, 285, 287

VP-16. *See* Etoposide

W

WAGR syndrome, 89

Wakes, 475

Weakness, 253

Websites, 524–528
    learning disabilities, 381

White blood cells (WBCs), 258, 492
    absolute neutrophil count (ANC),
      258–259, 261
    stem cell transplant, and, 289, 299, 301

Wide-field fundus photography, 61
Wigs, 255–256
    as deductible medical expense, 430
Wilms tumor, 89–96
    diagnosis of, 90
    genetic factors, 89
    signs and symptoms, 88
    staging, 91
    treatment, 93
    who gets, 89
Withdrawal by children, 347, 352

X

X-rays
    bone growth x-rays, 135
    conventional x-rays, 138
    external radiation, 274

Y

Yoga, 7, 357
Young adult survivors
    health insurance, 453
    safe sex, 450
    treatment summary, 451

Z

Zantac, 264
Zofran. *See* Ondansetron

About the Authors

Anne Spurgeon, trained as a historian at the University of Wisconsin, is the parent of a long-term survivor of rhabdomyosarcoma, a soft tissue sarcoma. For more than 15 years, she served as the executive director of the Badger Childhood Cancer Network in Madison, Wisconsin. Its mission is to educate, support, serve, and advocate for children with cancer, their families, survivors of childhood cancer, and the professionals who care for them (*www.badgerchildhoodcancer.org*). Anne enjoys having adventures with her three interesting young adult children; kayaking the beautiful lakes of Wisconsin; reading history, anthropology, and science; and making and drinking craft beer.

Nancy Keene, a well-known writer and advocate for children with cancer, is the parent of a 24-year survivor of childhood cancer. She is one of the founders of the nonprofit Childhood Cancer Guides, and she has written many books for families of children with cancer, including *Childhood Leukemia; Your Child in the Hospital;* and *Chemo, Craziness, and Comfort.* She co-authored *Childhood Brain & Spinal Cord Tumors* and *Childhood Cancer Survivors.* She served as chair of the Patient Advocacy Committees of both the Children's Cancer Group (CCG) and the Children's Oncology Group (COG). In her spare time, she likes to read, hike with her dogs, and kayak in the Salish Sea.

Childhood Cancer Guides™

Questions Answered
Experiences Shared

When your life is turned upside down, your need for information is great. You have to make critical medical decisions, often with what seems like little to go on. Plus, you have to break the news to family, quiet your own fears, help your ill child and your other children, figure out how you are going to pay the bills, and sometimes get to work or put dinner on the table.

Childhood Cancer Guides provide authoritative information for the families and friends of children with cancer or survivors of childhood cancer. Our books cover all aspects of how these illnesses affect family life. In each book, there's a mix of:

- **Medical information**

  Dozens of experts on childhood cancer and survivorship contributed to these books to provide state-of-the-art information to help you weigh treatment options. Modern medicine has much to offer. When there are treatment controversies, we present differing points of view.

- **Practical information**

  After making treatment decisions, life focuses on coping with treatment and any side effects that develop. We cover day-to-day practicalities, such as those you'd hear from a helpful nurse or a knowledgeable support group.

- **Emotional support**

  It's normal to have strong reactions to a condition that threatens your child's life. It's normal that the whole family is affected. We cover issues such as the shock of diagnosis, living with uncertainty, and communicating with loved ones.

Each book contains stories from parents, children, and siblings who share, in their own words, the lessons they have learned and what truly helped them cope.

www.childhoodcancerguides.org

Other Books for Families

Childhood Brain & Spinal Cord Tumors
A Guide for Families, Friends & Caregivers, 2nd Edition

by Tania Shiminski-Maher, Catherine Woodman & Nancy Keene
ISBN 9781941089002, $29.95, 560 pages

Childhood Leukemia
A Guide for Families, Friends & Caregivers, 4th Edition

by Nancy Keene
ISBN 9781941089057, $29.95, 503 pages

Childhood Cancer Survivors
A Practical Guide to Your Future, 3rd Edition

by Nancy Keene, Wendy Hobbie & Kathy Ruccione
ISBN 9781941089101, $29.95, 452 pages

Your Child in the Hospital
A Practical Guide for Parents, 3rd Edition

by Nancy Keene
ISBN 9781941089996, $14.95, 176 pages

Our helpful guides are available at
an online bookseller or a bookstore near you.